ALSO BY D. D. GUTTENPLAN

The Holocaust on Trial

AMERICAN
RADICAL

AMERICAN RADICAL

---•◆•---

The Life and Times of

I. F. STONE

D. D. Guttenplan

Farrar, Straus and Giroux   *New York*

Farrar, Straus and Giroux
18 West 18th Street, New York 10011

Grateful acknowledgment is made for permission to quote from the following:
"September 1, 1939" by W. H. Auden, copyright © 1940 by W. H. Auden, renewed ©
by the Estate of W. H. Auden. Used by permission.
Isaiah Berlin, unpublished correspondence with I. F. Stone. Reproduced with permis-
sion of Curtis Brown Group Ltd, London, on behalf of the Isaiah Berlin Literary Trust.
Copyright © the Isaiah Berlin Literary Trust, 1975.
Michael Blankfort, unpublished correspondence with I. F. Stone. Used by permission
of Mrs. Michael Blankfort and the Howard Gotlieb Archival Research Center at Boston
University.
"St. Bartholomew's Eve" by Malcolm Cowley, copyright © the Literary Estate of Malcom
Cowley. Used by permission of Robert W. Cowley. Malcom Cowley's unpublished corre-
spondence with Isidore Feinstein is used by permission of the Newberry Library, Chicago.
"Boats in a Fog" copyright © 1925, renewed © 1953 by Robinson Jeffers, "Woodrow
Wilson," "Shine, Perishing Republic" copyright © 1934 by Robinson Jeffers, renewed ©
1962 by Donnan Jeffers and Garth Jeffers, from *Selected Poetry of Robinson Jeffers* by
Robinson Jeffers, copyright © 1925, 1929, renewed © 1953, 1957 by Robinson Jeffers.
Used by permission of Random House, Inc.
Freda Kirchwey, unpublished correspondence with I. F. Stone. Used by permission of
the Schlesinger Library, Radcliffe Institute for Advanced Study, Harvard University.
Robert Silvers, unpublished correspondence with Isaiah Berlin. Used by permission.
I. F. Stone's unpublished correspondence, copyright © the Estate of I. F. Stone. Used
by permission of Celia Gilbert, Christopher Stone, and Jeremy Stone.

Library of Congress Cataloging-in-Publication Data
Guttenplan, D. D.
    American radical : the life and times of I. F. Stone / D. D. Guttenplan.— 1st ed.
        p.   cm.
    Includes bibliographical references and index.
    ISBN-13: 978-0-374-18393-6 (hardcover : alk. paper)
    ISBN-10: 0-374-18393-7 (hardcover : alk. paper)
    1. Stone, I. F. (Isidor Feinstein), 1907–1989.   2. Journalists—United States—
    Biography.   I. Title

PN4874.S69 G88 2009
070.92—dc22
[B]
                                                        2009009667

Designed by Jonathan D. Lippincott

www.fsgbooks.com

1   3   5   7   9   10   8   6   4   2

For Alexander, who was there at the beginning

and for Zoe and Theo,
who arrived in medias res:

Like the poet's Ithaka,
you three have made these years
a beautiful journey

And finally, in memory of
Andy Kopkind,
whose voice is always in my ear

CONTENTS

PREFACE

To the *Meet the Press* audience on December 12, 1949, there was nothing
special about the confrontation between I. F. Stone and Dr. Morris Fishbein. As editor of the *Journal of the American Medical Association*, Fishbein was a well-known foe of what the AMA called "socialized medicine"
in any form; Stone, a sometime member of the *Meet the Press* panel
since 1946, could always be relied on for provocative, irreverent, and persistent questioning. The country's most influential physician had already
denounced national health insurance as "the kind of regimentation that
led to totalitarianism in Germany." When Fishbein also condemned compulsory coverage as "socialistic," Stone demonstrated why the show's producers considered him "a good needler": "Dr. Fishbein, let's get nice and
rough. In view of his advocacy of compulsory health insurance, do you regard Mr. Harry Truman as a card-bearing Communist, or just a deluded
fellow traveler?"

The arguments over national health care did not advance much in the
next sixty years, but for I. F. Stone that broadcast marked a kind of limit.
After a career that saw him rise to national prominence not only on television and radio but as a correspondent for the *Nation* and a columnist for
PM—the legendary New York tabloid that refused advertisements and
revolutionized American newspapers—he was about to disappear. Not literally, of course. For the moment, Stone still had a job, though his latest
employer, New York's *Daily Compass*, had fewer readers than the same
city's Yiddish *Daily Forward*. And if the days when his habit of sauntering

into various New Deal agencies and making free with the phone—and the files—were behind him, he still had friends in Washington, some of whom were even willing to be seen talking with him. But it was to be another *eighteen years* before I. F. Stone was next on national television. And though he lived to an age when political punditry dominated Sunday morning broadcasting, he was never again invited back on *Meet the Press*.

A decade earlier, Stone had already developed as much "access" as any journalist in the country; his patrons included Felix Frankfurter, the Harvard Law professor and future Supreme Court justice, and Thomas "Tommy the Cork" Corcoran, the president's political fixer. During World War II, Stone worked closely with Walter Reuther and other union leaders in proposing plans to increase production of aircraft and arms; his exposés of the Alcoa Aluminum trust's war profiteering and the Standard Oil Company's cozy cartel agreements with the German firm I. G. Farben brought him kudos from the chair of the special Senate Committee to Investigate the National Defense Program, Harry S. Truman. After the war, Stone's undercover journey accompanying Jewish survivors of the Nazi Holocaust as they defied the British blockade of Palestine made front-page headlines; his reports under fire from the new state of Israel made him a hero to America's Jews.

And then, slowly, he vanishes. He opposes President Truman's loyalty program and the establishment of NATO, supports the Marshall Plan, and is denounced by the Communist *Daily Worker* for reporting favorably from Yugoslavia, whose leader, the former partisan fighter Josip Tito, declares his country's independence from the policies imposed in the Balkans by the Soviet Union. In February 1950, speaking at a rally against the hydrogen bomb, Stone begins, "FBI agents and fellow subversives . . ." The bureau will soon put him under daily surveillance. Although he is the author of four books, each one more successful than the last, when he writes another, on the Korean War, no publisher in America will touch it. Returning to New York in 1951 after a year in Paris as foreign correspondent for the *Compass*, he can't get his passport renewed. By the time that paper closes its doors in 1952, he is effectively blacklisted as a reporter; not even the *Nation* will give him a job. He is forty-four years old and relies on a hearing aid to make out any sound below a shout. He writes, "I feel for the moment like a ghost."

For some time he lives in a kind of internal exile. The American reporter more closely identified with the Jewish state than any other sits in Washington, D.C., in a rented office waiting for the phone to ring. When, after three years, he realizes that he hasn't had a single visitor apart from building maintenance workers and the mailman (who has been secretly sharing Stone's mail with the FBI), he gives up the office and works from home. Starting with a tiny fragment of his old magazine and newspaper audience—too few at first even to cover expenses, let alone pay his salary—he decides to launch his own newspaper. *I. F. Stone's Weekly* gives him a platform from which he can rally his fellow heretics, attack their persecutors, and, most of all, encourage resistance. "Early Soviet novels used a vivid phrase, 'former people,' about the remnants of the dispossessed ruling class," he writes. "On the inhospitable sidewalks of Washington these days, the editor often feels like one of the 'former people.'" Not all of his subscribers appreciate the irony, but for readers who want a radical perspective on current events free from sectarian distortion and distraction, the *Weekly* has no competition. Throughout the long nightmare of the American inquisition, whenever citizens stand up to claim their rights, I. F. Stone is there. Somehow he survives.

And slowly, almost imperceptibly, his audience returns. In 1956, thanks in part to a landmark legal victory by his brother-in-law, Leonard Boudin, he is again granted a passport. Able at last to go back to Israel for the first time in years, he returns via Moscow, eager to see whether Khrushchev's secret speech to the Twentieth Party Congress is really a harbinger of genuine reform. Comparing himself to "a swimmer under water who must rise to the surface or his lungs will burst," he declares: "Whatever the consequences, I have to say what I really feel after seeing the Soviet Union . . . *This is not a good society and it is not led by honest men.*" Yet Stone is a long way from respectability. On Cuba and on domestic civil rights his positions are far to the left even of most liberals, and his opposition to nuclear testing and to the American interventions in Guatemala and Southeast Asia place him well outside the cold war consensus. Though his initial enthusiasm for Fidel Castro is tempered after three trips to Cuba (and a spell in a Havana jail), his continuing support for students who want to travel there and make up their own minds (in defiance of U.S. law) and for blacks rising up in the American South brings him to the notice of a new generation of readers "bred in at least modest comfort" and looking uncomfortably at the world they are to inherit.

It is this generation and its response to the Vietnam War that plucks I. F. Stone from the dustbin of history and places him, once again, on the front ranks of American activism. Before the incident in August 1964 in the Gulf of Tonkin that gives rise to the large-scale involvement of U.S. forces in Vietnam, the *Weekly*—after ten years of struggle—has barely 20,000 subscribers; after two years of war in Vietnam, the figure has risen above 30,000; in 1969, a single appearance by Stone on *The Dick Cavett Show* brings 5,000 new subscribers, pushing the total above 70,000. In April 1965, when Stone is the only journalist asked to speak at the first March on Washington to End the War, Lyndon Johnson has no need to wonder how many divisions I. F. Stone has. The president can look out the window to see 25,000 protesters on the White House lawn.

Popular Front columnist and New Deal propagandist. Fearless opponent of McCarthy and radical pamphleteer. Scourge of official liars and elder statesman to the New Left. The fourth act in Stone's career sees him retire from the *Weekly* in 1971 to become a contributing editor to the *New York Review of Books*—and an avid amateur classicist out to solve one of the great mysteries of Western civilization: how it came about that the ancient Athenians, inventors of democracy and originators of the humanist ideal of free speech, put a man to death merely for speaking his mind. Published as the author turns eighty, *The Trial of Socrates* is an international best seller, making Stone, politically still an unrepentant radical, into a kind of national treasure whose death is marked by all four of the network evening news broadcasts.

To think for yourself is the hardest thing for a journalist. Yet I. F. Stone managed to do it, day after day and week after week, for fifty years. He may have been shocked into independent thought—in his case by the Nazi-Soviet pact, which marked the end of Stone's hopes for a genuine Popular Front embracing Communists, Trotskyists, liberals, and unaffiliated radicals—but however he began, he retained his independence. Unlike many of those who would later oppose him from the right, Stone never succumbed to the romance of American communism. But he was genuinely terrified by fascism, and he welcomed any ally in the fight against Hitler—even, when Stalin changed sides again, the Soviet Union. After 1945, Stone put most of the blame for the cold war on his own country, seeing that it was the stronger power, and on the Democratic Party's failure to sustain the New Deal faith in economic justice at home or resist the temptations of empire abroad. He defied conventional wisdom in urging the left to support Dwight Eisenhower's efforts to extricate the country from the war in Korea and to avoid entanglement in China or Vietnam, while he despised Richard Nixon, whom he labeled a "slick kind of Arrow-[shirt]-collar ad" Fascist. Still, when President Nixon made his historic opening to China in 1972, Stone, remarking that "there is nothing that a good newspaperman, like any Hegelian or Marxist historian, cannot foresee as inevitable once it has happened," confessed that he found it "exhilarating to be reminded again how unpredictable human behavior can be." The "Peking-Washington rapprochement," he declared, "is the most startling event of its kind since the Nazi-Soviet pact."[1]

Along with his independence of mind, Stone's capacity for surprise was one of his greatest assets. "I have never been able to figure out just what not being surprised is supposed to prove," he wrote in 1957 after the Soviet launch of its spacecraft *Sputnik* stunned the world. "A mummy is immune to surprise." Perhaps it was the memory of his chagrin over the Nazi-Soviet pact that saved him from the incorrigible smugness endemic among today's punditocracy. Certainly it is difficult to imagine our own Sunday morning Solons so cheerfully acknowledging the inevitability of error and inconsistency: "If you're going to be a newspaperman, you are either going to be honest or consistent," Stone told a young admirer. "If you are really doing your job as an observer . . . it's more important to say what you see than to worry about inconsistency. If you are worried about that, then you stop looking. And if you stop looking, you are not a real reporter anymore. I have no inhibitions about changing my mind."[2]

Stone remained a real reporter all his life. For him that meant a deeply ingrained skepticism about the claims of power—as in his famous quip, repeated through many variations, that "every government is run by liars." Yet his skepticism never degenerated into cynicism, nor did he indulge in the knee-jerk contrarianism that so often passes itself off as independence of mind. Stone understood that what journalism is really good at is answering empirical questions, that the best investigative journalism demands the skills not of an economist or a philosopher but of a good police reporter. Was there a North Vietnamese attack on the American destroyer *Turner Joy* in August 1964 or not? Can underground nuclear explosions be detected from more than one hundred miles away? Did the Limited Test Ban Treaty actually reduce the number of tests? These are questions that admit of simple factual answers—though in all three cases Stone's fellow reporters showed little interest in even asking the questions. As he often remarked, one reason that Carl Bernstein and Bob Woodward were able to follow the Watergate story all the way to the Oval Office was that they were working the police beat, not the White House.

"I tried to get my stuff from the horse's mouth—or the other end, at any rate," Stone said near the end of his life. But it would be a mistake to take Stone's modesty at face value, or to miss the immense intellectual confidence behind his passion for getting the facts straight. "The search for meaning is very satisfying, it's very pleasant, but it can be very far from the truth," he warned a pair of student journalists. "You have to have the courage to call attention to what doesn't fit. Even though readers are going to say, 'Well two weeks ago you said this.' So you did. And maybe you were wrong then, or partly wrong, but anyway you've just seen something new that doesn't fit, and it's your job to report it. Otherwise you're just the prisoner of your own preconceptions.

"You have a point of view, and you have a passionate belief," he continued. But, he told them, you also have an obligation to be fair, and to be prepared to accommodate uncomfortable truths. To describe this process of constant adjustment to reality, Stone used a deeply unfashionable word: "dialectical."[3] "A lot of people in this town," he told the writer William Greider in April 1988, "thought of me as Karl Marx's baby brother." Stone, like Marx, wrote to change the world. He was also, for all his ink-stained self-deprecation, perfectly at home amid the mainstream of European thought; not for nothing was he invited by Jean-Paul Sartre to write for *Les Temps Modernes*. But Stone's deepest roots were in his native ground: the deceptively plainspoken sophistication of Benjamin Franklin, the distilled outrage of William Lloyd Garrison, Tom Paine's appeal to revolutionary common sense, the unyielding dignity of Frederick Douglass, and above all Thomas Jefferson's view of a free press as the keystone of American liberty.

Stone enjoyed the celebrity that came to him at the end of his life. He and his beloved wife, Esther, who met on a blind date on a Philadelphia street corner and who survived the lean years together partly through her genius at running the *Weekly* on a shoestring and a promise—she took over the business side so he could concentrate on the reporting—danced the frug at the Peppermint Lounge and hobnobbed with stars at the Cannes Film Festival. They also shared the bemused satisfaction of seeing the onetime political leper celebrated from Paris to San Francisco. "I told my wife years ago," Stone says in the 1973 film *I. F. Stone's Weekly*, "I said, 'Honey, I'm going to graduate from a pariah to a character, and then if I last long enough I'll be regarded as a national institution.'" He lasted long enough.

In January 2008 on the *CBS Evening News*, Katie Couric asked John Edwards, then running for the Democratic nomination as president of the United States, to name the one book, other than the Bible, he would consider "essential to have along" as president. Edwards chose *The Trial of Socrates* because, he said, of the way Stone treats "the challenges that are faced by men about character, about integrity, and about belief systems." Four years earlier, when Edwards told ABC's George Stephanopoulos that *The Trial of Socrates* was his favorite book, the pundit Robert Novak led a pileup of right-wing bloggers professing outrage at his choice. Edwards may just be a stubborn character. After all, Stone's continuing status as a hate figure for the American right was attested as recently as August 2007, when President George W. Bush attacked Stone by name in a speech to the Veterans of Foreign Wars. But it is also true that, in the decades since his death, I. F. Stone has indeed become a national institution. This is the third biography since his death. In 2006, Peter Osnos, who began his journalistic career as Stone's assistant on the *Weekly* before becoming a foreign correspondent for the *Washington Post* and later the founder of PublicAffairs Books, published a selection of Stone's journalism. In March 2008, the Nieman Foundation for Journalism at Harvard announced plans to award an annual I. F. Stone Medal for Journalistic Independence as the culmination of a yearly "I. F. Stone Workshop on Strengthening Journalistic Independence." There is little chance that Stone will ever disappear again.

Despite his fame, Stone's actual life remains a chapter in the hidden history of the twentieth century. Indeed, it would be only a slight exaggeration to say that it is precisely Stone's status as a kind of journalistic totem that keeps him, like an Egyptian pharaoh, immured in a monument of his own devising. So it is not as clear as it should be that Stone was not only, or merely, or even primarily, a great reporter. He was also and always a radical, an irritant to those in power—for his uncanny ability to seize on and publicize the most inconvenient truths, and for his vociferous objection to the existing order, for his intransigent dissatisfaction with a society that forces its children to go to war in order to pay for college and that allows the earth to be spoiled and the sick to go without medicine so corporations and those who own them can continue to pile up treasure without let or hindrance.

I. F. Stone was a troublemaker all his life. From his youth as a soapbox orator for the Socialist Party to his middle-aged mockery of Harry Truman, John Foster Dulles, and J. Edgar Hoover, to his dying words in support of the students who risked death on Tiananmen Square by demonstrating against the Chinese government, he always relished a good fight. The list of his causes is itself a fair index of the rise and fall of American radicalism: equality for African Americans, government assistance for the poor, economic justice for farm laborers and factory workers, a left united in opposition to fascism (whether the jackbooted European variety or the "chrome-plated American fascism" Stone saw behind the repression of the 1950s), support for colonial independence and opposition to an American empire, industrial democracy and workers' rights, universal health care, the abolition of nuclear weapons, justice for Palestinians as well as Israelis, a negotiated end to the cold war, and, most of all, the right to dissent.

As Stone aged, his manners softened. In the tempest of the 1950s, harassed by the State Department, followed by the FBI, blacklisted by the mainstream media, and ridiculed by many liberals, Stone refused to trim his sails. But when the storm passed and Stone encountered his former antagonists in more peaceable climes, he was nearly always willing to forgive, if not to forget. His geniality and his increasing focus, in his final years, on injustices in the so-called Socialist world made it easy to overlook the man who'd proposed a government takeover of the automobile industry to equip the air force during World War II; suggested that a German John D. Rockefeller would have been interred, rather than merely interned, for trading with the enemy on the same terms as the American tycoon did; and who, long before the sit-ins and freedom rides, regularly chided American blacks not for their restiveness but for their patience. The I. F. Stone who wrote scathing critiques of Soviet psychiatry in the

New York Review of Books gradually eclipsed, if not effaced, the man who denounced American interference in Cuba as criminal and who described the war in Vietnam—"this distant slaughter of a small nation"—not as a heroic crusade or even a quixotic gesture, but as "genocide."[4]

Perhaps especially today, when a snide tone or a hectoring manner seems to serve as an emblem of commitment, any reader who happens upon Stone's calm, forensic, yet devastating critiques of American politics and institutions is likely to be shocked by the depth of his radicalism. Stone was no catastrophist; he didn't yearn for things to get worse in order to get better. He was always happy to support reform whenever reform was possible—and genuine. He cherished the Constitution, felt proprietary pride toward the Bill of Rights, and took for granted the necessity for liberals and radicals to work together on common goals as simple Popular Front common sense. Even in the depths of the McCarthy era, Stone never lost faith in the long-term prospects for democracy, telling himself, "Well, I may be just a Red Jew son-of-a-bitch to them, but I'm keeping Thomas Jefferson alive." And in the short term, he was always ready to stand and fight.

It is this I. F. Stone, the radical I. F. Stone, who has at least as much to teach us as the patron saint of investigative reporting. If journalism was his medium, his message was unfailingly political. Indeed, it was his immersion in the political battles of his day, his experience of the anguish of the Depression, the exhilaration of CIO organizing campaigns in the steel and auto industries, the brutal violence of Kentucky coalfields, the promise of the New Deal, and the cruel foreclosures of the cold war that shaped his historical sensibility and lifted his best journalism above the ephemeral score-keeping and score-settling of his long-forgotten rivals.

Shorn of its political engagements, Stone's career is reduced to a kind of performance, like a veteran ballplayer or a distinguished actor. And shorn of his history, he becomes merely a figurehead for a set of attitudes or political positions, a way to prop up our prejudices by showing how his views on any subject resemble our own. (Much of what is written about Stone brings to mind my favorite baseball joke, about the feared batter Ty Cobb. Two fans are in a bar watching a game. One asks: If Ty Cobb were still alive, how do you think he'd do against today's pitchers? Maybe .220, says the second fan laconically. The first fan is outraged by such a low estimate: How can you say that? Ty Cobb was the greatest hitter in baseball! Yes, comes the reply, but you have to remember—he'd be over a hundred years old.) I. F. Stone, too, would be more than a hundred years old. So perhaps it is time to stop asking "What would Izzy say?" and consider instead why he still matters.

Stone's ability to continue writing and to remain both radical and independent is itself a major achievement. I write these words near the end of a decade during which our country was again covered in darkness, trapped in the quagmire of a war begun on dubious grounds and whose ignominious end is still barely imaginable. Dissent has again been equated with treason, while domestic prosperity has been laid waste to finance an overweening president's imperial arrogance. In the words of the prophet Jeremiah, "The harvest is past, the summer is ended, and we are not saved." In such times, Stone's life and writings can again serve as a beacon to rally the republic and to remind us that radicalism is as American as the Boston Tea Party, and that we who stand on the side of Daniel Shays, or the abolitionists, or Eugene Debs, or the Wobblies, or Franklin Roosevelt, or the Congress of Industrial Organizations, or Rosa Parks, or Women Strike for Peace, or any of a dozen other causes, some lost, some respectable, and some now forgotten, have at least as much right to call ourselves genuine patriots as those who opposed them. As his critic, competitor, and longtime friend Murray Kempton said, when reading I. F. Stone "we soon come to understand that, among its many other uses, his work is a handbook on how to survive as a guerrilla."[5]

And when the tide turns, Stone's various flourishings will remind us to seize the day, to face our tasks undaunted, and to focus less on the minor differences of doctrine that may divide us and more on what we can accomplish together. I. F. Stone never forgot the healing impact of the New Deal's flawed and faltering efforts toward economic justice. He never forgot that as well as planting trees, saving banks, taming rivers, bringing electricity to the rural South, paving thousands of miles of roads, and building hundreds of public structures from amphitheaters to zoos, Roosevelt's bold, persistent experimentation repaired the spirit, building the nation that would go on to defeat fascism. Nor did he forget the coalition that pressed the president, and the country, to keep moving left. When shipyard workers in Gdansk rose up in 1980 against the Soviet-imposed work rules the Polish government had decreed, Stone was thrilled; he'd been a supporter of the strike at the Cegielski locomotive works in

Poznań, and that was in 1956![6] But he must have been especially pleased by the name the Poles gave to their movement: Solidarity. I. F. Stone knew a lot about solidarity. He'd seen the American left tear itself apart when solidarity gave way to suspicion and recrimination, but he never forgot what solidarity had achieved, either on the line at the Fisher Body plant in Flint, Michigan, or at lunch counters across the South or in demanding an end to the war in Vietnam. It was his memory, and his confidence, as much as his analysis of events that made a deaf, reedy-voiced, myopic old man such a powerful figure.

This is a book about a man who lived through extraordinary times. Our times. He was a very great reporter, and like all great reporters a great noticer. Which is our good fortune, because taken together his writings amount to as vivid a record of those times as we are likely to get. Was the man himself extraordinary? Where did he come from? What formed him? What does his life and work tell us about journalism? About politics? About our country? Those are some of the questions I set out to answer on the following pages.

AMERICAN
RADICAL

One

FEINSTEIN'S PROGRESS

———— ◆◦◆ ————

I was a natural-born reporter. I was a real bird dog right from the
beginning.   —I. F. Stone

Before he was anything else he was a newspaperman. He was the eldest
son, a first-generation American, a schoolboy, a Jew. He was all of those
things without choosing. The newspaper was his.

It was called the *Progress* and cost 2¢ (marked down from a nickel).
The first edition appeared in February 1922. On the front page, under a
half-column attack on the Hearst newspaper chain for "malignant propaganda against Japan," were the editor's initials: I. B. F. Isadore B. Feinstein. The "B" was a fiction—his first assumed name. He was fourteen
years old.

As befitted its high-minded title, most of the six unnumbered pages
that made up the *Progress*, volume one, number one, were devoted to
editorial exhortation or to poetry. A speech from *Antigone* (credited to
"Saphocles") warning that "money . . . lays cities low" was followed by a
demand to "Cancel the War Debts." Arguing on behalf of "every individual in the United States, more or less," the young writer tried his hand at
economics: "The war debt is the chief cause of the business depression.
Why? Because the war debts lower the rate of foreign exchange and increase the value of the American dollar."

The *Progress* showed a playful side as well, publishing "A. Nut. E.
Poem. (by an Animus)" along with jokes, humorous headlines, and a fea-

ture on "Unusual Occupations" credited to the *New York American*—a Hearst paper, but then, good features were hard to find.

Pragmatic, precocious, enterprising (the first issue included eleven display ads), sophomoric—were it not for the career that followed, there would be little reason to take note of Feinstein's *Progress*. Here was scant trace of the mature, wised-up style, the Talmudic relish for documentary evidence, the acidulous provocations and devastating deadpan that enlivened every issue of *I. F. Stone's Weekly*. In a young man, high ideals are hardly more remarkable than high spirits. Still, in light of what would come after, it is perhaps worth recording that from the very first he was immune to the charms of the parochial. Hearst, the Versailles Treaty, the economy—these were the causes that excited this fourteen-year-old's passion. The only local element in the *Progress* was the advertising—which, so far as addresses are given, seemed to all come from shops on the same street as the editor's house.

Tucked away discreetly on an inside page was an ad for the United Department Store, "B. Feinstein, Prop." B. Feinstein was the editor's father, and though the presence of the paternal name might have given readers (who were mostly neighbors) the impression of an indulgent, even proud parent supporting his son's venture, the truth was more complicated.

•

There is a Yiddish expression that perfectly captures the career of Bernard Feinstein, at least in the eyes of his eldest son: *Asakh melokhes un veynik brokhes* (Many trades but few blessings). More poignant than the English jack-of-all-trades (but master of none), the Yiddish phrase has a sense of hard circumstance, of fatality, mixed in with the dismissal. Born in Gronov, the Ukraine, in 1876, Baruch Feinstein had already served a number of years in the tsar's army before fleeing the country to escape being sent to the Far East. One family story has him making his way across Poland on foot, but there is general agreement that after stops in Hamburg, Liverpool, and Cardiff, he boarded a ship in London and landed in Philadelphia on April 12, 1903. He was a peddler.[1]

"At that time," Louis, his youngest son, recalled, "they were building the Main Line [of the Pennsylvania] Railroad from Philadelphia out to

Paoli . . . and the Polish workers didn't have a chance to go to shops. My father went up and down the line, selling watches out of a suitcase."[2]

Somewhere along his travels, Baruch Feinstein became Bernard. He was becoming Americanized in other ways as well. In the old country there was Shabbat—the Sabbath—a day devoted to prayer and study. In the New World, Bernard Feinstein had his Saturdays to do with as he pleased, and he seldom spent them in synagogue. Like hundreds of thousands of his fellow immigrants who flocked to Coney Island, Atlantic City, or Asbury Park, Bernard Feinstein used his leisure time for leisure. On one trip to the Jersey Shore in the summer of 1906, he was walking along the beach when he met a friend, Dave Novack, a recent immigrant from Odessa. Novack introduced the young peddler to his father, Zalman, and his little sister, Katy, a sewing-machine operator in a shirt factory.

An extremely dapper man who sent his wife and children out to work while he stayed home studying Torah, Zalman (or Solomon, as he soon became) Novack was a traditional Jewish patriarch. His house on South 10th Street in South Philadelphia was strictly kosher. He'd taken his wife's family name—Novack—as a mark of respect for the father-in-law who supported his studies, not a feminist gesture.

Bernard's father, born Judah Tsvilikhovsky, had also changed his family name. Most Russian Jews took second names (aside from the Hebrew patronymic) only when they were ordered to do so by the tsarist government. Alexander III instigated a wave of officially sponsored pogroms, and since the measure was designed to make it easier for the Jews to be taxed and their sons drafted, resistance was widespread. If a family had four sons, three would be drafted. But if a family had only one son—or appeared to have a single son—he was exempt. Judah Tsvilikhovsky's father had four sons; their last names were Tsvilikhovsky, Burrison, Steelman, and Feinstein.[3]

In March 1907, Katy and Bernard were married in Philadelphia. She was twenty; he was ten years older. At first they lived with her parents, and, at least in the beginning, Bernard and his father-in-law got along well enough. Bernard continued in his secular ways, but after they moved into a home of their own, on nearby South Wharton Street, the young couple kept a kosher kitchen so that the Novacks would feel comfortable when they came to visit.

Isadore Feinstein was born in his parents' house on December 24,

1907, nine months after their wedding. His birth certificate lists his father's occupation as "salesman." His father's name is given as "Barnet Feinstein."

Like many American cities after the turn of the century, Philadelphia was really two largely separate aggregations. There was the somewhat parochial, patrician backwater where, on a 1905 visit, Henry James was struck by "the absence of the note of the perpetual perpendicular, the New York, the Chicago note." For James, Philadelphia's endless array of row houses "seemed to symbolize exactly the principle of indefinite horizontal extension and to offer, refreshingly, a challenge to horizontal, to lateral, to more or less tangential, to rotary, or better still to absolute centrifugal motion."[4] A photograph of center city Philadelphia from that same year perfectly captures this bucolic prospect: Though the City Hall clock shows it to be a quarter before two in the afternoon, the streets are practically deserted. In the foreground, where a contemporary picture of New York would have been crammed with traffic of all sorts, a herd of sheep is being driven down the middle of South Broad Street.[5]

Just a few blocks farther south was the area known as Little Russia, where in 1910 the greater part of Philadelphia's 90,697 Jewish immigrants lived and worked.[6] It was in this community that the Hebrew hymn "Adon Olom" (Lord of the World) was composed; here also lived the author of "Hatikvah" (The Hope), the Zionist anthem. Most of the Jews in Philadelphia arrived at about the same time as Bernard Feinstein and by 1910 were already the city's largest single ethnic group, making up nearly a fourth of the immigrant population. By the time the United States entered World War I, more than 200,000 Jews lived in Philadelphia, surrounded by enclaves of Irish, Polish, and Italian immigrants.

Though they were spared the indignities of tenement life, the immigrant families jammed into row houses along the blind, bandbox alleys of South Philadelphia were a world away from the contented burghers of Rittenhouse Square. Even those with good jobs were often hard-pressed. But there were also stirrings of resistance. In May 1909, the city was paralyzed by striking street railwaymen. When a settlement with the streetcar monopoly broke down the following February, Philadelphia's central labor union called the first general strike in modern American history. Thousands of nonunion workers walked off their jobs in solidarity.[7]

For those without regular work, times were especially tough. As an occupation of last resort, peddling became increasingly popular. "From

Monday to Friday," says one account, "the roads along the Delaware River . . . were clogged by Jewish peddlers."[8]

It may have been this sharpening competition that drove the young Feinstein family to light out for the West. But there were other factors as well. "The story, I don't know whether it's apocryphal or not, is they had to move so that my father could get my mother away from her mother," recalls Louis Stone. One version of this family tale has Katy Feinstein clinging to her mother's apron strings. Others blame the continuing tension between the militantly secular Bernard and his devout father-in-law. Yet another element was Katy Feinstein's postpartum depression, which was evidently serious enough for Isadore to spend months at a time with his Novack grandparents.

In 1911, Bernard, Katy, and young Isadore moved to Richmond, Indiana. Here the Yiddish-speaking boy entered kindergarten. Toward the end of his life, he made light of the day he "went out into the street and started talking *mame-loshen* [literally 'mother tongue,' i.e., Yiddish] to the schoolchildren."[9] To his own children, though, Stone spoke of Richmond as his first encounter with anti-Semitism.[10]

It was also his first encounter with small-town America. Located at the junction of the Chesapeake & Ohio and the Pennsylvania railroads, Richmond's manufactures extended from the American Seeding Machine Company's agricultural implements to William Waking Company's "bicycles, water closets and bathtubs." Three daily newspapers served the town's 22,300 inhabitants. More to the point, Richmond had twelve dry goods stores. Above one of them, at 1101 Sheridan Street, lived the Feinsteins—but not for long.[11]

Perhaps it was the lure of the railroad line that brought Bernard Feinstein so far into the American interior. Or perhaps, as his grandson Jeremy suggested, "it was just an immigrant's mistake." Certainly—and this may have been Bernard's intention—they were a very long way from their families and from the familiar shtetl culture of Little Russia. Barely a dozen other Jews lived in Richmond, and though a city directory listed his business as "dry goods"—a traditional Jewish trade throughout the South and Midwest—in reality Bernard still spent much of the year as an itinerant peddler.[12]

The Feinsteins bought their combined house and store in 1911. By June of the following year, they'd sold out to Abraham Harsh, a coal dealer and one of the few other Jews in town. But the Feinsteins stayed on in

Richmond through two family milestones. On September 6, 1912, Marcus Feinstein (known through childhood as Max) was born. His birth record lists the father's name as "Bernhardt." And in January 1913, "Bernard" Feinstein and his wife became American citizens. Once these proceedings were complete, the family returned to the East.

What could five-year-old Isadore make of such a trek? An adventure? An odyssey? A retreat? For Bernard, though it ended in disappointment, the move to Indiana was a decisive break with his past. The Feinsteins might be Jews without money, but there would be no return to the ghetto. His children would grow up to be Americans. Yet for Katy, the end of their rural exile was an enormous relief. "My father went out peddling with a horse and buggy," said Louis Stone. "Mother used to tell this story about how terrified she was when he was away and she had to feed the horse. We had a barn behind the house, with one of those old-fashioned split doors. Well, she would run up to the door with some hay, open the top, throw in a handful, slam the door shut, and run back to the house." The long train journey, if it left him with nothing else, must have impressed Isadore with the size of his country, its varied landscape, and its vast unsettled expanses. The lesson that his father was a failure he would have many opportunities to learn.

Only a year after their return from Indiana, the Feinsteins moved one more time. Bernard, who'd been struggling to support his growing family as a butcher in Camden, New Jersey, heard of an opportunity to take over a small dry goods store in nearby Haddonfield. "A Mr. Fowler sold the store to my father," Louis Stone remembered. "Then Fowler opened up a new store across the street. They were our competition—catty-corner across the street." Luckily for the Feinsteins, the American economy was about to receive a huge boost from events half a world away.

•

Haddonfield's history has been peaceful, if not uneventful since British redcoats and tattered Continentals marched through her streets.
—"Haddonfield: A Sketch of Its Early History" by Isadore Feinstein, 1931

The Feinsteins lived above the shop. Known variously as the Philadelphia Bargain Store, Ladies and Gents' Furnishings and Shoes, and the United Department Store, the family's new home was on the busiest corner in Haddonfield. Four plate-glass windows stretched for sixty feet along East Main Street, beckoning customers inside with an ever-changing display of cut-rate women's fashion, men's clothing, shoes, sewing patterns, bolts of fabric, and notions—small, useful items, usually for sewing. A heavy wooden barrel filled with pickles was hidden away on the back porch, but from the front, where a pair of hitching posts flanked a large water trough for the benefit of nearby farmers who rode their horse-drawn wagons into town on weekends to shop, little set the Feinsteins apart from their neighbors.

Though Camden, with its clamorous shipyards and huge Campbell's Soup factory, was only five miles away—a 5¢ ride on the trolley that ran down Haddon Avenue, alongside the store, before turning onto Main Street—Haddonfield on the eve of the world war was a very quiet little town. Named for Elizabeth Haddon, a wealthy Quaker who began farming there in 1701, Haddonfield remained primarily agricultural. A two-minute journey outside town in any direction brought open vistas of wheat, corn, horses, and cows.[13]

For a small boy, the town was in many ways a paradise. "In the woods around . . . where I grew up," remembered Isadore's brother Max, "there were favorite swimming holes. It was great fun to swing out over the water on a rope tied to a high tree branch . . . There was choose-up baseball in the large field between the school and the Presbyterian Church that fronted on Main Street . . . and pick-up football . . . on a lot beside the Friends School on Haddon Avenue down past the cemetery . . . The cemetery was just across the street from the rear of our store . . . [and] when it snowed we sledded there or . . . skied on barrel staves."[14]

Even his bookish older brother enjoyed fishing in Evans Pond or wandering through the surrounding woods with a dog-eared copy of Keats, Shelley, or Emily Dickinson shoved into his back pocket. Home from his rambles, Isadore would curl up in the big green wicker rocking chair that stood at the rear of the shop. Often he also could be found in the dining room located behind the store, hunched over the piles of books that covered the whole of the round wooden table or staring through his thick round eyeglasses out the window and across Haddon Avenue to the firehouse, or perhaps at the two buttonwood trees in front of Milask's ice cream parlor. George Washington was said to have stood under those very trees, reviewing his troops. Behind the dining room was the kitchen, Katy Feinstein's fief. From here the smell of Jewish delicacies like knishes, *knaidlach*, and kreplach, her special chicken with kasha *varnishkes*, or fruity fragrant strudel and hamantaschen would go wafting up the dining room stairs to the rest of the house.[15]

For all its idyllic quality, though, the Feinsteins' life in Haddonfield was oddly insular. Bernard read a Yiddish newspaper; Katy still kept a kosher kitchen, which meant taking the trolley into Camden to a kosher butcher whenever she wanted to buy meat or poultry. Both parents spoke Yiddish at home. Indeed, Katy, who was a lively, relatively cultivated woman in Yiddish, was barely literate in English. There were only a handful of other Jews in Haddonfield—too few for a minyan, the quorum of ten men needed to hold a service, let alone to organize a synagogue. Not that Bernard would have gone. Instead, he and Katy spent practically every weekend in the family Maxwell driving the children to visit one or another of their numerous relatives scattered throughout the Philadelphia area. Many, like Izzy's favorite uncle, Ithamar "Shumer" Feinstein, still lived in the city.[16] But the rich, contentious communal life of immigrant Jewry—the world of Irving Howe's The World of Our Fathers—was one that young Isadore Feinstein barely knew.

Until the 1930s, Haddonfield didn't even have a Catholic church. Racially, Stone recalled later, it was practically "a Southern town." And while most of the Quakers who still dominated Haddonfield probably viewed the Feinsteins as harmless exotics, all of the town's Jews lived behind a wall of complete social segregation. Izzy's brother Max desperately wanted to be accepted. "There were only three classmates who like me were Jewish, but they were not part of the 'in' crowd so I shunned them," he admitted in a draft memoir. "Nonetheless, the cruel, childish taunts of 'Kike' and 'Christ Killer' continued into the teens, and though I might hang out with the drug-store crowd I was not invited to their parties."

"They used to tease me, 'Is he a door or is he a window?'" recalls Isador Rosenthal, who went through the Haddonfield school system at the same time as the Feinstein boys. "They didn't know a Jew from Adam. Some thought Jews had horns. Every time there was a Jewish holiday that we observed, I had a note to the teacher," he remembered.[17]

Describing Isadore Feinstein as "a loner," one of his high school classmates explained, "He never went to any of our parties." Was he invited? "Oh, no." A Jewish classmate remembers being barred from the YMCA, though he might indeed have felt out of place at the hilarious doings at YMCA Camp Ockanickon as described in the local paper: "Popular Confectioner in

Familiar Impersonation Convulses Campers With Laughter . . . It was the campers' first acquaintance with Mr. Hires, who entertained . . . with his Jewish impersonation . . . He looked exactly like a Jewish peddler would look if he wandered into camp with his neck-tie on."[18]

The Feinstein boys, sons of a Jewish peddler, were also barred from the fortnightly dances at the Artisans Hall. Indeed, most of the anti-Semitism they encountered in Haddonfield was on the level of social discrimination or ethnic stereotyping. But there were more virulent strains that the town's mask of placid contentment didn't completely conceal. In the 1920s, stickers appeared on trolleys, buses, and buildings all over Camden proclaiming: EVERY LOYAL AMERICAN KNOWS WHAT KKK STANDS FOR. Certainly Bernard Feinstein knew; when the Ku Klux Klan marched down Main Street, he stood silently on the store's front steps staring at the hooded procession. (Bernard's gesture of defiance was not without risk. The next day his son Louis, not yet ten, greeted Haddonfield's conspicuously tall chief of police with a cheerful, "Hi! I saw you in the parade yesterday.") Edward Cutler, who attended Hebrew school with the Feinstein boys, remembered an even more oblique response to local anti-Semitism. His mother sometimes sent gentile customers out of their dry goods store (also on Main Street) with a cheery "Good-bye—*brecha fis!*" (break a foot).[19]

From a very early age, Isadore Feinstein knew he was somehow different. "I was lonesome. I was a kind of freak," he recalled. Even as a grown man, he never entirely lost "the little boy's awe for those who could sing in school the line 'Land where my fathers died' without feeling awkward about it." By all accounts, school gave young Isadore a great many reasons to feel awkward. "I think we were cruel to Izzy because he was a loner," a classmate recalled. "He was very intellectual, but he never got down to our level, where we had fun."[20]

He also came from the wrong side of the tracks. The railroad running along Atlantic Avenue cut Haddonfield in half, with the most desirable homes on the west side. The Feinsteins lived in "the commercial section" on the east side. Shy, Jewish, bespectacled, physically clumsy, and relatively poor, Isadore devised two strategies to help him survive at school. One was humor, particularly humor directed at authority figures. Several classmates remembered his barbed exchanges with teachers. A particular triumph was the day he convinced his classmates to devour Limburger cheese—or, in one telling of the story, cloves of raw garlic—and then closed all the classroom windows in order to torment their hapless teacher.[21]

Far more often, though, Isadore would simply withdraw behind the covers of a book. A fascination with print was one of his earliest memories. "Before I learned how to read I would sit on the trolley car with a book in front of me and make believe I was reading and move my lips. And then one of the biggest thrills of my life was in those first-grade readers, with the lovely pastel illustrations showing a bird on the windowsill, and the words underneath it saying, plain as day, 'The bird sat on the windowsill,' and being able to figure it out was just tremendous."[22]

Other boys collected toy soldiers or marbles or stamps. The pride of young Isadore's collection was "a facsimile edition in color of *The Marriage of Heaven and Hell.*" Blake, Wordsworth, and the other English Romantic poets were a source of immense pleasure his entire life, as were Emily Dickinson and Camden's own bard. "While I was in high school Walt Whitman was a great influence in my life. I really feel that from him I got a feeling of naturalness and purity about sex," he recalled. Thanks to his fluent Yiddish, which helped with the German, Heine's *Buch der Lieder* was another early favorite.

His family worried that Isadore "buried himself in books," with reading "almost his sole activity in childhood or early teens." His own recollections make it clear, however, that while escape from the demands of his family or the taunts of his schoolmates might have been a motive, what he found in the library was nothing less than liberation. Starting with a sentimental education, he read his way from omnivorous curiosity to deeply held conviction. At first he looked primarily for vivid imagery and compelling rhythm. "I remember the thrill of reading Marlowe's *Tamburlaine*, with that wonderful line, 'Is it not passing brave to be a king and march in triumph through Persepolis?'" he said. Empathy soon steered him in new directions: "I can remember coming home from high school and lying on the couch at home over my father's store, eating pretzels and reading *Don Quixote* and bursting into tears at the moment of tragic lucidity when Don Quixote wavers and sees that he has been living in a world of illusion."[23]

When Isadore was twelve, his reading took another turn. Jack London's *Martin Eden* gave Isadore "my first glimpse of the modern world." Again and again in later life Stone would point to London's novel as "my introduction to radicalism" and "the book that first got me started" on the road to socialism. If so, it was an odd beginning. "You make believe that you believe in the survival of the strong and the rule of the strong. I believe. That is the difference," proclaims the book's eponymous hero. "I look to the state for nothing. I look only to the strong man, the man on horseback, to save the state from its own rotten futility." London himself was a lifelong socialist, but *Martin Eden* is a portrait of the artist as a young fascist.[24]

"The world belongs to the true noblemen, to the great blond beasts," says Martin Eden. Izzy Feinstein was no blond beast. Yet it is not hard to see how London's anguished young man spoke to—and for—his adolescent reader:

> Who are you, Martin Eden? . . . Who are you? What are you? Where do you belong? . . . You belong with the legions of toil, with all that is low, and vulgar, and unbeautiful. You belong with the oxen and the drudges, in dirty surroundings among smells and stenches . . . And yet you dare to open the books, to listen to beautiful music, to learn to love beautiful paintings, to speak good English, to think thoughts that none of your own kind thinks . . . Who are you? and what are you? damn you! And are you going to make good?[25]

To speak good English! For a boy whose earliest memories were of being teased for speaking in a foreign tongue, this must have been more intoxicating than any vision of the cooperative commonwealth. To think thoughts none of his own kind thinks. And headiest of all, the challenge, compounded of doubt and defiance: Are you going to make good?

To make good . . . to speak good English. Malraux's dictum that "the life of culture depends less on those who inherit it than those who desire it" never found a more willing exponent. Already primed by his reading of Emerson and Thoreau, the boy picked up the gauntlet in a voracious program of self-cultivation. He ranged widely: from Heraclitus to Hart Crane, Milton to *Moby-Dick*. He was also developing a taste for books that exposed the conflicts and conventions of everyday life. A cousin who visited the Feinsteins the summer before Isadore turned thirteen remembered: "Iz took me fishing and gave me a copy of Upton Sinclair's *The Jungle* to read." *Martin Eden* led Isadore to Herbert Spencer's *First Principles* and from there to the works of Charles Darwin. Spencer made a particularly strong impression on his young reader, though Spencer's vision of inexorable social evolution was seemingly less persuasive than his atheism, his faith in progress, and the sheer confidence of his taxonomy. Progress and its enemies were themes that would occupy Stone for the rest of his life, but his own emerging sense of politics owed much more to another item on his teenage reading list, the Russian anarchist Peter Kropotkin's *The Conquest of Bread*. "When you go into a public library," Kropotkin says, in an argument that surely resonated with his young reader, "the librarian does not ask you what services you have rendered to society before giving you the book, or the fifty books, which you require; he even comes to your assistance if you do not know how to manage the catalogue."[26]

"I fell in love with Kropotkin," Isadore recalled.[27] According to Kropotkin, "ours is . . . anarchist communism, communism without government—the communism of the free."[28] In time, Kropotkin would lead the young radical on to Marx, Bukharin, and Lenin. His developing analytical mind—the same faculty that found inspiration in Spencer's leaden prose—eagerly took up the tools of Marxist analysis and even, for a brief period, the far blunter implements of proletarian revolution and a Soviet-style planned economy.[29] That was much later. His initial enthusiasm for Kropotkin—for, as he put it a half century afterward, the Russian prince's "wonderful vision of anarchistic communism, of a society without police, without coercion, based on persuasion and mutual aid"—came from the same source as his passion for Shelley and Keats. He was a Romantic long before he was a radical, and he took up poetry years before he turned to pamphleteering. Only one of his poems was ever published: a sonnet in his high school yearbook. The banner he raises is of sympathy, not social revolution:

And then when all is past and darkness come
Men hearing the words that I have said
Shall say: "Here is another heart like ours
That spoke for those who spoke not and were dumb."[30]

•

"I was a politically conscious schoolboy of nine when America entered the First World War," Stone once wrote. "A young Irish Catholic friend and I . . . had been the only opponents of intervention." Whether or not this picture of a pint-sized Eugene Debs is factually correct, there is no doubt the war contributed to Isadore's growing sense of isolation. Not over the conflict with the Central Powers, since he was, he recalled, "caught up in the general enthusiasm which greeted the declaration of war, when frankfurters were patriotically renamed 'liberty sausages' and no decent American would play Bach or Beethoven." And his isolation at school was already well established. What was new was an awareness of tension in his own family—often with himself at the center.[31]

The war years were good years for the United Department Store. Rationing imposed its own challenges—Mrs. Feinstein sent the boys from shop to shop in search of a little extra sugar for her baking. But the wartime measures and the boom in the Camden shipyards also sent a steady stream of customers to the Feinsteins. Family fortunes didn't change overnight, and Bernard was no spendthrift. Discarded sewing patterns, Max recalled, were still "consigned to our bathroom. We never saw rolls of toilet paper until we moved away from the store." The family still rented out one of the upstairs bedrooms to a dentist, a Pennsylvania Dutchman named Orville Meland whose German helped broaden Isadore's Yiddish. As his business continued to grow, however, Bernard found himself relying more and more on his wife and sons. Soon Katy was spending so much time in the store that the family hired a full-time maid.[32]

Unlike his brother Max, who delighted in helping behind the counter, sweeping and washing the wooden floor, and carefully "dressing" the display windows—"you crawled in, set up your front display, and slowly backed out, filling the space as you went"—Izzy was a sullen and unwilling salesman. Told to *gib actung*—to watch the customers and make sure nothing was stolen—he often would be found reading instead. The boy's unmistakable disdain for the shopkeeper's life frequently brought down his father's wrath upon his head. His mother nearly always came to Isadore's defense.

Katy Feinstein adored her eldest boy. On Friday nights, when Katy, who didn't share her husband's atheism, lit Shabbat candles and the family said the traditional Sabbath prayers, she always made sure her firstborn got the choicest parts of the chicken. "Izzy was Mom's favorite," Max remembered. It was Katy who sent the boys into Camden for Hebrew lessons at Beth El Synagogue.* At first Bernard also indulged his eldest. He

---

*The rabbi who tutored the boys, Solomon Grayzel, later had his expert testimony cited in *Abington v. Schempp* (1963), the Supreme Court decision declaring Bible reading and the Lord's Prayer in public schools to be unconstitutional.

even arranged for him to receive additional Hebrew tuition from his brother, Shumer.

As a grown man, Stone fondly recalled "the memory of a warm home, the smell of cooking and books—there were always books aplenty at Uncle Shumer's. There was loveable Tanta Elka coaxing you to eat more, and Uncle Shumer, framed always in a certain majesty, calm, dignified, patient—a veritable Jove of an uncle." To an admiring small boy, this uncle was an ideal surrogate father: "full of the grandest stories, answering the hardest questions . . . When God walked with the sons of men, He must have walked with such as my Uncle Shumer." Stone would never describe his own father in such heroic terms.[33]

Bernard was certainly capable of exuberance. When the armistice was announced ending the Great War, he ran across Haddon Avenue to the volunteer firehouse to toll out the news on the fire bell, cheerfully paying the $5 fine for a false alarm. He was also interested in less momentous events, taking both the *Camden Courier* and the Yiddish paper *Der Tag* (The Day). "You could always tell the politics of a Jewish household in those days by which Jewish paper they subscribed to," Stone once explained. "If they were Communists they got the *Freiheit*; if they were socialists they got the *Forvitz*, the *Forward*; if they were religious they got the *Morning Journal*; if they were liberal they got the *Tag* . . . We took the *Tag*." In his father's case, the choice of paper may have had less to do with politics than family loyalty; Max Sobolofsky, who edited the *Tag* until his death in 1920, was Bernard's first cousin—a fact that, significantly, he seems never to have mentioned to his fractious firstborn.[34]

Bernard could be generous as well. "I remember my father taking us to Philadelphia to see the Yiddish Art Theatre," Stone told an interviewer, relishing the memory of Romain Rolland's *Wolves* and Sholem Asch's *God of Vengeance*. Outward displays of affection were rare, but Max remembered being favored with "skates that were always the best to be had and a bicycle and an expensive leather jacket." Such gifts, he knew, were "the benefit of Pop's experience and problems with Izzy." Their younger brother Louis put the matter succinctly: "Izzy and his father did not get along."[35]

The boy's reluctance to help out in the store, his pointed lack of interest in "the business," was one source of tension. Bernard and Katy's frequent quarrels may have been another. As he became more successful,

Bernard began looking for new business opportunities, leaving the day-to-day running of the store in Katy's hands, a turn of events she bitterly resented. Most ordering was done from salesmen who visited the store on their rounds, but two or three times a month Katy would have to "fill in." Bundling baby Louis under her arm, she would set off by trolley to Camden, take the ferry to the foot of Market Street in Philadelphia, then proceed by subway or another trolley to the wholesalers in Little Russia to replenish the store's stock of shoes, overalls, trousers, dresses, hats, or yard goods. Each time she'd return exhausted from the effort. "She would cry that her feet were sore and her bunions throbbing," Louis remembered. "Yet there were customers to be waited on and, behind the store, cooking to be tended."

There is no evidence that Katy and her beloved Izzy explicitly encouraged each other's resentments. It was years before the full extent of Katy's distress became known. But that the boy chafed under his father's authority was obvious. Fortunately, that authority was frequently in abeyance. Every summer Katy took the boys away for a few weeks, either to a small lakeside inn nearby or to Atlantic City, where they usually stayed at the Majestic Hotel. It was there, under a table in the hotel parlor, that the fourteen-year-old Isadore came upon a stack of back issues of the *Nation* and the *New Republic*. Whether the credit for inspiration goes to Herbert Croly's "just far enough left of the liberal consensus to be stimulating" *New Republic* or Oswald Garrison Villard's marginally racier *Nation*, or neither, somehow the boy had found his vocation.[36] Here were Mark Van Doren and Edmund Wilson, Lincoln Steffens, Ludwig Lewisohn, Walter Lippmann—all of them "making good," all of them writing "good English." And some of them were Jews.

Bernard's asthma also gave his son periodic breaks from paternal authority. The search for a healthier climate once sent Bernard on a cruise to Central America; another time he spent a few weeks recovering his breath amid the White Mountains of New Hampshire. Shortly after Isadore's fourteenth birthday, when his father left on yet another of his convalescent journeys, the boy wasted no time. With the help of a few school friends and the indulgence of a bemused local printer who "opined between meditative squirts of tobacco juice that I would come to a bad end," the *Progress* was born.[37]

Two names were listed in the first issue as "Owners and Editors":

Isadore B. Feinstein and Gerhard Van Arkel. Tall, confident, popular, and descended from a famous general in the French and Indian Wars, Garry Van Arkel, in many ways young Feinstein's antithesis, was his closest, perhaps his only, childhood friend, and the two remained friends for more than sixty years. Every morning the two of them walked to school together—"the long and the short of it," their classmates said. In volume one, number one, the division of labor was roughly even, with Van Arkel contributing a note on recent German inventions and a serialized story about a bicycle racer. But any doubts about who was running the show were dispelled in the next month's issue.[38]

The masthead of the March 1922 issue of the *Progress* proclaims Isadore B. Feinstein to be "Editor-in-Chief, Business Manager, Advertising Manager," and superintendent of "The Scrap Head," the paper's humor section. Van Arkel has been demoted to "Assistant Editor, Literary Editor" while another crony, Francis Fitzpatrick (probably the other World War I dissenter), is listed as "Special Articles." Volume one, number two also includes three poems by Gwynneth Walker, a shy, bookish Welsh girl who, like the editor in chief, "never had a date in high school," and who, like both Feinstein and Fitzpatrick, lived on the unfashionable east side of town. Despite the increase in personnel (and in pages, from six to twelve), the *Progress* was less a *journal des refusés* than a one-man band. The layout, with its conservative type and format—the main front-page headline reads EDITORIALS—comes straight from the liberal weeklies. The content, as in the first issue, is perhaps most sympathetically described as idiosyncratic. One thing it wasn't, the editor in chief's later claims notwithstanding, was radical.

"I am," he declared in an article hailing the Woodrow Wilson Foundation, "neither a Democrat nor a Republican. This paper is a freelance in politics, but I must say to the disconcernment [*sic*] of some of my readers that while Wilson was the thinker, and . . . Harding is the small-town provincial . . . even he too is imbued with the same idealist enthusiasm that urged Wilson onward." Leaving aside the naïve assessment of Warren Harding, the young editorialist's portrait of Wilson contains not a hint of the contempt that radicals felt for the president who, having campaigned for reelection in 1916 on a peace platform, promptly committed the United States to war. Nor is there a suggestion of rage at the idealist who condoned the arrest, conviction, and imprisonment on a trumped-up "espionage" charge of the Socialist Party leader Eugene Victor Debs, and who also slipped the leash on Attorney General A. Mitchell Palmer's notorious Red Scare, when in the wake of the Bolshevik revolution in Russia thousands of American radicals and pacifists were arrested and hundreds deported. Instead, we have a martyr, "crucified on the cross of politics."[39]

More than half a century later, Stone's admiration was undimmed. Wilson, he told a young interviewer, is "still one of my heroes. I know all of the bad things about him, but he still adds up as a great man, great president." Besides the League of Nations and "the enormous amount of progressive legislation" in Wilson's first term, Stone cited Wilson's manner: "He spoke with dignity, and didn't talk down. Greatness is a quality, it's an imponderable. And when you see it, you know it's there, it's hard to describe, but it's real . . . Woodrow Wilson had it. And Roosevelt, Franklin D. Roosevelt had it. But no other president I've seen had it."

One figure Stone did change his views about was Mohandas Gandhi. "The American Negro needs a Gandhi to lead him, and we need the American Negro to lead us," he was to write prophetically in 1955, and in his later life he often described himself as an early supporter of Gandhi. But he was less admiring in 1922, when, in the midst of the first satyagraha campaign against British rule, the cocky teenager assured his readers, "If there is any knifing to be done in India, Gandhi will do it."[40]

Despite its shortcomings, the paper sold well. Possibly it was the Literary Department that attracted readers. Here, in addition to syndicated stories the young editor ordered through the mail, which came in lead strips he cut apart with a hacksaw before taking them to the printer, appeared such fictional works as "Love vs. Pugilism" by Isadore Feinstein. Once again the tone is self-assured, though now in the guise of a hard-boiled newshound: "At that time I happened to be a reporter on the New York Morning Journal. I was green, eager for a story. It was not a case of enthusiasm, it was a case of necessity. If I did not get a story I would surely be canned."

Or perhaps the people of Haddonfield were moved to pity (or amusement) by the sight of the bespectacled publisher furiously pedaling his bike through town, trailed by his nine-year-old brother, the two of them struggling to carry heavy stacks of papers to the train station to be foisted on commuters en route to Camden or Philadelphia. Every weekday

morning that winter, Izzy and Max were there at the station, selling papers. By the second issue the price had risen to 3¢ a copy; the editor also
offered to pay contributors 25¢ for a column of material. By the third issue, there was even a notice optimistically offering a full year's subscription for 25¢. Alas, it was not to be.

In volume one, number three, the editor saw progress everywhere triumphant: "William Jennings Bryan's new role as a modern Torquemada
failed," the paper crowed, "when the Kentucky Legislature turned down
the bill to prohibit the teaching of Darwinism, agnosticism, atheism
and evolution in the public schools." Traditions were questioned: "Why
should a party stay in power when its only purpose is to stay in power?
Parties are no longer the organ of a part of a people, they have become
simply hereditary things like blue eyes and cancer." Shibboleths were
sent packing: "It is about time for a few changes in our over-revered constitution," thundered the future First Amendment fanatic. "Why not give
the President the powers of a premier?" the future scourge of presidents
proposed modestly. "Give him the power to dissolve Congress and ask for
another election."

Though Van Arkel was still on the masthead, the *Progress* was now
"owned and published by Isadore B. Feinstein." The responsibilities of
sole proprietorship left him no time for fiction, and a serial from the
McClure syndicate filled the gap. The paper also left its editor with little
time for his schoolwork. He received failing grades for the semester in
English composition and geometry. His father, returning from his convalescence to find that his eldest son had become a newspaperman who
thought of the store as his newsroom (the third issue listed the store's
phone number in the masthead), was livid. A huge ad urging "Buy at The
United Department Stores and Get Your Money's Worth" made little
impression on Bernard, who declared the paper closed. "The Big-Town
Round Up"—the serial adventures of "the most likeable puncher who
ever rode through sagebrush," promised in the May issue—had to be
postponed indefinitely.[41]

The April issue was the last of Feinstein's *Progress*. Bernard's authority
extended that far. But if he hoped to turn his son's attention back to
school, he was to remain disappointed. In his junior year, the boy failed
English, French, and first aid, and passed Latin only by the skin of his
teeth. "I had four years of high school Latin and I absolutely hated it.

They were cramming it down my throat—here I was, a bookworm and a lover of poetry, hating Latin!" he recalled. Outside the classroom, he'd read happily for hours; inside the classroom, he had a reputation as a hopeless oddball. Captain of the chess club in his sophomore year, by his senior year he had as little as possible to do with his fellow students. Even the senior trip to Washington, D.C., held little pleasure for him. On a visit to the Library of Congress he tried to impress his classmates by wagering he could ask for a book the library didn't have. He won the bet with a work of Chinese philosophy (years later he realized he'd misspelled the author's name), but his pedantry didn't win him any friends. "He was so intellectual," one classmate recalled, "and we were interested in having a good time."[42]

•

One afternoon, around the time his father put an end to the *Progress*, Isadore was working behind the counter in the store when he got into an argument with a customer. Her name was Jill Stern and though she lived in an imposing brick house just down Main Street, she and her family rarely came into the shop. The Sterns preferred to place their orders by telephone, and their penchant for having a single spool of thread or a packet of needles delivered was something of a running joke among the Feinsteins. The Sterns were also considered faintly ridiculous for another reason: Though they were Jews, they attended the local Quaker meeting and sent their children to the Friends' School.

Just how the dispute began is unknown, but soon Isadore was berating Mrs. Stern for being "an assimilationist" while she was taxing him with ignorance of Jewish history. Taken by the boy's spirit and struck by his obvious intelligence, Jill Stern made her young antagonist an offer: "Come up to our house some time. We have a lot of books."[43]

At first glance, Juliet Lit Stern—or "Big Jill," as she was known at home—made an unlikely teacher. Her uncles owned Lit's, the largest department store in Philadelphia. Her husband, J. David Stern, was publisher of the *Camden Courier*. With her own two children she could be distant, peremptory, difficult. But she had reserves of patience as well. A few years earlier, when the family lived in Springfield, Illinois, her son Tommy had a young friend named Robert Fitzgerald. Jill Stern taught the future translator of Homer how to read. Now she turned her formidable energy to the education of Isadore Feinstein.

She started by lending him books. But she also talked with him about his reading, argued with him, even gave him gifts. First Heinrich Graetz's massive *History of the Jews*, then collections of literature and the history of art. Most important, she took him almost as seriously as he took himself. Her encouragement was rewarded by a kind of puppyish devotion. He wasn't in love with Mrs. Stern—she was too much older and too matronly for that. And for all his brashness, he was still quite shy in some things. But he spent more and more time in the Sterns' library and less and less time behind the counter of his parents' store.[44]

Though his absences were noted—and resented—by his younger brother, his parents did not object. His mother's indulgence he could always count on. And while his father remained bitter that his oldest son showed no desire to follow in his footsteps, for Bernard, too, the world beyond the United Department Store was beginning to beckon. His son was besotted with books. Bernard chased a different grail: land. In the spring of 1923, in partnership with Isaac Milask, who owned the town's ice cream parlor, Bernard bought his first lot. By the end of the year he'd bought four more—some with his landsman Milask, some on his own. The news that a bridge was to be built over the Delaware River linking Camden and Philadelphia set off a South Jersey land boom as frenzied as the market in Miami frontage, and Bernard may have simply been too busy getting rich to keep Isadore penned behind the counter. By June, Bernard had made enough money for a down payment on a lot in the prestigious Haddon Estates section of town, not for speculation but as the site of his family's future home.[45]

When the *Public Press*, the local weekly whose print shop had also produced the *Progress*, offered its former client a job as high school correspondent, this time his father had no objection. Soon Isadore moved to the *Post-Telegram*, daily rival to the *Courier*, where they needed someone to cover the high school teams. And so, like Ben Hecht, Damon Runyon, and Ernest Hemingway, Isadore Feinstein began his professional newspaper career as a sportswriter.

Hopeless as an athlete, handicapped even as a fan, as a reporter he was a natural. On his first assignment, a basketball game, "I got there in the middle . . . at the half," he remembered later. Bad practice for a sportswriter, but then what police reporter ever arrives before the crime? "I began by asking, 'What's the object of the game? Show me what they do. What are the goals? Was there anything dramatic?'" Versed in the essentials and with a quick fill on the first half, "I wrote a very good story— very colorful." He was paid 10¢ an inch, but the real payoff was being back in print.

Then, one Saturday night toward the end of his junior year, he had a visitor at the store: J. David Stern. Big Jill's husband had heard so much about this extraordinary young man that he'd come to see for himself. Stern had produced his own mimeographed newspaper as a boy, and he may have recognized his younger self in the awkward yet oddly cocky Jewish teenager. He also probably noticed that the Feinsteins' store was just across the street from Haddonfield's fire station, police station, and town hall—an ideal location for news gathering. "Would you like to be my Haddonfield correspondent?" he asked. Would he! From that moment, Bernard's influence on his son was at an end. From now on, it was Stern whose approval the young Feinstein sought, and Stern whom he would battle for his independence. The approval came almost immediately.

"The second day of the job, I didn't have any news . . . and I ran into Mr. Pennypacker of the historical society." The society was trying to raise money to repair a plaque commemorating Elizabeth Haddon. Could the young reporter help? Telling the story later in life, Stone said he "wrote a story about how an elderly gentleman who had been campaigning to raise money to fix up the plaque was horrified one night when he thought he saw the ghost of Elizabeth Haddon try to polish it up." He claimed to have been afraid this fabrication would cost him his job but also claimed that the story ended up "atop page one with a two-column head and a byline," an unlikely triumph given that in the 1920s the *Courier* hardly ever used bylines in news stories. Whether the grown-up newspaperman's account of his first "pipe job" is itself partly fictional matters less than his evident glee in the telling, and in his success. He may have been an apprentice, but he was no acolyte. A newsroom, he knew even at the age of fifteen, is not a church.[46]

Nor was it a classroom, and for this, too, young Feinstein had reason to be grateful. His senior year was a series of humiliations. His grades had improved, with "Excellent" marks in English and ancient history, but his overall average was only "Fair." He graduated forty-ninth in a class of fifty-four, and his ambition to attend Harvard, printed next to his picture in the yearbook, had to be abandoned. The birth in May of his sister, Judith, might have protected him from his parents' disappointment, but there was no buffer to soften his classmates' ridicule. "The sad part about his 'wisdom,'" the *Shield* noted mockingly, "is that we Seniors find it too profound for our mental capacity to grasp." Thanks to open admissions for area high school graduates, he managed to gain a place at the University of Pennsylvania.

"Why do you want to go to college?" Stern asked him. "That's a waste of time for somebody like you. You ought to work for me." But he was already working for the *Courier*. And Stern, who liked to style himself a tough newsman, was, as his young protégé knew, a graduate of Penn and the University of Heidelberg. "Knowledge is power" was the motto the sixteen-year-old reporter chose for his page in the *Shield*. Now he wanted the kind of knowledge he couldn't find in a newsroom. He decided to major in philosophy.[47]

•

Though its football team did compete in the Ivy League, the University of Pennsylvania in 1924 had very little in common with institutions like A. Lawrence Lowell's Harvard or Columbia under Nicholas Murray Butler. Most of the 1,250 members of the class of 1928 were commuters, and if Penn's policy of taking any local high school graduate prepared to pay the $400 tuition meant that, unlike F. Scott Fitzgerald's Princetonians, few Pennsylvanians would be instantly recognizable from the way they stood at a country club bar, it also meant that rather more of them were Jews. At precisely the moment when elite colleges were imposing restrictive quotas to keep Jews out, as Lowell did at Harvard, Penn had perhaps the highest concentration of Jews in the Ivy League.

"Concentration" is the right word. Though the "A" houses, the fraternities that dominated campus social life, had little in common with Harvard's patrician "final" clubs, Yale's secret societies, or Princeton's elegant eating clubs, they were similarly and firmly restricted to gentiles. Since Jews were welcome to enroll at Penn, but any Jew seeking a place on the football team or a position on the *Daily Pennsylvanian* would be rebuffed, Penn's Jewish students tended to congregate in a few places: Those with social inclinations and money joined "B" houses, the polite name for Penn's Jewish fraternities; the rest sought refuge in various arts groups.[48]

As a freshman, Isadore Feinstein had neither money nor social ambition. Some members of his class were to achieve later distinction, among them William Brennan, a future justice of the Supreme Court. Feinstein knew none of them. Instead, taken ill at the end of his first semester, he withdrew from the university without having completed a single course or having made a single friend.

When he returned to the campus in September 1925, he threw himself into his studies, taking two advanced English courses—and receiving "Distinguished" marks in both—as well as French, history, and philosophy. His inability to pass trigonometry, however, was a persistent reminder of his past difficulties. There were fresh social humiliations as well. In the spring of his sophomore year, he put his name down on the list of applicants to the Philomathean Society, a campus literary group. Candidates were required to give a talk on the author of their choice; Izzy's subject was Robinson Jeffers, whose first book of poems, *Roan Stallion*, had been published that fall.[49]

He began in a halting voice. Short, chubby, with a round dimpled face behind thick glasses, his hair unkempt and shirttails hanging out, he was not an impressive speaker. Nor was Jeffers a conventional choice for this self-selected band of young aesthetes, though it is easy to see what drew this particular reader. Jeffers's ecstatic connection with nature, his bold appropriation of classical themes in poems like "The Tower Beyond Tragedy," and his firm assurance that

> *Sports and gallantries, the stage, the arts, the antics of dancers*
> *The exuberant voices of music,*
> *Have charm for children but lack nobility; it is bitter earnestness*
> *That makes beauty . . .*

were all in keeping with his young admirer's deepest beliefs. Though the verse was well beyond Izzy's competence, the sentiment expressed in "Woodrow Wilson (February 1924)"—the conviction that "Your tragic quality / Required the huge delusion of some major purpose to produce it"—was not.

Intoxicated by the poet's sprung rhythms and clashing consonants, Izzy never noticed he was losing his audience. No record exists of his talk, no way to know whether he read to them from "Shine, Perishing Republic":

> *While this America settles in the mould of its vulgarity, heavily*
> *thickening to empire,*
> *And protest, only a bubble in the molten mass, pops and sighs out,*
> *and the mass hardens*

If he did, perhaps he drew some consolation from the poet's advice: "boys, be in nothing so moderate as in love of man, a clever servant, insufferable master," for when he finished his rambling presentation, the tense silence was broken only by a single pair of hands applauding. These belonged to Seymour Blankfort, a tall, skinny, well-dressed New Yorker from a wealthy family who'd bought his own copy of *Roan Stallion* a few weeks earlier.[50]

While the candidate withdrew to College Hall, his fellow undergraduates voted by putting white or black balls into a box. All but three were black. Blankfort, one of the three, volunteered to break the news. "I told him that I admired his speech, that I was also a partisan of Jeffers, but that too many of the other members had not yet heard of the poet," he recalled.

What Blankfort didn't say is that he suspected anti-Semitism might have been a factor. Although "there were a few Jewish members, among them my roommate Seymour Siegel—I worried lest Izzy's appearance might be held against him . . . Moved by the look of disappointment on Izzy's face, and knowing that he was a commuter student from Camden, I invited him to use my room at the dorm any time he wanted to. We shook hands and he left."

Early the following Sunday, Blankfort "was awakened by a knock on the door." It was Izzy. "I scarcely recognized him in my half-sleep as he invited me to have breakfast with him at the Horn and Hardart's on Broad Street . . ."

Chatting on the way to the restaurant, Blankfort realized he'd found a kindred spirit. "Izzy was the fullest alive person I'd met up to then. He exclaimed over every bird call and the morning sky over the Schuylkill River; he talked of the great things he had been reading, Hardy's poetry as well as Jeffers', Livy, Horace—he loved Horace. And Gibbon's history."

After breakfast, as they walked along the river, Isadore showed Blankfort his method for expanding his Latin vocabulary. "In one pocket he had slips of paper with Latin on one side and the English translation on the other. As we walked he took the slips out, one by one, glanced at both sides and put the slips in the pocket on the other side of his jacket."[51]

Feinstein, who'd been spending his days alone in the library and his nights working at the *Courier*, gained more than just a friend who shared his interest in advanced poetry. Socially polished and intellectually confident, Sy Blankfort had made himself the center of a circle of bright young men (and a few women) who were passionate about theater, music, politics, and poetry—and for whom passionate talk about all these things was the cord that bound them together.

Aside from Blankfort and his roommate, and their fellow New Yorkers Sidney Cohn and Shepard Traube, there were the Philadelphians Walter Hart, Samuel Lipshutz, Chester Rabinowitz, and now, Isadore Feinstein. All of them were Jews. Cohn was studying law; Lipshutz, who changed his name to Grafton, was soon to sell his first essay to the *American Mercury*, the bible of undergraduate sophistication. Traube and Hart were committed to the theater. Blankfort, interested in everything, also acted as a kind of older brother to the group's mascot, Nathalie Bodanskaya, a street urchin from New York City's Lower East Side whose singing in the Henry Street Settlement had won her a scholarship to the Curtis Institute in Philadelphia. Brought into the group by Blankfort, Izzy soon became its acknowledged intellectual star.

Partly, his authority came from his reading, particularly when the talk turned to politics. "He was a confirmed socialist," Blankfort recalled, "who had read Hegel and Marx; naturally he despised Hoover and was hopeful about the Soviet Union." Mildred Gilbert, who came into the group as Sidney Cohn's girlfriend and stayed to marry Shepard Traube, remembers Izzy being "so well informed about everything." But the force of his personality was equally important.

"What impressed me most," said Blankfort, "was his great spirit and vast reading; he had an independent and stubborn point of view about things." Newspaper work also added to his cachet. The rest of the group might be learning about the world through books and in the classroom; Izzy was attending night school at the university of the streets, or at least the copydesk. Blankfort wrote plays at Penn, Traube directed, and Hart acted, but Izzy was reviewing Shaw's *Captain Brassbound's Conversion* as drama critic for the *Camden Courier*. "The play, already grown old-fashioned and of little interest in its theme . . . is yet as pleasing and mirth-provoking a comedy as that skillful craftsman Shaw could create."[52]

The cultivated air of sophistication was mostly façade. Accompanying Sidney Cohn on a trip to New York in the summer of 1926, Isadore rode the subway for the first time, all the way to the end of the line and back again, then reported, "Hey, you can go all day long for just a nickel!" Returning to Camden, he panned *Six Characters in Search of an Author*: "Luigi Pirandello has taken the good old-fashioned blood and thunder melodrama, covered its nakedness with the cloak of a time-worn problem and decorated it with some scraps of little force and no originality." Then he boasted about it in a letter to Blankfort. He was trying very hard to impress a friend: "Went to a grand booze party Sunday night with Jack, Sid and brunette and met a nymphomaniac restauranteure (female of course in case you don't know what an N. is), a police chief, a doctor from Iowa and his bride and had a hell of a good time."[53]

His assignments at the *Courier*—and its sister paper the *Morning Post*—were mundane: general assignment, rewrite, Camden city hall. Aside from his stints on the drama desk, his biggest "plum" was to cover the opening of the Camden Bridge: "President Coolidge arrived shortly after 3:30 P.M., stepped out of his automobile while Mrs. Coolidge remained inside, shovelled six spadefuls of dirt around a Vermont maple sapling on the plaza, smiled, climbed back into his car, and left Camden at 3:55 P.M. No one present heard the president utter a single word during the brief ceremony." Yet he was having the time of his life.

"I get up at six every morning to go to work and get home around six thirty and believe me I'm too damned tired to do much studying," he wrote to Blankfort. Instead, he was becoming a person of influence: "If you're in Paris or if you get a chance for a good news story, write it and send it to me and I'll get you space rates on it." A man on easy terms with famous writers: "Saw [Benjamin] De Casseres in New York . . . we chatted till 1:30. Told me of going to see Jeffers in California and met another young poet Sam Loveman." But he hadn't forgotten his friends: "chance I will be Dramatic Editor of Camden Evening Post next season, if so you will have shot at dramatic criticism. Walter Hart I've seen several times . . . Plan him for staff if I get job."[54]

Though he admired a few members of Penn's philosophy department, they must have seemed cloistered indeed in comparison with de Casseres, an essayist, critic, and member of Alfred Stieglitz's Photo-Secession movement, who'd run for mayor of New York in 1915 on the Smash It ticket advocating legalized prostitution and gambling and the sale of liquor twenty-four hours a day. "Long live Socialists, Anarchists, Nihilists, Communists, Diabolists, Impressionists, and anybody anywhere who is in favor of something somehow somewhere sometime," de Casseres had written—a fair imitation of a bohemian credo.[55]

For young Feinstein, bohemianism was a pose, but it was a pose he worked at. "My brother . . . used to wear his hair long and these four-in-hand ties with a very big knot," Louis Stone recalled. "This caused some consternation with my father. Especially because he didn't get those ties from my father's store. He went to Wanamaker's [in Philadelphia], and my father felt Izzy was saying the store wasn't good enough for him."

To his generation of college students, wide ties were a kind of badge of nonconformity—as long hair, shaved heads, torn jeans, or nose rings would be for later generations. Nonconformity to what? That was still an open question. Their generation was, wrote Izzy's contemporary Malcolm Cowley, in "transition from values already fixed to values that had to be created. Its members . . . were seceding from the old and yet could adhere to nothing new; they groped their way toward another scheme of life, as yet undefined; in the midst of their doubts and uneasy gestures of defiance they felt homesick for the certainties of childhood." If their allegiances were still mostly unformed, their aversions were more pronounced. They were avid "debunkers," a word that entered the language in 1923. "Civilization is barbarism clothed and housed," wrote Isadore Feinstein in his sole contribution to the *Junto*, Penn's literary magazine (S. Blankfort, editor). "Virtue is fashionable vice," he announced. "Truth is a lie grown respectable." Respectability was precisely what he didn't want.[56]

Describing to Blankfort his adventures with "a sweet little brunette who works on the paper, has a deuced lot of sound sense, lives utterly out of my world—beauty, dizziness, etc.—has a lovely body, is hot as hell," he concluded, "and I'm going to drop her soon for fear the thing's getting too serious. I'd love to have her as a mistress but she's not the kind who was made for it (not enough intellect, independence) born to be a wife and mother." Which was another item he could do without. Or so he thought.

•

If Philadelphia's bohemians and bourgeoisie had any common ground, it was the stretch of Broad Street outside the Academy of Music. There, every Saturday afternoon during the concert season, the line would form for 50¢ gallery seats. Disheveled college students, proper housewives, cultured clerks, and wide-eyed worshippers of the Philadelphia Orchestra's charismatic conductor Leopold Stokowski—or "Stokey," as he was affectionately known among initiates—gathered for a period of enforced fraternization.

In the fall of his third year at Penn, Isadore Feinstein found himself on the line with a classmate waiting for two girls. "We were supposed to be meeting someone else," remembered Helen Goldberg. Though Izzy was a last-minute substitute, he made an immediate impression on Helen's friend, Esther Roisman. "I could tell by the expression on her face she was taken with him," she said. "He made quite a fuss over her and asked her to go out the next night."[57]

Esther Roisman was eighteen, the oldest daughter of a moderately prosperous west Philadelphia businessman. "My father was president of the Home Preserving Pickling Company," said Esther's sister Jean. "That means he had a truck driver and a secretary and two girls who would fill the jars with pickles—and ketchup. We were competing with Heinz." A dark-haired, dark-eyed beauty whose mother had died when she was eleven, Esther had lots of beaux. "Young men would pick her up in big cars," said Jean, "and they'd go into the city to parties. And suddenly she was going with this funny-looking guy with very thick glasses and carrying a ton of books."

Thanks to his summer of newspaper work, Izzy owned a Tin Lizzie. "The kind you had to crank," said Jean, who was not impressed. Neither was Mr. Roisman. "Her father criticized his appearance," Helen remembered. "He didn't look like anything," recalled Eleanor Milgram, another school friend of Esther's. "He was very small and skinny and he wore very thick glasses. He was very unimpressive. Her father just didn't like him. He would not permit him to come to the house . . . so they would meet at her friends' homes."[58]

What did Esther see in him? A picture taken a few years later shows a man not entirely bereft of physical charm. With his full mouth, intense gaze, wavy hair, cigarette smoke curling elegantly upward past a wide, thoughtful brow, Izzy looks more like a young poet than a newspaperman. That may indeed have been his appeal. Other young men sent her flowers. He sent her verses:

I who kiss you cannot tell
People of your honeyed mouth;
Northern birds a secret keep
Their winter's refuge in the south.

Nor can I tell it in the wood
For there the bees might overhear
And leave their own flower-loves unkissed
To feed upon my dear.

Some of the twenty-year-old poet's efforts were silly:

Ah don' need no sugar, since ah met mah sweet,
Ah don' even need molasses foh mah buckwheat.

Some were more serious:

I am a dark place and you the light have driven out darkness
I am a sad room and you a glad song have come through the window
have driven out sadness.
. . . I am the beggared sky and you a spendthrift goddess have thrown
me a handful of silver stars.

All of them took him closer to the kind of commitment he'd scorned only a few months earlier.[59]

"Just finished Shaw's preface to *Getting Married*. Read it before you marry," he'd advised Blankfort the previous summer. "Wow of a lot of sense!"[60] Behind the Jazz Age diction lay a Jazz Age sensibility: pleasure-seeking, self-conscious, disillusioned. There wasn't, after all, such a huge gap, at least in intent, between Isadore Feinstein's carefully wrought paradoxes ("Civilization is barbarism clothed and housed") and Ernest Hemingway's declaration: "I was always embarrassed by the words sacred, glorious, and sacrifice." To the novelist, who paid for his illusions in a wartime field hospital, sham sentiment was "obscene." The young newsman came by his own detachment far less expensively, but he, too, wanted an end to pretense. Hence his enthusiasm for the Irish iconoclast. "What they call love," Shaw writes, "is an appetite which, like all other appetites, is destroyed for the moment by its gratification . . . [and] no profession made under its influence should bind anybody."

Romantic or rationalist? Anarchist or aesthete? In his reviews and in his letters to Blankfort, his tone is cool, his excitement tempered by irony. Perfect pitch for a newsman but less than adequate for lovemaking. His poems to Esther show another side: vulnerable, passionate, engaged. "This is just a bit like plunging into the dark," he writes in a letter accompanying two poems. "Sometimes I think: maybe by Saturday you'll have gotten over your liking for me and not care much about seeing me again. Can I phone you Thursday night?" Shaw's self-assured lover is nowhere in sight.

Even the young lover's taste in poetry accommodated contradictory ideals. He'd risk ostracism for a rule breaker like Robinson Jeffers or spend his early morning hours in the library wrestling with Thomas Hardy—"gnarled as oak trees, one grapples them with the mind," he wrote in praise of Hardy's verse—but whenever Sidney Cohn broke into a recitation of Swinburne's "The Garden of Proserpine," Izzy joined in happily:[61]

> From too much love of living,
> From hope and fear set free,
> We thank with brief thanksgiving
> Whatever gods may be
> That no life lives forever;
> That dead men rise up never;
> That even the weariest river
> Winds somewhere safe to sea.

Isadore Feinstein was not the first young man to find himself at odds with himself. Reporter, student, lover, cynic, poet, critic, free-thinking Jew—mostly he kept his multitudes contained. But it took effort, and sometimes the strain was too much. In 1926, he was sent to cover a meeting of the Camden Rotary Club. "There was a visiting professor speaking," he recalled years later. "He'd been to Italy and he was talking about the wonders of Fascism and how it made the trains run on time. And I was so angry I got up from the press table and denounced him . . . 'Why don't you tell the other side of the story?'—about the murder of [Giacomo] Matteotti."* The professor complained to the *Courier's* business manager, but thanks in part to David Stern's own antifascism, the young reporter kept his job. Still, a line had been crossed.

A year later he crossed the line again, this time by walking right out of the newsroom.[62] In the summer of 1927 a flu epidemic had left the *Courier* extremely shorthanded. So when Izzy asked if he could go to Boston to cover the executions of the celebrated anarchists Sacco and Vanzetti, scheduled for August 10, the city editor turned him down. The refusal was not for lack of interest in the case. Stern's *Courier* was the only paper in the Philadelphia area to favor the condemned radicals, but to the nineteen-year-old reporter this was no ordinary assignment. One way or another, he was going to Boston. "I quit the paper . . . and walked out of the city room with a $5 bill and an extra pair of socks to hitch-hike my way," he recalled.[63]

Like his debut as a sportswriter, Isadore Feinstein's entry onto the stage of radical politics occurred in medias res. Indeed, the failed robbery of a Bridgewater, Massachusetts, shoe company for which Bartolomeo Vanzetti was first convicted had taken place on Isadore's twelfth birthday, and he was only barely into his teens when the immigrant fishmonger Vanzetti and his friend the shoemaker Nicola Sacco were convicted of murdering the guard and paymaster during a holdup of another shoe company in South Braintree. Both men were anarchists, a fact that might have brought them to his notice, but he made no mention of the case in the *Progress* or, for that matter, in any of his few surviving letters, poems, or journalism from the period.

This is not unusual. The *New Republic*, the journal most consistently sympathetic to the condemned men, ran a single story on the case in 1924, none at all in 1925, and only one before May 1926, after which the

---

*An Italian socialist and opponent of Mussolini murdered in June 1924. Isadore Feinstein's interest in and knowledge of the affair stemmed from his acquaintance with Gaetano Salvemini, the anti-Fascist writer and historian who had fled Italy in 1925.

magazine ran ten more reports before the end of the year. Even Gardner Jackson, the young *Boston Globe* reporter whose involvement in the case began with the trial in 1921, didn't actually join the Sacco-Vanzetti Defense Committee until the summer of 1926. The vain struggle to save the two men, said Jackson, "subsequently became the major directional influence in my life."[64] By the summer of 1927, with the two anarchists in the shadow of the electric chair, their fate had become a cause célèbre around the world.

Walking off the job to keep vigil for the condemned men was also not so unusual. In Colorado, hundreds of miners quit in protest; in Rochester, New York, 16,000 workers answered the call for a general strike; in New York City, between 75,000 and 400,000 people stayed home from work on August 9. That same day police resorted to tear gas to quell rioting in Chicago and fought pitched battles with thousands of protesters marching on City Hall in New York and the American embassy in London. By the time Izzy reached New York, there was rumor of a reprieve; the stay was officially granted shortly before midnight on August 10.[65]

There are conflicting versions of Isadore Feinstein's efforts to be present at the Boston vigil.[66] But there is no mistaking the lasting significance of the young reporter's outraged sympathy. In the December 1971 final issue of *I. F. Stone's Weekly* (as in numerous previous interviews), he cited the episode as his first association with organized protest. Decades after the executions, Gardner Jackson could still remember "those early morning hours—the cool air, a sense of complete desolation." Feinstein was not Jackson; his involvement in the campaign to save Sacco and Vanzetti was much more peripheral—at most the matter of a few weeks. And yet we can see a definite turning point. In May, he'd sent a letter to Esther listing eight "Reasons for going to college." It was a tender polemic; he even mailed her applications. "People who can manage go to college," he declared. By November, he was a dropout himself. Soon afterward the former Shavian bachelor was engaged to be married.[67]

There is no neat causal connection between these events, yet it seems clear that Isadore Feinstein returned from New England a changed man. Before he'd been both idealist and cynic, no more serious about politics than he'd been about his weekend jaunts to Atlantic City. Passionate, yes, but not committed. Afterward, he—and a whole generation of young idealists—knew that in America, political dissent could have fatal consequences. More than that, he knew something a subsequent generation of young radicals would have to learn for themselves in Kent, Ohio, and Jackson, Mississippi: that the establishment was prepared to commit murder to preserve its hold on power.

Back in Philadelphia, his friend Sy Blankfort poured his grief and anger into a poem. "A Final Appeal" was published in *America Arraigned!*, a collection of verse protesting the verdict.[68] Though in distinguished company—Edna St. Vincent Millay and Witter Bynner were fellow contributors—Blankfort was not much of a poet:

> *Winds of the world give answer,*
> *Answer in sweeping song.*
> *Winds of the world, we ask you,*
> *How Long? How Long?*

Possibly the outrage was still too fresh. A year later, in Malcolm Cowley's "For St. Bartholomew's Eve," the tone is still frantic, blind with rage. Already, though, the grief has started to congeal into a cold, hard, angry defiance:

> *March on, O dago Christs, while we*
> *march on to spread your names abroad*
> *like ashes in the winds of God.*

It is this defiance—this sense of a commitment undertaken with full knowledge of the possible risks—that marked a generation of American radicals. "The effects of the Sacco-Vanzetti case," Cowley wrote in the 1930s, "continued to operate in a subterranean style, and after a few years they appeared once more on the surface."[69] Too young to know the Arcadian innocence of their Greenwich Village predecessors like Mabel Dodge or Floyd Dell, these "pre-depression radicals"[70] were neither dreamers nor economic determinists, at least not for long. The crucible of the coming Depression was to shape Isadore Feinstein along with the rest of them, though only to a point.

For his generation, neither poetry nor "planning" nor even "the proletariat" would ever be at the center of their politics. Their subject was power—brutal yet essential. For the best of this generation, the ambiguity would always be there. But they had few illusions about the fate of the powerless. "They have clubbed us off the streets," John Dos Passos wrote in *U.S.A.* "They are stronger." In the contrapuntal rhythms of Dos Passos's staccato sentences those desperate weeks in Boston became a kind of Passion:

> our work is over   the scribbled phrases   the nights typing
> releases the smell of the printshop the sharp reek of newsprinted
> leaflets   the rush for Western Union stringing words into wires
> the search for stinging words to make you feel who are your op-
> pressors America
>   America our nation has been beaten by strangers who have
> turned our language inside out who have taken the clean words our
> fathers spoke and made them slimy and foul
>   their hired men sit on the judge's bench they sit back with their
> feet on the tables under the dome of the State House they are ig-
> norant of our beliefs they have the dollars the guns the armed
> forces the powerplants
>   they have built the electricchair and hired the executioner to
> throw the switch
>   all right we are two nations

Dos Passos finished on a note of despair: "we stand defeated America."[71] For Isadore Feinstein, "the search for stinging words" was just beginning.

Two

PUBLISHER'S APPRENTICE

———•◆•———

We were all what Teddy Roosevelt stigmatized as muckrake journalists.
—I. F. Stone, 1982

The Depression came early to Philadelphia—softly, on stockinged feet, whispering of layoffs and lockouts, bread lines and bankruptcy. At first, in the Jazz Age clamor of Philadelphia's 1,100 bars, amid the short-skirted, flat-chested glamour of the city's defiantly wet downtown, the Depression was easy to overlook.

The policemen knew. In 1926, with the graft from Prohibition still flowing strong—strong enough so that the question of the day for the reporters who hung around City Hall was, "How rich is a rich policeman?" and the answer, "Any cop with a six-figure bank account"—4,000 families were evicted, mostly for defaulting on first mortgages.[1] Two years later, 9,000 families in the "City of Homes" had seen their belongings piled on the sidewalk. In 1929, when most of the country was still convinced the Wall Street crash was just a market correction, Philadelphia's finest officiated at 12,000 evictions.[2]

The millworkers knew, too. Textiles were Philadelphia's biggest industry, but by 1927 demand was so slow that one job would be finished before the next order came in.[3] Fashion was partly to blame. It didn't take much material to clothe a flapper; the fad for short skirts meant that the market for cotton socks sagged, too. And while the vogue for hardwood floors might have been good news in the Pacific Northwest, demand for Philadelphia broadlooms began to unravel.[4] As owners struggled to keep costs down in the face of competition from Southern producers unhindered by the need to pay a union wage, Philadelphia's weavers were told to stay home one day a week, then two days, then three.[5] Even the makers of seamless stockings, as essential for the soignée young woman as a beaded bag and cigarettes, felt the effects of falling prices. Lights were going out all along Allegheny and Richmond avenues as mill owners locked their gates and waited for better times. *Fortune* described an "invisible city-wide collapse that began in 1925."[6] In April 1929, more than 10 percent of Philadelphia's workers were already unemployed, and prosperity was not around the corner.[7]

Did Isadore Feinstein know what was coming? He had spent a few weeks after Sacco and Vanzetti's execution trying to get a job on a New England farm. But the beginning of the school year found him back in Philadelphia. At Penn, he managed to persuade the university to allow him to continue on general probation. The real difficulty lay in persuading himself that a college degree was worth the effort.

In his letter to Esther the previous May, he'd hinted at a certain ambivalence, even while encouraging her to apply. "Your fear that going to college may teach you more than is compatible with happiness is groundless," he assured her. "College is not that good." The same letter shows a disdain for credentials—"An ass plus an A.B. remains an ass"—but it is the disdain of a man for whom the credential remains within reach. He started his junior year taking courses in philosophy, economics, Latin, German, and the dreaded mathematics.[8]

He also had a new job. When "I came back to Philadelphia, [I] went around to the *Inquirer*—the Jersey editor was a Napoleonic little guy with glasses on a string. I said, 'Could you use a good man?' He bristled and said, 'I could use half a dozen,' and I said, 'Well, here's one.' So he hired me."[9] He still spent his mornings in the library. "I would leave school and go over to Camden to the office and do rewrites from 1:30 to about 5, hop the bus back to Philadelphia, sit on the copy desk and edit and write headlines for the Jersey edition until about 11 o'clock at night."[10]

On November 22 he left school for good. "It was just too much. I was making about 40 bucks a week—this was in 1927, and 40 bucks a week was a lot of money in those days."[11] His transcript says simply: "Withdrew (Financial)." In later years, Stone preferred to stress the lure of the newsroom: "I thought I might teach philosophy but the atmosphere of a college faculty repelled me; the few islands of greatness seemed to be washed by pettiness and mediocrity. The smell of a newsroom was more attractive."[12]

He could certainly have picked a more fragrant newsroom. Though it had not quite reached the nadir it was to attain in later years under the Annenbergs,* in 1927 the *Inquirer* was still an awful newspaper. Its days as chief cheerleader for the Philadelphia Police Red Squad were yet to come. Nor was the night rewrite desk of the paper's suburban edition a prime locale for *Front Page*–style human drama. But as a perch from which to observe the exercise in mass delusion that would constitute stand-pat Republicanism's response to the deepening Depression, the *Inquirer* was ideal. And in a city where, seven years and one union contract later, the minimum salary for a reporter was still only $20 a week, $40 a week was indeed a lot of money.[13]

Though he tended to emphasize his impatience with "the spinster atmosphere of a college faculty," it was the money that gave nineteen-year-old Isadore Feinstein if not the courage of his conviction, at least the wherewithal to follow his predilections.[14] His father was still busily buying property and in any case had neither the interest nor the authority to keep his oldest son in school. But it must have been a considerable boost to the young reporter's confidence to find himself so comfortably on his feet after walking out of David Stern's newsroom in August.

In the spring of 1928, an incident occurred that might have been calculated to dispel any lingering doubts about his decision to leave the academy. A young Penn instructor in philosophy, Solomon Auerbach, made a speech comparing the American and Soviet educational systems. After a viva voce by four senior members of his department, Auerbach was told his contract would not be renewed. "It is incompatible," explained the department chairman, Edgar Singer, "for a teacher to express his views on public issues and at the same time retain the critical state of mind necessary for research and teaching." Sy Blankfort was so outraged

---

*Moses Annenberg started out as hired muscle in the Chicago newspaper circulation wars of the early twentieth century, then parlayed a fortune from a racetrack wire service into ownership of the *Inquirer* in 1936. Like his sometime business associate Al Capone, Annenberg was eventually convicted on federal tax-evasion charges and died shortly after his release from prison in 1942. His son Walter, who had his own indictment on tax charges dismissed in exchange for his father's guilty plea, became a significant donor to the Republican Party and was appointed ambassador to Great Britain by President Richard Nixon.

he put a black-edged death notice for "Free Speech" on the opening page
of the *Junto*. He recalled, "A group of us were [Singer's] admiring students, among them . . . I. F. Stone. The fine reasonableness of [Singer's]
views as well as their breadth, the clarity with which he spoke and wrote
of Bruno, Vico and the moderns, and the liberalism with which he
weighed the great questions of justice and evil won our hearts as well as
our minds . . . We felt betrayed."[15]

That same issue of the *Junto* featured Isador [*sic*] Feinstein's "Paradoxical Meanderings of an Eclectic Plagiarist Obviously Suffering from
Metaphysical Inebriety," a fairly crude effort whose interest lies not in the
young writer's still unsuccessful attempt to hone an aphoristic style, but
in being his last piece of prose juvenilia. He wrote love poems for Esther.
He appears to have sent some poems to the *New Masses*.[16] In prose, however, he was now strictly professional. By the summer of 1928, Isidor
Feinstein (his byline) was back at the *Camden Courier* with a regular slot
in the paper's critical rotation. Theater, film, vaudeville, even the passing
circus ("Pepito . . . is clownishness raised to an art") drew his attention.[17]

For a man who would one day have to fill four pages a week with his
own opinions, it was an invaluable apprenticeship. Like any journalist, a
reviewer has to be able to get down what he sees, vividly and succinctly:
"She sings 'mammy songs' in the manner of an auctioneer and shouts 'kiss'
like a college cheer leader."[18] But unlike a legman out covering a fire, the
critic has to make sense of his own responses. And in an era when it was
"somehow discreditable for a reporter to show any sign of education and
culture," when, in H. L. Mencken's phrase, a newspaperman was considered "laudable when his intellectual baggage most closely approaches
that of a bootlegger," the review pages were largely exempt from such
strictures. The *Courier* was a middle-brow broadsheet, hence young
Feinstein's warning to readers considering an evening at Chekhov's *The
Sea Gull*: "Being Russian, it is a difficult play," but "a play that must
arouse sorrow, pity, wonder and understanding."[19] In a rave for Frank
Capra's *Submarine*, he found the underwater sequences "as good as anything in *Potemkin*, as fine as anything the movies have done."[20]

His reviews from the *Courier* show a young man exhibiting more ease
with himself and his culture than he actually feels but, of necessity, slowly
growing accustomed to his borrowed authority. From the very first, there is
the note of confident assertion: "Like certain persons who believe clothes
make the man, Max Reinhardt seems to think that lighting makes the

play."[21] As a novice, the pans may come more easily, but he can praise as well: "O'Neill has put Babbitt behind the footlights," he writes of *Marco Millions*, hailing the play's "poetic quality."[22] Stefan Zweig's *Volpone* is "better than Ben Jonson." The reviewer is trying on different voices: Zweig's Mosca is "a man in whom servitude and the deceits imposed by his master have bred a well-dissimulated bitterness."[23] George Farquhar's *The Beaux' Stratagem* has an impressive formality; in its time, the young critic quips, "Nobody said: 'Gee, kid, you're the pip,' and no girl answered after a blasé jab at a wad of gum to hide her flutters: 'Yeah? Say, who ya givin' the needles?'"[24]

With his critical manner slipping from Olympian to demotic, he was clearly still having a hell of a good time: "For the rustic Camdenite from, say, the bucolic fastnesses of the Third and Eighth wards and who has been reading about Philadelphia's graft probes, vice probes, gang probes, police probes and even probe probes, the picture at the Fox this week [*Me, Gangster*] might well have been named *Home Life in Philadelphia*."[25] Being well paid for working on his chops was pleasant enough; he also enjoyed his growing influence. Seymour Blankfort got to interview a Follies showgirl, while Walter Hart, appearing in a play reviewed by their friend Feinstein, protested that "Iz, not knowing much about acting, thought I was wonderful and . . . was foolish enough to write as much in his newspaper."[26] He was fortunate even in his enemies, and could boast of being banned from Philadelphia's Erlanger Theatre by Florenz Ziegfeld himself.[27]

On many of his first nights, he would pick up two house tickets at the box office, one for himself and one for Esther. Her family was slowly becoming resigned to the impetuous young man with thick glasses. One evening in 1928, the pair drove off to a different destination: a Socialist rally. The principal speaker was the party's new standard-bearer, Norman Thomas. Thomas's efforts during the 1926 Passaic textile strike had made him the hero of a famous New Jersey free-speech fight; he was an accomplished, inspiring orator. But for Esther, the climax of the meeting came when her escort rose to speak.[28]

•

When Isadore Feinstein joined their ranks, the Socialist Party was midway on a transit from obscurity to oblivion. Sixteen years earlier, with Eugene V. Debs heading the ticket, 879,000 Americans had voted Socialist; the party's rolls listed an all-time high of 118,000 members.

Debs had not won the election, of course. But the Socialists did manage to add the mayoralties of Butte, Montana; Berkeley, California; and Flint, Michigan to their long-standing control of Reading, Pennsylvania; and Milwaukee, Wisconsin. The thousand-odd Socialists elected in 1912 included state legislators, city aldermen, and one member of congress, Victor Berger of Wisconsin. Before World War I tore the party apart, J. A. Wayland's *Appeal to Reason* broadcast the Socialist message to more than 700,000 readers every week. In New York, the *Jewish Daily Forward*, with its circulation of 150,000, was the flagship of the party's foreign-language press. Across the country there were five Socialist dailies in English and eight in other languages; 262 English and 36 foreign-language weeklies; and twelve monthlies. But by 1928 these had gone.[29]

There is no need for a lengthy reprise of the lugubrious saga of factional battles, personality conflict, and genuine political courage that is the history of American socialism. Suffice it to say that when Isidor Feinstein joined the Camden local, there were fewer than 8,000 members "on the books" in the entire country, and nearly half of these were in foreign-language federations. New Jersey was so starved for recruits that the comrades elected their youngest member to the executive committee of the state party before he was even old enough to vote.[30]

Riven by the war, the Socialists had also been decimated by the 1919–20 Palmer Raids, when, without warning and without warrants, agents of the Justice Department's Bureau of Investigation (under the command of the young J. Edgar Hoover) orchestrated the largest mass arrest in American history, a dragnet that caught up more than 10,000 Communists, anarchists, Wobblies, pacifists, Socialists, and unaffiliated opponents of conscription. Foreign-born Reds such as Emma Goldman and her lover, the writer and anarchist Alexander Berkman, were simply deported; the Milwaukee congressman Victor Berger, duly reelected on the Socialist Party line in 1918, was convicted of sedition and sentenced to twenty years in prison. By 1928, the Socialist Party was further crippled by divisions between the surviving old guard, whose faith in "the inevitability of gradualism" made it suspicious of any form of activism, and, especially after the death of Debs in 1926, a younger, more militant generation centered around the charismatic Norman Thomas.[31]

Indeed, it was Thomas's first presidential campaign that drew the young newspaperman into the party. "I worked for Norman Thomas on the 1928 campaign. I had a very great admiration for Thomas because he knew an awful lot about America . . ." Stone recalled that he particularly "admired [Thomas's] capacity to deal with American problems in Socialist terms, but in language and specifics that made sense to ordinary Americans."[32]

As a wager on which track the locomotive of history would arrive, Stone's decision to join the Socialists was spectacularly ill-advised. But as a vehicle for his own entry into American political life, the Socialist Party was in many ways an inspired choice. Under Norman Thomas, the Socialists were embarked on a struggle whose goals were, at the time, scarcely less radical than those of the Communist Party, but whose language and approach owed far more to the Populists and other strands of indigenous American radicalism than to the lessons of bolshevism.

Despite his meteoric rise in the New Jersey hierarchy, Isidor Feinstein did not remain in the Socialist Party long enough to influence its ideological orientation. He was, however, exposed to what might be called the party's "movement culture,"[33] which at least among Thomas supporters was one of earnest engagement on the left, with little appetite for sectarian sniping. (The old guard were more suspicious of Communists and also more credulously attached to the American Federation of Labor.) As Thomas himself admitted, in the 1920s the Socialists would probably "have voted to join Lenin's new Communist International party had he not tried to dictate the rejection of our own leaders."[34]

This good-humored collaboration was worlds apart from the political cockfighting that shaped so many New York intellectuals on street corners in Williamsburg or the Bronx, or across the tables of the City College cafeteria. But then Camden wasn't New York. It wasn't even Philadelphia. "You see, in a small town there are only a few radicals," Stone recalled, "and you're all friends whether you're an anarchist, a communist, a socialist or whatever, and you regard the other people all as comrades."[35]

The fact that Stone began as a follower of the American Socialist Norman Thomas rather than the Russian Bolshevik Leon Trotsky or even the Machiavellian American Communist Jay Lovestone was to have a decisive influence on his own sense of the political landscape. In the 1960s, Stone and Thomas would rekindle a friendship that had been considerably affected by the cold war, but whatever the differences between the two men, certain articles of the Socialist creed remained with Stone for the rest of his life. The first was an affirmation that "the United States . . . was a stronghold of Utopian socialism even before Marx."[36] In a movement often derided as foreign, the Socialists' easy confidence in their native ground was, for the son of immigrants, a source of vital sustenance. It allowed Isidor Feinstein to feel as entitled as anyone to Floyd Dell's realization "that it is, astonishingly enough, we who are American: that Debs and Haywood [William "Big Bill" Haywood, leader of the Industrial Workers of the World, or Wobblies] are as American as Franklin and Lincoln."[37]

His baptism into the lees of American socialism also gave the young radical a conviction that, while others on the left might be (and often were) misguided, a fervent insistence on ideological purity was no way to make a revolution. Not that revolution was, in 1928, high on his list of priorities. Certainly no higher than good talk, good company, his own ambition, and his deepening romance with Esther. As it happened, there was one place in Philadelphia where a young Socialist could indulge a fondness for easygoing comradeship, literature, professional recognition, political discussion, and even young love all at the same time.

•

It may well have been the Socialist connection that first brought Isidor Feinstein to the Leofs' big "white brownstone" at 322 South 16th Street. Dr. Morris Vladimir Leof—known to all of Philadelphia's intelligentsia simply as "Poppa," except for his common-law wife, Jenny, who called him "M.V."—was the head of the city's Socialist Institute. An apprentice cigar maker who put himself through medical school by selling bananas, Poppa Leof held a regular Sunday night salon for radicals of any stripe.[38]

But it may also have been the theater that drew Izzy and Esther to 322. There were nights when virtually the whole of the Russian Inn, a restaurant on Locust Street near the Academy of Music popular with musicians and theater people, moved en masse to the Leofs' after closing time. Madelin Leof, Poppa's daughter, was a close friend of a young actress named Jo Blitzstein, whose brother Marc had been writing music for Jasper Deeter's experimental Hedgerow Theatre out in suburban Rose Valley. Deeter had employed practically all of Izzy's circle from Penn—Blankfort and Shepard Traube backstage, Walter Hart in several major roles—and was the beneficiary of numerous rave reviews in the *Courier*.

In May 1928, Maddie Leof stunned Philadelphia when she married not Marc Blitzstein, her contemporary in age, but his father, Sam, who promptly moved into 322.[39]

"Here," says one account of the period, "gathered the young intelligentsia in rebellion against parents who were illiterate and ran chicken stores and fruit stands."[40] Not all of those in attendance were young. "Everybody who came to Philadelphia who was anybody came to the Leofs'," said Samuel Grafton, at the time an editorial writer for the *Courier*'s sister paper, the *Philadelphia Record*.[41] "Clifford Odets read his plays sitting on the floor at 3 o'clock in the morning with all of us falling asleep. Sholem Asch was there. Stella Adler came. All the people there were either artists or friends of artists, that kind of people. And Esther and Izzy were there—a lot," recalled Jean Boudin, who was herself introduced to 322 by her sister.[42]

Just because they were sociable didn't mean the Leof-Blitzsteins weren't serious about their radicalism. The first racially integrated party in Philadelphia was held at 322. And John Frederick Lewis, the patrician owner of the Academy of Music, so admired Poppa Leof that he lent him the building from time to time for benefit concerts. If the heady mix of politics and culture that was to emerge in *Waiting for Lefty* and *The Cradle Will Rock* owed much to the atmosphere of 322, the house also served as an important way station for political refugees eager to alert Americans to the dangers of fascism. It was probably at 322 that Isidor Feinstein first encountered Gaetano Salvemini, the Italian historian and journalist who had spearheaded opposition to the *fascisti* and, now in exile in the United States, continued to organize resistance. Salvemini's 1927 speaking tour had a crucial influence on his fellow newspaperman's view of Mussolini.[43]

"In the twenties, despite the fact that we had a lot of Italians in Camden, the *Courier* was antifascist," Stone recalled, crediting his acquaintance with Salvemini and other exiles as helping to shape the paper's response. The Duce's American admirers extended far beyond Italian Americans. William Randolph Hearst gave the dictator a contract for twenty-six articles at $1,500 apiece—raised to $1,750 after the invasion of Ethiopia. Two Harvard professors, Irving Babbitt and George Santayana, both published paeans to Mussolini's leadership. The South Bend, Indiana, car manufacturer Studebaker named its 1927 model the

Dictator, while in Hollywood, Columbia Pictures released *Mussolini Speaks*, a film narrated by Lowell Thomas that took in $1 million at the box office, combining propaganda with profit. As late as 1933, an association of American Jewish publishers named the Fascist leader one of the world's twelve "greatest Christian champions" of Jews.[44]

The apprentice newsman's welcome by the regulars at 322 must have strengthened his confidence in his own judgment. Bohemians they might have been, but in philistine Philadelphia the denizens of 322 were the cream of the city's intellectuals, and his association with them may also have eased his acceptance by the Roismans. Esther's older brother, Charles, preferring photography to law, had already embarked on a lifelong involvement with the jazz scene in New York. Certainly the Roismans had become reconciled to the inevitability of their daughter's marriage, and on July 7, 1929, Esther and her young man stood together under a chuppah at Beth El Synagogue in Philadelphia and pronounced the seven blessings of the traditional Jewish wedding service.

The bride wore a white satin gown and a tulle veil, and carried a sheaf of calla lilies. The groom wore a tuxedo, with a white carnation in his lapel.[45] Jean Boudin, who was her sister's maid of honor, recalled that the couple were given $1,000 as a wedding present from the bride's family. "I remember she bought these red crystal glasses that were $15 apiece." If her sister's extravagance impressed itself in her memory of the time—the stock market crash was less than four months away—so did another aspect of the wedding festivities: "We had his family over, and I particularly remember the mother was very jolly and attractive."[46]

•

The Depression reached Camden the same way as everything else did—over the bridge from Philadelphia. In the frenzy of anticipation before the Camden Bridge opened to traffic in 1926, choice building lots had been changing hands for thousands of dollars a front foot. A local promoter, J. Robley Tucker, hired the electric news zipper at Times Square in New York to spread the message: "Greater Camden, The City of Opportunity." Hotels, office buildings, and factories were flung up on sheer speculation, and the county road gangs widening and repaving the old White Horse Pike brought a horde of small property developers in their wake.

"In the 1920s, every butcher, baker, and candlestick maker got into the real estate business," said Louis Stone. "My father built six stores in Haddonfield, ten stores and a theater in Clementon, and he bought land all along the White Horse Pike." While Izzy spent his spare moments writing speeches and memoranda for Norman Thomas, Bernard Feinstein's faith in speculative capitalism remained unshakable. When his partner Milask, perhaps heeding the signs of impending collapse, decided to withdraw from the Camden property market, Bernard simply bought him out.[47]

Bernard Feinstein didn't know. The Camden Bridge was going to turn the city into a bedroom suburb of Philadelphia, magically transforming grim urban lots into dazzling castles for the commuting clerks of the metropolis. But by the late 1920s, Philadelphia's economy was far too frail to regenerate itself, let alone Camden. And those commuters who did live across the Delaware preferred to do so in newly built suburbs, far from the stink of Camden's docks, especially since, thanks to the very bridge that was supposed to be the city's salvation, they could now go straight through Camden directly to downtown Philadelphia without the need to stop or shop. Shrewd investors got out of Camden even before the bridge opened. Bernard, who may have been counting on the Wall Street boom to turn things around, was still buying in 1929.

For a reporter in Camden, there were plenty of signs of the coming hard times. The shipyards that were the city's main employers laid off thousands of workers long before October 1929. Camden's hospitals, in a building boom of their own, dedicated new facilities for maternity and child care, but at the same time "one out of every ten children placed in the city's day care centers known as baby farms died from the unsanitary conditions."[48] The city's workforce relied on Campbell's Soup, RCA Victor, and New York Ship, and by the late 1920s even Campbell's was letting men go.[49]

But Isidor Feinstein wasn't primarily a reporter. "When I knew I was getting married I went to the managing editor and I said I'm getting married, and unless I get a five-dollar raise I'm going to quit. So he gave me a five-dollar raise."[50] He also got a new job: promotion manager. The advertisements he wrote ran in the *Courier* every day, but his byline seldom appeared. Even when he returned to the news side, he wrote about transportation and local government, not poverty and despair. And he kept up his reviews. Under Isidor Feinstein's byline, tragedy in 1930 meant *Richard III*, not rising inventories, the disastrous Smoot-Hawley tariffs, or unemployment.[51]

George Seldes, the *Chicago Tribune*'s legendary correspondent, described the period between the crash and the election of 1932 as "two parts and an interlude; first comes the effort to do nothing, then the effort to do everything."[52] At a time when the apparent breakdown of the capitalist system was on every front page, Isidor Feinstein's major contributions to public discourse concerned the relative merits of plays on the Philadelphia stage, with the odd movie or book review thrown in. As a critic he was becoming more urbane: "those quintessential wigglings of the brows, that sudden lifting of the chin, the delighted mischievous little laugh at her own joke, the way of speaking that ripples like a permanent wave that go to make up that theatric spectacle: Ethel Barrymore."[53] But it would be stretching things to say that a two-paragraph plug for a stage version of the proletarian picaresque *Jews Without Money*, by Michael Gold, editor of *New Masses*, shows a radical intelligence at work. Nor does his remark that Robert Wilder's *Sweet Chariot* "expresses the American colored man's hurt at being unwelcome in the only country he feels is home, his protest of injustice and slight" reveal a particularly acute grasp of what the novice critic calls "the Negro problem."[54]

Still, he had become a competent reviewer, hailing Lynn Fontanne's "passionate, careful" Elizabeth and Alfred Lunt's "fiery" Essex in Maxwell Anderson's *Elizabeth the Queen*. He had even developed an eye for good acting, lavishly praising the young Helen Hayes and a "lovely and appealing" ingenue named Bette Davis, while finding Lee Strasberg's manner "a little startling."[55] But his reviews showed scant enthusiasm for engaging with larger questions. In Shaw's *Apple Cart*, George Seldes saw a parable of capitalist excess: Shaw's villain "had the monopoly of junk and it was the duty of manufacturers to make cars and shoes and fountain pens and tables and pianos which must rapidly fall to pieces; the whole purpose of industry was to create ultimate rubbish." Attending the same production, Isidor Feinstein saw "merely a polished restatement of contemporary commonplace" from "England's bearded parlor revolutionary."[56]

A similar compulsion to display his own superiority kept him from treating the films he reviewed as anything other than celluloid theater. He saluted George S. Kaufman's play *Once in a Lifetime* not only for its "three acts and seven scenes of the most excruciatingly funny, devastating, downright gorgeous satire we ever hope to see," but also as "a slow and deliberate dismemberment of the talkie industry" and a definitive demonstration of film's inferiority.[57] This was the era of *Little Caesar* and *Public Enemy*, a time, according to Arthur Schlesinger Jr., "When the Movies Really Counted." In his essay "The Gangster as Tragic Hero," the critic Robert Warshow reveals a sea change in American attitudes to success underlying the Depression's most popular genre. The gangster, says Warshow, "is what we want to be and what we are afraid we may become," his rise and fall an indictment of rugged individualism.[58]

Though the signs of the times were there to be read, in 1930, according to Seldes, "misery, joblessness, and discontent had not yet come to the pitch of affecting the whole nation; they affected only the miserable, the jobless, and the discontented."[59] Comfortably ensconced on the *Courier*'s review page, Isidor Feinstein may well have resisted the gangster film's bleak certainty that, in Warshow's phrase, "there is really only one possibility—failure." With his stint as promotion manager confirming his anointment as David Stern's fair-haired protégé, the young journalist had only his socialist convictions to divert attention from his own glittering career to the human wreckage piling up around him. Until the night the Depression came after his mother.

Katy Feinstein had been distressed for months. It was bad enough when her husband's property business went well, leaving her responsible for running the store. Then, just as her adored eldest son moved out of the family home, Bernard's investments started to turn sour. First the speculative lots went. Then the rental properties. Then the new house—"a beautiful house, just finished, which we never moved into," said Louis Stone. It was to be several months before they lost the store, but late one night in 1930—"just before I was supposed to be bar mitzvah"—Louis Stone was awakened by his mother's cries: "My mother came and told me she'd taken poison. Lysol. I was an old Boy Scout and I remembered something to do. I pushed her to vomit. And then of course I woke my father and he took her to the hospital, and what happened then I don't know. But I remember that my sister and I sat there in the middle of the night looking out the window and wondering whether we would ever see Mother again."

Katy Feinstein was taken to Kirkbride's Hospital, a sunny, relatively cheerful asylum on the outskirts of Philadelphia. She returned home after a few weeks, but she would never be completely well again. With Bernard still struggling to fend off bankruptcy, the task of ferrying Katy to and from the hospital fell on her youngest son, Louis. The middle son, Max, also came home from college at Chapel Hill to lend a hand.* Katy's favorite son, the one she'd always defended from his father's temper, visited "occasionally . . . not very often," remembered Louis, who was quick to add that Isidor had "just gotten married" and had "sent money to help keep the family."[60]

Viewed from the outside, I. F. Stone's career as an apprentice journalist is the story of an almost effortless rise. It is also a story strikingly out of tune with the temper of his times. In one way, that dissonance was real: He succeeded at every newspaper job he turned his hand to, from general assignment drudgery to rewrite to reviews, and would soon be given more freedom than any other daily editorial writer in America. All at a time when the ranks of the unemployed grew month by month to a massive army of despair.

Yet his own father would soon be a conscript in that army. And while I. F. Stone never mentioned his mother's illness to any of the dozens of interviewers who came to profile him over the years, his response to the Depression could hardly have been unaffected by the knowledge that his own mother was unhinged by it. Though he enjoyed a certain amount of luxury, in later life favoring cruise ships and expensive hotels for vacations, holidaying in Venice and the Aegean rather than Miami or Atlantic City, he was always marked by the careful attention to his own finances that set apart people of the Depression generation, recycling columns into books and paying off his mortgage well ahead of time. But the emotional toll of those terrible years remained deeply buried.

Whether he felt guilt or anger or whether he marked it down as yet another of his father's failings, or perhaps a combination of all of these, is less significant than the tight and persistent silence from a man who otherwise delighted in public attention. In the millions of words he set down during the course of his lifetime, there is not one mention of his mother's

*Max, who'd been editor of his high school yearbook, went into business to produce Haddonfield's first city directory. In addition to the usual columns of names, addresses, and telephone numbers, the 1930 volume featured an introduction by his older brother.

ordeal. Even within the family, the facts of Katy's illness remained shrouded in shame—and silence. A niece who endured her own mother's suicide attempt recalls Izzy and Esther's solicitude and compassion. But the news that her beloved uncle had firsthand knowledge of what she'd been through came as a complete surprise to her.[61]

•

In *The Brass Check*, his exposé of the venality of American journalism, Upton Sinclair asks us to spare some compassion for the understandably misinformed O. Henry, "who, being an American, got his ideas about life from the newspapers." In Sinclair's view, American newspapers were corrupt, trivial instruments of mass delusion, factually unreliable and politically dishonest, subject to the whims of greedy publishers and fearful advertising managers. Doubtless they were. But for Isidor Feinstein the newsroom was more than just a refuge from his parents' despair, more, even, than the scene of his real higher education. The newspaper was his route into the world.

This is true, in a way, for every young reporter. Ben Hecht, who wrote the screenplays for *Underworld* (1927) and *Scarface* (1932), started out as a picture chaser in Chicago. "The picture chaser," he wrote, "was a shady but vital figure. It was his duty to unearth, snatch, or wangle cabinet photographs of the recently and violently dead for his paper." Despite such unpromising beginnings—Hecht also recalled a colleague "who was taking a correspondence course in embalming (hoping thus to rise in the world)"—he soon found himself transfigured into a big-city reporter, "a casual figure, full of anonymous power."[62]

The *Camden Courier* was considerably more genteel than the Chicago tabloids where Hecht served his apprenticeship and that he and Charles MacArthur immortalized in *The Front Page* (1931). Still, while the young Feinstein may have never shared a spittoon with Hildy Johnson, he did share the *Courier's* drama desk with Pierre de Rohan, a man who had been run out of the state of Connecticut following a conviction for bigamy.[63] And if, on the *Courier*, he remained a "skinny, thin-lipped black-haired youth [who] always seemed to be nervous, one of those nail-biting types . . . [who] boasted of his loose tie, of his uncut and uncombed hair," he had one advantage that the fictional Walter Burns and

Sinclair's all-too-real hardened cases did not.[64] He worked for a publisher who relished a good fight and happily described himself as "a maverick." To his young protégé, J. David Stern was "a newspaper man who felt an obligation to the underprivileged and against injustice and against the arrogance of great wealth and concentrated economic power."[65] He was, in a word, a muckraker.

President Theodore Roosevelt's invocation of Bunyan's man with a muckrake had not been intended as a compliment. The president's outrage was prompted by the publication in the March 1906 issue of *Cosmopolitan* of "The Treason of the Senate" by David Graham Phillips. But while they lasted, the muckrakers managed to illuminate the nature of American life and the exercise of power in America with a clarity that electrified the public, encouraged engagement, and enraged the powerful from the salons of St. Louis to the boardrooms of Standard Oil. No wonder Roosevelt was irritated.

In part, muckraking was a method: A progressive writer of a slightly earlier period, Henry Demarest Lloyd, described it as a journalism that "has been quarried out of official records, and . . . is a venture in realism." In his pioneering *Wealth Against Commonwealth* (1894), Lloyd laid out the main lines of attack: "Decisions of courts and of special tribunals like the Interstate Commerce Commission, verdicts of juries in civil and criminal cases, reports of committees of the State Legislatures and of Congress, oath-sworn testimony given in legal proceedings and in official inquiries . . . such are the sources of information."[66]

Muckraking was also an attitude, a faith that if only a writer could, as Upton Sinclair described his aim, "make the people believe what 'everybody knows'—then he will be recognized in future as a benefactor of his race."[67] How were the people to be convinced? They were to be given what Ray Stannard Baker, a writer on *McClure's Magazine*, a muckraking stronghold, termed the "unpalatable facts." If "proof was piled upon proof, certainty was added to certainty," said Baker, "even the prosperous and naturally conservative jury of the whole people [would be] thoroughly convinced."[68] It is a faith at least as old as the Gospel of St. John—"And ye shall know the truth, and the truth shall make you free"—and as rooted in American soil as Jefferson's University of Virginia, whose library is adorned with the verse in Greek over the portico. Journalists from Mark Twain to H. L. Mencken have been prominent dissenters from this credo, but

Lloyd and Baker were believers. And though Lloyd was a lone activist ahead of his time, the true muckrakers—Ida Tarbell, Baker, Steffens, and the others—were also "the leading edge of a political movement."[69]

The relationship between political movements and the journalism that both sustains and is sustained by such movements is complex. And, as always in American history, our view of insurgent movements is often occluded by what Lawrence Goodwyn, the historian of American populism, calls "the condescension toward the past . . . implicit in the idea of progress," which we unconsciously tend to bring to protests that appear to have failed. Yet, as Goodwyn points out, "movements of mass democratic protest . . . represent a political, an organizational, and above all, a cultural achievement of the first magnitude." Goodwyn's analysis of "the evolving stages" whereby "intimidated people" generate the "psychological authority and practical means" to challenge "culturally sanctioned authority" illuminates a recurring theme in our national life. Besides, it was the Populist critique of the economy that gave the facts so painstakingly assembled by the muckrakers their significance. And it was this same critique of the economy, shorn of some of its more simpleminded nostrums, that was to reappear with such force during the 1930s in, among other venues, the editorial pages of J. David Stern's newspapers.[70]

•

By his own admission, J. David Stern liked to stir things up. So when his friend Albert Greenfield approached him in 1928 and offered to finance the acquisition of the Wanamaker family's moribund *Philadelphia Record*, Stern was delighted.

The *Record* itself was no great prize. Once the city's leading newspaper, its circulation had declined steadily from nearly 200,000 at the turn of the century to barely half that, in a period when the dominant *Bulletin*'s sales had risen to well over half a million. But Stern, who liked to make money almost as much as he liked to make trouble, knew how to use exposés and provocative editorials to boost circulation. He also had two assets even more useful than his superb news judgment. One was his wife's family. Then, as now, the department stores whose patronage is a newspaper's lifeblood made their advertising decisions in a herd. Stern's confidence that, short of calling for an outright boycott or divorcing Jill, nothing he did would lose him Lit Brothers' business allowed him to give his natural boldness free exercise. His second advantage, his association with Albert Greenfield, meant that he sometimes had to rein in his indignation, but it also gave him access to the innermost vaults of Philadelphia's power structure.

A banker and real estate developer, Greenfield had served on the City Council. At the time, like most elected officials in Philadelphia, he was a Republican. Indeed, when William Vare, the city's Republican boss, decided in 1926 that he wanted to cap his career with election to the United States Senate, Greenfield gave his old friend $125,000 of his own money and raised most of the rest of his war chest himself. In the primary (the only election that mattered in Pennsylvania), Vare faced Governor Gifford Pinchot, a Theodore Roosevelt–style Progressive, and George Wharton Pepper, an ornament of the Union League Club whose campaign was bankrolled by the Mellon family. Vare lost all but two of the state's sixty-seven counties, but his 228,000-vote margin in Philadelphia alone was enough to win the primary and guarantee his election in November.[71] Unfortunately for Vare, the Senate refused to allow him to take his seat, citing allegations of fraud and bribery but perhaps even more offended by his machine politician's lack of deference.[72]

In 1928, Greenfield was a delegate to the Republican National Convention. The Republican Party had welcomed him, but he was an upstart and a Jew, and when, in September 1930, the collapse in the city's property market led to a run on Greenfield's bank, Philadelphia's WASP establishment, which had banded together to prop up a number of their own banks earlier in the year, offered Greenfield moral support but little else. By December he was bankrupt.

Greenfield's campaign to rebuild his fortunes rested on two pillars. He had managed to hold on to some of his interests in department stores; he also became chairman of Lit Brothers. And politically, he decided to change horses. Greenfield turned his back on the Quakers and Episcopalians who had permitted Vare to run Philadelphia for them (yet allowed his bank to go under) and made common cause with the rising Irish Catholics who were determined to breathe life into Philadelphia's all but defunct Democratic Party.[73]

For the first three decades of the twentieth century, Philadelphia's Democrats had effectively been a wholly owned subsidiary of Vare's machine, trading complete political docility for a fixed share of patronage and spoils. Statewide the situation was scarcely better. Between 1893 and 1931, Democrats lost ninety-five of ninety-six state elections in Pennsylvania; in 1928, a Democratic candidate for governor, making a realistic appraisal of his chances, withdrew from the race to campaign instead for election as Grand Exalted Ruler of the Elks.[74]

Greenfield's chief political ally was a prosperous Irish builder, John B. Kelly, who had become a local celebrity thanks to his prowess as an Olympic oarsman. ("Handsome Jack," as he was known, later achieved even greater fame as the father of his even handsomer daughter, Grace.) The pair's wealth, enormous range of contacts, and considerable political acumen soon gained them control of the party machinery. To reach the voters, though, they would need a newspaper—ideally, a crusading newspaper. J. David Stern's office at the *Record* became their war room.[75]

Their campaign was still in its early stages when Stern brought Isidor Feinstein over from Camden in September 1931. Like a AAA ballplayer sent to the major leagues, Stern's protégé had to earn his position. In Camden he had been a utility player. Now he wanted to write editorials. He'd already done a few as a substitute.* Now he wanted a spot in the starting lineup. First, though, he needed to relearn the city from the streets up to City Hall. Stern put him on general assignment, working nights.[76]

By the end of 1931, nearly everybody in Philadelphia knew there was a Depression. More than 15 percent of the workforce in a city that called itself "the workshop of the world" were unable to find jobs. A federal survey of nineteen major cities showed more severe unemployment only in Cleveland and Detroit. The number of evictions jumped from 12,000 in 1930 to 18,000 in 1931. In his first two weeks at the *Record*, Isidor Feinstein wrote three stories about local banks closing, one of them an account of a mass meeting of 10,000 depositors.[77]

In years to come, historians would debate whether revolt or resignation was the more significant response to such desperate times.[78] Without the luxury of such reflection, Philadelphians formed their own judgments. The labor organizer and pacifist A. J. Muste joined forces with

---

*In one, slipped into the paper while the regular editorialist was recovering from his New Year's excesses, we can hear the beginnings of a distinctive voice (and a topic that continued to engage Stone half a century on): "WILL THESE 8 NEW DEATHS END OUR HYPOCRISY ON NICARAGUA? Eight more Americans slain in Nicaragua. Is this war? Nothing of the sort. Merely a peace-time campaign against bandits. At least, the State Department calls them bandits; certain Nicaraguans call them patriots. You can take your choice." *Courier Post*, January 3, 1931.

Emil Rieve of the American Federation of Hosiery Workers, making Philadelphia a stronghold of Muste's new organization, the Conference for Progressive Labor Action. The Communist Party's Trade Union Unity League also made a big effort in Philadelphia, but with markedly less success: The Marine Workers Industrial Union called a citywide dock strike—but forgot to tell the workers until the morning of the strike;[79] on March 6, 1930, "International Unemployment Day," only 150 demonstrators answered the party's call for a "Red Thursday" show of force at City Hall Plaza. Despite such fiascoes, city authorities remained jittery. In November 1931, a friend wrote to J. Hampton Moore, the mayor-elect, informing him that the Pennsylvania National Guard was already drilling to "meet the possible mob rule that might take place during the hard times expected this winter" and urging that the city's police force be similarly prepared.[80] Moore took up the suggestion; for good measure he also banned demonstrations on City Hall Plaza, where on December 11, 1931, a crowd of 18,000 men and women had successfully demanded the cancellation of an increase in property taxes in a march instigated by the editorial pages of the *Record*.

With his gaze firmly fixed on the city's bond rating, Mayor Moore cut municipal workers' salaries by 23 percent, and fired half the employees of the Department of Public Works.[81] Relief was unnecessary. "There is no starvation in Philadelphia," he declared. The *Nation* responded with "Mass Misery in Philadelphia," one of a series of articles written by Mauritz Hallgren, a Baltimore *Sun* editor, assessing the impact of unemployment. Hallgren quotes an unnamed reporter for the *Record*: "Behind the lace curtains . . . lies the picture he [Moore] didn't see. Gaunt children, sunken eyes, ten-year-olds nineteen pounds under weight. Children in rags, without sufficient clothes to permit their attendance at school. Children without shoes . . . Starvation in Philadelphia today is an accumulative starvation; starvation through undernourishment; slow starvation from insufficient food."[82]

After three weeks covering horse shows, church conferences, bank failures, Prohibition, a visiting Italian premier, and a speech at the Elks' lodge, Isidor Feinstein was

> dying to do editorials. And I knew there was no editorial writer on Saturdays. So one Saturday morning I woke up at 4 o'clock, went

in to town, bought the morning papers, nobody was around, and by 9 o'clock I had written an editorial and put it on Stern's desk.

He came in at 9 and found it there. He was very mad at me . . . because he liked to write his own editorials . . . He didn't want me muscling in. He was very nasty about it. I was all shaken up. I thought, 'You son-of-a-bitch! I'm going to keep pestering you, you bastard, until you make me editorial writer.' I didn't know what he was going to do, and I went to work in the newsroom on my usual rewrite and reporting, and next morning when I came in, on Sunday (every day they would magnify one editorial, put it in large type and put it in the window) there was my editorial, so I was really thrilled.[83]

On the front page of the *Record* for October 15, 1931, a headline urges: "Tell the Truth About the Banks." Like all the paper's editorials, this one is unsigned. But its tone, subject matter, and timing, appearing two days after Isidor Feinstein's final assignment as a reporter, suggest that his apprenticeship was over. He had a platform. Now he needed to find his voice.

•

As Philadelphia entered the winter of 1931, the city's director of public safety banned Socialists from the premises of any textile mill. Asked to justify the exclusion, he replied, "Well, you know how it is—you start talking Socialism and go from that to a lot of things."[84] Isidor Feinstein had been talking socialism for some time. But as the mass misery in Philadelphia and the rest of the country steadily worsened, he found himself wondering whether socialism was enough.

At first, he kept any doubts to himself. As the newest member of Stern's editorial stable, he was busy writing on a wide range of topics, from the enforcement of Prohibition (which he thought fostered corruption) to the risk of a military confrontation in the Far East. By the end of 1932, however, three issues came to dominate his thinking: the disastrous failure of private relief efforts in Philadelphia, the coming presidential election, and the spread of fascism.

Since at least the nineteenth century, Philadelphia had relied on private philanthropy to feed and house the poor. Philadelphians took justifiable pride in the relative generosity of the city's provision, including the country's first large-scale school breakfast program, feeding 8,000 children every weekday and 4,500 on Saturdays and Sundays. Should altruism fail, the *Record*'s new editorial writer was ready with "Let the Rich Who Don't Give For Pity Give For Social Insurance," a timely reminder that "Revolutions are made on empty stomachs."[85] When private fundraising ultimately proved unable to keep pace with the Depression, the city's elite appointed a Committee for Unemployment Relief, headed by Horatio Gates Lloyd, a partner in the Drexel merchant bank, to distribute whatever state aid became available. In 1931, the state legislature authorized the city to borrow $3 million to aid the jobless. The money lasted a year. A further $5 million from the combined campaign of the Catholic, Jewish, and Protestant charities was gone in three months. With the number of applicants continuing to grow at the rate of 2,000 families a week, in April 1932 the Pennsylvania Supreme Court upheld the legality of using state funds for relief. But Philadelphia's share, $2.5 million in direct aid, lasted only two months.

On June 20, 1932, when the money ran out, another editorial on the front page of the *Record* declared: "The Lloyd committee is through. For fifty-seven thousand families to whom the committee has meant life itself, STARVATION is 'just around the corner.' The Committee for two years has fought the wolf away from the doorsteps of Philadelphia's worthy poor. It has tapped and exhausted every available source of succor. And now its funds are gone." For ten agonizing weeks, the 57,000 families were left to shift for themselves. At the end, even Horatio Gates Lloyd joined calls for direct federal relief.[86]

Philadelphians joined a growing chorus of voices urging President Herbert Hoover to act. One proposal that seemed to offer a way around the federal government's reluctance to take responsibility for the poor was for an early payout on money promised to veterans of the Great War. A Bonus Army of some 15,000 jobless veterans soon assembled on Anacostia Flats, a swampy district in Washington across the river from the Capitol, and the House of Representatives voted to authorize payments. But when the Senate defeated the bill, Patrick J. Hurley, Hoover's secretary of war, sent federal troops under the command of General Douglas MacArthur to evict the veterans. If the Hoover administration was an-

swering even the veterans' entreaties with tanks, bayonets, and tear gas,
how likely was it to rush to the aid of ordinary men and women?[87]

Clearly there would have to be a change in Washington before
Philadelphians could expect relief. But what kind of change? In an
August 1932 editorial entitled "The Red Bogeyman Again," the *Record*
ridiculed Hoover's claim that "Red agitators" were in charge of the Bonus
Army: "Blaming it on the Communists enables the Hoover Administration to pose as the Nation's Savior From Bolshevism." But the paper went
on to note that such talk "also enables American Communist leaders to
coax more funds from Moscow by leaping into the limelight as a Fearful
Menace to American Capitalism, forcing a frightened President to call
out the army, leading an enormous mob on the seat of Government and
preparing to turn Washington into another Leningrad."[88]

The *Record*'s lofty disdain for American Communists received a shock
three weeks later, when Mayor Moore's refusal to meet with representatives of the Unemployed Councils, many of them Communists, sparked
"the Battle of Reyburn [City Hall] Plaza" between demonstrators and the
police.[89] In October, the Communists, still barred from City Hall, staged
a rally at the Philadelphia Arena that drew 7,000 people. "Red Rally in
Arena Dwarfs G.O.P. Show," reported the *Record*, pointing out that the
audience for a Republican rally at the same venue a few days earlier numbered under 3,000.[90]

As tribune of a resurgent Democratic Party, the *Record* was delighted by
any evidence of Republican disintegration, but J. David Stern's tolerance
for Communists stopped well short of enthusiasm. So long as the party
remained both marginal and respectable, the *Record* could be counted on
to defend it. "No Red Menace in Phila.," proclaimed a typical *Record*
headline, adding the reassurance that "Communists Here Number 9000,
But Are Careful to Keep Within Law."[91] Despite the frequent provocations of Mayor Moore's police, the party retained its law-abiding demeanor. But as the presidential election drew nearer, its relegation to the
sidelines of American life began to seem less certain.

The American Communist Party deserves only part of the credit for
this turn in its fortunes. A series of purges had reduced its numbers from
some 15,000 in 1923 to about half that in 1930.[92] Those who remained
were burdened with the Comintern's proclamation in 1928 of the "Third
Period" since the Bolshevik revolution—an epoch that was supposed to

see the final collapse of capitalism and usher in proletarian rule world-wide. With their assumption of power believed to be imminent, Communists were enjoined to even greater degrees of ideological vigilance, particularly against "social fascists." The theory was ornate, but in practice a "social fascist" was anyone who, by advocating any reform short of the party's vision of revolution, was effectively working "to keep intact the structure of capitalism and the capitalist state."[93]

Just when the Depression seemed to confirm the validity of their analysis, American Communists were put in the position of being unable to take yes for an answer. And yet many Americans were moving to the left. Izzy's friend Sy Blankfort followed what was becoming a well-traveled path. Blankfort went to the Soviet Union immediately after his graduation from Penn. Three months later, he returned to begin graduate work in psychology at Princeton but soon dropped out to devote himself to a new kind of political theater. In 1931, he produced *Merry-Go-Round*, a scathing satire of New York City politics written by a pair of young Yale graduates named Albert Maltz and George Sklar. (The play opened at the Province-town Playhouse; Walter Hart directed.) By this time, Blankfort, who had dropped Seymour in favor of Michael, his middle name, was living in Greenwich Village, where his intelligence, poise, radical commitment, and family money soon brought him to the attention of V. F. Calverton.[94]

There is no better illustration of the perversity of Communist Party policy in the early 1930s than the career of V. F. Calverton. Born George Goetz, he took the name Calverton in the wake of the Palmer Raids, when many radicals adopted pen names, to protect his job as a Baltimore schoolteacher. In the mid-1920s, Calverton's attempts to Americanize Marx won him plaudits from Socialists and Communists alike. For a time he even managed to write a column for the Socialist *New Leader* while remaining a regular contributor to the *Daily Worker*. Attacked by the CPUSA as a Trotskyist in 1928 and as a "social fascist" in 1931, Calverton nonetheless repeatedly pledged his fealty to the party line. Indeed, the magazine he founded and edited, the *Modern Quarterly*, carried the name of the party's general secretary, Earl Browder, on the masthead until 1931. Calverton endorsed William Z. Foster, the Communist candidate for president in 1932, even though Foster had personally attacked him in his book *Toward Soviet America*.[95]

Michael Blankfort joined the *Modern Quarterly* in the autumn of 1932 as literary editor: "I became a greedy hanger-on to Calverton's circle of friends on Morton Street [in Greenwich Village]. A burly man with an addiction to curved pipes and sweepings of tobacco, he was a lapsed semi-pro baseball player . . . with an all-embracing passion for what he'd read and a passion to become a new Renaissance man all by himself. He was insatiable in his hunger for approval, and would make friends with anyone who was willing, whether or not they agreed with his politics, literary criticism or social theories."[96]

To the young critic Alfred Kazin, Calverton's deficiency in pessimism of the intellect—Kazin later described him as "a remarkably unsubtle Marxist critic even for the times"—was more than compensated for by his unshakable optimism of the will: "George really did believe that all the 'modern' disciplines, sociology and psychology and anthropology, would connect with Marxism to carry all of man to his destiny. The Stalinist critics of the mid-Thirties spoke of necessity, but George's favorite word was 'liberation.'" Kazin, who like Blankfort was taken up by Calverton at the beginning of his career, describes a "round, kindly, swarthy, eager man" who "could be as concerned about a new writer's struggles, as hopeful and friendly about the slightest piece I wrote for the magazine, as an admiring relative."[97]

Of course, Blankfort was encouraged to bring his friends to Calverton's weekly soirées. In a way, these gatherings were even more important than his magazine. After the party's anathema, Communist intellectuals like Joseph Freeman, Granville Hicks, and Michael Gold no longer wrote for the *Modern Quarterly*, but they were still happy to come to Morton Street, where, under the benevolent gaze of Calverton's longtime lover, Nina Melville, they frequently found themselves in the company of Max Eastman, Sidney Hook, Bertram Wolfe, and other sworn foes of Stalinism. It was as close as postwar Manhattan ever came to the broad-church bohemian radicalism of 322, and when Isidor Feinstein tagged along with Blankfort on a visit to New York late in 1932, he felt right at home.

Calverton took to the young newsman and immediately set about recruiting him for the magazine, which was on the verge of going monthly. He was well aware that Feinstein could be of use as more than just a contributor—indeed, his young friend had promised to write an editorial in the *Record* promoting the *Modern Monthly* as soon as the first issue appeared. Calverton tactfully left those arrangements in the hands of his new advertising manager, Sidney Cohn, another member of the Penn circle. Instead, he invited "Iz" to "start on one of those two articles we discussed the other night."[98]

He didn't have to ask twice. It may have been David Stern's vehement support for Franklin Delano Roosevelt (his new editorialist voted for Norman Thomas). It may have been Stern's regular denunciations of "dictators of the left and right." Or it may simply have been that Stern's paternalistic interest in his career had begun to chafe. By the time of Calverton's invitation, Stone was already looking beyond the *Record* for outlets where he could write to suit his own views, in his own voice.

One publication he particularly hoped to crack was the *American Mercury*. For his generation of college men, H. L. Mencken's cynical hauteur represented the acme of intellectual sophistication; publication in his magazine was a rite of passage. And Mencken would have every reason to welcome a writer on what the *Mercury* itself had recently proclaimed "a newspaper man's newspaper." Indeed, the magazine's celebration of the *Record* stressed the crucial role played by the editorial page in producing a paper that "delights the literates of the town." Moreover, Stone's editorial colleague at the *Record*, Sam Grafton, had been writing for the *American Mercury* even before he graduated from Penn.

"The *Record*'s formula for attracting and holding attention is so simple that the layman must wonder why it is not tried oftener. It consists, first, in taking a definite editorial stand on one side or the other of every debatable subject covered in its news columns."[99] The article in which this comment was made did not mention Feinstein's name, but as Stone remembered with gratitude many years later, Mencken "was a great editor, he never bought names." What he did buy, and publish in May 1933, was "A Gentleman in Politics," a profile of the Pennsylvania governor, Gifford Pinchot, "a Great Liberal in a Tight Corner," by one Isidor Feinstein.[100]

Though his efforts to prevent the despoliation of public lands during the Taft administration had made Gifford Pinchot a hero to many, Isidor Feinstein was never among his admirers. He'd first interviewed Pinchot as a reporter for the *Camden Courier* during the 1926 Senate campaign, dismissing him in a letter to Blankfort as "the old Roosevelt progressive type—dead, dead, dead." Pinchot's conduct in the governor's office provided little basis for a more favorable view: "His lances are still aimed, with convenient harmlessness, at Entrenched Wealth, the Plutocracy, and other decrepit hobgoblins of the Bull Moose era. A large portrait of

Roosevelt I is said to hang in his study . . . like that of Karl Marx over the worktable of Stalin."[101]

As a work of political reportage, the article was more than competent, linking Pinchot's reluctance to let the state fund relief payments to his lingering hopes for a seat in the U.S. Senate and his cultivation of the distinctly un-Rooseveltian Republican boss Joe Grundy. But in its rhetoric— Pinchot "is America's outstanding example of a type beatified by lady civics teachers and adoring Anglophiles"—it was not just good imitation Mencken. It was superior imitation Mencken. The state supreme court's decision authorizing relief payments, wrote Feinstein:

> seems to have broken the great Liberal's heart . . . He still weeps copiously over the unemployed and Pennsylvania's inability to help them—while boasting in the *New Republic*, of the State's magnificent highway programme, that "it is quite within the means of so rich a State as Pennsylvania." In a recent message on relief, he found that "the Commonwealth has a clear and sacred duty to do what it can and all it can to help its own people." But he also discovered that to touch the fat highway fund would "break the implied contract of the State with the users of the highways." The "implied contract," obviously, outweighs the "sacred duty."
>
> Gifford will pave his way to the Senate yet, even if he has to put macadam on every cowpath in the State to do it.[102]

Nowadays it is Mencken's fate to be widely venerated while remaining mostly unread. But in the first half of the twentieth century, his was the dominant voice in American journalism. Even today, a columnist making sport with a politician will often find that, though the words may be new, the tune is Mencken's. That Isidor Feinstein should work in the same key barely signifies. What matters more is the speed with which he abandoned that key, and what he abandoned it for. A month after Isidor Feinstein made his first (and last) appearance in the *American Mercury*, the incoming administration of Franklin Roosevelt was appraised in the pages of the *Modern Monthly*: "It was felt that he [FDR] was for the common people, that he would feed the hungry, that he would show Wall Street where it got off. Wall Street got off very well." The author's name was Abelard Stone.

Why the pseudonym? The title of the article gave one clue: "Roosevelt

Moves Toward Fascism." Such a dark view of the newly inaugurated president's intentions was hardly the party line at J. David Stern's *Record*,
which as the *American Mercury* noted "could probably set up a strong
claim to being the first Roosevelt-for-President paper in the country." A
further explanation for the young writer's disguise can be found two paragraphs into his argument: "The historian, looking back from the vantage
point of the future, will see two roads open and one closed to the American people on March 4, 1933. *The road to a Soviet America, the one way
out that could make a real difference* to the working classes, was closed"
(emphasis added).[103]

•

The short, unhappy life of Abelard Stone, Communist polemicist, lasted
just four months. "Roosevelt Moves Toward Fascism" was followed by an
acerbic, radical commentary on the latest congressional investigation into
J. P. Morgan & Co., which argued that "only a workers party and a Communist party can achieve a fundamental change and destroy the financial
oligarchy." In August, a house ad promised Abelard Stone on the National
Industrial Recovery Act (passed in June 1934) in a forthcoming issue, but
it was not to be.

    This was, in every respect, a bizarre episode. Even Stone's apparent en-
dorsement of the Communist line, with its deliberate echo of William Z.
Foster's campaign slogan "Toward Soviet America," was odd. The 1932
presidential election had marked a high point in relations between intellectuals and the Communist Party. In *Culture and the Crisis*, their October 1932 "Open Letter to the Intellectual Workers of America," Matthew
Josephson and James Rorty quipped that the Democratic Party headed by
Franklin Roosevelt "is the logical alternative of the Republican Party, just
as Tweedledum is the logical alternative of Tweedledee—for the same
job." The "interests of a truly human society," they argued, required
"workers in the professions and the arts" to "join in the revolutionary
struggle . . . under the leadership of the Communist Party." Writing after
the election, Abelard Stone, echoing Josephson's dismissal, concluded
that the country "fumed at Tweedledum and looked with hope to Tweedledee." Josephson (who would soon become a friend of the Feinsteins)
had called the Socialist Party "the third party of Capitalism," a view en-

dorsed by Malcolm Cowley, John Dos Passos, Sidney Hook, Edmund Wilson, and Lincoln Steffens.[104] Indeed, it was Dos Passos who remarked that to support the Socialists in the present crisis was like drinking near beer. Yet as recently as 1932, Isidor Feinstein, like John Dewey, Reinhold Niebuhr, and Oswald Garrison Villard, still preferred near beer.

The timing of Stone's apparent embrace of the Communist line was also extremely odd. In January 1933, just after the election, the Communist Party launched a particularly vicious attack on Calverton. His continuing sympathy for Leon Trotsky after the former Red Army commander's split with Joseph Stalin made him odious to the Comintern; Calverton's willingness to challenge the American party hierarchy finally rendered him intolerable. In "The Marxism of V. F. Calverton," the longest article *New Masses* ever published, written by two of his former students from Baltimore, he was accused of crimes ranging from plagiarism to being a "maturing fascist," an "open collaborator of the ruling class," and a "sex racketeer."[105]

That Calverton remained open to Communist arguments after such an assault is testimony to either his tolerance or his desperation. But after all this had happened, for Abelard Stone to use the July 1933 issue of Calverton's magazine as the venue for his own endorsement of the Communist Party line that finance capital "must . . . inevitably stand behind the throne of the Republican and Democratic parties, behind the Socialists if they come to power, behind any party that proposes to work within the framework of capitalism" verges on the perverse.[106]

What are we to make, then, of "Abelard Stone"? Peter Abelard—medieval scholastic, partisan of rational inquiry, who fell in love with his pupil Héloïse, seduced her, secretly married her after their son was born, and was castrated by her uncle—joined with Stone, an abbreviation (mutilation?) of Feinstein. Guilt over the use of a pseudonym? But name changes were a Feinstein (Tsvilikhovsky) tradition. A sentimental gesture toward Esther? Their first child, Celia Mary, was born the previous September. (Upon hearing the news, Michael Blankfort sent a telegram: "Welcome to the grandmother of the American revolution!") Or was it perhaps a private joke, a wink at the dialecticians of Union Square, a gesture of personal resistance as oblique as his choosing what in the party's eyes was a Trotskyist rag to recite his catechism?

His friend Blankfort, moving ever closer to the party, resigned from the

Modern Monthly in August 1933. "It does not redound to my credit as a revolutionary, although it may to me as a friend," he wrote Calverton, "that I did not leave the magazine when I most disagreed with it; the Trotzky episode.* I did not leave because my loyalty was greater than my conviction." Blankfort's wife was a party member; so were his new friends Maltz and Sklar. And if Blankfort himself never formally joined, by that autumn his "loyalties" and his convictions were no longer in conflict. "With George Calverton and his circle," Blankfort explained in an unpublished memoir, "I would be an acolyte in the shadow of the brilliance of older men . . . With [Maltz and Sklar], I was an equal, a fellow pioneer."[107]

Abelard Stone also disappeared from the *Modern Monthly*. Like Blankfort, Isidor Feinstein was still moving to the left, but not on the same road. In the end, Abelard Stone was retired for the same reasons that called him into being: the young writer's continuing search for his own voice and for a place where that voice could make itself heard. Politically, he left the magazine for the same reason he first sought a place on its pages: the rise of fascism.

Until at least November 1932, he was a Socialist. Six months later, he apparently saw little to choose between Norman Thomas and either Herbert Hoover or "the Hyde Park radicalism of Mr. Roosevelt." What happened to change his mind? On January 22, 1933, Isidor Feinstein reviewed a pair of books analyzing recent events in Germany for the *Record*. He treated both of them favorably, but the author of one, Oswald Garrison Villard (a Socialist comrade), came in for special praise: "Villard, in a passionate and fact-crammed book . . ."; "Villard after a brilliant analysis of Hitlerism concludes that should the German Nazi leader come to power 'the loss to Germany would be incalculable' . . ." The reviewer ended on a reassuring note: "Fortunately neither Villard nor [the second author, the *Chicago Daily News* correspondent Edgar] Mowrer thinks highly of Hitler's chances at dictatorship . . . And both believe Hitler's decline and his party's breakup inevitable should he assume power and be called upon to make good on his inconsistent and impossible crazy quilt of a program."[108]

Adolf Hitler was sworn in as chancellor of Germany eight days later.

---

*He was referring to Calverton's autumn 1932 attack on Stalinism, the theory of "social fascism," and "the tactic of making various outsiders, especially those close to the Party, scapegoats for inner factional fights."

The *Record* was still hopeful: "Position without power may weaken Hitler," who, in the editorialist's view, is but a tool of "the Junkers and industrialists." Or "the Nazis may be emboldened to attempt full seizure of power, an attempt that would almost certainly plunge Germany into civil war. Or the trades unions, Social Democratic, Centrist and Communist, may join before it is too late."[109] But by April 1933, when the byline Abelard Stone made its first appearance, the situation was very different.

Abelard Stone's debut in the *Modern Monthly* was a critique of the same two books reviewed by Isidor Feinstein in the *Record*. Though many phrases recur, and though both books "may be recommended to those seeking a rehash of the facts about the German Republic," this time the "liberal limitations of" Villard and the nature of Mowrer's job (as a newspaper reporter) "keep either of them from getting very far from the regulation liberal explanation." The writer thought that David Stern's liberalism, like that of Oswald Garrison Villard, had its limits, and clearly the constraint of his employment on the *Record* made a pseudonym prudent. But the deeper source of radical energy and radical anger that gave voice to Abelard Stone can be seen when he turns on his formerly brilliant comrade:

> Mr. Villard almost admits what is now so clear—the betrayal of the German working classes by the Social Democrats—when he says of their conduct in the revolution—
>
> "So from being too destructive, the leaders were not destructive enough . . . They might well have taken leaves out of the Russian book *without, however, resorting to the cruel and bloody ruthlessness of the Soviets* . . ."
>
> The italics, as they say, are mine but the explanation of just how capitalists and landowners were to be eliminated without "the cruel and bloody ruthlessness of the Soviets" must be left to Mr. Villard.[110]

The text was betrayal at the dawn of the Weimar Republic, when Germany's Social Democrats joined forces with the old regime to strangle the 1918–19 revolution. But the subtext is unmistakable: Again in 1933 the Socialists, still blinded by their hostility to communism, failed to act to prevent the Nazis from coming to power. Stone's scorn for "Germany's fake Socialists" is even more emphatic in a *Record* editorial, also from

April 1933, accusing the Social Democrats of being "ready to 'play nice' if Hitler will permit them an occasional dip into the government feedbag."[111] When Heywood Broun, whose syndicated column balanced Walter Lippmann across the *Record*'s editorial page, resigned from the American Socialist Party, he advised his readers: "in getting out of the Socialist Party one should leave by the door to the left." The Socialist Villard, wrote Abelard Stone, showed a "lack of realism," a common fault among liberals, who, "when deception is too transparent, usually help out by deceiving themselves, or reading Walter Lippmann."[112] Isidor Feinstein was taking the door to the left.

There was no Damascene conversion—just an apparent hardening of options. The view that Roosevelt's first moves were harbingers of fascism, though heretical to the likes of David Stern, was fairly common among the American left. Norman Thomas and Reinhold Niebuhr voiced similar reservations. History would prove them wrong, just as it was wrong of Stone to explain Hitler's rise to power by Socialist betrayal. But if you believed both these things in the summer of 1933, the implication was clear enough.[113]

And yet Isidor Feinstein never joined the Communist Party, even though his position on a number of issues was so close to the party line as to be indistinguishable. By allowing him complete freedom, V. F. Calverton had brought "Iz" closer to the party than he would ever be again. But in rejecting Calverton as a renegade, the Communists also lost Abelard Stone. Another road opened for Isidor Feinstein. Within three years he would be an intimate in the highest councils of the New Deal. His brother Max, now known as Marc, did join the Communist Party. So did his brother Louis. Even their little sister, Judith, eventually became a Communist. Isidor Feinstein never did. Instead, he moved to New York.

Three

MANHATTAN TRANSFER

———•◆•———

The rumor of a great city goes out beyond its borders . . .
———The Federal Writers' Project, *New York Panorama*

A straphanger who picked up the *New York Evening Post* on the way home from work on Monday, December 11, 1933, held a very different newspaper from the stolid, lethargic tabloid he would have read the previous Friday. Over the weekend the paper had grown into a broadsheet with a new masthead, a new owner, and a new attitude. The most prominent item on page one was a letter, on White House stationery: "My dear Dave: I want you to know how glad I was to hear that you had bought the New York Evening Post."

Franklin Roosevelt had ample cause for gratitude. Since the end of Joseph Pulitzer's *World* (swallowed by Scripps-Howard in 1931), the nation's largest city boasted not a single liberal newspaper.* With losses in excess of $1 million a year, the *Post* wasn't a financially compelling proposition.[1] But J. David Stern and his friend Albert Greenfield, now a rising power broker in the Democratic Party, saw a political opening. "I am 100 percent behind President Roosevelt," Stern pledged.

When Isidor Feinstein heard that Stern had bought the *Post*, he didn't

———

*Though Joseph Medill Patterson's *Daily News* was at this point still technically a supporter of the New Deal, Patterson's choleric populism was already showing signs of the *News*'s impending swing to the right.

hesitate. "Izzy high-tailed it up there without telling anybody," recalled Sam Grafton, whose more orderly transfer to New York took place six months later.[2] The twenty-five-year-old hopped a train to New York and presented himself at the *Post*'s offices at 75 West Street as the paper's new editorial writer the day before Stern's first issue went to press. His chutzpah was rewarded with an assignment to write the front-page editorial explaining the paper's new policy.

Fortified by a quick perusal of Allan Nevins's recently published history of the paper, he reminded readers that in its 132-year history, the *Post* hadn't hesitated "to throw in its lot with insurgent Barnburners, Locofocoes, and Mugwumps." The new management, he promised, intended to continue the tradition of a "fighting, independent, liberal newspaper." But the editorial also made the paper's allegiance to Franklin Roosevelt subject to terms and conditions: "The POST will support the New Deal as long as that New Deal offers hope of alleviating mal-distribution of wealth, which is our fundamental ill, and of restoring economic health and social justice."[3]

In time the difference of emphasis between Stern the gung-ho New Dealer and his more skeptical young editorial writer widened into an irreparable breach. In 1933, however, Isidor Feinstein was still Stern's favorite. With three papers to run, the publisher was happy to let this energetic young man take charge of the *Post*'s editorials, happy to endorse his efforts to restore the glory days when "fighting editors and fighting owners gave power to its editorial page."[4] It was several years before Stern noticed that his protégé put editors before owners.

If the newly minted New Yorker's syntax hinted at insubordination, his conscious thoughts were on mastering his job. "I was just thrilled to death to be in the big city at last," Stone later recalled. He was also terrified: "I'd walk along under the Ninth Avenue El to the paper and I'd start to vomit like a pregnant woman from excitement."[5]

Isidor Feinstein's eagerness to get to New York wasn't just professional. In 1932, the United Bargain Store had finally closed its doors. Too proud to claim bankruptcy, Bernard Feinstein had picked up his pack and gone door-to-door selling silk stockings until all his creditors were paid off.[6] A year later he'd moved his family to the Logan section of west Philadelphia. The loss of the store pushed Katy into a manic period. "She would buy yard goods and she would make aprons," said Louis Stone of his mother's attempt to contribute to the family's precarious finances. "She was a very good seamstress. She'd do all kinds of things with a sewing machine. But when she became manic, she wouldn't work with care. She'd make an apron, and it wouldn't match up with the pattern. She'd make a whole heap of these aprons, and she'd try to sell them door-to-door. She was hard to control."[7] When Katy went into the hospital this time, she was taken not to the cheerful Kirkbride's but to Norristown State Hospital, a grim, over-crowded institution where patients were often left unsupervised.[8]

With Bernard and Katy living nearby, the pressure on their eldest son had become intense. Squeezed between filial duty and the demands of his career, already chafing under the strictures of Stern's editorial policy, for Isidor Feinstein the opportunity to move to New York was more than an opening; it was a lifeline.

•

When Isidor Feinstein installed himself at the *Post*, New York was still poised on the brink of becoming the "world city" celebrated by the anony-mous bards of the Federal Writers' Project.[9] The infrastructure was in place: Robert Moses's gleaming parkways bringing workers and pleasure seekers into the metropolis, or outward to the beaches of Long Island, were newly opened. So were the Amalgamated Houses on Grand Street; the Century, the San Remo, and the Majestic on Central Park West; and the Manhattan office towers whose names alone—the Chrysler Building, the R.C.A. Building, the Empire State Building—seem to evoke the hero-ism of urban life.[10]

New York's transfiguration had been under way for some time. "After the war," wrote Dos Passos, "New York . . . Nobody can keep away from it."[11] Between 1910 and 1930, the city's population doubled, as a flood-tide of immigrants and arrivistes turned New York from a city to *the* city, the Big Apple of the jazzman's eye, a mecca for talent and ambition, an entrepôt of ideas, a cosmopolis.[12] In the 1920s, Manhattan was already moving—there was a renaissance up in Harlem and plenty of money to be made on Wall Street—but it still had competition: not just London, still arguably the world's financial center, or Paris, capital of the nineteenth century and, for the second decade of the twentieth, home to the most important voices in American literature, but also Chicago, birthplace of the *Dial* and the *Little Review*, home to *Poetry*, a city with its own pre-tensions to cultural preeminence. New York's undisputed primacy was forged on the anvil of economic calamity. The 1920s had provided the raw material, but it was the Depression, with its unprecedented demands, shifting alliances, and desperate experimentation, that made the city. And it was New York—pragmatic, confident, cosmopolitan—that turned a small-town newspaperman into a big-city reporter.

New Yorkers in the 1920s were beginning to entertain advanced ideas in music, literature, theater, and painting, but the city's politics were still a jungle of patronage and corruption where the Tammany Tiger, symbol of Manhattan's Democratic machine, roared unchallenged. Under Mayor Jimmy Walker, the brilliantined, tuxedo-clad front man for Tammany who as a young man peddled songs in Tin Pan Alley, New Yorkers had a government described as "high, wide, and handsome."[13] But in March 1931, Governor Franklin Roosevelt had appointed Judge Samuel Seabury to investigate, and Seabury's revelation of widespread corruption had forced Walker to resign in September 1932. When Isidor Feinstein arrived on the scene, New Yorkers had just elected Fiorello La Guardia—a half-Italian, half-Jewish Republican socialist congressman from East Harlem—to City Hall.

A veteran of the campaign to save Sacco and Vanzetti and a former lawyer for the Amalgamated Clothing Workers, La Guardia, with his mixed parentage and membership in the Episcopal church and the Masons, was, in Robert Caro's splendid phrase, "practically a balanced ticket all by himself." Pugnacious, passionate, able to rouse a crowd in seven languages— appearing before a legislative committee on rent controls, La Guardia announced: "I come not to praise the landlord but to bury him"—the Little Flower offered the *Post*'s new editorialist his first chance to shine.[14]

"There was a Tammany Hall hack coming up for reappointment, and La Guardia had just been elected," Stone recalled.

[The mayor] was one of my heroes—one of Stern's heroes, too. Stern called an editorial conference . . . Of course, I was the youngest guy there. And I was the only guy there that wasn't a New Yorker. But I knew the conference was coming, so after work the night before I went to the library and got out all the clippings on this fellow. The next day Stern called on me last as the junior member, and I proceeded to give a thorough review of the man's career, point out all the issues, and Stern was so proud that this kid he'd brought up from Philadelphia knew more than anyone else on the paper.

The resulting editorial—confident, well informed, and full of reservations about the reappointment of Tammany Transportation Board chairman John Delaney—pleased the publisher so much he put it on the front page.[15]

All three of Stern's papers shared editorials (as well as national advertising, which was why the *Post* became a broadsheet). But for his first six months in New York, Izzy was on his own: "I [practically] wrote the whole goddamned editorial page . . . And edited the mailbag and letters to the editor and the side stuff." His colleagues didn't like being shown up by "the kid," but Izzy had no choice. He had to become an expert on New York and its problems, he had to acquire this expertise quickly, and, if he was to be respected, he had to do it without asking a lot of questions in the newsroom. Once again he'd arrived in the middle of the game. Luckily for Isidor Feinstein, this time he could consult a program.

"I'd done publicity for Norman Thomas. And Norman Thomas did a wonderful book on New York at about that time." Published in 1932, *What's the Matter with New York* is indeed an extraordinary book. "Among the intelligentsia," say Thomas and his coauthor, Paul Blanshard, "it is smart to be cynical concerning all forms of democracy and especially local democracy. A man who discusses intelligently the color line in South Africa and the freedom of India will consider a street-car franchise in Brooklyn beneath his mental range." To correct this prejudice, the two Socialists marshaled an astonishing range of arguments. "In Russia under the leadership of a remarkable group of intellectuals, the city proletariat has not only overthrown the old order in the city but has carried to a bewildered and often reluctant countryside a coercive gospel of socialist salvation. So the city which to the shepherd and peasant has always been the symbol and home of a predatory culture appears in a new role as the pioneer of a system that challenges old acquisitive standards."[16] Here was a novel use for the prestige of the Russian Revolution: not to encourage submission to the Comintern but as evidence that the city, in Populist and Progressive mythology generally depicted as Sodom, could also function as the cradle of revolt.

From the realpolitik acknowledgment that "only a party machine can defeat a party machine" (which must have been music to David Stern's ears) to their classic muckraker's analysis of the city's subway finances, Thomas and Blanshard offered raw material for a dozen crusades and hundreds of editorials. Zoning rackets, sweetheart contracts, city franchises, pier rights, insurance commissions, interest-free bank accounts—the whole gaudy array of what the Tammany Hall founder George

Washington Plunkitt called "good honest graft" was anatomized and explained. For a young man suddenly obliged to consider Brooklyn streetcar franchises very much within his purview, the book was a godsend. The authors' verdict on the new president, "a nice person who once graduated from Harvard, has a good radio voice, and is as sincere as old party politics will permit," while in retrospect as wide of the mark as their admiration for the Soviets' "coercive gospel of socialist salvation," must at the time have only enhanced their credibility with the young editorialist.[17]

Norman Thomas was already a *Post* ally on one of David Stern's more dramatic policy shifts: the boycott of German-made goods. In May 1933, before Stern had bought the paper, the *Post* (like every other New York daily) had opposed the call by Samuel Untermyer, a prominent New York lawyer and founder of the Non-Sectarian Anti-Nazi League, for a boycott in response to Germany's new law barring Jews from German universities and from the civil service. Terming the proposal "a bad weapon," the *Post* editorial warned, "All boycotts 'hurt business' . . . This action by American Jews may well tend to drag America into a form of opposition to Germany that it might not care to take." But Norman Thomas refused to let the boycott be dismissed as a "Jewish" matter, leading hundreds of demonstrators to Macy's carrying placards that read: 'Macy's Buys German Goods, We Want No Fascism Here.' Stern's *Philadelphia Record* had been one of Untermyer's earliest backers—a stand which, when Stern reiterated his backing in the *Post*, initially cost the paper all its Macy's advertising.[18]

Certainly when Mayor-elect La Guardia, announcing his first six appointments, named Paul Blanshard as commissioner of accounts, a position allowing him to look into the finances of all city departments, the *Post* cheered: "La Guardia is living up to his promises."[19] That same day the paper's editorial writer, taking a leaf from Thomas and Blanshard, described the pension arrangements made by the outgoing mayor, John P. O'Brien, as "a new form of graft."[20] The explosion of mayoral wrath that resulted was gleefully recounted on the next day's front page:

> The Mayor read. Then saw red. Then telephoned personally . . .
> He didn't like the editorial, and he didn't like editorial writers, either. "That editorial was libellous and somebody should go to jail for it," he said in the loudest of Mayoral voices. "The man who wrote it should be thrown off the paper."

As it happened, it was the author of the editorial whom the Mayor was addressing. The author, a quiet man of 110 pounds, received the dictum with all the deference due exalted office, suppressing, out of high respect, his natural tendency to argue the point.[21]

After less than a week in the job, he already had the mayor of New York calling for his head. Isidor Feinstein had arrived. Esther and baby Celia soon joined him in New York, and the family settled at 1 West 68th Street, a small apartment building on the corner of Central Park West whose other tenants included Blanche Walton, a patron of modern music. Walton's two guest rooms overlooking Central Park were their own miniature artists' colony, housing at various times Béla Bartók, Henry Cowell, Ruth Crawford, and her husband, Charles Seeger.

The Asia scholar Jonathan Mirsky,* who grew up in the building, remembers Esther's total focus on her husband—"she worshipped him"—and the warm welcome she extended to any of her children's friends. The Mirskys were "lefty Jewish intellectuals," he said—his father, Alfred Mirsky, was a pioneering molecular biologist and his mother, Reba Paeff Mirsky, a musician and author of children's books—and the two families became close. Mirsky's older sister, Reba Goodman, recalls the way "whenever Izzy took a bath he always had Esther sit with him to keep him company"—an image of domestic harmony that was in contrast to her own parents' more difficult marriage.

•

Michael Blankfort had arrived, too. While his best friend courted controversy at the *Post*, Blankfort was fomenting revolution in Greenwich Village. Backed by a $2,000 check from John Hammond, the producer of Benny Goodman and Billie Holiday, in December the Theatre Union opened its first production, *Peace on Earth*. Written by Albert Maltz and George Sklar, the antiwar drama was directed by Blankfort. "We hoped to make radicals out of the audiences, and further than that we hoped to make communist sympathizers out of the radicals," he recalled.[22]

---

*Nearly seventy years after they became neighbors, Mirsky was named the first I. F. Stone teaching fellow at the University of California, Berkeley.

Of course, many of those in attendance on opening night at Eva Le Gallienne's Civic Repertory Theatre were already converted. One was Charles Shipman. Like Maltz and Sklar, Shipman was a Communist. In fact, under his party name, Manuel Gomez, he'd been one of the founders of the Mexican Communist Party. An American-born Jew, Shipman was also a talented actor, and in a break from his work for the Comintern joined the theater union, again under the name Gomez—this time to avoid scandalizing his bosses at the *Wall Street Journal*, where he wrote a stock market column.[23]

It was probably Blankfort who introduced the two newspapermen. A few weeks after *Peace on Earth* opened—"received by the labor press and audience with enthusiasm but by the Broadway critics with anguish"[24]— Shipman had a visitor at the *Journal*: "Izzy came to my office with his managing editor [Ernest Gruening], whom I had heard of, but never met, and . . . promptly offered me the *Post*'s financial editorship."[25]

By the time Shipman arrived at the *Post*, Gruening, a former editor of the *Nation*, had left it. "I reported directly to Stern, who ran the paper himself. Instead of a conventional financial section covering stocks and bonds, he wanted pieces about everyday money matters and economic problems, written from an FDR point of view. Then, without warning, he presented me with a bold new masthead for my section: 'The New Deal in Business.'" Shipman resigned.[26] But his friendship with the man who recruited him remained unaffected.

This was not unusual. Though theoretically the Communist Party was at the height of the "Third Period," a time when good Communists were supposed to be vigorous in denunciation of any leftist outside the party, Isidor Feinstein was not a member of the party and was not bound by party discipline. He moved comfortably in party circles, and had "family and friends" in the party, but "I always tried to keep away from ugly, blind, suicidal infighting on the left," he recalled decades later. "The idea of being subject to party discipline and told what to do, or what to think, or what to write was absolutely repugnant to me."[27]

A one-man united front, Izzy had brought the tolerant comradeship of the Leof-Blitzstein household at 322 with him to New York. "I tried to befriend everyone. I had socialists, communists, Trotskyists, Lovestoneites and liberals for friends. My door was open."[28] Just before he'd left Philadelphia, he'd joined the Newspaper Guild. "Heywood Broun came down and organized us" [at the *Record*, the first major daily to sign a guild contract]. In the fledgling guild, too, liberals and leftists of all stripes managed to work together. But he soon found that New York was not Philadelphia: "The radicals were distracted by the most ugly nasty sectarian quarrels. They would hate each other and fight even within the parties— the different parties—for lousy little $50 a week jobs." His enthusiasm for a "Soviet America" was fast becoming a thing of the past: "You know, it wasn't just Stalin. There were a lot of little Stalins in the Party. I don't want to mention anybody's name,* but there were some pretty horrible people, and they acted like little Stalins right in New York."[29]

Izzy had been in New York just three months when he found himself on the sidelines of a conflict that strained his determination to avoid sectarian bitterness and underlined the terrible consequences of a left divided against itself. The setting was Madison Square Garden, but, as in his departure from the Socialist Party, the background was German. Austria's Christian Socialist premier, Engelbert Dollfuss, had been ruling by decree ever since he'd dissolved the country's parliament in March 1933. Despite numerous offers of cooperation from the Austrian Social Democrats, who proposed an anti-Nazi front, Dollfuss made common cause with the Fascist Heimwehr (Home Guard) and, in February 1934, he moved to crush Austria's Social Democratic Party and all other political parties. With the Austrian left still at the barricades, the *Post* ran an editorial attacking Dollfuss and calling for "a broad united front . . . to save Austria from the Nazis."[30] New York's labor unions organized a rally against Dollfuss at Madison Square Garden on February 16, but what was intended as a show of labor unity and solidarity soon degenerated into a melee when Communist hecklers accused Austrian Socialists of "disarming and deserting" the workers. As New York's united front against fascism turned into a free-for-all, one speaker could be heard above the fisticuffs. Frank Crosswaith, an African-American Socialist, shouted that the Communists were pigs "who will always remain pigs because it is in the nature of Communists to be pigs."[31]

A *Post* editorial written by David Stern himself was equally forthright: "Communists staged a disgraceful spectacle in breaking up the Austrian

---

*Foremost among the names he did mention was V. J. Jerome, editor of the *Communist* magazine and the party's longtime cultural commissar.

protest meeting at Madison Square Garden . . . Had some other organization used the same tactics to break up a united anti-Fascist meeting in
the same way, the Communists would have found no epithet too vile for
such 'traitorous' conduct."[32] The editorial went on to quote a former president of Germany's Federation of Clothing Workers: "It was precisely
such spectacles as that staged here today that led to the triumph of
Hitlerism in Germany." Isidor Feinstein might have agreed with that,
but not with the editorial's assertion that "only Nazi hoodlums could
have equaled . . . the Communists." By now he was virtually obsessed
by what he saw as the German and Austrian left's failure to unite against
the Nazi threat, which is why the CPUSA's plunge down the same sectarian road pained him so much. In the fights he cared about most—the
battle against hunger, exploitation, and the spread of fascism at home and
in Europe—he thought of Communists and liberals both as potential
allies. "You might, at one and the same time, laugh at the *Daily Worker*
and their stuff on Stalin and Russia, [but] here in America, they were
comrades."[33]

"Millions of Americans want reforms more basic, measures more liberal than those which the New Deal has so far developed," declared a *Post*
editorial. Officially, the Communist Party was still deaf to this "thunder
on the left," being committed to what it called "the United Front from below"—in Izzy's words, "a fake United Front,"[34] according to which party
members were supposed to support the aims of other radical groups while
subtly suggesting that rival leaders lacked the organizational know-how to
achieve them. "It was really an effort to take over their rivals," he said.[35]
But many Americans both in and out of the Communist Party were not
deaf to the thunder on the left.

•

For American radicals, the long, hot summer of 1934 was in some ways
the best of times. Franklin Roosevelt's inauguration the year before had
released an extraordinary outburst of reforming energy, symbolized by the
explosion of "alphabet agencies" that made up the early New Deal: among
them an Agricultural Adjustment Administration (AAA) to stabilize farm
prices, a Civilian Conservation Corps (CCC) to put the jobless to work
building roads and planting trees, a Public Works Administration (PWA)

to manage public projects, the Tennessee Valley Authority (TVA) to tame a river and bring electricity to the rural poor, and presiding over it all the National Recovery Administration (NRA) with its codes and blue eagle to put the nation's industrial economy back on its feet.

"We have two problems," Roosevelt had told a Boston audience in October 1932. "First, to meet the immediate distress; second, to build up on a basis of permanent employment." By the end of his legendary "hundred days" the first objective had been largely met. Roosevelt's inaugural "bank holiday"—little more than Hoover's proposed moratorium with a more upbeat name—had succeeded in restoring public confidence, and the subsequent frenzy of federal activity signaled that the era of government indifference to public misery was over. But the nation's problems were proving far more intransigent than the country's mood. AAA paid big farmers who agreed to plow under surplus crops—though "surplus" was itself a loaded term in a country where hunger was still widespread—but offered nothing to small farmers or sharecroppers. Nor was the CCC wage of $1 a day much help to a starving family. Federal mortgage relief kept lenders afloat but had little impact on repossessions. And after a year of "bold, persistent experimentation," nothing FDR tried succeeded in generating jobs.

"The first wild wave of hope under the New Deal had receded," wrote Alfred Kazin.[36] Six million workers had been unemployed for more than a year; two and a half million had been out of work for over two years.[37] And as the tide of liberalism receded, the seeds of revolt began to put up shoots.

In Toledo, Ohio, employees at Electric Auto-Lite went out on strike after management refused to recognize the union, though workers had been guaranteed the right to organize under Section 7A of the National Industrial Recovery Act. The company turned to the courts for an injunction to stop the picketing, and the National Guard was called in. But A. J. Muste's Lucas County Unemployed League defied the injunction, and after hand-to-hand fighting broke out, the city's Central Labor Council called a general strike.[38]

That July, when police tried to break up a strike of West Coast ports called by the International Longshoremen's Association leader, Harry Bridges, a general strike paralyzed San Francisco for three days. And in Minneapolis the International Brotherhood of Teamsters local, led by the Trotskyist Dunne brothers, shut down the city with a general strike despite the opposition of national Teamster officials and in the face of brutal police violence. In one skirmish, two workers were killed and sixty-seven wounded. Many of the casualties were shot in the back.[39]

All three of these strikes achieved their immediate goals. Indeed, whatever the limitations of Roosevelt's reforms, workers throughout the country seemed to take the New Deal's promises to heart even when their leaders did not. This was particularly true of the right to organize.[40] By the end of 1934, one and a half million workers had been involved in some 1,800 strikes—most over the issue of union recognition. Not all were successful. In the North Carolina Piedmont, 300,000 members of the United Textile Workers walked out in September, but the union was still unable to gain a firm foothold.[41] For the men and women involved in these struggles, though, there were gains beyond any tally of wins or losses. For them, the waves of strikes racking the country were the birth pangs of a movement. Before Minneapolis, the writer Meridel Le Sueur had "never been in a strike . . . I felt my feet join in that strange shuffle of thousands of bodies moving with direction, of thousands of feet, and my own breath. As if an electric charge had passed through me, my hair stood on end. I was marching."[42]

This movement did not yet have a name. It never would have a coherent ideology. But it did have what might be called an ethic of solidarity. Thus Meridel Le Sueur, a Communist, underwent her political baptism in a strike led by Trotskyists, and later in 1934 she joined the staff of the Minnesota Labor School, sponsored by the Minneapolis local of the International Ladies Garment Workers Union, led by the Socialist stalwart David Dubinsky.[43] The prospectus for *Arise*, a magazine put out by the Socialist Rebel Arts group in 1934, lists the Trotskyist poet John Brooks Wheelwright, the Communist cartoonist Art Young, and the radical lyricist E. Y. "Yip" Harburg along with the Socialist functionaries James Oneal and Sol Levitas.

In campaigns against lynching in the South and in efforts to organize farmworkers on the West Coast, rank-and-file radicals of all persuasions discovered an ability, often an eagerness, to work together even when their leaders were divided by official hostilities. This was especially true of college students. At eleven o'clock in the morning on April 13, 1934, hundreds of thousands of students across the country put down their books and walked out of classes in a Student Strike Against War. The strike had been called by both the Communist-led National Student League and the Socialist Student League for Industrial Democracy, and was probably the most significant national harbinger of what was to become the Popular Front. (Indeed, by the end of 1935, the two groups would merge to form the American Student Union.)[44]

There were local outbreaks as well. At the finale of a Young People's Concert in Philadelphia, the orchestra's conductor, Leopold Stokowski, led the audience in singing the "Internationale."[45] The renegade Socialist Upton Sinclair's End Poverty in California (EPIC) campaign, while rejected by the leaders of both the Democratic and Communist parties, drew enough grassroots support to gain him victory in the state's 1934 Democratic gubernatorial primary. Like Franklin Roosevelt, David Stern rejected Sinclair's efforts to steer the Democrats leftward. "Liberalism seeks the middle of the road," scolded the *Post*. A month earlier, the paper had warned that any spread of San Francisco's general strike "would be a national calamity."[46] But when a similar coalition of communists (small *c* and capital *C*), Socialists, and assorted agitators in New York became engaged in a battle with Fiorello La Guardia's police commissioner, the *Post* weighed in on the side of the radicals.

Hostilities began on May 26, 1934. The location was relief headquarters* in Manhattan. A delegation from the United Action Committee (UAC), an organization of white-collar workers on relief, demanded a meeting with the city's deputy welfare commissioner to press for restoration of work-relief pay cuts, more public works jobs, and the opening of more relief bureaus. Instead, the demonstrators were met by a platoon of riot police, who waded in with clubs and fists. Several protesters were arrested and charged with incitement to riot. The following day, when a group was being arraigned, "at a signal from the magistrate, police hidden in rooms adjoining the court cleared it of spectators and staged an attack so brutal that two reporters intervened."[47] The reporters were from the *Daily News* and the *Daily Worker*, and while both papers reported the facts, the *News* editorial page derided talk of police brutality: "So long as the Red minority keeps trying to force its will on the majority by violence,

*Although in many cities "outdoor relief"—payments to those who were not living in almshouses or other institutions—was either nonexistent or left to the discretion of private charities, New York actually had a municipal relief system.

the police will have to use necessary force, mixed with their usual good judgment of course, to block the Reds."[48]

The *Post*, however, made the incident into a cause célèbre. Handicapped by the lack of a reporter on the scene, the *Post* had other assets, chief among them the wide acquaintance of its new editorial writer. Isidor Feinstein had already criticized Commissioner John F. O'Ryan for his men's frequent application of the nightstick to the skulls of New York's hungry and jobless, on one occasion defending a Communist relief worker, a slim, feisty woman who'd been arrested for attacking a policeman after she'd tried to prevent a beating.[49] "Because I was not sectarian," he recalled, "I was able to line up liberals, radicals, Trotskyites, Communists, Lovestoneites, et cetera, in a joint campaign to get rid of O'Ryan."

Throughout the summer, the *Post* editorial page kept up a steady barrage against the commissioner. O'Ryan's defenders, including La Guardia, pointed to the presence of Communists among the UAC leadership to justify the claim that the police had been provoked. But the mayor, who had described the UAC demonstrators as "yellow dogs" in May, began to reconsider after the commissioner's men beat up an Amalgamated Clothing Workers picket line. "O'Ryan Must Go" thundered the *Post*.[50]

The coup de grâce, administered by Isidor Feinstein, came not in an editorial but in a page-one news story: "I broke a story that really hurt him. I dug up the fact—there was a book by Elizabeth Dilling called *The Red Network*. I discovered that the Red Squad [the police department's Alien and Criminal Squad] was using that as its handbook, and one of the Reds listed in La Guardia's Red Squad handbook was Fiorello H. La Guardia! We put that right on the front page, quoting the Red rogues' gallery picture of this dangerous radical."[51] O'Ryan resigned soon afterward, and La Guardia, declaring that "economic issues cannot be settled with a nightstick," banned police from carrying clubs during daylight hours.[52]

The *Post*'s triumphant campaign against police brutality was significant for several reasons. The coalition Izzy put together of organized labor, Communists, radical intellectuals, and middle-class civil libertarians was soon to serve as a model for Popular Front organizing in New York, and its orchestration of mainstream press outcry and street protest was to become a hallmark of Popular Front tactics, as would the UAC's mix of Communists in some leadership positions but a largely non-Communist rank and file. This lesson of what could be accomplished by a diverse but united left was not lost on him. In the meantime, a dispatch from the front line headlined "How to Make a Riot" launched the young author onto the pages of the *New Republic*. The magazine's Contributors column credited him with making "the editorial page of [the *Post*] one of the high spots of New York journalism."

Success attracted celebrity. The Feinsteins' apartment on Central Park West became a gathering place for radicals of varying degrees of commitment. Some, like the former Communist vice presidential candidate Benjamin Gitlow and the freelance radical publicist Benjamin Stolberg, stayed only briefly before resuming their journeys to the far right. Others, like the Alabama senator Hugo Black, the *Nation* editor Max Lerner, and the *New Republic* editor Malcolm Cowley, were in for the longer haul.[53] And though Isidor Feinstein was energetically scaling the heights of political journalism, neither his hospitality nor his attention was restricted to those in a position to help his career. The young Arnold Beichman had just graduated from Columbia, where he'd edited the student newspaper, the *Spectator*, and been one of the leaders in the Student Strike Against War, when he was given a tryout on the *Post*'s editorial page. Beichman recalled, "The very first one I wrote—boom!—he took it right that day. Izzy was so taken with me, he took me to dinner with his wife, and afterward, he took me to meet Michael Blankfort, which was awesome to me, because he was a playwright, and had written for the *New Masses*."[54]

"We lived like kings," said Samuel Grafton, who joined the *Post* in June 1934. "I was making $125 a week. We had an eight-room apartment on Central Park West that cost $75 a month. We had a Japanese butler, he cost $50 a month. I had a car. In those days you could park outside a Broadway theater, see a show."[55] Though the Feinsteins also lived well, they had other obligations. "When we lost our business . . . lost everything, Izzy came to our rescue," Louis Stone remembered. "There was a period when he was paying our rent." Even so, Izzy and Esther managed to employ a full-time maid and, when Esther became pregnant again in early 1935, a woman to help look after the children.

Central Park West was a long way from the welfare office or the San Francisco docks or the streets of Minneapolis. But the cost in human misery of capitalism's boom-and-bust cycles was never, for Isidor Feinstein, a mere abstraction. It is easy in retrospect to ridicule the mix of culture and politics that was being born in New York in the early 1930s as naïve (about

Stalin), sentimental (about the working class), and sadly inattentive to the virtues of high culture (as opposed to the ersatz verities of Earl Robinson oratorios or Pete Seeger's Almanac Singers). Richard Rovere described the "cultural tone" of the 1930s as "deplorable because it was metallic and strident. Communist culture was not aristocratic; it was cheap and vulgar and corny."[56] It was a tone mercilessly satirized by Michael Blankfort in his first novel, when the hero, a former fellow-traveling screenwriter, is reminded of a poem he'd published in the *New Masses*:

> *This is our joy, that we are part of you.*
> *This is our song, the one you sing.*
> *This is our task, the freeing of you.*
> *This is our life, your life.*

"It's pretty bad, isn't it? What did I call it?" the screenwriter asks. The answer sums up Blankfort's retrospective disillusionment: "To Sacco and Vanzetti, to Tom Mooney,* to Angelo Herndon"†—a whole calendar of Communist martyrs.[57]

Yet it is wrong to dismiss the culture of the Popular Front as one long hootenanny. Not only does that belittle considerable achievement, from the music of Marc Blitzstein to the reportage of Martha Gellhorn to the poetry of Langston Hughes. It also rides roughshod over what it meant to the vast majority of Americans who, perhaps for the first time, saw their own lives represented with all the verve and sophistication of a Duke Ellington or the passion and pathos of a John Garfield. The culture of the Popular Front is often caricatured as crude, Soviet inspired, and relentlessly middle-brow. It could be all those things, but it could also be subtle, daring, and as American as cherry pie—or "Strange Fruit." It was a culture that arose out of the interweaving of political activism, cultural experimentation, and desperate circumstance. For Isidor Feinstein, as for many others, that interweaving was not just a stance, or a "tone"—it was a personal necessity.

---

*Mooney, a San Francisco union activist, spent twenty-two years in prison after being framed on charges of planting bombs. An international campaign eventually won his pardon in 1938.

†Herndon was an African-American organizer for the Unemployed Council in Georgia, where in 1932 he was tried and convicted under a state sedition law and sentenced to twenty years in prison. He was released after two years, and in 1937, his conviction was overturned by the Supreme Court.

•

Close readers of the *New York Post* editorial page during the years 1934 and 1935 might have noticed a kind of split personality. In national politics, the paper was solidly Democratic; locally, the *Post* backed the Republican La Guardia. But given the warm relationship between FDR and the mayor, that contradiction was more apparent than real. Pro-labor, anti-Hearst, tolerant on race—on all these issues the *Post* spoke with a consistent voice. Like most publishers, J. David Stern rode his hobbyhorse. "He was hipped on money," recalled Sam Grafton. "If you could change the currency from the gold standard, it would solve everything. He was a print-money man. We catered to him from time to time and wrote editorials about it." Catering to Stern's hostility to the nascent - alliance between Communists and the rest of the left was more difficult.

To Stern, the CP couldn't do anything right. Did the party's International Labor Defense (ILD) successfully mobilize thousands of people around the world to protest against the legal lynching of the Scottsboro Boys*? As far as Stern was concerned, no credit was due "the silly cavorting of Red demonstrators," nor was anything accomplished by "the spirit of class warfare."[58] Did the Comintern come out in favor of religious freedom for all anti-Fascists? "Too Dumb to Be Dangerous," said the *Post*, calling the move "as meaningless as a Nazi pledge to respect the religious beliefs of Nazis."[59] Both Stern and his longtime lieutenant, the *Post*'s managing editor, Harry T. Saylor, were vociferous in their disdain for "parlor pinks and Communist sympathizers."[60] Stalin, the Soviet Union, and the CPUSA were, in Stern's view, synonymous, and as evil as Hitler or the Nazis.

Yet the same editorial page that printed Stern's "Communism and Fascism are new labels, but the founders of this country knew them under other forms" also warned, "They talk Americanism but they mean Fascism"—one of many *Post* denunciations of Massachusetts Congressman John McCormack's new Special Committee on Un-American Activities.[61] "Special privilege in America has always had its bogeymen," the

---

*Nine young black men falsely accused of raping two white women and sentenced to death by an all-white jury in Scottsboro, Alabama, in April 1931. Feinstein closely followed the case.

Post noted. "In the first years of the Republic they were 'Jacobins.' Today the bogeymen are 'Communists.' Anyone who wants to organize labor, or shield the consumer, or protect civil liberties, or strengthen regulation, or end financial excesses is called a 'Communist.'"[62]

While David Stern himself could have written the *Post*'s ringing declaration that "the Constitution protects Communists and Fascists as well as Republicans and Democrats," only Isidor Feinstein would insist on acknowledging that "the Communist and Socialist Parties are the only ones interested in organizing the unemployed and workers on relief . . . The result is that our relief-worker organizations are largely controlled by one or another of the fifty-seven varieties of radicals: right, center, left and R.P.C.* Socialists, official Communists, Right Opposition Communists, Left Opposition Communists, Lovestoneites, Trotskyites, American Workers Party, I.W.W., etc . . . *It must also be recognized that such organizations do a lot of good*" (emphasis added).[63]

The *Post*'s divergence on communism reflected a genuine ambivalence about any measures beyond middle-of-the-road liberalism, but the party's line on radical cooperation was scarcely more coherent. Officially the party was still hostile to Franklin Roosevelt and deeply suspicious of the New Deal—as were many non-Communist commentators, from Norman Thomas and Reinhold Niebuhr to Max Lerner, who in 1935 wrote that "the logic of the New Deal" was increasingly becoming "the naked fist of the capitalist state."[64] That didn't prevent individual party members like Nathaniel Weyl or Lee Pressman from coming to Washington and working very hard to make the New Deal succeed.[65]

Well before the rise of Hitler or the election of FDR, some American Communists favored a more collaborative policy. Even as orthodox an apparatchik as Michael Gold, the *New Masses* scourge of social fascism in literature, came back from Moscow in 1930 to urge "it was of vital importance to enlist all friendly intellectuals into the ranks of the revolution. Every door must be opened wide to the fellow-travelers."[66] After 1933, with the consequences of sectarianism played out every day on the streets of Berlin and Vienna, many radicals, including Isidor Feinstein, walked through those doors. As Mark Naison argues, "It did not take much persuasion to make a Jewish printer or a Croatian steelworker hate Hitler, or

---

*Revolutionary Policy Committee, a short-lived caucus on the left wing of the Socialist Party.

a black school teacher denounce Mussolini, or an Austrian refugee actor raise funds for victims of the Dollfuss regime." And for intellectuals, especially Jewish intellectuals, "the myth of Soviet philo-semitism gave Communists a special panache."[67]

There were also plenty of reasons for a pragmatic line much closer to home. American Communists trying to organize tenant farmers found themselves walking the same fields and facing the same terror at the hands of the landlords and their hired gunmen as Socialist organizers. From the textile mills of the Carolina Piedmont to the factory farms of the San Joaquin valley, radicals breathed the same tear gas, felt the same clubs on their backs, and feared the same guardsmen's bullets, regardless of party affiliation. Irving Howe, no cheerleader for the Popular Front, observed: "There was a genuine urgency behind the clamor for a united front. Consider the feelings of socialists in Arkansas and Tennessee, who were trying, at the risk of their lives, to organize sharecroppers: didn't it make sense to work with anyone sharing their immediate objectives, no matter which idiotic theories Stalin advanced and his New York followers repeated? Or the socialists unionizing the automobile plants in Michigan: could they refuse out of hand to cooperate with communists who were also trying to organize the industry?"[68]

Ironically, it was V. F. Calverton's *Modern Monthly* that laid the theoretical groundwork for a rapprochement on the left. In the same June 1933 issue that had featured Abelard Stone's hankering after a Soviet America, the Trotskyist theoretician B. J. Field called for a "united front for immediate ends" in which he urged leftists to "March separately, Strike unitedly."[69] As Calverton's excommunication attests, the party was not yet ready to respond to such overtures. And though the Comintern in June 1934, facing the prospect of a right-wing government in France, ordered the French Communist Party to unite with the Socialists "at any price," the implications of such a move didn't filter down to Union Square for quite a while.[70]

A movement was finding its feet, but the Party still refused to join the party. At the climax of Clifford Odets's play *Waiting for Lefty*, audiences around the country rose up shouting, "Strike! Strike! Strike!" By the spring of 1935, *Lefty* had been performed in fifty cities and been banned in Boston, New Haven, and Newark; Isidor Feinstein thought the play deserved the Pulitzer Prize.[71] Though Odets was, at the time, a card-carrying

Communist, the party's cultural commissars panned his play. In June 1935, the critic Kenneth Burke, another *Modern Monthly* contributor (who, like Calverton, had no appetite for apostasy), gave a speech to the American Writers Congress on "Revolutionary Symbolism in America," proposing that the left base its rhetoric on "the People" rather than "the Worker." Burke's modest proposal, more a tactical suggestion than a profound disagreement, brought swift condemnation from party apparatchiks. Yet before the year was out, his "populist" heresy became Communist orthodoxy.[72]

The CPUSA didn't officially embrace a "united front against fascism and war" until July 1935, after Georgi Dimitroff, famed for his defiance as a defendant in the 1933 Reichstag Fire trial, announced the end of the party's confrontationist stance in a speech before the Seventh World Congress of the Communist International in Moscow. The *Post*, which had saluted Dimitroff's "courage and cleverness" in 1933, was predictably ambivalent.[73] Isidor Feinstein expressed relief that events in Germany had "taught the Left a lesson [and] . . . led Moscow to modify its policy, to subordinate revolutionary aims, and to offer cooperation to 'capitalist' nations and 'capitalist' parties for the sake of a firm stand against war and Fascism." But David Stern, though opposed to fascism, was more concerned about war. Wary of the Popular Front on political grounds, he was also opposed to any alliance that might draw the United States into a European war. When Mussolini's legions threatened Ethiopia in the summer of 1935, the *Post*'s indignation was decidedly muted: "It's too bad about the Ethiopians, but they'll have to take care of themselves."[74]

The new Soviet Constitution of December 1936, with its Bill of Rights promising freedom of speech and conscience as well as the right to employment and to a secure old age, also drew a conflicting response from the *Post*. The paper's chief editorial writer hailed the "good impression made by the new Soviet Constitution and recent moves in the direction of more democratic government." But to Stern, the Soviets' "pretense at Democracy—almost as far-fetched as Hitler's pretense that he derives his authority from a popular referendum"—was just so much "borsch."[75] He was more favorably impressed by Moscow's sudden admiration for the New Deal. Dimitroff himself had laid down the new line: "The most reactionary circles of American finance capital, which are attacking Roosevelt," are the prime movers behind "the fascist movement in the United

States." Anyone who continued to view the New Deal as a step toward fascism, said Dimitroff, was guilty of a "stereotyped approach."[76]

The CPUSA hierarchy now quickly adapted to the call for cooperation on the left and to a view of the New Deal that put it to the right of the Socialist Party, just as it would be quick to return to sectarianism when Moscow changed its tune. Still, even if the party's Popular Front policies were, as Irving Howe charged, "conceived in bad faith and executed with bad faith," they enabled a degree of political effectiveness and cultural participation that Howe himself, writing fifty years later, called "the most promising approach of the American left, [the] one that apparently came closest to recognizing native realities."[77] While the Popular Front may have come as news to party headquarters on Union Square, it merely gave official sanction to practices that, from Harlem to Harlan County to Hollywood, were already well established at the grass roots.[78]

Yet if the movement that became known as the Popular Front was hardly called into being by party fiat, Moscow's benediction was not without significant consequences. Within the CPUSA, as Maurice Isserman and others have argued, Earl Browder's declaration that "Communism is Twentieth Century Americanism" provided "a bridge by which the children of immigrants could adapt themselves to the culture of the New World without renouncing the ideals that had sustained their parents."[79] Party membership rose from fewer than 15,000 in June 1933 to around 75,000 in 1938. In 1935 alone, more than 19,000 new recruits filled out party cards—a figure that rose to 25,000 in 1936, the first full year of the official Popular Front.[80]

With Franklin Roosevelt designated Fellow Traveler Number One, Isidor Feinstein found the atmosphere at the *Post* more hospitable, but the change did not happen overnight. In December 1935, a *Post* editorial put Russia near the top of the list of countries in thrall to "the Totalitarian God." Only Hitler, said the *Post*, "has managed to outdo the Bolsheviks in brutality."[81] But if David Stern's distrust of the Soviet Union remained, his hostility to the CPUSA, now enlisted as a dedicated cadre in the New Deal, seemed somewhat diminished. The *Post* now reserved its ire for reactionaries such as Hearst or "chunk-headed Tories and turncoat liberals."[82] The decline in sniping at his left flank allowed the paper's chief editorial writer to concentrate on his latest crusade: corruption in the American labor movement.

•

In September 1935, Isidor Feinstein made his debut in the *Nation* with a two-part series on racketeering in the American Federation of Labor. Starting from the premise that "powerful and militant unions are made all the more necessary . . . by the growing menace of fascism," he proceeded to give a vivid account of "the crushing of democracy in the trade unions by racketeers and the labor politicians who support them." The first article detailed the methods employed by a Teamster delegate named Arthur "Tootsie" Herbert and his brother Charles, a delegate of Local 440 of the Official Orthodox Poultry Slaughterers of America, to maintain control over the New York poultry market. In a classic piece of muckraking based on public records and a *Post* investigation, Feinstein traced the high cost of chicken in New York city markets first to a gangster monopoly enforced by murder and bombing, then to corrupt unions, and finally to "a criminal network that reaches high up into the Tammany organization."[83]

The language was colorful—"a veil was cast over Mr. 'Tootsie' Herbert's first steps on the ladder to success by the removal of his record and fingerprints from the Police Department"—but the moral was plain: "the A. F. of L. leadership is usually lined up on the side of the racketeers, for those who oppose the racketeers are always stigmatized as 'reds' no matter how pale their actual political convictions or affiliations may be." In his second installment, he described union elections "that make Tammany look genteel." This time the roll of dishonor ranged from the gangster-led painters' union and the equally corrupt Electrical Workers to metalworkers, dockworkers, and movie projectionists. Contrasting the swift "expulsion of 'radical' or 'Communist' groups within the ranks" to the AFL leader William Green's indulgent treatment of even convicted racketeers, the articles added up to a blistering indictment whose only heroes were Sidney Hillman of the Amalgamated Clothing Workers, Harry Bridges of the International Longshoremen's Association, and Louis Weinstock, an insurgent in the painters' union.[84]

In the late 1930s, the federal government was to begin a decades-long fight to deport Bridges as a Communist, and in the 1940s Weinstock became a pillar of the Russian War Relief, but, as the heroic depiction of the anti-Communist Hillman should make clear, Izzy's "Racketeering in the A.F. of L." was hardly a Communist-inspired venture. (For one thing, the *Na-*

tion's labor- and industry editor, Margaret Marshall, later to become the literary editor, was a staunch anti-Stalinist.) Rather, his effort as a muck-raker in the house of labor was a harbinger of changes that would soon turn the American labor movement upside down. After decades of exclusive crafts-dominated "business unionism," forces within the AFL were pushing hard for change. These forces, encouraged by the obvious breakdown in the capitalist order that the Depression had revealed, yet frustrated because existing labor organizations seemed unable to meet the challenge, had been growing in strength for several years.

The Communist Party represented only a fraction of labor's insurgent ranks, but it was a crucial fraction, running like a red thread not only through Isidor Feinstein's cast of characters but through the whole of what would soon become the Congress of Industrial Organizations. The CPUSA's embrace of the Popular Front and its speedy abandonment of its earlier, disastrous dual-union policy (embodied in the Trade Union Unity League, which had tried to start CP-controlled unions alongside existing unions) brought thousands of experienced, militant union activists back into the mainstream of American labor, veterans who acted as catalysts for a massive surge in organizing in the steel, rubber, and automobile industries. But (with a few possible exceptions, such as Harry Bridges) the leaders of this surge were not Communists; they were men like Hillman, or the Socialist Reuther brothers, Victor, Walter, and Roy, of the United Automobile Workers, or the fiercely anti-Communist David Dubinsky.[85] Fiercest of them all was John L. Lewis, indomitable head of the United Mine Workers.

Back in the 1920s and early 1930s, Lewis had fought his own battles with the Communist-led National Miners Union for dominance in the coalfields of Kentucky and Pennsylvania. The autocratic Lewis had emerged victorious, but by 1934 times were so hard in towns like Centralia and Shamokin, Pennsylvania, that only a thriving trade in "bootleg coal" stolen from company-owned mines by unemployed miners kept UMW members from starvation.[86] Though patently illegal, the bootleg coal industry (in 1934 alone, bootleggers took some 4.5 million tons of coal worth more than $40 million) was tolerated by Pennsylvania's newly elected Democratic governor, George Earle—not surprising in light of the fact that, ranked in order of their respective contributions to Earle's victory, Lewis would probably come right behind J. David Stern and Albert

Greenfield, and that Lewis's lieutenant, the UMW secretary-treasurer Tom Kennedy, was now lieutenant governor.[87]

If any single incident can symbolize Lewis's role in the transformation of the American labor movement, it was his confrontation with the barons of the AFL at the federation's convention in Atlantic City in October 1935. A lifelong Republican, Lewis was suspicious of Democrats (small *d* or capital *D*). But his decision to use the New Deal as an organizing tool—"The President wants you to join a union," UMW placards urged— had brought 90 percent of the nation's soft-coal production under UMW auspices. Now Lewis put his considerable bulk squarely behind a resolution calling for a massive organizing campaign in steel, auto, meatpacking, and other mass-production industries. Traditional AFL practice in the case of new industries was to organize workers into "federal" locals, which would then be dissolved as workers were parceled out to the various crafts unions. Assessing the effects of this policy, the Lewis-backed resolution noted "that after fifty-five years of activity and effort we have enrolled . . . approximately three and one half million members of the thirty-nine millions of organizable workers is a fact that speaks for itself." Given the AFL's structure, the resolution was doomed, but during the debate, William Hutcheson, president of the carpenters' union, called Lewis a "big bastard." Lewis knocked Hutcheson to the floor with his fists.[88]

Isidor Feinstein's exposure of corruption in the AFL hierarchy to the readers of the *Nation* and the *New York Post* constituted a series of small blows in the same fight. The abuses he documented demanded radical action. On November 9, 1935, Lewis, Hillman, Dubinsky, and the leaders of five other unions announced the formation of the Committee for Industrial Organization. Though technically under AFL sponsorship, the CIO set its own course, very much guided by Lewis, launching an immediate organizing campaign on an industrial (as opposed to crafts) basis. Lewis, who suddenly had a pressing need for trained, committed organizers, evidently remembered his old adversaries with respect, if not affection. (Besides, he knew that party members were used to following orders.) Communists flooded into the CIO at both the local and national levels, where, for example, Len De Caux edited the *CIO News* and Lee Pressman, who had recently been fired from the Agricultural Adjustment Administration, became general counsel of the Steel Workers Organizing

Committee. At least sixty SWOC organizers were party members; the drive to unionize the auto industry also relied on Communists such as Wyndham Mortimer and Roy Travis.[89]

In later years, all parties to this bargain had reasons to deny it: the Communists out of fear for their jobs or their unions, Lewis and his fellow CIO leaders to distance themselves from organizers who had become political liabilities, and, perhaps most vehemently, anti-Communist liberals who wanted to defend the labor movement from guilt by association. At the time, however, Lewis made no bones about the terms of the arrangement. "Who gets the bird," he asked in reply to concerns about his new associates, "the dogs—or the hunter?"[90]

Most of the time, Fiorello La Guardia was similarly insouciant. Never as dependent on the CP as Lewis, the mayor was nonetheless prepared to recognize the party's utility. His protégé and former campaign manager, Congressman Vito Marcantonio, would never have made it to Washington without the party's troops to knock on doors and pass out palm cards. La Guardia and the Communists also had enemies in common, such as the East Coast Longshoremen's leader Joseph Ryan, one of the chief villains of Isidor Feinstein's series, who "sent Jimmy Walker a message to come back to New York."[91]

Given La Guardia's total disdain for loyalty to any political party, his relationship with the Communists was bound to be stormy. When one such tempest arose over the party's agitation for increases in relief, Isidor Feinstein returned to the *New Republic* to accuse the city of "Spying on the Jobless." Once again based on a *Post* campaign—and quoting "a suppressed document, photostats of which are in possession of The New York Post"—the article offers "a glimpse of the terror that is slowly being built up against the unemployed." This time Feinstein's targets were La Guardia and the welfare commissioner, William Hodson, "a social worker of long experience and rather liberal reputation." Exposing the existence of a "Red list" of radicals to be dropped from city relief projects, Feinstein's overheated rhetoric suggests that he may have been trying to persuade himself as much as his readers that this really added up to "Tsarist methods."[92] What it does show is that, forced to choose between "responsible" liberals and radical "agitators"—in Commissioner Hodson's words, "people who refuse to be gentlemen"—Isidor Feinstein cast his lot with the agitators.

•

Thomas Gardiner Corcoran also had a soft spot for agitators. Son of a Pawtucket, Rhode Island, lawyer, Corcoran blazed his way from Brown University to Harvard Law School in the mid-1920s, where his quick mind and felicity of expression brought him to the attention of Felix Frankfurter, the first Jew on its faculty. Frankfurter's eloquent and courageous effort to save Sacco and Vanzetti earned him the admiration of a generation of students and the hatred of many of his colleagues. A friend and adviser to Franklin Roosevelt since the president's days as assistant secretary of the navy, Frankfurter became probably the most important talent spotter for the New Deal, sending scores of bright young lawyers to Washington, where they were known as Felix's Happy Hot Dogs. For his special favorites, the most incandescent intellects, there was an appointment even more prized than the plum jobs at the Reconstruction Finance Corporation or the Departments of State or Agriculture or Interior, which were certainly within his gift. When Thomas Corcoran came to Washington in 1926 as law clerk and secretary to Supreme Court Justice Oliver Wendell Holmes Jr., he entered the company of Frankfurter's anointed ones.

This was a brotherhood that required a talent for flattery. ("When Felix walked in the door, there wasn't any question who was boss," recalled the lawyer Joseph Rauh, a junior member of the order.)[93] It was a brotherhood that prized daring above deference. (When Holmes died in 1935, his will directed that his Commonplace Book, in which among other things he had written the titles of the 3,475 books he had read, be burned. Corcoran, who was at Holmes's bedside, smuggled out the heavy black volume and had it sent by courier to the Harvard Law library.)[94] It was a brotherhood that valued intellectual toughness. (Frankfurter was "cocky, abrasive, and outspoken," said Alger Hiss, another Holmes clerk, as was Hiss's brother Donald.)[95] It was a brotherhood animated by the belief that the real power in Washington was, in Frankfurter's phrase, exercised "from behind the scenes." And from the outside, it was a brotherhood that could look very much like a conspiracy. Even so friendly a chronicler as Arthur Schlesinger Jr. couldn't help noting Corcoran's "boundless talents as a manipulator and an *intrigant*."[96]

Raymond Moley, a professor at Columbia Law School and member of the original Brain Trust of academic advisers to Roosevelt's 1932 campaign, thought Corcoran was "committed to the 'class-struggle' view of history." Put off by the president's increasing willingness to antagonize big business, Moley became one of the New Deal's most ardent critics. He used to quote Corcoran: "Fighting with a businessman is like fighting with a Polack. You can give no quarter."[97] But Moley had been supplanted in FDR's favor by the brilliant, accordion-playing Irishman (Corcoran was so lace-curtain he didn't drink, taking up the accordion to provide a cover for his abstinence at Washington parties), so he was hardly a reliable judge.[98] Neither was the Republican congressman Fred Britten who, furious at being outmaneuvered by Corcoran, denounced "the scarlet fever boys from the little red house in Georgetown."[99] The impatient Corcoran was no Communist. It was just that, like John L. Lewis, he needed people who could get things done.

When in the spring of 1936 Isidor Feinstein wandered into his office on K Street, Corcoran soon found a use for the short, rumpled, tousle-headed newsman. Izzy wanted a favor. Attached since 1932 to the Reconstruction Finance Corporation, Corcoran was known as the president's "fixer"—a tag that, though it unfairly slighted his work in drafting such key bills as the Public Utilities Holding Company Act, the Security Act of 1933, and the Securities and Exchange Commission Act of 1934, accurately reflected his influence. Feinstein wanted Corcoran to do something about the Florida governor, David Sholtz, who'd refused to prevent violence against union organizers in the citrus fields. Claiming that Sholtz had ties to gamblers ("his take is reputed to be close to a million dollars a year") and to the Ku Klux Klan, he asked Corcoran's help in passing an antilynching bill to "open up the situation."[100] This he did not get. Sholtz was a Democrat, and "Tommy the Cork" was not yet up to attacking members of the president's own party.

It is likely that Izzy had come to see Corcoran at Frankfurter's urging; as the *Post's* legal specialist he'd written to Frankfurter in praise of his writings on labor injunctions—the beginning of a warm correspondence.[101] And though he wouldn't help with Sholtz, Corcoran was sympathetic. There was something about the reporter's furious energy, his combination of indignation and generosity, that Corcoran liked very much. Benjamin Cohen, Corcoran's shy, studious, melancholy alter ego, liked Izzy, too. Another Jewish peddler's son, Cohen had spent his childhood in Muncie, Indiana, before a brilliant career at the University of Chicago brought him to Harvard and, inevitably, to the attention of Professor Frankfurter.[102] Officially Cohen was attached to the Public Works Administration; in reality, and in partnership with Corcoran, he was the New Deal's foremost legal draftsman.

As was his habit, Corcoran began by flattering his young friend, soliciting the newspaperman's views on administration policies. A stream of *Post* editorials started arriving in the next day's mail. Before long Corcoran was peppering "Dear Iz" with suggestions for new editorials that would be helpful to the president's goals. "Dear Tom" was not disappointed. The writer who once aped Mencken and thought Roosevelt a "slick salesman" now found Mencken "a querulous Tory" whose attack on the president "doesn't come off."[103] And he agreed to help find a job at the *Post* for yet another of Frankfurter's young men, Samuel Beer, a returning Rhodes Scholar who'd just finished a stint at the Resettlement Administration courtesy of Lee Pressman (another Happy Hot Dog). "Corcoran knew Izzy quite well," Beer recalled. "Izzy got me a job as a police reporter. That summer he was reading Virgil—on his vacation!"[104]

Like many New Dealers, Beer worked double shifts: After his day job in Resettlement, he'd do political chores for Corcoran, editing pamphlets, drafting speeches. "I never saw Corcoran with fewer than two telephones at one time. He had a suite of rooms at the old Powhatan Hotel, where he always kept the blinds down. And he had two secretaries: Peggy, who worked for him during the day at his official job, and a male secretary who helped him at night with political stuff," said Beer. "I usually saw him at night. I'd bring something in, he'd rework it right away and send it over to the White House."[105]

On a Saturday night in June 1936, Beer listened as 100,000 people cheered their throats raw in Philadelphia's Franklin Field in response to a campaign speech of Roosevelt's that Beer had helped to draft. Roosevelt's pledge to end the rule of "economic royalists," and his declaration that just as 1776 had been necessary to wipe out "political tyranny," so in 1936 the enemy was "economic tyranny," seemed to signal an opening to the left.[106] At the very least, there was an opening for Isidor Feinstein, now an ardent convert to the virtues of "peaceful, even halfway, reform and revolution."[107]

The ties that bound the once-dismissive radical newsman ever more firmly to the New Deal were a mixture of the personal and the political. Thoroughly charmed by Corcoran (and by "the beautiful Peggy," the future Mrs. Corcoran), he also saw a kindred spirit in Cohen, the awkward, idealistic Jewish intellectual. Nor was he immune to the intoxications attendant on proximity to power, replying to Michael Blankfort's complaint of an aching sacroiliac with the news that Felix Frankfurter—"What a swell guy he is, Mike!"—was a fellow sufferer.[108]

Gratitude may also have played a part. Bernard Feinstein owed his job at the Home Owners Loan Corporation, which got Izzy's father off the streets as a peddler, to Corcoran's influence. And in the spring of 1936, the young editorial writer may have also been glad for a reason to stay late at the office or spend his weekends commuting to Washington. His second child had been born the previous November. Unlike his sister Celia, Jeremy Judah Feinstein was a difficult baby, colicky and asthmatic. "They had this baby who screamed constantly and was almost choking to death all the time," said Esther's sister Jean Boudin. "It was almost impossible. They had a terrible time, and then Esther got pregnant again about eleven months later." Her brother-in-law, she recalled, was usually too busy working to be of much assistance at home.[109]

By the end of 1936, his identification with the New Deal was sufficiently strong for "Izzi" to complain indignantly to "Tom" that John J. O'Connor, a Democratic congressman from Manhattan's "Gashouse" district,* was an obstacle to "our policy." Corcoran prized loyalty, and when O'Connor told the *Daily News* that a *Post* editorial attacking his New Deal credentials was "libelous," Franklin Roosevelt himself came to Izzy's defense, publicly stating that the *Post* editorial expressed his own sentiments precisely. At least as important, though, was the way the president also seemed increasingly receptive to radical measures.[110]

Franklin Roosevelt's landslide reelection victory in 1936 was seen by his supporters both as a vindication of the New Deal and as a signal to proceed with what the *New Republic* termed "the greatest revolution in our political history." With the oblique endorsement of the Communist Party (whose confusing slogan "Defeat Landon at All Costs—Vote for Earl Browder" at least had the virtue of putting first things first), the left

---

*Named for the plants, on the Lower East Side of Manhattan, that heated coal to make gas.

(except for the Socialists, ever faithful to Norman Thomas) united behind the president. In New York, the Popular Front even had its own line on the ballot; endorsed by Lewis, Hillman, and Dubinsky as well as La Guardia and Louis Weinstock, a new entity called the American Labor Party rolled up 282,000 votes for Roosevelt. As the *Post* observed, it had been "the dirtiest campaign since Civil War days," with Hearst papers across the country demanding that voters repudiate "the Red New Deal with a Soviet seal." But Hearst's red-baiting had been decisively rejected. "I can see no interpretation of the returns," wrote Heywood Broun in the *Nation*, "which does not suggest that the people of America want the President to proceed along progressive or liberal lines."[111]

With Democrats now firmly in control of both houses of Congress, there was only one obstacle to the forward march of the New Deal: the Supreme Court. The first sign of trouble came when the Court overturned the Railroad Pension Act of June 1934, which had set up a comprehensive retirement plan for railway workers. Then in May 1935 the justices unanimously ruled the National Industrial Recovery Act of 1933 unconstitutional in a case involving a Brooklyn kosher chicken wholesaler. Though freeing Roosevelt from a program that had become a political liability (the NRA's thicket of regulations was widely unpopular), the Court's narrow interpretation of what constituted interstate commerce threatened the whole edifice of New Deal regulation, most of which made the federal government a referee between the competing interests of capital and labor. "The big issue is this," Roosevelt told reporters. "Does this decision mean the United States government has no control over any economic program?" In January 1936, the president's fears seemed realized when the Court struck down the Agricultural Adjustment Act of 1933, ruling the New Deal's entire agricultural reform program unconstitutional.[112]

Both Corcoran and Cohen had been heavily involved in drafting a law that tried to advance New Deal aims at the state level, but when in June 1936 the Supreme Court, on a five-to-four vote, held the New York State minimum wage law unconstitutional, a battle became unavoidable. The election returns were barely in when Corcoran gave "Dear Izzie" his most important assignment: to write a book that would strip the Supreme Court of its mystique, a muckraking essay laying bare the history of special interests and specious reasoning that characterized a Court that had turned the Bill of Rights into a charter for economic exploitation. For the first and last time in his life, Isidor Feinstein rode into battle not as a paladin of the powerless or a gadfly, but as an insider, a confidential agent of the "party within a party" that served the president's purposes.[113]

Given the run of Corcoran's "little White House" office, and with a full set of U.S. Reports (containing all the Supreme Court's decisions), over one November weekend in 1936 Feinstein produced an eight-page outline for "It's a Wise Founding Father: What Bench and Bar Have Done to Our Constitution."[114] Corcoran sent the prospectus to Felix Frankfurter, who not only pronounced it "excellent" but advanced $250 from his own pocket to cover the author's living and traveling expenses (later repaid him by Lincoln Filene, the Boston merchant).[115] Feinstein's prospectus listed four possible remedies, three of which he discussed at some length: to pass a constitutional amendment ending judicial supremacy, to use Congress's power to regulate the Court's jurisdiction, or to pass a constitutional amendment "so that the people may amend the Constitution by national referendum." The fourth alternative, in its entirety, read: "Pack the Court, but you never know what a man will do once he is on the Court."

The writing went very fast, but events were running even faster. On November 23, the Supreme Court split four–four in a decision that upheld the New York State unemployment-insurance act.* Writing in the Post, Isidor Feinstein called the decision "a lucky toss of the judicial dice," arguing that "in the very act of giving the victory to liberalism the Supreme Court exposed the fundamentally irrational and bizarre nature of the process through which it sifts the aspirations of our democracy . . . Why should the future of the country depend on the way Mr. Justice Hughes and Mr. Justice Roberts happen to feel when they get up three weeks from next Monday?"[116] It was a prophetic question.

By mid-December he'd sent Corcoran a draft of the first half of the book. By the new year the manuscript was complete, but on February 5 the author was forced to revise. Isidor Feinstein wasn't the only one taken by surprise by the president's announcement that he planned to "pack the court" by increasing its size and appointing up to six new justices. Ben

---

*Justice Harlan Stone, who was ill, had abstained. Supporting the New York law were Chief Justice Charles Evans Hughes and Justices Louis Brandeis, Benjamin Cardozo, and Owen Roberts.

Cohen read about it in a newspaper on the train to New York; he took the next train back to Washington. Corcoran, given a day's warning, tried in vain to warn the president that Justice Louis Brandeis, leader of the Court's liberal wing, would be unalterably opposed. Even Felix Frankfurter refused to speak up in support of the president's plan.

That unhappy task now fell squarely on Isidor Feinstein. With his least-preferred solution now the president's policy, he used the pages of the *Post*, where loyalty to Roosevelt was still a cardinal virtue, to refine his rationale: "The Supreme Court has been 'packed' for years with safe, conservative majorities," he wrote in an "open letter to Congress" on February 8. "Those safe, conservative majorities brought on the Civil War. Those safe, conservative majorities have stood in the path of almost every major piece of social legislation enacted by the elected representatives of the American people. To suit their ends, those safe, conservative justices have twisted the Constitution itself beyond recognition."[117] He reprised the theme in the next day's *Post*: "Let's figure that Mr. Roosevelt has 'set a precedent for packing the Court which other Presidents, less able and sincere, might eagerly follow.' What then? What's the worst that could happen? The worst that could happen is that the Supreme Court would be reduced to what the Constitution intended it to be—our highest court of appeal. It would no longer be what the Constitution never intended it to be—an autocratic super legislature overriding the other branches of the Government and the will of the people."[118]

In March, just as Feinstein's manuscript was on its way to Covici, Friede, his publishers,* the Supreme Court upheld the District of Columbia's minimum-wage law, reversing its own decision of the previous June and requiring Feinstein to make further revisions, but also offering a vivid illustration of "the maze of inconsistencies that is our constitutional law." Justice Roberts had changed his mind, "and, by changing his mind, changed 'the Constitution.'"[119]

When it did finally appear, *The Court Disposes* proved an impressive synthesis of legal and political history; given its provenance, it was also a remarkably radical document. "The Court and the law," argued the

---

*During its nine-year life, Covici, Friede managed to publish Dreiser's *An American Tragedy*, Hecht and MacArthur's *The Front Page*, and Steinbeck's *Tortilla Flat* as well as nonfiction titles such as James Wechsler's *Revolt on the Campus* and John Spivak's *America Faces the Barricades*.

twenty-nine-year-old author, "are primarily concerned with the rights of property, and of those who own property. The law does not protect one's right to eat, or to work, or to have babies, though these answer to fundamental needs in human nature." As for those liberals who saw the Court as a bulwark against fascism, "The Court can scent communism several centuries downwind, in a federal income tax or a minimum wage for chambermaids . . . If the Court were our only safeguard, the *Heil* and the goose-step would have established themselves here long ago."[120]

The arguments themselves were not new. Indeed, the author credits a long list of sources, including Louis Boudin,* whose *Government by Judiciary* he'd reviewed in the *Philadelphia Record* in 1932: "the story of how the Supreme Court has steadily widened its powers, made itself supreme over Congress, the President and the States, encroached further and further into the domain of law-making and now blocks progress by welding the economic and social prejudices of individual judges into the supreme law of the land"—a fair précis of *The Court Disposes*.[121] What was new was the sense of political urgency: "So bold and daring has the Court become in circumventing acts of Congress and nullifying or emasculating amendments to the Constitution" that "Democracy must curb the Supreme Court or the Supreme Court, instrument of our great concentrations of economic power, will destroy Democracy."[122]

The tone of the two books was also very different. Louis Boudin was a founder of the American Communist Party, author of *The Theoretical System of Karl Marx*, and a distinguished legal scholar.[123] *The Court Disposes*, however, was "a book by a layman for laymen." Salted with journalistic wisecracks—"Laissez faire, like castor oil, is something one prescribes for others"—it showed in its more serious passages the deepest vein of native American radicalism. The debt to populism is made explicit in a quotation from the Minnesota Farmers' Alliance, followed by the author's own summary: "The vast trusts which began to dominate our economic system between the 1870s and the 1890s had finally begun to dominate the Courts. On them now sat men who had been the servants of these trusts. The fabulous wealth that poured from the continent at the touch of these great

---

*Esther Stone's sister, Jean, was married to Leonard Boudin, Louis's nephew. Louis's daughter, Vera, married Sidney Cohn.

combines . . . represented an irresistible power, able to twist newspapers, legislators, lawyers and judges to its purposes."[124]

The reviews were mostly favorable. Matthew Josephson, writing in *New Masses*, called it "the most sensible and lucid tract" on the Court controversy by "one of our ablest young journalists."[125] The Harvard Law professor and expert on constitutional law Thomas Reed Powell found "Mr. Feinstein's detailed account of the Supreme Court and minimum wage legislation . . . an effective lethal instrument."[126] The *New Republic* and *Nation* reviewers both liked it, and the *Nation* even ran an excerpt before publication.[127] But it was Arthur Pierce, J. David Stern's senior editorial writer, who in the course of an extremely positive review put his finger on the book's insoluble handicap: "It is unfortunate that this brief but brilliant book has not been available since the beginning of the Supreme Court controversy."[128]

By the time *The Court Disposes* came out in April 1937, the court-packing plan was fatally stalled. Roosevelt's attack on the Court had alienated many of his admirers, and the president's disingenuous explanation that he merely "sought to aid overworked courts by adding new judges to the bench," though parroted by Isidor Feinstein, was universally dismissed. In May, the New Deal foe Justice Willis Van Devanter retired, giving Roosevelt the chance to name Senator Hugo Black, a populist from Alabama, in his place. The New Deal now had five firm votes on the Court. Social Security, the Wagner Act, and the Tennessee Valley Authority were all safe. In July, the bill to add new members to the Supreme Court was recommitted, but this face-saving procedure fooled no one. Though he was at the height of his power, Roosevelt had been defeated.[129]

And yet it moved: Roosevelt's threat to pack the Court really did bring about what amounted to a revolution in constitutional law. The *Post* editorial calling the result a "defeat more glorious than many victories" may have been, in part, an attempt at self-justification by its author, but Isidor Feinstein's recognition that the "unprecedented series of reversals which were the Supreme Court's reply" to Roosevelt's challenge were the campaign's most durable legacy was extremely prescient.[130] His personal accounting was even more positive. *The Court Disposes* didn't sell many copies or make its author much money, but it solidified his standing both as an intellectual and as a New Dealer. Corcoran passed along compliments from Judge Samuel Rosenman, the president's confidant. He also asked Izzy to draft a series of four speeches—"the sooner the better."[131] Felix Frankfurter brought him to Harvard to speak to his class. He was also invited to serve as a delegate to the second American Writers Congress, a fact he casually mentioned in a note to his new friend Matthew Josephson.[132] *The Court Disposes* may not have made his fortune, but it certainly made his name.

Four

POPULAR FRONT

—◆◆◆—

What is a name in our revolutionized and revolutionary world? A number
for those who do nothing, a sign or a motto for those who work or fight. The
one that I was given I made all by myself, after the fact, by my own efforts.
—George Sand, *Histoire de ma vie*

For a man who still hadn't celebrated his thirtieth birthday and who practiced the craft of journalism without benefit of column or byline, Isidor
Feinstein was, by the summer of 1937, becoming remarkably well known.
The Court Disposes helped. So did the *Post*'s unique position as the only
pro–New Deal paper in the country's cultural capital. David Stern's appetite for crusading journalism attracted a number of talented writers,
from Kenneth Crawford in Washington to the labor editor, Edward Levinson, a veteran Socialist Party activist, to a cub reporter named Ruth
McKenney, whose stories about her sister Eileen were beginning to appear in the *New Yorker*. Sam Grafton, more adept than his editorial stablemate at bending to the proprietor's whims, was busily carving out a niche
as chief cheerleader for the New Deal.

Izzy's role was different. While Stern considered Grafton "a natural
born writer," he found his colleague "more of a student," prized for his
skill as a quick study and a penetrating analyst rather than as a phrase-
maker.[1] Outside the paper, Izzy was also coming to be seen as an origina-
tor of ideas, a man who knew his own mind and who was, for that reason,
worth cultivating. Like his friend Tommy Corcoran, he was equally com-

fortable talking high policy or street-level politics. Nor was he a stranger to the currency of favors. Malcolm Cowley asked Izzy to help find a job for his nephew. And in the summer of 1937, Izzy used his contacts (probably Corcoran) to get Bernard Feinstein a temporary job at the Philadelphia Mint. He then asked Corcoran to help get the mint job made permanent, an effort that also called on favors from Stern and Senator Joseph Guffey, the Pennsylvanian whose efforts to stabilize the coal industry made him an ally of both Franklin Roosevelt and John L. Lewis. He sent an out-of-work friend to Washington to see the SEC commissioner Jerome Frank—whom he knew through Corcoran, of course—and, when the ever-cautious Frank failed to hire the man, wrote him an indignant letter.[2]

The New Deal's favorite radical, he was never quite considered "one of us" by organizationally minded leftists. Yet in late 1936, when a group of anonymous Republicans offered Earl Browder $250,000 to have the CP either nominate or endorse Roosevelt, the Communist leader took the story to Isidor Feinstein.[3] Trusted (if not liked) by Trotskyists, sympathetic to (if no longer a member of) the Socialist Party, and with family ties to the CP, he was becoming a crucial intermediary among various elements on the sectarian spectrum of the American left and, more important, between the self-conscious radicals and the equally fractious but much broader elements of the body politic who answered to the label of "liberal."

His friendships with Malcolm Cowley and Max Lerner gave him increasing access to the pages of the *New Republic* and the *Nation*, and in the years to come he would use that access to speak out in a voice less restrained by the confines of daily journalism, less burdened by the need for the boss's approval or the fear of alienating influential advertisers. Acerbic, demotic, streetwise but not cynical, it was a voice that could resonate in union halls and public meetings as well as the inner councils of the New Deal. The force of its logic might be described as "Popular Front common sense"—the voice of Isidor Feinstein, on an outing with his daughter Celia to buy her a typewriter, turning on his heels at the sight of striking department store clerks and announcing, "We don't cross picket lines."[4] And though it was a voice that would be heard in the marble corridors of Washington, D.C., its rhythm remained the Yiddish-inflected syncopation of Manhattan sidewalks.

•

To Isidor Feinstein and his friends, the League of American Writers Congress in June 1937 was practically a Penn reunion. Michael Blankfort was on the league's National Council. Walter Hart, Sam Grafton, Edith Grafton, Shepard Traube, and Mildred Traube were all members. Sidney Cohn, who wrote only legal briefs (he had become a partner in Louis Boudin's firm), didn't belong, but his brother-in-law, Benjamin Algase, was the league's accountant.[5] The daily program of panels, workshops, readings, and lunches ended with the Penn contingent gathered at Algase's Manhattan apartment, drinking and talking late into the night.[6]

But the daytime sessions were not so cordial. A small group of writers led by the novelist James T. Farrell opposed the league—and the whole Popular Front—for lending the Communists cultural legitimacy at the very moment when Stalin was presiding over the destruction of culture in the Soviet Union. Farrell, a Trotskyist whose proposal at the 1935 Congress to close the proceedings by singing the "Internationale" had been approved by the delegates (the Trotskyists, Socialists, and Communists all sang slightly different lyrics), had since become an implacable foe of his former comrades. (But he was not, at least in 1937, an implacable foe of Isidor Feinstein. Earlier that year Farrell had asked Feinstein for help after one of his novels was banned for obscenity by the New York Society for the Suppression of Vice, and by authorities in Philadelphia and numerous other cities. Izzy's response, in a letter to Farrell's publisher, was a blurb suitable for framing: "I hear the vice people have their snout in James T. Farrell's 'A World I Never Made.' I hope it's true. It will increase his sales and he deserves a wider audience . . . Mr. Farrell is an Irish-American Zola, but a Zola who doesn't have to refer to note-books. The smut hounds didn't like Zola either.")[7] To Farrell and his fellow Trotskyists, nothing happening at the congress or in the world was as important as the purges and show trials that had been taking place in the Soviet Union since the assassination of Stalin's close collaborator Sergei Kirov in December 1934.

One of the most durable myths about the 1930s is that fellow travelers and other leftists who participated in coalitions with Communists kept silent about the Soviet purges in order to avoid offending their comrades.[8] The record is more complicated. As early as December 1934, for example, Isidor Feinstein pointed out that "while radicals the world over protest the People's Courts by which Hitler's Reich is murdering its opponents without the shadow of a real trial, the Soviet Union adopts the same tactics in dealing with" Kirov's alleged killers. His *Post* editorial optimistically described the first purge as "an isolated case and more of a personal grudge than a terroristic counter-revolutionary movement," but, he warned, "terror is a weapon that corrupts those who wield it."[9]

After Grigory Zinoviev, Lev Kamenev, and the other defendants charged with complicity in Kirov's murder had been tried for treason, convicted, and sentenced to jail, the *Post* concluded that "Stalin is using the Kiroff assassination as an excuse for weeding out anyone who disagrees with his views."[10] That Stalin was acting like a dictator was not exactly a surprise.[11] And though the Trotskyists (and their American literary fellow travelers) might disagree, in Izzy's view, when it came to civil liberties, "Trotsky was not a whole lot different from Stalin . . . Trotsky in power was very draconian in dealing with problems of labor and labor discipline."[12] Still, as someone committed to the Popular Front, he definitely found the trials disturbing, particularly after Zinoviev and the others were put on trial a second time in August 1936, now accused of conspiring with the Nazis to try to kill Stalin as well as having murdered Kirov, and, after "confessions" in open court, were all sentenced to death. Indeed, he said as much in print. "The latest stories of a terrorist plot by Old Bolsheviks who have been in jail for more than a year, and of a link between Hitler and Trotzky, seem fantastic. The good impression made by the new [1936] Soviet Constitution and recent moves in the direction of more democratic government are threatened by the Trotzky-Zinoviev-Kamenev 'plot' stories."[13]

Hampered by the desire to give the Russians the benefit of the doubt and by an extreme reluctance to draw darker conclusions, Izzy searched desperately for information that would "make sense" of the trials. One afternoon in the summer of 1937, his search took him to Nathaniel Weyl. In the early 1930s, Weyl had joined the Communist Party as a member at large, meaning that his dues were paid directly to the Political Bureau in New York and his membership was kept secret. As an economist in the Agricultural Adjustment Administration, he'd been assigned to a secret party unit whose members included Harold Ware, Lee Pressman, and, according to Weyl, Alger Hiss. Though nothing happened at his unit meetings that Weyl could call improper, his discomfort over the need to maintain secrecy led him to leave the government and work for a while as director of the party's School on Wheels, a mobile classroom that tutored farmers in communism, before joining the *Post* as a reporter.[14]

> Izzy came to me with the request that I put him in contact with someone who could give him the true Soviet explanations of Stalin's actions as contrasted with the nonsense that Moscow was disseminating to the general public. If he had been in the party he wouldn't have gone to me. He would have gone to Browder. I thought of him as a fellow traveller.
>
> My own position was somewhat ambiguous. I was a member at large of the CPUSA. My wife and I had read the official transcript of the trials and concluded that the accused men had been judicially murdered. However, we thought that the communist movement was the most powerful world force against Nazism, and, therefore, that we should not join the public critics of Stalin.
>
> We arranged a meeting for him at our apartment with "Hans," a German refugee who was a member of the ECCI [Executive Committee of the Communist International]. I don't remember exactly what "Hans" told him. He may have used the Tukhachevsky story—about a conspiracy against Stalin among the Russian general staff, who were in cahoots with the Germans. Izzy left with a smile—which may mean he believed it, or it may mean he was just being polite.[15]

For a while, Isidor Feinstein managed to remain agnostic about the extent of Stalin's crimes. The effort it cost, and the mental accounting involved, can perhaps be glimpsed in a *Post* editorial he wrote in January 1937, after the well-known Bolshevik Karl Radek and sixteen other defendants were accused of treason:

> The Moscow trials require one to believe either (1) that Leon Trotzky is a monster or (2) that Joseph Stalin is a monster. And no ordinary monsters. For either Trotzky or some of his followers have plotted with German and Japanese emissaries to dismember the Soviet Union so that they might overthrow Stalin, or Stalin

has staged the greatest frameup in world history to discredit Trotzky . . . In all, thirty-three men have confessed. Almost all of them were old revolutionaries, men who had faced death and torture. One must believe either (1) that their confessions are true, or (2) that not one of the thirty-three had the courage to let out a protest before the assembled representatives of foreign powers and the foreign press. Not one.[16]

In June 1937, with charges now laid against Marshal Tukhachevsky and the rest of the Red Army high command, Izzy's credulity stretched even further, overcoming his previous qualms: "We have no reason to doubt the truth of the charges against the eight Soviet generals . . . The character of the generals specially appointed as judges makes it impossible to believe that the eight were framed in a struggle between the Communist Party and the Red Army."[17] The possibility that Stalin himself might be responsible, that terror instigated at the top might have corrupted the entire process, was apparently too monstrous to consider. That this was a willed agnosticism there can be little doubt. But there is a difference between agnosticism and apology. "Revolutions," Izzy had written in January, "do not take place according to Emily Post. The birth of a new social order, like the birth of a human being, is a painful process."

Another durable myth about the 1930s would have us believe that in this debate the Trotskyites had "clean hands."[18] As if their having been on the losing side of a power struggle conferred moral supremacy.* As if the fastidious disdain for compromise and coalition that rendered Trotsky's New York admirers immune to the charge of Stalinism was anything more than an attempt to dignify their political marginalization. The poet Archibald MacLeish, angered at the Trotskyist argument that Writers Congress participants were "dupes," replied: "The man who refuses to defend his convictions for fear he may defend them in the wrong company, has no convictions."[19] Isidor Feinstein agreed with MacLeish.

The world in 1937 was not a place where a politics of "clean hands" could be practiced. And nowhere was this cruel necessity more apparent than in the country whose cause prompted MacLeish's passionate en-

---

*This is a distortion of the argument advanced by Trotsky himself in *Literature and Revolution* on the relative position of oppressed and oppressor.

gagement, a country whose very name was, for Isidor Feinstein and his friends, a kind of shorthand for all the reasons they bothered to make the effort to remain agnostic, why they joined groups like the League, why many of them maintained, if not silence, what seemed at the time like a sense of proportion about the magnitude of Soviet crimes. Spain.

•

As a matter of political taste, Isidor Feinstein always preferred the French Front Populaire to Spain's Frente Popular. The French coalition—winner of the parliamentary elections of May 1936, with the Socialist Léon Blum as prime minister—may have lacked the utopian zeal of the Spanish Republicans who first came to power in 1931, lost a bitterly fought election two years later, and, after forming a coalition that extended from anarchists through Socialists and Communists to Basque and Catalan nationalists, returned to power in January 1936. While the Frente Popular stripped the Spanish nobility of its privileges, tried to nationalize the railways and banks, set out to redistribute latifundias, and, in areas controlled by the anarcho-syndicalist CNT (Confederación Nacional del Trabajo) or the dissident Communist POUM (Partido Obrero de Unificación Marxista), to bring about immediate social revolution, the Front Populaire contented itself with pay raises for French government workers, a forty-hour workweek, and nationalization of the arms industry. The French may have seemed gray, cautious, moderate, even bureaucratic in comparison to the heroic struggle being waged on the other side of the Pyrenees, but in their most critical task—keeping the government out of Fascist hands—the French left came through. Even before General Francisco Franco led his troops in revolt against the elected Spanish government in July 1936, precipitating open civil war, Isidor Feinstein warned, "a constructive program is needed to maintain the alliance in power. The Spaniards do not seem to have evolved such an alliance."[20]

With an eye firmly on the ever-present threat from the right, the *Post* praised the French Front Populaire government for its moderation, for "doing a much-needed 1933 Roosevelt job." To make sure readers—and advertisers—got the message, the paper quoted "an outstanding department store executive" just returned from Paris to certify: "France seems to be safely emerging from a bloodless, constructive revolution."[21]

The news from Spain was not so reassuring. But for once, David Stern and his radical young editorialist found themselves in complete agreement, at least at first: "Democracy is fighting for its life in Spain. Fascist Germany and Fascist Italy are doing their best to knife it . . . Believers in democracy the world over should rally to the defense of Spain before it is too late. Protests later will be futile."[22] Stern's fear of American involvement in European crises led to some evasions. "There is no longer any excuse whatsoever for refusing to sell arms to the Government in Madrid," proclaimed an editorial that summer. Since Hitler and Mussolini were both aiding the Spanish rebels, the *Post* urged "France and England" to "call Hitler's bluff by shipping arms and munitions into Spain for the Government."[23] But on the question of whether the U.S. government ought to take similar action, the *Post* kept silent.

Time and again the *Post* berated the "democratic Powers of Europe" for allowing "nonintervention" to turn them into "passive allies of Hitler and Mussolini." Stern didn't balk even at an editorial praising the Soviet Union, which had become the Republic's main source of arms and ammunition, for refusing to play along. But that the American government did nothing to stop what the *Post* described as "the rape of Spain"—refused even to prevent U.S. oil companies from selling to Franco on credit—was repeatedly overlooked.[24] This silence papered over a genuine difference of opinion. Stern, who wanted the United States to stay out of any European war, favored "mandatory neutrality legislation" barring the sale of arms "to any belligerent."[25] His lead editorial writer thought it crucial to stop fascism in its tracks, lest the same methods "be applied tomorrow in Czechoslovakia, the next day in France."[26]

The *Post*'s silence also covered the fact that enormous pressure was being brought to bear on Stern to drop his support for the Spanish Republic. While Franco's Falangists were no more popular with most Americans than Mussolini's Fascists or Hitler's Nazis, there was one powerful exception: the Catholic church. The American Catholic hierarchy stoutly supported the Roman Catholic church in Spain in its implacable antagonism to the Spanish Republic. The buildup of historic enmity between the church and the democratic forces that had formed the Republic meant, on one side, Republican actions that went well beyond disestablishment to confiscation of church property, church burnings, and, in some cases, murder; and, on the other side, the Vatican's blessing of Franco's Army of Africa troops (many of whom were in fact Muslim) as "crusaders."[27] In the United States, the church hierarchy and the Hearst newspapers cheered on the Falangist rebels. Hearst could be ignored; the church could not.

So few American newspapers had a good word to say about the Spanish Republic that the exceptions, like the *St. Louis Post-Dispatch* or Stern's three papers, were conspicuous. Stern not only published Isidor Feinstein's editorials but sent George Seldes, legendary foreign correspondent and author of two muckraking studies of the press,* to Spain as a special correspondent reporting on both the war and the distorted coverage of the war in the U.S. press. The archbishop of Philadelphia, Dennis Cardinal Dougherty, called on Catholics to boycott the *Record*—a call that was echoed in the *Tablet*, the Brooklyn diocese's weekly newspaper, and from pulpits in all three of Stern's markets. "Priests had driven our newsboys from their stands at the entrance of churches where Catholics customarily bought their Sunday papers after mass," he remembered later.[28] The *Post* wasn't just losing readers. The Straus family, still bitter at Stern's support for the anti-Nazi boycott campaign, canceled all of Macy's advertising (only recently returned to the *Post*) and increased linage in the Hearst papers by an equivalent amount.[29]

Nor was his bottom line the only place Stern was vulnerable to pressure. Albert Greenfield, his friend, financial backer, and political collaborator—part owner of the *Record* and a director of both the *Post* and the *Camden Courier*—was also a close friend and personal financial adviser to Cardinal Dougherty. A frequent dinner guest at Greenfield's home, Cardinal Dougherty even arranged for his friend to become a papal knight, Commander of the Order of Pius IX—the first American Jew to be so honored. With the Philadelphia archdiocese issuing pamphlets charging that "J. David Stern applauds murder of priests and rape of nuns," the cardinal's good friend Greenfield could hardly avoid raising the matter with his other good friend and co-owner.[30]

In his young editorial writer's view, Stern's resistance to these anti-Republican pressures ultimately cost him the *Post*.[31] As late as the winter of 1937, the paper was hailing Republican victories in Teruel and Madrid, where, under the slogan "*¡No Pasarán!*" the Loyalists had saved the besieged capital, with a "Salute to Heroes." Perhaps in recognition of the sacrifices that were being made by the Abraham Lincoln Battalion and

---

You Can't Print That (1929) and *Lords of the Press* (1935).

other American volunteers of the International Brigades, still under fire in the Jarama valley, the editorialist's rhetoric departed somewhat from *Post* norms: Though the "monocles of Downing Street" might obscure the truth—that the do-nothing policy of Great Britain and France, "the democratic powers," was "crucifying the Spanish Republic—the workers of the world sense the significance of Spain's agony." Still, the Popular Front exuberance was tempered by an insistence that Spain "is not a religious struggle."[32]

In the spring of 1937, infighting in Spain between the syndicalist CNT and dissident Communist POUM on one side and the Socialist PSOE (Partido Socialista Obrero Espanol, whose leader, Francisco Largo Caballero, was prime minister) and the Catalan Communist PSUC (Partit Socialista Unificat de Catalunya) on the other broke into open warfare on the streets of Barcelona. The Comintern's heavy-handed suppression of this civil war within the civil war turned the British volunteer George Orwell, whose comrades in the POUM bore the brunt of the repression, into a staunch anti-Communist. John Dos Passos, whose *Big Money* was to be voted novel of the year at the Writers Congress that June, went to Madrid in April to help organize a shipment of arms to the Loyalists, but the discovery that his friend and translator José Robles had been executed by the Republican secret police as a Fascist spy sent Dos Passos out of Spain—and out of the left.[33]

At the *Post*, the Spanish government's suppression of the Barcelona revolt was greeted with relief. Stern was so delighted to be able to draw a line under "church burnings and murders of the clergy by thoroughly irresponsible Leftist groups" that the *Post* completely misrepresented what was happening in Spain. The *Post* described the replacement of Largo Caballero's government with a new cabinet headed by the Socialist Juan Negrín—a government that excluded POUM and announced a policy that the civil war had to be won before any social revolution could be carried further—as a move "closer to democracy and farther away from Left radicalism." Instead of recognizing Negrín's ministry for what it was, a cynical Comintern calculation designed to appeal to "the democratic Powers," the *Post* told its readers that "the Government of Spain, far from turning Communist . . . is moving toward the Right."[34]

Did Isidor Feinstein know any better? "We knew there were anguished choices," he said many years later. "We knew the POUM were being treated badly and the anarchists were being treated badly. On the other hand, there had to be discipline in the war. We didn't know what to do."

David Stern had run out of nerve. When the American economy went back into recession in the fall of 1937 and the *Post*'s finances went from chronic to critical, the publisher's outspoken support for the Spanish Republic became a luxury he could no longer afford. In a truce arranged by Albert Greenfield, Stern issued a personal apology for his newspapers' coverage of the civil war in Spain, published in the Philadelphia diocese's *Catholic Standard and Times*.[35] The boycott of his papers ended, but the bitter cost of his engagement with the Popular Front stayed with David Stern for some time.

•

One night in the summer of 1937, while he was still working as a police reporter on the *Post*, Sam Beer went with his friend and patron Izzy Feinstein to the apartment of the composer Marc Blitzstein. Blitzstein had invited Izzy to see an "oratorio" version of his new "proletarian opera," which had just closed after a two-week run.[36] Originally commissioned by Orson Welles and John Houseman for Project 891, the WPA Federal Theatre Unit in New York, the show nearly became a victim of one of Franklin Roosevelt's periodic attempts to balance the federal budget. A defiant Welles had gone ahead despite the lack of funds, only to find the Maxine Elliot Theatre padlocked on opening night. While the actors Will Geer and Howard da Silva entertained the audience on the sidewalk, Welles and Houseman hired the Venice Theatre, twenty-one blocks away. After a procession across midtown Manhattan, and with Blitzstein seated alone on stage at a rented piano, and with the cast delivering their lines from the audience, since union regulations forbade the actors from appearing onstage, the curtain finally rose on *The Cradle Will Rock*—a landmark in the history of American theater.[37]

Though it was set in "Steeltown U.S.A," the background to Blitzstein's allegorical epic had really begun on January 29, 1936, in Akron, Ohio, when tire builders at Firestone Rubber stopped the assembly line and sat down by their machines. Used at first as a tactic to settle shop-floor disputes, the sit-down strike spread from the United Rubber Workers to the rest of the CIO. As the labor journalist Louis Adamic noted, the sit-down, though not a "purely American invention," was "pragmatic" and "a bit anarchic, which also helps to make it truly American."[38] Publicized by reporters like Adamic, Ruth McKenney (whose novel *Industrial Valley* centered on the Akron strikes), and her *Post* colleague Edward Levinson, the sit-down quickly became the winning weapon in labor's arsenal. From 48 sit-downs in 1936 involving some 88,000 workers, the tactic exploded on American industry in 1937, with 477 strikes involving nearly 400,000 workers.[39]

Blitzstein began composing his opera in the summer of 1936—just as John L. Lewis was kicking off a campaign to organize the steel- and autoworkers. As Lewis knew, the two industries were linked not only by manufacturing relationships but by emotional and psychological affinities as well. Time and again activists on the Steel Workers Organizing Committee would report that the ethnically divided steelworkers "hesitate to stick out their necks. 'Wait till you win the auto strike. Then we'll join.'"[40] As an example of what the ethic of solidarity could achieve, the great strikes that, in Levinson's phrase, "broke the back of General Motors' resistance to unionism and, incidentally, held the fate of the steel unionization drive in their grasp," still stand as a triumph of Popular Front common sense.[41]

Developed in Akron, the sit-down was perfected in Detroit. On January 12, 1937, the United Auto Workers were sitting in at General Motors' Fisher Body Plant Number 2 in Flint, Michigan, when a squad of police tried to rush past the picket line. After losing millions of dollars in the Depression, GM had enjoyed a boom year in 1936, and 1937 promised to be even better—but only if the company could get the line moving. The auto industry's highly segmented production made it especially vulnerable to the sit-down; in Flint, the strikers had managed to tie up production so that instead of making 15,000 cars a week, GM could turn out only 150.[42] But if the stakes were high for the company, the UAW's back was to the wall. As the police moved in, firing buckshot, they were met with a fusillade of nails, coffee mugs, and two-pound steel car hinges. The retreating police were sped through the town's frozen streets by streams of water from the factory fire hoses. Immortalized as the Battle of the Running Bulls, the union's victory at Flint forced the pace for both CIO organizers and their adversaries. At the beginning of February, the strike spread to Chevrolet; after ten days of sit-down, President Roosevelt publicly backed calls for GM to negotiate with the UAW.

In the eight months following the union's breakthrough at GM, UAW membership went from 88,000 to 400,000.[43] And on March 2, 1937, just as Blitzstein was starting rehearsals on *The Cradle Will Rock*, U.S. Steel signed an agreement to recognize the Steel Workers Organizing Committee. The corporation that "set the pattern for American heavy industry" had become a union shop before a single plant had been struck; the infant CIO had outstripped the fifty-six-year-old American Federation of Labor.[44] Blitzstein's hero Larry Foreman's chant, "Good-bye, open shop in Steeltown! Hello, closed shop!" seemed prophetic.[45]

The auto and steel campaigns were a watershed for the CIO, and their effects on American radicals were equally dramatic. Socialists like Levinson (who'd been publicity director for the SP and worked on the party paper, the *New York Call*, before going to the *Post*) and Victor Reuther (an organizer at Fisher Number 2) were ecstatic. But as the hub of American radicalism, it was the Communist Party that had the most to celebrate. Wyndham Mortimer, a party member, directed the Flint organizing drive and represented the UAW at the final negotiations. Henry Krauss, the UAW's Flint publicist, was a Communist, as were key members of the strike committee.[46] The CP also helped to create the political conditions that made victory possible.

In the past, employers had used goon squads to break strikes, backed up by court injunctions and the National Guard. In Michigan, however, Governor Frank Murphy now refused to allow troops to act as strikebreakers. Murphy's restraint—and Roosevelt's studied neutrality—doubtless took account of the disclosures coming out of Senator Robert La Follette Jr.'s Committee on Civil Liberties, which happened at that very moment to be examining the "labor spy racket" in the automobile industry. "The announcement by John L. Lewis that the UAW would seek a collective bargaining agreement with GM obviously spurred our work," wrote La Follette's chief counsel, John Abt, who had been recruited into the same CP unit as Lee Pressman and Nathaniel Weyl.[47]

La Follette's committee was back in the news in May, after the SWOC's drive at Republic Steel in Chicago ended in police gunfire. "Steel Mob Halted" was the *New York Times* headline for what would later be known as the Memorial Day Massacre. La Follette's investigators revealed that every one of the ten unarmed demonstrators killed by police bullets had been shot in the back. They also discovered that the Republic Steel management had bought ten times as many gas guns and twenty-six times as many shells as the Chicago Police Department.[48] Given Blitzstein's deliberately incendiary style and controversial subject matter, the Federal Theatre administrator decided that government sponsorship of his opera would be too dangerous.[49]

Despite its difficult birth, *The Cradle Will Rock* opened in triumph; indeed, the production was so successful that Welles and Houseman transferred the show to their new Mercury Theatre. It was this "oratorio" version—with the actors back on stage, but without scenery and with Blitzstein's piano in place of an orchestra—that Feinstein saw in workshop with his friend Sam Beer. That November, Blitzstein, who was also a CP member, served as musical director for *One-Sixth of the Earth*, a pageant that filled Madison Square Garden with the party faithful, "all of them," the *Daily Worker* reported, "guided by but one resolve, their love and devotion for the Soviet Union!"[50] With greetings from Stalin and speeches by CPUSA officials, the pageant, held at the height of Stalin's terror, is, in retrospect, a grotesque spectacle.

The Cradle Will Rock is something else. It was dedicated to the German playwright and poet Bertolt Brecht and influenced heavily by Brecht's collaborator Kurt Weill (their 1928 *Threepenny Opera*, a Marxist reworking of John Gay's *Beggar's Opera*, was a worldwide hit).* But Blitzstein's own hard-boiled prosody is at the service of a musical vocabulary that ranges beyond Weimar Germany to Beethoven and "Boola Boola." If *One-Sixth of the Earth* was intended for a CP audience, *Cradle* aimed at, and attracted, a broader crowd.

Who were they? The composer Virgil Thomson, reviewing the Mercury production, described *Cradle*'s audience as "roughly the leftist front: that is to say, the right-wing socialists, the communists, some Park Avenue, a good deal of the Bronx, and all those intellectual or worker groups that the Federal Theatre in general and the Living Newspaper in particular have welded into the most formidable army of ticket buyers in the world. Union benefits, leftist group-drives, the German refugees, the Southern share-croppers, aid to China and to democratic Spain, the New York working populace, well-paid, well-dressed, and well-fed, supports

---

*Blitzstein's translation of *The Threepenny Opera* opened on Broadway in 1954. Kurt Weill's wife, Lotte Lenya, won a Tony for her portrayal of the prostitute Jenny.

them all."[51] Twenty years on, the remnant of this audience was to form the readership for *I. F. Stone's Weekly*.

The historian Ellen Schrecker draws a useful distinction between the Communist Party and a "movement" that she does not name but that I have been calling the Popular Front. In traditional accounts written during the cold war, the movement is the tool—witting or "innocent"—of the party. In conventional liberal accounts, whose aim is to certify the movement's ideological wholesomeness, the emphasis is on the party's marginality.[52] In fact, as Schrecker properly stresses, the party was at once the movement's "institutional core" and yet largely dependent on it for its political influence and, in American terms, its moral authority, though the movement's aims—ranging from an end to the poll tax, which systematically disenfranchised Southern blacks, to industrial unionism and the fight against fascism—never extended to a "Soviet America."[53] The lines weren't always clear. Matthew Josephson was movement, but his wife, Hannah, was party. So was Michael Blankfort's wife, Laurie. Both Isidor Feinstein and his brother Marc, a reporter for Federated Press, the left-wing labor news service, followed the rise of the CIO with intense professional and personal interest. And as Philadelphia friends of Blitzstein, both might have seen *Cradle*. But only Marc would have attended the Garden pageant. Marc was party; Izzy was movement.

Drawing strength from the victories of the CIO, and a sense of urgency from the war in Spain, the Popular Front marked not a retreat from radicalism (or a watering down of principle) but a recognition of the movement's progress. Its shift from sectarian to populist rhetoric was not some stratagem but an acknowledgment of the transition from an embattled subculture to a significant mass movement.[54] Within the Communist Party, the Popular Front "turn" seemed to license Earl Browder's efforts to move the CP away from a Bolshevik model, where power was to be seized from the margins of society, toward a social democratic politics in which the machinery of the state might actually be used for radical ends.[55] More important, such apparent openness allowed "movement" radicals to feel that on the central questions—industrial democracy and racial tolerance in America, antifascism in Europe—party members were responsible and reliable comrades.

That such confidence turned out to be misplaced was to have tragic consequences. But if, in the long run, disillusion with the Popular Front meant the end of the party as a significant force in American life, the legacy of the movement was far more durable. You could see it in the campaigns to end lynching and abolish the poll tax; you could hear it in Louis Armstrong's version of the *Threepenny Opera* song "Mack the Knife" (adapted by Marc Blitzstein); there would be times and places when you could just about taste it.

The Popular Front was not a mechanism or even a mind-set but a movement: fluid, protean, with disparate sources and diverse effects. To stress its politics over its culture, or vice versa, is to misunderstand the phenomenon. Politics was one bank of the stream. Culture—from Aaron Copland's *Fanfare for the Common Man* to Duke Ellington's *Jump for Joy* to the Food, Tobacco and Allied Workers' hymn "We Shall Overcome"— was the other bank. But the Popular Front was the stream itself.

James Agee's sharecropper epiphanies, Langston Hughes's Harlem nocturnes, Orson Welles's narrator in *Citizen Kane*, Steinbeck's Exodusters—there was no single Popular Front voice. To discern the common elements, we first must get past the caricature drawn by critics like Dwight Macdonald and Lionel Trilling, whose personal discomfort with workers and the great unwashed spilled over into their critiques of popular (and Popular Front) culture.[56] From our perspective, what is perhaps most remarkable about these voices is what they took for granted: an easy, confident radicalism (or notably sanguine radical pessimism) and a faith in the expressive possibilities of the American vernacular. Isidor Feinstein wrote not in the stilted subtexts of sectarian infighting, or even in the defensive ironies of the typical *Nation* or *New Republic* columnist, but in the frankly majoritarian cadences of daily newspaper editorials. "It might take some steam out of the Southern filibuster against the anti-lynching bill," he advised *Post* readers, "if it were extended to cover all violations of civil rights, North as well as South. After all, the Chicago police on Memorial Day killed more people . . . than were lynched in the entire South in the year 1937."[57]

Isidor Feinstein had found his voice. The Popular Front gave it reach and power—an audience, an analysis, an influence. It also gave him an asset that was to endure even when, in the 1950s, his audience disappeared and his influence became imperceptible: The Popular Front gave him courage. This courage could look like a kind of innocence or naïveté, but the cub reporter who walked off the job to protest the execution of

Sacco and Vanzetti already knew too much about power to be anybody's dupe. Instead of an insouciance he never had, the Popular Front gave him a hard-won sense of political possibility.

If at times he seemed to hold that sense of the possible aloft, like a banner or a totem, when other men saw only cynicism and defeat, perhaps that was because he knew what the Popular Front's ethic of solidarity could do—not just in factories or welfare offices or coal towns, not just for tire builders or longshoremen or steelworkers, but for a scared, pudgy newsman with two kids, one more on the way, and a boss who leaned on him.

The threat of fascism scared Isidor Feinstein the way nothing ever would before or after. It scared him out of the Socialist Party; it scared him into the Popular Front. To understand how much he valued what he found there, to appreciate what the Popular Front gave him, and why he remained rooted in the values of the Popular Front long after the political conditions that gave it birth had passed from the scene, we first need to understand that fear.

•

Franklin Roosevelt's decision to balance the federal budget in the spring of 1937 had consequences far beyond the confines of "Steeltown U.S.A." Besides putting thousands of writers, artists, actors, carpenters, painters, and construction workers back on the street, the president's cuts in the Public Works Administration and the Works Progress Administration also pulled the safety net out from under an economy that was, by October, heading for a fall. The "Roosevelt recession" saw stock prices plunge farther and faster than they had in the Depression of 1929.* Panic on Wall Street soon spread to the rest of the country, as unemployment rose to nearly one in five workers, a level last seen in the grim winter of 1933.[58]

For the newly organized unions of the CIO, the effects were especially devastating. With production down 40 percent in rubber, 50 percent in autos, and 70 percent in steel, hundreds of thousands of new union members were laid off. Without some renewal of government stimulus, all the gains of the last few years would soon be nullified. In the *Nation*,

---

*Economists are no more in agreement on the factors responsible for the "Roosevelt recession" than they are for the crash of 1929. There is, however, consensus that Roosevelt's attempt to balance the federal budget was at best ill timed.

Isidor Feinstein called for "direct government action . . . to put idle men and idle materials together."[59]

Four years earlier, Franklin Roosevelt assured Americans they had nothing to fear but fear itself. Now the president's appetite for experimentation seemed spent, his political vigor consumed by his recent battles with Congress over the Supreme Court, reorganization of the executive branch (another defeat), and the effort to impose a federal minimum wage (which passed only after the White House agreed to exempt domestic workers and farm laborers). With the nation desperate for leadership, Interior Secretary Harold Ickes noted despondently, "The President acted like a beaten man."[60] But if the administration remained paralyzed, others were willing to act. This time, the thunder was on the right.

Despite the New Deal's manifest failure to get the economy up and running again, the Communist poet Joseph Freeman's assertion, during a debate at the Writers Congress, that "we are living in a period when our basic job is to preserve those conditions under which a congress such as this can be held at all" found echoes throughout the Popular Front.[61] When in October Roosevelt gave a speech advocating that the United States "Quarantine the Aggressor," making veiled references to the dangers posed by Germany and Japan and expressing implicit sympathy for developing collective security arrangements among the "peace-loving nations," American Communists responded with renewed declarations of fealty.[62] The far right, however, viewed the country's economic crisis as a call to arms.

Charles Coughlin, a Catholic priest whose popular weekly radio broadcasts from Michigan's Shrine of the Little Flower shifted from "Roosevelt or Ruin" in 1932 to an alliance with Louisiana's governor Huey Long and, following Long's assassination in September 1935, support for the third-party candidate William Lemke in 1936, took a vow of silence following Lemke's humiliation at the polls. Returning to the airwaves in 1937, Coughlin's calls for strong leadership now mutated into full-throated fascism, with Jew-baiting, which had barely been a motif in the earlier days when Coughlin drew 80,000 letters a week, a principal theme.

No longer a political threat to the president, Coughlin could still cause trouble. His print organ, *Social Justice*, gave sanction to the thugs of the Christian Front, a group whose frank advocacy of violence brought it particular notoriety in New York, where Front members delivered racist street-corner tirades in hopes of provoking Jewish passersby.[63] *Social Justice* also took over from Henry Ford's *Dearborn Independent* as chief American publicist for that classic of anti-Semitic paranoia *The Protocols of the Elders of Zion*. Though Coughlin's Catholicism kept his followers, many of whom were Irish or German Americans, from joining forces with the virulently anti-Catholic Silver Shirts, led by William Dudley Pelley, or the North Carolina racist George Deatherage's Knights of the White Camellia, all these American Fascists admired Adolf Hitler, not least for his outspoken anti-Semitism.

With hindsight it may be easy to dismiss the threat of a Fascist uprising in the United States. But in 1937—a year before Nazi thugs destroyed German synagogues and Jewish-owned shops in the terrible pogrom known as Kristallnacht but two years after the Nuremberg Laws had already deprived German Jews of their civil rights—a time when, flanked by Nazi and American flags, speakers at a German-American Bund rally led a packed Madison Square Garden in chanting *"Heil Hitler!"* and when the robed and hooded troops of Michigan's Black Legion openly flogged CIO organizers, the threat was harder to gauge.[64]

Nor could fascism be dismissed as un-American or even unfashionable. For every Samuel Dickstein,* who eventually persuaded the House to create a special committee on un-American activities to investigate American fascism, or Jerry Voorhis, who tried to expose the danger, Congress had unabashed racists who scarcely bothered to disguise either their bigotry or their broader sympathy with fascism—its Theodore Bilbos, John Rankins, and Jacob Thorkelsons. The Black Legion might be rabble and Senator Bilbo a rabble-rouser, but Lawrence Dennis,† a Harvard-educated State Department veteran who advocated *The Coming American Fascism*, as his book put it, was no gutter politician.[65] Neither was Philip Johnson. Heir to a famous American fortune and curator of architecture at the brand-new Museum of Modern Art in New York, Johnson attached himself first to Huey Long and then to Father Coughlin before setting up his own band of "grey shirts."‡[66]

Harold Ickes, who despite his Bull Moose Republican background

---

*According to Allen Weinstein and Alexander Vassiliev's 1999 study *The Haunted Wood*, Dickstein, the prime mover behind the creation of HUAC, was on the Soviet payroll from 1937 to 1940.

†Gerald Horne's 2006 biography *The Color of Fascism* reveals Dennis as an African American who "passed" as white.

‡The high point of Johnson's career as a Fascist intellectual must have been his jaunt to Poland in 1939, where, as a correspondent for *Social Justice*, he followed the invading Wehrmacht. Though he expressed neither regret nor remorse for this episode, Johnson's postwar rise to the pinnacle of American architecture—and New York society—was remarkably unhampered.

considered himself "the only New Dealer" in the cabinet, took the right-wing resurgence seriously enough to raise the issue with the president a number of times.[67] Ickes asked a researcher named Irving Brant, who followed the native Fascists, to draft some speeches on the threat. Isidor Feinstein knew Brant, too.[68] But Izzy was in no need of instruction on the dangers of fascism. Since his days on the *Camden Courier*, he'd watched fascism fill the void left by exhausted parliamentarians in Italy and Germany. Fear of fascism in Spain coarsened his rhetoric: "Only the writer who draws his sustenance from the caved-in teat of a decayed past can be a Fascist," he declared in *Writers Take Sides*, a League of American Writers pamphlet published in 1938. It also simplified his politics: "Criminal disunity among liberals and the Left helped fascism to victory in Italy and Germany. The Popular Front has made it possible for the people of Spain to fight the greatest battle against fascism the world has yet seen . . . We must never forget that the barricades of Madrid are barricades everywhere—in defense of freedom, of culture, and of humanity."[69]

As long as those barricades held, he knew where he stood. Isidor Feinstein had taken his side. But what if they were breached? Not just in Spain, where the situation looked increasingly desperate, but in the United States. In New York. On Wall Street. In 1934, Major General Smedley Butler (Ret.), former commandant of the Marine Corps, told congressional investigators he'd been approached by a group of New York brokers and asked to raise a Fascist army. Most newspapers, hostile to Roosevelt and the New Deal in the first place, buried this news, but J. David Stern, who'd known Butler as Philadelphia's crusading police commissioner in the 1920s, put the story on the front page of the *Record* and the *Post*. Isidor Feinstein warned *Post* readers:

> They did it in Italy. They did it in Germany. They did it in Austria. They will try to do it in America.
>
> Their talk will be of "liberty," but it will be liberty to plunder labor, consumer and investor without check from the ballot box, the press, the pulpit or the agencies of free government.
>
> They'd like to do it here if they could get away with it. They'd like to turn all America into a Pennsylvania company town where everything and everybody are controlled by the company and no one dare protest or speak."[70]

In 1936, most Americans had preferred a man in a wheelchair to any savior on horseback. But a year later, with the economy in crisis again, big business smelled blood. Ickes, Corcoran, and the rest of the New Deal's inner circle girded up for a fight, though not everyone relished the battle. When talk of the "Jew Deal" and "President Rosenfeld" first became staples of the country club as well as the lunch counter, Jerome Frank, the Chicago-born Jew who had gone from the AAA to the SEC, asked staffers "to recommend lawyers who are not Jews."[71] Isidor Feinstein, however, had no intention of walking away from the coming struggle for the soul of the New Deal. For that matter, he felt increasingly compelled to speak out on the very issue that brought the country's disparate right-wingers their greatest public response: the charge that America was being manipulated into another European war.

But he was also very much afraid. Whether Isidor Feinstein was worried more by home-grown fascism and anti-Semitism or by the rise of fascism in Europe is impossible to say. However, there is no doubting the strength of his fear—if not for himself, then for his family, especially his children. He may not have changed many diapers, but, perhaps spurred by his own father's failures, he wanted his children to have a safe, secure home. And so, in the fall of 1937, he did something that he felt guilty about at the time and would always partially regret, even though in some ways it was crucial to his continued effectiveness and later success. We know he regretted it because he said so.[72] His guilt is suggested by the fact that he initially bungled the job.

In September 1937, an article in the *Nation* attacked the idea of American neutrality in world conflicts—a stated goal of President Roosevelt's foreign policy and David Stern's editorial policy—as "a dangerous myth." The writer began on a personal note: "I hate fascism. My heart is with the Spanish Loyalists." He asked readers to imagine

an America geared to fight a peace rather than a war, pouring out millions for construction, clearing slums, ending floods, halting the deserts encroaching on our Western plains, building a new America, a richer, happier America, while the Old World, in a frenzy, spills its blood and treasure.

The prospect is inspiring. But is it possible? I doubt it. It can be reduced to blueprints. It is as simple as arithmetic. It is sane and it is sensible. But it won't work. True, we mobilize for war. Why not for peace? But we make a profit on war. There are dividends in war . . . Peace with isolation means a loss, and our boards of directors are not convened to pass altruistic resolutions . . . The problem would be to produce more, to distribute it better, and to do this quickly. That spells socialism of one variety or another. Would we give up profit for peace? I doubt it.[73]

Who was this "I"? The byline, Geoffrey Stone, had never appeared in the *Nation* before. For a piece whose rhetoric was so dependent on the writer's personal authority, this was paradoxical—as was the absence of any explanation by the magazine's editors. Just how paradoxical was made excruciatingly apparent the following week, when the magazine's letters page ran—without comment—the following:

Dear Sirs:
Your new contributor, Mr. Geoffrey Stone, is of course as much entitled to the use of his name as I am to the same name, but perhaps the fact that I preceded him in published authorship will allow me . . . to point out that I did not write the article in this week's *Nation* beginning "I hate fascism. My heart is with the Spanish Loyalists." As will have been plain to any *Nation* readers who may have seen articles and reviews signed by me in the *American Review*, the *Commonweal*, and elsewhere, it is Marxism that I hate, and my heart is with the Spanish Nationalists.
Geoffrey Stone, Assistant Editor, the *American Review*

Feinstein's next move was worse. According to a story that soon became part of *Post* legend, one morning the young editorial writer strode up to the managing editor and announced, "I am no longer Isidor Feinstein. I have decided to change my name. From now on, I won't have you call me Izzy. I have decided to call myself Abelard Stone." The managing editor looked up and, after a brief pause, replied, "Okay, Abie."[74]
Why such awkwardness? After all, Izzy's father and grandfather had both changed their names (from Baruch to Bernard and from Tsvilikhovsky to Feinstein). And for a Jew with any kind of public visibility or aspiration, the name change was as much a part of Americanization as

dropping Yiddish for English. This was the era, after all, that saw Julius Garfinkel become John Garfield and Billy Chon (né Chonofsky) give way to the urbane William Shawn. How else could "a shy, introspective Jewish kid named Arthur Arshawsky," as he described himself, emerge as "a sort of weird, jazz-band-leading, clarinet-tooting, jitterbug-surrounded Symbol of American Youth" named Artie Shaw? That such metamorphoses were not necessarily regarded as shameful, even on the left, can be seen from the case of Itzok Granich, mild-mannered Hebrew school dropout, who became Mike Gold, the *New Masses'* feared literary enforcer. No one could have accused the man who wrote *Jews Without Money* of trying to "pass"—his new name functioned as nom de guerre as well as nom de plume.[75] But Isidor Feinstein's new name was both, and he was also trying to allow his children, at least, to pass.

The name he finally made for himself, I. F. Stone, first appears in the *Nation* dated October 2, 1937, the same day that Esther gave birth to their third child, Christopher David Stone, named for the author of *Tamburlaine*. But Christopher, as his father knew, is Greek for "Christbearer." In his *Nation* debut, I. F. Stone pays tribute to "the resistance faith has always shown to faggot." Citing recent attacks on the Roman Catholic church in the Hearst press and in Germany, the author describes Christianity as sympathetic to the oppressed and "in this sense . . . inevitably Marxist . . . From Lollard to Leveler, common men have drawn radical conclusions from their Bibles . . . Democracy, humanitarianism, and utopian socialism, all derive from the enthusiasm with which the lower classes, as learning revived and printing spread, turned to Old and New Testament for solace and guidance."[76] Such a robust and venerable radical institution could surely afford shelter or at least camouflage to his own family. He would never disguise the fact that he was Jewish, he assured his *Post* colleague Nathaniel Weyl, but he saw the change as "protection for his children."[77]

Christopher Stone's birth certificate lists his mother and father as "Esther Stone" and "I. F. Stone." That December Izzy petitioned a New York court to "shorten and anglicize" his name and the names of his older children. In a separate petition, Esther Miriam Feinstein became Esther Mary Stone.[78] His brothers and sister all changed their names as well. "He said he didn't want to turn a reader off who might be anti-Semitic, right away, before he ever read the article," Louis Stone explained. "If the byline is I. F. Stone, people would read on . . . So we had a talk and we all agreed to go along with that." This display of family unity was spoiled by Bernard, however, who preferred to remain a Feinstein.[79]

Freed completely from the shadow of paternal authority, Isidor F. Stone ("I have a memory of him telling me the *F* stands for 'no middle initial,'" Jeremy Stone recalled) was to gain renown sufficient for several of his friends to claim credit for the change. Michael Blankfort, George Seldes, and Jill Stern all believed they had provided either the inspiration or the final abridgment.[80] But Bernard was not the only dissenter. The day Izzy first entered the newsroom as I. F. Stone, the *Post*'s financial columnist Sylvia Porter (who had shed her maiden name of Feldman upon her marriage to Mr. Porter) greeted him: "Good morning, Mr. Phone-stone."[81] Westbrook Pegler, the sportswriter turned sage of the Hearst chain, and Cordell Hull, Roosevelt's secretary of state, were both to use Izzy's name change in efforts to discredit him. The level of hostile comment was high enough that Stone felt the need to explain himself to Felix Frankfurter, whose own last name was a frequent target of right-wing witticisms.

His friend responded sympathetically. "I can only say about your metamorphosis that I can imagine all the pangs through which you went," Frankfurter replied, "and, knowing you and your purposes, I bow to your judgement. Izzy by any other name, etc., apparently isn't the truth."[82] Izzy needed the reassurance. He probably needed the camouflage as well, because by the end of 1937, I. F. Stone, though still publicly committed to "collective security," a stance that already put him at odds with his employer, was privately convinced that war with fascism was not only inevitable but welcome.

The emergence of I. F. Stone was more than just the birth of a byline. An editorial writer, no matter how influential, is still essentially the creature of his employer. Isidor Feinstein had long chafed under the restrictions imposed by J. David Stern, and as I. F. Stone he wasted little time in declaring his independence.

Opposition to collective security was "sustained emotionally," he pointed out, by drawing a parallel between the situations in 1937 and in 1914. This was done countless times on the editorial pages of the *Post*, but Stone attacked the premise head-on in the *Nation*. "The Germany of 1914 dreamed, as does the Germany of 1937, of a greater Germany. But the Germany of 1937 and the Italy of 1937 have new weapons. There is first the virus of anti-Semitism . . . Injected into the democratic powers, it sets Frenchman against Frenchman, Englishman against Englishman, American against American." The second weapon, he informed *Nation* readers, is "the bogey of communism."[83]

Here, too, his tone was a far cry from the even-handed denunciations of Stern's *Post*: "The Russia of 1937, though still in many respects absolutist, as all Russian governments have been for centuries, is nevertheless the scene of the greatest social experiment of our time. Under the most difficult circumstances—lack of capital, lack of literacy, lack of international security—its ruling party is seeking to transform the most backward of the great European nations into the most advanced." Acknowledging "a hunt for and extermination of suspected dissident elements that has left the outside world bewildered," he argued that "the rise of fascism in Germany has led the Communist doctrinaires to abandon their intransigent position of the past—a position that helped Hitler to power in Germany—and to seek the help of democratic countries" in maintaining peace.

Once again he sensed a hardening of options: "The European democracies themselves, caught between their national interests and the pro-fascist feeling all too common among their upper classes, fumble and falter as fascism advances. Today it is Madrid. Tomorrow it will be Prague. How long before it knocks at our own doors?"

And once again, he was moving to the left. "The experience of the Spanish republic shows that when that time comes there will be only one place to which anti-fascists can look for aid in the event that they must fight for their liberties and their lives. I shall not mention the bogyman by name."[84]

As Alfred Kazin wrote of this period: "Even for those who knew the [Soviet] trials were wrong, the danger was Hitler, Mussolini, Franco. And because the Fascist assault on Spain and the ever-growing strength of Hitler had made the United Front necessary, I found myself more sympathetic to the Communists. They had, they had just had, they still seemed to have, Silone, Malraux, Hemingway, Gide, Rolland, Gorky, Aragon, Picasso, Éluard, Auden, Spender, Barbusse, Dreiser, Farrell, while the Socialists seemed to have only their own virtue. I was tired of virtue, and now wanted to see some action."[85]

As Abelard Stone, Isidore Feinstein had blundered into the claustrophobic, marginal arena of sectarian infighting that he deplored—and quickly made his exit. As I. F. Stone, he moved into the mainstream of the Popular Front. For a time, it seemed as if the entire New Deal was moving along with him.

•

"Organized wealth, which has controlled the government so far, seizes the opportunity to decide whether it is to continue to control the government or not." The date was November 6, 1937. The setting was the White House. The speaker was the president of the United States.[86] Perhaps because it so admirably accorded with their own prejudices, the theory that the country's economic woes were the result of a big-business conspiracy—a "capital strike"—had numerous adherents in both the Popular Front and the New Deal.[87] They may have been correct.

America's Sixty Families, Ferdinand Lundberg's muckraking study of the plutocracy, had just been published—and favorably reviewed in the *New Republic* by I. F. Stone. Applauding Lundberg's treatment of "the irreconcilable conflict of our age," namely, "the existence of economic sovereignties so vast that they overawe the State," Stone felt Lundberg was unfair to "progressives of the past" and "too trusting" of the New Deal.[88] But Harold Ickes, a veteran brawler who'd learned to play political hardball on the streets of Chicago, thought Lundberg had identified the true cause of the recession, and, encouraged by Corcoran, Cohen, and the president himself, he said so to a national radio audience in a speech on December 30. Charging that the country was at the mercy of a "general sit-down strike—not of labor—not of the American people—but of the sixty families," Ickes warned of "the irreconcilable conflict" between "the power of money and the power of the democratic instinct."[89]

Though the echo may have been a coincidence, at the least it suggests a convergence of views. And though they may have differed in their assessments of the man Izzy referred to as the "squire of Hyde Park," the reporter and the cabinet curmudgeon also agreed on what was at stake in the current crisis and on the relevant historical precedent. "There are many similarities between the Jacksonian period and our own," wrote I. F. Stone. Reviewing Marquis James's recent biography of the master of the Hermitage, he found Jackson "as little fitted by his class position to be the leader and the symbol of the struggle for political democracy as Franklin D. Roosevelt was to be the leader and symbol of the present movement toward social democracy."* It was "popular aspiration," he declared, that "harnessed Jackson and made him great . . . The time lifted Jackson up, as it did Roosevelt."[90]

Two weeks after the review appeared, Ickes listened to the president's complaint about "organized wealth." As the cabinet meeting broke up, he passed Roosevelt a note: "This looks to me like the same kind of fight Jackson made against the United States Bank." The president replied: "That's right."[91]

Publicly the president remained silent. But in the same week Ickes issued his warning about a "big-business Fascist America," another New Deal insider was even more explicit in charging that "certain groups of big business" were engaging in "a strike of capital" to "liquidate the New Deal." Robert Jackson was head of the Justice Department's antitrust division. At the time he made his remarks, in two speeches at the end of December, he was also well known to be a particular favorite of President Roosevelt, who told his political operatives to talk up Jackson as a possible candidate for New York governor—an ideal position from which to campaign for the White House in 1940. The "Jackson boom" was closely managed by Tommy Corcoran, faithfully assisted on the pages of the *Post* by I. F. Stone.[92]

Jackson's harsh portrait of the nation's economy as "an impossibly long ladder of a few great corporations dominated by America's 60 families," though far from the received view even at the Justice Department, was something of an article of faith among two sets of New Dealers. One group has been described as "a party within a party." Self-consciously conspiratorial, its members were "linked to one another through an informal pattern of friendships and intellectual associations. Groups of them gathered in restaurants for weekly dinners . . . They held private meetings on Sunday afternoons to discuss the contours of administration policy. They attended dinner parties at one another's homes, often to meet with a visiting journalist or scholar sympathetic to their aims. They passed books

---

*Both Stone's review and James's biography of Jackson were part of a broad revival of interest in the seventh president that was to find its apotheosis in Arthur Schlesinger Jr.'s *The Age of Jackson*, published in 1945.

and articles back and forth. They sent each other frequent letters offering encouragement and advice."[93] The second group were members of the Communist Party.

Few if any of the "liberal crowd," as Corcoran called his true-believing cronies in the administration, were members of the Communist Party. But given the sheer magnitude of its administrative ambitions, the New Deal created an immense demand for new functionaries—by one estimate more than a quarter of a million new bureaucrats had arrived in Washington in 1933 alone.[94] And though the party's preferred image was of the dedicated, courageous factory worker, communism now had considerable appeal among white-collar workers—architects, teachers, social workers, even lawyers—exactly those groups which, hit hard by the depression, rallied to the banners of the New Deal. Thanks to the lingering effects of McCarthyism and the CP's habitual duplicity, we may never know the extent to which the party was literally, as Ellen Schrecker puts it, "a junior partner within the New Deal coalition."[95] New Dealers and Communists shared a taste for conspiracy and a sense of themselves as embattled crusaders against a powerful established order, and there is no question that many experienced Communist organizers brought personal dedication and, thanks to the Popular Front, political direction to the haphazard experiment that was the New Deal.

Franklin Roosevelt was of course no fonder of Communists than John L. Lewis was. But his administration, like the CIO, needed capable operators. He also needed to mobilize public opinion. "You must *force* me to act," he repeatedly told liberal supporters. The party's armada of letterhead organizations might not have been broadly based (though during the Popular Front, many party "fronts" did become genuinely popular), but groups like the Civil Rights Congress or the American Student Union or the League of Women Shoppers were repeatedly able to generate publicity and raise public awareness on issues important to New Dealers.

Conservative politicians like the AAA administrator George Peek and reactionaries like the Texas congressman Martin Dies used the charge of "Communist influence" to try to derail the New Deal's efforts to reform the capitalist system. In the early 1940s, Dies sent Robert Jackson a list of 1,121 alleged Communists in the government, a list that one historian has characterized as reading "like a Who's Who of Popular Front Washington [with] the names of many of the New Deal's best and brightest lawyers and bureaucrats," but only two people lost their jobs.[96] Though we now know beyond serious doubt that some Communists in government service would also be encouraged to spy for the Soviet Union, there is no evidence to suggest that most Communist cells in Washington, despite their secrecy, were anything more than political ginger groups or talking shops. Corcoran, Ickes, and the other New Dealers knew that Communist support arose not out of secret sympathy or an identity of aims but from mutual utility. Under Earl Browder, party members were encouraged to work within the institutions of the state to further causes like union recognition or justice for Southern sharecroppers.

This was the signal political achievement of the Popular Front: to create, amid all the adverse historical, social, and ideological conditions for which America is famous, and at a time when world events were far from propitious, a sense of optimism, even inevitability, about the future of progressive, reforming, even revolutionary politics. This political confidence, which shifted his tone from shrill to sure footed, set the work of I. F. Stone apart from the writings of Isidor Feinstein. Writing in January 1938 in the *New Republic*, he admonished William Allen White, a foe of the CIO and critic of the New Deal, to take the long view: "We barricade ourselves and Mr. White against despair with the thought that history is less logical than man; cuts its own patterns; picks its own instruments; eludes our formulas; is perverse, eccentric, whimsical. Sometimes it leaps . . . Sometimes history creeps (and this is where we come in)."[97] This is the voice of a man who is not only confident of his place on the train of history, perhaps in one of the more comfortable carriages, rather than the locomotive, but determined to enjoy the view as well.

And why not? Besides the *New Republic*, whose pages seemed open to him whenever he had something to say, he was becoming a frequent contributor to the *Nation*. At the same time, his *Post* editorials on New York City's transit finances resulted in an invitation to Washington to testify before a subcommittee of the Senate Judiciary Committee.[98] This February 1938 trip was a triumph: His testimony that a revision of the federal bankruptcy law, pending before Congress, could endanger the city's 5¢ subway fare prompted the New York senator Robert Wagner to press for changes in the bill. The whole campaign was featured on the *Post*'s front page for three days running—with the stories bylined "I. F. Stone." And though the SEC chairman, William Douglas, was out of town, Izzy was able to meet with Corcoran, Cohen, and the SEC commissioner Jerome Frank. From his base at the *Post*, his influence now extended from the inner councils of the New Deal to the outer reaches of the Popular Front.

Yet within a year he was to lose that base, and within two years he was off the train of history—this time for good.

•

The trouble started less than two weeks after his return from Washington. Stone might still joke about a report in *Pravda* that Soviet newspaper editors were being purged "as enemies of the people for allegedly deliberate typographical errors" and because they gave "full freedom" to reporters: "If Crime No. 1—typographical errors—is serious, Crime No. 2—editorial freedom—is doubly serious."[99] But with the *Post*'s finances going from pale pink to deep red, David Stern was no longer smiling.

On February 15, 1938, the *Post* declared war on the Popular Front. "There can be no united front for democracy with the enemies of democracy," argued Stern. Though reasonable on its face, Stern's premise quickly degenerated into the claim that communism was "more dangerous" than fascism and that "the 'united front'—union of liberals with Communists against Fascists—is a greater threat to democracy than the frontal attack of reactionaries."[100] Stern's opening salvo, which took up two full columns on the *Post*'s front page, was supposedly prompted by Stalin's call for the "political help of the working class of bourgeois countries to [aid] the working class of our country in case of military attack"— neither a novel nor particularly provocative statement by the Soviet leader. Certainly I. F. Stone believed that his boss's warning to "resist all efforts of Communists in disguise to entangle liberals in 'united front' efforts" had more to do with falling revenues than fear of revolution.

If Stern was trying to pick a fight with the left, he didn't have long to wait. That very night the publisher attended a dinner party at the home of George Seldes, who denounced the editorial to his face.[101] At the paper the next day, Stone was equally vehement. In the past, Stern had always been the most forbearing of bosses. "I was a very hard guy to handle," said Stone. "I'd always fight back and give him a big argument. Because we were old friends, and he was a great guy, he would let a guy talk back to him, and holler."[102] This time was different, partly because Stern felt himself in a corner financially and partly because the shouting match over this editorial soon became public.

"Once there was a liberal paper in New York City and now there is none," Heywood Broun informed readers of his column in the *New Republic*. Broun moved swiftly from the general to the personal: "In the Red-Baiting Handicap (one mile and a furlong for colts and geldings) J. David Stern was a slow starter . . . [yet] as they charged across the finish line it was evident that Stern had won by a head." Behind the horse-racing metaphor was a furious attack. Stern had been the first publisher to sign a Newspaper Guild contract. "There never has been a time," wrote Broun, "when J. David Stern was not eager and ready to bleed subcutaneously for a good cause." And his papers were easily the most contentiously liberal in the country. But "J. David," scoffed Broun, "was playing the wolf only until such time as he could be measured for sheep's clothing."[103]

In normal times, Stern might have shrugged off Broun's barbs; he might even have welcomed the publicity. But Stern, as Broun well knew, was almost as dependent on the union's goodwill as he was on advertisers' patronage. Stern had recently begun negotiations with the guild over the deep pay cuts he needed to keep the paper solvent.* Under the circumstances, the guild president's hostility was potentially dangerous. The fact that Broun punctuated his tirade with praise for I. F. Stone's work—"personally, I always felt that the editorial page was the chief attraction"—probably didn't help.

The situation at the *Post* was hostile but not yet terminal. One reason may have been that in the spring of 1938, David Stern temporarily discovered the virtue of solidarity. The agency for this realization was Frank Hague, boss of Jersey City and self-appointed scourge of the CIO. For more than twenty years, Frank ("I Am the Law") Hague's grip on power in Hudson County had easily justified his sobriquet: Juries, judges, prosecutors, and tax assessors were his instruments. His critics found themselves assessed to the point of penury, denied the right to vote, and, if they were persistent critics, arrested on trumped-up charges.[104] Though Franklin

---

*Broun's biographer, Richard O'Connor, reports city room gossip that Broun himself engineered the guild's approval of the pay cuts, which took effect in September. Though Broun's fondness for sharp turns lends the rumor some plausibility, given the absence of any other evidence and given the pitch of Broun's hostility, it lacks basic credibility.

Roosevelt studiously ignored Hague's antics (stayed perhaps by the knowledge that in 1932, when his own margin in the whole of New Jersey was only 30,000 votes, Hague carried Hudson County by 117,000), David Stern not only published three of the region's leading newspapers but actually lived in New Jersey. When the *Post* dared to differ with a mayoral edict banning CIO organizers from Jersey City's streets, sidewalks, and parks, Hague issued a further ukase ordering the city's two hundred newsdealers to remove the paper from their stands.[105]

In the ensuing free-speech fight, Stern found himself in harness with Norman Thomas, the American Civil Liberties Union, the CIO, and the Communist Party—the whole of the Popular Front to the left of the New Deal. For a while, it looked as if Stone's constitutional expertise would save his job. Certainly there were not many newspapermen who could command the respect of Felix Frankfurter, quarrel on equal terms with Jerome Frank, conspire with Corcoran and Cohen, and write with Stone's fond authority of Benjamin Cardozo that "he was the master of a style that always illumined but sometimes dazzled."[106] Hague's own red-baiting may even have shamed Stern into calming down—momentarily. "We hear about Constitutional rights, free speech and the free press," Hague once said. "Every time I hear those words I say to myself, 'That man is a Red, that man is a Communist.' You never heard a real American talk in that manner."[107]

Still, there was no getting away from the widening gap between David Stern and his principal editorial writer. For the moment, though, there was little Izzy could do. He bombarded Freda Kirchwey, the *Nation*'s editor, with suggestions for editorials and also proposed writing a column for her.[108] At home, he and Esther began to economize, subletting their apartment in the city and moving the family to a bungalow in Northport, Long Island, in the summer of 1938. The commute to work gave Izzy a chance to read the papers in the morning and work on freelance projects in the evenings. On weekends he took the family for drives in Rin Tin Tin, a battered 1932 Dodge, or they all strapped on roller skates.[109]

He also embarked on a frenzy of freelancing, writing for the *New Republic*, *Current History*, and the *Southern Review* as well as the *Nation* and the *Post*—and, on Maddie Josephson's advice, pitching stories as far afield as the *Virginia Quarterly*. Northport's tranquil atmosphere was a good place to work, and the Stone family was joined for the summer by

Izzy's old Penn friend Chester Rabinowitz (soon to become Roberts) and his wife, whose rented bungalow up the hill from Izzy and Esther also housed Walter Hart and his wife. But Izzy's "headoverhellishly heels" busyness had another spur as well. On a visit to his doctor earlier in the year he'd been told that he was losing his hearing. Though none of Stone's letters that survive from that year so much as mention his impending deafness—even when, as in his correspondence with Blankfort, they give a detailed account of his "wheezes, sneezes, twinges" and the whooping cough epidemic that also helped push his family out of the city for the summer—the prospect must have weighed on his mind.[110]

Signs of his darkening mood and his mounting political and personal desperation can be seen in the longest essay he wrote at Northport, a 5,400-word demolition of Jerome Frank's book *Save America First*. Though he'd warned the SEC commissioner earlier in the summer that he was writing "a destructive job," Frank seems not to have taken the warning seriously. And, perhaps out of recognition that Frank is really a stand-in for other targets, Stone begins by conceding that the book is "brilliant, stimulating and informing even when one disagrees with it." But he soon goes on the attack. Frank's thesis that the Depression was "a mental, not an economic phenomenon" is summarily dismissed: "It will take more than a combination of Christian Science and specious anthropological analogies to end the paradox of want amid plenty." The second pillar of Frank's argument, that "America's prosperity requires relative isolation," prompts this brutal rebuttal: "He is, like most of the isolationists, Anglophobiac; a belated critic of British Imperialism. Their reaction to the crimes of Hitler and Mussolini is to protest the raw deal England handed Ireland, Egypt, India and the Sultan of Zanzibar a century ago. The apologists of Fascism use the same line of argument."[111]

Izzy seems not to have cared very much for Jerome Frank. He'd already had a run-in with him over Frank's refusal to hire his friend George Brounoff. (On the promise of an interview with Frank, Izzy had lent Brounoff the $10 train fare to Washington only to have him shunted off to an assistant who gave him a form to fill out but no promise of a job.[112]) But the fury in Stone's prose suggests that Frank's book was only a proxy for a man whose arguments against structural economic change and in favor of American isolationism he couldn't yet confront directly: J. David Stern.

That such a confrontation was in the offing Stone could no longer doubt. The free-ranging banter of happier days had been replaced by a frosty formality. When the financially pressed publisher of the *Post* and his former protégé needed to communicate with one another, they did so via Harry Saylor, the managing editor, an old-fashioned newsman deeply suspicious of intellectuals in general and I. F. Stone, whom he thought held "an exalted opinion of himself," in particular.[113] Preparing for the inevitable, Stone worked through his summer vacation, doubling for the absent Sam Grafton as well.

He also rode the wave of CIO organizing a bit further. Gerhard Van Arkel, his friend since their days together in Haddonfield editing the *Progress*, had abandoned journalism for law and was now a staff attorney for the National Labor Relations Board. Acting on complaints from the United Mine Workers, the NLRB's efforts to force Harlan County, Kentucky, mine owners to obey the Wagner Labor Relations Act had already resulted in the conviction of two coal companies. But as the CIO quickly discovered, even though the NLRB could prevent companies from firing union members, it couldn't force them to sign a union contract. So the Roosevelt administration decided to try a new weapon: In the summer of 1938, fifty-five defendants—coal companies, mine operators, and the county sheriff and twenty-two of his deputies—were charged in federal court with violating the Civil Rights Act of 1870 by depriving Harlan miners of their right to organize.[114]

After the first jury deadlocked (with a majority in favor of conviction) in August, the Justice Department moved for a retrial. In the meantime, the CIO mobilized its friends in the press. Following in the footsteps of John Dos Passos, Theodore Dreiser, and his friend Malcolm Cowley—who had all been in Kentucky on a 1931 Communist-sponsored fact-finding mission—Stone went to Harlan County to report on conditions there. Beyond his predictable outrage at the coal companies' tactics—there was little chance Stone would side with the "thugs for J. H. Blair"—his dispatches from the CIO's front line are notable for two reasons. The first was his retrospective scorn for "the ineffectiveness of the famous Dreiser–Dos Passos investigation: [Despite] mass meetings in New York City . . . [where] protests were drawn up and money collected . . . the operators were undeterred. By autumn of 1931, twelve miners had been killed, two reporters had been shot, a relief kitchen . . . dynamited." The result: "Unionism in Harlan was crushed."[115]

More striking still was his endorsement of the "unrelenting pressure of inquiry and prosecution by the Government this year." Surveying the effect of exposure by La Follette's committee—once again used to soften up a CIO target—followed by NLRB and Justice Department intervention, Stone was optimistic. The legal situation might be stalemated, but the result, he predicted, would be "a far cry" from the vain battle that gave "Bloody Harlan" its fame. "Whatever the outcome of the new trial . . . Harlan is changing for the better . . . The rights of labor are slowly winning recognition." Not even the combined might of "absentee owners U.S. Steel, International Harvester, Ford, Aluminum Company and Peabody" could resist this Popular Front–New Deal coalition.[116] I. F. Stone's faith in what, writing in the *Nation* that August, he called the "Roosevelt Revolution" was vindicated a few weeks later when the Harlan County Coal Operators' Association signed a UMW contract.[117] The tide was still running to the left.

His report from Harlan County was just one of a series of unsigned articles he wrote for the *Nation* that summer while filling in for the vacationing Max Lerner. And, though he was still trying to avoid a final rupture with the *Post*, Izzy was deeply grateful when Lerner, quitting the *Nation* in September, arranged for his summer substitute to take over his half-time job. "This has been a terribly unhappy year for me on the *Post* which has been going right fast," he wrote to Michael Blankfort's new wife, Suzy, "and the *Nation* gives me a substantial oar to windward."[118]

Stone's debt to Lerner was intellectual as well as practical. Reviewing his benefactor's *It Is Later Than You Think* (an obvious quid pro quo), he hailed "the first book of a man destined to a foremost place among American political thinkers." His enthusiasm for Lerner's anatomy of "the feelings, doubts, dilemmas, hesitations, beliefs, and gropings of the contemporary middle-class Leftist intellectual" seems sincere. He quotes the climax of Lerner's diatribe with evident relish: "His symbol is the swivel chair—whether that of editor, columnist or professor—and the best thing about it is that it can turn in so many directions. His ammunition is abstractions. His tenacity is nil."[119]

"Only a man's relatives," Stone remarks, "can make him so furious." Or, he might have added, a man's boss. Hence his delight at Lerner's slap at liberal isolationists, whose hopes "rest on the premise that the fascists will keep promises they make in being bought off from breaking other promises previously made." But where "Lerner would like to take capitalism from the capitalists—but peacefully," his successor demurs: "History doesn't work that way."[120] To I. F. Stone, capitalism was bankrupt. In the long term he wanted socialism, not "capitalist collectivism." His immediate objective, especially after the Munich Conference of September 1938, was equally abhorrent to David Stern. In a letter to Maddie Josephson enclosing his *Nation* blast at appeasement (and asking the writer to support Mike Blankfort's application for a Guggenheim fellowship), he closed with a terse P.S.: "pray for war NOW."[121]

The final breach with Stern came in January 1939. According to Stone, "There was a strike at a Brooklyn department store. There was secondary picketing, and [Stern] wanted me to write an editorial saying that it was unconstitutional." Stone, who'd recently given several talks to department-store unions at the invitation of his friend Sidney Cohn, refused. "I said, 'Look, the Supreme Court recently upheld secondary picketing. I can't write that!' So he was really sore. 'Goddammit, I need that editorial to get the department-store advertising.' And I said, 'Goddammit, why didn't you tell me that in the first place? I've been in a whorehouse long enough to know what one's supposed to do!' I don't think I ever wrote the editorial."[122]

According to Samuel Grafton, it was Izzy's acerbic manner, not his principles, that cost him his job.

> One day Izzy and I were haggling a little over who was to write a particular editorial. And finally it was agreed that I would write it. Izzy, who never let the grass grow under his feet, decided to go off on an errand or something, and Harry T. Saylor, the managing editor, came in and said, "Sam, I'd like to write that editorial." So, Saylor wrote the editorial. The next morning, we had an editorial conference, and Iz took off: "That was a lousy editorial, poorly written, etc." I was trying to signal him, but he thought I was trying to get him to take it easy on me. So then it struck me—enough of this. I leaned back, lit a cigar, and let nature take its course . . . Izzy was fired that day."[123]

Actually, Stone was never fired; he was simply transferred to the news desk and given nothing to do. Stern later claimed he was distressed by

"Izzy's juvenile attitude" toward subway finance—his insistence that the city should let the private transit companies go bankrupt before allowing them to raise fares.[124] But Stone's *Post* campaign had been a resounding success. Besides, Stone's transfer was in January; he hadn't written a word about the subways since "Wall Street Goes Socialist"—a tidy piece of muckraking but hardly the *Communist Manifesto*—in the *New Republic* in August 1938.[125] A more likely trigger was a fight between the *Post* and the New York College Teachers Union over charges of Communist domination. The paper's pronouncement on January 21, 1939, that unions should stay out of politics would have been anathema to any partisan of the CIO.[126]

In later life he claimed "it was fun to be back on the street." This cheerful picture is completed by the assertion that "on the first day, I got a page-one story."[127] But Newspaper Guild records show that I. F. Stone was banished to the newsroom on January 23, and his byline did not appear on the *Post*'s front page at any time that month—or later. (He may well have conflated his transit stories from a year earlier, perhaps the fruit of a previous, temporary banishment, with his final transfer out of editorials.) There was little bravado in his complaint to the union, which accused Stern and Saylor of trying to humiliate him into quitting in order to avoid paying severance. "As editorial writer I was subject only to the editor, and my advice was sought and friendship cultivated by persons high in the City, State and Federal governments; as reporter I am subject to four City editors, to the news editor, and to the managing editor as well as to the editor and publisher . . . In the newsroom, too, I have been kept 'on ice' . . . usually with nothing at all to do."[128]

"I do not deny the management's right to discharge me, nor do I ask reinstatement." All he asked was his severance pay—after ten years in Stern's employ, a considerable sum. Lulled by his apparent rapprochement with Stern during the fight with Hague the previous year, Stone had moved his family to "an enormous house" in the Richmond Hill section of Queens at the end of September 1938. His *Nation* pay would "keep us all in food and clothes," he had thought, but keeping that job, let alone maintaining the contacts and visibility that might land him another editorial job, depended on a freedom of movement barred by his chair-warming duties at the *Post*. Increasingly dependent on a bulky hearing aid, his chances of getting a reporter's job on another daily paper were, at that point, negligible.[129]

Stern, who after years of losses had decided to sell the *Post*, refused to pay. In the legal wrangle that followed (during which neither side made mention of his deafness), Izzy was represented by the Newspaper Guild's counsel Abraham Isserman,* with assistance from Louis Boudin. Though his new duties were nonexistent, Izzy's salary remained $115 a week, more than double what his fellow reporters and rewrite men were getting. Stern claimed this was evidence of good faith; Izzy argued that it was designed to embarrass him. The arbitrator, Francis Biddle, agreed with the publisher.[130]

I. F. Stone never got his severance from the *Post*. He did, however, get the last word. When Stern finally managed to unload the paper in July, his former employee wrote that the sale "again demonstrates that freedom of the press is nine-tenths rhetoric." Though faulting "the *Post*'s baiting of reds and the Soviet Union," its call for "regulation of labor unions" and "an ignominious run-to-cover on Spain," Stone was personally generous to Stern: "Although New York City's numerous liberals and powerfully organized workers would seem a natural market for a progressive, pro-labor daily, the same economic forces that killed the old *Globe* and the *World* have proved too much for one of the country's most enterprising publishers."[131] It was an epitaph he would have occasion to remember more than once.

•

A freelance writer in need of regular employment is like a courtesan in search of a husband. There is the same necessity to keep one's attributes on display, the same habit of calculation, and the same need to keep material considerations hidden behind a mask of pliable, easygoing amiability. That the whole process remain unacknowledged is essential if self-respect is to be maintained.

His friends tried to help. George Seldes wrote to Harold Ickes asking him to give Izzy a job. Ickes was interested—until an underling, describing "Feinstein" as "a bright emotional writer of fixed views," reminded him that Izzy had been "the author of a number of . . . editorials to the effect that Ickes' PWA is snarled in red tape."[132] Freda Kirchwey promised a

---

*Isserman, who later represented the Communist Party in the Dennis case, was the uncle of the historian Maurice Isserman.

full-time spot as soon as the money became available; in the meantime, she urged Izzy to take a job he'd been offered as press secretary to the Federal Housing Administration, while continuing to write for the *Nation* on the side.[133]

Instead, he took a six-month research job with the Institute for Propaganda Analysis, a think tank funded by the American Jewish Committee and the Goodwill Fund, a foundation set up by Edward Filene, the father of his *Court Disposes* benefactor. He also moved his wife and children to a small house in Forest Hills, gave the family's German maid her notice, sold their beloved Rin Tin Tin, and tightened the family belt by about $100 a month. Though all three children now slept in the same room, the only complaint came from four-year-old "J.J."—disappointed that his father wasn't going to become a policeman like the little boy next door's father.[134]

Attached to Teachers College at Columbia, the institute sought to "help the intelligent citizen detect and analyze propaganda." The editorial director, Harold Lavine, was a good friend of James Wechsler, now the *Nation*'s labor correspondent, and like Wechsler had recently left the Young Communist League. In the 1940s, these ex-Communists would become very anti-Communist, but in May 1939, when I. F. Stone reported for work at the institute, there appeared few grounds for disagreement among the "large numbers of independent progressives for whom," wrote Wechsler, "the growth of fascism was the central fact of political life."[135]

This "central fact" helped make the spring of 1939 swing time for the Popular Front. On Broadway, Harold Rome's *Pins and Needles*, a musical revue staged by the International Ladies Garment Workers Union, was in the second year of the longest run in Broadway history. A celebration of CIO values—"No court's injunction can make me stop / Until your love is all closed shop" went the lyrics of "One Big Union for Two"—*Pins and Needles* put real garment workers on stage, while songs like "Chain Store Daisy" put the workers' lives in the spotlight. Determined to have it both ways, the show satirized the conventions of Tin Pan Alley even as it depended on audience knowledge of those conventions to give a number like "Sing Me a Song of Social Significance" its satirical bite.[136]

Downtown, at Barney Josephson's nightclub Café Society, the songs of social significance came with a jazz beat. Featuring left-wing comedians like Jack Gilford and Izzy's friend Zero Mostel, the stride pianist

Meade Lux Lewis, the singers Lena Horne and Hazel Scott, and Teddy Wilson's band, the club's lineup changed nightly. But for nine months in the spring and summer of 1939, every show ended the same way: "lights out, just one small spotlight" on Billie Holiday, singing the ballad of a lynching, "Strange Fruit."[137]

What with rent parties in Harlem and dances to raise money for the Scottsboro Nine and benefits for the Spanish Loyalists, the Popular Front gave a lot of jazz musicians their first steady work. "We used to play for all the communist dances," said Dizzy Gillespie.[138] In Philadelphia, Gillespie recalled, the players often finished with a jam session at Charley Roisman's apartment. Roisman, nicknamed "Professor Bogus," was Gillespie's lawyer and Esther Stone's big brother.[139]

Even the *déshabilleuses tentatrices*, as Izzy liked to call the artistes at Minsky's, were enlisted in the cause. In May 1939, an advertisement in the *Nation* showed a scantily clad Gypsy Rose Lee over the teasing caption: "Clothes? Any Old Clothes?" It seems the celebrated stripper was chair of the Clothing Division of the Spanish Refugee Relief Campaign.[140] But partial as he was to burlesque, Izzy was more of a literary man. Like most of literate America that year, he'd been reading John Steinbeck's *The Grapes of Wrath*. For Stone, the novel was of interest partly as background for his next assignment: an exposé of the Associated Farmers.

Though wreathed in rural pieties, the Associated Farmers, Stone told readers of the IPA bulletin *Propaganda Analysis*, was little more than a "front" for West Coast banks, utility companies, railroads, and big growers to prevent migrant pickers and cannery workers from joining labor unions. Stone traveled to California and Oregon to interview group members and their adversaries. He befriended Carey McWilliams, who had just published his own survey of California agribusiness, *Factories in the Field*. As California's commissioner of immigration and housing, McWilliams was an invaluable source for Izzy, who did his best to return the favor: "Steinbeck's *Grapes of Wrath* here finds its sequel," he wrote in a *Nation* review. "And who would understand and help the Joads must read *Factories in the Field*."[141]

Warning tenderhearted readers that "charges of 'Communism' and 'Communist agitation' are justified," since "the Communists . . . long had the field of migratory farm labor to themselves," Izzy recounted the struggles of the Cannery and Agricultural Workers Industrial Union, whose organizers had been shot, beaten, tarred and feathered, and, convicted under California's Criminal Syndicalism Act, imprisoned in San Quentin. "Whatever the theories of government and society to which these leaders subscribed, the result of their organizational work seems to have been a humble and lawful one. Gregory Silvermaster,* former Director of Research for the state's Emergency Relief Administration, estimated that as a result of the strikes led by this union, the general level of wages for unskilled farm workers was lifted from 15 cents an hour to 25 cents an hour."[142]

I. F. Stone's attack on the false populism of the Associated Farmers, like Isidor Feinstein's exposé of AFL racketeering, was very much in tune with the left wing of the American labor movement. Reporting on what had already been accomplished in Harlan County, which he had called a "Roosevelt Revolution," he allowed himself to hope what others feared, that "the New Deal was a genuine revolution, whose deepest purpose was not simply social reform within existing traditions, but a basic change in the social, and above all, the power relationships within the nation. It was not a revolution by violence. It was a revolution by bookkeeping and lawmaking."[143] Most of the time, though, he despaired of Roosevelt's moderation, of the president's reluctance to confront big business. Declaring himself "dubious of attempts at 'cooperation' among government, industry, labor and consumers," he lamented, "Liberals never learn."[144] The Supreme Court's March 1939 decision to outlaw sit-down strikes only sharpened his radicalism. Even at the *Nation*, his skepticism about Roosevelt's determination on the home front put him to the left of the magazine's editorial board, prompting a warning from Freda Kirchwey to "use due tact and discretion in regard to the subjects you write about in editorial columns."[145]

But for all his impatience with the tempo of the New Deal, opposition to fascism remained the bass line of Stone's politics, and here Roosevelt's caution was in harmony with his own view. "I am not anxious to see this country commit itself too soon or too rigidly so long as pro-Fascist elements are at the controls in England or France," he wrote in June 1939. Still, his faith in the president's step-by-step approach was not limitless. "It

---

*Nathan Gregory Silvermaster was to make headlines in the 1940s as the purported leader of a Soviet spy ring whose members were alleged to include Assistant Treasury Secretary Harry Dexter White and the White House aide Lauchlin Currie.

is possible to wade," he agreed, "but one should be prepared to swim." The danger was clear: "Adolf Hitler is out to dominate the world, and may do so unless we recognize that security is indivisible, and that like the Thirteen Colonies other nations must hang together—or separately . . ." So were the pitfalls of impulsive action: "I would [not] hand a blank check signed 'Uncle Sam' to the umbrella man from Birmingham [Prime Minister Neville Chamberlain] . . . The safest course," argued Stone, "would be to give F.D.R. enough elbow room to steer with skill and safety."[146]

I. F. Stone was a radical, not a liberal, and he understood the difference, as did liberals like Freda Kirchwey, Communists like the literary critic Granville Hicks, and ex-Communists like James Wechsler. But with the Nazi takeover of Czechoslovakia in March 1939 and Franco's announcement the following month that Spain would join Germany, Italy, and Japan in the Anti-Comintern Pact, dwelling on such differences seemed suicidal.

In May, when the Committee for Cultural Freedom, founded by the philosopher Sidney Hook in opposition to the Popular Front, published a "Manifesto" in the *Nation*, it was Freda Kirchwey who questioned the group's purposes. Describing the signers as "honest but not innocent," Kirchwey, noting that "the only important feature of the present manifesto is its emphasis on Russian totalitarianism," had little doubt the group "intended to drop a bomb into the ranks of liberal and left groups in the United States." She recognized that "the Communist Party is a nuisance or a menace to all its opponents. Whatever its line may be, its tactics are invariably provocative and often destructive . . . The result has been to create a fund of bitterness on the left which can be drawn upon whenever a convenient occasion arises." So she understood the impulse "to create a clear division on the left by relegating members of the Communist Party and the vague ranks of its sympathizers to outer totalitarian darkness."[147]

But Kirchwey believed it should be resisted—not just because Communists "have helped to build up and to run a string of organizations which serve the cause not of 'totalitarian doctrine' but of a more workable democracy," not because "in the name of the fight against fascism, they have committed themselves to an almost uncritical acceptance of the status quo," but because "the Communists in their present phase seem to me to share the larger hopes and fears that animate most other people who stand to the left of center . . . Add to this the fact that they oppose with obvious sincerity all forms of racial discrimination, and the total score is one that forces me to question the whole premise" on which the committee was organized. "Instead of signing any such document, I should like to plead for an era of good-will and decency."[148]

Sidney Hook replied with a blaze of dialectics: "If you are opposed to all gangsterism, it is neither principled nor strategic to extenuate the crimes of one gang rather than another." This prodded Kirchwey to the point of asperity—"One cannot but envy the man who is able to dispatch his social problems so easily"—but she reiterated her view that for all its faults, not least its many attacks on the *Nation*, "the Communist Party and its press . . . have also fought for decent conditions for workers and the unemployed, for equality of rights for Negroes, for relief and aid to the victims of the civil war in Spain." Kirchwey admitted the issue was "confused and troubling," but she stood her ground: "It is not necessary for liberal lambs and Communist lions to lie down together. Enough if they will move ahead toward their common objectives without wasting time and strength in an attempt to exterminate each other along the way."[149]

As a statement of Popular Front common sense, a credo for fellow travelers, Kirchwey's plea for "factional disarmament" on the left could hardly be bettered. But by the end of the summer the current of feeling on the left was moving so fast that Kirchwey's reminder that "there is virtue in merely refusing to shoot" was seen in some quarters as insufficiently vigorous. Her argument rested, after all, on an implicit distinction between the Soviet Union and American Communists. The latter she would defend; of Stalin she would say only that his government had "stood consistently for justice and non-aggression in international relations." And her suggestion that "Communists have developed a sort of double mental book-keeping by means of which they are able to account jointly for their love of Stalin and their adherence to the New Deal" was doubtless too acute for comfort.[150]

In August, the Popular Front shot back. A letter that was in effect a countermanifesto, addressed "To All Active Supporters of Democracy and Peace" (the barb was in the third word), warned:

> On the international scene, the fascists and their friends have tried to prevent a united anti-aggression front by sowing suspicion between the Soviet Union and other nations . . . On the domestic

scene the reactionaries are attempting to split the democratic front by [encouraging] the fantastic falsehood that the U.S.S.R and the totalitarian states are basically alike.

Some sincere American liberals have fallen into this trap, [but] to make it clear that Soviet and fascist policies are diametrically opposed . . . we should like to stress ten basic points in which Soviet socialism differs from totalitarian fascism.

The first point was a proud affirmation that "the Soviet Union continues as always to be a bulwark against war and aggression." The nine others were a predictable mix of the plausible ("the Soviet Union considers political dictatorship a transitional form"), the irrelevant ("the Soviet Union has emancipated women and the family, and has developed an advanced system of child care"), and the outrageously false ("it has eliminated racial and national prejudice within its borders").[151]

For most of the 400 signers of this letter, it is probably fair to say that the first basic point was the only one that mattered. The arguments were crude, the signatories were mostly the usual party suspects, just as many of those who endorsed the Committee for Cultural Freedom were Trotskyists.* Indeed, many of the countermanifesto's signers (but not I. F. Stone) had also signed "a statement by American Progressives" defending the Moscow trials a year earlier. (Maxwell Stewart was the only *Nation* editor to do so, but he was in distinguished company, including Nelson Algren, Marc Blitzstein, Malcolm Cowley, Dashiell Hammett, Lillian Hellman, Granville Hicks, Dorothy Parker, Irwin Shaw, and, to his eternal regret, John Garfield.)[152] This new letter defending the Soviet Union, opposed by Freda Kirchwey and the *Nation* editorial board, was also signed by I. F. Stone. "I signed," he told her, "because I wanted to see Russia in alliance with the West against Hitler."[153]

Popular Front optimism or wishful thinking? By the time the letter appeared in print in the August 24 issue of the *Nation*, the question was moot. On August 22, it had been announced that the Nazi foreign minister, Joachim von Ribbentrop, was flying to Moscow the next day to sign a nonaggression pact with the Soviet Union. The Popular Front was dead.

---

*William Carlos Williams, who had helped edit . . . *And Spain Sings*, a collection of ballads published by the League of American Writers, somehow managed to sign both.

Five

WAR YEARS

Stone is a clever little Jew who has to wear an acousticon.
— Harold L. Ickes, *The Secret Diary*

"Where did you hear that I felt a sense of 'personal betrayal'?" Izzy asked Michael Blankfort. "Personal betrayal would be ludicrous, yet while I kick back at the description, maybe it has truth in it. I have recovered—but no more fellow traveling."[1]

Like a shell which, in the moment of detonation, illuminates the battlefield even as it causes immense damage, the Nazi-Soviet pact and its aftermath shed a harsh, unforgiving light on the American Communist Party, whose leaders had spent the previous weeks ridiculing rumors of any rapprochement. Now they were stunned into silence. The *New York Post*, like the *Times*, *Daily News*, and *Herald Tribune*, all put the pact on the front page. But the *Daily Worker* had no story at all; reporters who called at party headquarters were told that Earl Browder and other party officials were "out of town."

Richard Rovere, a *New Masses* editor, left the party; so did Granville Hicks and numerous other intellectuals. Disaffection among the rank and file varied; in New York, many Jewish Communists who had been drawn to the party by its leadership in anti-Fascist campaigns found the pact difficult to stomach. The Scottsboro defense attorney Samuel Leibowitz,*

---

*Leibowitz was never a member of the Communist Party or even a fellow traveler, but his campaign was built—and would break—along Popular Front lines.

whose campaign for Brooklyn district attorney had drawn assistance from both I. F. Stone and his brother Louis, dropped out of the race.[2] But to a veteran CIO organizer in the Midwest or a Communist working with sharecroppers in Alabama or tobacco and textile workers in the Carolinas, the pact was just a piece of paper whose abstract importance mattered far less than the shared risks and shared triumphs of daily political struggle.[3]

Defections of high-profile intellectuals from the party have led some historians to overestimate the pact's effect on American Communists; in fact, most party members weathered the storm.[4] If the pact put an end to the Communist Party's influence in American life, that was due chiefly to the almost physical revulsion to it felt by the party's numerous sympathizers who made up the vast majority of the Popular Front.

There were, to be sure, some efforts at accommodation. When Billie Holiday moved from Café Society to Kelly's Stables in 1940, she added Harold Rome's "The Yanks Aren't Coming" to her set. The Almanac Singers Lee Hays, Pete Seeger, and Woody Guthrie dropped calls to arms like "Viva La Quince Brigada" in favor of pacifist anthems:

Oh, Franklin Roosevelt
told the people how he felt.
We damn near believed what he said.
He said, I hate war
and so does Eleanor,
but we won't be safe till everybody's dead.[5]

I. F. Stone's response was more typical. Like Richard Rovere, who considered the Munich conference as having been "a signal for Hitler to move eastwards," he blamed Prime Minister Neville Chamberlain for Britain's "interminable delay in negotiating" a mutual defense pact with the Soviet Union.[6] But Stone's fury was reserved for Stalin, "the Moscow Machiavelli who suddenly found peace as divisible as the Polish plains and marshes," and for his "apologists-after-the-fact" on Union Square. Scorning the Communist Party's new "imperialist war" line depicting British opposition to Hitler as merely a clash of rival imperialisms, he informed *Nation* readers, "It is still a war against fascism, despite Mr. Chamberlain, and anti-fascists should urge repeal of the embargo" on arms sales that Congress had imposed by the Neutrality Acts of 1936 and 1937.[7]

How much of Stone's anger derived from personal embarrassment is impossible to say. He didn't regret having signed the *Nation* petition, he told Freda Kirchwey, "though I wouldn't sign it now and told Corliss Lamont to take my name off a few days after the pact."[8] The closest he came to a public mea culpa was an admission, in the *Nation*, that "the future of Russo-German relations is a no man's land into which the prophet ventures at his own risk. More than one seer has been blown to bits, and most of us are already shell-shocked." But that was in an unsigned editorial.[9]

"Among fellow travellers," wrote Granville Hicks, "there is almost complete disillusionment, with bitterness varying according to the closeness of the travelling." Hicks described a correspondent, "a man who worked with the party for years and last summer was ready to join." Hicks never named his man—almost certainly I. F. Stone—but quoted him at length:

> My attitude toward the CP is one of distrust. The party bet its pants, shirt and G-string on Russia (and those of everyone who accepted its analysis and followed its line) and lost to the last stitch. It clings more desperately than ever to the Russian connection as the be-all and end-all of its existence, and insists that people continue to trust Russia (i.e. to take on faith what it says about Russia) and accept lines built on what it thinks is Russia's orientation. Those who peddle a gold brick twice over ought not to be surprised if they get the door slammed in their faces. The whole Russian connection has become an absolutely gratuitous nuisance and a stumbling block.[10]

In the *Nation* in October, Izzy called the Nazi-Soviet pact "a blackmailer's peace," adding, "two months ago Hitlerism was a menace to world civilization. Now Izvestia says, 'One may respect or hate Hitlerism, just as any other system of political views. This is a matter of taste.' Thus Marx is wedded to Savarin."[11] Writing to Michael Blankfort the next week, he was equally caustic:

> I'm off the Moscow axis. They aren't playing a bad game for themselves. The Ukraine and White Russia is better off under them. But the Pravda editorial on the Poles causing the war and the Izvestia editorial on liking or disliking Nazism "a matter of

taste" . . . have turned my stomach and the party and its organs
have stunk pretty badly in their efforts at explanation . . .

A new Jesuitry is visible in these interminable and contradictory "explanations." A new Catholicism is growing up in Communism as directed from Moscow, with its own Pope and its own
heretics, bitterly persecuted and pursued. The ease with which
party members flip-flop on instruction and are all against Nazism
one day and British Imperialism the next is indicative of the robot
quality the party creates.[12]

Until August 22, 1939, Stone, Hicks, and their comrades in the Popular Front had been red figures on a red ground. The whole political ter-
rain seemed to be open on the left. Now they were figures in a blasted
landscape visible only in shades of gray. What had once been a movement, a mighty stream, now seemed more like a collection of islands.

After the German invasion of Poland, some writers responded by
withdrawing to the interior.

> *I sit in one of the dives*
> *On Fifty-second Street*
> *Uncertain and afraid*
> *As the clever hopes expire*
> *Of a low dishonest decade*

W. H. Auden disowned not only his own fellow traveling but a whole
decade of political commitment.

Trotskyists, who had never been part of the Popular Front, reacted to
its collapse with predictable schadenfreude. (Trotsky himself, however,
was far less sanguine, seeing in the pact a "capitulation" that strengthened
fascism.) Dwight Macdonald, a recent émigré from *Fortune* magazine
to *Partisan Review*, called for "revolutionary action against the warmakers." Arguing that workers in the West should put insurrection at home
ahead of defeating fascism overseas, Macdonald joined the Socialist
Workers Party. Within a few months he had jumped again, this time to
Max Shachtman's Workers' Party, leaving it after only a few months but re-
taining his belief that American entry into the war would mean fascism at
home. Macdonald's allegiance to what a biographer has called "revolu-

tionary socialism in one editorial office" was shared by the young Irving Howe, who as editor of the Workers' Party weekly *Labor Action* exhorted his readers, "The only way to fight against Hitlerism is for American workers and farmers and unemployed to take over the government." A month after the fall of France in 1940, Howe declared, "No conscripts for Wall Street's War!"[13]

For the Trotskyists (and the right-wing Social Democrats in whose ranks so many Trotskyists ended up), only a public recantation would suffice, and only if the heretic's former views were renounced in full, preferably under the banner of the Committee for Cultural Freedom. In late October 1939, weeks after the Wehrmacht had invaded Poland, James T. Farrell sent a furious letter to Freda Kirchwey accusing her of harboring "two Stalinists on your editorial board." That Stone had, weeks earlier, dismissed any defense of the pact as "wishful thinking" and had, only days before Farrell's denunciation, used another signed *Nation* editorial to declare that "the hammer-and-sickle, as well as the umbrella, is linked with the swastika in responsibility for the attack on Poland," was clearly not good enough for Stone's former friend.[14]

Stone might have been a Stalinist on the *Modern Monthly*—at the very least, a small *c* communist. But in the years since, he'd been no more than an enthusiastic fellow traveler. Yet Farrell's error—his conflation of the Popular Front with the Communist Party, and his assumption of Stone's implied fealty to the Soviet Union—was not confined either to Trotskyists or to the confusing period immediately after the pact. "The literary united front has disappeared," wrote Granville Hicks in July 1940. "Not only many of its new recruits but also some of its veterans have left the Communist Party; there has been a sharp revulsion against the Soviet Union."[15] As a former Stalinist himself, it suited Hicks both to overstate the importance of the party within the Popular Front and to equate cooperation with the party with admiration for the Soviet Union. To gauge the effect of the pact on particular actors, you'd really need to know not just where they ended up but where they started from.

September 1, 1939, found I. F. Stone not in a dive but in a coffee shop, having breakfast with Max Lerner. The news that Hitler had invaded Poland, which they heard on the radio at the *Nation* office, was hardly a surprise.[16] Neither man had ever been a big fan of Joseph Stalin or the Soviet Union, yet for them, the 1930s would never be "a low dishonest decade." Stone had, like every other anti-Fascist (excluding the Trotskyists), been grateful for Russia's apparent willingness, in Spain and afterward, to contribute more than rhetoric to the fight against Hitler, Franco, and Mussolini. He had also, like most fellow travelers, been willing to trade a certain ideological forbearance for the stamina and organizational know-how Communist Party comrades brought to the battles for industrial democracy and racial equality. Years later he regretted having kept silent about Loyalist excesses in Spain.[17] But in the fall of 1939, he saw Hitler on the march in Europe and the New Deal under fire at home. There was no time to cry over spilled borscht.

•

Disillusioned but not despairing, I. F. Stone soon found he was not the only intellectual left homeless by the disintegration of the Popular Front. The group that gathered in Max Lerner's apartment in October 1939 ranged from Hicks and Rovere and Joseph Lash (who'd resigned as executive secretary of the American Student Union over the pact) to Malcolm Cowley and the economist Paul Sweezy—the two members least hostile to the Communist Party and the Soviet Union.

Taking their inspiration from the German New Beginnings group that had sprung up after the Nazis took power, they agreed to call themselves the Independent Left and to meet again in a few weeks. Beyond that they agreed on very little. Rovere wanted "a neo-Marxist movement, one not cursed by the incubus of Stalinist foreign policy."[18] His fellow ex-Communist Hicks also hoped for "something like the Party," as did the teachers' union president Ernest Simmons. Sweezy wanted to issue "an out-and-out Socialist manifesto," while Malcolm Cowley just wanted to "discuss what we ought to believe now that Marxism has collapsed."[19]

Lerner wanted influence "on people in key positions"; Hicks wanted "names with prestige, thus money, thus members."[20] Theirs was an approach which, in an essay written the week of the group's first meeting, Stone derided as trying "to affect events by memorandum rather than by manifesto."[21] Like his *Nation* colleague James Wechsler and the writer Leo Huberman, who were also members of the group, Stone wanted action.

They met at least once more, at the *Nation* offices in November. But the Independent Left were already going their separate ways—some to the surviving shells of the Popular Front; some, like Wechsler and Huberman, toward the CIO; and some, like the writers Kyle Crichton and Matthew Josephson and the critic Newton Arvin, out of political life altogether. Though little more than a footnote in the history of the Popular Front, the episode marked an important conjunction in I. F. Stone's intellectual career.[22] In a period when many on the left seemed to lose their bearings, he'd found colleagues who, whatever their differences, trusted his good sense and good faith. And while the group was soon overtaken by events, several of the dramatis personae would recur in his life repeatedly over the next two decades.

"I've got my debts cleaned up," Izzy wrote to Michael Blankfort, "and more money in the bank than we ever had before . . . enough to keep us going six months in case of need. On that basis I'm going to try and become a writer."[23] That resolve, too, was overtaken by events. On November 30, the Soviet Union, having six weeks earlier invaded Poland and swallowed half its territory, and having forced Latvia, Estonia, and Lithuania to sign "mutual assistance" pacts, invaded Finland. So much for a quiet exit from the train of history.

George Bernard Shaw blamed the invasion on American support for the Finns, telling reporters that of course the Soviets had to defend themselves from "other Great Powers."[24] Lillian Hellman refused to allow a benefit performance of her play *The Little Foxes* for Finnish war relief.[25] But Freda Kirchwey had no doubt who was at fault: "The horrors that fascism wreaked in Spain," she wrote, "are being repeated, in the name of peace and socialism, in Finland." I. F. Stone also invoked what was, for fellow travelers, a devastating comparison. The "attack on the Spanish Republic," he wrote, was "strikingly parallel to the attack on Finland." The Finns, he summed up, "are fighting for their homeland; the Red Army is an aggressor; morale is on the Finnish side."[26]

By January 1940, Izzy's freelance idyll was over. A planned book on the Associated Farmers never materialized. Nor did a project on "man's war-like nature"—though he and his brother Louis did spend some happy hours in research at the New York Public Library. Still, the time wasn't completely wasted. Several of his *Nation* pieces written during this period display a newfound frankness toward the Socialist motherland. He describes Romania's efforts to head off "an expected Soviet offer of 'mutual assistance' in which Bulgaria, Hungary, and Russia will mutually assist each other to slice off those sections of Rumania which were taken from them after the last war."[27] Reviewing a recent biography of the feminist pioneer Fanny Wright, he compares "her starry-eyed" *Views of Society and Manners in America* with Beatrice and Sidney Webb's *Soviet Communism: A New Civilization*—the fellow traveler's Baedecker.

This essay also contains an implicit rebuttal to those who argued that, having been wrong about Stalin's foreign policy, the Popular Front should simply fold its tents in disgrace:

> the handsome, headstrong, and sometimes giddy Fanny . . . played a leading role in the period during which the common man in America won the right to vote and free schooling for his children. She helped organize American labor for the first time for political action. She occupies an honorable place among the pioneers of modern socialism . . . Fanny, like many social pioneers, often slid into the faddist. Sometimes she seemed the social worker. It is not difficult to sneer. But it is not the sober or the prudent who provide the ferment that precedes and accompanies a great period of change."[28]

Stone also grappled, in a tentative way, with two themes that were to preoccupy him for much of the next five years. "Portrait of a Dollar-a-Year Man," an attack on Earle Bailie, a Wall Street fox sent to guard the Treasury chickens, inaugurated a whole rogues' gallery of muckraking profiles exposing the self-dealing reality behind the self-serving rhetoric of the new breed of businessmen-administrators. The rise of the dollar-a-year men, who in many cases replaced New Dealers forced out by the Red Scare that swept Washington after the Nazi-Soviet pact,[29] filled Izzy with dismay. But their business-as-usual mentality made them easy targets, and Bailie's prompt resignation was only the first of many official scalps to Izzy's credit.

Unfortunately, his November 1939 attack on the Évian conference, "Mercy and Statesmanship," was far less effective.[30] (Convened in the summer of 1938 at the behest of Franklin Roosevelt to discuss the situation of Jewish refugees from Nazism, the conference offered neither the hope of refuge nor even a forthright condemnation of German conduct. A bill the following year by Senator Robert F. Wagner of New York and Representative Edith Rogers of Massachusetts that would have waived U.S. immigration quotas for 20,000 German Jewish children under the age of fourteen died for lack of support either in the Senate or from the White House.) Despite heroic efforts by Freda Kirchwey and the *Nation*, it was several years before Washington awoke to the perils facing "non-Aryan" refugees from the Third Reich.[31]

Like many coalitions formed in the confused months after September 1939, the American Investors Union, Izzy's new employer, was soon to fracture along ideological lines. The idea was simple enough: to provide small investors with the same independent, in-depth analysis available to Wall Street insiders. Each month the AIU magazine, *Your Investments*, promised to examine the financial reports of companies held by AIU members. The AIU staff also promised to analyze new issues on the market and to campaign for legislation to protect small investors. But with a staff of two—the editor, I. F. Stone, and a business manager—each issue was an exercise in cutting corners.

The AIU's parent, the Consumers Union, was a classic Popular Front organization, formed in 1936 by employees of Consumer's Research after a strike over union representation ended in a lockout.* The AIU's executive director, Bernard J. Reis, had resigned from the board of Consumer's Research during the strike; he'd also written a book whose call for a union of investors had been endorsed by Isidor Feinstein.[32] Reis was an accountant, and by the time the first issue of *Your Investments* appeared, his own board of directors—an amalgam that included communists, fellow travelers, socialists, the muckraking author George Seldes, and John T. Flynn, an America First supporter (and *New Republic* editor)—was content to leave the details to Reis.

---

*It can be argued that the present-day consumer movement is one of the more durable legacies of the Popular Front. The Consumers Union and the League of Women Shoppers, founded about a year earlier, were "front" groups in exactly the double sense explicated by Michael Denning—though organized by a Communist core, the broader membership, which formed the "front" in the sense of façade, soon found itself part of a battlefront or political alliance. In the groups that survived for any length of time, that "front" often took the members into positions far from party control or even party interest. Though the league, whose founders included the novelist Josephine Herbst, the reporter Leane Zugsmith, and Louise Waterman Wise, was a casualty of the postwar Red Scare, both Consumers Union and Consumer's Research survive, at least in letterhead form—Consumers Union as publishers of the respected and successful journal *Consumer Reports*, and Consumer's Research under the wing of the National Journalism Center, a project of the American Conservative Union.

"When Bernie was interested in a particular company he would gather up all the information he could get, give it to Izzy, who would spend a day or so analyzing it and then (he was already quite deaf at that point) he would dictate to me a first draft that required no editing whatsoever," recalled Shirley Kasdon, the magazine's business manager.[33] The pace left little time for investigative reporting, but according to Kasdon this arrangement was deliberate: "Reis was involved with an attorney who filed a lot of stockholder suits," she said. "When you subscribed you were sent a letter saying that since we were following what was happening in the corporate world, if they would tell us what securities they owned we could advise them if something was happening that was of interest to them. As a result, we had a file of thousands of people and what stocks they owned, and as you know, to bring a stockholder suit you need to be a stockholder."

Kasdon suspected that Izzy suspected Reis's motives, she remembered, "because he was a very shrewd guy."* But if Stone had suspicions, he kept them to himself. What he did reveal to Kasdon was a sense that his relationship with Esther was under some strain. One evening after work, Izzy came to Kasdon's apartment for a few drinks. "He made a pass at my roommate," she recalled.[34]

Stone's unhappiness also showed up in his prose. He wrote the whole of each issue himself, and though he could be lively at times—no mean feat when writing about corporate governance or steel capitalization—his attempts at punchy copy often descended to a kind of (unintentional) parody of *Time*-ese: "Revealing was the address of Dr. Benjamin M. Anderson before the California Bankers Association . . . Pessimistic are the conclusions he advanced . . . Highest are the temperatures."[35]

His immersion in corporate balance sheets was to prove useful, as would his closer acquaintance with "grand larceny as practiced by the better classes."[36] But when the famous tenor Lawrence Tibbett asked Stone to come work as his speechwriter in the summer of 1940 at a salary of $250 a week, he didn't have to think twice.

Tibbett, head of the American Guild of Musical Artists, was in the

---

*Reis later achieved fame—or infamy—as an executor of the estate of the artist Mark Rothko. He and his fellow executors were sued by Rothko's heirs for financial chicanery. After fifteen years of litigation, Reis was found guilty of conflict of interest and negligence, and fined.

midst of a vicious battle with James Petrillo, newly elected president of the American Federation of Musicians. The dispute centered over who had the right to represent instrumental soloists—a group neglected by the AFM, which focused on orchestra and band players. But there were political overtones. The AFM's powerful New York Local 802 had long been a fiefdom of organized crime.[37] Efforts to clean up the local, spearheaded by Communists, had been only partially successful.* And Petrillo's autocratic leadership, though in the classic AFL mold, was a godsend to the opposition. "They stole my people and I'm going to get them," he declared. "They're musicians and they belong to me."[38]

Petrillo issued an ultimatum that summer: If the soloists didn't join the AFM by Labor Day, his musicians would boycott any venue where the soloists appeared. Such tactics, scolded the *Nation* (in an unsigned editorial written by Izzy), "played into the hands of labor's worst enemies."[39] By the time matters came to a head, Tibbett had been elected president of the American Federation of Radio Artists.[40] His speechwriter had moved on as well. Freda Kirchwey, finally making good on her promise of a full-time job, asked Stone to set up a Washington bureau for the *Nation*. At $90 a week plus $15 for expenses, to be reduced to $75 a week once he'd established himself as a freelancer, the salary was less than half his speechwriter's pay.[41] But with Washington in the grip of third-term fever, the offer put him right in the center of the action. On September 9, 1940, his daughter Celia's eighth birthday, the Stone family moved to Washington.

•

"As an appendage and ward of the government," the writers of the 1942 *WPA Guide* proclaimed, "Washington lives and has its being in an atmosphere predominantly political."[42] Though he, too, had taken up residence in an atmosphere predominantly political, I. F. Stone never became either an appendage or a ward of the government. He was, of course, no stranger to the capital. Indeed, one of Stone's qualifications for the job was his extraordinary access to the New Deal. Creekmore Fath, a Texas

---

*Resentment at the party's efforts to influence the union led two brothers, Jack and Harry Thorne, to form the Christian Front, the group whose street-corner provocations were applauded by *Social Justice*.

lawyer who had come to Washington to work for the California Democrat John Tolan's House committee on migratory labor, recalls Izzy and Esther as fixtures of the capital's New Deal dinner circuit. "At any one time you'd see fifteen or twenty of them at Hugo Black's house, or Virginia Durr's house, or the Stones' house."[43]

Politics were to make him a pariah, but in the early 1940s Stone's natural gregariousness and left-wing views made him particularly congenial company for the group of young, mostly Southern liberals whose doyenne was Virginia Durr. Between her husband, Clifford Durr, an Alabama native who had come to Washington in 1933 to work for the Reconstruction Finance Corporation, and her brother-in-law, the senator and later Supreme Court justice Hugo Black, Virginia Durr's connections covered most of New Deal Washington. Over drinks at Seminary Hill, the Durrs' house in Alexandria, Izzy and Esther often encountered Clifford's colleague Abe Fortas; Clark Foreman from the Department of the Interior; the National Youth Administration head, Aubrey Williams; and his assistant, a young Texan the others called "the drugstore cowboy" because of his affectation for boots. His name was Lyndon Baines Johnson.[44]

Though President Roosevelt wouldn't acknowledge it for another three years, by the time the Stones arrived in Washington, Dr. New Deal was already being elbowed aside by Dr. Win-the-War. Tommy Corcoran, whose efforts on behalf of FDR's policies made him a lightning rod for New Deal critics, and who resigned his position at the RFC to concentrate on Roosevelt's 1940 campaign, found himself exiled from the government. Ben Cohen was similarly, though less brutally, marginalized.[45] Izzy's friendship with the Durrs and their circle afforded him continuity of access to an administration very much in transition. It did something else for his career as a reporter: It allowed him to remain an outsider in Washington.

This seems paradoxical, especially in light of the later careers of such consummate capital operators as Abe Fortas and Lyndon Johnson. But in the early 1940s, the group that gathered at Seminary Hill constituted yet another of Washington's interlocking conspiracies. Though culturally Southern—and proud of it—these men and women were mostly liberal on race, sympathetic to the CIO, and unanimously opposed to the poll tax, the very bulwark of Bourbon power in Washington (Virginia Durr was vice chair of the National Committee to Abolish the Poll Tax). In time, some of them succumbed to the blandishments of power. But when Izzy first met them, they were acutely conscious of their heretical status and welcomed kindred spirits with a uniquely Southern mix of personal warmth and evangelical fervor.

Another thing that Stone had in common with his new friends was a disdain for the fresh wave of anticommunism that passed through Washington in the wake of the Nazi-Soviet pact. "My husband thought the Communist Party was ridiculous," Virginia Durr recalled. "It was so badly run."[46] But in the Deep South even a hint of liberalism on race was enough to get you labeled a Communist—a tactic that men like Theodore Bilbo, Martin Dies, and John Rankin had recently imported into the halls of Congress. So when the American Civil Liberties Union decided it could no longer tolerate the presence on its board of Elizabeth Gurley Flynn, a Communist who had been one of the organization's founders, the fact that I. F. Stone leaped to her defense did him no discredit as far as the Durrs were concerned. The coalition that Stone put together to protest the ACLU's action was testimony to the range of Stone's contacts across the whole left of the political spectrum. Issued in the name of Robert Morss Lovett, governor-general of the Virgin Islands, the open letter "to defend civil liberties in the Civil Liberties Union," which Stone had drafted, was signed by Wechsler, Gardner Jackson, Carey McWilliams, Theodore Dreiser, and the Columbia University professors Franz Boas and Robert Lynd.

The same traits that drew the Durrs and their friends to Izzy also marked off the limits of intimacy. "Tex" Goldschmidt and Abe Fortas may have been Jews, but they were Southerners born and raised. To his Washington friends, Izzy was a New Yorker, the actual circumstances of his birth and education overshadowed by his metropolitan aura. Virginia Durr "remembers particularly" a dinner at the home of Michael Straus, aide to Harold Ickes: "Izzy was so brilliant, so funny, so bright."[47]

Operating more like a foreign correspondent than a bureau chief, Stone was able to set his own agenda. Working for a weekly also gave him the luxury of time—to dig up scoops, to develop new contacts, or simply to satisfy his intellectual curiosity. His attempts to pay a courtesy call on the Soviet ambassador in October and November were rebuffed.[48] He had better luck at the Washington Cooperative Bookshop, whose manager, Larry Hill, ran a combination emporium, community center, debating society, and literary salon. A visitor to the bookshop might run into anyone in Washington from the New Deal to points leftward, and Izzy soon became a habitué.[49]

Nothing better illustrates how quickly Izzy found his niche in Washington and how adroitly he leveraged access as a reporter into influence on policy than his role in what became known as the Reuther Plan.

By the end of 1940, everyone in Washington knew that the United States needed to produce more airplanes. President Roosevelt had been saying as much for years: In November 1938, just after Kristallnacht, the president, believing that only airpower would deter Hitler, told his advisers he wanted an air force of 12,000 planes and the capacity to produce a further 24,000 planes a year.[50] In May 1940, Roosevelt asked Congress for 50,000 planes a year. The fall of France the following month, and the Battle of Britain, which was still raging as the Stone family moved to Washington, only made the need for planes more obvious.

But in 1940 the American aviation industry was still in its infancy, and as infants go, aviation was a spoiled brat. Curtiss-Wright, the largest domestic manufacturer, produced well-built, handsome aircraft—at the rate of ten a day! Organized around high-quality boutique production, the aircraft industry, in its entire history from the Wright brothers' flyer to the latest Boeing, still hadn't managed to produce 50,000 planes. After the lean years of the Depression, aircraft manufacturers were now reveling in a five-year backlog of orders and had neither the incentive nor the ability to produce at anything like the rate needed to catch up with the Nazis.[51]

Only the automobile manufacturers had the machinery, and the expertise, to deliver the volume needed. That, presumably, was why the president had appointed William Knudsen, president of General Motors, as head of the Office of Production Management. "The [auto] manufacturers," wrote the New Deal economist turned journalist Eliot Janeway, "were willing to take on any and all jobs thrown at them—but as contractors outside their own plants, not as manufacturers inside them. Inside their plants they proposed to continue making automobiles."[52] The year 1941 was expected to be the most profitable in the history of the automobile industry, and no one was in a hurry to leave the banquet. Nor did anyone in Washington have the political will to force them from the table. In 1940, Roosevelt had an election to win. In 1941, the administration still treated its dollar-a-year men with the same delicacy it displayed toward the French navy, where it was feared that any failure of tact might prompt a shift from hostile neutrality to active sympathy with the enemy.

"To the manufacturers' astonishment and anger," wrote Janeway, "the answer came not from Washington, but from Detroit. It announced the debut of Walter Reuther."[53] With his brothers Victor and Roy, Walter Reuther had been an activist in the Socialist Party and a supporter of Norman Thomas's 1932 presidential campaign. A skilled tool and die maker, he had spent 1933 with Victor working in Gorki in the auto factory that Henry Ford had built for the Soviets. Reuther's suggestion now was as simple as it was bold: allow the automakers to continue building 5 million cars a year, but put the industry's excess capacity to work producing aircraft using assembly-line methods. The scale of Reuther's ambition was evident in his plan's name: 500 Planes a Day.

One strand of Reuther's scheme came from his firm machinist's grasp of Detroit production possibilities; another aspect was rooted in Rome, where in 1931 Pope Pius XI had issued his encyclical *Quadragesimo Anno*. Within the largely Catholic leadership of the CIO, the pope's vision of corporativist collaboration among workers, employers, and the state was hugely influential. The CIO president, Philip Murray, was particularly enthusiastic about what he called "Industrial Councils," which he envisioned as made up of an equal number of representatives from management and labor, chaired by a government representative, and put in charge of each vital industry.[54] But where Murray's proposals were abstract and vague, the Reuther Plan offered a "detailed blueprint" for producing desperately needed fighter planes and for putting defense industries on a firmly social-democratic basis.[55]

Though a Jewish ex–New Yorker might make an unlikely mouthpiece for such a vision, Stone had long been thinking along similar lines. In 1938, when he was still at the *Post*, Izzy argued that any "long view" of air defense must begin from the realization that "the real weapon is the plane factory, not the plane."[56] Just before he moved to Washington, he had written a three-part series in the *Nation* on "Aviation's Sitdown Strike," exposing the aircraft industry's devotion to lengthy backlogs (and windfall profits) rather than increased production. The last installment, "How to Build 50,000 Planes," called for nationalization of the industry.

Edward Levinson, a former *Post* labor editor now working as Reuther's political lieutenant, brought Stone and Reuther together. Part of the interventionist wing of the Socialist Party, Levinson had been sent to Detroit by Sidney Hillman to help Reuther maintain his balance with the CP, which was still a major force in the UAW.[57] Reuther's argument was forthright: Instead of waiting until new, purpose-built aircraft factories like Willow Run could be completed and brought on line, why not use automobile plants, which had already been forced to make drastic cuts in production, to start producing planes right away? Murray had been urging the government to treat each industry as a series of plants rather than separate corporations. Now Reuther was calling for a detailed, plant-by-plant inventory of surplus capacity to be matched with specific plans for retooling idle machinery to make Spitfire parts. Given a six-month delay in retooling for the 1942 model year, Reuther was confident that Detroit could turn out 500 planes a day.

The Reuther Plan, revealed first to *Nation* readers by I. F. Stone in December 1940, also made the front page of the *New York Times*.[58] But Stone's scoop was only half the story; as he admitted four decades later, the plan itself "went through my typewriter."[59] With Stone's authorship a secret, Reuther became the toast of New Deal Washington. Jerome Frank hosted a breakfast at the Cosmos Club so the union leader could drum up support from an audience that included Lauchlin Currie, Tommy Corcoran, and Leon Henderson, an economist who had fought his own battles with the auto industry at the National Defense Advisory Council's price division. Hailed by "all-outers" such as Harry Hopkins, Treasury Secretary Henry Morgenthau, and Sidney Hillman (in his capacity as codirector of the Office of Production Management), the plan was also endorsed by Under Secretary of War Robert Patterson and, more cautiously, by Donald Nelson, the former Sears, Roebuck executive who chaired the Supply Priorities and Allocations Board.[60]

"There is only one problem with the program," Morgenthau told Reuther. "It comes from the 'wrong' source." Most of the opposition to the Reuther Plan was couched in technical grounds: the impracticality of converting civilian plants or the fine tolerances needed for aviation or the impossibility of pooling production facilities.[61] It didn't help that Knudsen, the real power at OPM, had been president of General Motors when Reuther, as head of the UAW's GM department, led several successful strikes against the auto giant. "We had to stall," Knudsen later admitted, "and say it couldn't be handled." Knudsen's successor as GM president,

Charles E. Wilson,* was more frank, complaining that Reuther's proposal to give labor an equal say in production would "destroy the very foundations upon which America's unparalleled record of accomplishment is built."[62]

Reuther and his supporters kept the plan alive for more than a year. According to Bruce Catton, who worked as Nelson's press aide, right up to January 1942 it still "seemed quite possible that the Reuther plan might win by simple default. And if it did . . . This was not labor standing by the edge of the desk, hat in hand, gratefully accepting the opportunity to make a suggestion here and there; this was labor declaring that it had just as much responsibility for winning the war as management had and asserting that, on the whole, it possibly had just about as much to contribute. It was a revolutionary proposal."[63]

Pearl Harbor ended Reuther and Stone's push for "democracy in the economic sphere" even as it vindicated the practicality of their vision. The auto industry was now entirely, not partially, converted to military production, retooling with a speed that not even Reuther would have imagined possible. Within a few months the industry was sharing manpower and even factory space to a degree far greater than anything called for in Reuther's supposedly utopian scheme. True, these plants were mostly turning out tanks and trucks, not planes, but within a year two-thirds of all prewar machine tools had been converted to aircraft engine production. And at least at first, the dollar-a-year men and military procurement officers ran the process without much interference from labor.[64]

But the fight on the home front was far from over. In retrospect it is hard to argue with the conclusion that "instead of an active participant in the councils of industry, the labor movement had become, in effect, a ward of the state."[65] At the time, though, for I. F. Stone and many others, the social and economic transformations imposed by the war seemed to offer a chance to redeem the thwarted promise of the New Deal. If organized labor hadn't yet won a seat at the table, the unions were still very much in the game. As was Izzy.

Stone was also in the front row of the Social Security Building audito-

---

*Known as "Engine Charlie" Wilson to distinguish him from General Electric chairman Charles E. Wilson, who was known as "Electric Charlie" Wilson.

rium on the day in late December 1941 when Leon Henderson finally announced the end of domestic car production. With car sales booming,
carmakers were still reluctant, and so Henderson agreed to allow a few
more weeks of production even after Pearl Harbor. John Kenneth Galbraith, who was on Henderson's staff, recalled that "the excuse was that
this delay would allow the using up of components that would otherwise
be wasted. The decision being indefensible, Henderson went over his defense in detail." At the press conference, "Henderson was detailed, volu-
ble, persuasive. There was silence when he had finished" until Izzy raised
his hand. "Henderson tried not to see him, tried again, and failed. Stone
asked, 'Mr. Henderson, may we assume that this was a deal?'"[66]

How could Stone be so sure? Because a few days earlier there had
been a showdown between Wilson and Knudsen in the same building.
That meeting was closed to the press, "but in the hallway outside was a
small group of reporters, including I. F. Stone, who wore a hearing aid,
then constructed with a separate receiver to be clipped to a coat pocket
and a wire running up to an earpiece. Stone pressed his receiver flat
against the conference room door [and] turned up the volume . . . [Stone]
heard [Wilson] say Detroit had a seventy-five-million-dollar inventory of
engines and bodies and drive shafts and chromium bumpers, and at least
they should be able to assemble these existing parts into new cars."[67]

•

The Reuther Plan might not have had much impact in Detroit, but it did
get I. F. Stone one place he was very eager to be: on the front page of *PM*.

It is not known whether, during the period he contested his dismissal
from the *New York Post*, Stone ever made his way to the Publications Research suite at the Plaza Hotel. Even if he did, it is unlikely that the man
to see, the novelist Dashiell Hammett, would have offered him a job.
Stone was an experienced newspaperman, and experienced newsmen
were exactly what Ralph Ingersoll, the man behind Publications Research, didn't want. At least not at first.

Ingersoll believed that American newsrooms were filled with "young
men and old hacks, worked too hard for them either to become well-
informed or to improve themselves . . . There *are* men of talent writing
news," he recognized, "particularly amongst the younger men," but gener-

ally speaking, they are "not allowed to use their talents."[68] Ingersoll was going to change all that.

A graduate of Hotchkiss and Yale in an era when a few semesters of college marked a reporter as suspiciously intellectual, Ralph McAllister Ingersoll had worked briefly for Hearst's *New York American*, quitting when an editor changed his copy to fit the owner's politics. Hired by Harold Ross during the early years of the *New Yorker* largely on account of his social connections (his great-uncle, Ward McAllister, had coined the term "the 400" to denote the number of people who could fit into Mrs. William Astor's ballroom), Ingersoll made the magazine's "Talk of the Town" section a must-read for café society. Lured by Henry Luce to Time, Inc., in 1930, Ingersoll quickly turned *Fortune* (where he hired James Agee) into a showcase for fine writing and penetrating reportage on American industry. When Luce's first marriage fell apart in 1935, Ingersoll held the reins at *Time*; as a reward, Luce put him in charge of launching *Life* in 1936, where he inaugurated a new era in photojournalism.[69]

Declaring himself the enemy of "the curse of newspaper writing," with its rigid formulas and "tortuous tell-all" lead paragraphs, Ingersoll set out to redeem "the spiritual degradation" of reporters forced to toe an owner or advertiser's line. Instead of semiliterate "legmen" whose chief qualification for the job was a shared social (and sometimes family) background with the policemen and firemen who were their primary sources of information, and who phoned in their reports to office-bound "deskmen," Ingersoll wanted writers who would be able to take advantage of an unprecedented freedom to report what they saw and felt—and thought. Commercial pressures wouldn't be a problem, since Ingersoll's paper would accept no advertising. Instead, the new paper would sell for a nickel—two cents more than the competition—because, pledged Ingersoll, "it will be worth it." When in 1940 he asked Hammett and Lillian Hellman, friends who had been members of Ingersoll's Marxist study group, to help him screen potential staffers, Ingersoll hoped to recruit about 150 people. More than 11,000 applied.

Ingersoll's new hires were expected to write vigorous, colorful, compelling narratives. City room veterans were at a distinct disadvantage. Instead, Ingersoll raided the slick magazines, poaching Louis Kronenberger from *Time* to serve as drama critic, Cecelia Ager from *Variety* to review movies, as well as the *New Yorker* writers Dorothy Parker and James

Thurber (not to mention Lillian Ross, whose career as a *New Yorker* profile writer lay ahead of her). With Hammett sitting in at the copydesk, and Ben Hecht himself writing features, the young, literate, but unformed Ivy Leaguers and cub reporters who made up most of the staff could be forgiven for thinking they'd taken "the fast elevator" to newspaper heaven.[70]

To Penn Kimball, former chairman of the *Princetonian* and a Rhodes Scholar at Oxford, "it sounded like the dream paper."[71] Kimball joined James Wechsler, former editor of the *Columbia Spectator*, who in turn recruited Arnold Beichman, his successor at the *Spectator*. Ken Stewart quit his job at the *New York Times* to work for the new paper, one of many who sacrificed salary and security to join Ingersoll's bold experiment.* Hodding Carter wasn't just the editor of the *Mississippi Delta Democrat Times*—he owned it. But Carter, who'd carried a gun after writing articles critical of Huey Long for his hometown paper in Hammond, Louisiana (and had been fired by the Associated Press for "insubordination"), couldn't resist a good fight, and in the summer of 1940 he, too, found his way to the hot, cramped, dirty offices Ingersoll rented above the Munyer Printing and Engraving Company on the corner of Sixth Avenue and Bergen Street in Brooklyn.

Freedom from editorial straitjackets—and the promise of a good fight—were just part of what made *PM* so exciting. The name itself had a kind of hard-boiled mystique. Even today, nobody really knows whether *PM* was an abbreviation for "Picture Magazine" or "Photographic Material"—or simply referred to the time of day the first edition rolled off the presses Ingersoll shared with the *Brooklyn Eagle*. There was no doubt what *PM* stood for, though: "We are against people who push other people around, just for the fun of pushing, whether they flourish in this country or abroad." Ingersoll had no patience with Gray Lady–like pretensions to objectivity: "We shall hardly be unbiased journalists. We do not, in fact, believe unbiased journalism exists."[72] At a time when even David Stern thought the CIO was a threat to the republic, *PM* was unabashedly prolabor. Also pro-FDR, pro–civil rights for blacks (James Baldwin was a copyboy), proconsumer (one of many types of journalism

---

*Arthur Gelb, who became managing editor of the *Times*, may be the only person who got his job at the *New York Times* through *PM*. A college dropout and graduate of DeWitt Clinton High School in the Bronx, Gelb was a disappointed candidate for *PM* when the kindly woman in charge of personnel offered to recommend him for a night copyboy's job at the *Times*.

pioneered by *PM*), and very vocally prowar. From the first issue in June 1940, when the *Daily Worker* and the Republican right were still harmonizing on "The Yanks Aren't Coming," Ingersoll waged a relentless campaign exposing Nazi aggression with the repeated page-one refrain, "What are we going to do about it?"[73]

One answer, promoted by the paper as "the most important defense-production development of the present emergency, and the most important labor story as well," came on December 22, 1940, under the byline of I. F. Stone. Every day for more than a week Stone kept *PM*'s readers up to date on the Reuther Plan: what was in it, how FDR would respond to it, who opposed it, why the British liked it.[74] Curiously, the only detail omitted from this chronicle was the reporter's own role in formulating the plan. Instead, Stone, with his foot now firmly in the *PM* door, branched out with an exposé of government favoritism toward the Ford Motor Company, particularly in the contract to build the army's new "midget car" (better known to posterity as the Jeep). By January 1941, Stone was billed as a *PM* "special correspondent"; in February, his succession of exclusive stories broadened to editorials as well, including a stinging attack on the House Committee on Un-American Activities and its chairman, the Texas congressman Martin Dies: "In Germany one dare not reflect on Hitler. In Russia one dare not reflect on Stalin. In Italy one dare not reflect on Mussolini. Shall it be said that in America one dare not reflect on Dies?"[75]

By the time Stone came aboard, *PM* had already weathered its first near-death experience. Ingersoll's original intention was to raise $10 million. On advice from his bankers he lowered his sights to half that. But when the first issue went to press on June 18—and then sold out in a matter of hours—he'd managed only $1.5 million. Ingersoll's backers were a mix of the *Social Register* and Dun and Bradstreet: Harry Cushing, John F. Wharton, John Hay Whitney, and the heirs to the A&P supermarket (Huntington Hartford II, who bought himself a cub reporter's job), John Deere tractor, and Wrigley chewing-gum fortunes all took shares. The ad men William Benton and Chester Bowles came aboard, as did the publisher M. Lincoln Schuster, Julius and Lessing Rosenwald (of Sears, Roebuck), and Mrs. Louis Gimbel. "If we are half as good as we think we are," Ingersoll told his investors, *PM* "will make us rich." The former *Fortune* editor cast his crusade as a paying proposition: "We do not believe we can call ourselves a success in this civilization if we cannot persuade [the public] to make us as rich, say, as the men who manufacture . . . Life Savers."[76]

In his own terms, Ingersoll was in trouble almost immediately. Daily sales of *PM* settled in at less than half the 200,000 needed to break even, and though 60,000 New Yorkers had sent in advance subscriptions, the forms were discovered only months later, rotting in a storeroom.[77] Luckily, one of Ingersoll's backers had no need for greater wealth. Marshall Field III owned a town house in Manhattan, an estate on Long Island, racing stables in England and Kentucky, and a 13,000-acre hunting preserve in South Carolina.[78] He also shared Ingersoll's dream of a paper that "would say the things that needed to be said," the kind of paper reporters fantasize about at "bull sessions over glasses of beer." When Field bought out the other shareholders in September 1940—at 20¢ on the dollar—he declared, "I'm not supporting a newspaper, I'm supporting an idea."[79]

As a newspaper, though, *PM* changed forever the way American newspapers looked—and read. Before *PM*, newspapers didn't run complete radio (or television or movie) listings. Nor did they cover the press. Until *PM* asked him to chronicle the life of his patient "Baby Lois," Benjamin Spock was an unknown pediatrician. Jimmy Cannon was a private at Fort Dix when *PM* published his tales of army life.

Printed on coated paper with special quick-drying ink, *PM* could run pictures bigger and more boldly than any other daily. Margaret Bourke-White, another of Ingersoll's hires from *Life*, joined Arthur "Weegee" Fellig to record not just the naked city but the whole spectacle of metropolitan life, from Coney Island to Carnegie Hall. The artist Ad Reinhardt drew for it, as did Saul Steinberg and the cartoonist Crockett Johnson, whose *Barnaby* made the paper a daily necessity even for readers who loathed *PM*'s politics.* On the editorial page, a young illustrator, whose only previous claim to fame was his work for Flit bug spray, lent his pen to Ingersoll's campaign to prod the United States out of its isolationist lethargy: "Said a bird in the midst of a Blitz / 'Up to now they've scored very few hitz, / So I'll sit on my canny / Old Star Spangled Fanny . . .' / And on it he sitz and he sitz." Theodor Seuss Geisel's attacks on Hitler, Tojo,

---

*Tallulah Bankhead called *PM* a "filthy, rotten, Communist" rag but admitted she sent her maid to buy it so she could keep up with *Barnaby*.

and their American apologists weren't subtle. When the North Dakota senator Gerald Nye endorsed the Fascist Gerald L. K. Smith's magazine *The Cross and the Flag*, "Dr. Seuss" drew Nye as a horse's ass. But they were funny—and as memorable in their way as the Cat in the Hat or the Grinch Who Stole Christmas (a character whose look owes a lot to Seuss's Hitler cartoons for *PM*.)[80]

•

In the spring of 1941, *PM* declared war on the Axis powers. Any staff who objected, said Ingersoll, could become "noncombatants" exempt from war-related assignments. What Ingersoll didn't say was that this was actually the paper's second front. *PM*ers had already been at war for months—with each other. Weeks before the first issue appeared, an anonymous "blind" memorandum made the rounds of the city's newsrooms describing Ingersoll as "an adventurer on the make" who, though "not sold on any political ideology . . . appears to have fallen in with CPers, and to have become impressed by their energy and ability . . . to get things done." The memo named names, with staffers described as either party members (coded CP) or sympathizers (coded S). There were some mistakes. Wechsler, who in the months since the Nazi-Soviet pact had become vociferously, even obsessively anti-Communist, was listed as a sympathizer. But his fellow labor reporter Amos Landman, who joined *PM* from the *Daily Mirror*, was indeed a party member, as were the investigative reporter Leane Zugsmith, her husband, the New York Newspaper Guild president Carl Randau, and most of the others listed.

Conceived during the palmiest days of the Popular Front, *PM*'s actual birth coincided with the low ebb of Communist influence. Perhaps for that reason, Ingersoll saw little to fear from the party or its adherents. Besides, some of Ingersoll's best friends were Communists. They never held his membership in the Racquet Club against him. "If what is meant by a Communist sympathizer is a man who sympathizes with *some* part but not all of the Communist Party line," Ingersoll wrote in a memo to his staff, "then I would be willing to state unequivocally that I have not knowingly hired a man who is not a Communist sympathizer. What *PM* is not," he went on, is a party organ; and "if I catch" anyone "doctoring *PM*" to reflect any party line, "I will put him out on his ear as fast as I can throw him."[81] Just to show his red-baiting critics he wasn't spooked, Ingersoll ran a summary of the blind memo in *PM*—with all the names included.[82]

I. F. Stone shared Ingersoll's assessment of the Red menace. Stone had contempt for the CPUSA's attempts to paint Stalin's realpolitik in heroic colors, but what really worried him were far more influential obstacles to his and Ingersoll's main priority, preparing Americans for the fight against Nazism—dollar-a-year men like the shoe manufacturer Francis Murphy, whose favoritism to his own company cost the army millions of dollars and consumers tens of millions, or the Mellon trust, whose determination to preserve Alcoa's monopoly on aluminum, even if it kept the RAF waiting for planes, was the subject of a double-barreled exposé by Stone in *PM* and the *Nation*.[83]

Not everyone at *PM* agreed with Stone's or Ingersoll's priorities. Indeed, the first major battle on the internal front reached its climax when Stone was still just a freelancer. The central figure was Leo Huberman, and the incident reveals both the high stakes and the low cunning that doomed the financially beleaguered *PM* to perpetual sectarian sniping. Four years older than Stone, whom he knew from the New Beginnings group, Huberman was, at least on paper, the ideal man to head *PM*'s pioneering labor desk, with extensive union contacts developed while writing *The Labor Spy Racket* (1938). But his difficulty meeting a daily deadline, exacerbated by his inability to type, made him an obvious target during Ingersoll's first round of layoffs in December 1940. Since everything at *PM* was instantly interpreted in political terms, the dismissal of Huberman, an avowed Marxist (though not a party member), was seen as a victory for the anti-Communist forces, particularly since James Wechsler, leader of the paper's anti-Communist caucus, now became labor editor. "We all thought that young Wechsler ran to Ingersoll, lusting after [Huberman's] job," recalled Penn Kimball, who as chair of the Newspaper Guild grievance committee "became front and center the defender of Leo Huberman."[84] Wechsler himself felt his appointment was "intended . . . to dramatize that anti-communists were at last taking over the paper," and he bolstered his position by bringing his cronies Beichman and Harold Lavine under his wing.

With Stone writing from Washington, and not yet formally on staff, the affair could easily have passed him by but for one further complication: union politics. Ken Crawford, *PM*'s Washington bureau chief, was also president of the American Newspaper Guild and a staunch member of the union's anti-CP wing (as was his successor as president, *PM*'s Washington correspondent Milton Murray). Meanwhile, Tom O'Connor, the paper's national editor and former president of the Los Angeles Guild, and Carl Randau, *PM*'s deputy foreign editor and president of the New York Guild, were equally active on the union's left (as was Randau's New York successor, and *PM*'s radio editor, John T. McManus).[85] With matters so finely balanced, control of both the New York Guild and the national office hinged on the outcome of the battle over the guild unit at *PM*.

The political battle lines were blurry, and the overlay of journalistic and commercial competition makes it even harder to disentangle the strands of hostility aimed at the new daily. The editorially reactionary *Brooklyn Eagle*, for example, had the largest Communist cell in the New York press,* which led anti-Communists to see dire significance in the fact that *PM* used the *Eagle*'s downtime. And though the *New York Post* was the anti-Communist guild faction's main base, *Post* staffers also viewed *PM* as their paper's only rival for liberal readers.

Himself a guild stalwart, I. F. Stone played no part in the Huberman affair (which was resolved in a face-saving deal that gave Huberman back pay from when he was fired, in May, to when he "voluntarily" resigned, in December).[86] Stone had, in any case, no appetite for ideological infighting,† preferring, as he wrote in an October 1941 *PM* eulogy for Justice Louis Brandeis, "the power of a fact." Like many of his obituaries over the years, Stone's description of Brandeis is also an essay in self-portraiture: The "Attorney for the People" derived his strength, Stone wrote, from his "vast appetite for the concrete details of any situation or problem, and his intellectual patience. [Brandeis] believed in the reasonableness of human beings and the possibilities of reaching them by persuasion."[87]

---

*At the time, most of the city's papers had party cells, many large enough to publish their own shop papers combining press criticism, office politics, and gossip. On publication day for *Better Times*, the shop paper at the *New York Times*, "the office loses its Olympian dignity. There are laughter and curses. Everyone marvels at the disclosures," reported George Seldes. However, Amos Landman, who was vice president of the *PM* guild unit and had been recruited into the party when he worked at the *Daily Mirror*, where the party published the *Hearst Worker*, told me that *PM* never had a cell.
†Unlike Richard Rovere, who in his memoir *Final Reports* described Huberman as returning "to the Stalinist fold" but who at the time wrote at least two letters to Ingersoll declaring his "high regard for Huberman's knowledge and integrity."

Izzy's reluctance to be drawn into *PM*'s internal warfare didn't mean he was aloof. Leon Edel, who left the war desk of the Canadian Press Association to become *PM*'s night editor, recalled Stone as "gregarious, and curious, and very popular with the staff . . . His figure gave an effect of roundness; one would have caricatured him by drawing a series of circles." Stone's roundness, Edel added, "wasn't obesity; he had considerable bounce in him." On his visits to the New York office, Stone often joined the future biographer of Henry James for a sandwich. "He knew the neighborhood, and took me to the old equivalent of good fast food places. He gave me the sense then, and always, of a person who took possession of everything that interested him . . . Washington was his kingdom; yet he knew the byways" of New York. In the summer of 1941, Stone invited Edel to join him and Esther and the children at a house he'd rented on Fire Island. "We didn't talk of the current news which absorbed him, but about novelists—Proust, James Joyce . . . Even then Izzy liked to talk about the Greek philosophers," Edel recalled.[88]

Washington on the eve of war was a "30-ring circus," Izzy told Michael Blankfort; he was "busier than all hell . . . but having such fun!"[89] Keeping his distance from his bosses in New York and Brooklyn suited Izzy. But his evident detachment from office politics made him enemies as well. For James Wechsler, Stone's refusal to enlist in the ranks of the guild's anti-Communists was the beginning of a lifelong animus.

The morning of FDR's third inauguration, January 20, 1941, *PM*'s front page showed a line of ragged, jobless men. Eleven years after the Wall Street crash, four years after the Roosevelt recession, and the promise of American prosperity still rang hollow. In the first half of 1941, a fresh wave of strikes hit heavy industry, and on June 5 the entire California CIO came out in sympathy with a Communist-led strike at the North American Aviation plant in Inglewood. On June 9, Roosevelt sent in 2,500 troops with fixed bayonets to seize the factory; Secretary of Defense Henry Stimson ordered California draft boards to cancel the deferment of any striker who refused to return to work.[90] Despite its push for war, *PM* defended labor's right to strike—a position it maintained throughout the war. But the CP's overnight switch on June 22 from industrial militancy to lockstep loyalty certainly made Ingersoll's life easier. "When the Nazis invaded Russia in June, 1941," Wechsler grumbled, "Ingersoll really got the old Popular Front gleam in his eye."[91] And Ingersoll wasn't the only one.

For Wechsler and other ex-Communists, the American party's battle-field conversion was just another grotesque example of its subservience to Moscow. But by the summer of 1941, most Americans had come to accept the inevitability of war. When the Almanac Singers literally changed their tunes, with Woody Guthrie now asking,

Tell me what were their names, tell me what were their names,
Did you have a friend on the good Reuben James?

(in a ballad commemorating an American destroyer torpedoed by the Germans in October 1941), there were plenty of people happy to sing along. "Since the Fall of France," Stone had written to Mike Blankfort back in January, "I have become a warmonger." As far as he was concerned, the Russians had now joined his fight.[92]

"The involvement of Russia," thundered Dwight Macdonald and Clement Greenberg, "does not change the issues."[93] Only the Communist Party claimed it did. What changed was the distribution of forces both at home and abroad. Operation Barbarossa, Germany's invasion of Russia, meant that American opposition to the war was now limited to the Republican right, John L. Lewis, pacifists like Norman Thomas, and the Trotskyist groupuscules that lingered on after Trotsky's assassination the previous August. As for the war in Europe, Stone pointed out that "by his attack on the Soviet Union [Hitler] has 'landed' a huge anti-Nazi army on the Continent . . . Hitler had hoped that dislike for Stalin's ideological table manners*—and, conversely, Soviet dislike for ours—would keep the leadership of the Western free countries from effective united action, and it may."[94]

The view that antifascism once again trumped anticommunism—elementary Popular Front common sense—found adherents far beyond the narrow circle of *Nation* and *PM* readers. *Time* magazine may have been entertained by the prospect of "two vast prehistoric monsters lifting themselves out of the swamp." The *New York Times* might quote Harry Truman: "If we see that Germany is winning, we ought to help Russia, and if Russia is winning, we ought to help Germany, and that way let them kill

---

*As his language here suggests, while Stone considered opposition to fascism a moral imperative, it is probably fair to say that in his view a hatred for Stalin was more "a matter of taste."

as many as possible."[95] Franklin Roosevelt pledged immediate aid to the Soviet Union. And in London, George Orwell changed his tune, too: "The Russians acknowledge seven hundred thousand casualties . . . I never thought I should live to say 'Good luck to Comrade Stalin,' but so I do."[96]

So determined were American Communists to prove their good citizenship that the party's leader, Earl Browder, still serving a prison sentence after being tried and convicted of passport violations in the wake of the Nazi-Soviet pact, issued a no-strike pledge. And in July 1941, when the Justice Department indicted twenty-nine Minneapolis Teamsters on conspiracy charges under the newly passed Smith Alien and Sedition Act, the party uttered not a word in protest. But that may have been because the Dunne brothers, who led Teamster Local 544 and had balked at the union's no-strike pledge, were also mainstays of the Trotskyist Socialist Workers Party. It fell to I. F. Stone to note that on the Justice Department's estimate, "1/260 of 1 percent of the people of this country belong" to the SWP, yet according to the indictment the Trotskyist leaders, "unless placed in jail, may overthrow the government of the United States, a task which would seem to call for more than a handful of men." Stone made two serious points: The arrests were a political favor for Dan Tobin, president of the International Brotherhood of Teamsters and a Roosevelt ally.* They were also a dangerous precedent. He took special delight, though, in reporting what the conspirators actually did when observed at union headquarters. "They went to the Gaiety, a local burlesque house," Stone quoted the prosecutor. "He said each admission cost 75 cents and the government wants to know who paid for the tickets."[97]

On Sunday mornings, Izzy liked to slip out of the house while Esther and the children were still sleeping and read through the Sunday papers in his office at the National Press Building. On December 7, 1941, he "first heard the news from the elevator man . . . The ticker at the Press Club, normally shut off on Sunday, carried the first flash telling of the Japanese attack."

As he shuttled from the War Department to the Navy Department, Stone "encountered a sense of excitement, of adventure, and of relief that a long expected storm had finally broken. No one showed much indigna-

---

*The Dunnes' real crime, said Izzy, "was leaving the A.F. of L. for the C.I.O." In his assault on the refractory local, Tobin made use of a rising young tough named Jimmy Hoffa.

tion. As for the newspapermen, myself included, we all acted a little like firemen at a three-alarmer.

"This is really world war," he told *Nation* readers, "and in my humble opinion it was unavoidable and is better fought now when we still have allies left."[98] The long wait was over.

•

The outbreak of war brought I. F. Stone something that had previously eluded him: respectability. He'd had influence in New York from the day he joined the *Post*; in Washington, New Dealers considered him an important ally. And over the years his contacts had widened considerably. Garry Van Arkel, his oldest friend, was general counsel to the NLRB. Francis Biddle, who'd denied Izzy's bid for severance pay, was now attorney general. Abe Fortas was under secretary of the interior. And through Freda Kirchwey, Stone was soon on familiar terms with Fortas's boss, Harold Ickes, as well. Nor had his old friends forsaken him. He still had lunch with Felix Frankfurter, still saw Tom Corcoran regularly. Out of office, Corcoran was the busiest influence peddler in Washington; his ability to funnel donations to helpful congressmen from the Houston builders George and Herman Brown or Samuel Zemurray, president of the United Fruit Company, ensured his calls were still returned promptly.[99] Shocked by Pearl Harbor, America finally began to mobilize. And as a leading advocate of radical mobilization, I. F. Stone finally found a national audience.

Walter Reuther had kept Stone's name off the Reuther Plan. But when the CIO leadership published the pamphlet *The CIO and National Defense*, they put I. F. Stone on the cover with his coauthors Philip Murray (president of the CIO), James Carey (its secretary), and John Brophy (director of its Industrial Union Councils). The pamphlet's aim, Stone wrote, was "to correct the impression that the labor movement is opposed to national defense," an impression fostered in part, he added, by the actions of unions "reputed to be influenced by Communists during the 18 months when the umbrella flew over the Kremlin." The Russians have now "learned the same bloody lesson in appeasement as the British." In the meantime, Stone argued that thanks to union victories over longtime foes Henry Ford and Tom Girdler of Republic Steel, "the cave-men of industry," American workers "know they have something to fight for; they know democracy is not a myth."[100]

Stone's first book, *The Court Disposes*, had been published too late to influence the court-packing fight. His second book, *Business as Usual*, was, if anything, a bit premature, coming out in the fall of 1941. Yet it was precisely the book's urgency that lent it power and credibility. For *PM* and *Nation* readers, Stone's facts were familiar: the lag in aircraft production, Alcoa's all-out effort to protect its monopoly, the sit-down strike of capital to block an excess-profits tax. "Democracy has lost one battle after another trying to appease its enemies and by antagonizing its friends," warned Stone. What was new, particularly after Pearl Harbor, was the sense of crisis. "Only by building a new America can we save America."[101]

Reading these lines with what the historian E. P. Thompson has called "the enormous condescension of posterity," it is almost impossible to recognize what Stone was doing. By 1941, Izzy was no wide-eyed romantic. He was a hard-bitten newsman who had firsthand knowledge of Franklin Roosevelt's unerring instinct for expedience and temporization. Stone's good friend Clifford Durr, recognizing that private capital wasn't interested in expanding defense capacity, carved out, from his office in the Reconstruction Finance Corporation, a Defense Plants Corporation that would finance, build, and own new manufacturing facilities. Knowing the whole idea would be anathema to his boss, Jesse Jones, a one-man bottleneck when it came to government spending, Durr simply didn't tell him. Eliot Janeway wrote:

> Each morning the War Department would telephone its latest applications to Durr . . . the legal staff would begin reducing the daily batch to contract form before lunch; the papers would be ready for transmission to the War Department by the end of the day; and the company with the contract would have its construction-and-tooling-up money the next day. No team of administrators has achieved as much. This conspiracy of administrative efficiency—it was nothing less than a conspiracy—was three months old before Jones discovered what had been going on.[102]

When he did, Durr had to resign. But the DPC survived to become

> the most important source of capital investment in the nation during the war . . . As early as 1943, the government had invested over $15 billion, nearly two-thirds of it through the DPC, to build some

of the newest and most efficient manufacturing facilities in the United States. DPC plants controlled virtually all the nation's synthetic rubber and magnesium [important in aircraft construction] production, nearly three-quarters of the aircraft production, more than half the aluminum production . . . and important segments of steel, pipelines, barge production and other industries.[103]

Stone's view that winning the war would require a social revolution wasn't wishful thinking. He'd seen it happen. Whether it would continue, whether the inevitable expansion of American wealth and power and productivity could be controlled and channeled in the public interest—that was the home front on which I. F. Stone would fight his war.

Michael Straight, editor of the *New Republic*, saluted Stone's "admirable analysis." Lewis Corey, a cofounder (with Reinhold Niebuhr and A. Philip Randolph) of the interventionist Union for Democratic Action, said *Business as Usual* was "timely" and written "with superb journalistic skill." Even Dwight Macdonald was moved to praise: "Mr. Stone is an excellent reporter; his Washington letters for months have been the only bit of journalistic *terra firma* in that slushy mushy quagmire of liberal yearnings the *Nation* has become. His long account of the Mellons' aluminum monopoly and its extraordinary—even to a hardened Marxist—record in the 'defense' effort is the best thing in the book." What bothered Macdonald was Stone's belief that Dr. Win-the-War could serve progressive ends. "How much longer can you continue to believe that Messrs. Churchill and Roosevelt are on your team?"[104]

If Macdonald only knew. The most significant comment on *Business as Usual* came not in a review but on the back cover: "This is the first book to show the way in which monopoly practices and big business control hamper mobilization . . . This book is absolutely essential in the public interest.—Senator Harry S. Truman, Chairman of the Senate Committee Investigating Defense."

PM, which serialized *Business as Usual*, now offered Stone steady work, and it was just as well. In the weeks after the book came out, the paper had suddenly stopped taking his pieces, citing budget problems. Stone's own finances were dire—he'd gone so far into debt writing the book, he told Freda Kirchwey, that he was trying to sell an article to the *Reader's Digest*. His mother, hospitalized in Philadelphia, had also taken a turn for the worse. Kirchwey was sympathetic: "I respect profoundly your need to make money," she wrote, advising him to "be sure to strain out" of his article "any hint of leftness." But she didn't offer to give back the $15 a week the *Nation* cut from his salary when he'd started freelancing for *PM*. Nor, despite repeatedly badgering Roosevelt's secretary, Stephen Early, was she able to get the *Nation*'s Washington correspondent White House press credentials.[105]

On January 2, 1942, Izzy had lunch with Harold Ickes. Ickes had written to thank him for an inscribed copy of *Business as Usual*, and although he didn't say so in the note, Ickes was pleased with the way Stone handled the aluminum story, for which he'd been the prime source. A deadly bureaucratic infighter (as his long tenure in office attests), Ickes, Freda Kirchwey told Izzy, was "full of dope [and] absolutely unrestrained in his speech—as long as you protect him."[106] Ickes was also an empire builder, and as petroleum administrator helped launch Stone on one of the biggest stories of his career.

"Stone seems to know pretty well what is going on here in Washington and is a fearless writer," Ickes recorded in his *Secret Diary*. "I told him about the rubber set-up."[107] Back in the 1930s, the German cartel I. G. Farben had entered into a series of partnerships with Standard Oil. One arrangement concerned tetraethyl lead, a gasoline additive essential to the production of high-octane aviation fuel. Standard, which owned half of the patents on lead production, agreed to build a plant for its German partners. Before the new plant was ready—at a time when there could be only one customer for large quantities of aviation fuel in the Reich—Standard sold Farben 500 tons of the additive just in time for the Nazis' seizure of Czechoslovakia. And though war was fast approaching, Standard gave its German partners the rights and technical know-how to manufacture synthetic rubber. In principle, the cartel agreement was a two-way street. But when the Americans asked for the rights to Farben's more advanced Buna synthetic rubber process, Hermann Göring's Air Ministry balked. The Nazis also made sure Farben's American partners were never informed of German breakthroughs in producing synthetic oil.[108]

These cartel arrangements first became public when Assistant Attorney General Thurman Arnold, who had just signed a consent decree with Standard on an antitrust action, was summoned to testify before Senator Truman's committee. Primed by Ickes, Stone was ready with a series of exclusives. So incendiary were Stone's reports that his *Nation* editors made cuts "in the interest of protecting us from libel." Freda Kirchwey also warned Izzy against "editorializing."[109]

Ralph Ingersoll felt no such qualms. On April 5, *PM* published an open letter from Izzy to John D. Rockefeller Jr., reminding him that during the Teapot Dome scandal "you stepped in and forced the resignation" of Standard Oil's chairman. "We think it your duty," Stone told Rockefeller, to remove the current chairman, president, and vice president of Standard for "acting as international economic collaborators of the Third Reich." The next day, Stone was back: Had Standard's officers "been acting in Germany for us, rather than here for Germany, they would consider themselves lucky to be interned. The Nazis would have been more likely to inter them." In all, *PM* ran six letters from Stone in a single week. "Mr. Rockefeller, you owe no explanation to an obscure scribbler in the press," Izzy conceded in the final installment. "But . . . there are people who have lost their sons because the Japanese are well supplied with oil. There are people who may lose their sons because we are so inadequately supplied with rubber."[110]

The general manager of Esso marketers told Rockefeller that gasoline sales were down as a result of Standard's poor image. Rockefeller himself was so distressed by the *PM* series that he hired the pollster Elmo Roper to survey public opinion. And in case Standard's major stockholder thought Stone was finished, the Senate Committee on Patents, whose chief investigator was Izzy's friend Creekmore Fath, announced hearings on the synthetic rubber patents. "Izzy was there for every session of the committee," said Fath. By the end of the year, Standard had a new president and a new chairman.[111]

Harold Ickes was delighted with the outcome of Stone's rubber series. But he was less thrilled when, over lunch in June, Izzy told him he was taking three months off to write a book on "big oil." Ickes was no puritan; his extramarital affairs were an open secret in Washington. But he abhorred corruption, and the suggestion that any of "his" men, many of whom still had their salaries paid by the big oil companies, might be anything other than devoted public servants struck Ickes as the height of impertinence. So when Izzy returned from his hiatus in September 1942 and compared Ickes' staff unfavorably to the dollar-a-year men at the War Production Board, Ickes wrote Stone a letter saying, "I resent this delib-

erate slur." Then, at the end of September, when *PM* published a series
of Izzy's articles on "the run-around given our Russian allies on aviation
gas," and took credit for prodding Ickes into action, the petroleum administrator exploded. In a blistering letter to Stone he wrote:

> At last Col. Robert Rutherford McCormick, the tin soldier expert
> of the CHICAGO TRIBUNE, has a rival. McCormick claims he
> "introduced ROTC into the schools"; he "introduced machine
> guns into the Army . . ." But all these modest claims are as noth-
> ing compared with the front page of *PM* for September 29, where,
> in big black print, one may read: "PM Expose Gets Action On
> Aid To Russia in Eighteen Minutes." If you could accomplish
> so mightily within what, in effect, is a split second, you are being
> wasted where you are. I am going to suggest to the President that
> he draft you who knows so well how badly things are being done
> here . . . I hope that the President will not delay in putting this
> incomparable "go-getter" to work before the Russians get him."[112]

In his diary, Ickes admitted later, "I have no doubt we could have ex-
pedited this transaction very much indeed," but when the Washington
congressman John Coffee introduced a bill calling for an investigation of
PM's charges, Ickes "cautioned him not to rely too implicitly upon what
he might get from Stone. I pointed out that Stone was more interested in
tearing down than in building up; that he is not so much a newspaper reporter as a muckraker."[113]

The problem wasn't Izzy's approach to evidence. He didn't always
have all the facts—nobody who writes to a daily deadline can afford to
wait that long—but he was as careful as any reporter and more willing
than most to admit his errors in print.

As for his take-no-prisoners approach, when turned on targets like
Jesse Jones or the reactionary congressman Eugene Cox, "a beneficiary of
Georgia's poll tax," Izzy's ferocity was part of his effectiveness. Cox was a
member of Speaker Sam Rayburn's "Board of Education"—a group of colleagues that met after hours in an unmarked, unnumbered room on the
House side of the Capitol to trade favors and sip the Speaker's whiskey—
and a power in the House of Representatives. To Stone, Cox was "one of
the intellectual hookworms who infest the Southern end of the Demo-

cratic Party," and when Izzy learned that the congressman had taken an illegal $2,500 fee from a Georgia radio station at the same time he'd launched an attack on the Federal Communications Commission, he broke the story in *PM*.[114] Cox retaliated by naming himself chairman of a committee to investigate the FCC; he also proposed an amendment eliminating the commission's funding. But the FCC, one of the New Deal's last redoubts, fought back in a campaign organized by commissioner Clifford Durr, who'd joined the agency after he was forced out of the Defense Plants Corporation. Durr sent the evidence of Cox's illegal fee directly to Rayburn. Izzy's attacks in *PM* were repeated and amplified by the *Washington Post*, whose publisher, Eugene Meyer, was no fan of Cox. When Cox was forced to resign from the investigation in October 1943, Izzy had another scalp on his belt—and the New Deal chalked up another victory.[115]

The problem was that Izzy was just as willing to attack his friends. Despite the inauspicious start to their relationship, he genuinely admired Francis Biddle, who was not only a liberal but, as Freda Kirchwey reminded Stone, an important supporter of the chronically cash-strapped *Nation*. Yet when Biddle approved an order to deport Harry Bridges, the Australian-born leader of the West Coast longshoremen's union, Stone went after him with such fervor that the *Nation* lopped the end off his piece. "I am not trying to protect Biddle," Freda Kirchwey wrote to Izzy. "I do think however that we should give the guy a chance."[116]

Kirchwey also spiked Stone's critique of the War Department's push for antistrike legislation, this time on the advice of her friend Edward Greenbaum, a New York lawyer serving as a brigadier general attached to the department.* And she found his on-and-off feuding with Harold Ickes distinctly unnerving. When Izzy bridled at Ickes' sacred-cow status, Kirchwey warned him not to make Ickes a "sacrificial goat" either: "Don't make him into one of those little images that primitive people stick pins into to express their hatred of somebody. Just because he is a liberal," she added, "you naturally expect more of him than of an ordinary officeholder . . . This is a humanly understandable feeling. But it is politically foolish."[117]

Stone simply refused to be governed by prudence or silenced by consid-

---

*What Kirchwey didn't know was that Greenbaum's partner, Morris Ernst, who had led the fight to expel Elizabeth Gurley Flynn from the ACLU, was not only an enemy of Stone but also a friend of J. Edgar Hoover and a longtime confidential source for the FBI.

erations of loyalty. And with editors he didn't particularly respect, he could be extremely touchy about his copy. He clashed continually with Robert Bendiner, managing editor of the *Nation*. Bendiner, who quit the magazine in 1943, was moving out of the left, but their constant bickering was usually personal rather than political, and on Bendiner's side aggravated by the knowledge that Izzy had gone after his job.[118] With Kenneth Crawford, *PM*'s Washington editor, he took a different tack and simply ignored him, filing his stories directly to the paper's national desk in New York. Crawford didn't like it, but since Izzy wasn't on staff there wasn't much he could do about it. The managing editor, John Lewis, who took over running the paper after Ralph Ingersoll joined the army in late 1942, did finally put Stone on a regular salary, but he still filed directly to New York.

Ingersoll had written most of *PM*'s editorials. Lewis hired Max Lerner to replace him in New York, with Izzy, who had done guest editorials in the past, now writing regularly from Washington. Perhaps surprisingly for two such famously abrasive personalities, this irregular arrangement never broke down. Izzy was delighted to have his old friend on board, and though their political paths would diverge, he was also genuinely respectful of Lerner's ability. "I know I will enjoy working with you," he wrote Lerner. "I want you to enjoy working with me . . . But I am sometimes gauche, tactless, overeager . . . I'm not a sensitive plant. You are a good teacher. You're a better writer than I am . . . I can take criticism and I like it. I know you could teach me a lot, and you'll find me very willing to be taught."[119]

•

Izzy was now working the equivalent of two full-time jobs. He wrote a Washington letter for the *Nation*, plus one signed and at least one unsigned editorial in the magazine most weeks—on top of three columns a week for *PM*. At home, Izzy "was *le roi soleil*," recalled his daughter, Celia. Her father was happy to share his passions. "When I was ten," she said, he gave "me some Robinson Jeffers to read, saying 'To be a great poet is the greatest thing in the world.'" Most of the time, though, his family had to accept that Izzy's work took priority. "We were all of secondary importance. When father napped, we tiptoed; when he was hungry, we ate; when he needed an outing we were packed into the car (we children, carsick; mother, exhausted from the preparations) and driven off for long hot rides to the beach accompanied by his cheery calls to the back seat, 'Isn't this fun, kids?' If the teacup wasn't filled to the brim he raged as though he had uncovered a plot to destroy him."[120]

Sometimes he spread himself too thin. Bendiner complained bitterly that he was "duplicating coverage . . . This trailing after *PM* is getting serious."[121] At the same time, Izzy was simply becoming too big for the *Nation*. His journalism led to more and more frequent speaking engagements. In October 1942, he spoke at Carnegie Hall for the Artists' Front to Win the War. Orson Welles was the master of ceremonies. The keynote speaker was Charles Chaplin. That December Izzy chaired a Union for Democratic Action forum on the first year of the war. And he regularly gave talks at the Washington Cooperative Bookshop.[122]

He was also willing to stand up for unpopular causes. In the spring of 1942, the *New Masses* announced that Izzy would chair the Washington rally of the Citizens Committee to Free Earl Browder. Stone's seventeen-year-old sister, Judy, an activist in her high school chapter of the American Student Union, came down from Philadelphia to hear her brother speak. Her high school friends were even more impressed when he turned up at a meeting of the American Youth Congress that same night.[123] After Roosevelt commuted Browder's sentence at the end of May, Stone wrote, "There remains only the prosecution of the Trotskyites in Minneapolis to haunt our speeches about free government."[124]

What about Executive Order 9066? Signed by the president in February 1942, the order led to the internment of more than 110,000 first- and second-generation Japanese Americans. I. F. Stone wrote not a single word in protest—indeed, his remark about Browder suggests that at the time he didn't even notice the most massive violation of civil liberties by the federal government in American history. Or was it that the internment was partly organized by his friend Abe Fortas and rationalized by their mutual friend Hugo Black? Black's December 1944 opinion upholding the constitutionality of the order (to which Felix Frankfurter concurred) on the grounds that "time was short" and "military authorities feared an invasion of the West Coast" drew only a mild demurral from Stone.[125]

Far from being a First Amendment fundamentalist, Izzy repeatedly chided the Justice Department for its failure to prosecute such "pro-Axis termites" as Gerald L. K. Smith and Elizabeth Dilling, author of *The Red Network*, who had been indicted on sedition charges. Nor, in his many quarrels with Freda Kirchwey, did he ever object to her campaign to curb the Fascist press in the United States; he was equally untroubled by Ralph Ingersoll's *PM* crusade to ban Father Coughlin's *Social Justice* from the mails. Even his defense of Harry Bridges rested "on the fact that he and the Communist Party, whatever their motives, are now doing their best to support the government in its war effort . . . If its position changes, its legal position will also change."[126] Stone believed that Francis Biddle was willing to deport Harry Bridges out of "weakness"—a reluctance to confront conservatives. So it is worth recording that it was Biddle, not Stone, who spoke up against interning the Japanese.[127]

Fascism at home and abroad still scared Stone in a way that communism never would. To Izzy, Martin Dies and John Rankin and J. Edgar Hoover were all clear and present dangers. He happily defended the Socialist Workers Party not out of political sympathy but because these "Ishmaelites of the left" could "hardly have mustered sufficient force to seize the dog pound in Minneapolis."[128] He had more affection for the American Communist Party—after all, not just some of his best friends but also some of his relatives were party members—but the party, too, had very little power. (And seemingly it used what influence it did have to enforce national unity. In April 1942, the *Daily Worker* attacked Izzy's cartel and patent revelations for sapping corporate morale![129]) The Soviet Union was a different story. Unlike the *Collier's* writer who in December 1943 pronounced it a "modified capitalist set-up . . . evolving . . . toward something resembling our own democracy," Stone never pretended that the Soviet ally was a democracy. He would probably have agreed with Douglas MacArthur's view in February 1942 that "the hopes of civilization rest on the worthy banners of the courageous Red Army."[130] He certainly believed that if the Soviet Union were defeated, as many in Washington expected—or hoped—Britain would be unable to hold out until the United States could mount an effective European campaign. And he turned his pen against anyone who would deny the Russians adequate supplies. But when Harold Ickes, Helen (Mrs. Ogden) Reid, and Thomas and Florence Lamont joined Paul Robeson, Charles Chaplin, and Edward G. Robinson (and one hundred other notables from Louis Adamic to the inventor Dr. Vladimir Zworykin) at the Congress of American-Soviet Friendship in November 1943 to celebrate "American-Soviet Cooperation," they had to do without the presence of I. F. Stone.[131]

So did the National Press Club. One day in April 1943, Izzy sat down in the club dining room with a guest. Elmer Davis, director of the Office of War Information, was giving a speech in the auditorium and the club was crowded. A page came up and told Izzy he was wanted on the phone. This turned out to be a ruse. William H. Hastie, Izzy's luncheon guest, was a former federal judge. He was also black, a former dean of Howard University Law School, and he had recently—and noisily—left a job as aide to Secretary of War Stimson. "Reactionary policies and discriminatory practices," Hastie told the *Chicago Defender*, "were the immediate cause of my resignation."[132] The club manager informed Izzy "that we would not be served. I said that as a member of the club I insisted on service for my guest and went back to the table. There we sat unserved until two o'clock, when we left for a Chinese restaurant.

"It takes a little while," Stone wrote, "to catch on to the extent that Washington is a Jim Crow town. Although the Negro press reaches 4,000,000 readers every week, its correspondents are barred from the House and Senate press galleries and from White House press conferences." I. F. Stone may have overlooked the injustice done to Japanese Americans. He sent his children to the district's segregated public schools, and when he and Esther bought a house in Washington, their deed contained a restrictive covenant preventing the property from "being sold to, or occupied by or used for residence or any other purposes by negroes, or persons of negro blood, commonly called colored persons." He had no close black friends. But the mistreatment of fellow journalists galled him, and that a man like Hastie should be snubbed by "the third-rate advertising men and fourth-rate politicians who belong to the [press] club" filled him with rage.

"Under the constitution of the club special meetings must be called on petition of twenty-five members." When Izzy managed to obtain only "nine signatures, and a diverse collection of arguments from well-meaning people who agreed with me but . . . ," he resigned his membership.[133]

•

His sense of solidarity with the oppressed may well have been awakened by an incident a few months earlier. I. F. Stone never found press conferences very rewarding. The general clamor often rendered his hearing aid useless, and at the State Department, the words themselves were liable to be opaque at the best of times, frequently designed to convey a false impression. But at Freda Kirchwey's behest he had put a lot of time into understanding the department's various factions, though he never produced the survey she'd hoped for.* Since the earliest days of the war he had closely followed events in France, and was a warm admirer of the Free French government in exile that General Charles de Gaulle had set up in London after the French capitulation to the Germans in June 1940. So when Secretary of State Cordell Hull used language that seemed calculated to offend de Gaulle, demanding that the "so-called Free French navy" hand back French territory it had seized from the Germans to the collaborationist government of Marshal Philippe Pétain, Stone's own language was far from diplomatic: "Cordell Hull, [with] a stupidity that calls for his removal from office . . . could not have chosen a better way to undermine the confidence of oppressed peoples everywhere . . . Some way should be found to let the world know in decisive fashion that the undemocratic little clique of decayed pseudo-aristocrats and backsliding liberals who dominate the State Department do not speak for the American people."[134]

Criticizing the State Department was bad enough. Praising the upstart Office of Strategic Services, which at least seemed willing to work with the French resistance, was worse.[135] But what was finally unforgivable was Izzy's uncanny ability to report what was really happening inside the department. In February 1942, his exposé of secret deals to ship oil and mining equipment to Franco's Spain sent the diplomats scurrying to plug the leak—until Joseph Rauh, a young lawyer in the Bureau of Economic Warfare, confessed that he had been Stone's source.[136] When Izzy reported the U.S. ambassador to Bolivia's efforts to scupper a new code guaranteeing workers' rights, the secretary of state denied the story; when Izzy then published a summary of Hull's own cabled instructions to the ambassador, investigators were again called in—this time without success.[137]

Izzy was also (as was Churchill) a merciless critic of the "Darlan deal"—the military agreement in November 1942 to recognize Admiral Jean-François Darlan, Vichy's military commander in French North Africa, as high commissioner there in return for French cooperation with the Allied invasion, which had begun days before. Darlan's assassination in

---

*Stone eventually fobbed off this chore on a resentful Robert Bendiner.

December and his replacement by General Henri Giraud, a sworn foe of de Gaulle, did not change things. *PM* was especially outraged at the State Department's delay in renouncing the Nazi imposition of the Nuremberg Laws on French and North African Jews in the area that had now fallen under Allied control. In January 1943, Izzy also faulted Hull for permitting the appointment of Marcel Peyrouton, who as Pétain's interior minister had introduced the Nuremberg Laws in France, to be governor-general of Algeria.[138] So when Izzy turned up at a State Department press conference to ask Hull whether President Roosevelt had personally approved the Peyrouton appointment, he was hardly an unknown quantity.

Yet when Izzy rose to speak, the secretary of state interrupted him. "What is your name?" asked Hull. "Stone," Izzy replied. Hull: "I thought it was. You have some other name, too, have you not?" Izzy answered again: "That is my name, Mr. Secretary." Unabashed, Hull said simply, "I thought so. Go ahead."

Shaken, Izzy asked his question, which Hull refused to answer. Then, recovering, Izzy asked, "Would you care for a statement on my name?" To Hull's response that he was not interested in his name, Stone replied, "I think you stepped out of bounds." Nor did he accept Hull's claim that he was "trying to find out to whom I am talking." Instead he continued, "I said my name is Stone. You made a further remark that I think was uncalled for and untrue."[139]

On the floor of the House, the Mississippi demagogue John Rankin denounced Stone twice on successive days, first for inciting "crackpots" critical of Hull and then as "Bernstein or Feinstein . . . one of the pen pushers on this communistic publication known as *PM*."[140] Michael Straus, press aide to Harold Ickes, saw a chance to initiate a thaw in his boss's relations with Izzy. Though wary at first, Straus had come to consider Stone "one of the most useful, courageous, and hard-socking correspondents in this town." Back in October, Izzy had run into Straus and complained that his life was "miserable" because Ickes "disdain[ed] his respects." Straus urged his boss not to let Izzy "suffer any delusions of persecution." But at that very moment Ickes was writing yet another long letter of complaint to Freda Kirchwey. After Izzy's run-in with Hull (whom Ickes detested), Straus sent his boss another memo. Ickes wrote the very next day, never mentioning the incident but simply expressing wry gratitude for a recent *Nation* piece Izzy had written praising his department "without a single 'but,' 'however,' or intimation . . . 'I could do it even better if.'" Stone was pleased: "You know I think you are a wonderful guy. But you insist on that 'love me love my dog' attitude . . . So, like Ivory Soap, my affection and admiration remain only ninety-nine and forty-four one hundredths per cent pure."[141]

Izzy's penchant for embarrassing the State Department also brought him renewed attention from the FBI. He initially had come to the bureau's attention in the traditional fashion for a journalist—by writing something critical of J. Edgar Hoover. As early as 1936, an eagle-eyed agent had flagged Stone as the author of a *New York Post* editorial intimating "that the FBI is carrying on OGPU* tactics [and] that the Director is anti-labor and anti-union." His efforts in support of the Spanish Republic were duly noted, as was an informant's description: "The Director will recall that Stone is not his correct name. He is of Jewish descent and [redacted] advises that he is very arrogant, very loud spoken, wears thick, heavy glasses and is most obnoxious personally."[142]

In July 1943, the *Nation* published two articles that ensured Stone's place on J. Edgar Hoover's private enemies list. The series was titled "Washington Gestapo," and the author was identified as XXX, a "minor government executive helping to run one branch of a war agency." XXX argued that "the Civil Service Commission and the F.B.I. . . . are undermining Washington's strength and will to fight" through ham-handed character investigations. By taking affirmative answers to questions such as "Does he think the colored races are as good as the white?" or "Does he seem to have too many Jewish friends?" as evidence of subversion, these investigators were "being used as a club . . . to beat liberals out of town."[143]

In an editorial note, the *Nation* said that XXX's "identity has been revealed only to our Washington editor, I. F. Stone, who as a friend of long standing is able to vouch for his absolute reliability."† That was enough for

---

*Ob'edinennoe Gosudarstvennoe Politicheskoe Upravlenie (Joint State Political Directorate), a Soviet forerunner of the KGB.

†Robert Bendiner and Freda Kirchwey had both repeatedly asked Stone to trust them with XXX's identity. Stone sent Bendiner a telegram saying that if his own guarantee was "unsatisfactory, please mail them [the articles] back." A handwritten note on the bottom of Izzy's reply to Freda Kirchwey suggests XXX was Edward F. Prichard, an official in the Office of Economic Stabilization who had been Felix Frankfurter's first clerk on the Supreme Court. The FBI never did discover who XXX was, but Hoover may have had his suspicions. In 1945, he put a wiretap on Prichard, persuading President Truman that he was both a New Dealer and an inveterate leaker. When Truman fired him, Prichard returned to his native Kentucky, where after he admitted stuffing ballots in the 1948 election Hoover took personal

J. Edgar Hoover to send handwritten "action" memos asking, "Who is this guy? H" and "What is his name? H," prompting a full-scale biographical summary whose mix of fact, gossip, and misinformation (Stone, "whose true name is Isadore Finklestein") would be reiterated dozens of times in the coming years.* Hoover also got his friend Morris Ernst to write a letter to the *Nation* "to let you know that I have yet to hear of a single violation of the [*sic*] basic civil liberties. This is close to a miracle . . . The position of J. Edgar Hoover with respect to wiretapping sets a new high standard for the constabulary of the United States."[144] Izzy was not convinced. "Like most miracles," he said, replying on behalf of XXX, "this does not stand up too well under examination."[145]

•

Izzy's rapprochement with Harold Ickes produced another string of scoops. One, published in late March 1943, an exposé of how Jesse Jones had negotiated a deal between the RFC and Alcoa to build a hydroelectric dam in Canada using U.S. government funds, allowed him to smite two favorite targets at once. Ickes, who leaked the material to both Izzy and Drew Pearson, author of the syndicated "Washington Merry-Go-Round" column, was especially pleased when Jones blamed Milo Perkins, a bureaucratic rival, for the leak.[146] But the interior secretary's evident delight in his own deviousness led to a final breach with Stone.

In May, Ickes told Stone he had another scoop for him. "He knew I hated the oil trust," Izzy recalled, and "I hated the State Department. He slipped me a document, a very good story about an aviation gas plant in Mexico, but I just was leery of it, so I went down to the State Department, as much as I hated them, to check it out, and discovered that . . . [Ickes] was really grinding the axe of Ed Pauley, a California oil promoter. So I printed the fact that he tried to plant the story on me. He was sore as a bull."[147] Ickes was indeed so angry that he summoned Stone to his of-

---

charge of the investigation. Prichard, his marriage and career destroyed, was sentenced to two years at the federal penitentiary in Ashland. See Tracy Campbell, *Short of the Glory: The Fall and Redemption of Edward F. Prichard, Jr.* (Lexington: University of Kentucky Press, 1998).

*One error that was eventually corrected was the remark, noted in Stone's file at the time of the "Washington Gestapo" controversy, that "Isidor Feinstein had applied for a Special Agent's position in October 1935."

fice, then threw him out. He wrote later to apologize, and Izzy took back "the charge of 'planting' . . . I must have sounded like an insufferable Pharisee and prig." But the damage was done. Stone never really trusted Ickes again, and the next time Ickes had a complaint about one of Stone's stories he took it to John Lewis, *PM*'s managing editor.[148]

Izzy's attitude toward Franklin Roosevelt was much more forgiving. He forgave the president his dilatory approach to race relations, his endless compromises and concessions to the right, even his apparent contempt for his allies on the left. But Roosevelt's refusal to back Vice President Henry Wallace in his long-running feud with Jesse Jones brought Stone's language to a white heat:

> Franklin D. Roosevelt has again run out on his friends . . . In 1937 this craven tactic drove from progressive ranks one who might have been America's ablest labor leader instead of the dark menace that he is today. In 1944 it will probably cost Henry Wallace the Vice-Presidency, the New Deal its most promising leader. When the firing grew hot in the Little Steel strike, Roosevelt turned impartially on the workers who believed in him and those who shot them down . . . The man who created the New Deal seems intent on destroying it before he leaves office."[149]

But when it became apparent that Roosevelt had no intention of leaving the White House, Stone's anger cooled. "In the field of social and economic reform," he conceded, Roosevelt barely "enabled us to catch up with the England of Lloyd George and the Germany of Bismarck's Monarchial [sic] Socialism . . . It was only war that saved the second Roosevelt Administration and world capitalism from a new depression." Even so, he counseled, "it is our job to push the President, but not to push him over a political precipice . . . Maybe I'm wrong, but I think the place for us to push between now and election is the common man's doorbell."[150]

Izzy knew very well the president's power to cloud men's minds, and he struggled hard to resist. What he couldn't resist, and didn't want to, was the belief that as long as Franklin Roosevelt was in the White House, the causes he held most dear were far from lost. Roosevelt was infuriatingly unreliable, but that very inconstancy enabled his supporters on the left to hold on to the hope that if the political wind shifted, and if they were able to rally their forces sufficiently to appeal to the president's sense of expediency, if not idealism, he might abandon his tack to starboard. "It is easy," Stone reminded *Nation* readers, "to identify ourselves emotionally with 'the people.' At the moment the people are not identifying themselves with us."[151]

"Is the outlook for liberals hopeless?" Izzy wondered. "Not at all." For keeping his hopes alive Stone was prepared to forgive the president almost anything. He forgave him his Machiavellian maneuvering in North Africa. (Izzy was exceptionally well informed about this thanks to Garry Van Arkel, now working for the OSS as Arthur Goldberg's deputy in North Africa. When Van Arkel, who thought America's policy in French North Africa was "disastrous," found his complaints about Giraud's regime falling on deaf ears at Allied HQ, he simply passed the details on to his old classmate.)[152] He forgave him his perverse (and uncharacteristic) loyalty to Cordell Hull, and when in the fall of 1944 Hull emerged as a strong backer of the Dumbarton Oaks treaty setting up a postwar United Nations organization, Izzy was even inclined to forgive Hull. "At this moment in our national history," Izzy wrote in *PM*, "Hull is in many ways an indispensable man . . . *PM*, as its readers know, does not like Hull." But, Izzy argued, precisely because the secretary was "the idol of the right-wing Southern Democrats" and because "by now, the Republican Party is so committed to Hull," these traditional isolationist blocs "could hardly refuse [to] support . . . any treaty of international co-operation he advocated."*[153]

Though it stuck in his throat, Izzy even forgave Roosevelt his failure to aid the Jews of Europe. For most of the American press, the fate of the Jews under Nazism was "beyond belief," and when details did emerge they were often dismissed as Zionist propaganda or recycled atrocity sto-

---

*However temporary, Stone's grant of absolution to Hull was too much for James Wechsler, *PM*'s new Washington bureau chief. Wechsler called John Lewis in a fury, shouting that the editorial "contradicted everything *PM* had said and stood for . . . He said that it was more of Izzy Stone operating behind his back and getting things into the paper on his own." Wechsler was mortified, saying the editorial "raised the question in Washington: Which page of *PM* do you read? Do you read Wechsler or do you read Stone?" Sadly for Wechsler, his editors believed more people read Stone. Wechsler's demand that Izzy be fired was ignored. Instead, Lewis nominated Stone's work for a Pulitzer Prize. See Kenneth Stewart, "The People Who Made *PM* and the *Star*" (manuscript), Kenneth Stewart Collection, American Heritage Center, University of Wyoming, pp. 88–91.

ries from World War I.[154] To this chronicle of willed indifference, the *Nation* and *PM* are among the most distinguished exceptions. In December 1942, *PM* published a lengthy summary of Rabbi Stephen S. Wise's account of the Nazi program of extermination. Wise's dossier, which *PM* reported had been presented to Roosevelt at a White House meeting with American Jewish leaders, included detailed information on the liquidation of the Jews of Warsaw, the murder of 24,000 Latvian Jews, and the establishment of "extermination centers" at Mauthausen and "at Ozwiecim [Auschwitz] near Cracow," where eyewitnesses reported the building of "giant crematoriums."[155] A month later, the *Nation* began a series on "The Jews of Europe," intended to "impress on the conscience of free men the vastness and the ghastliness of the Jewish tragedy in Europe."[156]

A few weeks later, Izzy weighed in:

> The Jews of occupied Europe could do with a little less pity and a little more help. We are tired of statements from Washington and London deploring the mass murder of the Jews by Hitler and declaring the moral conscience of the world is shocked. The truth is that the moral conscience of the American and British governments, always flexible, is not so much shocked as blunted. For when definite measures are proposed to help the victims of these horrors, the State Department and the British Foreign Office, though ever so politely, turn away.[157]

In March 1943, Freda Kirchwey was at her most eloquent:

> Seven or eight thousand Jews a week are being massacred. The ghetto of Warsaw, two years ago the dumping ground for Jews from all over occupied Europe, is now depopulated. Every Jew is dead. In Cracow, where 60,000 Jews lived, 56,000 have been killed . . . In this country you and I and the President and the Congress and the State Department are accessories to the crime and share Hitler's guilt. If we had behaved like humane and generous people instead of complacent, cowardly ones, the two million Jews lying today in the earth of Poland and Hitler's other crowded graveyards would be alive and safe.[158]

When Stone went to the State Department or to the British embassy, he saw men with blood on their hands. Not only Jewish blood. He hammered away at Britain's refusal to release Gandhi and Nehru from prison, and at the American failure to send food aid to India's millions, starved by their imperial masters.[159] But the world's indifference to the murder of European Jewry was something he took personally. In case there was any doubt of what was at stake, in August 1943 *PM* published a chart, "What Has Happened to the Jews of Europe," showing an estimated 1.7 million murdered Jews. The paper also published a detailed report on the crushing of the Warsaw Ghetto revolt and an account of the gas chamber at Treblinka.[160] So in June 1944, when the opportunity presented itself to save the remaining Jews of Hungary, Stone put whatever influence he had on the line:

> This letter, addressed specifically to fellow-newspapermen and to editors the country over, is an appeal for help . . . I have been over a mass of material, some of it confidential, dealing with the plight of the fast-disappearing Jews of Europe and with the fate of suggestions for aiding them, and it is a dreadful story.
>
> Anything newspapermen can write about this in their own papers will help. It will help to save lives, the lives of people like ourselves . . .
>
> The essence of tragedy is not the doing of evil by evil men but the doing of evil by good men . . . It is a question of Mr. Roosevelt's courage and good faith. All he is called upon to do, after all, is what Franco did months ago, yes, *Franco*. Franco established "free ports," internment camps, months ago for refugees who fled across his border."[161]

For all its passion, Stone's plea went largely unheard amid the news of the Allied landings on the beaches of Normandy. "D-Day served to remind us," Izzy wrote, "that we are heavily in debt to the man in the White House as well as to the boys on the beaches."[162] Once again, Roosevelt was forgiven, though in August, when the president expressed his "abhorrence" at the plight of Hungary's Jews, Izzy remarked tartly, "There is something more abhorrent than evil . . . It is an unwillingness to do more than indulge in a sentimental gesture when confronted by human suffering."[163]

Roosevelt's inability to see the Jews' suffering outside the political cal-culus he used for everything else drove Izzy to the brink of despair. But only to the brink. If Dr. Win-the-War had forced Dr. New Deal into hid-ing, at least Izzy was perfectly at home among the conspirators. "In some ways a liberal newspaperman in Washington today is a kind of guerrilla warrior," he wrote in April 1945, "watching for a chance to get at the truth." He described "a kind of underground . . . made up of left-of-center newspapermen and officials. The underground carries on in ways well known to sophisticated Washington newspapermen. It operates on well-placed leaks to trusted correspondents, to progressive members of Congress, to New Dealers employed by Congressional investigating com-mittees. Victories that could not be achieved by normal administrative processes . . . are often achieved by leaks."[164] So long as Roosevelt re-mained in the White House, Izzy and his band of shadow warriors felt they had a fighting chance.

Exactly a week later, on April 12, Stone was in *PM*'s new office, a con-verted shoe factory at the corner of Hudson and Duane streets in Man-hattan, when the bells signaling a "flash" rang on the United Press machine. "There was a commotion in the newsroom. A copy-boy ran out of the wire room . . . That first flash, 'The President died this afternoon,' seemed incredible; like something in a nightmare, far down under the horror was the comfortable feeling that you would awake to find it was all a dream. The Romans must have felt this way when word came that Caesar Augustus was dead." *PM* put out an Extra and ran Izzy's editorial on the front page. "It is hard to believe that fighting heart is stilled, that buoyant spirit quenched . . . Not a few of us cried yesterday when the first flash came over the wire."[165]

Six

UNDERGROUND TO PALESTINE

———◆•◆•◆———

I learned in Israel what men here once learned at Lexington—not to
scare easily.   —I. F. Stone

For a man whose world was about to collapse around him, I. F. Stone entered the Truman era in remarkably high spirits. "Those newspapermen
who have had personal contact with Truman (this writer among them)
have confidence in him," he assured *PM* readers. "I talked with Mr. Truman several years ago and liked him immediately and instinctively . . . He
is a good man, an honest man, a devoted man."[1] In part, Stone's affectionate tone reflected the national outpouring of goodwill toward the former
haberdasher from Missouri who suddenly found greatness thrust upon
him. During his first three months in office, Truman's approval rating
reached 87 percent—higher than his predecessor's had ever been. And
though Izzy was far from a confidant, he actually did know Truman, who
as both senator and vice president had been one of the most accessible
politicians in Washington.

President Truman was much harder to see, and Stone may in part
have been making a bid to stay in a former source's good graces. But his
faith in Truman's intentions, his assurance that Truman "will surprise the
skeptical," was sincere. The world in the spring of 1945 offered ample
grounds for optimism of the will. Fascism was in retreat: "The Red Army,
like an avenging juggernaut in a cloud of clamorous smoke and flame,
is advancing toward the final destruction of Nazism, the overthrow of

Hitler, the end of the Third Reich," Izzy had exulted (this was in February 1945).[2] However faltering at first, four years of war production under the aegis of the Wagner Act and the War Labor Board had seen union membership double in the United States. An August 1945 Gallup poll found that 79 percent of Americans thought the "law guaranteeing collective bargaining" was a good thing.[3]

Though still a faithful member of the Newspaper Guild, Stone had long passed the point of needing anyone else's help in salary negotiations. His *Nation* pay remained $75 a week; he also earned $150 a week from *PM*—more than any other writer on the paper except its theater critic, Louis Kronenberger.[4] John Lewis, who found Izzy "a *prima donna* and a difficult man to get along with," nonetheless valued him as "a money player," and for Ralph Ingersoll he was simply indispensable—a steady pro amid the paper's sectarian snipers and a "journalist whose reputation is respected in Washington."[5] Increasingly in demand as a speaker on topics ranging from Indian independence to Nazi war criminals, he'd become a figure of influence among his fellow journalists as well. In his long fight against Martin Dies, chair of the House Committee on Un-American Activities, Izzy found an ally in the gossip columnist and broadcaster Walter Winchell. When Dies subpoenaed Winchell's radio scripts in April 1944, Izzy rushed to defend him, and when the *Daily Mirror*, Winchell's regular employer, refused to print a column Winchell wrote in April 1945 attacking British interference in Greece—a cause that would soon be Stone's as well—it ran instead in *PM*, where Winchell, under the thinly disguised byline "Paul Revere II," soon became a regular contributor.[6] Financially, politically, and in terms of his access to and influence on more mainstream journalists, the dawn of the Truman era saw Izzy at the height of his powers. But as Winchell observed, "Nothing recedes like success."

Still, when I. F. Stone pushed through the crowds straining against the plush ropes outside the San Francisco Opera House on April 25, 1945, and made his way to the press gallery for the opening of the United Nations Conference for International Organization, he had reasons to be cheerful. The setting itself, with its Maxfield Parrish decor and lofty interiors, was meant to be awe-inspiring—a fitting backdrop for statesmen from forty-six nations who were meeting to decide the fate of the world. Hollywood glamour was also present. "Your correspondent, as goggle-eyed as any movie fan," he admitted to *Nation* readers, "was introduced to Charles

Boyer by a member of the French delegation and later that night . . . to Edward G. Robinson. 'Well,' Robinson asked, with that overtone of quiet menace for which he is famous, 'is our side going to win?' It was definitely an 'or else' question, and I hastened to assure him all would be well."[7]

But who exactly was "our side"? Izzy wasn't really afraid of Robinson, to whom he'd been introduced by Mike Blankfort, recently demobbed from the army and now a successful Hollywood screenwriter. (Mike's cousin Henry Blankfort had written the screenplay for *Tales of Manhattan*, a 1942 film that starred both Robinson and Boyer.) Blankfort flew up from Beverly Hills to share his friend's room at the Palace Hotel, press headquarters for the UN conference.[8] But Izzy was increasingly troubled by the sense that this conference, held while the world was still at war in order to build the framework for a durable peace, was in terrible danger. Looking around at the delegates, Stone saw "those same old codgers to whose fumbling we owe World War II . . . These men lost the last peace, and unless they are replaced they will some day lose the next one."

Not even the jubilation over Germany's surrender, announced on May 8, 1945, could allay Stone's worry that certain members of the American delegation regarded the conference less as an occasion to safeguard the peace than an opportunity to prepare for the next war—this time against the Soviet Union. With the Yalta Conference only two months past, and the Potsdam Conference two months in the future, the San Francisco meeting took place at a time of disillusionment on both sides. Isaac Deutscher was probably right to describe the wartime alliance between the Western powers and the USSR as a "marriage of convenience" in which "the thought that divorce was inevitable had been in the mind of each partner from the beginning." But for those, like I. F. Stone, who had danced at the wedding and hoped the partnership could endure, the idea of a breakup was almost unbearably painful. In March, on Stalin's orders, sixteen leaders of the London-based Polish government in exile had been lured back to Poland for "talks" with the Soviets and then seized and taken to Moscow; their fate was unknown in the West for two months until *PM* broke the story in the middle of the San Francisco conference; Stone thought "American progressives" upset about this news should "keep their shirts on."[9] He prescribed similar patience regarding the Yugoslav partisan leader Josip Tito's claims on Trieste; Tito's Partisans had liberated the city from Germany's control on May 1, but their powers there were challenged by the Allies, who arrived two days later.

Izzy was less detached, however, when it came to "my own people, the Jews, millions of whom still want and need a national home in Palestine." Whether out of distilled resentment over Britain's obstructive behavior toward Jewish refugees—a government white paper in 1939 had cut off their access to Palestine, limiting immigration to 15,000 a year—or political hostility to Churchill's efforts to maintain Britain's imperial grip in Greece, India, and the Middle East, Izzy had little sympathy with British claims. Instead, he warned that unless Truman was "prepared to take up Mr. Roosevelt's role and mediate between the Russians and the British," the president was in danger of becoming "the tail to Mr. Churchill's giddy new kite."[10]

Stone's concerns about Churchill's eagerness to force a showdown with Stalin were shared not just by numerous other journalists and activists on the left, but by a significant number of American diplomats as well. They may not have amounted to more than a small minority in the State Department, but the early spring of 1945 marked a high point of internal conflict within the American political establishment. On one side were those who urged forbearance toward the Soviet Union and toward Stalin's determination to ensure a buffer of "friendly," if not outright puppet, governments in the nations on Russia's western and southern flanks that the Red Army had liberated from German occupation. This same group also tended to favor a "hard peace" for Germany and Japan, and were skeptical if not hostile toward Chiang Kai-shek and the Chinese Nationalists. Their opponents were dubious about Stalin's actual wish to have peaceful coexistence with his erstwhile Western allies, and they advocated a "soft peace" for Germany and Japan, tending to oppose the idea of prosecuting German industrialists for war crimes or plans to break up the zaibatsu, the giant cartels that controlled the Japanese economy.

This internal struggle, and how it was played out at San Francisco, preoccupied Stone and his companions at dinner one evening. Sidney Roger, a Voice of America commentator for Asia, recalled, "I first met Izzy at Julian Friedman's house during the San Francisco conference. Julian worked at the State Department with another man in setting up the conference. The other man was Alger Hiss. Julian invited a bunch of us to come meet I. F. Stone."[11] Friedman's boss in the China affairs division of the VOA was John Carter Vincent, a career diplomat who had vociferously criticized Joseph Grew, ambassador to Tokyo at the time of Pearl Harbor and a leading advocate of a "soft peace" for Japan. Vincent, like

Owen Lattimore, Sidney Roger's boss at the Office of War Information, was one of the several diplomats and scholars with extensive experience in the Far East who before the war had called for a U.S. policy favorable to China, then under the rule of the Nationalists but torn by civil war; many of them now argued that the United States needed to recognize the importance of the Chinese Communists in China's resistance to the Japanese occupation.[12] In February 1945, the *Nation* had published an attack on Grew and his former assistant, Eugene Dooman, now head of the State Department's Bureau of Far Eastern Affairs, claiming that they had been guilty of an "execrable mistake in judgment" in minimizing the threat posed by Japan in 1941 and were just as off base now when they urged the United States to rely on the same Japanese business leaders and bureaucrats to make peace. Titled "Dangerous Experts," the *Nation* screed ran under the byline "Pacificus," a pseudonymous government official who, like XXX, made contact with the magazine via I. F. Stone.[13]

Besides the China hands, Izzy found another circle at the conference who were to become increasingly important to him in the months and years to come. These were the Zionists. Though Stone was acutely sympathetic to the plight of Europe's Jews, in 1945 he was, he acknowledged, "like most American Jews, neither a Zionist nor an anti-Zionist."[14] His old boss David Stern had become an important backer of the Committee for a Jewish Army, a Philadelphia-based group devoted to the establishment of a Jewish militia to help defend Palestine, then still under British mandate, from Germany. The CFJA's founder, Peter Bergson,* was a member of the Irgun, an underground Zionist group that advocated using armed force to push the British out of Palestine. In 1943, when Bergson founded the Emergency Committee to Save the Jews of Europe, Stern was again an enthusiastic supporter.[15]

Until this point Stone had been an observer, not a participant, in the debates over Zionism that had riven American Jewry, splitting the American Jewish Committee (in 1945, still anti-Zionist) from the (pro-Zionist) American Jewish Congress. Both these groups sent several representatives to San Francisco, some of whom were accredited as advisers to the American delegation; this was as close as the Jews came to having an of-

---

*Bergson, whose real name was Hillel Kook, was a nephew of Avraham Kook, who became the first chief rabbi of Israel.

ficial status at the conference. But there were twenty groups claiming to speak for the Jews, from Irgunists to the staunchly anti-Zionist American Council for Judaism, and their kaleidoscope of conspiracy and conflict constantly shifted as they shuttled from hotel to conference hall, button-holing delegates and trading information.

Even for Izzy, a veteran traveler through the sectarian minefield of the American left, navigating among the World Jewish Congress, the Jewish Labor Committee, the American Jewish Trade Union Committee for Palestine, the Hebrew Committee of National Liberation, the New Zion-ist Organization, the World Zionist Organization, and both AJCs required considerable tact. Jesse Zel Lurie, executive director of Americans for Haganah (a support group for the mainstream but still underground Jew-ish militia in Palestine), introduced Izzy to Teddy Kollek, Haganah's man in New York (and later, 1965–93, mayor of Jerusalem).[16] Izzy also met frequently with Eliahu Elath, a representative of the Jewish Agency for Palestine. Russian-born and educated at both the Hebrew University in Jerusalem and the American University of Beirut, Elath explained the behind-the-scenes politicking around the issue of United Nations trustee-ships. Elath's mission was to try to head off changes to the Palestine mandate that had been proposed by the Arab League, a campaign in which *PM* was happy to assist.[17] As Izzy talked late into the night with Elath, who had himself worked as a journalist in Beirut, or his colleague Gershon Agronsky, editor of the *Palestine Post*, or Si Kenen, who handled public relations for the American Jewish Conference, the American newsman began to be drawn to these men and their cause.

Returning to Washington at the end of May, Izzy was buoyant. I've "fallen in love with the U.S.A. all over again," he told *PM* readers. The fledgling United Nations organization itself was "not much to write home about, but . . . it is a beginning." There was, he thought, "a fighting chance to maintain peace," especially since so many of his own reserva-tions about events in San Francisco were shared by commentators whose views presumably reflected the foreign-policy establishment.[18]

"We cannot police the Soviet Union and we must not flirt with the idea," warned Walter Lippmann, the influential *Herald Tribune* columnist, whose denunciation of America's "steamroller tactics" in support of admit-ting the dictator Juan Perón's Argentina was as strong as anything in the pages of *PM* or the *Nation*. Like Izzy, Lippmann thought the United States should "mediate" between Britain and the Soviet Union, and urged Truman to resist Churchill's attempts to get America to "underwrite" the British empire, particularly in Greece, where he was a persistent critic of British efforts to restore the monarchy. And it was *Time* magazine, not I. F. Stone, that condemned the United States for playing "a straight power game" over Latin America "as amoral as Russia's game in eastern Europe."[19]

Izzy's sense of benevolence, of being profoundly in tune with his country and his times, extended all the way up to the White House. "Reading over the papers, talking with old friends, catching up on the press releases, give one the impression—which is also in part a hope—that the new President has begun to get his bearings and to chart his course," he wrote in late May. Reviewing Truman's proposals to lower tariffs and to provide unemployment insurance for workers displaced by the end of hostilities in Europe, Izzy saw "an emerging pattern of policy that promises well for the future. If Truman can begin to chart as skillful a course in foreign as in domestic policy, he will serve our country well."[20]

•

I. F. Stone's first warning that the political ground rules were about to change came on the afternoon of June 6, 1945. Six people connected with *Amerasia*, a fortnightly foreign-policy journal published in New York City, were arrested under the Espionage Act. The arrests, which made front-page news across the country, were the culmination of an investigation that had begun in February after an OSS officer noticed one of his own classified reports, on British policy in Thailand, reproduced almost verbatim in the pages of the magazine. OSS agents broke into the *Amerasia* offices in March and discovered a large cache of government documents, many stamped "Top Secret." The State Department asked the FBI to investigate further, and Hoover's men soon bugged the home of *Amerasia*'s editor and publisher, Philip Jaffe, a self-made businessman who used the fortune produced by his greeting-card company to fund his interest in left-wing causes. Jaffe, who'd traveled to Yenan with the China scholar Owen Lattimore in 1937 to meet Mao Tse-tung and Chou En-lai, had long nurtured intellectual as well as political ambitions; besides Lattimore, *Amerasia*'s editorial board included such prominent Far Eastern experts as Edwin Reischauer and Kenneth Colegrove.[21]

Initially targeting Jaffe and his assistant editor, Kate Mitchell, the FBI surveillance operation soon grew to employ seventy-five agents in round-the-clock shifts. The sheer size of the operation made it difficult to conceal. Federal agents broke into the *Amerasia* office on six occasions; the FBI tapped the phones of Emmanuel Larsen, a State Department employee, the navy lieutenant Andrew Roth, and Mark Gayn, a journalist who wrote under contract to *Collier's Magazine* and the *Chicago Sun*. On May 28, Jaffe took a room at the Statler Hotel in Washington, which the FBI bugged. The next day Jaffe was visited there by Lieutenant Roth and his wife, Renée. Jaffe and Roth were in the middle of an argument when Renée interrupted to say that she'd discovered something that looked like a hidden microphone. Both men ignored her, but the FBI agents listening decided it was time to move in. Eight days later, on June 6, Roth, Gayn, Larsen, Jaffe, Mitchell, and John Stewart Service, a young State Department China expert whom Jaffe had been wooing for his magazine (and whose earlier meeting with Jaffe had also been picked up by the bug at the Statler), were all arrested and charged with espionage. Bail was set at $10,000 apiece, and though Jaffe put up the money for himself, Mitchell, and Gayn (all arrested in New York), the other three (in Washington) were on their own.

As it happened, the argument picked up by the FBI's hidden microphone was over I. F. Stone. Jaffe had been tipped off that the United States was about to lend $186 million in gold to Chiang Kai-shek's Nationalist Chinese government. Hoping to "squash" the deal, Jaffe wanted to leak the story to Drew Pearson but was having trouble reaching him. Roth suggested he give the story to his friend Izzy Stone. Jaffe, whose self-importance was inextricably linked with his enthusiasm for the Soviet Union, objected: "Stone doesn't get that sense of defending the Soviet Union all the time. How can a real radical, or liberal even, not have that . . . ? It's the workers' government, the one shining star in the whole damned world, and you got to defend that with your last drop of blood and Izzy Stone hasn't done it all the time and there is no excuse for it!"[22]

Roth, who spent four days in a D.C. cell waiting for his mother to raise his bail money, may still have had Jaffe's harsh words in his mind when his jailers announced he had a visitor. "It was Izzy. His was the first friendly face I'd seen in days," Roth recalled. A graduate of CCNY, Roth had arrived in Washington in December 1942 shortly after the navy sent him to Harvard for an intensive Japanese course. Outspoken, energetic, and extremely gregarious, he soon numbered Drew Pearson, Izzy, and the *PM* reporter Frederick Kuh among his friends. "The first thing Izzy said was, 'When you get out of here we'll get together and talk about how to fight this.' Izzy got me my lawyer, Bill Rogers, who'd lost a son in the war and practically adopted me."[23]

Stone had gone on the offensive even before he'd visited Roth. "The first point to be kept in mind," he wrote in an editorial published on June 8 and signed by "I. F. Stone for the Editors of *PM*," is that, "although these six are charged under . . . the Espionage Act, they are not accused of acting as spies." They had been charged under a section of the act that made it a crime to conspire "to defraud the US in any manner or for any purpose." Stone also pointed out that Roth had been charged as a civilian, rather than by a court-martial. The defendants might well have been in possession of classified documents, but "the State Dept.," Izzy argued, "is constantly leaking material to favored reporters . . . Progressives in that Department (a very tiny handful) leak to . . . people like yours truly. Naturally the Department regards leaks in the former class as legitimate discussions of facts and policy. But so does the other side. Is the leak to be a right-wing monopoly?"[24] In the *Nation* the following week, Izzy argued that the *Amerasia* defendants were merely "engaged in . . . the favorite Washington pastime of letting 'confidential' information leak out. If this is a crime, all but a hopelessly inefficient minority of Washington's officials and newspapermen ought to be put in jail."[25]

Thanks to the Freedom of Information Act, we now know that while most of "the Six" were playing inside baseball according to well-established rules, scoring points by assisting their allies in government and leaking information designed to discredit others, Jaffe apparently did have Walter Mitty–esque fantasies of becoming a Soviet agent. (That he was deficient in tradecraft can be deduced from the fact that once, after being approached in May 1945 by a man claiming to be working with the Soviets, Jaffe's next move was to drive to the Yonkers home of the CPUSA chairman, Earl Browder—shadowed every step of the way by the FBI!) At the time, though, even the rock-ribbed Republican *Herald Tribune* followed Izzy's lead, dismissing the arrests in an editorial titled "Red Baiting."

Press sympathy for the *Amerasia* defendants grew by an order of magnitude after Joseph Grew, now acting secretary of state, told the *New York*

Times that the arrests were just the first fruit "of a comprehensive security program which is to be continued unrelentingly in order to stop completely the illegal and disloyal conveyance of confidential information to
unauthorized persons."[26] Though it had no factual basis—the arrests had
occurred only after the FBI had committed several illicit burglaries and
conducted wiretaps of equally dubious legality—Grew's statement certainly represented his fondest wish. His protégé, Eugene Dooman, told
John Carter Vincent that he hoped Julian Friedman, Service's friend and
Vincent's subordinate, would soon be under arrest as well.[27] Major General Patrick Hurley,* American ambassador to China and a vehement
supporter of Chiang Kai-shek and the Nationalists, had been saying for
months that a cabal of "un-American elements" in the State Department
was plotting against him; now he announced a "clean out" of the U.S. embassy in Chungking.[28]

In August, a grand jury in New York voted to indict Jaffe, Larsen, and
Roth not for espionage but on the lesser charge of illegal possession of government documents; the other three defendants were never charged at all.
Jaffe, who agreed to pay a fine, argued that at most he had been guilty of
"an excess of journalistic zeal"—a claim accepted by the Justice Department.[29] Larsen, whose name and notes were on many of the documents,
pleaded no contest (and Jaffe paid Larsen's $500 fine as well). When Am-
bassador Hurley surprised Truman by resigning in December 1945, charging that "a considerable section of our State Department is endeavoring to
support Communism generally as well as specifically in China," Truman
was furious, denouncing the "son-of-a-bitch" at a cabinet meeting. By February 1946, when the government quietly dropped all charges against
Roth, "America's Dreyfus Case," as Drew Pearson called it, appeared to
have fizzled. Izzy commended Roth's "excellent new book, *Dilemma in
Japan*," to *PM* readers. And with Dean Acheson replacing Grew as under
secretary of state, John Carter Vincent heading the Bureau of Far Eastern
Affairs at State, and John Stewart Service cleared for reassignment and
back in Japan, the tide of fear seemed to have turned.[30]

As long as Americans still faced combat in the Pacific, the claims of
common sense, even Popular Front common sense, were hard to refute.

---

*As Hoover's secretary of war, Hurley had given Army Chief of Staff General Douglas MacArthur the
order to evict the Bonus Marchers in the summer of 1932.

"It is true" admitted I. F. Stone, "that the Chinese Reds are—Reds. But this is a war," he continued, neatly turning the "effete" charge against the right, "not a weekend house party. It cannot be fought in priggish accord with the *Social Register* of politics. There is no more reason for shying away from the help of the Chinese Reds in the war against Japan than there was shying away from the help of the Russian Reds in the war against Germany."[31]

The Stone family was spending a long weekend on Fire Island in August when the news came from Hiroshima. Like most Americans, Izzy's first response was relief that the use of an atomic weapon would bring the war in Japan to a quick end. Even *PM*'s editorial cartoonist allowed himself a mocking one-panel drawing of a completely blank landscape with a speech bubble saying, "So Sorry." The theme of giving the Japanese their just deserts was repeated on the editorial page, where John Lewis suggested that "while we are dropping atomic bombs, why not drop a few on Tokyo, where there's a chance to run up our batting average on the royal family." Within less than a week, though, Izzy was voicing misgivings: "The atomic bomb was the logic of war carried to an extreme which many people (the writer included) felt abhorrent."[32] He hoped that Russia's imminent entry into the war against Japan meant not just a swift end to the fighting but "closer . . . unity among the Big Three." But the timing led him to suspect that the bomb had taken Stalin by surprise. Was Truman's decision to use it intended to send a message to the Soviet Union as well as Japan? One thing was certain: If the United States no longer needed Russian—or Chinese—assistance to win the war in the East, a key brake on the juggernaut toward a new world war had just been removed.[33]

•

"To judge from the cables I read before I came here . . . [the] Negev shouldn't have been a healthy area for a wandering American correspondent of obvious Jewish lineage to have met an Arab chieftain," I. F. Stone told the readers of *PM* in November 1945. "The Jews are in a sense invading [the] Negev and by all accounts there should have been tension, especially since I encountered the Sheikh—and mounted his camel— outside the most westerly of the new Jewish colonies, Gevulot."[34] The Zionist contacts that Stone had made at the UN conference had pressed him to come to Palestine and see for himself. But so long as hostilities continued, travel was difficult, and Izzy's post was on the home front. By the end of October, though, with the fighting over and Washington returning to peacetime politics as usual, he was on board the *Queen Elizabeth* bound for London, Cairo, and Palestine.

Stone's departure was prompted by Earl Harrison, an acquaintance from his Philadelphia days and dean of the University of Pennsylvania Law School. A former U.S. immigration commissioner, Harrison had been sent by President Truman in the summer of 1945 to investigate the condition of displaced people in Europe, "particularly the Jews." He'd found 100,000 Jews living in German and Austrian camps—in many cases their former concentration camps—subsisting on a diet "composed principally of bread and coffee." He also reported that most of these survivors wanted to go to Palestine. Harrison's report, delivered to Truman in late September, concluded, "As matters now stand, we appear to be treating the Jews as the Nazis treated them, except that we do not exterminate them."[35]

Stone spent five days in London, staying in a Bayswater flat and talking with everyone he met, from cabbies to cabinet ministers. In December, he wrote that he heard "an undercurrent of feeling about America. Perhaps resentment is too strong for it. But world power has passed from London to Washington . . . The role of a dependent and suppliant is never a pleasant one." He liked Britain, "both the land and the people . . . a fair-minded, courteous, humane and patient folk . . . I have some harsh things to say of British official policy and some British officials, but that and they are not the same as the British people."[36]

The sheer pleasure of foreign reporting seemed to invigorate him. Nearly everyone he met—"a very fine young Palestinian Arab" barrister in London, an Egyptian publisher in Cairo, a Sephardic Jew in Greece, a Maronite politician in Beirut, a British engineer in Haifa, Mohamed el Organi (the Negev sheikh), and "above all the young men and women of the Jewish colonies I visited, the grandest young folk I have ever met"—called forth a sympathetic response.[37]

When he reached Palestine, his reporting was precise, vivid, and responsive to the country's immense variety: "My first impressions of Jerusalem were the whiteness of the buildings, the stone and stucco cleanliness, the streets crowded with folk of every kind—Chassidic Jews with ear locks and fur hats; European Jews, some obviously German, with horn-rimmed specs; dignified town Arabs with red tarbooshes; country Arabs with flowing kaffiyeh head dress and desert robes; monks in cowls and Ethiopian Christian prelates in tall, black hats, like magi. And everywhere peace."[38]

Stone knew he was walking into an intense propaganda battle, and he did his best to resist what was expected of visiting reporters and American Jews. "I did not go abroad to write what I might have written at home," he promised. Instead, he recounted a series of surprises. Though a confirmed atheist, the former Isidore Feinstein acknowledged that he found himself immensely attracted by the life of the Yishuv, the Jewish community of Palestine. "It is the one place in the world where Jews seem completely unafraid . . . In Palestine a Jew can be a Jew. Period. Without apologies, without any lengthy arguments as to whether Jews are a race, a religion, a myth, or an accident. He need explain to no one, and he feels profoundly at home; I am quite willing to attribute this to historic sentimentality but it remains nonetheless a tremendous and inescapable fact."[39]

Equally inescapable, however, at least to Stone, were the Arab inhabitants of the land, of which there were "more than a million . . . Palestine is their home. They love their country. Any equitable and lasting solution of the Palestine problem must take these Arabs and their feelings into account." He agreed with Jewish claims that, materially, the Palestinian Arabs had benefited from Jewish immigration. But he "did not find a single Arab who favored a Jewish state," nor "a single Jew who claimed to know" one. The result was "deep political disagreement, but . . . no hatred between Arab and Jew."[40]

Whether this "huge reservoir of goodwill" could be harnessed depended largely on the British—and here Stone's own optimism ran dry.

> To talk with Coptic Christians in Egypt or Maronite Christians in the Lebanon is to begin to understand that what Britain is playing in the Middle East is not an Arab, but a Moslem game, with the dual hope of keeping India divided and the Arab world united (under British control) . . . But just as the desire to build a Moslem bloc does not deter the British from shooting down Moslems in Indonesia, so its highly advertised fear of Arab uprisings does not deter it from the firmest stand against Arab aspirations wherever Britain's own interests are at stake.[41]

Stone had been revolted by the squalor of British rule in Egypt: "In the Muski, the ancient quarter of Cairo, I saw a sight one cannot forget—flies feasting on the corrupted eyes of little children . . . The *fellah* [peasant] lives on the Nile and the *pasha* lives on the *fellah*."[42]

Stone reserved his harshest language and his biggest surprise for his fellow American Jews. He thought that Palestinian Jewry was going down a "blind alley" in its failure to achieve a political understanding with the Arabs. And he was clear about the danger of the Jews' insistence on a state of their own: "I wish to say just as strongly that political agreement will be impossible so long as a single Jewish state in Palestine is demanded." He now believed that the Jewish campaign in America on behalf of Israel was based on half-truths, "and on this basis no effective politics can be waged and no secure life built for the Yishuv."[43] He confessed that he found it painful to write as he did. "I am a Jew. I fell in love with Palestine. I want desperately to help the homeless of Central and Eastern Europe to find a home there . . . I do not blame them for refusing to accept minority status in an Arab state. Under present circumstances that would leave all their magnificent accomplishments to the kind of *pashas* and *effendis* who rule Egypt . . . But equally I do not blame the Arabs of Palestine for fighting against minority status in a Jewish state."[44]

Stone's solution was a binational state inside a broader Arab federation, in which Jews who wanted to leave Europe could find a home, and whose Arab citizens would retain their own religious, civil, and political rights, and where neither people would dominate the other. He knew this was not what most Palestinian Jews wanted, but despite his deep sympathy for their cause, "I felt myself painfully impelled to disagree with majority opinion in the Yishuv." He also recognized that the proposal had still less support among Palestinian Arabs. Undeterred even by "the cost of unpopularity in the American Jewish community," Stone insisted that a binational state was not a compromise but "the only just solution . . . The Arab problem is the central problem for the Yishuv."[45] It was a theme the coming years would give him ample occasions to develop.

Though I. F. Stone may not have become a Zionist in the conventional sense, his trip to Palestine gave him something he thought he'd lost forever in August 1939—a cause. Also, at a time when the audience for radical journalism, or radicalism of any kind, was increasingly beleaguered and beset, it gave Stone's readers a reason to stick with him, and it gave him entrée to an audience far beyond the concentric circles of *PM* and the *Nation*.

At *PM* the effect was immediate: Stone's reports from Palestine in November 1945 lifted the paper's circulation to profitable levels for only the second time in its history.* (His bosses at *PM* were so eager to keep sales up that when Izzy became ill with a stomach complaint in December, just after his return to the United States, they put him up in a hotel room for a week so he could continue writing. Even so, he had to take a ten-day break before he was well enough to write the last two installments at the end of the year.) Izzy's stunning debut as a foreign correspondent also may have helped Ralph Ingersoll make up his mind about how to handle James Wechsler. Like his boss, *PM*'s national editor had been a reluctant draftee, and as a returning veteran was entitled to his old job back. But when Wechsler returned to his desk in January 1946, he also demanded a raise and the right to hire two reporters "of his own choosing." Ingersoll pointed out that the paper still lost $5,000 most weeks and proposed trimming the Washington bureau instead. Wechsler responded with "savage personal attacks" on Stone, "with whom he disagrees politically." Ingersoll then "informed Wechsler we could meet none of his demands."[46] Wechsler didn't go quietly, charging in an article for the *New Leader* written by Ken Crawford,† his predecessor as national editor, that "although not himself a Communist, he [Ingersoll] has continuously yielded to Communist pressure."[47]

In early 1946, Ingersoll could still laugh off such detractors. He even considered asking Izzy to fill in as national editor after his return from the Middle East, but then balked "because he is not an executive." Besides, Stone was now making news as well as reporting it. When, in February, Truman nominated Ed Pauley, the California oilman who'd helped engineer his nomination as vice president, to be under secretary of the navy, Harold Ickes resigned in protest at "government by crony." Izzy's column

---

*The first had been during a seventeen-day newspaper strike in the summer of 1944—immortalized for a generation of New Yorkers by the image of Mayor La Guardia reading the funny pages over the radio—when *PM*, which reached an early agreement with the unions, had no real competition.
†Crawford's account of Wechsler's departure was published under the pseudonym "Karl Collins." A veteran of the *New York Post* and the *Philadelphia Record*, Crawford had a long-simmering antipathy to Izzy, who he said "compensated for minor deviations by re-embracing the [Communist Party] line before his condition could be diagnosed as chronic."

pointing out Ickes' selective blindness to oilmen in his own department made his old sparring partner apoplectic. At his farewell press conference, Ickes derided Stone's reporting as "psychopathic" and "untruthful." As *Time* recorded, "chubby I. F. ('Izzy') Stone, of the *Nation* and Manhattan's hyperthyroid *PM*," had the last word: "Though not always a devotee of the Marquis of Queensbury," Stone wrote, Ickes was "the best all-round brawler in the public interest the town has seen in many years."[48]

Stone's admiration for Ickes was unfeigned; so was his regret at the departure of one of the two remaining New Dealers in the cabinet. "Mr. Truman and the little band of mediocrities who have become his advisers are trying to follow the New Deal program in a kind of fog," he complained. "The present White House crowd talks the New Deal language, but as though it were a foreign tongue, imperfectly understood."[49]

•

The telephone call that sent I. F. Stone on the greatest adventure of his life came in April 1946. "I was in the press gallery at Hunter College in the Bronx," temporary home to the UN Security Council, listening to Sir Alexander Cadogan, the British representative, make "a professionally astringent argument designed to prevent action against Franco. An usher tapped me on the shoulder."[50]

Picking up the phone, Stone recognized the voice of Joe Boxenbaum, an American he'd met in Palestine: "How would you like to meet some boys who volunteered to serve as seamen for the illegal immigration?"

"Call me back in fifteen minutes," Stone replied, and after asking John Lewis, *PM*'s managing editor, for the rest of the day off, he took the subway to Penn Station and then boarded a train to Cream Ridge, New Jersey, to inspect a pair of rusting hulks, the corvettes *Beauharnois* and *Norsys*, recently sold as scrap by the Canadian navy. Renamed the *Josiah Wedgwood* and the *Haganah*, the two ships had been covertly bought by a mysterious outfit known as F.B. Shipping.* Until now the immigration of Jews to Palestine over and above the tiny quota of "legal" immigrants allowed in by the British (the Aliyah Bet) had relied on professional sailors

---

*According to Akiva Skidell, the Polish-born U.S. army veteran who helped arrange the deal, "F.B." stood either for Fanny Barnett, wife of the owner of the Hotel Fourteen at 14 East 60th Street, which served as the unofficial Zionist residence in New York, or, more simply, for "Fuck Bevin"—a reference to the British foreign minister, Ernest Bevin.

attracted by the prospect of high pay for hazardous duty. ("Illegal" ships were liable to seizure on the high seas; crew or passengers who resisted could be, and sometimes were, shot.)[51]

"This ship," said Boxenbaum, pointing to the *Josiah Wedgwood*, "will be the first to be manned by American Jewish boys who volunteered their services . . . Some are experienced sailors. Others are going to sea for the first time." Izzy joined the volunteers for a round of drinks. Many were veterans of Habonim (the Builders) or Hashomer Hatzair (the Young Guards), rival Socialist Zionist youth groups. At least one young New Yorker recognized *PM*'s star columnist—who sprung his own surprise: Instead of a feature about the ships, said Izzy, "I'd like to go along and write the whole story of the voyage from the beginning to the arrival in Palestine."[52]

The *Wedgwood* was due to sail at dawn the next day, and it was only with some difficulty that Izzy was persuaded to wait until the ship reached Europe and was ready to take on its cargo of refugees instead of rushing home to pick up his passport and a few clean shirts. He quickly managed to acquire a visa for Palestine. Esther and the children knew where he was going, and so did Ralph Ingersoll and John Lewis—no one else. Freda Kirchwey was out of the country, but on the insistence of his contacts in the Haganah, who feared a leak to British intelligence, his other *Nation* colleagues were told that Izzy was taking a leave of absence to cover the Paris peace conference.

"Izzy wouldn't tell me why he was in Europe or where he was going," complained Victor Bernstein, *PM*'s war correspondent. He spent a week in London talking with friends such as Richard Crossman, a Labour MP and editor of the *New Statesman*. (Crossman had been instrumental in persuading the British members of the Anglo-American Committee on Palestine to support the recommendation that 100,000 Jewish displaced persons be admitted to Palestine immediately, and conversations with him and others convinced Stone that Foreign Minister Bevin "had no intention of keeping his promise" to admit the refugees. Further disappointment awaited him on the Continent, where the *sheliakh*, or Haganah emissary, warned him of "unforeseen delays" in getting him on a ship, which might leave from any number of ports. After collecting visas for every country on the Mediterranean—and Poland and Austria—he boarded the *Orient Express* for Munich, where Bernstein, who was covering the International Military Tribunal, drove with him to Nuremberg.[53]

The two reporters heard Baldur von Schirach, leader of the Hitler Youth and former gauleiter of Vienna, "explain that he was one of the Jews' best friends." But it was the testimony of Rudolf Höss, commandant of Auschwitz, that made the deepest impression. One knew when the people in the gas chambers were dead, said Höss, "because they stopped screaming." As Stone later told his readers, "My parents were born in Russia. Had they not emigrated at the turn of the century to America I might have gone to the gas chambers." No longer "a newspaperman merely in search of a good story," Stone now viewed himself "as a kinsman, fulfilling a moral obligation to my brothers."[54]

Fed up with waiting for a ship, Stone joined a trainload of Jewish DPs en route to Bratislava. At the border between Czechoslovakia and Poland, he noticed something about the Jews heading west: "There was one striking difference between these Jews from Russia and those pouring into the underground from the European countries which were under Nazi domination or influence. Out of the Soviet Union alone came the miracle of whole Jewish families. Only among these refugees did one see fathers and mothers with children."[55] In weighing up the historical accounts years later, Stone was never quite able to dismiss the thousands of Jewish families saved, however inadvertently, by the Soviets.

After weeks on this underground railroad, Stone finally joined the *Josiah Wedgwood* in Vado, an Italian port town on the Ligurian coast. Besides the crew of American Jews ("as odd a collection of seamen as ever sailed the seas . . . The captain and the first-mate were . . . ex-Wobblies"), Izzy had two new companions. The "gentle, slender, dark-haired woman who was the widow of a gifted Italian Jew" is named only as "Mrs. A-" in Stone's account, where he describes her simply as "my Italian translator." Ada Sereni was actually a key operative in the Mossad Le'Aliyah Bet (Organization for Illegal Immigration), the secret underground network bringing Jews to Palestine. Her husband, Enzo Sereni, whose father had been physician to the royal house of Savoy, had immigrated to Palestine as a young man and was, like Stone, an advocate of a binational state.[56] In 1944, caught parachuting behind German lines with the British Special Operations Executive, Enzo Sereni had been executed in Dachau. Stone also camouflaged the identity of his second friend, "a man known locally as Phil," claiming that "before I quite knew what I was doing I hired him as a second translator and general handyman. He spoke virtually all the East and Central European languages . . . and assured me that he could make himself generally useful."[57] No doubt. In reality, Yehuda Arazi, code-named "Alon," was the highest-ranking Jewish agent in Italy, wanted by the British for his role in "confiscating" 5,000 rifles from the Palestine police on behalf of the Haganah in 1943 and known as the King of Ruses for his talent for disguise and deception.

Late in June 1946, the three drove up the coast to Savona, where on a moonlit stretch of deserted beach the *Wedgwood* was to rendezvous with its cargo. Italy's ports were still under the control of the British, who were determined not to allow any ships to leave for Palestine, but as Sereni knew, Savona was a Communist town where the British were not popular.[58] Shortly after midnight, a convoy of twenty-four British army trucks, "borrowed" by Arazi, began to pull up on the gravel, depositing some 1,200 DPs and their bags. But the *Wedgwood* didn't arrive until three a.m., by which time either the crowds or the frantic ship-to-shore signaling had also attracted the attention of the carabinieri.

Arazi takes up the tale: "Ada, Stone and I tried to persuade them not to obstruct us. In the meantime the ship finally pulled in to shore and we got the policemen's consent to let the people get on board."[59] Stone pulled out his "most impressive" ID, "a red State Department card with a gold American eagle on it," and demanded the name and rank of one of the police officers. "I began to hand out Camels, and the carabinieri were visibly softened."[60] However, when Izzy pressed the officers to "let these people go," he and his two "interpreters" were taken to police headquarters in Savona. There, "Yehuda explained in English," Sereni recalled, "that in America there are two important people, Truman and Stone, and that if the Italians don't treat us well then Stone will make a big fuss."[61]

Worried that he might be searched for incriminating documents, Izzy asked to use the bathroom, emerging resplendent in his green war correspondent's uniform with shiny gold "U.S." insignia on the lapels. Yet not even this awesome sight was sufficient to prevent the Italian prefect from telephoning British military headquarters to boast of the capture of an illegal ship. Suddenly Izzy began to shout that his hearing-aid battery had gone dead and that the replacements were in his bags, now aboard the *Wedgwood*. Suspicious, the Italians refused to let Stone leave to retrieve his bags but finally consented to allow "Phil," the translator, to go in his place, writing out a pass to get him through police roadblocks. Once on board, Arazi told the captain "to wait until I leave, and then cut the ropes and sail away, even if they start shooting at you."[62]

Back at the police station, Arazi found a chaotic scene. Stone and Sereni were gone. "All the carabinieri were running back and forth. Total mayhem. I asked the [prefect] what was the matter, and he said, 'The American escaped.' Fifteen minutes later Stone and Ada came into the room followed by a whole procession of carabinieri. Both of them were laughing."[63] It seemed they had simply gone next door for coffee. Now Stone challenged the Italians either to arrest him—threatening dark consequences for such shabby treatment of a distinguished American journalist—or let him go. He also demanded to speak with the American ambassador. But when the call came through, it wasn't the ambassador but British military headquarters in Genoa on the line asking if he was willing to be questioned about the ship. "I'm working for my paper, not British intelligence," Izzy yelled, slamming down the phone. In the middle of this commotion, word reached the station that the *Josiah Wedgwood* had cut her moorings and sailed off. Feigning outrage, Izzy threatened to lodge an official complaint against the police. Holding his head in his hands, he shouted that thanks to them he'd come all the way from America for nothing, concluding his tirade by declaring, "I'm walking." The astonished Italians released the distraught American and his "translators."

"We didn't so much walk as we flew away," recalled Sereni. "And it was six o'clock in the morning."[64]

Thanks to Izzy and his friends, the *Wedgwood* and her human cargo reached Palestine safely. In late June, Izzy managed to board her sister ship, the *Haganah*, in the French port of Sète, west of Marseilles. Hoping to avoid the fate of the *Wedgwood*, which the Royal Navy had seized at Haifa, the 1,015 passengers (and one reporter) aboard the *Haganah* were to be transferred to another ship on the high seas about one hundred miles off the coast of Palestine. For the eight days he was aboard the *Haganah*, Izzy's only worries were a short bout of seasickness and the guilt he felt at having a bunk in the officers' cabin instead of sleeping in the rough wooden bunks stacked four and five deep in every bit of space belowdecks. "Despite the discomforts and shortcomings, there never was a gayer ship on the high seas," Izzy wrote. "Our decks looked like Orchard Beach or Coney Island on a hot Sunday. They were packed with people in every possible costume, from bathing suits to the black mohair vests of the . . . orthodox men."[65]

But when he saw the *Akbel*, an ancient wooden-hulled freighter about half the length of the *Haganah*, Izzy's heart sank—especially when the *Akbel*'s Turkish skipper tried to flee from the rendezvous. Among the *Haganah*'s passengers were several veterans of the FPO (Faraynigte Partizaner Organizatzye, the United Partisan Organization founded by Abba Kovner, the legendary resistance fighter), and after nine of the "huskiest men," several "with pockets which bulged interestingly," were sent to negotiate with the Turkish captain, the refugees were rowed aboard.⁶⁶

Conditions on the *Akbel* were dire: "The ship was unstable and overcrowded," recalled Bezalel Drori, who as ranking officer of the Palyam (the marine unit of the Palmach, the Jewish special forces) was in command of the operation. "There was not enough air coming in, so it was necessary to rotate the people who stood on the deck with the people who were inside all the time. There was a severe shortage of water and food."⁶⁷

During the night, Stone took a turn packed belowdecks stripped to the waist. He found the air "sickening, the noise almost unbearable." After two hours of heat and exhaustion punctuated by fistfights among men clambering to gain a place on deck, Izzy emerged badly shaken. "I confess with shame that I never again volunteered to go down into the hold. It was more than I could take." Morning brought further misery. The captain, perhaps unhappy with the previous day's negotiation, had steered the ship away from Palestine, and they were now off the coast of Cyprus, where a British destroyer loomed less than a mile to starboard. Stone hailed the destroyer, HMS *Virago*, explaining that there were sick passengers on board the *Akbel* and asking for a tow to Haifa. But after sending a boarding party and learning that the *Akbel* had neither sufficient food nor water, the British steamed away. "The second day and night on the Turkish cargo boat was the worst I ever spent," Izzy reported. Ignoring the captain's repeated SOS calls, and Izzy's shouts over the megaphone, the *Virago* waited until the *Akbel* passed the entrance to Haifa harbor before taking over and towing the vessel into port on July 2. The quarantine officer explained that owing to the mass arrest of the Zionist leadership three days earlier, the Athlit detention camp in Haifa was full. "You people will be held in the harbor." Stone also learned that there were two cases of suspected bubonic plague aboard the ship. At this point he decided he'd had enough and pulled out his U.S. passport with its British visa for Palestine.

"You must be the only legal passenger on board," said the British officer. Stone said that he was, explaining he'd come to report on the Jewish immigration. The officer asked him whether, now that he knew what conditions were like, he'd do it again.

"Sure," Izzy replied. "I had a wonderful time."[68]

•

The front page of *PM* for Monday, July 15, 1946, featured a two-column photograph of a smiling I. F. Stone descending the steps of the plane that brought him back to New York. His series "Through Europe's Underground to Palestine," which ran in *PM* from July 22 to August 30, sent the paper's circulation above 200,000 for the first time since 1940. The CBS program *We the People* introduced Izzy to radio audiences from coast to coast. And Joseph Gaer, former editor in chief of the Federal Writers' Project and publicity director for the CIO, signed up the celebrated correspondent to write a book version for his new publishing company, Boni & Gaer.

With the publication of *Underground to Palestine*, Stone finally gained a national audience. "He risked his life to get this story" proclaimed the full-page ad in the *New York Times*, which also quoted Albert Einstein: "Like a genuine artist, I. F. Stone has described what he saw and lived through." "The book lives and breathes," pronounced the *Herald Tribune*. Meyer Berger, probably the most accomplished stylist to write for the *New York Times*, saluted his fellow newsman's restraint: "Mr. Stone does a quiet and simple reporting job in this story . . . In it were all the elements that might tempt a reporter to flood his pages with hysteria in type. He has escaped that temptation." Even Elsa Maxwell, the *New York Post* society columnist famed as the "hostess with the mostest," gushed, "Go, get a copy and read it. You cannot help being moved and enriched at the same time."[69]

In the *Nation*, Bartley Crum, a San Francisco lawyer and member of the Anglo-American Committee for Palestine, wrote that with his book Stone "did something which no official could possibly do . . . I hope that every member of the Senate Foreign Relations Committee will read *Underground to Palestine*. The publisher should see that Ernest Bevin and Clement Attlee have copies." In fact, Stone had already sent Bevin a copy. The inscription read, "To Ernest Bevin, on whose conscience this should not lie lightly."[70]

Bevin never replied. But then the Foreign Office had followed Stone's

Palestinian odyssey with dismay from the very beginning. His presence on board the *Akbel* had triggered an exchange of telegrams between His Majesty's high commissioner for Palestine and Lord Inverchapel, the British ambassador in Washington, sniffily pointing out that as "Stone was granted a visa for Palestine in May . . . it was unnecessary for him to resort to clandestine methods of entry." Inverchapel wanted to know whether Stone "did in fact sneak in as he claimed." If not, the British could "use this fact to deflate his publicity heroics."[71]

Yet despite the uniformly stellar reviews, Stone's book earned him little money. Billed as "the story of how the Haganah is saving the Jews of Europe," the *Times* advertisement had promised that "a large part of the money from this sale will be used to further the work of Haganah." And Stone had been only too happy to help; indeed, the book was dedicated to "those anonymous heroes, the *Shelikhim* of the Haganah." Feted by Jewish groups around the country and a featured speaker at the national convention of Hadassah, the Zionist women's organization, Stone was taken to lunch by "friends in the Zionist movement" and offered a lavish publicity campaign to help sell his book—and the Haganah.

There was just one condition. "There was one sentence, I was told . . . that had to come out." In its entirety, the offending sentence read: "I myself would like to see a bi-national Arab-Jewish state made of Palestine and Trans-Jordan, the whole to be part of a Middle Eastern Semitic Federation." Stone refused. "That ended the luncheon and, in a way, the book."[72]

Stone did receive a warm letter from Judah Magnes, the California-born president of the Hebrew University in Jerusalem, who chided the American for describing himself as only a reporter. "What a reporter—keen, deep, and above all identifying yourself with the suffering!" Magnes urged Stone to hold fast to his support for a binational state.[73] He also had a reply of sorts from his most important reader. In January 1947, Stone sent a copy to the White House, inscribed "To President Truman, Who has done more than any other occupant of the White House to help these unfortunate people. Respectfully, I. F. Stone." A blurb from Senator Truman had decorated the jacket of *Business as Usual*; now President Truman had his secretary, Rose Conway, respond with a note to "acknowledge the receipt of your book."[74]

For the sake of Palestine, Stone tried as hard as he could to give Truman the benefit of the doubt. But events in Washington and in Europe made the effort increasingly difficult. In September 1946, just a few weeks after his series concluded in *PM*, Stone was once again personally caught up in the headlines. As with the departure of Harold Ickes, the issue was President Truman's fidelity to his predecessor's policies. This time the head on the block belonged to Henry Wallace, the last New Dealer in the new administration and, to his supporters, the rightful heir of Franklin Roosevelt.

As secretary of commerce, Wallace had lent the weight of his own considerable political following to Truman's efforts to maintain full employment during peacetime. If the leader of American "progressives" (as the not-quite-a-coalition of labor unions, Popular Front groups, civil rights campaigners, Communists, fellow travelers, and anti-Communist liberals now called itself) had doubts about the wisdom of Truman's threats to seize striking coal mines, or to use the army to break a railroad strike, he kept them to himself. But on foreign policy, Wallace spoke out.

In March, with Truman looking on benignly, Winston Churchill made his famous "Iron Curtain" speech at Westminster College in the president's native Missouri. Billed as a frank résumé of Soviet conduct in Eastern Europe, the speech was also an invitation to form a postwar Anglo-American alliance that Wallace—and Stone—viewed as a dangerous departure from Roosevelt's policy of not getting embroiled in defending British imperialism.

Stone's experiences in the Middle East helped him discount Churchill's lofty rhetoric. In Cairo he had spent time with George Polk, a young CBS correspondent who'd been reporting on the civil war in Greece and on Britain's brutal treatment of elements in what had been the Greek resistance to the German occupation of their country during the war years. A decorated veteran of Guadalcanal, Polk was in Athens in December 1944 when the shooting started between British soldiers and the EAM (Greek National Liberation Front), a republican coalition whose Communist-led partisans in ELAS (People's National Liberation Army) had borne the brunt of the fighting against the Nazi occupation. Though the EAM would have won any fair postwar election, Churchill was determined to restore the Greek monarchy (cousins of Britain's royal family) to the throne, and by early 1946 British troops were fighting shoulder to shoulder with the Security Battalions, a collaborationist militia established during the Nazi occupation by Greece's quisling government,

and Polk was broadcasting "the roundup of persons even vaguely suspected of not approving the government and not loving the king."[75]
Churchill during the war had hailed "those gallant guerrillas" of ELAS;
now he condemned them as "miserable banditti."[76] Though the Tory
leader had been turned out of office the previous summer, in America his
influence seemed undiminished.

So when Henry Wallace, speaking at Madison Square Garden on September 10, 1946, warned that "to make Britain the key to our foreign policy would be the height of folly," Izzy heard only common sense. He
shared Wallace's fear that "British imperialist policy in the Near East
alone, combined with Russian retaliation, would lead the United States
straight to war." And Wallace's assurance that "just two days ago, when
President Truman read these words, he said they represented the policy
of his administration," was something Izzy desperately wanted to be true.
Indeed, according to his reports on the ensuing crisis, the president *had*
gone over Wallace's speech, "page by page and line by line," which was
why Truman had evidently endorsed it in a news conference before Wallace spoke. But then a frantic cable from Paris, where Secretary of State
James Byrnes and Senator Arthur Vandenberg had just launched a "get
tough" policy in dealing with the Soviet Union, prompted Truman to back
away, and after the fact, he claimed that he'd meant to endorse only Wallace's "right to speak," not the contents of his remarks. Yet as Izzy reported, far from being taken by surprise by Wallace's views, Truman had
promised Wallace to meet with Stalin himself if Byrnes's mission to Europe failed. Indeed, the president had known of Wallace's position since
July, when Wallace had written him a letter saying that U.S. actions "must
make it look to the rest of the world as if we were only paying lip service
to peace at the conference table." The text of that July letter, leaked to
Drew Pearson but first published in full by Izzy in *PM* on September 16,
pushed Truman to demand that Wallace take a vow of silence on foreign-
policy questions. When Wallace refused, Truman fired him.[77]

The loss of Henry Wallace was a key factor in the Democratic rout
that November, when Republicans took control of both houses of Congress for the first time since 1928; among the Republican freshmen were
Richard M. Nixon and Joseph R. McCarthy. Wallace's departure also
cleared the way for a bipartisan foreign policy. At the moment it didn't
have a name, but it did have a theorist. In February 1946, George F. Ken-

nan, chargé d'affaires at the U.S. embassy in Moscow, sent his famous "Long Telegram" to the State Department arguing that Soviet communism represented "a political force committed fanatically to the belief that with the U.S. there can be no permanent *modus vivendi*; that it is desirable and necessary that the internal harmony of our society be disrupted, our traditional way of life be destroyed [and] the international authority of our state be broken."[78] Kennan was to elaborate his ideas in a pseudonymous article in *Foreign Affairs* in July 1947, suggesting that, far from accepting a stable share of power with the United States, the Soviet Union was an inherently aggressive regime that could be contained only by "the adroit and vigilant application of counter-force at a series of constantly shifting geographical and political points."[79]

In the fall of 1946, "containment" was still just a theory. Indeed, so wide open was the debate about U.S.-Soviet relations that when Sava Kosanovich, formerly Tito's minister of information and now Yugoslav ambassador to the United States, and the nephew of the scientist Nicola Tesla, appeared on a new radio program to answer questions from various journalists meant to represent the spectrum of American opinion, I. F. Stone was one of his interrogators. Broadcast on Friday evenings over the Mutual network, *Meet the Press* featured "four of the country's ace reporters . . . gathered around the press table." Martha Rountree, the show's producer, tried to have "somebody for the guest, somebody against the guest, someone middle of the road, and somebody from a wire service who was neutral." With a panel that included Ken Crawford, a fervent anti-Communist who'd gone from *PM* to *Newsweek*, and Lawrence Spivak, publisher of the increasingly right-wing *American Mercury*, Izzy had his work cut out for him providing "balance." Invited initially thanks to his reporting on the Wallace debacle (his first broadcast was on the day Wallace resigned), Stone soon became part of the program's regular rotation. "If we had somebody who was a conservative on, we'd put Stone on," said Rountree. "He was a good newspaperman, he did his homework."[80]

•

I. F. Stone was no apologist for Moscow. Indeed, the *Daily Worker* had condemned his championing of Tito's "deviationist" government in Yugoslavia and attacked his reporting from Palestine as pro-Zionist. He was, however, becoming increasingly convinced that the greatest danger to American liberties came from Washington, and particularly from J. Edgar Hoover. When, in October 1946, Hoover told the American Legion convention to be on guard against American Communists' "sly propaganda and false preachments on Civil Liberty," Izzy dismissed the speech as "melodramatic bunk by a self-dramatizing dick." Noting that the FBI chief had never roused himself to denounce "the menace of racism, or anti-Semitism," Izzy argued that it was "hysterical nonsense to build up the Communist Party, which can't elect a dog-catcher outside New York City, into Public Enemy No. 1. The party's been on the decline ever since the Nazi-Soviet pact, and its intellectual antics descend to lower levels daily."[81]

Once again Izzy's criticism of Hoover brought renewed attention from the FBI. In a series of memos dating from immediately after the article, the bureau summarized his contacts with groups such as the Joint Anti-Fascist Refugee Committee (formed to aid fugitives from Spain), the CIO Maritime Defense Committee, and the Independent Citizens Committee of the Arts, Sciences and the Professions. But being one of the very few journalists willing to take on Hoover publicly had its benefits. In November, Izzy and Esther were invited to dinner with Mr. and Mrs. Harry Dexter White. White, an economist who had been an assistant secretary of the treasury under Roosevelt, had just been appointed by Truman as an American director of the International Monetary Fund. It had been White who, with his British counterpart John Maynard Keynes, had drafted the blueprints for the IMF and the World Bank, the twin pillars of the postwar economic order. Flattered by the invitation, Izzy never knew that the entire dinner took place under FBI surveillance.[82]

The target wasn't Izzy but his host. Both Whittaker Chambers and Elizabeth Bentley, two former Communists who had confessed to spying for the Soviet Union, had told the FBI that White, too, was a Soviet spy. Although Chambers made repeated attempts to warn American officials about a Communist underground operating in Washington, his credibility was hampered by the fact that his story seemed to change with each telling.[83] Bentley, an alcoholic who turned to espionage out of passion for a Russian lover, not ideology, was also originally suspect.[84] But the FBI, noticing the overlap between their accounts, and possibly encouraged by the Truman administration's less conciliatory stance toward the Soviet

Union, instituted surveillance on Bentley's former contacts. Besides White, the list included two other economists, the presidential aide Lauchlin Currie and Nathan Silvermaster—both longtime sources for Stone. Still another economist, William Remington, told investigators that Bentley had initially pretended to be a researcher for *PM*, asking him if he "knew Izzy Stone or [Kenneth] Crawford." Remington replied that he'd heard of them.[85]

Stone was of course unaware of the extent of Hoover's interest in him. But the changes in Washington's political climate were impossible to miss. In January 1947, Carl Marzani, an ex–OSS officer, was arrested and charged with perjury for having fraudulently denied former membership in the Communist Party. Marzani admitted lying but said his superiors were well aware of his past, which was virtually incontrovertible. A month before Pearl Harbor, William Donovan, head of the OSS, had asked Milton Wolff, commander of the Abraham Lincoln Brigade, to recruit veterans of the Spanish Civil War to serve with British commando units being prepared for operations in occupied Europe. When the United States entered the war, Donovan took Wolff's recruits into the OSS, and Marzani was one of them.[86] Moreover, as Izzy pointed out in *PM*, Marzani was arrested after he had left government service and hence could pose no possible threat to security. He had, however, recently set up a company making films for the labor movement. The Hearst press had already gone after him for *Deadline for Action*, an exposé of banking and cartels that he'd made in cooperation with the United Electrical Workers, Izzy reported.[87]

A week later, five union officials were fired from their jobs at the army's Aberdeen Proving Grounds without being granted either a hearing or a chance to see the evidence against them; they were told only that they were suspected of being Communists. In his *PM* editorial "Portrait of a Witch Hunt," Izzy didn't dispute the army's right to fire them if they were Communists; he merely insisted that "accused persons in loyalty cases [have a right] to know exactly what they are supposed to have done and when."[88] This may not have been a popular stand, but taking it was not yet an act requiring political courage. Secretary of War Robert Patterson responded to Izzy's series on the Aberdeen firings by inviting him over to the War Department for an exclusive interview.[89]

As Stone recognized, however, it was the arrest of Gerhart Eisler that marked the first hard frost in the long winter of American repression. A German intellectual who had visited the United States in the early 1930s as a representative of the Comintern, Eisler had fought in Spain, then fled to France, where he was interned in a Vichy concentration camp from the fall of France in June 1940 until the summer of 1941. En route to Mexico, where he had been granted political asylum, Eisler was detained as an enemy alien at Ellis Island and refused an exit permit. He spent the war years in Queens living on the generosity of his brother Hanns, a composer working in Hollywood,* and on a meager stipend he received from the Joint Anti-Fascist Refugee Committee. In 1946, Eisler finally received his exit permit and was about to set sail for Germany when Hoover, convinced he was a "key figure in Communist activities in the United States," got his permit revoked. But charging Eisler with a crime was not so simple. Instead, in February 1947, he was summoned to testify before the House Committee on Un-American Activities (HUAC). A steady diet of tidbits leaked from the FBI kept press interest high. *Newsweek* called Eisler "the Number One Red agent" in the United States; his estranged sister, Ruth Fischer, wrote a series of five articles for the Hearst press on "Gerhart Eisler: The Career of a Terrorist." Two days before he was scheduled to testify, Eisler was arrested, charged with conspiracy to overthrow the U.S. government, perjury, passport fraud, and tax evasion, and imprisoned again at Ellis Island, where he was denied bail. When he did appear in front of HUAC, he refused to testify unless he could first read a sworn statement. In his maiden speech in the House, Richard Nixon moved to cite Eisler for contempt; the motion passed 370–1.[90]

Interestingly, Stone did not immediately leap to Eisler's defense. Though he ridiculed the government's attempts to link Eisler to the Canadian atom spy ring recently in the headlines,[†] he also cautioned "that the rest is a frame-up I am not convinced." Fascinated by what he called "this fierce family quarrel between Stalinist brother and Trotskyist sister," Stone felt the stakes were too high for pretense: Eisler's partisans

---

*Hanns Eisler's score for *Hangmen Also Die* was nominated for an Oscar. The film, dramatizing the 1942 assassination of the Nazi governor of Czechoslovakia, Reinhard Heydrich, was the only Hollywood screenplay written by Eisler's longtime friend and lyricist Bertolt Brecht. Their fellow refugee Fritz Lang directed.

[†]In the spring of 1946, Allan Nunn May, a physicist who worked on the Canadian side of the British atomic weapons program, confessed to spying for the Soviet Union.

in the Communist press "can't make a revolution," he warned, "but they can certainly set off a counter-revolution that will smash civil liberty and the whole progressive movement in America." He continued,

> Here in America the conspiratorial habits of a petty handful of Communists may soon provide excuse and occasion for a repetition, on a far more dangerous scale, of the Red scare that followed the last war. It would be better for all concerned if the Communists came fully into the open, ended all the penny-dreadful . . . playing at revolution and then fought, as free men in a country still free, for the maintenance of legal standing as another legal minority party.
>
> No politically sophisticated person believes that the Comintern has been abolished in more than name. The Russians cannot have the cake of conspiracy and the penny of cooperation at the same time. That is an issue the Kremlin must face . . . I can hear the screams from Union Square already.[91]

Joseph Starobin, foreign editor of the *Daily Worker*, rose to the bait, denouncing Izzy in his pages, but such subtleties were lost on Hoover. A clipping from *PM* of an I. F. Stone article published later in the year that argued that by targeting federal employees the government risked "destroying the realities of freedom without touching its forms," bears the FBI director's handwritten scrawl: "The theme song of Eisler when he spoke in N.Y. Thursday night. I wonder who writes whose material! H."[92]

On March 12, 1947, President Truman told a joint session of Congress, "It must be the policy of the United States to support free peoples who are resisting attempted subjugation by armed minorities or outside pressure." Whom did the president have in mind? Churchill had proclaimed in his "Iron Curtain" speech, as he surveyed the nations of Central and Eastern Europe, now wholly dominated by the Soviet Union, that "Athens alone—Greece with its immortal glories—is free to decide its future at an election." But the government of his successor, Clement Attlee, was strapped; British aid to Greece, Truman was told, would end on March 31. Now Truman wanted $400 million from Congress to prop up the governments of Greece and Turkey. Dean Acheson warned congressional leaders that if Greece went Communist, "like apples in a barrel . . .

the corruption would infect Iran and all the East." Afterward, Senator Arthur Vandenberg told Truman, "If that's what you want, there's only one way to get it . . . scare hell out of the country."[93] The containment of Soviet power and influence was now the official policy of the U.S. government, and it had a new name: the Truman Doctrine.

Nine days later, the president issued Executive Order 9835 establishing the Federal Employees Loyalty and Security Program. Stone described this measure as "an experiment in American fascism." Under its provisions, any federal worker could be dismissed if there were "reasonable grounds for belief that the person is disloyal," but the order did not specify what "disloyal" meant, nor did it allow the accused the right to confront the evidence—or his or her accusers. By May, the FBI had begun "name checks" on two million federal workers, from stenographers to cabinet secretaries. Any finding of "derogatory information"—supplied by a disgruntled coworker, for example, who remembered a sympathetic comment about Spanish Loyalists, or membership in the National Lawyers Guild, or attendance at a wartime rally saluting Russian troops—led to a "full field investigation." Decades later, Clark Clifford, Truman's special counsel, admitted that the entire program was drafted with the 1948 elections in mind. "It was a political problem," he told Carl Bernstein (whose father, Al Bernstein, represented hundreds of members of the United Federal Workers of America in loyalty proceedings). "We did not believe there was a real problem. A problem was being manufactured."[94]

What was real was the fear. "I flew down to Washington," Izzy reported in July 1947, "to see what I could learn about the firing of 10 employees last week by the State Department. To go back to Washington is like going back into a country under the shadow of a terror. It's not the heat that makes Washington so uncomfortable these days, it's the hysteria."[95]

•

The epidemic of cowardice was even more striking to a man returning, as Stone was, from a capital filled with soldiers, whose every street seemed cut by barricades and where, on passing through the barbed wire surrounding every public building, "they pat your pockets and under your arms for guns." Jerusalem in the spring of 1947 had been a city literally under siege. Two years after the end of hostilities in Europe, British authorities were still struggling to turn back the tide of Jewish immigration; mounting Jewish frustration led to greater sympathy for the terrorists of the Irgun Zvai Leumi and the Stern Gang, whose campaign of bombings and shootings did little to calm Arab apprehension. Yet Stone reported, "I get no sense of fear among the people in the streets, Arab or Jewish. Where one feels the fear is among the British, who have shut themselves up for safety in barbed wire ghettoes."[96]

British paranoia was sufficiently acute for Stone to be detained and searched when he entered Palestine at Lydda Airport in February 1947 equipped with a valid British visa and advance clearance from the embassy. Among the documents removed from his pockets were a letter from Kermit Roosevelt introducing Stone to the chief of U.S. Military Intelligence in Jerusalem, a letter in Arabic from Azzam Pasha, secretary general of the Arab League, presenting Stone to the Egyptian ambassador in Washington—and Esther Stone's grocery list! A quick trip to the bathroom had allowed Izzy to dispose of "a complete list of all Jewish illegal immigrant ships and their sailing dates" he had tucked inside his sock before landing.[97]

In March, just as President Truman was announcing his Loyalty Program, Stone set off to Cyprus with a group of illegal immigrants deported by the British. Though he had obtained clearance this time from both the British army and navy, he was refused permission to land or to cable his report and was forced to return with a shipload of "legals" who, after being held six months in camps on Britain's Mediterranean island colony, were now being permitted to proceed to Palestine. "Only Max Beerbohm could do this . . . spectacle justice," he wrote. The desperate Jews are carted back and forth "like zoo exhibits in the cages of these ships" making "squalid chambermaids of His Majesty's Army and Navy."[98]

Through all his tribulations, Stone retained great sympathy for the beleaguered British Tommy. But the British government was absolutely right to regard him with suspicion. Since his adventures the previous year, the Stone household had become a way station on the Jewish underground railroad.

"We had people from Haganah at the house lots of times," Christopher Stone recalled. "People would come by who Dad knew. Bomb makers. Irgun guys. He knew a group that used to ship guns from Baltimore harbor. I remember a guy at dinner telling a story about blowing up a British garage. The bomb was connected to the hand brake and on the way out the guy running the garage struck up a conversation. The fuse was about a minute and a half, and the conversation went on almost forty-five seconds." And Zev Meir Siegel said that he and many of the rest of the American crew aboard the *President Warfield*—an Aliyah Bet vessel better known by its new name, the *Exodus**—were recruited "at a meeting at the home of the journalist I. F. Stone."[99]

So when Stone took off for Palestine again in early May 1948—his fourth trip in as many years—he was treated by the Yishuv's government-in-waiting not as a foreign correspondent but as a *chaver*, a comrade. Ever since the United Nations vote in favor of the partition of British-mandate Palestine the previous November, the country had been in a state of unofficial civil war. Lydda Airport, still controlled by the British, was closed to commercial flights. Any doubts Stone might have had about the imminence of formal hostilities were settled on the plane to Tel Aviv, when he recognized a familiar face (whose identity he withheld from *PM*'s readers).

David "Mickey" Marcus was a former federal prosecutor who had been Mayor La Guardia's commissioner of corrections. A 1924 graduate of West Point, the New Yorker returned to uniform in 1940 and after Pearl Harbor was appointed commandant of the Army Ranger school. Though he spent most of the war as a staff officer, Marcus saw combat on D-day, when he volunteered to parachute into Normandy with the 101st Airborne. His last post before returning to civilian life was as head of the Pentagon's War Crimes Division, and when Marcus was approached by the Haganah for help in finding an American officer to organize and train the nascent country's armed forces, he nominated himself. As a colonel in the U.S. army reserves, David Marcus was forbidden to wear the uniform of a foreign country, so he became "Michael Stone" for the duration.

I. F. Stone arrived just in time to watch David Ben Gurion, the new premier, proclaim the establishment of the Jewish state in a ceremony at the Tel Aviv Museum on May 14. Jerusalem was already under siege, and

---

*When the *Exodus* and its 4,515 passengers approached Haifa in July 1947, the British, tired of shuttling refugees back and forth to Cyprus, decided at Ernest Bevin's suggestion to deport the emigrants back to France. However, the French government's refusal to cooperate with British plans meant that the *Exodus* had to sail on to Hamburg, in the British occupation zone of Germany. The resulting international outcry is widely viewed as a crucial factor in forcing Britain to relinquish its mandate in Palestine.

though Jewish troops had taken Jaffa, Haifa, Acre, and Tiberias, the Arab Legion, a well-trained, well-equipped force under the command of the British general John Bagot Glubb, had seized the Etzion bloc, a group of four settlements guarding the southern approach to Jerusalem. Izzy slept through his first air raid, on a Sabbath morning in Tel Aviv. But a few days later, covering the fighting in the Negev, he lay "scared and helpless in a ditch" while bombs and incendiaries landed all around and Spitfires from the Egyptian air force "swooped down to strafe us with machine gun and cannon fire."[100]

Though "sobered and shaken" by his baptism of fire, Stone recovered his nerve sufficiently that, back in Tel Aviv and "restive under [the] restrictions of barfly-and-handout journalism [and] tired of waiting for the promised official Cook's tour to the front," he set off—by taxi—with another reporter. "We wanted to see how close we could get to the front lines and how near the Egyptians really were." They were joined along the way by Wolfgang von Weisl, a doctor who had been a lieutenant in the Austrian imperial artillery in World War I, an activist in Vladimir Jabotinsky's Revisionist Zionist movement, and an early admirer of Benito Mussolini;* he was currently editing an Irgunist newspaper. Dropped off a few miles from Gaza, Stone and his companions hitched a ride with an armored car full of Israeli riflemen back to the Negev front, where he again came under fire, this time both from the air and from a nearby police fortress that the departing British had turned over to the Arabs. Stone survived the raid unhurt, but five settlers were killed and another had a leg blown off.[101]

By early June, the tide of battle had turned decisively in favor of the Jewish state. Though both sides accepted a UN truce proposal, Israel now had control of the Galilee from Nazareth to the Lebanese border as well as a land corridor connecting Jerusalem to the territory allotted to the Jews under the UN-sponsored November 1947 partition plan. Contrary to the impression in I. F. Stone's dispatches, Israel's defenders were never outnumbered. With about 29,000 soldiers under arms on May 14, the combined forces of the Haganah, Irgun, Stern Gang, and the Palmach were roughly equal to the invading troops from Iraq, Egypt, Lebanon,

---

*In 1936, Wiesl joined with Lev Nussimbaum, a fellow admirer of fascism Italian-style (and, under the pen name Kurban Said, the author of the best-selling novel *Ali and Nino: A Love Story*), to write the polemical tract *Allah Is Great: The Decline and Rise of the Islamic World*.

Syria, and Transjordan (supplemented by a few hundred volunteers from Saudi Arabia, Libya, and Yemen). But with the white paper now a dead letter, Israel was admitting more than 10,000 immigrants a month. Some were exhausted Holocaust survivors, but others, like the "big, blond, six-foot Russian Jew" Stone interviewed days after he disembarked and who had served as a Red Army flamethrower in the battles of Moscow, Leningrad, and Vladivostok, were seasoned combat veterans.

Between immigrants and general mobilization, by early June the Israelis had more than 40,000 troops in the field; six weeks later the total had risen above 60,000.[102] And though Stone's reports constantly underlined the unfairness of the UN arms embargo, which let Britain supply the Arab states with weapons while cutting off military aid to Israel, he didn't mention that the Israelis, unlike their opponents, were able to produce their own armored cars, light machine guns, and land mines.[103] Nor did he report—though it could hardly have escaped his notice—another significant fact about the embargo: that for his own reasons Stalin had decided to ignore it, allowing the Czechs, whose nation was now under his control, to sell Israel heavy machine guns, rifles, and millions of rounds of ammunition. In May 1948, the Czechs also sold the Israeli government several dozen fighter aircraft, bringing Amman and Damascus within range and giving the Jewish state control of the skies. (Until these were delivered, Israel had been forced to send captured German Messerschmitts into the air against Egypt's British-supplied Spitfires.)

As the June 11 cease-fire deadline approached, the battle for Jerusalem itself still raged. The Arabs held the Old City, including the Jewish quarter; the Israelis clung to most of the New City, a larger geographic area that included the wealthy Arab neighborhoods of Katamon and Talbiyeh, the German colony, and most of the larger hotels. But Arab control of Latrun, a strongly built police fort that dominated the Jerusalem–Tel Aviv highway, meant that Jewish forces in the city were completely cut off. Two attempts had been made to dislodge the Arab Legion from the fort. Both ended in failure—and in the highest Israeli casualty figures of the war. Finally Ben Gurion asked David Marcus to take command of the campaign to break the siege. Marcus ordered that a series of goat paths through the hills be paved and turned into a "Burma Road," like the route that allowed the Allies to bring supplies from Burma to China during World War II, to bypass Latrun. Working only at night and constantly exposed to hostile fire, his forces barely completed the road before the truce. To keep food, water, and ammunition flowing into Jerusalem, Marcus also organized a human mule train of volunteers with pack and rifle whose last run was accompanied by I. F. Stone. "Workers came from the factories of Tel Aviv and the docks of Haifa to risk their lives nightly in this grueling march. To stumble and slip across these rocky defiles in the starlight with these men, to see the gray shapes ahead of one bowed under heavy packs like silent ghosts moving forward in a lunar purgatory, was to see a demonstration of determination which filled a Jew with pride headier than the cold mountain air."[104]

"I was the first correspondent to reach Jerusalem after the cease fire," he boasted in *PM*. But his sense of triumph was cut short by an encounter on the way. "At a junction this side of Bab el Wad I passed a Tel Aviv bound jeep carrying the rough wooden casket containing the body of Col. David Marcus." Early on June 11, just a few hours before the truce came into effect, Marcus, unable to sleep, had wrapped himself in a sheet and gone for a walk. On his return, Marcus apparently failed to understand the Hebrew-speaking sentry's demand for the password. Panicking, the guard shot the New Yorker through the heart.[105] The news that an American named "Stone" had been killed caused considerable anxiety for Esther until Ralph Ingersoll, who knew Michael Stone's true identity, telephoned and told her Izzy was unharmed.

At the memorial service for Marcus in Jerusalem, Stone ran into Robert Capa, the Hungarian-Jewish photographer and one of the founders of Magnum, the photographers' cooperative. It was Capa who famously observed, "If your pictures aren't good enough, you aren't close enough." Covering Israel's war for independence brought I. F. Stone closer to Zionism than to any of his life's other causes. At home with the movement's leaders, from Chaim Weizmann and David Ben Gurion to Moshe Sharrett and Goldie Meyerson (later Golda Meir), in a way he'd never been with Franklin Roosevelt, he shared in the young country's hopes and perils, and risked his life to tell the story of Israel's turbulent birth.

In *This Is Israel*, a big, beautifully laid out coffee-table book that combined Stone's reportage with Capa's photographs, the new state is described as a "lusty baby" nearly strangled in the cradle by the "wicked midwives" of the Foreign Office and the State Department. Published in the fall of 1948 to coincide with the first anniversary of the UN vote for partition, *This Is Israel* is an affectionate, intimate portrait. Based on his dispatches for *PM* and the *New Republic*, Stone's text portrays the Jewish David contending with an Arab Goliath. No mention here of Deir Yassin, the Arab village whose inhabitants, almost all of them women, children, and old men, were murdered by Jewish forces just a few weeks before Stone arrived in Israel. (In August 1949, Stone was to describe Deir Yassin as a village "whose Arabs were massacred by Irgunists with Biblical ferocity, a shameful page in the history of the Jewish war of liberation."[106]) Instead we read: "Ill-armed, outnumbered, however desperate their circumstances, the Jews stood fast. The Arabs very early began to run away." Or, later on, "Some 350,000 Palestinian Arabs fled eastward and northward from the Israeli armies, in many cases abandoning homes and fields out of sheer fright without attack."[107]

However incurious* he may have become about the fate of Palestine's Arab population, Stone was still troubled by the extent to which Zionism remained "an auxiliary weapon of imperial expansion." And if, this time, he neglected to reiterate his preference for a binational state, admitting that "Hitler and the crematoriums [made] the Jewish people everywhere Zionist in their sympathies," his sardonic acknowledgment of reality stopped well short of the convert's fervor.[108]

He remained a socialist—indeed, his heroic portrait of Histadrut, the Israeli labor federation that owned factories and ran construction cooperatives, is a vindication of socialist planning in wartime. And he realized that outside of Israel "socialists considered Zionism old-fashioned, almost quaint; with the revolution all would be well with the Jews. They fought anti-Semitism, but they rejected the notion of the Jews as a people, with a right to national aspirations of their own." Maybe they were right. But at the moment, "Events affirmed what liberalism denied."[109]

•

When I. F. Stone returned from Palestine in the summer of 1948, he entered a political landscape so transformed as to be barely recognizable. *PM*, the newspaper that had made him a household name, printed its

---

*To be fair, this was a singularly difficult war to cover from both sides. "You fell into a category," wrote Kenneth Bilby, the *Herald Tribune* correspondent, "Arab or Jewish, soon after arrival and it became immutable."

last issue on June 22.* Ralph Ingersoll had resigned in 1946 after an exasperated Marshall Field, tired of *PM*'s losses, reversed the paper's no-ads policy. Now Field himself bailed out, practically giving the paper to Bartley Crum and Joseph Barnes, a foreign correspondent for the *New York Herald Tribune*. Crum, a pro-FDR Republican, was a lawyer for some of the Hollywood Ten, a group of writers and directors, all current or former Communists, who, when summoned before HUAC in 1947, had refused to cooperate on First Amendment grounds. The new paper, published from the same building at the corner of Duane and Hudson streets, with a substantially identical staff to *PM*, was called the *New York Star*.

"I had known Crum through some Communist connections," Stone told Andrew Patner. Crum and his wife, Gertrude "Cutsie" Bosworth, had given many parties at their San Francisco home during the United Nations conference where Izzy's fellow guests often included Harry Bridges, the screenwriter Dalton Trumbo (a member of the Hollywood Ten), the actor and singer Paul Robeson—and Adlai Stevenson, a young diplomat who served as press secretary at the conference.[110]

But it was Palestine, not politics, that cemented Stone and Crum's mutual regard. A member of the Anglo-American Committee on Palestine and part author of the report, prepared at the request of both governments, that prompted President Truman to urge the British to admit 100,000 Jewish refugees to Palestine without delay, Crum was an influential voice among supporters of the Jewish cause. It wasn't just his position as editor of the *Star* that made Crum the obvious choice to write the foreword to *This Is Israel*.

Crum was also a prominent backer of Henry Wallace's third-party candidacy for the presidency in 1948. Despite all his reservations, so was I. F. Stone: "In thirty minutes, cross-legged, saying 'Oom' with alternate exhalations, I can conjure up a better third-party movement than Wallace's . . . Yet with only seventy shopping days left until elections, I find I'm still for Henry Wallace."[111]

About Wallace's electoral vehicle Stone had his doubts:

---

*Only a few months earlier, at a State Department press conference, a correspondent from one of the big New York papers was persistent in his questioning. There came a stage whisper from the rear: "Who does that fellow think he is? The rich man's Izzy Stone?"

I yield to no man in the variety and number of my objections to Henry Wallace's Progressive Party. I don't like yogis and I don't like commissars. I condemn the way Stalin combs his hair and I disapprove the way Molotov blows his nose. I can't help cheering for Tito, and when socialism comes I'll fight for the right to spit in the nearest bureaucrat's eye. I own a house in Washington and I don't want proletarians trampling my petunias on their way downtown to overthrow the government by force and violence. I wouldn't want my sister to marry a Communist, and force me to maldigest my Sunday morning bagel arguing dialectics with a sectarian brother-in-law.[112]

But he admired the former vice president enormously and considered him "the heir to Roosevelt, a giant in the pygmy world of the Left."[113] He also hoped that a significant vote for Wallace might restrain the rush to military confrontation with the Soviet Union. He recognized, however, that with the Red Army blockading West Berlin, and with Stalin having unleashed "an old-fashioned Russian orgy of suspicion of foreigners, intellectuals, and any kind of dissent" inside the Soviet Union, there was scant hope of any immediate thaw in U.S.-Soviet relations.[114] Nor was Stone an admirer of the American Communists who "are doing the major part of the work of the Wallace movement, from ringing doorbells to framing platforms."

"I know that I'm a dupe," he admitted, "and ought to have my ideological tires checked at the nearest FBI service station. I know that if the Communists came to power I'd soon find myself eating cold *kasha* in a concentration camp in Kansas *gubernya*." It was not the Progressive Party candidate's dubious allies who prompted Stone to rally to his standard, but "Wallace's opponents [who] supply the best sales talks in his favor."[115] For Stone the 1948 election offered more than just a choice of delusions, though there were plenty of delusions to go around. What the election really offered Izzy was a choice of enemies.

Stone had had his differences with Henry Wallace, most recently over the Marshall Plan, which Stone had hailed as "a program in which every thoughtful American may take pride." The former vice president had expressed reservations. These arose, according to Stone, not from Wallace's own principles but rather from "the attitude of the Communist Party . . . The Communist position is to fight the Marshall Plan, period; to condemn it in advance, and to decide no good can come of it." Izzy argued that the plan deserved "the fullest support of all progressive elements," and was deeply disappointed by Wallace's failure to provide leadership. And he was scathing about American Communists' "attempts to read the mind of Moscow and to achieve a kind of theological consistency in their international movement."[116] But nothing he'd seen in the past decade had caused him to waver in his conviction that the real threat to American freedoms came from the right.

"Washington under Truman is a capital of confusion, incompetence, and reaction," Stone had told *Nation* readers during a brief return to the magazine's pages in late 1947.[117] Six months later, the outlook was darker still: "I cannot for the life of me, hard as I have tried, see what difference it makes at this stage whether the Democrats win or the Republicans."[118]

True, it had been a Republican Congress that passed the Taft-Hartley Act in June 1947, forcing labor union officials to take a non-Communist oath or lose the protection of the NLRB. (Garry Van Arkel, coeditor of the *Progress* and Izzy's oldest friend, resigned as NLRB general counsel in protest and helped to draft Truman's veto message.)[119] But Democratic votes had helped to override the president's veto, just as Democrats had controlled many of the thirty state legislatures that in 1947 passed their own laws restricting the rights of organized labor.[120] Even when Truman meant well, he was too weak to make a difference. And though the Republicans certainly tried to make anticommunism their issue, the impetus behind the Federal Loyalty Security Program came from the man whose signature gave Executive Order 9835 the force of law: Harry S. Truman.

The choices facing anyone who still believed in the values of the New Deal in the fall of 1948 were neither simple nor attractive. On one side were the "liberals"—many of them men and women Stone had worked with in the past, some of them people whose integrity and commitment he admired and whose good opinion he valued highly. When the anti-Communist Union for Democratic Action reformed itself as the Americans for Democratic Action, Izzy's former source, the lawyer Joseph Rauh, and his old sparring partner Leon Henderson were among those who joined Reinhold Niebuhr, John Kenneth Galbraith, Walter Reuther, and Eleanor Roosevelt in the new organization. On the other side were the "progressives"—including old friends like Clifford and Virginia Durr, the sculptor Jo Davidson, the actor Zero Mostel, the attorney Robert

Kenny (cocounsel with Bartley Crum for the Hollywood Ten), Lillian Hellman, and FDR's sons James and Elliott. Behind the Progressive Party stood the Communists, who, as Izzy noted publicly, supplied the organizational muscle and did their best to manipulate the party's platform. Behind the liberals stood a less occult but in Stone's view no less sinister alliance of Northern machine politicians, Southern bigots, and the kind of Chamber of Commerce patriots who viewed the New Deal itself as Communist-inspired and for whom Taft-Hartley and the Truman loyalty program were just a beginning.

The liberals barred Communists from their ranks; progressives, who refused as a matter of principle to impose such a ban, risked becoming "dupes," but Izzy evidently thought the risk worth running. After all, the other side endorsed Truman's intervention in Greece, and though they might express alarm at J. Edgar Hoover's methods, they shared his premise that America's hapless Communists were a menace and so could hardly dissent from his aims. Perhaps most important was the relative freedom Izzy's identification with the progressive cause offered him. Former radicals found that "loyalty" was provisional, needing to be affirmed and reaffirmed. The liberal posture, which demanded both pious nods to the right and anxious glances over the left shoulder, was not exactly conducive to forward progress.

As if to make sure his comrades knew just what kind of dupe they were getting, Izzy threw himself into the cause of James Kutcher, a $42-a-week clerk in the Veterans Administration in Newark, New Jersey. Kutcher, who had lost both legs to a German shell in the battle of San Pietro in 1943, was fired under the Loyalty Program for his membership in the Socialist Workers Party. Izzy pointed out that as a Trotskyist, Kutcher was unlikely "to steal the atom bomb and ship it to the Kremlin, except perhaps with mechanism attached to make it go off when Stalin turned the spigot on the office samovar."[121] Whether it was Stone's unforgivable lèse-majesté or his willingness to serve on the Kutcher Defense Committee with such unorthodox characters as A. J. Muste, Max Shachtman, C. Wright Mills, and Norman Mailer (whose first novel, *The Naked and the Dead*, had just been published), the West Coast party organ *Daily People's World* was predictably offended: "What is being touted as the 'case of the legless vet' and a 'test case' for civil liberties hasn't the remotest connection with the defense of civil rights."[122]

At another time the party's crass contortions might have been funny. But in the summer of 1948 the federal government indicted twelve leaders of the CPUSA under the Smith Act, which made it a crime "to knowingly or willfully advocate, abet, advise, or teach the duty, necessity, desirability, or propriety of overthrowing or destroying any government in the United States by force or violence." As Izzy had predicted years earlier, the burlesque farce of the "G-String Conspiracy" was now deadly serious. "The fundamental question," he warned of the prosecution unfolding in Judge Harold Medina's Manhattan courtroom, "is the effect of this trial not on the Communist Party but on freedom in America. If a guilty verdict is returned and stands on appeal, the Communist Party will have been made illegal. Then, as it dissolves or goes underground, the real terror will begin."[123]

For liberals, the 1948 election offered a chance to prove their anti-Communist bona fides by attacking Wallace and the Progressives. The goal may have been to dissociate the New Deal—and, not so incidentally, their own careers—from the taint of the Popular Front, but the effect was to lend aid, comfort, and moral authority to the inquisitors. Arthur Schlesinger Jr., for example, opposed the Smith Act—for being insufficiently direct. "The government," he argued, "should name the Communist Party as a criminal conspiracy, serving notice that all who remain associated with it would be subject to prosecution as co-conspirators." As for fellow travelers like Izzy, "they are the Typhoid Marys of the left, bearing the germs of infection even if not obviously suffering from the disease."[124]

The republic fought off the infection. Wallace polled just over 1,150,000 votes, but unlike Strom Thurmond, the South Carolina segregationist who led the Dixiecrat revolt and won thirty-nine electoral votes in four Southern states, the Progressive candidate didn't carry a single state. For I. F. Stone, Truman's victory was part of a long season of mourning that had begun in August 1947 with the death of his father, who succumbed to pneumonia. The following May, the body of George Polk, Izzy's friend from Cairo, had been found floating in the waters of Salonika Bay bound hand and foot and with a bullet hole in his head. And in August 1948, Harry Dexter White had suffered a fatal heart attack two days after appearing before HUAC to defend himself against accusations of spying for the Soviets.[125]

Izzy carried on, backing Simon Gerson, a reporter for the *Daily*

Worker, in his futile campaign to succeed Peter Cacchione, a Communist elected by the voters of Brooklyn to the New York City Council, who had died in November 1946. Gerson lost, too.[126] The Washington Cooperative Bookshop, an early addition to the attorney general's list of subversive organizations (making membership alone sufficient to render a federal employee's loyalty suspect), held a reception for Izzy and Esther to mark the publication of *This Is Israel*. One hundred guests attended, according to the FBI, which had an informant among them.[127]

Seven

THE GREAT FREEZE

———◦•◦———

The following rules are to be observed in order that we may hold the opinions that we should hold in the Church militant:

(1) We should put away completely our own opinion and keep our mind ready and eager to give our entire obedience to our holy Mother the hierarchical Church . . .

(13) To arrive at complete certainty, this is the attitude of mind that we should maintain: I will believe that the white object I see is black if that should be the decision of the hierarchical Church.

—Ignatius of Loyola, *The Spiritual Exercises*

When I. F. Stone arrived at the Connecticut Avenue studio of radio station WQQW in early January 1949, the telephone was ringing. "Izzy walked in," recalled Mairi Foreman, host of the Washington, D.C., station's morning interview program, "and the first thing he did was shout, 'Have you got any coffee?' He didn't seem to notice [the phone]. I picked up and it was Esther. 'Is Izzy there?' 'Yes he is. Do you want to speak with him?'" Esther told Foreman there was no point in her speaking to Izzy as he'd left the house without either his glasses or his hearing aid. "He won't be able to do anything!" Esther shrieked, her Minnie Mouse voice even higher than usual.

The Stones and the Foremans were old friends. Mairi had been women's editor of the *Toronto Star*. Her husband, Clark, a grandson of the publisher of the *Atlanta Constitution*, had joined the New Deal as FDR's special adviser on the economic status of negroes* and had also been head of the Power Division of the Public Works Administration and an assistant secretary of the interior under Harold Ickes. In 1938, along with a group of black and white activists including Mary McLeod Bethune, Eleanor Roosevelt, the Durrs, Frank Graham of the University of North Carolina, and Myles Horton, Clark Foreman helped to found the Southern Conference for Human Welfare, serving as the group's president from 1946 to 1948. More recently he had been national treasurer of the Progressive Party. Both Foremans were regulars at Virginia Durr's Sunday afternoon "teas."[1]

"Since I couldn't interview Izzy—he couldn't hear a word I said—I just turned the microphone over to him. For the next ten minutes he spoke nonstop, denouncing 'this lousy government,' the Smith Act prosecutions—I was sure we were going to get cut off. I was a nervous wreck."[2]

She needn't have worried. A star of the Progressive Party's rubber-chicken circuit of benefit dinners—only a few weeks earlier Izzy had joined Lillian Hellman, Jo Davidson, and Clifford Durr as speakers at a dinner honoring Henry Wallace—Izzy had become, thanks to his reports from Israel in the Nation and PM, a popular attraction on the kosher chicken circuit as well. Nor had his deafness prevented him from becoming a polished performer on Meet the Press. An exchange between Izzy and Senator Henry Cabot Lodge Jr. illustrates what that show's producer, Martha Rountree, meant when she said the newspaperman was "a good needler." The Massachusetts Republican had been asked whether he favored recognizing Franco's Spain:

> STONE: . . . what is your opinion as an American citizen?
>
> LODGE: My opinion as an American citizen and a U.S. Senator is—and I can't forget that I am a citizen and a Senator—is that we should not do anything unilaterally about Spain.
>
> STONE: I think you're ducking the question.
>
> LODGE: No, I'm not ducking the question. You asked me what I think we should do, and I've told you I think . . .

---

*Foreman took the post on condition that he be allowed to recruit a black assistant and then "work myself out of a job." His assistant, the Harvard-trained economist Robert Weaver, went on to become the secretary of Housing and Urban Development in Lyndon Johnson's administration—the first African American to hold a cabinet post.

STONE: And you haven't answered.

LODGE: Well, I'm going to—that's all the answer I'm going to give you, Doc!

Despite the appearance of mutual exasperation, Izzy's encounter with Lodge had been cordial enough—perhaps because the patrician senator had begun by describing himself as "a liberal" in favor of civil rights and even federal housing for the poor.[3] But not all of Izzy's radio targets were so amicable. In November 1949, he asked Congressman Walter Judd, a former missionary to China, if "Chiang Kai-Shek and his gang of crooks" hadn't made the Communist victory inevitable (Mao Tse-tung had proclaimed the People's Republic of China on October 1). "That's the line that's always been taken all these years by people of your persuasion," Judd replied.[4]

Chinese politics, specifically Kuomintang corruption, was also the spark that set off Izzy's most explosive appearance on *Meet the Press*. The guest on August 15, 1949, was Patrick Hurley, whose resignation as ambassador to China in 1945 had so annoyed Truman—and who had his own history with Izzy. Five years earlier, he had described Hurley in the *Nation* as "an 'oil general' . . . Still Harry Sinclair's lawyer and Washington Man Friday, Hurley operates in full military panoply out of his corporation law office in Washington, with his press agent commissioned a major. He is one of those who think Arabian oil too important to be left 'at the mercy of a local conflict,' the implication being that the conflict must be ended by liquidating the effort to build a Jewish home in Palestine."[5]

Hurley was testy even before Izzy started pressing him, quarreling with Marquis Childs, a columnist for the *St. Louis Post-Dispatch*. But when Izzy intervened, accusing Hurley of "making a long speech instead of answering [his] question," the general snapped; "You people went to Yalta and surrendered every one of those principles." When Izzy tried to say that he'd never been anywhere near Yalta, Hurley fixed him with a baleful glare: "You are noted. You are not for the United States. You've been for Russia all along. Don't kid an old kidder."

This was merely the preliminary bout. Izzy didn't retreat or feign outrage. Instead, he kept the heat on Hurley's evasions: "Why don't you answer a few questions instead of reading the Atlantic Charter at us?"

"Why don't you put your old party line on—and it's red," Hurley replied.

Perhaps in an attempt to restore some coherence, the newspaperman, still on the attack, shifted ground to the Kuomintang. "We've spent three billion dollars on the KMT . . . Did you ever see a bigger bunch of crooks than those guys?"

"Quit following the red line with me," returned Hurley. "You asked me if I—"

"I was asking you if you ever met a bigger bunch of crooks," Stone persisted. "You're an oil man. Did you ever see a bigger bunch of crooks— even in the oil fields of Texas or Oklahoma?"

"You go back to Jerusalem and I'll go back to the oil fields. If you don't want to fight then don't start with me, young man."[6]

This was too much even for *Variety*, whose arbiters of outrage found Hurley's remarks "not only off-base but entirely uncalled for."[7] The *Herald Tribune* agreed: "One of the great attractions of 'Meet the Press' is the liveliness and frequent acerbity of the discussions. But there are limits and Mr. Hurley went quite a distance beyond those limits." Any *Trib* reader curious about the target of this attack was left to wonder, however, as the critic John Crosby managed to report the incident without ever mentioning I. F. Stone.[8]

Meet the Press courted controversy. A year earlier, the *Time* editor Whittaker Chambers had appeared on the program and charged that "Alger Hiss was a Communist and may be one now"—the first time he made this claim outside the protection of congressional privilege, prompting Hiss to sue him for libel. (It was in response to this suit that Chambers produced the "Pumpkin Papers"*—evidence, according to Chambers, that Hiss had not only been a member of the Communist Party but also committed espionage.) The penitent "Spy Queen" Elizabeth Bentley was the program's first female guest. But the Stone-Hurley "slugfest," as the showbiz bible called it, attracted an unusual amount of attention for one very simple reason: It happened live, on television.

Though it was to become the longest-running show in television history, at the time *Meet the Press* had been seen for less than two years (the radio version had been on since 1945) when Izzy made his television debut on it in June 1949; the guest was Hans Freistadt, a young Commu-

*So called because the papers, a mix of State and Navy Department documents, were stored on five rolls of film that Chambers had kept hidden inside a hollowed-out pumpkin on his Maryland farm.

nist from the University of North Carolina whose insistence on the sanctity of dissent inside the Soviet Union Izzy greeted skeptically. Broadcast
live from WNBT in New York, the show went out over the NBC network—at the time barely a handful of stations—reaching nearly 900,000
homes.[9] This was a tiny audience even by the standards of early television, but compared to Izzy's heyday at *PM*, an appearance on *Meet the
Press* extended his reach by a whole order of magnitude; the radio audience was larger still. In 1949, his peak year as a panelist, Izzy was on eight
broadcasts (four each on radio and television)—all at a time when his
print readership was shrinking dramatically.

Back in 1946, when Izzy was first on the radio version of *Meet the
Press*, the guest was Sava Kosanovich, Yugoslavia's ambassador to the
United States. Izzy was an obvious choice as a panelist on a program
where "the left, the right, and the middle of the road are all invited to appear and answer questions." By November 1949, when Izzy and Ambassador Kosanovich sat down again, this time in front of the television
cameras, a great deal had changed. In 1946, Izzy's fellow panelists had
tried to paint Kosanovich as Stalin's lackey. But the television session took
place in the aftermath of Tito's refusal to accept direction from Moscow
and Stalin's decision to expel Yugoslavia from the Cominform (the cos-
metically renamed successor to the Comintern);* this time Izzy, who took
the same respectful approach to Kosanovich as he had in 1946, became a
target of the *Daily Worker*'s wrath.

When Izzy appeared on either the television or radio version in 1949,
he was described as "formerly of *PM* and the *Nation*, now of New York's
newest daily, the *Compass*." The *Star*, which took over from *PM* in the
summer of 1948, hadn't lasted long enough even to get a mention on
Meet the Press, closing its doors after just seven months. The corpse got
mixed reviews. "I liked *PM* much better than the *Star*," Izzy wrote. "The
trouble with *PM* was that the men running it lost their nerve in the cold
war. The trouble with the *Star* was that it never had any nerve to start
with. The men who ran the *Star* wanted respectability above all else and
subordinated their own radical views to this."[10] A. J. Liebling, the *New
Yorker*'s press critic, was kinder—partly, it seems, because he didn't think

---

*On November 28, 1948, the Cominform decreed that "the transformation of Yugoslavia from the
phase of bourgeois nationalism into fascism and direct betrayal of national interests is complete."

so highly of its predecessor: "A girl to whom I gave a subscription to *PM* in 1946 asked me after a time, 'Doesn't *anybody* have any trouble except the Jews and the colored people?' . . . I think the *Star* was making progress towards a successful changeover, although the process resembled changing clothes underwater." Liebling pointed out that the *Star* was the only New York daily to endorse Truman; he also credited the paper with bringing down the price of milk in New York City, and with a more lasting contribution to American life made by "a young *Star* cartoonist named Walt Kelly."[11] Kelly, the paper's art director and chief political cartoonist, launched *Pogo*, his chronicle of life along the Okefenokee, three months before the *Star*'s final edition.

Izzy had been writing three columns a week for the *Star*. When Joe Barnes called at the end of January 1949 to let him know the paper was closing, he told Esther, "Now I'll really get a chance to write that book," and went upstairs to take a bath. Izzy came down from his ablutions to find Ted Thackrey on the phone asking if he would join Albert Deutsch, his former *PM* stablemate, as a six-day-a-week columnist for the *New York Post*.[12] A veteran newsman who had edited papers in Cleveland and Shanghai, Thackrey had joined the *Post* in 1936 and was appointed executive editor by Dorothy Schiff in 1939 when she and her second husband, George Backer, bought the paper from David Stern. In 1943, Thackrey became Schiff's third husband and the *Post*'s editor in chief, returning the paper to the tabloid format it still retains. By 1949, Thackrey and Schiff's marriage was under strain. (Doubtless there were deeper rifts, but throughout the 1948 presidential campaign Thackrey's editorial page supported Henry Wallace—except for a column written by his wife and publisher, who campaigned for the Republican candidate, Thomas Dewey.)

Izzy's return was heavily promoted by the *Post*, which described him as "A Courageous, Crusading Newspaper Man" credited with a number of scoops but "best known for his more recent stories on Palestine." Still, perhaps sensing the precariousness of his new perch, Izzy put out feelers to Freda Kirchwey about returning to the *Nation*. He also tested the waters at the *New Republic*, recently moved to Washington by its owner and editor, Michael Straight, who was happy to commission specific articles but never offered Stone a job.[13]

Though his schedule at the *Post* left him little time for fresh exposés, Izzy managed to make waves. Opening arguments in the 1949 Smith Act trial of American Communists had barely begun when Izzy wrote irreverently, "I wish the defense of the 12 could be conducted with less noise and more sense. The government is making a martyr of the Communist leaders; their lawyers are making a martyr of the judge." The *Daily Worker* cried foul, but Izzy's position was clear enough: unflagging defense of the rights of Communists but no indulgence toward the party's self-inflicted idiocies. To individual Communists he was often quite friendly, happily accepting an invitation from the *Daily Worker* Washington bureau chief, Rob Hall (an old Alabama friend of the Durrs), to a lunch for *DW*'s foreign editor, Joseph Starobin, in February 1949, an occasion when more prudent colleagues found their social schedules unaccountably full.[14] But his sympathy stopped well short of genuflecting before "the brave working class advocates spitting manfully in the eye of the capitalist judge as they are dragged off to the counter-revolutionary gallows screaming defiance on their way." Izzy's mockery drew a swift (and predictable) response: "Working people," the *Daily Worker* warned, "have long since learned not to follow Mr. Stone's faith in the objectivity of class courts and class justice in capitalist countries."[15]

Union Square was even more agitated by Izzy's defense of Anna Louise Strong, an American journalist who had written sympathetically about the Chinese Communists and reported the Red Army's progress through Poland in 1945, but who in February 1949 had been expelled from the Soviet Union accused of being an American spy. Comparing her with Agnes Smedley, another publicist for the Chinese revolutionaries who found herself fending off charges of spying by both the Russians and the U.S. army, Izzy warned that communism's compulsion to devour even its friendliest critics would leave it in the hands of "the sycophant, the lickspittle, the yes-man, the apple-polisher, the guy who plays safe."[16] (Smedley herself phoned Izzy in a panic in February 1949. General Charles Willoughby, MacArthur's chief of intelligence, had just accused her of having been a Soviet spy, which may have been true—spying against Japan and Germany during the war. But ten days later the army was forced to issue a public apology. Smedley fled to England shortly afterward.)[17]

None of this prevented the writer Dwight Macdonald from including Stone on his list of "Stalinoid" dupes for agreeing to speak at the Cultural and Scientific Conference for World Peace held at the Waldorf-Astoria hotel at the end of March 1949. Hosted by the National Council of the Arts, Sciences, and Professions, an offshoot of the Progressive Party, the Waldorf Conference was indeed, as *Life* magazine breathlessly reported, "dominated by intellectuals who fellow-travel the Communist line."[18] Though Macdonald and Sidney Hook, who had been refused a slot in the conference program, organized an anti-Communist counterconference, Macdonald was also a delegate at the Waldorf meeting, where he found that "the American leaders of the Conference took a very cautious, critical-of-both-sides line." This left Macdonald in an awkward position. He wrote:

> I got quite a different impression of the Stalinoids talking to them face to face. It was possible to communicate, since we had a common cultural and even (oddly enough) political background: that is, we read the same books, went to the same art shows and foreign films, shared the same convictions in favor of the (American) underdog—the Negroes, the Jews, the economically underprivileged—and against such institutions as the Catholic hierarchy and the U.S. State Department. In contrast, I felt very little in common with the pickets who demonstrated against the Conference, who booed me as roundly as any other delegate (since their hatred was directed against all alien-appearing intellectuals) and who marched under the (to me repulsive) banners of religion and patriotism.[19]

The next few years posed hard choices for American intellectuals. Though the New Deal's promise of social justice remained unredeemed, and the advent of the atomic age lent a new urgency to the search for coexistence, many intellectuals simply stopped marching altogether. Some found peace in the church or made their own peace with the state. An ever-dwindling band followed the Communist Party. Urged to "watch your step," most discovered a new quietism. "There is only one sure way to avoid guilt by association and that is to avoid association," wrote Stone, who kept to his own course. Within days of the Waldorf Conference, Izzy spoke at a "Keep Spain out of the U.N." meeting organized by the Joint Anti-Fascist Refugee Committee, another group on the attorney general's list. Unbuttoning his shirt as he spoke, Izzy told the audience that when a friend had recently asked him if he was a liberal, he replied that he was

not. "I'm one of them damned Reds—and I've got my red woolen underwear on to prove it!" he shouted. The crowd roared with laughter. The
FBI men took down every word.[20]

•

The guest on the May 25, 1949, broadcast of *Meet the Press* was Ted
Thackrey, now editor of New York's newest paper, the *Daily Compass*.
Murray Davis, a reporter for the *New York World-Telegram*, kicked off the
questioning: "Mr. Thackrey, are you a Communist?"

Ted Thackrey was not and had never been a Communist. Until recently, he had been the editor of the *New York Post*. But when, shortly
after Truman's inaugural, Dorothy Schiff issued a memorandum citing
"irreconcilable differences on fundamental questions of policy" and appointed the thirty-three-year-old James Wechsler to the *Post* editor's chair,
Thackrey became an ex-husband as well as a former editor.[21] He was not
without resources, however, and on May 15 the first issue of the *Daily
Compass* rolled off the presses. To *PM*-starved New Yorkers, the *Compass*
was déjà vu all over again: The plant, premises, furniture, and fixtures of
the new paper had been scavenged from the *Star*, and so had most of the
staff. As for financial backing, Henry Wallace had arranged an introduction to Anita McCormick Blaine, heiress to the International Harvester
fortune. "In the company of Mr. Wallace, I called on Mrs. Blaine in
Chicago," Thackrey recalled. "After listening to my plans and looking at
my budget, she excused herself for half an hour of private vigil."[22]

Blaine's prayers may have been answered, but Thackrey's shoestring
financing made Ralph Ingersoll look extravagant. Indeed, if Thackrey had
managed to retain all of *PM*'s core 150,000 readers, the *Compass* would
have been profitable. But it still wouldn't have been much of a newspaper. Reporting the news costs money; investigating the stories behind
the news costs even more. From an opening week high of about 60,000
readers, the *Compass* bled circulation, settling all too soon at a stubborn
(and fatally unprofitable) 30,000–35,000. At that level even the Associated Press subscription—in Thackrey's words, "our single greatest news
asset"—had to be dropped.[23]

What the *Compass* did have was I. F. Stone. Columnist, capital dope-
tipster, editorial writer, crusading reporter, Supreme Court spoofer, for-

eign correspondent—during his first few months at the *Compass,* Izzy did everything but run the presses. "There was always tension in the house," Izzy's son Christopher recalled. "He worked six days a week trying to get the right story for page one. He was trying to write columns and do a lot of stuff on the side."[24] Soon there would be even more "stuff on the side."

In October 1949, the jury at Foley Square found the leadership of the American Communist Party guilty of violating the Smith Act by forming a conspiracy to "teach the principles of Marxism-Leninism" and advocacy of "overthrowing and destroying the government of the United States by force and violence." Not only were all eleven defendants sentenced to prison but every one of their six attorneys* was also cited for contempt of court and given a prison sentence.

With the Communist Party now effectively an illegal organization, the drumbeat of congressional investigations, which had been gathering force since the end of the war, reached a crescendo. The Nevada Democrat Patrick McCarran, powerful chair of the Senate Judiciary Committee, held hearings on Communist influence at the United Nations.[25] Within a year, McCarran no longer felt bound by even the tenuous chain of logic connecting the UN to the American judiciary; instead, he engineered his own legal charter, the Internal Security Act (usually known as the McCarran Act), and his own vehicle, the Senate Internal Security Subcommittee (known at first as the McCarran committee). The Senate Appropriations Committee delved into Communist influence on the radio. The House Committee on Un-American Activities took a break from its investigation of leftist infiltration in Hollywood to hear public testimony from Elizabeth Bentley and Whittaker Chambers; its chairman, J. Parnell Thomas, focused his attention on America's scientists. In September 1949, the committee had finally identified the hidden hub of subversion in the nation's capital: "Key Reds in Capital Reported in Hiding" was the Associated Press headline of a report that "key Communists in Washington have gone underground and are trying to infiltrate the government." Their home base: the Washington Cooperative Bookshop.[26] Izzy's response came in yet another talk at the bookshop. "I joined the bookstore tonight and have my card here to show for it," he told a gathering held to protest the Smith Act verdict. Once again, the FBI faithfully transcribed his remarks.

---

*One of the six, Abraham Isserman, had represented Izzy in his salary dispute with David Stern.

To readers of the *Compass*, Izzy's insouciance was at least as important as his analysis. New York City schoolteachers, unionized federal employees, CIO electricians—all were feeling the chill of an American inquisition. Stone's response was conditioned by his own history as a favored target of congressional red-baiters dating back to his 1943 tiff with Cordell Hull. He knew, both from his own reporting and from personal experience, that J. Edgar Hoover's animus against the New Deal and New Dealers long antedated the FBI's interest in espionage or subversion. In other words, Stone knew his enemies. He also knew that ridicule, not righteousness, was the deadliest weapon in his own arsenal.

At a Deadline for Freedom rally in April 1950 on behalf of the Hollywood Ten and the board members of the Joint Anti-Fascist Refugee Committee, who had also been convicted of contempt of Congress, Izzy's speech followed appearances by Paul Robeson, the film director Adrian Scott, and his fellow Hollywood Ten defendant the screenwriter John Howard Lawson. Bounding onto the stage accompanied by a midget hauling a huge red card, Izzy announced, "This is one of those card-carrying Communists I picked up at the State Department." The audience exploded with glee. When Izzy spoke at a similar rally a few days later, the inevitable FBI informant was scandalized: "His total disrespect for people on the national scene is remarkable."[27]

And genuine. In Stone's view, the New Dealers had been shouldered aside by "big-bellied good-natured guys who knew a lot of dirty jokes, spent as little time in their offices as possible [and] saw Washington as a chance to make useful 'contacts' . . . They were just trying to get along. The Truman era was the era of the moocher. The place was full of Wimpys who could be had for a hamburger."[28] Yet for all his contempt, Stone never hated Harry Truman. Genuine hatred was reserved for one man in Washington—J. Edgar Hoover—along with a fear that, though Izzy was careful never to let it show, ran through him like an electric current. Because Izzy knew what Hoover could do.

Hoover had destroyed the government careers of Izzy's friends Edward Condon and James Newman. "Dear George," Hoover wrote to George Allen, a Truman crony made director of the Reconstruction Finance Corporation (an appointment Izzy had opposed), "I thought the President and you would be interested in the following information with respect to certain high Government officials operating an alleged espionage network . . . on behalf of the Soviet Government." Hoover then listed the members of this "ring" aimed at "atomic energy"—including Henry Wallace; Under Secretary of State Dean Acheson; former assistant secretary of war John McCloy; Alger Hiss; Newman, who headed the Office of War Mobilization and Reconversion; and Condon, director of the National Bureau of Standards.[29]

Hoover was careful to cover his tracks, and this 1946 letter laying the kindling for a witch hunt sat undisturbed for decades in the Truman Library until Senator Daniel Patrick Moynihan's Commission on Protecting and Reducing Government Secrecy unearthed it in the mid-1990s.[30] But when, in March 1948, the HUAC chairman, Parnell Thomas, branded Condon "one of the weakest links in our atomic security," Izzy recognized the FBI director's hand. In the summer of 1949, the *Compass* published a series by Stone defending Edward Condon and attacking Hoover and the FBI for leaking unsubstantiated gossip and innuendo to the physicist's congressional tormentors. Though President Truman himself came to Condon's defense, the leaks and attacks continued through four different loyalty boards stretching over the next six years. The campaign against Condon was, in part, a reprisal for his forceful advocacy of the McMahon Act, which mandated civilian control of atomic energy. Thomas, who wanted the military to retain control, was a bitter opponent of the act.[31] The same tendency to turn policy disputes into loyalty investigations also drove Condon and Stone's mutual friend James Newman, who'd helped draft the McMahon Act, out of public service altogether. He had been Truman's science adviser and special counsel to the Senate subcommittee on atomic energy. Though described in Hoover's letter to Allen as "the ringleader of this alleged espionage network," Newman was never publicly scourged—possibly because he'd left government for journalism, and Hoover, bully that he was, feared negative publicity.*

Still, the relentless barrage of revelation, accusation, and guilt by association was as demoralizing as Hoover intended. Izzy couldn't have known the evidence against his friends—a peculiarity of the loyalty hearings was that the accused had no right to confront their accusers or to see the evidence against them—but he knew that what put men like Condon

---

*In 1946, Newman became an editor at the *New Republic*. His four-volume *The World of Mathematics*, first published in 1956, sold more than 150,000 copies. A few years later, Newman wrote the introduction to his friend Izzy's collection *The Haunted Fifties*. He died in 1966.

in jeopardy were not only their left-of-center views but also their left-of-center associations. (In Condon and Newman's case it was their friendship with Nathan Gregory Silvermaster, Izzy's old source from the Associated Farmers investigation and a man whose Communist sympathies had been an open secret since his student days.[32]) Izzy also knew that not all of the victims of the new inquisition were innocent.

At the same time Izzy rushed to defend Condon, he also wrote about another government employee accused not just of disloyalty but of actual espionage. Judith Coplon, who worked at the Foreign Agents Registration section of the Justice Department, had been arrested that March after a rendezvous with Valentin Gubitchev, a Russian who worked at the UN. The FBI found secret files in Coplon's purse, and she was convicted in two trials, one in Washington and one in New York.

When Coplon was first arrested, she had not actually passed any documents to Gubitchev, which made espionage impossible to prove. Instead, she was charged in Washington with illegal possession of government documents, but during her first trial it emerged that the FBI, in its haste to arrest her, had neglected to obtain a warrant. She was then charged in New York with attempting to pass the documents to an unauthorized person. During this second trial she fired her original counsel and hired Leonard Boudin. Her conviction in the second case was overturned on appeal after Boudin learned that the FBI had illegally wiretapped conversations between Coplon and her original counsel and exposed this government misconduct in open court.[33] Izzy began to comment on the Coplon case and Hoover's "vice-squad methods" only when his brother-in-law entered the scene, and he was naturally pleased by Leonard's triumph, particularly as it caused the FBI director enormous embarrassment. But his *Compass* columns on the case make no pretense of Coplon's innocence. Echoing the appeals judge Learned Hand's conclusion that Coplon's "guilt is plain," Izzy told his readers she had indeed been involved "in some kind of undercover activity inconsistent with her duties."[34]

Just as significant was Izzy's silence on a case that, from the steamy August afternoon when Whittaker Chambers first stood and took his oath to tell the truth, became a national obsession. I. F. Stone didn't like Whittaker Chambers. "No martyrdom was ever more lavishly buttered," he wrote of *Witness*, the *Time* editor's Manichaean memoir. Izzy was particularly revolted by the spy turned informer's public piety: "This man so suffocatingly ostentatious in his new-found Christianity is the kind of martyr familiar in its early annals—the kind who threw others to the lions and retired to a villa."[35]

But Izzy was not convinced by the defendant, Alger Hiss, either. He'd known Hiss for years—the attorney was yet another Frankfurter protégé like Tommy Corcoran and had been part of a group that included Lee Pressman and Gardner Jackson who had walked out of the Department of Agriculture in 1935 to protest Henry Wallace's refusal to prevent Southern farmers from throwing sharecroppers off their land. Another colleague at Agriculture, Nathaniel Weyl, who worked with Izzy at the *Post* in the 1930s, may well have told him privately what he later told the McCarran committee: that he, Hiss, and Pressman had all been part of the same Communist Party unit led by Harold Ware.[36] After Hiss was released from prison in 1954, he and Izzy became friends of sorts, though decades later Izzy said he'd originally thought of Hiss as a "climber and a snob."[37] Whatever his personal feelings, it seems likely that his total public silence on the question of Hiss's guilt or innocence, during the many months of Hiss's libel suit against Chambers, his indictment for perjury before a federal grand jury in New York, through the perjury trial's hung jury and then a second trial and conviction, arose not out of dislike for the man he'd once described as "youthful Alger Hiss" but because he simply didn't believe Hiss's denials.[38]

•

"I've had it with those people!" The telephone transcript, recorded secretly by the FBI in November 1949, doesn't reveal the identity of the person who had called Izzy and heard this outburst (and who was the apparent target of this illegal surveillance).[39] But there is no mystery about the cause of Stone's exasperation. A few weeks after his conviction in the Smith Act trial of American Communist leaders, John Gates, editor of the *Daily Worker*, appeared on *Meet the Press*. Lawrence Spivak was so eager to grill Gates that he relinquished his moderator's chair for the occasion and, taking the first question, jumped on Gates with both feet, quoting Lenin: "'We must be ready to practice trickery, deceit, law-breaking, withholding and concealing truth.' Do you follow that?"[40]

Izzy, who was also on the panel, got caught in the subsequent crossfire. Knowing that Gates would soon be in prison, "I didn't have the heart to do more than act as stooge or straight man. The poor guy had about as much chance as a sirloin steak thrown into a lions' cage," he recalled, but Gates didn't make it easy on either of them, with his resolute defense of the Moscow trials. When Izzy started to question this as well as Gates's claim that opponents of communism in the Soviet Union were treated better than he and his fellow defendants had been, Spivak accused Stone of "trying to break in and take you [Gates] off a limb."[41]

Reluctant to join the on-air pileup, Izzy vented his frustration not only on the telephone but in the *Compass*. Gates had been asked if the government had to wait "until its throat is being cut" to take action against subversion. That, Izzy pointed out, "is exactly the question Moscow relies on to excuse its own war on 'Trotzkyism.' The premises are not those of a free and stable society." As for Gates's invidious comparison between the trials in Moscow and on Foley Square, Izzy took a swipe at "the noisy clamor of the defense," insisting that "no political dissident in the U.S.S.R. could hope to get as much fair treatment as has been accorded the Communists even in the hysteria-haunted U.S. of this date." It was only to be expected, Stone added, that Gates would deny this. "These pious assertions, customary from Communists, are not to be dismissed as lies; they are the passionate embodiment of a will to believe encountered in any system of thought which commands deep devotion. Nevertheless they are contrary to fact, and therefore get in the way of rational action in politics."

More than the predictable idiocies of either American Communists or a tin-pot Torquemada like Spivak, what really annoyed Izzy was the realization that his own role on *Meet the Press* had changed. Comparing himself to the *"Hofjude,"* the "court Jew . . . kept around for amusement and useful errands" by German princes, Izzy wrote, "I seem to be the 'Hof' radical . . . Whenever some poor Red or near-Red is to be barbecued, I am invited on the program to give it some appearance of fairness, perhaps because there is no one left in the Washington press corps still willing to stick his neck out* in this capital of the land of the free and the home of

---

*Under the wry headline "Who's Afraid of the Capitalist Press?" the *Washington Daily News* columnist Tom Donnelly reported that Gates "did right well for himself the other night." When Donnelly's remarks were themselves quoted approvingly by the *Daily Worker*, an anxious friend in the State Department phoned Donnelly to say, "You better do something" about it. "I think I understand now," Donnelly wrote, "why so many people in this town feel you should watch every word, refrain from loitering in front of a certain book shop, keep off committees and never sign your name to anything but a check for a prosaic purchase at a department store." Donnelly's second thoughts ran under the headline "Some of My Best Friends Are Reactionaries."

the brave. [Since] I also like to ask embarrassing questions even of my friends and allies . . . I either look like a stooge or an enemy."[42]

It was about to get worse. Following the collapse of the Wallace campaign, the CIO voted in December 1949 to bar Communists or anyone who "consistently pursues policies and activities directed toward . . . the purposes of the Communist Party" from serving as union officers. Izzy thought the move suicidal. He wrote:

> I understand the rancors built up in the labor movement by past Communist tactics, but the more I see of the consequences flowing from the CIO's Red purge the more strongly I feel that it will end by seriously damaging the labor movement and stinking up the whole fight for civil liberties on which labor's own future depends . . . The fact that Communists have never been disposed to give their opponents a fair break on civil liberties in the trade union movement or elsewhere is no excuse for the use of similar methods by those who claim to be the champions of "democracy" against "totalitarianism."[43]

His prophetic bitterness was compounded by the fact that Walter Reuther, Philip Murray, and James Carey, all old comrades, were leading the purge.

"The Communists are a problem. It is hard for liberals to live with them," Izzy admitted. "But a liberal organization which makes anti-Communism a major tenet is apt to find itself feeding the hysteria it must—in self-preservation—fight." Those remarks were aimed at his friends and former friends now in the Americans for Democratic Action. His conclusion, though, applied across the whole of what had been the Popular Front: "I still believe that the Left will hang separately if it cannot hang together. I think the cold war is aimed much more at us here at home than at Russia . . . I am content to find myself still with the unrespectable, red as well as pink."[44]

Yet even though his allies often disappointed him, Izzy's enemies never let him down. On February 9, 1950, Joseph McCarthy, the hitherto obscure junior senator from Wisconsin, already under a cloud for shady campaign practices and whose previous bid for national attention had been on behalf of Nazi SS officers convicted of massacring unarmed civilians and U.S. POWs in Malmédy, Belgium, during the Battle of the Bulge, gave the Lincoln Day speech to the Women's Republican Club of Wheeling, West Virginia. Initial reports quoted McCarthy claiming he had the names of 205 "card-carrying Communists" in the State Department. The following day the number had fallen to 57, though when McCarthy repeated his charge on the floor of the Senate ten days later it had grown to 81. By the end of March, McCarthy narrowed his claim to one man, "the top espionage agent in the United States, the boss of Alger Hiss." His name, he said, was Owen Lattimore, and McCarthy pronounced himself "willing to stand or fall on this one."[45]

Owen Lattimore had never been a Communist. Nor was he in any sense Alger Hiss's boss. Director of the Page School of International Relations at the Johns Hopkins University, Lattimore was the most influential China scholar in the United States. During the 1930s, he had traveled extensively in China, including a visit to Mao in Yenan with Philip Jaffe. But he had also served as political adviser to Chiang Kai-shek and remained a close friend of the generalissimo, whom he described as "a great man," and Mme. Chiang.[46] Proving that Lattimore had on occasion been naïve or even shown poor judgment was not difficult. For example, in 1944, as a representative of the Office of War Information, he had accompanied Henry Wallace on a visit to Magadan, a Soviet forced-labor camp in Siberia. Lattimore's glowing account of the trip in *National Geographic*, in which he compared conditions favorably to life in the Alaskan goldfields, included this grotesque encomium to the camp commandant: "Mr. Nikishov . . . and his wife have a trained and sensitive interest in art and music and also a deep sense of civic responsibility."[47]

When Lattimore faced his accusers, however, the issue was his loyalty, not his judgment. The charge was treason, and though the setting was a Senate caucus room, there was no doubt Lattimore was on trial for his life. Stone was in the front row: "The Red hearing has become the American equivalent of the bullfight. This is how the crowd must feel in Mexico City or Madrid, waving to friends around the arena, tensely waiting for the bull to appear, the bright sand to be stained with gore."[48]

The main witness against Lattimore was Louis Budenz, former managing editor of the *Daily Worker*, looking "well-dressed and fatter than in his radical days," Izzy reported. A decade earlier, when Budenz faced criminal syndicalism charges in Chicago, Izzy had come to his defense.[49]

Now he listened to Budenz launch into "his familiar story of the Communist conspiracy with the glibness of a travelling evangelist describing the details of hell." His testimony included elements of farce, as when he claimed Earl Browder had put Lattimore in charge of making sure that Chinese Communists were referred to as "agrarian reformers." Millard Tydings, the conservative Maryland Democrat chairing the special committee investigating McCarthy's charges, asked if Lattimore had been "present at the meeting where this occurred."

> BUDENZ: Oh, no sir. He was not there.
> THEODORE GREEN (D-R.I.): Do you know Mr. Lattimore?
> BUDENZ: Do you mean personally?
> GREEN: Yes
> BUDENZ: I do not.
> GREEN: Have you ever seen Mr. Lattimore?
> BUDENZ: No sir; I have not.[50]

In June, just as Lattimore finished his testimony refuting McCarthy's charges, Izzy left Washington for Alabama. He had been writing about the Scottsboro Boys, nine black youths convicted in 1931 of raping two young white women, since his days on the *Philadelphia Record*. So when a "well-known Negro leader" phoned Ted Thackrey early in the spring of 1949 to say that one of the nine had escaped from prison and was holed up in New York City, Thackrey sent his star columnist. "I have him in an apartment in Harlem," was all Thackrey had been told. In New York, Izzy was taken to meet Haywood Patterson, still on the run from an Alabama prison farm, whom he found hiding out at the apartment of Earl Conrad, author of *Jim Crow America*, a muckraking look at life in the South.

Patterson's tale was gripping, and the story of his escape to New York would be a huge scoop. But "the more I listened, the more I felt it would be wrong to spill Haywood's story in a hasty series of newspaper articles . . . I called Ken McCormick, chief editor of Doubleday." Stone and McCormick knew each other from Fire Island.

The two men met for lunch at "at a restaurant I'd never heard of," McCormick recalled. Izzy "took out a little piece of paper, and he wrote down a name and held it up. 'Does that name mean anything to you?' It said 'Haywood Patterson.' He took out a match box and burned the piece of paper and put it in the ash tray." Stone warned McCormick that if he did as he suggested, the two of them would be "in a criminal position, because we're hiding an escaped convict and we're accessories after the fact." He then asked him to persuade Doubleday to put up $10,000 "to finance a very worthy book." McCormick agreed.[51]

The cash advance arranged by Izzy made it possible for Patterson to leave town with Conrad; it also financed the months it took Conrad to transcribe and edit the escaped convict's memoir. The publication of *Scottsboro Boy*, coauthored by Patterson and Conrad, was what sent Izzy south in the summer of 1950.[52] Now he was free to tell the whole story and to confront Alabama officials, from Governor James "Big Jim" Folsom to the superintendent of Kilby Prison, in his quest for a pardon for Patterson and parole for Andy Wright, last of the Scottsboro defendants still behind bars.[53]

"The South," Izzy reported on his return, "is a story the white man must write in Old Testament terms; only God and the Negro have a right to be forgiving about it . . . There are always excuses. The oppressed always have bad table manners and the oppressors always have their rationalizations." He had little faith in white liberals. "Nobody feels the cut in somebody else's skin. There were times when I found the rationalizations of so-called Southern liberals harder to bear than the subhuman savagery of the Negro-hater."[54]

Izzy's exasperation at the Communist Party's confrontational "labor defense" tactics at the Foley Square conspiracy trial didn't prevent him from acknowledging that the Scottsboro Boys would have long ago been lynched without the party's International Labor Defense campaign to save them, however exploitative or inept it had been.[55] Yet he also knew those struggles were part of the past. Now, he declared, blacks must take the lead themselves. "The Negro must free the white man, and the Negro can only do so if he fights for himself, and we support him." His journey to Alabama was a revelation, but only a partial success. Andy Wright got his parole; however, Izzy's request that Governor Folsom pardon Haywood Patterson was politely ignored. "I liked Folsom, and felt that there was no race hatred in him," Izzy wrote after a meeting where, though the governor himself refused to discuss either case, his men let Izzy know that the state of Alabama was "not interested" in Haywood Patterson. No pardon—but no pursuit either.[56]

Izzy returned to Washington just in time to attend the hearing that sent Edward Barsky, the Joint Anti-Fascist Refugee Committee chairman, and the novelist Howard Fast, a JAFRC board member, to prison for refusing to give HUAC the names of JAFRC contributors. Then on July 17, the Tydings committee reported, "We find no evidence to support the charge that Owen Lattimore is the 'top Russian spy' or, for that matter, any other sort of spy." The report, signed only by the committee's Democratic majority, labeled McCarthy's charges "false smears and headlines."[57] Not that it mattered. That same day the FBI arrested Julius Rosenberg, who was accused of delivering the secret of the atomic bomb to the Russians.

Three weeks earlier, on June 25, troops from the Communist Democratic People's Republic of Korea had crossed the 38th parallel into the territory of the Republic of Korea. (In 1945, the country, liberated from Japanese occupation, had been divided according to a UN decree, and by 1948 the opposing governments in the south and north had stabilized their control.) That January, Secretary of State Acheson had omitted Korea from a list of nations comprising the Pacific perimeter along which the United States would defend itself against "Asian aggression." North Korea's invasion of the South was widely, if mistakenly, viewed as Stalin's initiative, and Truman committed U.S. forces under the auspices of the UN to counter the attack. (Thanks to a temporary Soviet boycott of the Security Council in protest over the UN's exclusion of Communist China, the Security Council resolution to aid South Korea passed unopposed.) Though Truman labeled the intervention a "police action" to avoid the necessity for congressional approval, the United States was at war.

On August 3, Izzy spoke at the Capitol Hotel in Washington to the same group that had sponsored the Waldorf Conference. "You won't like to hear what I have to say so better prepare your tomatoes," he began. "I'm sorry to report to you that I couldn't find any proof to justify the Communist claim that South Korea started this war . . . North Korea started the war and North Korea was well prepared for such a war . . . Where did a little power like North Korea get such a strong war machine . . . ? The Soviet Union equipped North Korean Communist forces and the Soviet Union is behind the North Koreans in this war." Though Izzy also blamed the United States—"Wall Street is dreaming of world conquest and the Kremlin is dreaming of world revolution"—his remarks, according to the FBI informants present, "were applauded by only a small number of persons."[58]

Two weeks later, Izzy left on an El Al flight to Israel, not knowing whether he would ever return to the United States.

•

On the surface, Izzy's fifth visit to Israel in as many years was just a good reporter working his beat. This time he'd even brought company—his daughter, Celia, about to celebrate her twentieth birthday. The only one of his children who shared his passion for poetry, Celia was something of a favorite to her father. Given Izzy's obsession with work, this preference expressed itself mainly as a little extra warmth in the preoccupied smile he bestowed on all his children, or a little more indulgence on the rare occasions when one of them rebelled. But because she was the only girl, or perhaps simply because she was his oldest, Izzy was able to confide some of his fears.

"Father was afraid American intellectuals were going to be put in concentration camps," she recalled. "He told me that if anything happened he wouldn't be able to get me out of the country."[59] He also told her that the trip to Israel might not be just a visit.

Izzy's attraction to Israel had little to do with religion. He was a staunch atheist, and neither he nor Esther had ever shown any interest in Jewish ritual or observance. They'd never even celebrated Passover at home, going instead to Roisman cousins on the first night and to Grandfather Feinstein for the second seder. Then suddenly in 1948, flush with enthusiasm after the establishment of the state of Israel, he insisted that his sons, who were still living at home, begin to learn Hebrew. "We had a Hebrew tutor come to the house and teach us," recalled Christopher Stone, who even joined Young Judea, the youth movement for Reform Jews. Jeremy, about to turn thirteen in 1948, and narrowly saved from having to prepare for his bar mitzvah by the death of the pious relative for whose benefit the ceremony had been intended, remembered only "considering studying Hebrew."[60] But all three children have clear memories of their parents seriously contemplating emigration. And though she had escaped the attentions of the tutor, Celia, too, felt the pressure. When they landed in Tel Aviv in August 1950, Izzy bought her a book of Picasso reproductions with the captions all in Hebrew.

Izzy took Celia to Ein Hashofet, the kibbutz in the north of Israel where Arthur Koestler had once lived and that served as the inspiration for his novel *Thieves in the Night*. He also took her to Deganya, the first of the Jewish communal settlements, founded in 1910, and a hotbed of left-wing Labor Zionism. But the trip wasn't all holiday or even personal reconnaissance. The *Compass* wanted Izzy to find out whether there was any chance that a bloc of countries independent of both Soviet and American influence might be able to mediate an end to the fighting in Korea. In September, it asked him to fly immediately to India to interview Jawaharlal Nehru.

The Indian prime minister and the Jewish-American journalist did not hit it off. Despite Izzy's long history as an advocate of Indian independence, the country's appalling poverty disturbed him, as did the ruling Congress Party's "police-state mentality." There was also Nehru's record as an opponent of Israeli statehood. After two weeks Izzy returned to Celia in Israel. "He kept saying, 'That Nehru! Phew!' He didn't like Nehru," she recalled. But his personal distaste didn't prevent him from appreciating the immensity of Nehru's task or from realizing that if there was ever going to be an alternative to the cold war polarity it would have to be led by men like Nehru—and Tito.[61] So when the Yugoslav leader granted the *Compass* an interview in late October, Izzy was on his way to Belgrade.

In his first dispatches, Izzy is clearly dazzled by the partisan leader, whom he describes as a "hero of the fight against Fascism . . . a legendary figure." Indeed, he was so delighted to find a country where Communist Party members were actually willing to discuss their ideas freely, he seemed for a while to believe he had arrived in his Jeffersonian Marxist promised land. "Freedom of Speech Found in Yugoslavia," he assured *Compass* readers. He was also beguiled by the Yugoslav approach to industrial democracy. But after a couple of weeks, a more skeptical tone crept in. Perhaps he had had a discreet warning from the Yugoslav vice president, Milovan Djilas, still serving in Tito's government but already critical of his country's lack of democracy, and a frequent companion during Izzy's stay in Belgrade. Warning of the emergence of a "new privileged class," a variation on the thesis that would land Djilas a nine-year prison term in 1956, Izzy also lamented the Yugoslav government's "merciless mendacity" toward those it branded deviationists.[62]

The last leg of Izzy's tour took him to Paris to see Claude Bourdet, an-

other anti-Fascist hero. Bourdet had escaped from a German POW camp
to help found *Combat*, the underground newspaper of the non-Communist
French resistance. Captured again by the Nazis in 1944, he'd barely survived Buchenwald. Charles de Gaulle, who had enormous respect and affection for Bourdet, made him director of France's state radio network
in 1945, but Bourdet soon returned to print, founding the magazine
L'Observateur (later called *Le Nouvel Observateur*) in 1950. When Izzy
met him in the fall of 1950, Bourdet, a fervent defender of Tito's break
with Stalin, was well known as a *progressist*—the French version of the
non- (as opposed to anti-) Communist left. An advocate of France's withdrawal from Indochina, as he would later argue in favor of Algerian independence, he was also perhaps the most advanced thinker in what had
not yet become known as the Non-Aligned Movement.* Tall, tweedy,
erudite, and nearly as eloquent in English as in French, the fiercely independent Bourdet was a compelling figure. Even more than the man,
though, Izzy was attracted by Bourdet's milieu.

Compared to the spartan exigencies of daily struggle in Israel, Paris
was a feast for the senses. Never inclined toward asceticism, Izzy reveled
in the French capital's abundance of tastes, sights, and sounds. In particular he found himself captivated by the freedom to disagree, to debate,
and most of all to dissent, which his French friends seemed to take for
granted but which offered a striking contrast to McCarthy-era Washington. After all, when Bourdet made it clear he was well to the left of
de Gaulle—and even to the left of the French Socialists—no one suggested
he should be imprisoned or blacklisted or even denounced. Like his successor at *Combat*, Albert Camus, Bourdet's independence had been hard
earned—and the comparison with America's shabby treatment of its own
anti-Fascists made Izzy realize how estranged he'd become from his own
country. The passage of the McCarran Act in September 1950 made him
feel "like a man trying to shout into a hurricane." Viewed from Paris, the
United States seemed, he wrote in October, in the grip of a "Mad Hatter"
mentality, rushing headlong "toward Fascism and folly."[63]

---

*It took four more years before Nehru coined the term "nonalignment" during a speech in Colombo,
Sri Lanka, in 1954. The Bandung Conference, often considered the origin of the movement, was
held in Indonesia in 1955. And it wasn't until 1961, largely at Tito's instigation, that the first official
summit of the movement was held.

"He called up my mother," said Celia Gilbert, "and told her to sell the house and come to Paris." Izzy explained, "What really scared me was when Congress overturned Truman's veto of the [McCarran] Act establishing the Subversive Activities Control Board, the first thought police in American history. When that happened, I was afraid America was really going to go turn fascist. I even talked to Ted [Thackrey] about maybe we ought to establish a branch of the *Compass* abroad, to carry on the cause . . . if they really clamped down—and I thought they might."[64]

Esther Stone's outward deference to her husband's wishes masked a quiet confidence in her own judgment, and she decided to rent, not sell, the family's house in Washington. Meanwhile, Izzy learned that Le Clos des Metz, the former home of Léon Blum, France's Popular Front prime minister, who had just died in March, was available. "Dad ran into Mme. Blum in Paris," said Christopher Stone. "The house was in Jouy-en-Josas, near the École de Montcel," a boarding school where the Stones enrolled their sons as day students.[65] Celia, by the fall of 1950 already at Smith College, remained in the United States.

Stanley Karnow, who somehow managed to work as Paris correspondent for the left-wing weekly *National Guardian*,* while also stringing for *Time*, was a frequent visitor chez Stone. "The people at the *Guardian* were sectarians. I once proposed doing a piece on Arthur Koestler. They went berserk! They thought those people [former Communists] were worse than fascists. Izzy was not at all sectarian. Plus Izzy had these two worlds in Paris. He had a kind of left-ish world and a Zionist world," Karnow recalled.[66]

Christopher Stone remembers regular visits from Jo Davidson, the writer Pietro di Donato (author of *Christ in Concrete*), and the film director Carl Foreman, in self-imposed exile from Hollywood while his lawyer, Sidney Cohn, fought the blacklist. But most of the Stones' visitors were journalists. Kingsley Martin, editor of the British *New Statesman*, came often, as did Martin's assistant editor Richard Crossman. (On first sitting down to supper with the Stone family, Martin exclaimed, "A fine joint you have here!" Celia and her brothers thought he was praising the house,

---

*According to his FBI file, Izzy attended the paper's founding meeting at Lillian Hellman's apartment in May 1948, along with his brother Marc, who was for a while the *Guardian*'s business manager. But Izzy seldom wrote for it. Karnow, who did, described the *Guardian* as "nominally independent" while actually very close to the Communist Party line.

only to realize later that coming from London, where meat was still subject to rationing, the Englishman's appreciation was meant for the roast.)
Jean-Paul Sartre, who wanted Izzy to contribute to *Les Temps Modernes*,
was a more occasional visitor. It was Claude Bourdet, though, who
launched Izzy on the project that would take up most of his time in Paris.

The Frenchman asked Izzy to write a series of articles for *L'Observateur* on the origins of the ongoing conflict in Korea. Working from his
study in France, and forced to rely on the State Department's July 1950
white paper, the Paris edition of the *Herald Tribune*, clippings from the
New York Times, and the British and French press, Izzy noticed that accounts of the war produced for American domestic consumption diverged
considerably from those intended for European readers, regardless of political orientation. This piqued his interest, and he soon realized that he
could use this parallax effect—the apparent change in position of an
object when seen from two different vantage points—to his reportorial
advantage.

Izzy still had to produce six pieces a week for the *Compass* as well as his
work for Bourdet. "Because they didn't want to spend money on cables I had
to have my stuff at the post office . . . by 2 p.m. each day in order to get it to
New York the following day. So I was really hopping."[67] Somehow, though,
he managed to find time to enjoy Paris. When Chris, his younger son, turned
thirteen, Izzy marked his coming of age not with a bar mitzvah or even a trip
to synagogue, but by taking him to see the Folies-Bergère. Jeremy, two years
older, decided that total immersion in French was not for him. Instead, he
became his father's typist on what had by now become a book-length manuscript, *The Hidden History of the Korean War*.

"When the book was finished I went with him to London to try and
sign a contract with the *New Statesman*," Jeremy told me. "Before we
went to their offices he'd opened a British bank account, and on the way
back from the bank we passed a big sign outside a newsstand, TRUMAN
SACKS MACARTHUR. So when we got to the *New Statesman* he said, 'I feel
like the Venerable Bede,' meaning the book would never be published." It
was the summer of 1951, and the lease on Jouy-en-Josas was at its end.
"There was talk of going to Israel," Christopher Stone recalled, "up to the
last minute. He said, 'Bring me some tea and I'll decide.' When I came
back with the tea he'd fallen asleep!"

On June 15, Izzy, Esther, and the two boys sailed into New York harbor aboard the French liner SS *Liberté*. An official from U.S. customs came aboard ship to examine their passports.

"Is youse the Stone that writes for *PM*?"

"Yes, I am," Izzy replied, thinking, Oh, boy! Here's where I lose my passport. Unlike some of his worries, this fear was not at all far-fetched. Paul Robeson and the artist Rockwell Kent among many others had already had their passports taken away. Arthur Miller would soon be denied a passport to attend the premiere of *The Crucible* in London.

"*Zei gur gezint!*" [Yiddish for "Go in good health!"] said the official, who stamped the passport and handed it back to its astonished—and delighted—owner.[68]

•

His euphoria was short-lived. The State Department Press Association refused his application for membership. With the house in Washington still occupied by tenants, Esther and the children went to Fire Island while Izzy camped out at the Willard Hotel, making the long commute most weekends. But Washington depressed him, and whenever possible Izzy sent in his column to the *Compass* from the house on Fire Island. This made life difficult for the hapless copyboys, as Ralph Ginzburg, who was one of them, recalled: "Izzy habitually pushed a deadline. He pushed it harder than anyone I've ever worked with. And so the heat was always on me . . . I would show up, he would finish writing his column—or usually he would start writing his column." Then Ginzburg would race to the Western Union office (the Fire Island house had no telephone), returning to New York by ferry and railroad.[69]

On July 4, Izzy reflected on "a country scared into submission." Noting that "everywhere, in government employment, in the press, on the radio, in the movie business, in the labor movement, among professional people, one finds fear," Izzy remarked that "in Germany and Italy it was necessary to beat, torture, and imprison relatively few people in order to frighten the rest into silence."

Calling for "the conservatives and respectables . . . to see that if they do not begin to fight, all that was precious in America may well be lost," he admitted that forming a coalition to "stand and fight" would take more than just courage. Strong stomachs would also be required: "Some of us are closer to Minsk than to the Mayflower. Some are Reds. Some are folk whose skins bar them from many places . . . We are not quite the kind of people with whom one associates."[70]

Izzy knew what it was to be shunned. Though he had found *Scottsboro Boy* a publisher in a single phone call, his own manuscript on the Korean War was turned down by more than two dozen houses. Even his British friends seemed skittish, preferring to wait until the book came out in the United States, where editors were unanimous in finding Izzy's work important, and worthy of publication—by someone else.

In the fall of 1951, the Stone family was living in borrowed luxury: Through friends, they'd arranged to sublet an apartment at 1133 Park Avenue. Izzy, who had been reassigned to the *Compass* features desk, liked to walk to work downtown via Central Park. One day, outside the Central Park Zoo, Izzy ran into his old *PM* colleague Leo Huberman. "We were sitting at the cafeteria and Izzy walked in," said Paul Sweezy. Sweezy was an economist who had taught at Harvard; he and Huberman had just started the *Monthly Review*, a nonsectarian leftist journal. Izzy could hardly believe it when the two men asked if he knew anyone with anything interesting to say about the Korean War. "He told us about this manuscript he'd written that no one would publish. He told us in quite anguished detail about it. And the more he told us, the more excited we got. We said, 'Look, this thing has got to be published. Could you send it over?' The manuscript arrived at around four or five o'clock. We began reading it right away, and we got even more excited. We figured we'd raise the money somehow."[71]

Claude Bourdet told Izzy that his second article on Korea created a more frenzied response than anything else *L'Observateur* had ever published.[72] So when *The Hidden History of the Korean War* appeared in April 1952, Izzy had every reason to expect controversy. What he got instead, at least from the mainstream press, was silence, eerie and unbroken. At the *New Republic*, Michael Straight roused himself to declare the book "not reasoned dissent" and "a fictive report." A brief notice in *Foreign Affairs* warned readers that *The Hidden History* "at times verges on the official Soviet line."[73] Even the *Nation*'s reviewer found Stone's theorizing "tendentious." True, the *Daily Worker* reviewer saluted "a valuable work of polemical journalism in the best bourgeois tradition." *The Militant*, organ of the Trotskyist Socialist Workers Party, went further, praising the book in such terms that the *Compass* book page simply reprinted it verbatim.[74] But from the *New York Times*, the *Herald Tribune*, the *Saturday Review*, *Time*, or any of the dozen other publications that had positively reviewed *Underground to Palestine* and *This Is Israel* . . . nothing.

With one exception. On Sunday, May 11, 1952, before any other notice, a full-page attack on "this preposterous book" appeared in the *New York Post*, labeling it "a piece of bland and heavily documented rubbish." Recalling Stone's fury at the Nazi-Soviet pact, the reviewer wrote,

> I can recall no one from the period who was more outraged by that outrageous document than Stone. As *The Nation*'s Washington correspondent during the early years of the war, Stone was as good as the best and perhaps was the best. I do not know what happened to deflect Stone's promising career in the forties . . . For several years now, Stone has no longer been a promising journalist, or even a moderately good one. Zest, style and humor have departed his work, leaving it merely querulous . . . Stone's contribution to American journalism today is that of a man who thinks up good arguments for poor Communist positions.

The author of this screed was Richard Rovere. Now comfortably established at the *New Yorker*, Rovere was an unusual choice for the *Post*—indeed, he never reviewed for the paper again. "That was a hit job," explained Murray Kempton, a friend of both Rovere and Wechsler who had just begun his own long career as a *Post* columnist. "Wechsler summoned him to do it." In a letter to Rovere thanking him for his "effort . . . in a noble cause," Wechsler warned, "Too many of our silly readers will be quoting Stone as gospel unless this job is done."[75]

The reverberations from Rovere's exercise in character assassination lasted a long time. According to Kempton, there was a "rage at Izzy on the part of the anti-Communist left" dating from "the Korean War period. It ran very deep." Deep enough to generate a cloud of allegation and misperception easily sufficient to obscure what was, in fact, a relatively modest essay in the critical reading of contemporary sources. Over the years such a mythology has developed around *The Hidden History*—that Izzy contended South Korea invaded North Korea, or that he accused the United States of using nerve gas or "germ warfare" against North Korean troops*—that it is worth taking a brief look at what the book actually says.

The Hidden History of the Korean War is a history wrapped in an enigma. The history, however controversial at the time, is straightforward: When the war began, Secretary of State Dean Acheson told the United Nations the aim of intervention was "solely for the purpose of restoring the Republic of Korea to its status prior to the invasion from the North." By the time the Stone family had reached France, this objective had been achieved; after his brilliant landing at Inchon in September 1950, General MacArthur had pushed the North Korean army back behind the 38th Parallel. But instead of stopping there, U.S. troops crossed the 38th Parallel in early October 1950. The war continued for another three years, with MacArthur's race north drawing in the Communist Chinese and seeming to herald a much wider conflict. In the fall of 1951, with fighting stalemated on the 38th Parallel and Communist Chinese delegates en route to peace talks at the UN, MacArthur launched a "Home-by-Christmas" offensive that kept the fighting going for months without any significant change in the battle line but with thousands more dead on both sides. Throughout, Soviet military support for the North Koreans remained limited, even after U.S. fighter planes attacked a Russian air base forty miles south of Vladivostok.

"The Korean War book is a very good book," said Kempton. "His analysis of the progress of the war was impeccable. We misread the war—especially those of us who'd been soldiers in the Second World War. Izzy read the war better than any of the rest of us."

Korea also provided the occasion, if not the pretext, for a sharp rightward turn in American policy not just toward China, where Truman had ordered the Seventh Fleet to protect Taiwan, ending the U.S. military's

---

*Such claims still surface on the Internet, but while both North Korea and China did accuse the United States of using "germ warfare" in June 1952, and this propaganda campaign did have supporters on the American left, I. F. Stone was not among them. "Several readers have written in to ask what I think of the germ war charges in Korea," he wrote in the *Compass* on July 3, 1952. "The answer is that I do not believe them." He did, however, write that the use of "jellied gasoline bombs" (napalm) to obliterate the entire city of Sinuiju "makes me as an American deeply ashamed"—an admission perhaps sufficiently damning for Stone's detractors. Or was the provocation Stone's realization that such means wouldn't always be restricted to one side? "A terrible retribution," he wrote, "threatened the peoples of the Western world who so feebly permitted such acts to be done in their name. For it was by such means that the pyromaniacs hoped to set the world aflame" (p. 179).

hands-off policy, but also in Europe, where Washington's proposals for NATO now included ten divisions from a rearmed West Germany.[76] Though National Security Council Paper No. 68, the secret 1950 document advocating a more aggressive approach to containment, backed by an unprecedented increase in peacetime military spending, would remain classified for decades, the shift to a more confrontational military posture was, at least to Izzy, unmistakable.[77]

Equally obvious, at least from Paris, was the way the war spared the Truman administration any number of tough political choices. With military spending ballooning, there was no need to plan for a full-employment peacetime economy. Rescuing Syngman Rhee's regime in South Korea also allowed Truman to redeem himself from the opprobrium of having "lost" China, as right-wing Republicans claimed he had, though at the cost of tying the United States more closely to the Nationalist Chinese government on Taiwan. Indeed, the outbreak of fighting was so well timed from the point of view of both Rhee (whose party had fared disastrously in South Korea's first free elections, held just a month before the war began) and the China Lobby, which fiercely supported Chiang Kai-shek's regime in Taiwan, that Izzy, though never quite claiming that South Korea started the war, did suggest that Rhee provoked the North Korean invasion and that both he and MacArthur certainly welcomed it. "Was the war Stalin's blunder? Or was it MacArthur's plan?" Izzy wondered somewhat disingenuously.[78]

History shows that Izzy was probably wrong about how the war started. Certainly he underestimated the degree of coordination between Kim Il Sung's North Korean regime and Stalin.[79] We now know, in the historian John Lewis Gaddis's phrase, many things that Izzy could only surmise. And yet the enigma of when and how the Korean War began, and why the United States and the Soviet Union responded as they did to this proxy battle, remains mysterious. "What is striking about the Korean War," says Gaddis, writing after the opening of American, South Korean, and some Chinese and Soviet archives, "is the extent to which its outbreak, escalation, and ultimate resolution surprised everyone."[80]

Where *The Hidden History* really touched a raw nerve was Izzy's calm assumption that in pursuit of its political aims a group within the Truman administration was willing to allow (at the very least) an attack on South Korea to go ahead and then to deceive the American people about the real

objectives of American government policy. After the Gulf of Tonkin incident in 1964, wrote Eisenhower's biographer Stephen Ambrose in a preface to the 1971 reprint of *The Hidden History*, "Americans are ready to
believe things about their government that they would have dismissed as
Communist propaganda five years ago."[81]

Yet even today, after Vietnam, after the Iran-contra scandals, after the
9/11 Commission reports, Rovere's dismissal still does its work. There are
exceptions—most significantly Bruce Cumings, America's leading Korea
scholar, who not only explicitly acknowledged his debt to I. F. Stone in his
own two-volume study *The Origins of the Korean War* but also hand-
somely repaid it in a preface to the 1988 edition of *The Hidden History*.
Cumings described Stone's work as an inquiry into "empire and its
method," noting that the book seemed to have "nine lives, padding in on
the cat's feet of its shrewd author to unsettle the scribes of historical and
political orthodoxy."[82]

Maybe the end of the cold war has rendered such controversies purely
of academic interest (though for twenty-first-century readers, Izzy's account of China's phantom army, which, according to contemporary reports was supposedly utterly destroyed by MacArthur after Inchon, and
somehow rose "like Lazarus from the tomb" before Christmas, yet baf-
flingly "failed to 'aggress,'" can't but conjure up similarly elusive agents
of mass destruction alleged to exist in later times). And it is still hard
to better his description of "an Anglo-American partnership in which
one partner made the decisions and left the other to face the consequences." The British government, he wrote, could "threaten to withdraw
its troops if it did not like MacArthur's conduct of the 'unified command.'
But it could not recall or revise the blank check it gave him through the
United Nations. It could urge, it could suggest, it could protest, it could
deplore, but it could not instruct."[83] Nor has the passage of time rendered
obsolete Stone's sketch of American attitudes at the United Nations:
"The relationship of the United Nations to the Korean question had been
from the beginning marked by a strategy of *fait accompli* on the American side, and a quick and quiet acquiescence on the part of the United
Nations."[84]

Reflecting on the ostracism Izzy faced, Stephen Ambrose wrote: "It
took guts to publish this book in the McCarthy era." He didn't know the
half of it.

•

For I. F. Stone the "knock on the door" came on September 25, 1951, when Agent William Canfield of the State Department Security Division presented himself at the *Daily Compass* office and demanded that Izzy surrender his passport.[85] Izzy had expected to have his passport taken at dockside in June. The chemist Linus Pauling had just been refused a passport despite an invitation to address Britain's Royal Society. In Paris, Stanley Karnow held on to his passport only after Time, Inc., interceded on his behalf. Even Joseph Lash, confidant to Eleanor Roosevelt and one of the founders of Americans for Democratic Action, was refused a passport. Ruth Shipley, the head of the State Department's passport division, was notorious for the way she used her new powers under the McCarran Act to punish anyone whom she—or her good friend J. Edgar Hoover—deemed subversive.* Max Lowenthal, who'd known Izzy since the 1930s, found that even a close friendship with President Truman wasn't enough to erase the sin of having written a book critical of Hoover and the bureau.[86] Besides, Izzy's passport had expired earlier in September.

If the request was predictable, the response was not. To Canfield's amazement, Izzy sent him away empty-handed. "I said a passport was too valuable a piece of property to be handled in so unbusinesslike a way, and asked for a letter from the Department stating (1) its legal authority to withdraw the passport and (2) its reason for doing so."[87] He got his letter—in fact he got two letters, since, as he pointed out, the first letter gave the required authority but not the reason. However, it seems Izzy never did surrender his passport.

Izzy might well have assumed the move was in retaliation for his criticism of the Korean War. Dean Acheson's cable ordering the American consul in Israel not to extend I. F. Stone's passport was dated March 29, 1951, when the diplomatic stir created by Izzy's articles in *L'Observateur* was at its height.[88] And though Izzy concentrated most of his fire on John Foster Dulles, the Republican corporation lawyer who served as Truman's special envoy, reminding readers of the Presbyterian layman's amiable ne-

---

*Her older brother, A. Bruce Bielaski, had been FBI director in the Wilson administration. Her younger brother, Frank Bielaski, an investigator for the Republican National Committee in the 1930s, became director of investigations at the OSS and supervised the *Amerasia* break-ins.

gotiation with the Nazis on behalf of several New York banks ("if the Nazi regime offended his religious sensibilities, he gave no evidence of it") and depicting him as MacArthur's coconspirator,[89] he was hardly one of Acheson's admirers either. In Izzy's view, most of what Acheson said about China was foolish, and the department's premise that Peking was merely Moscow's tool wrongheaded; the resulting policy, Izzy wrote, showed "an absence of . . . vision and courage."[90]

The truth, though, was that Izzy's passport difficulties had nothing to do with Acheson, or Dulles, or even Korea. The roots of Agent Canfield's visit went back to the closing days of World War II, and to a private girls' school near Washington named Arlington Hall. And to Moscow. It was at Arlington Hall that Meredith Gardner, a lanky Texas-born linguist who had been recruited to the army's Signals Intelligence Service from the German faculty at the University of Akron, had turned his attention from Japanese codes to Russian. During the war, the Soviet embassy, like other foreign missions in the United States, communicated with its home country via commercial cable companies, which under wartime censorship rules supplied to the U.S. military copies of every cable sent. The Russians were aware of this but didn't mind because they used a two-step code system that, in theory, was completely unbreakable. Each message was first translated into a string of numbers using a codebook, essentially a dictionary with separate number strings for each word. Then these number strings were themselves turned into other number strings using a onetime pad—sheets of paper with random number sequences that were supposed to be destroyed after use (the recipient needed an identical sheet to decipher the message).[91] Onetime-pad ciphers are indeed virtually unbreakable, but the pressure to keep producing new one-time sheets after June 22, 1941, meant that some sheets were reused. This enabled Gardner to decipher some common phrases—for example, the code string used to signal the beginning and end of a non-Russian name (since names wouldn't be in the codebook, they had to be spelled out letter by letter).

In December 1946, Gardner deciphered a two-year-old cable containing a whole list of foreign names: Hans Bethe, Niels Bohr, Enrico Fermi, Edward Teller, Harold Urey—all under the heading "List of scientists engaged on the problem of atomic energy." Gradually, Gardner and his largely female team of cryptanalysts uncovered evidence that a network of Soviet espionage agents was working in the United States; the product of their efforts, code-named Bride (later Venona), was closely held by the army. In October 1948, the FBI was invited to send a full-time liaison to the project, but the slow and painstaking work was still not a very high priority—until August 1949, when the Soviet Union's first atomic bomb tests stunned the United States and suddenly put Arlington Hall into high gear.[92]

It was this decrypted cable traffic that led to the arrest of Judith Coplon, but the army's determination to keep its code-breaking achievement a secret proved a fatal handicap for the prosecution.* The British had better luck with the physicist Klaus Fuchs, a refugee from Nazi Germany and naturalized British subject who was already passing information to the Soviets when he arrived in the United States in 1943 to work on the Manhattan Project. Interrogated in late 1949 after being identified by the code breakers, Fuchs quickly confessed, leading investigators to his KGB courier, Harry Gold, whose information in turn led the FBI to David Greenglass. In June 1950, Greenglass confessed and implicated his sister, Ethel Rosenberg, and her husband, Julius.[93]

What does any of this have to do with I. F. Stone's passport? Also in late 1949, the code breakers at Arlington Hall deciphered a number of messages that had been sent by the KGB's New York station to Moscow in the fall of 1944 concerning contacts with American journalists. One cable described the efforts of SERGEJ—the codename for Vladimir Sergeyevich Pravdin (itself a pseudonym), New York correspondent for the Soviet press agency TASS and also a KGB officer—to cultivate an ac-

---

*The government kept the Venona Project a secret for fifty-three years. As Haynes and Klehr point out (*Venona*, p. 18), this secrecy "has seriously distorted our understanding of post–World War II history." They also note that "the Venona messages, if made public, would have made Julius Rosenberg's execution less likely" for the simple reason that Venona identified three other Soviet spies inside the Manhattan Project, each of whom made a far greater contribution to the Soviet atomic program than Rosenberg. But Klehr and Haynes do not grasp the full implication of the decision to keep Venona secret. As Moynihan notes (*Secrecy*, p. 70), "President Truman was never told of the Venona decryptions." Yet as Klehr, Haynes, and Moynihan all acknowledge, the Soviets knew almost immediately that their wartime cable traffic was being broken. Kim Philby, the British Intelligence liaison to Washington, was not only given access to Venona product but actually visited Arlington Hall in 1949! Indeed, Philby had barely arrived in Washington before the FBI consulted him about the possible identity of a Soviet spy in the British embassy code-named Homer. Quickly recognizing his friend— and fellow KGB agent—Donald Maclean, Philby was able to warn Moscow and arrange for Maclean and Guy Burgess, also working at the British embassy in Washington, to escape.

quaintance with "persons of great interest from a legal point of view. They are well-informed and, although they do not say all they know, nevertheless they provide useful comments on the foreign policy of the country. Among them SERGEJ is studying Joseph Barnes and I. Stone who, however, for the time being is avoiding SERGEJ."[94]

The assertion that Stone was "avoiding" the TASS correspondent caught the eye of Robert Lamphere, the FBI man assigned to Arlington Hall. In a message sent just a few weeks earlier and also deciphered in 1949, Pravdin's boss complained that "SERGEJ has three times attempted to affect liaison with BLIN* . . . [but] each time BLIN declined."[95] A further message reported on what happened when SERGEJ finally succeeded in making contact: BLIN admitted he'd been avoiding a meeting, "fearing the consequences," but now "gave him to understand that he was not refusing his aid, but [one should] consider that he had three children and did not want to attract the attention of the [FBI]."[96] In other words, at least according to Pravdin, BLIN was a target for possible recruitment by the KGB who did not immediately send the Russians packing. Could BLIN be I. F. Stone?

Lamphere certainly thought so. In a note dated February 1951, Lamphere wrote that "it would appear . . . I. F. Stone is identical with PANCAKE (BLIN)." He gave four reasons for the identification: Stone had been reported as avoiding Pravdin, as had BLIN; in 1944, Stone was Washington correspondent for *PM*, and BLIN was a correspondent; Stone, like BLIN, had three children; SERGEJ "was considering the recruitment of Barnes and Stone." His boss "recommended that Barnes not be recruited. The inference is quite clear that [the KGB] was not opposed to the recruitment of Stone."[97] It was probably this note that led to Stone's passport difficulties.

Not all of Lamphere's colleagues were convinced. The FBI's Washington field office noted that BLIN was described as "earning as much as 1500 dollars a month," while "the income of Stone . . . was considerably less than that."[98] The New York field office was even more skeptical, arguing that BLIN "must have been a person whose true pro-Soviet sympathies were not known to the public and his associates." New York concluded that "I. F. Stone would not appear to be identical with [BLIN]"

Blin is the Russian word for pancake.

and suggested that "Ernest K. Lindley was perhaps a better suspect."
(Lindley, who died in 1979, covered the Roosevelt White House for the
New York Herald Tribune before becoming *Newsweek*'s Washington bureau chief. FDR's 1932 speech calling for "bold, persistent experimentation" was written by Lindley, who also served on the National Security
staff in the Kennedy and Johnson administrations. Lindley's lasting claim
to fame, though, is probably as the inventor of the "Lindley rule" for
deep background briefings in which the source, and the very fact of
the conversation, are off the record but the substance of the conversation is not.) A few days later, New York again weighed in with the view
that since the evidence "tends to eliminate Stone entirely as a suspect"
further investigation would be unwarranted.[99] Here Washington disagreed: "Stone cannot now be eliminated from consideration."

The FBI was still debating when the *Liberté* docked in New York. Indeed, Izzy might not have been so relieved by the customs agent's welcome if he had seen the memo sent from the FBI's Washington field
office to the collector of customs advising that the FBI "is especially interested in Stone." Warning that "Stone should not be unduly detained or
otherwise made aware that the Federal Bureau of Investigation is interested in him," the memo nonetheless "requested that Stone's baggage be
searched."[100] In August, Hoover made up his mind, ordering New York
"to conduct a physical surveillance of Stone in order to . . . ascertain if
he is presently active in Soviet espionage work."[101] The FBI, which had
been keeping tabs on Izzy since the 1930s, started a new file: "I. F. Stone,
ESPIONAGE-R."

Fire Island, with its absence of cars, posed a problem, as did the lack
of a telephone at the Stone family cottage on Ocean Beach.[102] So, apparently, did the *Daily Compass*: "In view of Stone's profession and his
frequent castigations of the Bureau, it is felt that extreme caution is
needed . . . The large windows of the *Compass* office could easily be used
to detect a surveillance and perhaps even to take photographs of the sur-
veilling agent."[103] By September, though, when the State Department
asked for his passport, Izzy was living on Park Avenue, where "it is felt that
a more discreet and productive surveillance can be maintained."[104]

Was I. F. Stone the journalist known as BLIN? In 1995, when the
Venona decrypts were first released, the National Security Agency's official historian declared, "The identification really is not in doubt."[105] But

the available evidence, though suggestive,* is not conclusive.[106] And as even the NSA concedes, "The doubt concerns what happened next." BLIN appears only once more in the decrypted cable traffic—a summary of "correspondents who have contacts with military leaders"—when mentioned in the context of a report on BUMBLEBEE, the code name used for Walter Lippmann.[107] What happened to BLIN after that is still unknown.

Might Moscow have viewed Stone as a potential recruit? Of course. The Soviets' grasp of American political reality was as shaky as J. Edgar Hoover's. And though BLIN's tactic of avoidance and excuses rather than outright refusal might be merely an imaginative agent's rationale for failure, at worst, says the historian Ronald Radosh, the Venona decrypts prove "merely that one agent in the States says he approached Izzy and that Izzy was interested but was worried about taking the money. Even that could be attributed to [the] agent's desire to impress his boss."[108]

But what happened next to Stone is amply documented. Agent Canfield's visit to the *Daily Compass* was the visible tip of a massive undercover operation. A thirty-day mail cover allowing the FBI to open Izzy's mail was begun—and renewed every month for *the next two years*. FBI agents interviewed his neighbors at the National Press Building and recruited the doorman at 1133 Park Avenue to report on his movements. They also interviewed the former *Post* editor Harry Saylor, who described Izzy as "especially friendly with officials of the Newspaper Guild" and probably a Communist.

From the fall of 1951 onward, Izzy was the subject of daily physical surveillance. Agents followed him on the bus and subway, they followed him in and out of the Argosy Book Store and Brentano's, to the men's room at Grand Central Station (but waited outside until he finished), to the Automat and Horn & Hardart, and followed Izzy, Esther, and Celia to the Trans-Lux Theatre, where in March 1952 the Stone family saw Luis Buñuel's *Los Olvidados*.[109] The bureau even followed him on a trip to San Francisco, collecting from the hotel operator a list of his calls to such subversive organizations as United Airlines, an auto repair shop, and the Jewish Community Bulletin. The IRS combed through Izzy's tax returns, looking for Moscow gold.[110] FBI agents sifted the Stone family garbage (in bureauspeak, a "trash cover"). They also tapped the family telephone.[111]

---

*Despite its authors' claims to the contrary, the most recent discussion of BLIN's identity, in Haynes, Klehr, and Vassiliev's *Spies* (2009), is still inconclusive.

•

Did I. F. Stone, nearsighted and hard of hearing as he was, fail to notice the corps of clean-cut young men who now shadowed him virtually every waking hour of the day (though with Sundays off and only from ten a.m. to six p.m. on Saturdays)? "I never felt that there were FBI men on the corners watching him," said Jeremy Stone, at the time a student at the Bronx High School of Science.[112]

But there were. If he'd been born in Pinsk instead of Philadelphia, Izzy would have been denaturalized and deported.[113] Instead, he was put on the FBI's Security Index. "The idea," said a former FBI agent, "was to arrest everyone on the Security Index within twenty-four hours or as soon as possible, if there was a national emergency."[114] Seeking to demonstrate their own anti-Communist credentials in the fight over McCarran's Internal Security Act, a group of Senate liberals, led by Hubert Humphrey, had inserted a provision calling for "subversives" to be rounded up and held in concentration camps in the event of a national emergency.[115] Now I. F. Stone's name was on the list of potential detainees.

Many on the left seemed to be losing the will to fight. In one early issue of the *Monthly Review*, every single contributor preferred to remain anonymous.[116] Mike Blankfort had begun distancing himself from the Communist Party even before the Nazi-Soviet pact. When his friends Albert Maltz and George Sklar were blacklisted, Blankfort wrote privately to George Sokolsky, the Hearst columnist, explaining his disenchantment.[117] Called before HUAC in January 1952, Blankfort told Congressman Donald Jackson he'd never been a party member and therefore had no names to offer. Yet when Jackson asked if he had any relatives who were or had been Communists, Blankfort replied, "You are referring to my ex-wife, Laurie, and my cousin Henry—I have no knowledge of either."[118]

Izzy did not reproach his old college friend for naming even those two names to the inquisitors, perhaps because he remembered what it felt like to be afraid. But he didn't follow Blankfort's example either. "I. F. Stone, of the *Daily Compass*, made his eleventh speech attacking the Smith Act," the *Herald Tribune* warned its readers in November 1951. "I have heard of more sensational exposés," Izzy replied, noting that actually he had "made 12 speeches in nine cities against the Act since returning from abroad in June . . . They were not advertised as violin recitals. I did not pretend to be a lecturer sent out by the National Geographic Society. I did not claim to be a card-carrying Republican . . . Except for a few jokes in Yiddish, they were carried on in the English language."[119] When, a few months later, the *Trib* columnist Ogden Reid ran Izzy's picture under the headline "The Red Underground," Izzy's next *Compass* column, also headlined "The Red Underground," featured Reid's picture, captioned "Tribune Reporter," next to a picture of "Former Tribune Reporter" Karl Marx.*[120]

Far from signaling a retreat, Izzy's brush with the passport office seems to have made him more pugnacious. Though he never mentioned the incident in his column, where he was too busy attacking the China Lobby, by the end of September 1951 he had opened a new front in the fight against what, refusing the epithet favored by Schlesinger and the ADA, he insisted on calling "Trumanism." Shortly after the Supreme Court voted to uphold the convictions in the first Smith Act trial in June 1951, Izzy and a group of friends gathered at Ted Thackrey's apartment. Conversation turned to the ACLU, which since expelling Elizabeth Gurley Flynn had become more and more a bystander, seemingly content to remain on the sidelines as passports were seized, writers and academics subpoenaed, and wires tapped. Izzy was also deeply suspicious of Morris Ernst, the ACLU co-counsel who acted as J. Edgar Hoover's personal attorney.[121]

"The question was whether a new organization was needed," recalled James Imbrie, a retired banker present that evening, "with guts enough to fight the evils of McCarthyism without fear of being sullied by the label 'pro-Communist.'" Most of the group were opposed, but Imbrie, Izzy, and Henry Pratt Fairchild, an emeritus professor of sociology at New York University, favored immediate action. Joined by Paul Lehmann, a professor at the Princeton Theological Seminary, E. Franklin Frazier, chair of the sociology department at Howard University, and H. H. Wilson, professor of politics at Princeton, they founded the Emergency Civil Liberties Committee. Besides taking on cases—and causes—shunned by the ACLU, the ECLC was from the very beginning willing to take a more ag-

---

*Not that Reid was in danger of being blacklisted. His grandfather, Whitelaw Reid, had wrested the *New York Tribune* away from its founder, Horace Greeley; his father, Ogden Mills Reid, merged the paper with James Gordon Bennett's *Herald*; his mother, Helen Rogers Reid, was the *Trib*'s current publisher; and his brother, Whitelaw Reid II, was the paper's editor.

gressive approach. Clark Foreman, whose own passport had been seized earlier that year, was hired as director.[122]

"The ACLU did not take test cases all the way to the Supreme Court," said Edith Tiger, who came with Foreman from the Progressive Party and worked as his assistant. "Test cases were expensive; you had to stay with it . . . [But] Izzy felt this had to be done. He said, 'We'll do one of each kind of case.' Izzy didn't want it to come out of the left. This was a group of New Dealers."[123] They were also men who, either retired or with tenure, had little to fear from any blacklist. Yet "before we got under way, Izzy said to me, very quietly, 'Do you know what you're getting into?'" recalled Paul Lehmann. He had been a member of the Fellowship of Socialist Christians, a group founded in the early 1930s by Reinhold Niebuhr, and he thought he did know the risks. But the ECLC's lack of a Leninist past was no deterrent to the paladins of the newly revived American Committee for Cultural Freedom, who, though bitterly divided among themselves on whether McCarthy or Stalin posed a greater present danger to American culture, were energized by the prospect of a common enemy on the left.[124] No sooner had the ECLC announced its first public meeting than Lehmann and his fellow sponsors received letters urging them to withdraw. When they refused, the ACCF publicly denounced them, not as Communists or even fellow travelers but as "dupes."[125]

As the only ECLC board member not protected by wealth or tenure, Izzy faced intense pressures. He must also have been aware that the *Compass* itself was in desperate straits. Yet it was as if something inside, an internal censor weighing his words, calculating for prudence or personal advantage, had shaken loose. His attacks blazed with new ferocity: Robert Morris, chief counsel to the McCarran committee, was not just "the man who protects" the perjurer Budenz, but a master of "the ethics of the knife in the back."[126] Even to his friends, he seemed suddenly determined to speak his mind: "I was never persuaded by the campaign on behalf of the Rosenbergs . . . I have never been persuaded that the case was a frame-up." (He did go on to call the death sentence imposed on them by Judge Irving Kaufman "barbaric, savage, and way out of line with justice.")[127]

When the government sent Dashiell Hammett to jail for refusing to turn over the names of donors to the bail fund of the Civil Rights Congress, successor organization to the International Labor Defense, Izzy leaped to his aid: "If you pick a fight with a midget in a bar-room you ought to be able to finish it without getting your friends to hold his hands behind his back while you kneel down to give him an uppercut."[128] But when Hammett asked him to speak at a rally for V. J. Jerome, the party's cultural commissar and a defendant in the second round of Smith Act trials, Izzy declined: "I'd feel like a stultified ass to speak at a meeting for Jerome without making clear my own sharp differences with the dogmatic, Talmudic and dictatorial mentality he represents."[129]

Nothing so symbolizes Izzy's newfound independence, his determination not just to stay and fight but to speak his mind, as his response to the George Polk investigation. Greece's rightist government had announced a solution to his friend's murder—Gregory Staktopoulos, a Reuters stringer, confessed that he had killed the CBS correspondent on behalf of "the Greek Communist Party, in order to throw the blame of the murder to the Right, thus to defame Greece abroad and to stop the application of the Marshall Plan"—but Izzy was dubious. "Two months in solitary confinement may make a man tell the truth," he wrote in October 1948, "or it may make him say anything his jailers want him to say. This is one of the reasons for *habeas corpus*. That right does not exist in Greece."[130] Others shared Izzy's skepticism. Howard K. Smith, the CBS correspondent who had spent the most time in Greece after Polk, cabled that he thought it "highly improbable" that the Greek left would have killed Polk, and asked the network to mount its own investigation with him in charge.[131]

Instead, two separate press groups formed. The Newsmen's Commission to Investigate the Murder of George Polk, organized by the New York Newspaper Guild, called for "a full investigation . . . by a qualified team of correspondents and government officials." It was backed by Polk's family but had little clout and less money. Its sole staff member, Shana Ager,* daughter of *PM*'s film critic, Cecelia Ager, was paid $35 a week. The Overseas Writers Special Committee to Inquire into the Murder of George Polk, on the other hand, was a first-class operation. Chaired by Walter Lippmann and backed by the *Washington Post*'s publisher, Eugene Meyer, who raised more than $40,000, the committee included Marquis Childs, James Reston of the *New York Times*, Elmer Davis of ABC, Eric Sevareid of CBS, and Ernest K. Lindley, who asked his friend William

---

*Known in later life as Shana Alexander.

"Wild Bill" Donovan, head of the OSS until Truman disbanded it in 1945, to serve as counsel. CBS contributed $10,000 and the services of its Rome correspondent, Winston Burdett, who flew to Athens to monitor the trial.[132]

These, Lippmann boasted, were "men whose profession it is to have few illusions." And when, in July 1952, the Lippmann committee finally issued its report concluding that Staktopoulos "received a fair trial," most American journalists were happy to go along. Not I. F. Stone. In a devastating five-part series in the *Compass*, Izzy denounced the Lippmann report as a "feeble bit of whitewash" written by men "willing to hold back vital information rather than go to bat . . . on behalf of their dead colleague." It was years before Staktopoulos recanted his confession, decades before evidence of a frame-up came to light, and decades more before the full extent of collusion among Lippmann, Donovan, and the State Department became known. That anyone was still paying attention, after so many years, must in large measure be due to Izzy's furious indictment of what he termed "a double crime. One was the murder of the man whose body was found floating in Salonika Bay . . . The other was the success of the Greek and American governments in making an accomplice of this bunch of journalistic stuffed shirts."[133]

Izzy's wasn't the only voice crying "Whitewash!" John Donovan, Polk's opposite number at NBC, was fired by the network for refusing to resign from the Newsmen's Commission. Protests by Polk's cousin, a *Daily News* reporter named William Price, prompted the FBI to open a file on him; a few years later, Price was refused a passport. Neither man ever worked in mainstream journalism again.[134]

And I. F. Stone? For Izzy, the fall of 1952 was a frenzy of activity and indecision. In Boston he raised funds for Dirk Struik, an MIT mathematician indicted on state sedition charges. In the Bronx he appeared with Representative Vito Marcantonio at a rally honoring Elizabeth Gurley Flynn and three other women Smith Act defendants. In San Francisco he hung out with Vincent Hallinan, a prosperous lawyer turned Progressive Party candidate for president. And in Brooklyn he defended Mildred Flacks, a first-grade teacher at P.S. 35, in Bedford-Stuyvesant, who had been fired for refusing to answer questions about her political beliefs: "Are there hysterics so idiotic they believe she managed to inject Marxism-Leninism into minds grappling with alphabet blocks and how-to-do-sums-without-fingers?"[135] He wrote, "Watching the witch hunt in the schools is like watching a particularly revolting kind of murder, the kind in which a man is beaten to death before the eyes of a crowd too cowardly to interfere."[136]

Yet even on this topic, indignation was not the only string in his bow. When Yale University issued a stirring defense of academic freedom, Izzy applauded. But he also allowed a sneaking admiration for the "brash young right-winger, William F. Buckley, Jr.," whose manifesto *God and Man at Yale* prompted the university's self-examination. Calling Buckley "an able and engaging fellow, with a sharp eye for liberalistic bunkum," Izzy noted Buckley's defense of "free enterprise 'until something better comes along.' The man flatly denies he's a Communist, of course, but . . ."[137] With America gripped by an ice age of fear and political paralysis, Izzy was grateful for nonconformity wherever he found it.

His increasing impatience with orthodoxy made the 1952 election especially difficult for Izzy. The Democrats disgusted him: "I am sick and tired of the Trumanites, with their fake liberalism. The politicians among them live as unscrupulously on war hysteria as the cheap moochers among them live on the graft they get from selling favors . . . I do not think in this situation the Democrats are a lesser evil. In some ways I think the Democrats in their present stage are worse."[138] Not that he expected better from the Republicans. Eisenhower he'd always admired; he also felt the former soldier would be less easily led by his generals. But Nixon was another matter: "a young man who symbolizes a slick kind of Arrow-collar-ad Fascism, with a cynical contempt for the masses behind the histrionics of That Broadcast."*[139]

And the Progressives? The party he'd been willingly duped by in 1948 still "gives the isolated few who believe in peace and liberty a sense of not being alone. Its candidates and organization, whatever their shortcomings, deserve support."[140] Coming from a man who had been accused of "indulging in some plain and fancy red baiting" by the Progressive Party's secretary, C. B. Baldwin, this was generous praise,[141] but it stopped well short of an endorsement. The world had changed since Henry Wallace rallied his "Gideon's Army," and the Progressives, Stone felt, had not: "It

---

*Nixon's famous "Checkers speech," broadcast on September 23, 1952, in which he defended himself against charges of financial impropriety.

would be good for some Progressive Party people to try and remember that a man who wants peace is an ally. Period. It is not necessary to sell him a subscription to *Pravda*."[142]

Yet still he struggled. On succeeding days Izzy lauded the Democrats as the "Little Man's Party" and despaired because the "Dead Past Still Rules Dems" when it came to civil rights.[143] What finally got Izzy off the fence, and off his high horse of disdain for the Democrats, was the sense that, nationally, "this is one election year when my vote and voice will count . . . I am not going to run the risk of electing Eisenhower and Nixon" by voting Progressive. "This is, I realize, inconsistent with a great deal I have written, but that doesn't worry me either."[144]

Consistency was the least of his troubles. His all-out endorsement of the Illinois governor, Adlai Stevenson, not only put him at odds with American Communists (the party polemicist Alan Max spent three issues of the *Daily Worker* putting Izzy through the dialectical wringer) but also brought rebukes from old friends like Vito Marcantonio, whose attacks ran across the page from Izzy's column in the *Compass*. Izzy's announcement that the Progressive Party was now a dangerous distraction must also have made for a few awkward moments at the Corliss Lamont for Senate campaign headquarters. The son of the J. P. Morgan partner Thomas Lamont—who also happened to hold a mortgage on the *Daily Compass* machinery, plant, and fixtures—was running in New York on the American Labor and Progressive Party lines.* His campaign manager: I. F. Stone.[145]

On November 5, 1952, it was all over. Stevenson lost the election by nearly 7 million votes and carried just nine states. The Progressives, with a bare 140,000 votes, were destroyed as a party. Despite the best efforts of his campaign manager, who pronounced the candidate "firmly in [the] great Western libertarian tradition," Corliss Lamont wrote Virginia Durr that his result in New York "fell very far beneath what I had hoped for."[146] Like its star columnist, the *Compass* supported Stevenson. The paper itself had shut its doors two days before the election. Lamont had foreclosed.[147]

That April, Izzy had written to Freda Kirchwey offering her a column on the *Compass*. Kirchwey had declined. Now he wrote again, offering his

---

*As a mainstay of the Congress of Soviet-American Friendship, Corliss Lamont was the architect of the infamous letter proclaiming—on the eve of the Nazi-Soviet pact—the impossibility of any rapprochement between fascism and communism.

services to the *Nation*. When Kirchwey failed to respond, he followed up with a telegram, but Kirchwey "wouldn't say yes, she wouldn't say no." Other editors had no hesitation turning Izzy down, making him feel like some kind of "ideological Typhoid Mary."[148]

"My father had a recurrent nightmare," Jeremy Stone remembered. In the dream, some "they"—faceless and nameless—"just wouldn't let him work."[149] One winter afternoon after the paper closed, Stone sat at his old desk off the now empty city room on the third floor of the *Compass* building, formerly the *Star* building and before that the *PM* building, watching the snow fall on the corner of Hudson and Duane streets. He had gone from the inner councils of the New Deal to the outer darkness of American politics. No daily newspaper in America would hire him. He was forty-four years old. He began to type: "I feel for the moment like a ghost."[150]

Eight

COMING UP FOR AIR

———◆◆◆———

If STONE leaves the city of Washington by train or bus, he is to be taken by one man.

If he leaves the city driving his own auto, he is to be taken.

If he leaves the city by plane, he is to be put on the plane and [REDACTED] advised immediately, so that the appropriate office may be instructed to take up the surveillance on his arrival.

—Office memorandum, Federal Bureau of Investigation,
November 4, 1953

One night while they were still living at Jouy-en-Josas, the Stones received a visit from George Seldes, editor and publisher of *In fact*, a muckraking fortnightly newsletter he'd started in May 1940 with Richard Bransten, husband of the *PM* writer Ruth McKenney.* *In fact* was self-righteous, often shrill—A. J. Liebling wrote that Seldes was "about as subtle as a house falling in"—but at its height had more than 175,000 subscribers, most of them members of the CIO, whose unions subscribed in bulk. Seldes was the first reporter to highlight the link between smoking and cancer and the first to expose the hypocrisy of the press, flush with cigarette ads, which suppressed the story. He was also a pioneering media critic, legendary for-

———

*Bransten, who signed his *In fact* articles Bruce Minton, was the son of Morris Brandenstein, founder of MJB coffee in San Francisco. He and Seldes parted company in 1941. A financial backer of the *New Masses*, Bransten was expelled by the Communist Party with McKenney in 1946.

eign correspondent, and, at least in 1950, a tireless opponent of the blacklist which, combined with FBI harassment, cut *In fact*'s circulation down
to 55,000.[1] Seldes, who had just turned sixty, had decided to pack it in,
and wondered if Stone might be interested in taking over. At the time, Izzy
turned him down, but he never forgot the offer, or Seldes's explanation of
the economics of independent journalism.

"The Stones were friends of ours," Seldes recalled, "and we told them
exactly how we got started . . . Start on a small scale, don't have investments, and don't risk everything on it. Put a few ads in the *Nation* and the
New Republic, and if you catch on you're started."[2] Nor did Stone forget
that when *In fact* finally ceased publication in October 1950, Seldes had
kept his list of the 10,000 names who not only subscribed to the newsletter but also bought his books.

"There is no protest," Seldes had written upon closing *In fact*, "no indignation. People are frightened to death." Even the *Week*, the British
journalist Claud Cockburn's gossipy, muckraking journal—launched in
1933, scourge of the "Cliveden set" of British appeasers of fascism and
one of Seldes's chief inspirations—couldn't survive the postwar freeze.[3]
But Stone was determined to try. "He came to see me, and I gave him my
list of the book buyers," said Seldes.

What prompted Izzy's change of heart? From his friends in Israel he'd
learned a Hebrew expression often used to explain the country's survival
against the odds during the war of independence: *Ein breira*. No alternative.

A prospectus for the new venture went out in early November. In it
Stone reminded readers of his track record, and of the freedom he had enjoyed on *PM* and the *Compass*. But in asking their support to carry on the
good work, he omitted one crucial detail. "We sent out the first mailing for
the *Weekly* and realized we'd left out the price for a year's subscription,"
Jeremy recalled. A second mailing followed, offering "a 4-page letter size
miniature newspaper of uninhibited commentary and let-the-chips-fall-
where-they-may reporting from Washington and elsewhere, wherever
the news is hottest," for $5 a year. The new *Weekly*'s first office was at
401 Broadway; Izzy and his family were still living on Park Avenue, and he
was in no hurry to leave New York. Despite more than a decade in Washington, his sensibility remained less Beltway than Broadway. Christopher
Stone remembered: "He liked New York. He had friends. He loved his
fans. Dad hated Washington. I remember him being very bitter . . . But he

needed to be in Washington." The stories he'd made his own—the struggle for nuclear sanity in foreign policy and the battle "for the maintenance
of free institutions at home"—were being fought out in the corridors of the
capital, and, as he told prospective readers, "I want to stay in the fight."[4]

"Willing to return Nation full schedule letter and editorials as Washington editor for one hundred and fifty dollars a week," he cabled Freda
Kirchwey in late November. "I recommended to Freda that we do it," said
Carey McWilliams. He was the *Nation*'s California contributing editor
who had come to New York for "a few weeks" in 1951 to help edit a special issue on civil liberties and ended up working on the magazine for
twenty-five years. But Kirchwey "didn't think [Stone would] stay put in
Washington. Freda was worried that Izzy would run off to Israel or somewhere else and we couldn't afford that."[5] Nor were these concerns—or
even Stone's radical politics—the only obstacles to employment. Applying for a job at the *New York Times* in 1953, Daniel Schorr was told the
paper had a temporary freeze on hiring Jews as foreign correspondents
because the *Times* was short of non-Jewish correspondents to cover Arab
countries in case of a war in the Middle East.[6]

But it wasn't clear that Izzy could afford to set up on his own either.
David Stern had forced him out without severance pay, a deficit that neither
PM nor the *Star* would remedy. So when Ted Thackrey brought him back to
the *Post*, Izzy asked for $3,500 to be put in escrow, and he had kept this fund
when he went to the *Compass*. Walking downtown after lunch at the Museum of Modern Art with a friend, Izzy explained his money worries, adding
that he was determined "to keep on fighting if I have to crank out a paper on
a mimeograph machine in the cellar!" The friend, Arthur Weiner, offered to
lend him $3,000, enough to pay for another round of mailings and promo-
tion.[7] Using the Seldes list, *Compass* subscribers, and the *Monthly Review*
list of people who had bought *The Hidden History*, Marc Stone, acting as
business manager, sent out 30,000 letters between November 1952 and
January 1953. He also placed ads in the *Times*, the *Post*, the *Nation*, and the
National Guardian. Izzy kept a close watch on every dollar.

Sidney Roger, who came east on a lobbying trip for the longshoremen's
union that fall, said that when Izzy invited him to dinner his friend was
bursting with excitement about "his new publishing venture, to be called
I. F. Stone's Weekly . . . I reached in my wallet and gave him a $5 bill and
said, 'I want to be your first subscriber.' He put it in his vest pocket."

When the bill came, Izzy felt his jacket "and said, 'Oh, my God, I left my wallet at home!' The tab was about $4.50 for two of us." Roger pointed out the $5 bill. "He said, 'No, I've got a subscription in my vest pocket. I can't spend that money.' I paid for the dinner."[8]

In just three weeks that November, Izzy and Marc managed to bring in 3,000 subscribers for the yet-to-be-published *Weekly*. It wasn't enough. By the middle of December 1952, when the writer Harvey O'Connor sent in his check, the total had reached 3,495. It still wasn't enough. All this time Stone remained in touch with Freda Kirchwey, who still "wouldn't say yes, wouldn't say no. I finally got tired of waiting." In his last mailing, Stone warned readers: "I have no crystal ball and will not deal in predictions. I have no access to keyholes and will not dish up 'hot stuff.'" By January, he had just over 4,000 subscribers—about 1,200 short of what he needed to break even—but he was going ahead.[9]

Unlike Cockburn's *Week*, which really was produced on a mimeograph machine, or the strident certainties of *In fact*, volume one, number one of *I. F. Stone's Weekly* was a sober affair, printed on four letter-size pages of plain newsprint in conservative Garamond type. Just days before Eisenhower's inauguration, the editor-publisher took a parting shot at President Truman before moving on to more present dangers. "Who Will Watch This Watchman?" pointed out that "with much daring and few scruples, McCarthy can make himself the most powerful single figure in Congress and terrorize the new administration." Two years earlier, when Wisconsin's junior senator was still struggling for the nation's attention, Sidney Roger had invited Stone to speak at a San Francisco rally for the California Smith Act defendants. "America depends on us," Izzy had said to the crowd, and then he told them "a wonderful story from Aristotle. He asks the question: what happens when an army, that's running away, suddenly turns and starts to fight? [Aristotle] says what happens is that somebody gets tired of running and decides that since he might be killed anyway, he might just as well stop and fight and die honorably. And somebody else joins him. And a third guy, and a sixth guy. And pretty soon the whole darned army has turned around and is putting up a fight instead of running away."[10] Stone had gone from *PM* to the *Star* to the *Compass*, and from Washington to Tel Aviv to Paris to New York. But on January 14, 1953, when he took the first issue of the *Weekly* to the post office, I. F. Stone finally stopped running.

•

Izzy and Esther moved back to Washington in February 1953. Their son Chris came with them, but Jeremy stayed behind to finish his senior year at the Bronx High School of Science. The night before they left New York, the Stones went to see Arthur Miller's new play. In *The Crucible* Izzy felt he'd witnessed "a parable for our own haunted times"; he was particularly struck by Miller's line "but witches were purely imaginary, whereas today . . ."[11]

Of course, Izzy knew that Communists were real, and that Moscow's intentions were neither benign nor wholly rational. The trial and execution of the Czech Communist leader Rudolph Slansky for "Zionist activity" horrified him, and when the Russians claimed to have discovered a "Doctors' Plot," a conspiracy on the part of a group of Jewish doctors to poison the top ranks of the Politburo, he rejected the charges as "too hideous to be credible." Melodrama "sometimes occurs in real life," he allowed, but "the Soviets have a way of erecting possibilities into actualities and then staging trials to 'prove' what they fear . . . It is not enough to prove a man mistaken; he must be displayed as a monster . . . Their purpose is to warn the Jews of the Soviet world to break all ties with the West and to stifle all nationalist feeling 'or else.'"[12]

And he'd long since ceased to expect much from what he called "the vermiform appendix of American communism." Yet he refused to turn his back on his old comrades (or his relatives), partly out of respect for what they had been able to accomplish together: "The Popular Front, far from overturning the government by force and violence, made democracy work, proved that social reform was possible by peaceful means—and did so at a time when other countries were turning to dictatorship of right or left. It gave the workers and farmers of America new faith in their country and their society. It taught radicals who came to Washington a new respect for democratic processes as it taught not a few big business men a new respect for the meaning of free government." But mostly he believed the current fight was simply too important. "The question," he reminded his readers, "is not whether the Communists are part of an international movement; of course they are. The question is not whether these organizations named by the Attorney General are 'fronts'; let it be assumed that they are. The question is whether we are to abandon the standards and

I. F. Stone's Weekly

VOL. 1 NUMBER 1   JANUARY 17, 1953   WASHINGTON, D. C.   15 CENTS

Mr. Truman's Farewell Evasions

The warning to Stalin made the headlines. The warning to ourselves was played down. "War today between the Soviet empire and the free nations," Mr. Truman said in his last State of the Union message, "might dig the grave not only of our Stalinist opponents, but of our own society, our world as well as theirs." The outgoing President was apocalyptic in his picture of the war of the future. "Man could extinguish millions of lives at one blow, demolish the great cities of the world, wipe out the cultural achievements of the past . . ." Mr. Truman said "Such a war is not a possible policy for rational men."

But if a new war between the giants of East and West threatens their mutual destruction, if such a war is not a possible policy for rational men, then the alternative is co-existence. If the disputes of U.S. and U.S.S.R. cannot be settled on the battle-field without endangering the survival of civilization, then they must be settled somehow at the conference table. The conclusion is inescapable, but Mr. Truman managed again to escape it, as he has all through his years in the Presidency.

Mr. Truman fears war, but remains evasive about peace. The meaning of the H-bomb and the new weapons of destruction is that men must learn to live together on the same planet in mutual forbearance. What Mr. Truman should have said is that in the awful perspective of a new war no pains must be spared to negotiate differences between Washington and Moscow. But Mr. Truman's emphasis was on his old hope that if cold war and containment were continued long enough the Soviet regime would somehow crack up from within. Negotiation requires compromise, but there was in Mr. Truman's message the same self-righteous insistence that any settlement must be on our terms. Some years ago at press conference he made it clear that what he sought was unconditional surrender by Moscow as the price of ending the cold war. Mr. Truman set the mood and Mr. Acheson coined the phrase for it—"total diplomacy." It was to shut the door on negotiation and keep the heat on until the Soviets crumpled.

What happens to us in the meantime? Mr. Truman says we are being "hurried forward" in atomic research "from one discovery to another, toward yet unforeseeable peaks of destructive power." Will this safeguard our own security? "We must realize," Mr. Truman himself warns, "that no advance we make is unattainable by others, that no advantage in this race can be more than temporary."

The more terrible the weapons of destruction grow, the greater must become our fear, that the enemy also possesses them, the greater our frenzied effort to remain ahead. The atmosphere and momentum of an atomic arms race spell ever greater insecurity at ever greater cost. Like a new war, this too is no policy for rational men.

We can impose tension on the Soviet system only by imposing tension on ourselves. The tension which we hope will disintegrate the Soviet system from within may do the same to our own. Mr. Truman warns against "fear that breeds more fear, sapping our faith, corroding our liberties, turning citizen against citizen . . . Fear could snatch away the very values we are striving to defend." But how avoid that fear in a world of mounting tension, hate and war preparations?

To pursue such a policy with stubborn blindness while warning against its inevitable consequences is to give a drunken party and salve one's conscience with a lecture on alcoholism. "Already the danger signals have gone up," Mr. Truman says piously. "Already the corrosive process has begun . . . every diminution of our tolerance, each new act of enforced conformity, each idle accusation, each demonstration of hysteria—each new restrictive law—is one more sign that we can lose the battle against fear." It is also a sign that we cannot wage cold war on Soviet society without waging cold war on our own.

Mr. Truman thinks of himself as a liberal. It is at once something subtler and more human than hypocrisy which leads him to say, "We must take our stand on the Bill of Rights. The inquisition, the star chamber, have no place in a free society." The same capacity for inviting war in the name of peace made it possible for him to launch star chamber loyalty purges and peacetime sedition prosecutions while preaching civil liberties. The man who devoted most of his years in the White House to propagating alarm ends by warning us "The Communists cannot deprive us of our liberties—fear can."

But how make people accept the heavy burdens of cold war without injecting ever greater doses of fear and suspicion? If the purpose is to preserve liberty and safeguard peace, the cold war is no more rational than another world war would be. In any case the one, if continued, must lead inevitably to the other. At the Pentagon indeed these last words of Mr. Truman's must seem little more than smoke-screen to hide the full import of current military preparations from civilians.

Washington's Farewell Address had better advice than Truman's. Washington warned the new Republic—and the warning now seems prophetic—not to cherish "permanent inveterate antipathies against particular nations." Washington saw that hatred could be one of the most entangling of all entangling alliances. He said "the nation which indulges toward another an habitual hatred . . . is in some degree a slave. It is a slave to its animosity." Only negotiation, coexistence and peace can emancipate us from the campaign of hate and its hateful consequences.

habits of a free society, fleeing the risks of freedom for the deadlier risks of repression. The question is whether we are to relinquish the standards of Jefferson for those of Torquemada."[13]

In the winter of 1953, when *I. F. Stone's Weekly* made its debut, the American inquisition was at its height. The country was still at war in Korea. Republicans branded the New Deal "twenty years of treason" while Democrats and labor unions purged their ranks of Communists, former Communists, fellow travelers, and anyone unwilling to disavow previous sympathy for left-wing causes. At the annual Lincoln's Birthday luncheon of the American Civil Liberties Union, the ACLU cofounder Roger Baldwin was flanked on the dais by Robert Morris, counsel to the McCarran committee, and Vincent Hartnett, coauthor of *Red Channels*, the broadcasting blacklisters' bible.[14] Roy Cohn, the young prosecutor whose examination of David Greenglass sent the Rosenbergs to their deaths, sat among the honored guests. On J. Edgar Hoover's recommendation, Cohn had just been named counsel to Senator McCarthy. Meanwhile, Owen Lattimore was at home in Maryland preparing for yet another round of his ordeal—this time on perjury charges.

"I was in high school in Washington and 'things' were at their most hysterical pitch," Christopher Stone recalled. "I went along on a drive with my father . . . out to where Owen and Eleanor were living." The details of the conversation are long forgotten. But the toll exacted by the China scholar's tormentors made an indelible impression: "Lattimore had developed an awful tic—my father said afterward it was something new—and was in considerable pain. I am pretty sure he asked leave . . . to lie on the floor for his back." Lattimore maintained his dignity throughout. "He seemed, in fact, to be unaware of the tic that was scuttling across his face with a mean mocking life of its own."[15]

That winter Leonard Boudin was on a train to Washington for a meeting with his brother-in-law when the conductor called his name. At Izzy's suggestion, Leonard had begun to take cases for the Emergency Civil Liberties Committee. The two men had a deep respect for each other's abilities that survived a fierce, if fraternal, competition stretching over many decades. They also had very different relationships with their wives, a disparity that was about to grow more acute. The conductor told Leonard that his wife, Jean, Esther Stone's sister, was in St. Vincent's Hospital in New York. The family's housekeeper had found her in the kitchen of their

Greenwich Village brownstone with her head in the oven, a dish towel folded under her cheek, the gas left on; Leonard and Jean's two children, thirteen-year-old Michael and nine-year-old Kathy, had arrived home seconds later. Though Jean's suicide attempt was largely a response to Leonard's flagrant infidelity, Jean also knew that her husband had powerful enemies.[16] Attorneys like Harry Sacher and Abe Isserman who defended the rights of Communists—or even former Communists who refused to "name names"—found themselves cited for contempt and subject to disbarment proceedings.

And those were not the only targets. A whole generation of diplomats experienced in Far Eastern affairs, the "China hands," had been driven from office, blamed for America's inability to hold back the "Red tide" in Asia. Scientists like Izzy's friend Edward Condon learned that their contributions to the war effort counted less than ideological conformity or the political reliability of their prewar associates (or relatives). Hollywood had been under siege since the first HUAC hearings in 1947, when Lela Rogers told the committee how her daughter Ginger had been drafted as a mouthpiece for the screenwriter Dalton Trumbo's Communist propaganda—"Share and share alike, that's democracy!"—in the wartime weepy *Tender Comrade*.[17]

"You start out by wanting to keep your friends," the actor Lee J. Cobb told Victor Navasky. "In a totalitarian country they want you to betray your friends—and you persuade yourself that it is your duty." Cobb resisted HUAC for two years. For those two years he had no work, and two small children, and at the end a wife who was institutionalized. In the spring of 1953, he cooperated, naming twenty people. One of these was Philip Loeb, who played Papa on *The Goldbergs*, a popular series on CBS. Loeb's wife was dead; their son, who suffered from schizophrenia, was in a private asylum. After CBS canceled his show, Loeb never worked in television again. In 1953, Vincent Hartnett, his zeal undiminished by the ACLU's hospitality, wrote a feature in the *American Mercury* describing Loeb as "one of the loudest noises" on "New York's Great Red Way." At the time Loeb was scraping by in an $80-a-week revival; with no income to pay for private care he'd moved his son to a Massachusetts state institution. When Loeb attempted suicide, unlike Jean Boudin, he succeeded. And, as Cobb had told the committee, he never even knew Loeb to be a Communist.[18]

John Garfield wasn't a Communist. But he, like Cobb and Clifford Odets—who'd quit the party after *Waiting for Lefty* and had written *Golden Boy* for Garfield—had been a member of the Group Theatre and a reliable ornament on various Popular Front platforms. Garfield's formal education had ended in grade school, and when he first became a target of the blacklist he'd pleaded political naïveté, a claim that didn't satisfy his inquisitors. The actor was threatened with perjury unless he agreed to name names. "It killed him, it really killed him," his daughter Julie Garfield told an interviewer. "He was under unbelievable stress. Phones were being tapped. He was being followed by the FBI. He hadn't worked in eighteen months." The star of *Body and Soul* died of a heart attack in 1952 at the age of thirty-nine. Among the former Communists he'd protected with his silence was his wife, Roberta Seidman, who after Garfield's death married his lawyer, Sidney Cohn.[19]

One by one Izzy's friends and associates found themselves caught in the inquisitor's net. In March 1953, Julius Hlavaty, head of the mathematics department at the Bronx High School of Science and Jeremy Stone's teacher, was hauled before the McCarthy committee and asked to explain his registration in the American Liberal Party. Hlavaty, a Czech émigré, had agreed to make a Slovak-language broadcast for the Voice of America. McCarthy himself conceded there was no Communist propaganda in the broadcast, yet the teacher was examined on his politics, on his associations, and, by Senator Stuart Symington, on whether, "as a good American . . . you believe in God?" Denying present or recent membership in the Communist Party, Hlavaty pleaded the Fifth Amendment for 1948—a response sufficient to cost him his job. The hearing "was painful to watch," wrote Stone, one of only a handful of reporters in attendance. "A teacher was being ruined because he had done a favor for a government agency. A committee sated with victims took him apart indifferently, like a small boy taking the wings off a beetle."[20]

The following month, Izzy's friend Palmer Weber, like Clark Foreman a Southern liberal and activist in the Southern Conference for Human Welfare, was subpoenaed to testify before hearings on "Interlocking Subversion in Government Departments." During the war, Weber had been a staffer on the Senate's War Mobilization Committee; he was also the first white Southerner elected to the national board of the NAACP. Asked about his associations with the International Longshoremen's Association leader Harry

Bridges, Weber replied, "I will plead my privilege."* He gave the same reply to questions about Simon Gerson and John Abt. Robert Morris asked: "Mr. I. F. Stone is a frequent visitor at your home, is he not?" Weber replied: "I would not describe him as a frequent visitor. I know Mr. Stone."[21]

The ink was hardly dry on his subscription check to the *Weekly* when Harvey O'Connor got a telephone call from Roy Cohn summoning him to Washington. The author of *Mellon's Millions* and *The Empire of Oil* declined the invitation of a mere minion but soon received a subpoena from McCarthy himself. "This is the era of the Armageddon—that final all-out battle between light and darkness foretold in the Bible," the senator told adoring audiences. O'Connor, taking him at his word, gave no quarter.[22] A week earlier, Leo Huberman had tried to fence with Cohn. Asked, "Have you ever been a member of the Communist Party?" Huberman, under oath, replied that he had not. Cohn then asked, "Have you ever been a Communist?" prompting Huberman to wonder "What does that mean?" and then to elaborate: "Well, if you mean by a Communist one who believes in socialism, I do believe in socialism." Satisfactorily branded with a scarlet C, Huberman was dismissed. But O'Connor, accompanied by his attorney, Leonard Boudin, didn't even let McCarthy swear him in before stating his "objection . . . under the First Amendment to the Constitution. The committee has no authority to look into my books or political beliefs, and if my writings have violated any laws, that is the proper subject for the law enforcement agencies and this committee is not a law enforcement agency."[23]

Once sworn, O'Connor was asked by Cohn if, at the time he wrote his biographies of the Astors and the Guggenheims, he had been a member of the Communist Party. O'Connor objected to the question. Told by McCarthy that he could refuse to answer "only if you feel a truthful an-

---

*He refused to answer on Fifth Amendment grounds. The Supreme Court had ruled that a witness who refused to answer questions about past political associations on First Amendment (free speech) grounds alone could be jailed for contempt; the Court had also held that anyone who answered questions about his or her own political past could be compelled to testify about others—to "name names" (*Rogers v. U.S.*, 1951). Any witness who wished to avoid either jail or becoming an informer was forced to rely on the Fifth Amendment protection against self-incrimination, which aided McCarthy and his imitators, since they generally preferred to maneuver hostile witnesses into invoking the Fifth Amendment as often as possible. Such a stance almost always rendered the witness unemployable. Palmer Weber, who held a doctorate in economics from the University of Virginia, was one of a surprising number of blacklist victims who later made their fortunes in the stock market.

swer might tend to incriminate you," O'Connor said, "I feel that a truthful answer will not incriminate me." And when McCarthy directed him to answer the question, O'Connor replied, "I have answered the question." When Cohn repeated the question, O'Connor declined again: "How many ways do I have to phrase the damn thing?"[24] Like I. F. Stone, O'Connor was picking a fight.

The two men were political allies—toward the end of 1954, O'Connor was to become chairman of the ECLC—but their situations were far from identical. A former editor of the *Seattle Daily Call*, a Socialist paper, O'Connor was best known for his muckraking biographies. He'd also spent much of the 1930s as a foreign correspondent for the Federated Press, the labor news service that later employed Marc Stone. It was through the FP that O'Connor met his wife, Jessie, a journalist carrying the radical tradition (and name) of her grandfather Henry Demarest Lloyd, author of *Wealth Against Commonwealth*. An heiress to the *Chicago Tribune* fortune, Jessie Maverick Lloyd (the liberal congressman Maury Maverick was her uncle) owned ranchland in Texas as well as the estate in Little Compton, Rhode Island, where she and Harvey offered refuge and hospitality to generations of American radicals.

I. F. Stone's Weekly, however, started life with a net operating deficit of $5,600, and while Esther Stone was as supportive of her husband's new venture as any wife could be—handling the subscription and mailing operations so that Izzy could concentrate on reporting and writing—family finances were cut to the bone. (In December 1953, when Celia eloped with the young scientist Walter Gilbert to Elkton, Maryland, she phoned her mother, who was working at the *Weekly*'s new office at 301 East Capitol Street. A dazed Esther handed the phone to the bride's father. "Izzy got on the phone," his daughter remembered, "and I said, 'We're married.' And he said, 'Look, okay, you're married, you're not married, get the car down here. I have to get the *Weekly*s to the stands.'")[25]

And there was one more difference: Harvey O'Connor had an FBI *file*. I. F. Stone was an FBI *target*, a suspect in an ongoing espionage investigation. The *Weekly* may be the only radical periodical in American history born under the lens of daily FBI surveillance.

On October 12, 1953, two special agents followed Izzy to Angelo's Barbecue, where he "emerged . . . carrying a small package," then on to Gerhard Van Arkel's apartment. The following day a team of agents watched while "subject bought 2 papers and picked up dry cleaning." The next night the G-men trailed Izzy and Esther to the movies. When the Stone family moved to Washington, the FBI's "mail cover" moved with them, which meant that every subscriber or potential subscriber to the *Weekly* was soon noted by Hoover's men. Nor did the bureau relax its scrutiny of the Stone garbage cans, whose contents were duly inspected at D.C. Incinerator Number 2 in order not to arouse suspicion.[26]

In that respect, at least, the FBI's surveillance of I. F. Stone was a success. Neither Izzy nor Esther nor any of their children ever suspected the bureau's extraordinary level of interest. Hoover's men remained discreet, even when tailing Izzy taking Chris out for driving practice.* But then, they had been given explicit instructions: Under the heading IMPORTANT!! IMPORTANT!! IMPORTANT!! the FBI warned Stone's shadows:

> Stone has been a bitter critic of the Bureau in his writings and speeches for many years . . . This surveillance *must* be conducted with the utmost discretion. If there is a possibility that Agents have been or might be "made" the surveillance is to be dropped immediately. Stone is an intelligent and observant man and . . . if he does "make" the surveillance he will undoubtedly use his newsletter to good advantage in embarrassing the Bureau. This is a very delicate situation and consistent intelligent effort *must* be expended to insure that the surveillance is properly, and at all costs discreetly, conducted.[27]

(Ironically, the FBI's discretion came at a price. For years Hoover struggled to link Owen Lattimore with "Pacificus," the anonymous *Nation* contributor whose critique of America's policy toward Japan had so enraged certain diplomats. Indeed, it was the Pacificus connection that first put Lattimore in Hoover's sights. Now, with Lattimore on trial for perjury, the Justice Department's criminal division asked the FBI to interview I. F. Stone—the one man who could identify Pacificus. The reply—in Hoover's

---

*Such discretion was not standard procedure. In his *Going Away: A Report, A Memoir*, the screenwriter Clancy Sigal describes the pair of agents who, with monotonous regularity, turned up on his doorstep alternately threatening him and attempting to entice him to become an informant. And in *Loyalties*, Carl Bernstein, whose father, Albert, was a Communist lawyer, recalls the FBI standing outside his house during his bar mitzvah conspicuously noting down the license plates of the guests.

own handwriting—was emphatic: "We will not do so under any circumstances. If they want him interviewed, they will have to do so themselves.
H." As a result, neither Hoover nor the Justice Department ever learned
the identity of Pacificus: not Owen Lattimore but Andrew Roth, the navy
lieutenant unsuccessfully prosecuted in the *Amerasia* affair.[28])

Although Stone remained unaware of the extent of FBI interest in his
activities, he couldn't ignore his own transformation into an unperson:
"Early Soviet novels used a vivid phrase, 'former people,' about the remnants of the dispossessed ruling class. On the inhospitable sidewalks of
Washington these days, the editor often feels like one of the 'former
people,' a phantom out of the New Deal past."[29] There were exceptions,
cherished all the more for their rarity. He saw Van Arkel regularly, and
James Martin, the former Justice Department antitrust division lawyer in
charge of German cartels, was still willing to put his name down on paper
as a director of the *Weekly*.[30] Jennings Perry, a colleague from *PM* and the
Compass, sent in reports from the South. One day Izzy and Esther piled
the boys in the car and drove to Princeton to visit a charter subscriber:
"Albert Einstein bounded down the stairs," Jeremy remembered, "carrying a violin and wearing a sweatshirt. He saw dad and said, 'Ah, the subversive hero.'" Christopher recalled that at the end of the afternoon, as
Einstein walked them to the door, he said, "Do the boys have any questions? I will answer them if I can."[31]

More typical was an evening at Dick Dudman's house. Dudman
sought out Izzy in New York before going to Europe on assignment for
the *Denver Post* to report on conditions in camps for displaced persons
(DPs). "[Izzy] was very cordial, but he was also very blunt. He said he
didn't think I knew enough European history to do a good job." Undaunted, when Dudman became Washington correspondent for the *St.
Louis Post-Dispatch* in 1953, Stone "was one of the first people I looked
up. At that time, he was really a pariah . . . They just assumed he was a
Communist. He was really shunned by people. Once we gave a party at
our house in Cleveland Park. There were several other people, including
a guy who was with the government. Our other friend followed me into
the kitchen, and said: 'How could you invite me to your house at the same
time as I. F. Stone?'"[32]

"I will refer you to one of the best collections on the subject, which is
Mr. I. F. Stone's book on the Secret [*sic*] History of the Korean War." The

source of this testimonial was Victor Perlo, a New Deal economist named by Elizabeth Bentley as a member of the same Communist Party cell as Nathaniel Weyl and Alger Hiss, who in May 1953 found himself fending off the attentions of the Jenner committee, successor to the McCarran committee. Perlo's plug for I. F. Stone was a rare departure for a witness whose responses, following a routine he had already rehearsed before HUAC, were largely confined to variations of "I refuse to answer on the grounds that it might tend to incriminate me." (Perlo did admit uncertainty in relation to Korea. Not on the war, where he cited both Izzy and the *Daily Worker* on the likelihood that South Korea was never invaded, but on a more fundamental question: "I don't know whether [North Korea] is classified as a People's Democracy or not.")[33] With such endorsements, it took a brave man indeed to be seen in public with I. F. Stone.

•

Looking back from a comfortable distance of years, Stone described the 1950s as "haunted," a term encompassing both the climate of fear and the spectral source of that fear. More enlightened times have laid to rest many of that era's obsessions. Who now maintains the innocence of the Rosenbergs?* Or the "guilt" of Acheson? The letter-writing legions of the China Lobby have long been silent; Marvin Liebman, single-handed convener of the lobby's Committee of One Million, baptized in 1980 into the Catholic faith with William F. Buckley Jr. as godfather, went to his grave in 1997 an activist for gay rights. Yet a half century after its blue-chinned eponym drank himself to death, McCarthyism still rattles its chains. "McCarthy is not stupid," Stone warned when the senator announced his crusade—his first under a Republican president—against the Voice of

---

*"The ghost of the Rosenberg case," Izzy wrote after their execution in June 1953, "will haunt the United States for a long time to come." This was no idle prophecy. But long before Ronald Radosh and Joyce Milton's book *The Rosenberg File: A Search for the Truth* (New York: Holt, 1983) purported to settle the question, and even longer before the Venona decrypts settled the question for Radosh and Milton's principal antagonists, I. F. Stone advised those agitating for clemency for Morton Sobell to "free his case from the burden of using it to prove the Rosenbergs the victims of a frame-up." Izzy's July 1956 argument that "the Rosenbergs were treated a good deal more fairly here than Slansky and other Jewish victims of Stalin justice" was, harrumphed Cedric Belfrage's *National Guardian*, "demagogic word-slinging at the meanest level." In September 2008, Sobell told the reporter Sam Roberts that both he and Julius Rosenberg had passed classified information to the Soviets.

America. "He knows what he is doing. This is one of a series of little 'Reichstag fires' to light his way to power."[34]

Stone noticed two salient facts about McCarthy right away that seemed to elude many later commentators on the period. The first was that for all the prominence given to exceptions like Owen Lattimore and George Marshall, few of McCarthy's targets were "innocent liberals." "This was crucial," writes the historian Ellen Schrecker. "McCarthyism succeeded because the people it targeted were already political outcasts. They were Communists or ex-Communists. And, by the late forties and early fifties, the Truman administration, the Supreme Court, and most private citizens believed or claimed to believe that Communism was so alien to the American way of life that its adherents did not deserve to be protected by the Constitution."[35]

Izzy also knew that just as the Red Scare hadn't begun with McCarthy's speech in Wheeling, the -ism and its effects had a life independent of the career of one Wisconsin senator. "All too few will notice the key role the FBI has been playing in the witch hunt from J. Parnell Thomas to Joe McCarthy," Stone lamented, "and will continue to play behind the scenes as one adventurer succeeds another in the center of the stage."[36] When J. Edgar Hoover, whose men were supposedly following up a Senate report investigating McCarthy's finances, gave an interview describing McCarthy as "a friend," the national press buried the story. Perhaps, speculated the *Weekly*, because acknowledgment of the "Hoover-McCarthy axis must also spike the feeble popguns of those faint-hearted liberals whose anti-McCarthy line has been, 'Let the FBI do it.' This *is* how the FBI does it."[37]

Did Izzy have a particular popgun in mind? In April 1953, just a few weeks after the death of Stalin, McCarthy subpoenaed James Wechsler. The *Post* editor's friend (and McCarthy biographer) Richard Rovere painted the confrontation in heroic colors, claiming Wechsler "gave McCarthy as good as he got."[38] Stone was less admiring: "It is ironic that the first target of McCarthy in American journalism should be an editor who advanced his own career by deft use of anti-Communism in inner newspaper politics. One editor after another made James Wechsler a protégé only to be repaid with a self-serving Red smear." Wechsler did deserve credit, he argued, for pushing the ADA toward "a more liberal position than that advocated by his columnist, the ignominious Arthur M. Schlesinger, Jr.," whom Izzy (echoing Carey McWilliams) described as "a

Zalman (Solomon) Novack, Stone's maternal grandfather

Young pioneer: Isadore Feinstein as a boy in Indiana

The Feinstein family home and dry-goods store in Richmond, Indiana, as it looks today (© 1994 by Bob Statzer)

"I started talking *mama-loshen* to the schoolchildren": Isadore (foreground at right, in a sailor suit) in kindergarten in Indiana

Esther Roisman and Isadore Feinstein on their wedding day

As chief editorial writer of the *New York Post* in 1933, Izzy enjoyed unparalleled freedom at the age of twenty-five.

"Grand Central Station," the family's cottage on Fire Island, was a cherished retreat.

The Stone family in Central Park in 1936: (from left) Jeremy, Izzy, Celia, and Esther

Stone in Stuttgart with a U.S. serviceman and two *PM* readers, awaiting news of a ship to Palestine, May 1946 (Courtesy of Norma K. Eigles)

Underground to Palestine: Stone in a displaced persons camp, 1946 (Courtesy of the Haganah Archives, Tel Aviv, Israel)

The *Nation*'s office in the 1940s (Freda Kirchwey on the couch, Stone at the far right)
(Courtesy of the Schlesinger Library, Radcliffe Institute for Advanced Study, Harvard University)

"To be a great poet is the greatest thing in the world": Izzy with his daughter, Celia

Izzy's children with their grandfathers: (from left to right) Celia, Jeremy, Christopher, and their cousin Michael Boudin; Morris Roisman (rear left) and Bernard Feinstein (rear right)

On the town: Esther and Izzy at a dinner at the Waldorf-Astoria in the late 1940s

Ink in the blood: Stone and his siblings. (left) Louis and his wife, Deena; (center) Izzy and Esther; (right) Marc and his wife, Martha; (rear) Judy. All four siblings became journalists.

Stone in Saigon, April 1966 (© 1966 by Bill Wingell)

The hardest-working man in the news business: Stone with his reporter's notepad at the Moratorium to End the War in Vietnam, November 15, 1969

At Izzy's seventieth birthday party in 1978, Izzy and Esther (center) are joined by (from right to left) the novelist Kurt Vonnegut, Jr., Murray Kempton, the cartoonist Jules Feiffer (partially obscured), the broadcaster Jim Jensen, and the poet William Meredith. (© 1978 by Jill Krementz)

Collecting his A. J. Liebling Award in 1972, Stone said, "To be a pariah is to be left alone to see things your own way." (© 1972 by Jill Krementz)

La grande vedette du festival: Esther, Izzy, and Lina Wertmüller at the Cannes Film Festival, 1974

By the end of his life, the former iconoclast had become something of an icon. (© 1982 by Jill Krementz)

"Because history is a tragedy, not a melodrama": Stone inside the Jefferson Memorial (© 1982 by Sylvia Plachy)

McCarthy with a Harvard accent" using his column "to smear those liberals who have had the temerity to defend the rights of Communists, and
thereby organize a principled opposition to McCarthyism.

"Not much principle was left," Izzy continued, "by the way Wechsler
himself answered McCarthy." The *Post* editor handed over a list of associates from his days in the Young Communist League, plaintively requesting
his inquisitors not to make the list public—in vain—and asking instead
that the names be forwarded to the FBI. Among those Wechsler named
was the *Post* columnist Murray Kempton. "An editor who will inform on
his own staff 'to keep the record straight' is an editor who has allowed
himself to be degraded," wrote Izzy, perhaps with some satisfaction after
his own brushes with Wechsler. But the personal agenda never overshadowed his more serious point: "Once the Inquisition is accepted, it is futile
to protest that its victims should be chosen and broiled more carefully . . .
For if Communists are such cunning devils—to doubt the consummate
cunning of Satan was a particularly insidious form of heresy—then is it not
possible that Wechsler as a promising young Communist was ordered
many years ago in Moscow to pretend anti-Communism?"[39]

It was precisely the liberal impulse to genuflect before the heresy
hunters, Stone argued, that crippled effective resistance: "The right to
dissent was not established and will not be preserved by submitting cer-
tificates of conformity. McCarthy had no right to question Wechsler, but
McCarthyism cannot be fought effectively until men are prepared to
deny the right of Congress to interrogate any American, newspaperman
or not, anti-Communist or not, on his political beliefs."[40]

As if in illustration of this principle, concurrently with Wechsler's torment, Congressman Harold Velde, the Illinois Republican and ex-FBI
man chairing HUAC, issued a press release proclaiming that the witness
Cedric Belfrage, editor of the *National Guardian*, "has been, and may
now be, a member of the Communist Party." If this "stupendous discovery" was indicative of Velde's acumen as an investigator, Izzy quipped, he
was "no great loss to J. Edgar Hoover." But when Belfrage was arrested
and threatened with deportation a few days later, Stone jumped into the
fray. Not that it was much of a fray:

> The respectables look the other way. The *New York Times* spoke up
> for James Wechsler of the *New York Post* but the *Post* did not speak

up for the *Guardian*. True, Belfrage's case is more difficult; he neither confessed, recanted or informed. But the difference clarifies the real issue which must be faced if freedom of the press is to be preserved. Congress, under the First Amendment, may make no law abridging freedom of the press . . . The crucial question is whether a Congressional committee can do by indirection under the guise of investigation what it clearly could not do directly.[41]

For Izzy the issue was never McCarthy's *methods*, any more than it had been Dies's or Jenner's—or Truman's. The danger was the deliberate extinction of dissent, the destruction of what was later called "civil society," and the gradual, inexorable imposition of a social order dominated by the needs of corporations and their managers. Never one to mince words, Stone described McCarthy's goal as "a chrome-plated American version of Fascism," tracing the blacklist to a series of reports issued by the U.S. Chamber of Commerce immediately after the war that advocated "community action" to drive potential subversives out of entertainment and the professions. Intellectuals were a target, he argued, not because of any intrinsic propensity to radicalism but because "to break the intellectuals morally is part of the strategy of the witch hunt. The exaction of the informer's role helps to spread panic and distrust: this is as important as learning who else may be dragged into the pillory."[42]

Some were allowed their moral calculations in private. Harvey Wheeler, a fledgling lecturer in the political science department at Johns Hopkins with a newly minted Harvard PhD, wrote to Izzy asking for assistance in publicizing a booklet he'd put together on Lattimore's record as a scholar. Wheeler knew both Lattimore and Stone only by reputation. He recalled:

With strangers, people often conducted interior (virtual) dialogues that went something like: "Hi, I'm not a Communist . . . and not a Cold War liberal; not anti-liberal either . . . Actually I'm just a traditional First Amendment constitutionalist radical. Any chance you're the same kind of person? Or have I got to watch you, and stay in this meeting until adjournment to make sure you and a few friends don't start ramming through your private agenda?" But to ask any such thing out loud would be to . . . play the very litmus paper game one stood against.

Actual conversation, Wheeler said, "tended to be more elliptical."

Izzy insisted on a personal interview. "Stone questioned me closely—piercingly—an intense inspection." His manner, said Wheeler, was "deftly surgical, not impolite but not friendly." Wheeler's booklet was duly featured in the *Weekly*, but not before his department chairman gave him a choice: Worried that publication would bring McCarthy's wrath down on the whole university, the chairman told the young instructor that if he dropped the project he'd be given tenure; otherwise he should look elsewhere for work. Wheeler published.[43] (Johns Hopkins, true to its word, did not renew Wheeler's appointment. He went on to a distinguished career at Washington and Lee University.)

Harvey Wheeler was a young man. George Seldes was sixty-three when he received a subpoena from McCarthy as part of an investigation into U.S. Information Agency libraries.* His testimony in the summer of 1953 was taken in executive session and remained secret for the next fifty years. Seldes himself never mentioned it. The author of *Witch Hunt: The Technique and Profits of Redbaiting* had been waging war against McCarthy's predecessors long before Pearl Harbor; *In fact* had frequently pilloried Hearst's house inquisitor, J. B. Matthews, along with his boss, as Fascist propagandists. Yet when Seldes found himself across the table from Matthews himself, recently named executive director of McCarthy's staff, the old muckraker offered little resistance. He denied Matthews's suggestion that he had written "anti-Catholic books." Seldes also denied Roy Cohn's insinuation that he'd belonged to a Communist cell in Connecticut, claiming that "actually it was . . . due to [the] Communist attack on [*In fact*] that we had to suspend—that we went under." But he

---

*Among the other witnesses were Dashiell Hammett, who had recently finished serving his prison term for contempt for refusing to give the names of donors to the Civil Rights Congress bail fund, and Solomon Auerbach, whose expulsion from the University of Pennsylvania nearly thirty years earlier had brought protests from Stone and Michael Blankfort. Both men made use of their Fifth Amendment protections; only Hammett, the famous novelist, was made to testify in public session. That same month, perhaps as an insurance policy, Blankfort, who had already been a sufficiently cooperative witness before HUAC to be able to continue working in Hollywood, wrote an article published in the *American Mercury* on "The Education of a Jew," describing his own path from "Communist Marxism . . . back to the synagogue."

made no objection to either the general line of questioning or the committee's right to query writers about their beliefs. Asked by Cohn, "Do you know any Communist Party members?" Seldes stalled—"I have ulcers and am sort of the nervous type"—then went on to name Richard Bransten, his partner on *In fact*.[44]

For liberals the obligation to cooperate with government investigators was paramount; national security trumped individual liberties. So when William Frauenglass, a Brooklyn high school teacher who had been summoned by the McCarthy committee, wrote to Albert Einstein, the physicist's advice that he should refuse to testify landed on the front page of the *New York Times*. Urging "the revolutionary way of non-co-operation, in Gandhi's sense," Einstein argued that "every intellectual who is called before one of the committees ought to refuse to testify, i.e. he must be prepared for jail and economic ruin, in short, for the sacrifice of his personal welfare in the interest of the cultural welfare of his country . . . If enough people are ready to take this grave step they will be successful. If not, then the intellectuals of this country deserve nothing better than the slavery which is intended for them."[45]

Einstein was no cold war liberal. He had written to both President Truman and Judge Irving Kaufman asking for clemency for the Rosenbergs on the grounds that the scientific evidence against them, even if accurate, did not add up to the secret of the atomic bomb. And in 1951, when the African-American scholar and peace activist W.E.B. Du Bois was indicted under the McCarran Act, Einstein not only helped raise funds for his defense but volunteered to appear as a character witness without attracting opprobrium.[46] But counseling open resistance was different and, even for some of the physicist's admirers, a step too far. "One cannot start," the *Times* scolded, "from the premise that Congressional committees have no right to question teachers and scientists or to seek out subversives wherever they can find them . . . It is one thing to fight the investigations because of the manner of their procedure and another to oppose the right of investigation."[47]

"The fact is," the *Weekly* responded, "one cannot start from any other premise without making defeat inevitable." Einstein's statement was just what Izzy and the ECLC had been waiting for. The Supreme Court let the Hollywood Ten go to prison without ruling on whether the First Amendment forbade the government from inquiring into the beliefs of private citizens. The courts had also left open the question of whether, by functioning as a kind of grand jury without grand jury safeguards, the congressional inquisitors were in violation of due process. "Neither point can be tested," Izzy wrote, "until someone dares invite prosecution for contempt."[48] Harvey O'Connor and Corliss Lamont soon rose to the challenge.*

Nor was this Einstein's last word on the subject. Though increasingly frail, the physicist consented to a request from the ECLC to hold a conference in Princeton to celebrate his seventy-fifth birthday. Too ill to attend personally, Einstein agreed to answer a set of written questions on threats to academic freedom and the obligation of intellectuals and ordinary citizens in defense of the Bill of Rights. Many liberals were horrified. Norman Thomas wrote to Einstein warning him of the ECLC's "double standard." Refusing to be cowed, Einstein replied, "I see with a great deal of disquiet the far-reaching analogy between Germany of 1932 and the U.S.A. of 1954."

The world's most famous refugee from fascism wasn't going to line up with radicals if the American Committee for Cultural Freedom had anything to say about it. Reinhold Niebuhr, an ACCF member, wrote to Paul Lehmann urging the Princeton theologian to resign from the ECLC. And J. Robert Oppenheimer, who as director of the Institute for Advanced Study was, at least nominally, Einstein's boss, volunteered his services to the ACCF, where he had recently applied for membership. (Oppenheimer's security clearance had been suspended by the Atomic Energy Commission only a few weeks earlier.) Einstein told Oppenheimer he had already sent his written replies—more tactful, perhaps, than simply refusing to withdraw. But Sol Stein, the ACCF's new director, pressed Oppenheimer, claiming that American Jewish leaders feared the consequences of linking Einstein, who was also the world's most prominent Jew, with communism. Besides, said Stein, Einstein's association with

---

*Appearing before McCarthy, Lamont volunteered that he was not and never had been a member of the Communist Party; nor was he an employee of the U.S. government. Citing both the First Amendment and the committee's lack of jurisdiction, he refused to answer further questions, thereby inviting a citation for contempt, which he received. The ACLU, where he had been a board member for more than twenty years, eventually issued a statement supporting Lamont, but at the urging of Norman Thomas and Morris Ernst his name was removed from the list of nominees for reelection, thus propelling him into the arms of the ECLC.

the ECLC would only "help to spread the notion one hears so often nowadays about physical scientists being political babes-in-the-woods."[49] Oppenheimer tried again.

The Princeton conference went ahead, drawing letters of support from Nehru, Thomas Mann, and Bertrand Russell, who became a subscriber to the *Weekly* at the same time. "Do not mind my invisibility at the Princeton meeting," Einstein wrote to Izzy. "I am shooting only from ambush."[50] The physicist's name, if not his presence, assured considerable coverage. "Einstein Hits Probes as Peril to Freedom" was the *Philadelphia Inquirer* headline—though the story did point out, twice, that the ECLC "has no connection with the American Civil Liberties Union." The *New York Times* was similarly respectful: "Einstein Rallies Defense of Rights; In Replies on Eve of His 75th Birthday He Advocates Resistance to 'Inquisition.'"

Not the *New York Post*, however, where Murray Kempton described the ECLC as "unique among opponents of the witch-hunt because it welcomes witches and warlocks to its councils." Reporting that "I. F. Stone, a deviationist, told them that the Communists represent a monolithic spirit," Kempton remained far from impressed.* "I confess a certain reluctance to mention broomsticks parked outside any demonstration against a witch-hunt," he said, overcoming his reluctance sufficiently to note the presence of "Dirk Struik of MIT, a proud Leninist-Stalinist, and Dr. Barrows Dunham, a Fifth Amendment insuree." Kempton did have a good word for Harvey O'Connor: "Whittaker Chambers has said he wasn't a Communist when he knew him." On the whole, concluded Kempton, "Dr. Einstein was smart to stay home."[51]

•

"Buds are beginning to appear on the forsythia, and welts on Joe McCarthy," Izzy wrote in March 1954, following McCarthy's confrontation with the army general Ralph Zwicker and the broadcast of Edward R. Murrow's "brilliant TV attack on McCarthy."[52] Though forced to fire J. B. Matthews after his staff director published an article calling Protestant

---

*Henry Schwarzschild, at the time a young ACCF staff attorney who attended the meeting incognito, came away "with great admiration for Izzy's autonomy and civil courage vis-à-vis the left." (Schwarzschild to Guttenplan, January 21, 1993.)

churchmen "the largest single group supporting the Communist apparatus in the United States," McCarthy himself had appeared unstoppable. "The key to the situation developing in Washington," said the *Weekly*, "is that, though the Eisenhower Administration wants desperately to appease Mc-Carthy, McCarthy does not want to be appeased . . . This is a redoubtable gambler, playing for the highest stakes. His match is not yet visible."[53]

When McCarthy told General Zwicker, a decorated veteran of Normandy and the Ardennes, that he was "not fit to wear the uniform," the senator finally, fatally, forced President Eisenhower onto the offensive. While teachers, authors, scientists, and diplomats were apparently fair game, McCarthy would not be allowed to damage the honor and morale of the U.S. Army. McCarthy's ostensible target was Irving Peress, a dentist who had once been a member of the American Labor Party. Drafted into the army, Peress refused to answer questions about his political beliefs, served an uneventful year filling teeth at Camp Kilmer in New Jersey, and was routinely promoted* from captain to major. It was this promotion that General Zwicker was supposed to explain. One of McCarthy's aides, G. David Schine, had himself just been drafted, and feverish efforts by Roy Cohn to win his handsome colleague a deferment or an officer's commission had not succeeded. So it may have been that Cohn and McCarthy were simply seeking a lever, using the cry "Who promoted Peress?" to apply pressure all the way up to the secretary of the army.

The result was the Army-McCarthy hearings, held over 36 days from April to June 1954, and broadcast for 188 hours to what was then the largest television audience in history: 80 million Americans (out of a total population of just over 150 million) were estimated to have watched at least part of the proceedings.[54] When in July the Vermont Republican senator Ralph Flanders introduced a motion to censure McCarthy, which passed in December, Izzy wrote, "McCarthy the man is personally discomfited, but McCarthyism is still on the march."[55]

In September 1954, Congress passed the Communist Control Act, officially declaring the CPUSA "an instrumentality of a conspiracy to overthrow the Government of the United States" and declaring party members or members of "Communist-infiltrated" organizations, such as labor unions, liable to fine or imprisonment. The sponsors of this "noose for the labor movement," the *Weekly* noted bitterly, were all "liberal Democrats":

*Under the "doctor draft law," promotion was automatic after a year's service.

Hubert Humphrey, Paul Douglas, John F. Kennedy, and Wayne Morse.
"The Democratic party is in complete moral collapse, as far from Jefferson as the Republican Party is from Lincoln."[56] Which helps to explain
the most shocking headline in the early history of the *Weekly*: "Why I
Cast My Vote For Ike."

Stone had been a latecomer to the Stevenson banner in 1952, but on
the eve of midterm elections he not only acknowledged how he intended
to vote but also told readers,

> the United States and the world will be better off if the Republi-
> cans stay in power a little longer . . . Democratic leaders are so ob-
> sessed with the need to clear themselves of any suspicion of
> Communism, they and the trade union leaders supporting them
> are so ready to relapse into an arms race as an easy means of
> pump-priming that they have become the war party . . . It is an as-
> set in the struggle against McCarthy to have it fought out within
> the Republican party instead of between the two parties. When
> McCarthy has been put in his place and peace more firmly estab-
> lished, Democrats could safely come back and pick up where the
> New Deal left off.[57]

Stone's fondness for Eisenhower dated back to 1948, when he had written, "I like Eisenhower. Everybody seems to like him . . ." He recognized,
however, that the general's attractions were personal, not political: "Everyone is free to indulge the hope that Eisenhower probably agrees with him."
Izzy's admiration for Eisenhower's common sense and benign intentions
had grown considerably since his inauguration: "General Eisenhower is
proving much less bellicose than Captain Truman." And when it came to
coexistence with the Soviet Union—the single issue on which Izzy believed
the future of the human race was at stake—he challenged his readers to
look past their preconceptions: "At the risk of complete and total Leftist excommunication—from the ADA straight across the board through the
Communists to the Trotzkyists—I want to put forward a daring slogan in
the difficult and precarious weeks ahead: Back Ike for Peace."[58] Eisenhower's disentanglement from the war in Korea impressed him, as did the
president's reluctance to extend the Truman Doctrine to Indochina, where
Ho Chi Minh's forces had just defeated the French at Dien Bien Phu.

The presence of Richard Nixon was, as ever, a bar to any wholehearted embrace of the Republican administration. But the *Weekly*'s critical support for the president was itself far too radical for Hal Draper, editor of *Labor Action*, organ of the Independent Socialist League, Max Shachtman's post-Trotskyist sect. In "The Strange Case of I. F. Stone," Draper found "this apparently fantastic step [Izzy's endorsement of the Republicans] of considerable interest . . . because of the very harsh light it throws on a type of Stalinoid-liberal mentality." Izzy is "no theoretician" and therefore "unable to see that the alternative to supporting either Republicans or Democrats is to build a *class* movement of labor and, eventually, a class assumption of power by labor, i.e., a revolution."[59]

Draper's furious dialectics obscured a serious point: Most radicals experienced the 1950s as a series of assaults. In addition to the perpetual discouragements of American political life, the disillusionment that dedicated Communists felt after the death of Stalin in March 1953 meant that they could no longer rely on the Soviet Union for guidance. Meanwhile, the siege mentality engendered by McCarthyism left even the most independent radicals looking over their shoulders, wondering whether the relic of some ancient act of solidarity would mean the loss of a job, the betrayal of a friend, or the wreck of a marriage. None of the available choices was attractive, and most radicals opted for some form of withdrawal—either deeper into sectarian sterility or out of politics altogether. Stone did neither.

Unlike his old friend Max Lerner, who returned from a trip to Guatemala in June 1954 justifying the U.S.-sponsored coup against the elected government there on the grounds that President Jacobo Arbenz had "deliberately and with open eyes accepted Communist aid in shaping his policies and getting a popular base for his regime," Stone decried this "new and more dangerous form of dollar diplomacy."[60] Nor did Izzy share Lerner's enthusiasm for another of America's imperial ventures. Prompted by Leo Cherne, head of the International Rescue Committee (though founded in the 1930s to aid refugees fleeing fascism, by the time Cherne took over in 1951 the IRC had shifted its efforts to refugees from communism), in the spring of 1955 Lerner joined Arthur Schlesinger Jr. and Joseph Buttinger, one of the IRC's financial backers, on the American Friends of Vietnam, a letterhead group urging greater American involvement in that country's conflict. Stone remained wary, perhaps mindful of the French soldier's diary he had published in the *Weekly* in March 1954 under the prophetic title "Operation Cachis" (Operation Waste).[61]

Izzy's skepticism about the use of American power to shape the world toward liberal values set him apart from happy cold warriors like Lerner and Schlesinger. But he also harbored a deep pessimism about even the Eisenhower administration's ability to pursue its own aims. "In Indo-China . . . there is little doubt the White House is not only opposed to sending troops but wants to get those American technicians out" as soon as possible.* Nonetheless, he warned in March 1954, "If France backs out, we will step in, just as we stepped in to replace the British in Greece . . . Those circles in the Pentagon which believe Indo-China the key to Southeast Asia will yet find a way to intervene."[62] McCarthy himself was no longer a force, but Izzy still saw "on every hand evidence of terror in American life, freezing into fearful inaction all those on whom an alternative policy might be based. Though there is instinctive resistance to intervention in Indo-China, there is no peace movement, there are no peace meetings . . . A situation is building up in which inept men may be pushed by some unexpected turn of events into terrible decisions in sheer funk."[63]

It was this nexus of domestic terror and imperial inertia that the *Weekly*, with very little competition, tried to expose. Of course, the American inquisition was worth opposing on its own terms as a menace to liberty and civil rights, and as a bludgeon used by the right against any vestige of the New Deal coalition. Even ADA liberals knew that. But the climate of fear was also a deadly distraction from the opportunities in foreign policy—in China and East Asia as well as in Eastern Europe—opened by the death of Stalin in 1953. And to the Eisenhower administration's foreign policy, as to its buildup of nuclear weapons, opposition was either marginal or nonexistent.

For Izzy nothing so revealed the depths of America's blindness, or the abject paralysis of the country's liberals, as the public flaying of J. Robert Oppenheimer, father of the atomic bomb. At Berkeley, where he spent the 1930s building the country's leading school of theoretical physics, Oppenheimer had also been involved in radical politics, both as a supporter of the university teachers' union and as a donor to various Communist causes. His brother Frank briefly joined the party, and his wife, Kitty,

---

*The United States Military Assistance Advisory Group, Indochina, arrived in Vietnam in September 1950. This handful of officers, sent by President Truman to assist the French, had barely grown in numbers by 1954.

was the widow of a man killed in the Spanish Civil War and a close friend of Steve Nelson, the party's West Coast organizer. General Leslie Groves, the army officer in charge of the Manhattan Project, knew all about Oppenheimer's past when he appointed him the project's scientific director. Though J. Edgar Hoover kept up a barrage of memos throughout the war questioning Oppenheimer's loyalty, Groves believed Oppenheimer could be trusted. Besides, the physicist's charismatic leadership, with his encyclopedic understanding of the theoretical and practical problems, made him indispensable. After the war, Oppenheimer's achievements kept him involved in atomic weapons policy, serving as chair of the Atomic Energy Commission's General Advisory Committee.

In 1949, Frank Oppenheimer, who had worked with his brother designing the Trinity test of the first atom bomb, was called before HUAC, where he admitted to past membership in the Communist Party but refused to name others, which cost him his position at the University of Minnesota.* But Robert had cooperated with HUAC, appearing before a closed session in June 1949 where he disclosed the names of several former associates, even identifying one as "a dangerous man and quite Red." As a result, he kept both his position and his security clearance. In the spring of 1954, however, the AEC chairman, Lewis Strauss, arranged for Oppenheimer, who by then had left active government service to head the Institute for Advanced Study, to be stripped of his security clearance. Strauss, an extraordinarily petty man, seems to have been motivated largely by spite; Edward Teller (whose testimony against his former boss was probably the most damaging), by resentment over Oppenheimer's opposition to his pet project, the "super" or hydrogen bomb. Oppenheimer appealed, but in June 1954 an AEC board upheld the decision.[64]

"The most important conclusion to be drawn from the Oppenheimer affair," said the *Weekly*, "is that the United States is becoming a sick nation . . . Our allies must now take seriously into account the pathological state of our politics." Izzy blamed "two forces" for the attack on a distinguished scientist who, his war record aside, had already demonstrated a willingness to name names and been an energetic recruit to the ACCF. One was the FBI, which saw any evidence of leftist sympathy as an in-

*Frank's attorney was Clifford Durr. Virginia Durr said her husband took the case after Frank was refused representation by the Washington law firm of Arnold & Porter, which was willing to act only for those falsely accused of party membership.

eradicable taint; "the other stems from the Air Force, particularly from the Strategic Air Command," whose doctrine of massive retaliation had also been criticized by Oppenheimer. "The silence of the liberals is thunderous," Izzy lamented. "A great nation is being driven towards catastrophe like a herd of sheep, moved onward and held together by the nips and growls of a few fierce dogs."[65]

Stone expected more of his countrymen, and in particular he expected more from America's newspapers. So in the spring of 1955, when the powerful *New York Times*, which had, however gingerly, criticized McCarthy, found itself the principal target of James Eastland, new chair of the Senate Internal Security Subcommittee, Izzy hoped for a fight. Instead, he lamented, "The New York Times Opens the Gates to Its Enemies." Only a few months earlier, the *Times* publisher, Arthur Hays Sulzberger, had made a widely reported speech arguing that persecuting ex-Communists was cruel and unreasonable. Anyone who had left the party before 1948, said Sulzberger, should be entitled to "a sort of moratorium or some sort of political amnesty." The paper had also published numerous editorials reaffirming "our faith in the whole Bill of Rights—the Fifth Amendment included," lending credibility to the publisher's declaration that there would be no "witch-hunting" at the *Times*.[66] But when Melvin Barnet, a *Times* copy editor, told the Eastland committee that he had not been a Communist since 1942 but refused to answer questions about other people, citing the Fifth Amendment, the paper fired him before he had even left the witness stand. (Barnet had himself been "named" by the CBS newsman Winston Burdett. The two men had belonged to the same party cell at the *Brooklyn Eagle*; Burdett had also been the best man at Barnet's wedding.)

"How can the *Times* editorially support the Fifth Amendment," Izzy demanded, "and discharge those who invoke it?" His was a lone voice of outrage. The *Washington Post* advised that "for the repentant ex-Communist . . . the proper path is plain, although hard. He should be prepared to confess . . . including names of former associates." Should such disclosure subject old friends to "hardships," the *Post* urged an "appeal to the Senate committee's sense of justice and fair play." For Izzy this episode represented "the moral collapse" of both newspapers,[67] because by the summer of 1955 James Eastland's "sense of justice and fair play" was a matter of public record.

It was the Mississippi senator who, the previous year, had set up
a one-man inquisition in New Orleans in order to smear the Southern
Conference Educational Fund—an offshoot of Clark Foreman's Southern Conference for Human Welfare—as a Communist conspiracy. At
those hearings, neither Aubrey Williams, the fund's president, nor James
Dombrowski, its executive director, availed himself of Fifth Amendment
protection. During the New Deal, Williams had been head of the National Youth Administration; returning to his native Alabama, he was currently publisher of *Southern Farm and Home* magazine. When two
informants claimed to have met Williams at a Communist function
twelve years earlier, he challenged them to repeat their accusations outside the committee room: "I'll sue for everything you've got." Both declined the invitation.

The headlines, however, came from Williams's lawyer, Clifford Durr,
whose wife had also been subpoenaed. In a break with normal practice,
Eastland announced that Durr would be allowed to cross-examine Paul
Crouch, one of the government witnesses. The reason for this departure
became clear when Crouch, in an aside, remarked that Durr himself had
once been a Communist and that his wife "had full knowledge of the
Communist conspiracy." This was too much for Durr, who launched himself at Crouch, shouting, "You dirty dog! I'll kill you for lying about my
wife!" before being restrained by federal marshals and later taken to a
nearby hospital, where he was found to have suffered a mild heart attack.
Clifford Durr's chivalric gesture made the front page of the *New York
Times*. The accompanying photo, along with his willingness to defend
clients like Frank Oppenheimer, soon put paid to what remained of his
law practice.[68]

•

What brought Senator Eastland to New Orleans? Historical explanation
is an inexact science, but part of any answer, surely, would include the
fact that the parents of Linda Brown, a third-grader in Topeka, Kansas,
felt it unfair that her route to school extended for more than a mile, passing through a railroad switchyard, when there was a neighborhood school
only seven blocks away. Linda Brown was a black child, and on May 17,
1954, the day her parents' lawsuit was decided by the Supreme Court,

I. F. Stone was waiting in the press room. A light flashed summoning the reporters to the Court chamber. This was already unusual. Written copies of opinions were customarily sent down to the press via pneumatic tube. Izzy ran upstairs and crowded into the marble chamber to hear Earl Warren read out "in a firm, clear voice, and with expression" the central question: "Does segregation of children in public schools solely on the basis of race, even though the physical facilities and other 'tangible' factors may be equal, deprive the children of the minority group of equal educational opportunities?" Warren paused, then continued: "We believe it does." It was, wrote Izzy, "all one could do to keep from cheering, and a few of us were moved to tears."[69]

Arguments in *Brown v. Board of Education of Topeka* had begun in December 1952 and resumed the following December, and Hugo Black might have been the deciding vote. Indeed, it was out of concern for the pressures on her brother-in-law that when Virginia Durr faced Eastland in March 1954, she gave her name and testified that she had never been "under Communist discipline" before stating, "I stand mute" to every other question—itself a considerable sacrifice for the famously loquacious Alabaman. The Supreme Court's unanimous decision, two months after the New Orleans hearings, kept Justice Black out of the spotlight. But Eastland, who as the *Weekly* noted was running for reelection that fall, had other targets. The same *New York Times* front page that showed Clifford Durr surrounded by three federal marshals also showed Myles Horton being carried bodily out of the hearing room. Not even Paul Crouch* dared to suggest that Horton, a Social Gospel Christian, was a Communist; he was, nonetheless, a genuine revolutionary.

Horton had studied with Reinhold Niebuhr at the Union Theological Seminary in New York, returning to his native Tennessee in 1932 to found the Highlander Folk School. A unique institution where blacks and whites mixed freely, Highlander offered classes in leadership skills, history, literacy, and music. (It was Horton's wife, Zilphia, who taught "We Shall Overcome," the South Carolina tobacco workers' adaptation of the gospel standard "I Shall Overcome," to Pete Seeger.)[70] Besides Niebuhr,

---

*By the summer of 1954, so many inconsistencies had been revealed in his testimony that Attorney General Herbert Brownell put an end to Crouch's $9,000-a-year career as a professional informer—at which point Crouch wrote to J. Edgar Hoover suggesting the FBI investigate Brownell!

Highlander's advisory board included Norman Thomas and Eleanor Roosevelt. (Roosevelt's ties to Horton dated back to the first meeting of the Southern Conference for Human Welfare in Birmingham in 1938. Told that local law required blacks and whites to be seated on opposite sides of the hall, the First Lady moved her chair into the center aisle, to the considerable annoyance of Birmingham's young police commissioner, Eugene "Bull" Connor.)

I. F. Stone didn't know Myles Horton personally. But he knew what Horton was up against. In the wake of the *Brown* decision, eight Southern states established their own little HUAC-style investigating committees. As with Eastland, the pretext was communism, but the real aim was to smear and discredit the opponents of segregation. Through Jennings Perry, Izzy's old colleague from *PM* (and, during the 1940s, chairman of the National Committee to Abolish the Poll Tax) now writing for him at the *Weekly*, readers already had a ringside seat at the Eastland hearings. Then in the fall of 1954, Leonard Boudin told Izzy about his newest client, Carl Braden, a copy editor on the *Louisville Courier-Journal*. With some other friends, Carl and his wife, Anne, agreed to help a black war veteran and his family buy a house in a white neighborhood. When the house was dynamited, Louisville police arrested Braden, who was indicted under the state sedition law and accused of blowing up the house himself. The FBI made no effort to investigate the bombing, instead sending a parade of ex-Communists—none of whom had ever met Carl Braden—to testify about the subversive implications of the books found in the Braden home. "Mere possession of such literature," Commonwealth Attorney A. Scott Hamilton told the jury, "raises a presumption of guilt." Asked to make the case a "milestone" in ending "this setting whites against blacks," the jury convicted Braden, who was sentenced to fifteen years in prison.

"Tell Carl that I am proud to know him," began the letter Anne Braden received from Leonard Boudin. "I stand ready to do whatever you want me to do on appeal. Money is not a consideration. I will be glad to do this without a fee if need be." Leonard heard about the case from Clark Foreman, who in turn knew the Bradens through Palmer Weber. And when Anne Braden's plane stopped off in Washington, D.C., during a fundraising tour, I. F. Stone was there to meet her. "I said, 'They know who blew up the house,'" she recalled. "'It's just a frame-up. Nobody will print what we really know about it.' And he said, 'I'll do it.' I said, 'Well, the Louisville papers are afraid they'll commit libel.' And he answered, 'I'll commit libel for you. What's the use of having your own publication if you can't commit libel to do something good?' I'll never forget that." The *Weekly*'s spotlight on the "Nightmare at Louisville" was crucial in helping to raise the $40,000 to bail Carl Braden out of jail pending appeal—especially when even the *Nation*, after an initial sympathetic report on the case by Jennings Perry, ran an article during the trial accusing Carl of "conniving at a piece of Communist agitation" and another afterward blaming the defendants for having "invited the lightning."[71]

Izzy never did commit libel to help the Bradens. But in August 1955, just a few months later, when an all-white jury in Sumner, Mississippi, decided that fourteen-year-old Emmett Till had also invited the lightning, he didn't hesitate: "Emmett Till's broken body, with a bullet hole in the right temple and the gaping hole in the back of the head, as if broken in by a rock, testified to a maniacal murder . . . If [J. W.] Milam and [Roy] Bryant [the defendants] didn't kill Till, then who did?" Nor was his anger restricted to the South. "To the outside world it must look as if the conscience of white America has been silenced, and the appearance is not too deceiving. Basically all of us whites, North and South, acquiesce in white supremacy, and benefit from the pool of cheap labor created by it."[72]

Stone's awareness of racial injustice had deepened since the days when he and Esther bought their house in Washington without a word of protest at the restrictive covenant on the deed. Christopher Stone remembered "once going with Dad to a movie and he insisted on sitting in the 'colored' section." And when his father took the train south, "in those days the trains stopped in Washington, and you had to change to segregated cars. Dad refused. 'No, I'm black,' he said."[73] But he knew too much about white equivocation, including his own, to expect change "unless Negroes rouse themselves to make their indignation felt in some dramatic way . . . Were thousands of Negroes to converge on the Department of Justice and demand action against the murderers of Till, and of the other Negroes whose recent murders have gone unpunished in the South, such a demonstration would have an impact.

"The American Negro needs a Gandhi to lead him," Izzy continued, "and we need the American Negro to lead us. If he does not provide leadership against the sickness in the South, the time will come when we will all pay a terrible price for allowing psychopathic racist brutality to flourish unchecked." In Paris, a young American serviceman saw those words posted on a kiosk. "It was the kiosk outside the Café Deux Magots," said Robert Silvers, who in 1955 was stationed at NATO headquarters and working for the *Paris Review* in his spare time. "You could pick up *I. F. Stone's Weekly* there sometimes." Stone's attempt to link the American Negro's struggle for freedom with the tradition of nonviolent civil disobedience stayed with Silvers for a long time.[74] In part, perhaps, because on December 1, just two months after Izzy wrote his call for a "Negro Gandhi," Rosa Parks refused to give up her seat on a Montgomery, Alabama, city bus to a white man.

The previous spring, Myles Horton had written to Virginia Durr asking if she knew anyone in Montgomery who might be interested in coming to Highlander that summer. Virginia suggested Rosa Parks, secretary of the Montgomery chapter of the NAACP, who worked as a seamstress in a local department store and occasionally did sewing for the Durrs. With some discreet assistance from Aubrey Williams, the bus fare to Tennessee was raised and Rosa Parks spent several weeks at Highlander, attending workshops on school integration and meeting Septima Clark, a South Carolina woman who ran Highlander's Citizenship Schools, and other veteran activists.[75] After Parks was arrested and charged with violating the town's segregation laws, E. D. Nixon, head of the Montgomery NAACP, phoned the Durrs, asking if they would come with him to post bail. By this time Clifford's law practice was so moribund he was forced to admit, "Mr. Nixon, I don't have anything to make bail with." Nixon, who worked as a Pullman porter, said, "That's all right. I can get bail, if you'll just go with me."

Virginia Durr also helped behind the scenes to ensure that the Montgomery bus boycott, begun by Jo Ann Robinson and the Women's Political Council, was a success. Originally a one-day protest, the boycotters were encouraged by E. D. Nixon to continue until the city's bus system was integrated. The only similar campaign, a bus boycott in Baton Rouge, Louisiana, had collapsed after two weeks. And though the Montgomery Improvement Association did a heroic job of organizing car pools, very few blacks owned private cars. But Virginia Durr knew that Montgomery's white gentry couldn't do without their maids. She organized a pool of white women drivers, and when Mayor Tacky Gayle ordered them to stop, replied, "If Tacky Gayle wants to come out here and do my washing and ironing and cleaning and cooking . . . he can do it."

I. F. Stone quickly realized the significance of what was happening in Alabama—not just in Montgomery, but also in Tuscaloosa, where a white mob chased Autherine Lucy out of the state university while the governor and police looked on. It was the *Weekly* that first reported the reply of an old woman who turned down Aubrey Williams's offer of a lift: "I'm not tired. When I used to ride those busses, my feet rode but my spirit would walk. Now my feet walk, but my spirit rides." (Izzy used the story to underline the poverty of Adlai Stevenson's nervous sidestep on civil rights; asked to comment on *Brown*, Stevenson dismissed the "mere presence of children of two races in the same classroom.") And it was the *Weekly* that devoted two full pages to Jennings Perry's "First Hand Report from Montgomery," describing and quoting a local pastor: "His accent . . . less Deep South than [Ralph] Abernathy's, his congregation . . . a little better circumstanced, but his counsel is the same: 'There is not a tension between Negro and whites. There is only a conflict between justice and injustice.'"[76] In twenty-seven-year-old Martin Luther King Jr., America had found its Gandhi.

•

On the same day that Rosa Parks stayed in her seat, I. F. Stone received a letter from a Mrs. Dorothy Baker along with a check for a subscription to the *Weekly*. Normally, of course, Izzy welcomed subscribers with open arms. But Mrs. Baker's request was on behalf of her bosses, J. G. Sourwine and James Eastland, chief counsel and chairman of the Senate Internal Security Subcommittee. After considerable pressure from Senate Minority Leader Lyndon Johnson, an old friend of both Aubrey Williams and the Durrs, Eastland had agreed to cancel hearings he had planned for Birmingham.[77] Instead, the Mississippian headed north again, reopening his investigation of "subversive influence" on the press. Eastland's committee served more than seventy subpoenas—thirty of them to journalists on the *New York Times*. The initial hearings in New York were in executive session, and in Izzy's view, the *Times* again "knuckle[d] under."

The *Weekly*, which clearly had excellent sources inside the *Times* city room, reported that after being summoned one at a time to the personnel department, where they were served their subpoenas, employees were interviewed by Louis Loeb, the paper's counsel, who "made it clear that those on the *Times* who invoke the Fifth Amendment will be fired." Izzy scored the paper's hypocrisy by highlighting recent *Times* editorials that hailed the Fifth Amendment as "an important and historic element in the charter of our liberties" and defended a citizen's right to "associations . . . and thoughts which were nobody's business but his own."[78] (He put these quotations from the *Times* in a "box"; a regular feature of the *Weekly*, Izzy's boxes might contain short excerpts from speeches, government reports, court documents, or translations from the foreign press, and were often used to ironic effect.)

But the *Times* management's collaboration with the witch hunt, however deplorable, was not the principal issue. So on December 4, 1955, Stone had summonses issued to Sourwine; Benjamin Mandel, the committee's research director; and Senator Eastland and his eight colleagues on the Senate Internal Security Subcommittee in connection with a lawsuit filed in the federal district court in Washington that morning. *I. F. Stone v. Eastland* argued that the use of public funds to examine the contents of newspapers or magazines was a violation of the First Amendment. The suit asked for a judgment that surveillance of the press by the subcommittee was illegal and an order requiring Eastland to produce any dossiers on newspapers or newspapermen.

Stone didn't expect his "man-bites-dog" suit to get very far in court. Even so, all the Washington dailies carried reports—which included Eastland's declaration: "It's bunk." And a note from Izzy to "Jimmy" Wechsler enclosing the legal papers along with a copy of the current *Weekly* saluting the *Post* and Wechsler for editorials defending Melvin Barnet drew a warm reply from his old adversary.[79] In an open letter to William Randolph Hearst Jr., Izzy wrote, "I am about to be tagged out at first base," explaining that the government's motion to dismiss his suit cited *Hearst v. Black*, a twenty-year-old decision lost by Hearst's father, holding that the courts can't interfere with congressional committees.[80] Hearst Jr. never replied. But Stone's argument that "a few courageous publishers could save the press from a witch hunt" was soon borne out by action from an unexpected quarter.

Senator Eastland announced that in January he was taking his investigation back to Washington, and this time the hearings would be public. Six of the seven witnesses called the first day were employees of the *New York Times*; the seventh, David Fine, who ran a bookstore and movie house that sometimes showed Russian films, was forced to admit, in response to a direct question, that his bookstore carried *I. F. Stone's Weekly*. His brother Benjamin Fine, the *Times*'s education editor, whose series on the teaching of American history had been awarded a Pulitzer Prize in 1944 for public service, also testified, calling his yearlong membership in the Communist Party in graduate school a "tragic mistake." Once again Eastland's aim was to discredit a newspaper that, whatever its equivocations on civil liberties, had been a strong supporter of civil rights. This time the *Times* hit back.

The editorial was titled "The Voice of a Free Press." Written by the managing editor, Charles Merz, it arrived in Washington early Thursday morning, just as the *Weekly* was going to bed. It said:

> It seems to us quite obvious . . . that the Times has been singled out for this attack precisely because of the vigor of its opposition to many of the things for which Mr. Eastland . . . and the subcommittee's counsel stand—that is, because we have condemned segregation in the Southern schools; because we have challenged the high-handed and abusive methods employed by various Congressional committees; because we have denounced McCarthyism and all its works; because we have attacked the narrow and bigoted restrictions of the McCarran Immigration Act; because we have criticized a "security system" which conceals the accuser from his victim.

The editorial was reprinted in papers from the *Washington Post* to the *Minneapolis Tribune* (and by the *Times*, so pleased with its newfound courage it repeated itself verbatim on Sunday); Merz's old *New York World* stablemate Walter Lippmann endorsed the *Times* defi in his Tuesday column, ratifying what was rapidly becoming conventional wisdom. Congressional investigation of the press was finished.[81]

Slowly, unevenly, often unpredictably, the flames of the inquisition began to flicker and die. Perhaps the most bizarre episode involved one of McCarthy's star performers, a key witness in the Lattimore trial and the man who, in testimony leaked to Walter Winchell,* first charged that there were "over 100 dues-paying Communists" at the *New York Times*. His name was Harvey Matusow. The son of a Bronx cigar store owner, Matusow served in the army in France and Germany before dropping out of CCNY and drifting into the Communist Party. The party, he said, gave him "the feeling of belonging." In 1948, he won a free trip to Puerto Rico for selling a record number of subscriptions to the *Daily Worker* (later it emerged many of his subscribers had false names or bogus addresses). In 1950, he contacted the FBI and volunteered to inform. Matusow had sold records for Pete Seeger's People's Songs company and at one point even worked as a switchboard operator at CP headquarters in New York before being expelled by the party as an "enemy agent." But he soon discovered that for a professional informer embellishment paid better than actual recollection. Matusow's talent for colorful confession got him an editing job at the red-baiting newsletter *Counterattack* and a staff investigator's position with the McCarthy committee. Not even his claim to have identified 126 Communists in the *New York Times* Sunday department—which never had more than 100 employees—slowed his ascent.[82]

Then Matusow had a change of heart. In the fall of 1953, he gave the *Times* a signed affidavit admitting that his testimony against the paper—as well as the Boy Scouts, the Voice of America, the USO, and the YMCA—had all been fabricated. Instead of publishing the story, however, Sulzberger sent a copy to J. Edgar Hoover. The FBI did nothing, and Matusow, despite his own ambivalence, was still testifying before the Subversive Activities Control Board into the following spring. It was only when Matusow repeated his recantation in a meeting with G. Bromley Oxnam, the Methodist bishop of Washington, adding that he hoped to write a book about his experiences, that Matusow's victims learned of his plans. Eventually Matusow's search for expiation led him to Albert Kahn, a journalist turned publisher whom Matusow had himself named as a Communist in hearings investigating the Veterans of the Abraham Lincoln Brigade. Even before it was published, Matusow's *False Witness* was a sensation; the syndicated columnist Stewart Alsop said the book was

---

*The columnist who once wrote as "Paul Revere II" in *PM* had long since changed horses, becoming one of McCarthy's most visible—and vicious—outriders.

"likely to initiate a serious investigation of this new postwar profession of the informer." Among the book's many revelations was Matusow's account of how he had been coached by Roy Cohn to commit perjury. On February 3, 1955, at the Biltmore Hotel in New York, Matusow faced a barrage of hostile questions, many from reporters who had depended on him for their own lurid exposés of the Red conspiracy. The din threatened to drown out Matusow's statement when suddenly a furious voice silenced the room.

"What the hell's the matter with you bastards!" I. F. Stone got up from his seat in the front row of the press conference and faced his colleagues. "Why don't you want him to be heard? You call yourselves newspapermen! You make me sick! I've never seen such a shameful exhibition." The questions that followed, Kahn recalled, "were noticeably restrained. No one again interrupted Harvey's answers." The same compulsive delivery that once held HUAC spellbound at Matusow's tales of free love among the pines at Camp Unity now demanded that attention be paid to the Justice Department's whole roster of professional informers. "Either way you look at it," wrote Izzy, "the Congressional witch-hunters and the Justice Department emerge—those great investigators—with their pants down. Either they were suckers or something close to suborners of perjury." Most liberals agreed, and though Alsop covered his role in publicizing Matusow's recantation with ritual denunciations of his book's "pro-Communist" editors, Murray Kempton simply noted, "What is relevant about Matusow is not whether he lied then or is a liar now . . . What is undisputed fact is that he was either a liar then or a liar now. You and I didn't offer him as a trustworthy man; the United States government did." For a number of years, Kempton wrote later, his own work had been "suffused" by a theory, "the liberal theory . . . We stood, in that theory, fighting the massed weight of General Motors and United States Steel on the one side and the massed weight of Miss Elizabeth Gurley Flynn on the other."[83] Harvey Matusow's testimony in the second round of Smith Act trials in 1952 sent Elizabeth Gurley Flynn to prison; when he recanted, the balance, for Kempton and many others, began to tip.

The signals were still mixed. In January 1955, perjury charges against Owen Lattimore were finally dismissed. In March, the New York Newspaper Guild hosted a "coffee klatsch" get-together with I. F. Stone for

New York–area subscribers to the *Weekly*. And after years when his audiences seemed made up entirely of activists under threat of arrest or deportation or subpoena, Izzy was suddenly in demand again as a speaker, appearing at a synagogue in Manhattan, an integrated school in Delaware, and a union hall in Gary, Indiana, before making a tour of Winnipeg and Saskatchewan, where Premier T. C. "Tommy" Douglas personally welcomed him to "North America's only socialist state."[84] Of course, the same New York Guild—under pressure from the national leadership—dropped its protests against the firing of journalists who had taken the Fifth Amendment.

HUAC was a like a wounded bear—damaged but still dangerous. In October 1955, the committee subpoenaed Izzy's friend Zero Mostel. By this time Mostel had been on the blacklist for three years. A comedian whose career had begun at Barney Josephson's Café Society, Mostel often satirized public figures in his act, sometimes as the Red-hunting Senator Polltax T. Pellegra. Offered the chance to "clear himself" by naming others, he refused, citing not the Fifth Amendment or any other amendment but "religious" grounds. Then, risking a contempt citation, he asked the committee, "What if I did an imitation of a butterfly at rest? There is no crime in making anybody laugh. I don't care if *you* laugh at me." The FBI, convinced that Mostel was a Communist, wasn't laughing. But he didn't go to jail. Neither did Barrows Dunham (Kempton's "Fifth Amendment insuree"), a Temple University philosophy professor who refused to tell HUAC anything more than his name and the date and place of his birth. Fired from his job and cited for contempt, Dunham was acquitted in federal court a few days after Mostel's command performance. Still, it was another three years before Mostel returned to the stage, eleven years before Hollywood let him act again—and fifteen years before Dunham found another academic job.[85]

So when Leonard Boudin, speaking to the Emergency Civil Liberties Committee (and to the numerous FBI informers transcribing his remarks) in April 1955, said that the current situation was cause for "despair" and that he had "nothing but fear for the future," his brother-in-law might have agreed. Instead, Izzy told the group, "We have passed the crest of the crisis in civil liberties . . . There is much less to fear today." Indeed, he told them, "The biggest enemy we have to fight is our own despair. The witch hunt is on the defensive."[86] That June, the bureau sent its informants to the Broadwood Hotel in Philadelphia to report on Stone's speech to another ECLC conference. His topic: informants.[87] Izzy wanted the courts to stop evading the question of whether Americans could be fired—or deprived of passports—based on the testimony of faceless informers. And in November, the Ninth Circuit in San Francisco ruled they couldn't. For Izzy, and for the physicist Edward Condon, who knew from experience how hard it was to rebut anonymous accusers and who tipped Izzy to the importance of the case, this decision in *Parker v. Lester* was cause for celebration.[88]

Eastland was still a power in the Senate. Indeed, in March 1956 the voice of "massive resistance" to the federal courts became chairman of the Judiciary Committee. "Mad Hatter government," said the *Weekly*, noting that senators Wayne Morse of Oregon and Herbert Lehman of New York opposed the appointment "without a word of support" from Republicans or other Northern liberals. Nor had the Mississippian given up the Internal Security Subcommittee, which he used to harry Matusow and his publishers; the reformed informer eventually served four years for perjury. Yet Izzy was very far from despair. His nemesis Ruth Shipley had finally retired as head of the State Department's passport office. And in January, his friend Sidney Cohn had gotten the blacklisted director Carl Foreman, an admitted ex-Communist, a passport despite Foreman's refusal to "prove his sincerity" by naming names.[89]

On March 23, 1956, a chubby, bespectacled reporter in a slightly bedraggled suit and tie presented himself at the State Department. Proposing to visit Israel, France, Britain, Italy, and the Soviet Union (if he could get a visa), he completed the form and, perhaps with some trepidation, handed in his old passport. Besides the oath of allegiance (identical to the one he'd first signed in 1945) his application included two affidavits. In the first, written in his own hand, he did "solemnly swear that I am not and never have been a member of the Communist Party or of the Communist Political Association." The second simply attested: "Mr. Stone says he will surrender his passport if requested by State Dept."[90] Though he had no way of knowing it, the FBI had closed its espionage investigation months earlier. The bureau even vetoed an opportunity to plant an informant in the *Weekly* office.[91] In the event, his application was successful. Five years after the knock on the door, I. F. Stone had a valid passport.

•

For a reporter who was probably more closely identified with the Jewish state during the first few years of its existence than any other American journalist, the inability to travel abroad had been a crippling blow. His Zionist audience had kept Stone in the public eye just as the cold war denied him other platforms. And though he'd decided against emigrating, Israel continued to have a special place in his affections. Of course he would return as soon as he could. But why did he want to go to Moscow? And why now?

Stone's brief career as an apologist for the Soviet Union had ended in 1939. During the war, when antifascism was his animating political passion, he'd been deeply grateful for the efforts of the Red Army—though no more so than Eisenhower, MacArthur, or the publishers of the *New York Herald Tribune*. If what seemed to him small-minded sectarian quarrels or blind hostility to the Soviet Union threatened the war effort, he was quick to expose those responsible. Even after the war he had urged understanding of Russian fears of encirclement and been appalled by Truman's hard line. But he'd never thought of Stalin as anything but a brutal dictator. When he'd told Mike Blankfort "no more fellow traveling," he'd meant it. "Izzy was a socialist," said A. B. Magil, a former editor of the *New Masses* who met Stone in 1948 when Magil was covering Israel's war of independence for the *Daily Worker*. "He was critical of the Soviet Union."[92]

Yet like many others on the left, Izzy was reluctant to abandon the promise of the Russian Revolution. "The Soviet Union breaks with Stalinism," declared Isaac Deutscher in 1956, "in order to resume its advance towards equality and socialist democracy."[93] Could Deutscher, a Polish Jew who had been expelled from the Polish Communist Party in 1933 for criticizing Stalin and who had just published the first volume of his monumental biography of Leon Trotsky, be right? Like Deutscher's optimism, Stone's trip to the Soviet Union was motivated by a speech given by Nikita Khrushchev in late February 1956. At a closed session on the last day of the Twentieth Congress of the Communist Party of the Soviet Union, Khrushchev stunned the delegates by denouncing Stalin's "cult of personality" and admitting the enormous scope of his predecessor's crimes, including mass deportations and responsibility for the deaths of "many thousands of honest and innocent Communists."

Reports of the "secret speech"[94] began to filter out of the Soviet Union almost immediately, and though a full text wasn't published in the West until that June,* enough detail reached the United States to cause disarray among the faithful at Union Square: "Krushchev's [sic] revelation that Stalin was a bloody old tyrant, suspicious to the point of madness, may not lead to the liquidation of foreign Communist parties," Izzy wrote in late March, "but must strike them an irreparable blow. Their members may be devoted, but they certainly are exposed as knuckle-heads taught to believe whatever lies they were told from Moscow."

As a longtime critic not just of Stalin but of the whole "org" mentality of unquestioning obedience prevalent among party members, Stone believed that

> Stalin's exposure is Communism's self-exposure and the lessons are (1) that Russia is too backward a country to provide leadership elsewhere, (2) that the slavish conformity of the Communist parties to Moscow has stultified a whole generation of radical leadership, and (3) it is time for the Left to break away from all Communist influence and strike out on a new path determined by each country in its own conditions and traditions . . . The Communists stand exposed as prize idiots abroad and prize cowards within Russia; the hierarchy knew what was going on but dared not speak up. When Stalin growled, Krushchev danced the *gopak*.

Stressing the need for "critical detachment," he warned, "These are not lessons that Communists are capable of learning. They have lost the habit of independent thought."[95] He would have to go and see for himself. First, though, he needed to visit the land that was so much more the focus of his hopes and dreams.

The Israel that welcomed I. F. Stone in 1956 was another country from the precarious refuge he'd seen six years before. Prosperous, confident, "booming," the Jewish state boasted an army that "can win a new war now against all the Arab states combined." Izzy's friend Gershon

---

*By the *New York Times*, which was leaked a copy by the CIA. The CIA obtained it from Mossad, the Israeli intelligence agency. Viktor Grayevsky, a Polish Jewish journalist who was dating the Polish premier Edward Ochab's secretary, had given Ochab's copy to the Israelis in April.

Agron, the Philadelphia newspaperman who came to Palestine with the Jewish Legion in World War I and stayed on to edit the *Palestine Post* (later the *Jerusalem Post*), had just been elected mayor of Jerusalem. Goldie Meyerson, the former Milwaukee schoolteacher who had befriended Izzy on earlier visits and had appeared with him at Haganah fund-raisers in New York, was now Foreign Minister Golda Meir. Access was not a problem.

But the changes in Israel were minor compared to the transformation of Egypt. In 1948, King Farouk's administration had been too corrupt to pose much of a threat to Israel. A revolution in 1952 had abolished the monarchy and brought to power a group of young army officers whose leader, Gamal Abdel Nasser, was charismatic, intelligent, and capable of playing off Britain, the United States, and the Soviet Union against one another. Under Nasser, Egypt also served as a base for raids by Arab commandos, or fedayeen, against the Jewish state. And as Izzy noted, this time the Arabs were as likely to have Russian as British weapons; indeed, Moscow's energetic courtship of Nasser was on Stone's mind throughout this trip.

"War May Come at Any Time" was the headline on his first dispatch from Jerusalem in April. "Ben Gurion," he reported, "is almost cockily ready to take on the Arabs." Yet nothing he saw convinced him that war was inevitable or that, if war did come, the result would be anything other than a military victory for Israel. "But what good will a military victory do?" he wondered, before returning to a message that went as unheeded in 1956 as it had on his previous visits: "We must face up to the full human reality of Arab bitterness if we are to find peace again. We dare not let ourselves be corrupted by the easy robber ethics of conquest . . . Too many Jews delude themselves with the easy rationalization that the Arabs 'left voluntarily,' and that there would be no problem but for their leaders. People flee war when they can; they are bitter when they lose all they had. Is this so hard to understand?"

Reflecting on a visit to Kibbutz Lohamey ha-Geta'ot, founded by the survivors of the 1943 Warsaw Ghetto uprising, Stone was haunted by "the crimes men may be drawn to commit in the name of their *volk*." The Jews, he warned, "are at a crossroads in our history as a people. One way leads towards greater militarization and chauvinism; greater fear and hatred of the Arab. This will poison our relations with the Arabs within Israel and even with the Jews from Arab countries—if we do not treat the Arab as an equal we will not treat the Arabic Jew as an equal . . . We dare not treat the Arab as human dirt swept out of the land without dirtying ourselves." Stone arrived at Nahal Oz, a kibbutz northeast of the Gaza Strip, on April 18, 1956, just as the bombardment by Egyptian soldiers began, killing Israel's security chief, Roï Rutenberg. (Israel, retaliating the next day, shelled the market in Gaza, Izzy reported, "killing some 40 persons and wounding 100 others, mostly civilians.") He knew that what he was suggesting was immensely difficult—"a challenge . . . worthy of Isaiah's people." But the route was clear: "The road to peace lies through the Arab refugee camps"—as, perhaps, was the alternative. A half century later rockets are still falling on Nahal Oz.[96]

Back in Jerusalem, Izzy ran into Dan Wakefield, a young reporter whose coverage of the Emmett Till murder in the *Nation* he'd admired. Wakefield was in Israel trying to make a living as a freelance correspondent. He wasn't doing too well. "Izzy looked at my ragged appearance and skinny frame and said, 'Could I loan you a hundred dollars?' I said yes."[97]

Like the proverbial taxi driver, the Intourist guide was a staple of reports from the Soviet Union. Natasha, the young woman who escorted I. F. Stone in Moscow, did not disappoint. "She wanted first to know why Paul Robeson could not get a passport. I said I had criticized the government's action in refusing him a passport. She then wanted to know what I thought of the condemnation of the Communists in the United States. I said I had criticized that in public speeches and in my paper. She asked whether many people agreed with me and I said unfortunately not many did."[98]

Though he stayed in Moscow only six days, Stone managed to fill four issues of the *Weekly* with his reports. The first three show a veteran foreign correspondent using all his antennae. Everywhere he went—a collective farm outside town, a performance of the Bolshoi, a service at St. Basil's, the patient queue outside Lenin's tomb—yielded up its kernel of significance. The difficulty of conducting man-in-the-street interviews seemed to inspire him, and a whole parade of Russian types, from a traveling magician to a distinguished Soviet jurist to a pair of timorous Jews and a slick, party-line journalist, were duly pinned and cataloged. Some of these encounters—like the young man who blushed as he admitted membership in the Komsomol, the Red Army officer who said "the peasant here has a hard life," then added, pointing to his uniform, "I cannot speak freely," or the Jewish teacher of literature who agreed to a meeting and then turned up with a minder and said he couldn't stay because "he faced a heavy examination the next day in historical materialism"—hinted at disquiet.

In the fourth issue, having exhausted his stock of anecdote and analysis, he finally admitted he had been holding something back: "The way home from Moscow has been an agony for me . . . All the inhibitions of expediency have been urged upon me, the inhibitions of the most worthy expediency—the fight for world peace." It is as if all the arguments that kept him quiet in the 1930s, the ties of sympathy and loyalty, the political calculation that even now urged him to silence, had to be thrown off. "I hate the morass into which one wanders when one begins to withhold the truth because the consequences might be bad—that is, indeed, the morass on which the Russian Communist State is built."

"I feel," he wrote, "like a swimmer underwater who must rise to the surface or his lungs will burst.* Whatever the consequences, I have to say what I really feel after seeing the Soviet Union and carefully studying the statements of its leading officials. *This is not a good society and it is not led by honest men.*" The emphasis was his—and he wasn't finished.

"To blame the evils of Stalinism on Stalin," he continued, "is obviously inadequate . . . The average Communist was prepared to believe anything about anyone who differed with him in the slightest; the liquidation of the opposition was not just a duty but a savage pleasure. And if 'errors' were occasionally made, these were the unavoidable sacrifices of the revolution. This was the spirit the Communist movement bred. Stalin embodied that spirit." As for those, in Russia or the United States, who urged a "return to Lenin," he had news for them: "Stalinism followed naturally from Lenin's own brand of Marxism."

This was not a conversion. He still believed "not only [Russia's] people but her rulers want peace . . . But we will not help the Russian people by letting this crowd of leaders soft soap us."[99] It was merely a recognition, however painful, of the truth: The legacy of communism in

---

*Despite his dislike of Whittaker Chambers, Stone seems to have been influenced by his style. Compare the imagery here with a climactic passage in *Witness*: "I began to break away from Communism and to climb from deep within its underground, where for six years I had been buried, back into the world of free men . . . At the same time, I felt a surging release and a sense of freedom, like a man who bursts at last gasp out of a drowning sea."

the West was one of irredeemable subservience to Moscow, the very existence of Communist parties had become an obstacle to change, and
"nothing has yet happened in Russia to justify cooperation abroad between the independent Left and the Communists." It was also, for I. F.
Stone, a liberation.

•

By May 1956, the *Weekly* had become solidly if modestly profitable. But
Stone's candor on the Soviet Union lost him 400 subscribers, sending circulation below 10,000 for the first time in two years. He gave up the
office on East Capitol Street and moved the paper into his house, an
economy measure that was long overdue. "I realized," he told his son
Jeremy, that "not a single person came to the office who was not a maintenance man or a mailman." Now even some old friends deserted him.

"I am not greatly impressed," wrote Anna Louise Strong, "when I. F.
Stone finds Russians 'browbeaten' because they will not chatter with him
as freely as he desires."[100] The *Daily Worker*'s foreign editor, Joseph Clark,
took a break from the paper's own contorted self-criticism to attack Stone's
aspersions on Lenin. Meanwhile, J. Edgar Hoover personally ordered the
FBI to buy 300 copies of the May 28 *Weekly*, with its headline "Stalinism
Is Far From Liquidated." (Hoover, who had already arranged an FBI subscription to the *Weekly* in the name of "Irving Rubin," originally wanted
1,000 copies but feared such a large order would attract Stone's attention.
His G-men spent months trying to track down spare copies.)[101]

"I shot the works on Russia . . . with some trepidation," Stone admitted
in a letter to "Comrade Thomas," adding that cancellations to the *Weekly*
had been partially offset by new subscriptions. But even if the financial
impact of his reports was not yet clear, in every other way his decision to
hold nothing back gave him a tremendous lift. His warm correspondence
with the Socialist Party leader, initiated by a note saying, "It looks as if I am
liable to end up as I began, 'in the camp of Norman Thomas,'" was perhaps the most personally gratifying consequence of his trip.[102] Both the
Socialists and the Trotskyist Socialist Workers Party invited Stone to talk
to their members about the situation in Eastern Europe. And when the
Weekly sponsored a Bill of Rights Day Forum in New York, chaired by Izzy,
those who agreed to speak ran the gamut of the anti-Stalinist left, from the
pacifist A. J. Muste to Hal Draper from *Labor Action*.

Not all these men shared Stone's view (inspired in part by his reading of Nikolai Berdyaev's *The Origin of Russian Communism*) that "it began with Peter [the Great], not Lenin."[103] Nor would all of them have endorsed his conclusion, after three days in Warsaw on the way back from Moscow, that "Poland has begun to liberate itself," or his optimistic report that Poles "see no reason why socialism cannot be combined with freedom of thought and security of the person." Here, too, though, Stone was determined to write what he found: "I have nowhere in the world, East or West, not even in Tito's Belgrade in 1950, heard Communists talk as they are talking in Warsaw, without Communist clichés or party cant, and a good deal more freely than in the loyalty purge haunted government circles of Washington."[104] Yet the clarity and moral force of his reports on the Soviet Union seemed to inspire generosity even from recent adversaries like Draper.

Stone wasn't changing sides. He still thought Paul Robeson "a great artist, and a deeply sympathetic human being." The singer's "emotionalism and political immaturity have led him into a blind pro-Sovietism but that is his affair," insisted Stone, and "to deny him the right to travel . . . to put him in the pillory of a Congressional committee and let lesser men bait him, is more hurtful to American prestige than any intemperate statement he ever made." He still wasn't ready to weigh Stalin's crimes on the same scale as Hitler's, or to give denunciation of Soviet communism the same moral imperative he had attached to condemnations of fascism or Nazism. He never would.

He had, nonetheless, shriven himself of his fellow traveler's baggage, which may well have included a certain amount of guilt over his previous reticence. Stone was still ready to defend the rights of present as well as former Communists, but where once he might simply have savored the irony of the State Department's refusal to grant Max Shachtman a passport, now he rushed to the pioneering cold warrior's defense. Shachtman, a notoriously touchy archsectarian, may have felt a little patronized by Stone's remark that "though staunchly revolutionary in its ideology, [Shachtman's] Independent Socialist League constitutes a somewhat unclear and only microscopically present danger. It has 200 members. Technically speaking, the ISL originated as the Right opposition to the Left opposition to orthodox Communism." But when Stone described the ISL as "triply pariah—the government regarded them as Reds, the Reds as Trotskyists, and the Trotskyists as renegades," his empathy was obvious.[105]

There were limits, though, even to his newly enlarged sentiments. Not only did he disagree with Sidney Hook's pessimistic pronouncement that any "popular revolt" in Eastern Europe would "achieve heroism and martyrdom, but not victory," he found Hook's "insidious sophistry" on domestic repression—his argument that as conspirators rather than heretics, American Communists had forfeited their civil rights—repellent.[106] On the other hand (or perhaps on the same hand), Stone's own increasingly contemptuous references to the CPUSA were no bar to his deepening fondness for Earl Browder. Stone admired the deposed CP leader's* refusal to betray his former comrades or sell his story, even when his own wife was threatened with deportation. At the height of the frenzy over Oppenheimer, the *Weekly* printed Browder's bylined account of how Dewey and Taft had both welcomed Communist support in the 1930s; Stone also urged readers to contribute to Browder's defense fund.[107] As long as there was still a witch hunt, he would be on the side of its victims, not their persecutors.

Foreign affairs seemed easier. When a dispute at the Cegielski locomotive works in the Polish city of Poznań turned into a general strike just a few weeks after he returned to the United States, Stone was ecstatic: "The workers of Poznan deserve the widest support from abroad; this uprising is the test of the Polish regime. How it reacts will determine its right to survive." Note that he did not, yet, consider the regime illegitimate—probably owing to the influence of the poet Czeslaw Milosz, whom Izzy had befriended when Milosz had served as cultural attaché at the Polish embassy in Washington in the late 1940s. Milosz, living in self-imposed exile in Paris after 1951, made a series of broadcasts for the BBC in 1956, urging support for the reformist Communist government of Władysław Gomulka, a once banished Polish Communist who was invited back into power several months after the strikes. Readers who wanted to understand Poland, Stone wrote, should look to Milosz's *The Captive Mind* (published in 1953), "a first rate study of intellectuals under Stalinism."[108]

When Gomulka ordered the release from prison of the Poznań strikers in late October, Hungarian students in Budapest, inspired by the idea of

---

*Browder had been expelled from the party in 1946 for advocating more cooperative U.S.-Soviet relations.

obtaining similar freedoms in their country, took to the streets. The *Weekly* hailed the new dawn, "the 1848 of the Soviet World." As the revolt spread from Budapest to the rest of Hungary, drawing support from workers and eventually leading to the fall of the government, Stone was jubilant:

> For those of us who have all our lives regarded socialism as our ideal, it is humbling to see that the leading role in the convulsions sweeping Eastern Europe is being taken by the working class, and by the factory workers in particular . . . The workers rise against the workers' state. The epic of the Paris Commune and the Moscow Soviet is played out again in reverse . . . No condescending stereotypes about "bourgeois democracy" can hide the giant lesson of events—the worker needs the secret ballot, the opposition party, "due process" of law and the free press fully as much under socialism as under capitalism. Otherwise he has merely changed bosses.[109]

Perhaps in part because his attention was so fixed on events in Eastern Europe, Stone badly misread the simultaneous crisis unfolding over the Suez Canal. When Nasser, whose purchase of Czech weapons in the summer led the United States and Britain to renege on their pledge to aid in the financing of the Aswan Dam, announced his intention to nationalize the Suez Canal, Stone admitted, "I could not help but admire Nasser for his resourcefulness and daring in pulling a new rabbit out of his hat just when we had called his bluff." If Turkey could be trusted to control the Dardanelles, he wondered, "and the U.S. the Panama Canal, why can't Egypt control the Suez?" Writing from Israel in the spring, he had warned, "Britain would like to use Israel to overthrow Nasser and then to make a settlement at the expense of a weakened Israel." And even as late as August he believed that Israel would "under other circumstances be on Egypt's side in this dispute . . . Nasser is not a Hitler; he has gone out of his way to demonstrate publicly a friendly attitude toward the Jews of Egypt."[110]

But when Israeli troops crossed into Egypt on October 29, Stone's anticolonial scruples disappeared. Depicting British and French support for Israel as "Titoism suddenly spread to London and Paris," he said that it "was England's declaration of independence" from the United States. He termed the invasion a "satellite rebellion" like those in Poland and Hungary. "All we can hope for now," he wrote with cynicism worthy of any party apparatchik, "is if the deed were done, 'twere well—as Lady Macbeth said—it were done quickly. If Nasser could be toppled before the other Arab States join in the melee and Soviet zone 'volunteers' begin arriving to man those planes and tanks, peace might be patched up."[111]

By the following week, Soviet tanks were rolling through the streets of Budapest, and Izzy's breezy realpolitik lost its appeal. That he had underestimated President Eisenhower would take months, perhaps years, to emerge.* That he had let himself down, however, was all too clear:

> Because so many bonds attach me to Israel, I am ready to condone preventative war; I rejoiced when my side won. Though I preach international understanding and support for the UN, I found all the excuses for Israel that warring nationalisms always find to excuse breaches of the peace. Should they wait until the enemy is strong enough to attack them? . . . What better time to save Israel than in concert with Britain and France, on the eve of the American elections, and before the winter rains made the Negev and Sinai impassible for tanks? Israel's survival seemed worth the risk to world peace. And this is how it always is and how it starts, and I offer up the mote in my own eye.[112]

His mid-November report on the Soviet invasion of Hungary also began with an admission of fallibility: "It is not easy to understand the really momentous events of one's time while they are happening." Yet there was not a shred of evasion in his declaration that "Budapest is the biggest. Abandoned by the West, shunned fearfully by their Eastern neighbors, fighting the world's biggest army with home-made weapons, the Hungarians seem doomed and perhaps they are. But in another sense, they—alone—have brought the new Russian empire low . . ." Here the tone

---

*Historians now generally agree that it was not Khrushchev's bluster but Eisenhower's determined action—including a quiet but credible threat to force a run on the pound sterling—that forced the British and French to withdraw from Egypt.

shifts, first to a kind of mourning: "The world will never be the same when this prolonged battle and general strike is over. An era is dying, the era in which many of us intellectuals grew up, the era of the Russian Revolution, the era in which—for all its faults and evils—defense of that revolution was somehow the moral duty of all progressive minded men. That is over, and with it the companion notion—especially powerful in the East—that Russia is not an imperialist power." Refuting the libel, widespread among Soviet apologists, that the Hungarian rebels posed a danger "of a relapse into fascism," he fleshed out his indictment with specifics, including one, about Russian control of Hungarian uranium, from his old friend Claude Bourdet. And then his tone shifts again, voicing both a depth of anger and a certainty in his cadence that can only be called prophecy: "They [the Russians] will never live this down. Budapest is worse than the Khrushchev speech because the speech, for all its revealed horrors, bore the implied promise of real change for the better. Budapest months later demonstrates how unwilling the Stalinist bureaucracy is to make real changes at home and abroad. *What happened in Budapest will some day happen in Moscow*" (emphasis added).[113]

•

Stone was now officially anti-Communist, at home and abroad, but he was still a long way from respectability. When Louis Lautier, Washington correspondent for the National Negro Press Association, broke the color bar at the National Press Club, Izzy decided the time was ripe for him to rejoin. His decade in exile hadn't been absolute; he often visited Edwin Lahey, bureau chief for the Knight newspaper chain, in his office on the twelfth floor of the Press Club building.[114] Now, with Lahey's backing, as well as support from Dick Dudman, he applied for readmission. The membership committee gave its approval—only to be overruled by the club's board of governors.[115] Another quarter century would pass before he would try again.

Counterattack still thought him subversive enough to devote a whole issue to "I. F. Stone: His Niche and His Newsletter." And his continuing attacks on American Communists—"How the same people could excuse Slansky and the 'Doctors' Plot' and at the same time carry on the Rosenberg campaign as they did calls for political psychiatry," he wrote in July

1956—did not keep the Senate Internal Security Committee from denouncing him as "one of the eighty-two most active and typical sponsors
of communist-front organizations." In a way they had a point. The journalist who endorsed four Republican candidates in the 1956 elections
(including one Prescott Bush, of Connecticut, because "[Thomas J.]
Dodd, his Democratic opponent, was the chief architect of the Nixon-
like foreign policy portion of the Democratic platform"), still rallied his
readers to defend Steve Nelson, on trial for sedition in Pennsylvania and
various federal charges, as "perhaps the most long suffering and heroic
figure of this whole witch hunt period."

Yet he had moved, urging the veteran Communist to "consider long
and hard that justice is still possible in this country for oppositionists
whose counterparts in the Soviet Union would not have a dog's chance
even today. A Soviet Steve Nelson would be lucky to get to Vorkuta [a notorious gulag] alive."[116] America was also moving. From the very first issue, the *Weekly* functioned as a kind of underground telegraph of the
American opposition—not just on the blacklist or the liberal pieties of
the cold war, but on race, nuclear weapons, and FBI lawlessness. Clancy
Sigal, author of *Going Away*, the great book of 1950s disaffection and
disillusion, viewed the *Weekly* as a "life raft" for activists like his autobiographical hero—"a traveling salesman of resistance, Willy Loman with
leaflets." In a later novel, *The Secret Defector*, Sigal again elaborates on
his adventures in this "intellectual maquis" fighting "with paranoia and
defiance mixed in equal parts" against the phantasms that haunted the
1950s: "I'd parachute into the least likely places: Walla Walla, North
Platte, Mobile, Knoxville, Conneaut, Troy—anywhere readers of *I. F.
Stone's Weekly*, *Dissent*, or *Monthly Review* were prepared to give me a cot
for the night."[117]

The very juxtaposition of these three journals may seem jarring—an
indication of how tenacious the narcissism of small differences can be.
But it was true that in the late 1950s the momentary cessation of hostilities was sufficient even for such bitter enemies as Earl Browder and Norman Thomas to find common ground.[118]

The witch hunt still sent out flares, though. Izzy depicted HUAC's
subpoena of Arthur Miller as a comically desperate bid for publicity, worthy of the front page "only if the Committee pulls a real surprise—say, an
infra red photograph to prove that Miller tattooed atom bomb secrets on

Marilyn's lovely bottom." Is there, the *Weekly* wondered, "a red-blooded American boy from six to sixty who does not hope some day to marry Marilyn Monroe? Surely, as at Lexington, there is a point at which America will stand and fight." Arthur Miller, understandably, was inclined to treat the matter more seriously. His deferential posture toward the committee earned him a caustic review from the *Weekly*, where Izzy told readers that the playwright "came out of his own 'Crucible' poorly." Only Miller's refusal to name the other members of a Marxist writers' group, which earned him a citation for contempt of Congress, saved his dignity.[119]

Stone's appraisal may have been ungenerous, but it was consistent with everything else he'd written on the witch hunt. The general public viewed Miller far more sympathetically—one sign of changing times. Another was the fate of Robert Shelton, a *New York Times* reporter whom Eastland subpoenaed and who declined to answer any questions at all. (Shelton's refusal was entirely on principle; he never had any connection with the CP and had been subpoenaed by mistake.) The paper kept Shelton on even after he was convicted of contempt,* and Izzy, who usually had the press table to himself at such trials, found himself sharing the otherwise "empty courtroom" with the *New York Post*'s "brilliant columnist, Murray Kempton." In March 1957, Kempton and Stone met again, this time on the podium of a benefit for William Price, a former *Daily News* reporter (and cousin of George Polk) who was also on trial for refusing, on First Amendment grounds, to cooperate with the Eastland committee.[120]

Izzy felt confident enough about the future that in October 1956, when Dan Wakefield turned up on his doorstep to repay the $100 loan, he offered him a job as assistant to the editor. (Wakefield, who wrote one article on "tryout" for Stone, was about to accept when the *Nation* made him a staff writer.) Still too "red" for the Press Club or national television, in July 1957 Izzy was invited onto *Night Beat* on WABD-TV in New York, where the host, John Wingate, asked his views on men in public life. By the end of the year, the *Weekly*'s circulation was higher than it had been before the Moscow trip—and rising.

---

*Shelton became the *Times*'s pop music critic, a beat that in September 1961 sent him to Gerde's Folk City in Greenwich Village to catch a twenty-year-old unknown: "His clothes may need a bit of tailoring, but when he works his guitar, harmonica, or piano and composes new songs faster than he can remember them, there is no doubt that he is bursting at the seams with talent." Shelton's rave notice launched Bob Dylan's career.

Subscribing still took some daring. Cynthia Scollon was given a subscription by her boss, Irving Berlin. The composer of "God Bless America" never had a subscription of his own, though. "As a recluse he was very careful about what he put his name down on," recalled Scollon, who went to work for Berlin as a "twenty-three-year-old from an old Republican family" in upstate New York and was "hooked right away" by the *Weekly*. If his "girl Friday" forgot to bring in her copy, Berlin could always borrow one from his arranger, Helmy Kresa, who did subscribe in his own name.[121] Irving Caesar, who wrote the lyrics for "Swanee" and "Tea for Two," also subscribed, writing after one issue, "If you can get some boys to distribute a thousand copies on the streets of Washington . . . I will be happy to pay for it." There was, however, a caveat: "I prefer not to have my name used."[122] The man responsible for "Brother, Can You Spare a Dime" and the lyrics to "Somewhere Over the Rainbow" was another subscriber, but since he was already on the *Red Channels* blacklist, E. Y. Harburg had nothing to lose.

Tin Pan Alley furnished only a small portion of the *Weekly*'s growing audience. But so many of the rest were also in New York City that when Izzy threw a fifth-anniversary dinner in January 1958, he hired the Port Arthur restaurant on Mott Street. In a break with custom, the event was not a fund-raiser. Instead, the eponymous editor served as master of ceremonies for a Chinese banquet where 300 subscribers heard speeches from Edward Condon, Owen Lattimore, Earl Browder, Clark Foreman, and Leonard Boudin.

For Boudin, too, 1958 was to be a year of triumph. Ever since 1955, when he forced the State Department to issue a passport to Otto Nathan, Einstein's secretary, Boudin and the ECLC had been seeking the right plaintiff to take the issue all the way to the Supreme Court. Boudin's own passport had been seized, partly in retaliation for his efforts on behalf of Paul Robeson. But in June 1958, in the landmark *Kent v. Dulles*, the court ruled five to four that Boudin's client, the artist Rockwell Kent, had a fundamental right to travel that could not be taken away merely because of his alleged political associations or his refusal to sign a non-Communist affidavit.

Boudin's famous victory might well have made his brother-in-law jealous—at a triumphal brunch at the Boudin town house in Greenwich Village, Izzy supposedly chided Leonard to remember that while he and

Louis Boudin "studied Marx like the Talmud," Leonard's law books were mere "hammer and nails." But Izzy's teasing couldn't mask his pride in Leonard's ability.[123] Besides, the journalist brother-in-law was still basking in the glow of a recent triumph of his own, "the biggest scoop I ever got."

In the fall of 1957, the United States had conducted the first ever underground nuclear test, in the Nevada desert. This was an issue the *Weekly* followed closely. Izzy had been an early and vocal supporter of moves to ban nuclear weapons testing. Only a few weeks before, he had published a detailed account of the first Pugwash Conference—an international meeting of eminent scientists called at the behest of Albert Einstein and Bertrand Russell.[124] When George Kennan, in a text prepared for his 1957 Reith lectures on the BBC, opposed continued nuclear testing, Izzy put the news on his front page. (Kennan apparently deleted this comment when delivering the lecture, however.)[125] And when Edward Teller wrote an article published in *Life* magazine on "The Compelling Need for Nuclear Tests," Stone gave the Nobel laureate Linus Pauling (a Pugwash activist) two pages of the *Weekly* to puncture Teller's argument that there was no point in trying to agree on a test ban, since the Russians would simply test in secret underground.[126]

As Stone recounted it years later to the filmmaker Jerry Bruck, the tale illustrates the way Stone, with only his own guerrilla fighter's cunning and an insider's knowledge of Washington folkways, was able to outmaneuver not just other news organizations but also a government bureaucracy devoted to concealing the truth. (This was also probably the best précis, in his own words, of Stone's method.)

"The first underground test was held by the Teller crowd in order to show the possibility of hiding testing underground," he explained. "I wasn't out there, but I got the *Times* the next morning." The experiment, the *Times* reported, "seemed to have conformed with predictions of A.E.C. scientists that the explosion would not be detectable more than a few hundred miles away." But the paper's city edition, on Izzy's doorstep, "had a 'shirt-tail' [a brief story appended to the end of a news article] from Toronto saying Toronto had detected it. I went downtown and bought the Late City, and there were little shirt-tails, one from Rome and one from Tokyo, saying *they* had detected it. I thought, 'Gee, I wish I had enough money to cable those places and find out what's going on.' [Instead, I] put it down in the basement with all my back numbers of the *Times*, and waited."[127]

While he waited, Harold Stassen, Eisenhower's negotiator on nuclear issues, reached tentative agreement with the Soviets to allow monitoring stations every 600 miles. Two days later, Edward Teller appeared on *Meet the Press* claiming "disarmament is a lost cause" since it was "virtually certain" that the Russians would be able to cheat. (He also assured viewers that "world-wide fallout is as dangerous to human health as being one ounce overweight or smoking one cigarette every two months.") Within a week, the AEC issued its official report on the September test, saying the blast couldn't have been detected more than 200 miles away. "The obvious purpose," said Stone, "was to make a liar out of Stassen and undercut the agreement. When I saw it I went down to the basement, dug out that old *Times* . . . I thought, I've never been on a seismology story before."

At the Coast and Geodetic Survey branch of the Commerce Department, Izzy found his seismologist. "So I jumped in the car and went down there . . . I don't think they'd seen a reporter since there was a tremble from Mount Ararat when Noah's Ark landed." The government scientists were dubious about Tokyo and Rome, but they gave Izzy a list of nineteen U.S. and Canadian seismic stations, from Arkansas to Alaska, which had detected the September blast. Thanks to his investigation, the AEC eventually issued a correction disclosing that stations as far as 2,300 miles away had recorded the shock waves. Teller's argument was destroyed. The episode—which in Stone's many retellings ends with the AEC chairman Lewis Strauss, at a special hearing of Congress's Joint Atomic Energy Committee, being asked, "Wasn't it I. F. Stone's story" that prompted the AEC's correction—was one of his favorite anecdotes.[128] Forcing Strauss to admit the AEC's "complete inadvertence" was "my great moment," said Stone.

Izzy stayed on the story, and with the help of Edward Condon and other scientist friends he was soon exposing other AEC "inadvertences" on the dangers of fallout and increased levels of strontium 90 in milk—and revealing that the Pentagon, while claiming that continued testing was necessary to develop a "clean bomb," was also actively researching "radiological warfare"—the use of even dirtier, *more* radioactive weapons.[129] Bertrand Russell, already a *Weekly* subscriber, began a warm correspondence with the editor, who had been among the philosopher's few defenders years before when the *Brooklyn Tablet* forced him out of a position at City College.[130]

It wasn't just Lord Russell. The *Weekly*'s aggressive exposure of atomic mendacity brought Stone kudos and credibility from a whole new audience. In 1957, the Detroit Labor Forum asked him to speak on ending nuclear testing. He had given a similar talk to the Eugene Debs Forum in Chicago and the Women's International League for Peace and Freedom in Washington, where he commented on "the conspicuous absence of young people in the audience." But by the end of 1958, he'd become a favorite speaker of the National Committee for a Sane Nuclear Policy. SANE, as it came to be known, began life the previous year as a temporary project of the American Friends Service Committee. Under attack almost from birth—*Time* wondered "How Sane the SANE?" dismissing the group's campaign on the dangers of fallout as "Folks who listened to the horror stories without listening to the evidence"—SANE grew to 130 chapters with 25,000 members by the end of its first year.[131] SANE's chairman, Norman Cousins, came out of the United World Federalists, which had been decimated by red-baiting, and he was determined to make sure the new group criticized both nuclear powers. And though SANE did briefly function as a kind of foster home for many former Communists, they never had nearly as much influence within the group as Quaker pacifists like its cofounder, Clarence Pickett, or independent radicals like A. J. Muste and Bayard Rustin. More important, unlike the shell-shocked Old Leftists whom Stone usually addressed, his SANE audiences were young, confident, and, inspired by the example of Gandhi's satyagraha campaigns, increasingly willing to risk arrest.[132]

•

"The American Communist Party is dead for all practical purposes, though it can continue to live on, the way a mummy does," said John Gates, resigning from the *Daily Worker* a few days before the *Weekly*'s fifth-anniversary dinner.[133] The rusting hulks of the Old Left had run permanently aground, and not even the rising ferment of the late 1950s redeemed them from irrelevance. *I. F. Stone's Weekly* was still a reliable defender of their rights, still a fixture on coffee tables in "co-ops" from Brooklyn to the Bronx. But the editor's interest and passion were engaged elsewhere. After a decade of trying to hold the line against government repression, Stone now saw stirrings on a range of issues, from disarmament to desegregation. Like tiny waves far out at sea, the ripples scarcely troubled the placid surface of Eisenhower's America. Not "a movement," but movement nonetheless.

In New York City, a handful of radical pacifists, including Bayard Rustin, David Dellinger from the War Resisters League, and Dorothy Day, editor of the *Catholic Worker*, publicly defied orders to take shelter during Operation Alert, the annual nationwide civil defense exercise. In London, the Campaign for Nuclear Disarmament (CND), founded by Izzy's friend Kingsley Martin, editor of the *New Statesman*, staged a march to the British atomic weapons research center at Aldermaston; on Easter weekend 1958, more than 100,000 people joined the CND president, Bertrand Russell, in calling for an end to nuclear weapons. And at Katz's Drugstore in Oklahoma City in August 1958, a high school teacher named Clara Luper and twelve members of the local NAACP Youth Council sat at the store's "whites only" counter and ordered Coca-Colas. The sit-down, the CIO's winning weapon from the 1930s, was about to get a new lease on life.

At the same time, the Supreme Court decision banning segregation in public schools had forced Stone and other radicals to rethink their adversarial stance toward the state. The very federal government whose agents had tapped their phones, revoked their passports, and deported their comrades was now the best hope for imposing civil equality on recalcitrant state and local officials. The House of Representatives was useless; the *Weekly* described its hearings on yet another toothless civil rights bill as "white man's comedy, black man's agony," adding that "the battle will be won on the streets of Montgomery and Tallahassee, not in Washington." The Senate was worse. When John Kennedy made a much-admired speech favoring Algerian independence, the *Weekly* was scathing: "During the McCarthy era, the Senator from Massachusetts wrote a book about courage—the courage shown by other Senators on other occasions in history—but he himself did not practice what he described. When McCarthyism was the issue, his own profile was discreetly set in silence. It is characteristic that on the eve of a battle to enforce the rights of colored people in our South, Senator Kennedy should launch a crusade to help the colored people—in Algeria. He's a brave man away from home."[134] And when the Senate chamber rang with tributes to the sanctity of trial by jury—for those charged with civil rights violations—and Kennedy voted with the South, Izzy stripped away the rhetoric to reveal a racial divide. Since no Southern jury would convict segregationist officials,

> the problem was whether the Northern majority was to coerce the Southern majority or back down before it . . . To the Negro the question was simply whether he was or was not to be treated as a first class citizen. But to the white man, the good liberal white man of the North, the indispensable ally in the Negro's struggle, the question was whether he was going to be "fair" . . . How can one be fair to the oppressed without some unfairness to the oppressor? This is how the question honestly presents itself in a revolutionary period and the effort to win equality for the Negro in the South is a revolutionary enterprise.

The *Weekly* offered some tactical advice: "to turn the tables on the South, to put it in the wrong, to wage counter attack with a symbol and slogan as powerful as jury trial. The slogan to match it in our society is the right to vote . . . To invoke the right to vote as the South has invoked the right to jury trial would be to throw its ruling class on the defensive."[135]

What made the struggle for civil rights a "revolutionary enterprise" was not just the scale of the change but also Izzy's sense that Southern resistance had become open defiance of the law and that in the end the matter would have to be resolved by force. So when President Eisenhower, after long temporizing, finally sent the 101st Airborne to Little Rock to escort nine black students to Central High School in September 1957, Izzy, though acknowledging that "the white South was shocked at military 'occupation,'" recognized that "Negro reaction was of a different kind."

"The Negro," he reported, "felt like Cinderella. When a station wagon guarded by Army jeeps took little Negro children to and from school instead of leaving them to run a gauntlet of hate alone, the Negro felt that for the first time in American history he was being treated like a first class citizen." Being on the government's side was an unusual experience for Stone, and he tried not to let it go to his head. "Troops may be an answer in Little Rock but they will not prove an answer in Atlanta," he warned. However momentary, there was no disguising his elation: "The law never looked more truly majestic than it does today in Little Rock."[136]

Stone hasn't received much credit for his pioneering coverage of the civil rights movement.* Yet from the Scottsboro campaign onward he was one of the few white reporters to realize the enormous importance of the fight and one of even fewer capable of seeing not just the historic but also the international implications of America's efforts fully to enfranchise its black citizens. "Whether here or in Algiers," he remarked, "the white race just doesn't seem as civilized as it claims to be." For Stone, France's futile battle to hold on to its North African colony was a cautionary tale, corrupting the whole political system from "the Communist party as evident in its pampered Cadillac-borne god, [Maurice] Thorez [leader of the French Communist Party]," to unrepentant Pétainists on the far right: "In France, as elsewhere, the price of white supremacy turns out to be the liberty of whites and blacks." The United States is fortunate, Stone observed: "Our Negroes still want to be Americans like the rest of us . . . In the years ahead, as Black Africa develops, there will also develop in conflict with the whites of South Africa, of our South, and of North Africa, a fierce Negro nationalism, a racism in reaction against ours, that may win our Negroes away from the ideal of assimilation."[137]

Under *Brown*, the states had been told to end segregation "with all deliberate speed." In September 1958, when the Supreme Court decided what "deliberate speed" meant in Arkansas, Stone joined the early morning vigil outside the Court, then flew to Little Rock to report on the impact—and the obstacles: "After a night with a group of tortured Southern liberals one acquired a new view of Tennessee Williams; he began to seem a camera-like realist."[138]

Stone remained an observer (albeit a decidedly unneutral one) on civil rights, but he was very much a participant when the battle to protect civil liberties moved onto the offensive. At first Izzy thought Chief Justice Earl Warren's June 1957 ruling, in *Watkins v. U.S.*, that Congress has "no general authority to expose the private affairs of individuals" and that hearings conducted solely "to 'punish' those investigated are indefensible"

---

*The two-volume Library of America anthology *Reporting Civil Rights* contains nothing from Stone, who, despite his limitations as a one-man operation, produced vivid, insightful firsthand reports from Alabama, Arkansas, and the 1968 New York City teachers' strike, as well as perceptive portraits of activists ranging from A. Philip Randolph to Malcolm X. Perhaps Stone's comment, amid the elation of the 1963 March on Washington, that he found Martin Luther King Jr. "a little too saccharine for my taste," was insufficiently reverent, or perhaps he was simply too radical. Walter Rodney, who as sports editor of the *Daily Worker* did more than any other journalist to break baseball's color bar, is also consigned to the memory hole.

meant the end of the witch hunt. That turned out to be excessively optimistic. Still, Izzy sensed an opening.

"When the *Watkins* decision came down," Frank Wilkinson recalled,
he was working in Los Angeles with a group supporting individuals hauled
before HUAC or similar state committees. Wilkinson's own career had
been collateral damage in efforts made by private real-estate interests to
stop public housing being built in an area known as Chavez Ravine. He'd
been fired by the Los Angeles Housing Authority for refusing to tell the
California Subcommittee on Un-American Activities whether he was a
Communist.* "Izzy called me and said, 'It's time to start the abolition campaign.' Izzy also went to [the ECLC], and the next thing I knew I got a call
from Corliss Lamont asking if I would initiate this campaign."[139]

In February 1958, Izzy spoke at a Carnegie Hall rally on Regaining the
First Amendment. In March, *Esquire* saluted the *Weekly* as "the heady
champion of many American liberals," a sign that the battle was not as
quixotic as it looked. That August, when HUAC held hearings in Atlanta
and subpoenaed Carl and Anne Braden, Wilkinson flew down as the
ECLC's observer, whereupon he was promptly served with a subpoena as
well. At Wilkinson's first appearance before HUAC, in Los Angeles in
1956, he had refused to answer questions about his beliefs on First
Amendment grounds but had escaped prosecution. Now, in Atlanta, he
challenged "the fundamental legality" of the committee itself, leaving it
no choice but to cite him for contempt. The ECLC finally had the test it
wanted.[†] By the time Wilkinson's case reached the Supreme Court, the
New York Times had labeled the once-dreaded committee "ridiculous."
The *Times* also attacked HUAC's "usual policy of harassment of suspected Left-Wingers and dissenters" after it tried to force Linus Pauling
to turn over the names of people who had helped collect signatures on a
petition calling for a nuclear test ban. And on May 13, 1960, when col-

---

*Ry Cooder's 2005 album *Chavez Ravine*, a musical evocation of this lost community—now the site
of Dodger Stadium—includes a cameo narration by Wilkinson, who is also the inspiration for the
track "Don't Call Me Red." Ironically, as Robert Sherrill reveals in *First Amendment Felon: The Story
of Frank Wilkinson* (New York: Nation Press, 2005), the activist actually was a Communist, remaining in the party from 1942 to 1975.
†If the ECLC had known about his connection to the CP it might well have preferred a different
plaintiff, but according to Sherrill (p. 153), Wilkinson concealed his party membership from both
Stone and Clark Foreman.

lege students rioted outside HUAC hearings in San Francisco, the *Washington Post*, though regretting the violence, declared that "students ought to protest against a Committee of Congress which has long since ceased to serve any purpose but punishment by publicity. It is heartening to see American students behaving like American students."[140]

"That young people on the campuses are again a-stir on the great issues of our time" was hardly news to Izzy, who regularly reported as much in the *Weekly* and whose talks for SANE and Student SANE were making him a fixture on the college lecture circuit.[141] One of his rare local television appearances—on *The Open Mind* for WRCA in New York, where Stone had a strong local following—even drew a rave review from *Variety*: "Stone, who pulls no journalistic punches and is a badgering banderillero of the American press, provided most of the fireworks," said the paper, adding that it was Izzy's "pyrotechnics that put the torrid tabasco sauce" in the broadcast.[142]

Stone was also thrilled by "the spreading revolt of Negro college youth against segregated lunch counters." Finally American blacks were rising up to demand their rights, and in the wake of the Sharpeville Massacre in South Africa in March 1960—when police fired on thousands of unarmed blacks gathered in peaceful protest against that country's racist "apartheid" laws and at least eighty people were killed—he felt "fortunate that our own fellow citizens of color in their struggle for full equality appeal to common national heroes and ideals, to Lincoln and the Declaration . . . The American Negro asks only to sit with us and eat with us as a brother. He fights to end the humiliation of *apartness*. This is the secret of the wonderful sit-downs sweeping the South." Compared to the young activists of Greensboro and Nashville, the interminable congressional wrangling over civil rights was becoming "a white man's sideshow."[143]

One of the few legislators who escaped Stone's scorn was the maverick Ohio Democrat Stephen Young. First elected to Congress in the 1930s, Young, who entered the Senate in 1958, was famously ill-tempered, answering a constituent's critical letter, "Dear Sir: Some crackpot has written to me and signed your name." When the Emergency Civil Liberties Committee nominated Izzy for its Tom Paine Award in December 1959, he asked Young to give the keynote speech at the celebratory dinner. The "Americanism chairman" of the Ohio American Legion denounced the senator's acceptance, but Young, a decorated veteran of both world wars and a longtime legionnaire, held his ground: "I repudiate your resolution, Buster, and your pompous, self-righteous, holier-than-thou title." Though Eleanor Roosevelt and Bertrand Russell both cabled their regrets, the award dinner was heavily oversubscribed.[144]

But if things were looking better at home, the cold war was still freezing the heart of Europe, the French remained stuck in their Algerian quagmire, U.S. marines occupied Beirut "without consulting Congress," and "the Congo affair on top of everything else,"* Stone worried, "gives the world the atmosphere of a bar-room on the verge of a brawl."[145] Hoping to make a quick trip to Paris and Algiers, Stone applied to renew his passport. This time he left blank the questions on past or present membership in the Communist Party, explaining his refusal as "a matter of principle."[146] With the State Department still smarting from the *Kent v. Dulles* decision, Izzy got his passport anyway. Rumors that an Eisenhower-Khrushchev summit meeting was imminent kept him in Washington through the summer, but the spring of 1959 found him in Berlin, "a divided city in a divided world."

Stone's sense of the division was summed up in a pair of interviews. After his hasty departure from the United States in 1946, Gerhart Eisler had become vice president of the East German broadcasting system. Eisler "looked older but well," Stone reported from East Berlin, "and he spoke with that assurance and lack of party line cant one encounters in Communist circles only among officials securely near the top." The following day he met with Paul Hertz, the Social Democratic economics minister for the city of West Berlin. "Both men lived in exile in America. Both men are Jewish . . . For Eisler the lesson of German history between 1919 and 1933 is that the weakness of the Social Democrats was criminal, that a ruthless purge, Russian style . . . would have nipped Hitlerism at its roots . . . For men like Hertz, on the other hand, Eisler represents a force which helped to undermine the prewar Republic, which joined hands often with the Nazis . . . [and] which divided the left until it was too late." Between the old Bolshevik and the old Menshevik, Stone's sympathies are clearly with Hertz, "a living link" with Karl Kautsky and "the greatest days and names of German socialism."[147]

---

*The mineral-rich province of Katanga, backed by Belgium, tried to secede from the newly independent Congo. Pitting the country's former colonial rulers against the national liberation movement, the crisis threatened to become another cold war proxy fight.

Stopping in Warsaw, Stone found "slow retrogression" since his last visit, but in comparison with East Germany "Poland remains extraordinarily free. The 'revisionist' philosopher, [Leszek] Kolakowski, for example, still teaches philosophy at Warsaw University and is still a member of the United Workers' Party. The government is still full of Left Socialists who talk and think like socialists, not Communists, that is, as men who share the traditions of free society, and prize the virtues of persuasion over the shortcuts of coercion."[148]

All his life Stone held to the view that the way a society treated its dissenting intellectuals was an index of freedom. But he was also extremely susceptible to personal charm. When he returned to New York, the city was abuzz with talk of a recent visitor. Fidel Castro, the *Weekly* reported, was "one of the heroes of our time . . . like something out of the romantic Nineteenth Century. In the age of the atom bomb, when military force is supposed to be overwhelming, a handful of brave men take to the hills and wage a successful struggle to free their country from a dictator whose forces have been trained and armed by the Colossus of the North. Not since Bolivar has any man so thrilled the youth of Latin America."[149]

Or the North American press. "A Humanist Abroad" was *Time*'s verdict on the Cuban who had triumphed in the revolution against the corrupt regime of Fulgencio Batista only a few months earlier. "It would be a great mistake," declared Walter Lippmann, "even to intimate that Castro's Cuba has any real prospect of becoming a Soviet satellite"—a warning echoed from the *New York Times* to the *New Leader*, where Theodore Draper (Hal's older brother) described the Cuban revolution as "neither capitalist nor socialist."[150] Once again, Izzy wanted to see for himself.

•

He never did get to interview Castro. But in July 1960, I. F. Stone, cold-eyed chronicler of revolutionary illusions, went to Cuba and came back a believer. It wasn't as if he didn't know the risks. Only a month earlier, commending Huberman and Sweezy's *Cuba: Anatomy of a Revolution*, he cautioned that the book was "the product of a love affair . . . and as in most love affairs this did not generate objectivity."[151] So what were Stone's objective conclusions after two weeks on the island? "I believe Fidel Castro and his able group of young associates are bringing about a social revolution of an admirably humane quality with amazing swiftness and order . . . By comparison with the hysterical demagogy of the Arab States and the phoney Leftist oratory of Mexico, the Cuban leadership seems sober and restrained. Except for the absence of a multi-party press and a multi-party politics, Cuba seemed most like Israel in its ebullience. The cooperatives in the countryside, the devoted technicians in the government, reminded me strongly of *Eretz*."

Partly it was the change of air. "For almost two decades we have lived in a stale atmosphere of Fifth Amendment radicalism; no one is a Communist; few admit themselves Socialists, nobody owns up to reading Marx and practically everybody on the Left claims only to be a Liberal, nothing more; the word 'radical' is avoided as a bad word." Castro, by comparison, "is a man who has never hidden his intentions," a leader "who proudly avowed his revolutionary aims." The youthful guerrilla (Castro was then thirty-three), Stone assured his readers, was "pragmatic rather than doctrinaire. In this he strongly resembles Franklin D. Roosevelt, except that operating in a poorer country Fidel is more socialistic and U.S. pressure, by putting the economic squeeze on him, has been pushing him further Left . . . Talking with officials one found the same zeal and devotion that marked New Deal Washington."[152]

By his own account, Stone, who did not speak Spanish, only heard Castro on television. So how did he know? Late one night Stone was admitted to an office in the Cuban National Bank building in Havana. The official who greeted him "was the first man I had ever met whom I thought not just handsome but beautiful. With his curly, reddish beard, he looked like a cross between a faun and a Sunday School print of Jesus." Che Guevara greeted Izzy with a warmth the American found puzzling, until the young Argentine rebel explained that as an exile in Mexico in 1954 he'd learned that the U.S. embassy was buying up every copy it could of the Spanish edition of *The Hidden History of the Korean War* to keep the book out of circulation. In later years, Stone honored "the Shelleyan purity of Che's intentions." In the *Weekly*, though, he simply reported "from my meeting with Dr. Guevara and from the biographies of the top leadership, I believe the young men around Fidel are as unusual and gifted a group as those who made our own American Revolution and those who wrote the Constitution."[153]

Back in the United States, Stone joined the national board of the Fair

Play for Cuba Committee, a group founded in 1960 by Alan Sagner, an activist in the New Jersey Democratic Party, the CBS correspondent Robert Taber, and Carleton Beals. Though Taber was roughly Stone's age, and Beals, a journalist who had interviewed Mussolini, covered Augusto Sandino's revolt in Nicaragua in 1928, and reported on the first Scottsboro trial in 1931 for the *Nation*, was even older, the FPCC introduced Stone to a new generation of activists smitten, as he was, by the Cubans' seeming disdain for the political taboos of the 1950s. (Many of these young activists, like Sagner, were also *Weekly* subscribers.) In a way, the middle-aged Stone's espousal of the Cuban cause was as much a return to his own youthful romanticism as it was the result of any political analysis—an emotional commitment he shared with Sandra Cason, Al Haber, Tom Hayden, and other members of Students for Travel to Cuba, a campus group that invited him to speak. A triumph of hope over experience, Stone's Cuban adventure would not end happily. It also put him on a collision course with another attractive young man whose combination of vigor, charm, and disregard for political convention moved Izzy, almost against his will, from opposition to admiration. But then Stone's infatuation with John F. Kennedy, like his admiration for Castro, was only temporary.

Disappointment with Kennedy's lack of courage on race was just one item contributing to the *Weekly*'s "long held and indeed cherished anti-Kennedy bias." The senator's father, Stone reminded his readers, was an anti-Semite, a World War II defeatist, and a backer of Joe McCarthy. (Joseph Kennedy got his son Robert appointed McCarthy's counsel, yet for some reason this item never made Stone's bill of particulars. Perhaps Robert Kennedy's subsequent service on Senator John McClellan's Rackets subcommittee redeemed him. "The McClellan investigation," Stone remarked approvingly, "is doing for the labor movement what it demonstrably could not do for itself—expose the finest collection of phonies who ever fattened on a working class payroll." It is difficult to imagine the *Weekly* accusing anyone else but the Teamsters Union president, Dave Beck, of "stretching the Fifth Amendment beyond all reasonable bounds"—a reminder, perhaps, that Stone had exposed Teamster corruption when Robert Kennedy was still in grade school.)[154]

John Kennedy's main handicap, though, was his party. "If there is to be a settlement with the Russians, it will take conservatives to do it," Stone explained in an April 1959 article calling Richard Nixon "the key to peace." Democrats were too afraid of being seen as soft, and a speech Kennedy gave that was supposed to demonstrate the senator's toughness was, Stone thought, "a piece of wicked hysterical drivel." A year later, the *Weekly* was still describing Nixon as "the advocate of co-existence" while warning that Kennedy "moved leftward to defeat Humphrey, and . . . cut the ground out from under Stevenson. But if he's really that much of a liberal, why has he been such a favorite of Henry Luce?" After the conventions in the summer of 1960, Stone acknowledged "the promise of bigness in Kennedy," but watching the two candidates in their first televised debate left him "wishing for a commercial . . . I felt as if I had been smoking more and enjoying it less, and that neither Nixon nor Kennedy tasted as good as a cigarette should . . . On civil liberties, Nixon emerged more liberal than Kennedy."[155]

His visceral distaste for Nixon was as strong as ever: "There were moments [during the debate] when he tried to smile, which were downright frightening; he looked like an undertaker congratulating a steady customer on another death in the family." But this made Stone's inability to recommend either man all the more striking. Kennedy was "hopeless" on Cuba. Yet Nixon, the author of the hated Internal Security Act, "who was so ready for war over Indochina in 1954, how could one possibly vote for him?"[156]

Stone's gloom lasted through Kennedy's inauguration in January 1961. Warning that "the CIA may be preparing an invasion of Cuba," the *Weekly* cited a report of armed men training in Guatemala and asked, "Just what *are* we cooking up in the Caribbean?" Kennedy "gives every indication of being the greatest master of manipulative politics since FDR, no mean man at razzle-dazzle." But what did the president mean, Stone wondered, with his declaration that "We shall pay any price"?[157]

And then came John Kennedy's first press conference. "At the risk of alarming steady customers, inured to a weekly diet of apocalyptic pessimism, I must confess that I am becoming optimistic . . . I feel that for the first time since Roosevelt we have a first-rater in the Presidency, a young man of energy, zest and ability." It was, as Izzy put it himself, "as if the Prophet Jeremiah were caught cheering."[158]

Nine

THE IMPERIAL THEME

———•◦•———

I. F. Stone was not alone in greeting John Kennedy as a harbinger of renewal. The cohort of idealistic young men and women arriving in Washington in the winter of 1961 saw themselves not as a partisan changing of the guard, but as votaries responding to a call: "Ask not what your country can do for you—ask what you can do for your country."

At Harvard, where the *Crimson* proudly reported each new faculty recruit to the administration of "John F. Kennedy, '40," students packed a meeting of the Boston Fair Play for Cuba Committee three weeks before the inauguration to hear Izzy and Robert Taber urge the new president to embrace the Cuban revolution. Hadn't Kennedy himself (or Harris Wofford, the president's ghostwriter) written, "Fidel Castro is part of the legacy of Bolivar, who led his men over the Andes mountains vowing 'war to the death' against Spanish rule"? In *The Strategy of Peace*, a 1960 book designed to burnish the candidate's liberal credentials, Kennedy had attributed Castro's victory to "the frustration of that earlier revolution which won its war against Spain but left largely untouched the indigenous feudal order." The United States, said Kennedy, should have "given the fiery rebel leader a warmer welcome in his hour of triumph, especially on his trip to this country."[1]

Presumably the author had in mind something closer to the reception Harvard had given Castro in April 1959, when Dean McGeorge Bundy hosted a dinner for him at the Faculty Club, then escorted him to Soldiers' Field, where a crowd of 10,000 students applauded the Cuban leader's invitation to come visit the revolution.[2] Yet when Castro arrived in New York to attend the opening session of the United Nations shortly before the 1960 elections, neither Bundy nor Harvard's most prominent graduate was in evidence. Nikita Khrushchev made the journey up to Harlem, where the Cuban delegation was ensconced in the Hotel Theresa, and was photographed on 125th Street with his arms around Castro; Nasser and Nehru followed in the Russian's wake. Malcolm X, the Nation of Islam's Harlem minister, was another visitor. I. F. Stone, who pronounced Castro's UN speech a *"tour de force,"* joined the beat poet Allen Ginsberg, the sociologist C. Wright Mills, and 250 other invited guests at a reception for the Cubans in the Theresa's shabby ballroom, where Richard Gibson, a CBS colleague of Robert Taber and the network's first black correspondent, presented Castro with a bust of Abraham Lincoln. Even the party of Lincoln sent an emissary, the baseball legend Jackie Robinson, a supporter of Richard Nixon's presidential bid, who came to denounce Cuban "propaganda" but stayed to tell reporters Castro's presence had given Harlem "a real lift—a sense of pride." But from the junior senator from Massachusetts there wasn't so much as a PT-109 tie clip.[3]

Once he had the Democratic nomination in hand, Kennedy cut sharply to the right on Cuba, calling the island "a chink in our defensive armor" and warning that "an enemy stands poised at the throat of the United States." In response to Kennedy's taunt, "If you can't stand up to Castro, how can you be expected to stand up to Khrushchev?" it was the hapless Nixon who defended the United States for not dealing with Cuba as the Russians "dealt with the Hungarian patriots in the streets of Budapest." The comparison was as revealing as the speaker. After a decade of cold war immobility, the Hungarian uprising had made revolution respectable again. Though his brother's government didn't like Fidel Castro or his beard, Milton Eisenhower, the president of Johns Hopkins, hailed the Cuban as "a symbol of a noble revolution."[4] This was especially true for two groups making their own rapid—and symbolically freighted— journey from the margins of American society: African Americans and college students.

Richard Gibson's extensive contacts inside the black community—it was the Urban League that first approached CBS on Gibson's behalf— soon brought a wide range of prominent African Americans into the FPCC orbit. Gibson recruited James Baldwin, Langston Hughes, and the playwright Alice Childress for a special issue of the Cuban literary magazine *Lunes de Revolucíon* on black America; he also organized an FPCC delegation to the island that included the activist Robert F. Williams, the poet Leroi Jones, and the essayist Harold Cruse. Enthusiasm for the Cuban cause extended well beyond literary intellectuals; a campaign to promote black tourism featured the Brown Bomber himself. "Where else," asked Joe Louis, "can an American Negro go for a winter vacation?"[5]

By early 1961, the FPCC claimed "Student Councils" on forty college campuses. In the first three months of the year, there were debates on Cuba at Berkeley, Brown, Columbia, Wisconsin, Stanford, Swarthmore, and Yale as well as the universities of Kansas, Minnesota, Pittsburgh, and Washington. C. Wright Mills, the charismatic Columbia professor whose dissection *The Power Elite* was already a campus bible, set off on his own fact-finding trip to Cuba escorted by Robert Taber. *Listen, Yankee*, Mills's impassioned write-up of his revolutionary tourism, sold 400,000 copies in a matter of months. (While Taber and Mills were in Cuba, subscribers to *Fair Play*, the FPCC journal, were sent copies of the *Weekly* instead.)

I. F. Stone's increasing prominence as a campus speaker on the Cuban revolution saw him denounced yet again from the floor of the House of Representatives, this time by Gordon Scherer, the ranking Republican on the Committee on Un-American Activities. When Castro followed up his invitation to American students with an all-inclusive "Christmas in Cuba" package for only $100 (from Miami, or $220 from New York), an "informal goodwill delegation" of 326 students set off for Havana, visiting clinics and agricultural cooperatives, and attending a final party hosted by Castro himself just as the outgoing Eisenhower administration broke off diplomatic relations with the Cuban regime in January 1961. Despite the ensuing travel ban, the level of campus activity around Cuba was high enough to worry Arthur Schlesinger Jr. Now a special assistant to the new president, the Harvard historian told his boss that an attack on Cuba might draw volunteers "in José Martí and probably even Abraham Lincoln Brigades" to defend the revolution.[6]

The incoming administration's hostile intentions toward Fidel Castro's government were one of the worst-kept secrets in Washington. Back in October, when the *New York Times* columnist James Reston lamented that candidate Kennedy's bluster over Cuba could result in "another big splashy debate involving not only Cuba but Guatemala and the activities of the CIA, and a lot of other things that could well be left unsaid," and Walter Lippmann advised that "when a government goes into the political black market it must keep its mouth shut," and the *Washington Post* editorialized that "perhaps it is a mistake to talk about such matters publicly," *I. F. Stone's Weekly* put the question on the front page in thirty-six-point type: "What Do We Do in Cuba if We Win?" Even if the United States could dislodge the Cuban leader, Stone wrote, "what Castro has done for the Cuban peasantry can never be undone, and we will incur the hatred of all Latin America and risk world war if we try it."[7]

The arrival in Washington of McGeorge Bundy, Castro's Cambridge host, as head of the National Security Council did nothing to slow the administration's preparations for an invasion. Citing reports of "men trained in the camps of Miami, Orlando, Homestead, Fort Lauderdale and Fort Myers, Florida" and "swiftly built new air bases in Guatemala," Stone told his readers, "We are moving toward something much more fateful than a minor colonial police operation." Even as he cheered the promise of John Kennedy's dazzling first press conference, he warned, "It is by our attitude toward Cuba, not by promises of new aid, *manana*, that the Latin American masses will judge us. It is in this Lilliputian quarrel that I see the greatest danger."[8]

Izzy had excellent sources. One was David Kraslow, Washington correspondent for the *Miami Herald*. Kraslow, who shared an office with Ed Lahey, turned in an article about the CIA's training of Cuban exiles in a guerrilla camp near Homestead, Florida—a violation of the Neutrality Act. After *Herald* editors were summoned to a meeting with Allen Dulles, director of the CIA, who informed them publication would not be in the national interest, the story was spiked. Karl Meyer had been a student in H. H. Wilson's political science class at Princeton when Wilson invited his fellow ECLC founder to speak. "My father, Ernie Meyer, was a columnist on the [*New York*] *Post* when Izzy was an editorial writer. I introduced myself. Then in '56, when I started as a young reporter for the *Washington Post* . . . one of the first people I looked up in Washington, of course, was Izzy," Meyer recalled. Meyer went down to Cuba in 1958 and interviewed Castro. In early 1961, Gilbert Harrison, editor of the *New Republic*, sent galleys of Meyer's article "Our Men in Miami" to Arthur Schlesinger at the White House, who passed on the president's request that the story be held. It was. But the *Nation* published a report on U.S.-run training camps for Cuban exiles in Guatemala, a story later picked up by the *New York Times*. And the *Times* correspondent Tad Szulc produced a string of scoops that Izzy followed closely.[9]

Fighting had already broken out among the intelligentsia. When Nathaniel Weyl, another *Post* veteran from the 1930s, wrote *Red Star Over Cuba*, an anti-Communist screed describing Castro as a covert Soviet agent and the leader of a "Cult of Uncleanliness," the *Weekly* quoted Szulc's demolition of the book in the *Times* along with a similar catalog of errors in the *Wall Street Journal*. More serious was the news that Melvin Lasky, editor of *Encounter*, was sending Theodore Draper to take a second look. "Castro's Cuba—A Revolution Betrayed" was on newsstands and in faculty mailboxes in February 1961.* But by that time Stone himself had returned to Havana.

"I had expected," he told his readers, "to come back with news and interviews to show how easily and painlessly peace could be achieved between Washington and Havana . . . In the political realm—I might as well make a clean breast of this—I envisaged a declaration of ultimate free elections and ultimate restoration of fundamental political liberties." But the Cubans had confounded his expectations on every front. "There was an attitude toward the Soviet bloc which can only be described as a naive kind of infantile leftism . . . For the first time, in talking with Fidelista intellectuals, I felt that Cuba was on its way to becoming a Soviet-style Popular Democracy.

"The euphoria—and demagogy—appalled me," Stone admitted. While he declined to make excuses for his Cuban hosts, Stone also recognized that the United States bore some responsibility for the "general tightening up of controls" he found so disturbing. "Moderate, mixed-society solutions," he argued, "are only possible where countries are still able to deal with both sides in the East-West struggle . . . By our oil and sugar policies we have made Cuba completely dependent on the Soviet bloc . . . Castro's oil supply, his sugar market and now his industrialization program depend entirely on the good-will of the Soviet bloc."

---

*The appearance of this article, with its deliberate echo of Trotsky's 1937 indictment of Stalinism, offering readers a series of plausible rationales for abandoning Castro on the eve of an American-sponsored coup against him, was a striking example of what the CIA hoped to achieve by its covert sponsorship of "cultural" journals such as *Encounter*.

For Stone, a "wistful liberal pilgrim," to come "face to face in Havana with a full-fledged revolution, in all its creative folly and self-deceptive enthusiasm," was distinctly unsettling. "The Fidelistas," he worried, "are living in a dream world." But the rude awakening he saw on the horizon brought him no pleasure either. He returned to Washington "in that mood of awed and helpless wonder with which one looks on at the unfolding of an heroic tragedy."[10]

Why heroic? Over a long lunch in Havana, Izzy renewed his acquaintance with "Major Ernesto Guevara . . . the least demagogic, and the most sober, though perhaps also the most revolutionary, of all the Cuban leaders." Guevara's trust in Soviet benevolence was, Izzy thought, as misplaced as his admiration for Kim Il Sung. But American strategists who believed they could simply "read Che Guevara's little handbook on guerrilla warfare" and adapt his strategy "to *our* needs" were even worse. In a phrase that could serve as an epitaph for "counter-insurgency" failures from the Bay of Pigs to the Gulf of Tonkin and beyond, Stone asked, "Can you see a U.S. guerrilla knocking on a peasant's door late at night, 'Give me water; hide me; I bring a message from the United Fruit Company; we've come to take back your land'?"[11]

Like a guilty bystander, Stone saw his discomfort with Castro cited in what he acknowledged was a "brilliantly written" government white paper on Cuba in early April 1961 that rehearsed the rationale for U.S. intervention. "Of course the document is careful not to quote my repeated warnings against intervention in Cuba," he complained. The white paper, polished by Arthur Schlesinger Jr., was no more than "a smoother sales talk for the interventionist plans begun under Eisenhower and stepped up, I regret to say, under Kennedy."*[12] Though helpless to stop the drift toward attack, the *Weekly* did report on both the scope and personnel of the planned attack, telling readers that Cuban-exile commandos had been told by their American trainers "that 'if the invading forces were bogged down' the Cubans would be 'on their own.' From what

---

*Stone may well have been aware of Schlesinger's hand in the white paper, but he was almost certainly not aware that only a few weeks earlier, the nimble professor, in a top secret memorandum to the president, had advised *against* intervention: "At one stroke, it would dissipate all the extraordinary good will which has been rising toward the new Administration through the world. It would fix a malevolent image of the new Administration in the minds of millions." (Arthur Schlesinger Jr. to the president, February 11, 1961.)

little I can learn the administration also made the decision against permitting a large-scale invasion in favor of small landing parties of exiles." Izzy even named Frank Bender, deputy director of plans, as "CIA agent in charge" of the operation. This was no feat of investigative reporting. "It seemed foolish," Stone noted, "to telegraph the news of an invasion in advance. But this was not so foolish if the purpose was political, to force the administration's hand."[13]

When approximately 1,200 Cuban exiles landed at the Playa Girón— the Bay of Pigs—on the southern coast of Cuba on the morning of April 17, their hope was indeed to foment a counterrevolution and overthrow the Castro government. But the invaders found themselves pinned down on the beach, and when the U.S. government decided to cut its losses and declined to send air support, they were easily defeated by the Cuban army. By April 20, most had been captured or killed. And though it went to press nearly a week before the landings, the *Weekly* was still a better guide to what happened at the Bay of Pigs than the Associated Press, whose lead story for April 17 proclaimed: "Anti-Castro forces struck their long-awaited invasion blow for the liberation of Cuba Monday and claimed immediate successes . . . Amid a fever of rebel reports and rumors, anti-Castro spokesmen claimed thousands of Castro's militiamen had deserted him at the first shot and that the first thrust of the invaders carried to the area of Colon, astride central Cuba's main east-west highway."[14]

Stone seemed pleasantly surprised by the debacle. Painful as it was to watch Adlai Stevenson, Kennedy's ambassador to the UN, "defend the indefensible and deny the undeniable" while the outcome was still in doubt, for Stone the rebel defeat "turned high tragedy into low comedy." The "Kennedy honeymoon" was over. Rounding on Max Lerner and other liberals who "lined up so quickly—and so prematurely—with the war crowd," Stone remarked, "The deed *was* done quickly, but it's Macbeth who's dead." He saw little cause for lamentation.[15]

•

For Stone the most surprising—and encouraging—thing about the Bay of Pigs was the aftermath. The CIA may have done a better job of covering its tracks in Guatemala and Iran, but the Kennedy administration's re-

fusal to countenance governments that put American rhetoric on land reform and social revolution into practice was nothing new. The *Weekly*, in
company with the usual left-wing suspects, duly decried each intervention, but there had been little domestic fallout. Cuba was different.

In New York, a series of protests began on the day of the invasion with
2,000 demonstrators outside the United Nations and culminated in a
rally of 5,000 people at Union Square—the largest demonstration in the
United States since the execution of the Rosenbergs. Norman Mailer
publicly scolded the president he'd recently anointed as "Superman
Comes to the Supermarket":

> Dear Jack:
> I may have made the error of sailing against the stereotype that
> you were a calculating untried over-ambitious and probably un-
> deserving young stud who came from a very wealthy and much
> unloved family. I took a hard skimming tack against the wind of
> that probability and ventured instead into the notion that you gave
> promise of becoming the first major American hero in more than a
> decade . . . Wasn't there anyone around to give you the lecture on
> Cuba? Don't you sense the enormity of your mistake—you invade
> a country without understanding its music?[16]

In San Francisco, more than a thousand protesters picketed the Federal
Building and then marched en masse to the offices of Hearst's anti-Castro
Examiner, where a message from C. Wright Mills was read out: "Kennedy
and Co. have returned to barbarism. Schlesinger and Co. have disgraced us
intellectually and morally. I feel a desperate shame for my country." At Cor-
nell, 400 students protested on the steps of Willard Straight Hall, while at
Madison, 1,000 attended a rally sponsored by the campus Socialist Club.
At Harvard, where they seemed to take the administration's fall from grace
personally, a protest meeting of more than 300 students and teachers heard
H. Stuart Hughes, a professor of European history and the grandson of
Chief Justice Charles Evans Hughes, call on Schlesinger to resign. Professor William Yandell Elliot, on loan to the Kennedy administration from the
government department, was so affronted by the Harvard protest, which he
described to the *New York Times* as "one of 134 similar meetings all over the
United States," that he demanded, "If that isn't organized protest, what

is?"—which somehow implied that the whole wave of campus demonstrations must have been conjured up by Communists.[17]

Yet it was Walter Lippmann who said, "I don't think a democracy . . . should have secret training camps and secret armies and secret navies in foreign countries, all in violation of its own treaties and its own laws." Murray Kempton, after pronouncing his personal sympathy for the anti-Castro Cubans—"under ordinary circumstances, being no Fidelista, I should wish them well"—and reassuring his readers, "I do not propose to go to jail over this matter," remained sufficiently repelled by "this dirty business" to conclude "there is no excuse for Allen Dulles and John F. Kennedy. If you think there is, you are, believe me, wrong." Americans for Democratic Action nearly split over a motion proposed by James Wechsler to denounce the invasion.[18]

Even more striking was the response from the academy. That Mills and Hughes would join Kempton, Stone, and Norman Thomas in signing a protest letter in the *New York Times* organized by the Fellowship of Reconciliation was perhaps to be expected. An "Open Letter to the President" opposing "any further intervention in Cuba, direct or indirect," drafted by Thomas and signed by Stone and a long list of intellectuals including James Baldwin, A. J. Muste, Norman Podhoretz, Philip Rahv, David Riesman, and Edmund Wilson, could have been merely an indication of widespread respect for the Socialist leader.* (*Dissent* mailed out a special supplement written by the political philosopher Michael Walzer deploring the "criminal stupidity" of the operation. Walzer did not question the right of the United States to overthrow Castro, however, arguing instead that any future efforts would succeed only if they "take on a 'progressive' form.") But the same elite universities that had compromised with McCarthy and furnished both the CIA and the Kennedy administration with its best and brightest recruits suddenly emerged from a decade of silence. Some 70 members of the Harvard faculty signed a statement condemning the invasion. At Princeton—alma mater of the Dulles brothers—the total was only 38, but a letter drafted by Carl Schorske aimed

---

*John Roche, a Brandeis professor and leader of the opposition to Wechsler's motion in the ADA, resigned from the Socialists over the Thomas letter. Max Shachtman, whose Social Democratic Federation had just merged with the Socialists, stunned a Berkeley crowd protesting the Bay of Pigs by declaring his support for the invaders.

specifically at his fellow historians drew the signatures of 181 professors in 41 departments.[19]

Izzy knew not to read too much into these signs. Writing to Mike Blankfort he admitted "feeling about as depressed as I suppose I ever get." That March a five-to-four ruling by the Supreme Court sent Carl Braden and Frank Wilkinson to prison even though Braden had denied under oath membership in the Communist Party. "I was in Washington seeing a great deal of Izzy," said Wilkinson, "and he asked if I realized the decision was about to come down. I wrote a winning and a losing statement. Izzy said he wanted to read both. I met him in the cafeteria of the Supreme Court. He had a friend with him—Anthony Lewis [Supreme Court reporter for the *New York Times*]. They said both my statements were corny, so after the decision Izzy handed out a press release—which he'd drafted."[20]

Then in May, the Court, again divided five-to-four between "the strict constructionists—the liberals" and those, like Felix Frankfurter, who felt basic constitutional rights need to be "balanced . . . in favor of the state," held the Illinois bar was entitled not to admit a lawyer* if he refused to answer "the $64 question." In June, another five-to-four decision to send Junius Scales, a Communist who had quit the party after the events in Hungary in 1956, to jail for six years merely for having been a party member prompted Stone to turn on an old patron. In his first inaugural address, Thomas Jefferson had urged that Americans opposed to the "Republican form of government" be left "undisturbed, as monuments" to faith in reason. "Mr. Justice Frankfurter and his four colleagues," Stone fumed, "no longer have that faith." Stone's own appetite for the fight was undiminished. "Most of the time I'm a small boy reporter having a helluva lot of fun covering such a wonderful bunch of 10-alarm fires," he assured Blankfort. "But every once in a while the reality breaks through . . . above all the feeling that so few people cared."[21]

For all the protests, he feared "official Washington has learned nothing, on the contrary it has drawn all the wrong conclusions, from the failure in Cuba." The first was President Kennedy's appeal to the American

---

*George Anastaplo, described by the *Weekly* as "a brilliant young man," never belonged to any political party. Despite finishing first in a University of Chicago Law School class that included a future attorney general of the United States, a federal judge, and two U.S. congressmen, Anastaplo's principled stand meant that he remained unable to practice his profession for the rest of his life. Instead, he became a prolific writer on the law, an inspiring teacher, and a distinguished legal scholar.

Newspaper Publishers Association that "every newspaper now ask itself, with respect to every story . . . 'Is it in the interest of the national security?'" In other words, wrote Stone, "when the government lies, the press should fib." Citing CIA efforts to plant reports about defecting Cuban pilots bombing their own airfields, Stone pointed out that "it was not the enemy, it was our own people, this story was intended to deceive. Was it in the national interest to let the government deceive the American people?" he asked. "Down this road lies the garrison state."[22]

A resolution in the House labeling the Cuban regime "a clear and present danger" passed in May by a vote of 401–2; a similar motion in the Senate was opposed only by William Fulbright and Wayne Morse. Such congressional posturing was far less troubling than the evidence that Kennedy's Cuban misadventure had done nothing to diminish his enthusiasm for covert operations. Citing President Charles de Gaulle's difficulties with the French army in Algeria, Stone warned, "The lesson de Gaulle understood but Kennedy hasn't yet grasped is that when military men read Mao (and Che Guevara) and seek to turn their tactics to counter-revolutionary purposes . . . sooner or later they will be tempted to use at home, against their own people and government, the psychological warfare, the brain-washings, the cloak-and-dagger methods and the 'dirty tricks' they are allowed to utilize in colonial areas." His concern about "the dazzling latest military toothpaste for social decay" led Izzy to track down not only "an anonymous report on 'Special Warfare' . . . leaked to the *Army Navy Air Force Journal*" but also one of the officers cited most frequently as an expert in the field, Slavko N. Bjelajac. "When I reached Mr. Bjelajac by phone at the Pentagon, he admitted he had served with the Yugoslav Partisan forces under Mihailovitch," Stone learned. Bjelajac's experience fighting against Tito doubtless recommended him to the Pentagon, where his doctrine that "the battle must be waged for the minds and hearts of peoples" was echoed by the other special warfare expert named by the *Weekly*, "Brig. Gen. E. G. Lansdale, reputed to be the 'Quiet American'* of Graham Greene's novel."[23]

Characteristically, Stone was interested in the intellectual as well as

---

*Published in 1955, *The Quiet American* details an American intelligence agent's vain and ultimately murderous quest to nurture a "third force," neither Communist nor colonialist, in Vietnam.

combat background of these covert warriors, extending his reading from U.S. army manuals to "the chief theoreticians on our side" such as Roger Trinquier, a French veteran of Indochina and Algeria, whose book *Modern Warfare: A French View of Counterinsurgency*, recommending the use of torture, forced relocation of civilians, and "psy-ops"—psychological warfare tactics—had a considerable following at the Pentagon.

Stone's own sense of counterinsurgency, and also of the ongoing conflict in Indochina, owed much to Bernard Fall. The son of Austrian Jews murdered by the Nazis, Fall was only sixteen when he joined the French resistance. After the liberation of Paris in August 1944, Fall became an officer in the French army, and as a graduate student at Syracuse University in the 1950s had done fieldwork in Indochina, where his military background gave him unique access to French forces. He predicted their defeat in an influential March 1954 article for the *Nation*. In September 1959, Izzy invited Fall, then teaching at Howard, to lunch at the Hay Adams—the beginning of an important friendship for both men.[24] And of course Stone had lived in France while the French were losing their war; he'd heard optimistic generals before.

In May 1961, Izzy complained that no one noticed that the Pentagon's French experts

> not only failed to win by these methods in Algeria but have had to be scattered and suppressed by the French government because they began turning their "dirty tricks" against the French Republic. Nor does anyone stop to consider that these tactics and the men who would be in charge of them have just had an easy opportunity in nearby Cuba, and failed dismally. The same Joint Chiefs of Staff which lacked the competence to stage an invasion of Cuba, and the same intelligence agents who could not correctly evaluate the Cuban people—can they be expected to do better, let us say, in faraway North Vietnam?[25]

That same month Vice President Lyndon Johnson, visiting Saigon, described South Vietnam's President Ngo Dinh Diem as "the Winston Churchill of Asia." May 1961 was also when the United States sent 400 Green Berets as "special advisers" to train Diem's army in the new techniques of counterinsurgency.

•

Despite such portents, Izzy's depression didn't last. His advice was still ignored at the highest levels, but he was becoming less isolated. He and Esther now had a social circle wide enough that they could hold regular dinner parties where stalwarts like James Newman or the Dudmans would meet more recent acquaintances like Karl Meyer or Bernard and Dorothy Fall. Meyer often brought his friend Neville Maxwell, correspondent for the London *Times*. "I met my best friend, Amos Elon, the Israeli journalist, who had just arrived as a correspondent for *Ha'aretz*, at Izzy's table," Meyer recalled. Lawrence Stern, a young reporter for the *Washington Post*, was another regular, as was the labor journalist Sanford Gottlieb, who had been introduced to the Stones by Stanley Karnow in Paris. An admirer of Izzy's reporting on nuclear testing, Gottlieb was among those who responded to the first newspaper advertisement for SANE and soon became the organization's executive director.[26]

Gottlieb had grown up reading *PM*, but most of their new friends knew only the I. F. Stone of the *Weekly*. The Popular Front, the New Deal, even the Progressive Party were ancient history. Instead, they revered Stone for his candor, for his outspokenness, and above all for his fearless exposure of official lying. "You have to remember," said Gottlieb, "these were the days when radiation measurements were given in 'sunshine units.' Izzy's reporting on [the dangers of nuclear] fallout was critically important. He was the only one pointing out the lies coming from the Atomic Energy Commission."[27]

Two of the youngest voices around the Stone table belonged to a pair of congressional aides. Arthur Waskow and Marcus Raskin both worked for Robert Kastenmeier, a Wisconsin Democrat whose district included the university at Madison. Along with James Roosevelt, Kastenmeier, who was first elected in 1959, was a prime mover in a group known as the Liberal Project, a loose grouping of ten or twelve congressmen who hoped to break the Bourbon-Republican political stranglehold, enabling the country to move on civil rights as well as nuclear disarmament. The group became even looser after 1960, when half their number failed to win re-election, but by then Waskow and Raskin had put together a collection of essays, *The Liberal Papers*, including one of their own on "The Theory and Practice of Deterrence."[28]

"We decided to find out what these guys mean when they say 'deterrence,'" said Waskow. "What would it really take to do a general disarmament, and could any of this be achieved in stages?" Stone had long been interested in the same questions. He also had a more personal reason to be gratified at the direction of Waskow and Raskin's argument. His older son, Jeremy, a Stanford PhD in mathematics, had spent the previous two summers working for the RAND Corporation, an air force think tank. (Once again government agents sifted through Izzy and Esther's mail, this time at the behest of the Air Force Office of Special Investigations. In May 1959, Jeremy Stone's security clearance was withdrawn and he was interviewed about his relationship with Izzy. Eventually he was able to back up his assertion of loyalty to both father and country by pointing out the State Department's citation of the *Weekly* in the Cuban white paper.) In the summer of 1961, just after I. F. Stone termed the Pentagon's new civil defense program "a lunatic nightmare" designed to "make it possible to skirt closer to the brink" on issues like the division of Berlin, Jeremy announced his intention to take a job with the program's architect and chief publicist, Herman Kahn.[29]

"Now, my father knew who Herman was," said Jeremy, "and had written some very critical things about him, and Jim Newman had described him as a monster. But Kahn said he wanted all kinds at the Hudson Institute," the organization Kahn had made synonymous with his ideas about winnable nuclear war and other variations on "thinking the unthinkable," as the title of his 1962 book put it. "So I told my father . . . and he just said, 'You have to decide for yourself.' He may have been somewhat miffed, but he never gave me a hard time about it."[30]

Maybe not. But I. F. Stone didn't exactly let up on "Kahn and Kissinger and the other Pied Pipers of limited thermonuclear war." And in this fight, his young friends Raskin and Waskow were of crucial assistance. Just before he flew to Cuba, Izzy shared a platform with Raskin at a meeting of Washington SANE. He also gave a warm endorsement in the *Weekly* to "the brilliant little book of Arthur Waskow's, *The Limits of Defense*," a demolition of the "counter-force" doctrine in which each side targets its opponent's military forces rather than its cities. Tracing the notion to a Rockefeller Brothers Fund study whose author, the Harvard professor Henry Kissinger, had just become a consultant to the White House, Stone angrily derided "the idea of limited nuclear war" as "a delusion tailor-made for the needs of far-flung business enterprise: How to Push the Russians out of the Middle East Without Setting Fire to Standard Oil's Wells." Such wars, he sneered, presumably "would be won on points, like a tennis match." The *Weekly* headline for this tirade? "A Triumph of Herman Kahnism."[31]

Stone knew that progress on disarmament was impossible without the mobilization of a domestic constituency to balance the constant pressure on Kennedy and the administration from the military, defense contractors, and those whom David Riesman, a contributor to *The Liberal Papers*, dubbed "bomber liberals." The other side was both well organized and well funded. More than 30 million copies of the Pentagon's pamphlet *Fallout Protection: What to Know and Do About Nuclear Attack*, advocating home fallout shelters, were sent through the mails. In September 1961, *Life* magazine proclaimed, "How You Can Survive Fallout: 97 Out of 100 People Can Be Saved."[32] Yet even after the Bay of Pigs, there was considerable, if anecdotal, evidence that President Kennedy saw himself as a captive of, rather than a convert to, the cold war consensus. Certainly there were those at a high level in his administration who not only thought the United States needed to change course on a whole range of issues, from China to nuclear strategy, but also believed the president himself was open to argument, and were themselves prepared to argue for such change.

One of them was Marcus Raskin. A concert pianist who had once taught the composer Philip Glass, Raskin had abandoned music for public policy. It was Raskin, a graduate of the University of Chicago Law School, who had commissioned David Riesman, author of *The Lonely Crowd* and a former sociology professor at the University of Chicago, to write the keynote essay for *The Liberal Papers*. Riesman had been lured to Harvard by McGeorge Bundy; when Bundy took over at the NSC, Riesman immediately pressed him to hire the twenty-six-year-old Raskin.

At the interview, Bundy asked, "Well, Mr. Raskin, do you have a liberal theory of deterrence?" Raskin handed him "The Theory and Practice of Deterrence." Waskow and Raskin's ideas must have been in tune with Bundy's own analysis; he soon wrote to Riesman praising his protégé's "remarkably powerful and lively mind . . . flanked by both moral and physical energy." With any luck, wrote Bundy, "he should be at work here in another few days."[33] There was just one hitch—Raskin's security clearance. "Before the final clearance was given, Mac Bundy called me into his office and said there are several things that have been flagged by the FBI. It seemed the main problem was my friendship with I. F. Stone. I'd spoken on the same platform with Izzy at a SANE meeting. Bundy said, 'Well, you know he's a Communist.'" "I don't know that," Raskin replied. Bundy, who visibly blushed at Raskin's vehemence, dropped the subject.[34] Raskin eventually got the job, but the delay in his security clearance meant he didn't begin work until April 17, when the papers were full of the Bay of Pigs disaster.

Bundy ran the NSC as he'd run the Harvard faculty, with wide-ranging intellectual debate. Yet when Raskin, at his first staff meeting, which included a postmortem on the Bay of Pigs, responded to Bundy's remark that "Che learned more from Guatemala than we did," by asking, "And what have we learned?" he was told afterward, "Mac would prefer you not to come to meetings."[35] On disarmament, though, Bundy and the Kennedy administration still seemed open to persuasion.

So in February 1962, a group of students decided to show the White House there really was a constituency for peace. Tocsin, a Harvard-Radcliffe group, managed to get 4,000 students to turn out to picket the White House despite a heavy snowstorm. The Turn Toward Peace protesters were, the *Weekly* reported, "no longer the beatniks of the 50s nor the party-liners of the 40s. Both a new courage and a new maturity were visible." *Time* was equally respectful: "With demonstrations and proclamations—and also with moderate voices and measured argument—students across the nation are astir with a new enthusiasm, and in the process the anemic boredom voguish in the '50s has disappeared."[36] Marc Raskin, watching the proceedings from the Old Executive Office Building next to the White House, had a suggestion: "Why not send out some coffee?" The arrival of a liveried White House butler bearing a huge urn of hot coffee with the president's compliments was as much a public relations coup as the invitation for a delegation of students to meet with Bundy; Jerome Wiesner, the president's science adviser; Kennedy's speechwriter Theodore Sorensen; and Raskin. Todd Gitlin, a Harvard junior and Tocsin organizer who considered Raskin an ally, later described the meetings as "a dialogue of the moral with the deaf." At the time, though, it must have felt like the peace movement had finally come in from the cold.[37]

Raskin scarcely saw Stone during the period he worked at the White House, and in the spring of 1962 the two men flew, separately, to Geneva, where again they did not meet. Izzy went because there was an eighteen-nation conference on disarmament and he didn't want to wait for weeks to read the verbatim transcript. He also didn't trust the daily briefings: "The government information officer, to put it plainly, is a *mis*information officer; his job is not to inform the press, but to put across the particular version or distortion previously decided upon by the government for which he works . . . The Russians are past masters at this business."

Stone had been in Geneva the previous September, on "the dreadful morning the kiosks carried the news the Russians were resuming nuclear tests." He had condemned that decision as poisoning "not only the atmosphere of mankind, but its mind and soul, and its hopes." The American plan to follow the Russians ended a three-year moratorium on both sides and gave him "a sense of despair . . . The country accepts it with only scattered protest; even organizations like the National Committee for a Sane Nuclear Policy are numb and dumb." Yet he returned to the Palais des Nations, "a rest home for idealists," with a sense that some kind of treaty was not only possible but inevitable. For all the issues dividing the United States and the Soviet Union, "if a man doesn't want to marry a girl, he had best not enter into theoretical discussions with her father, mother and brothers on when, where and how they would be wed if he finally made up his mind to wed her."[38]

Raskin was also optimistic. Based on his "analysis and discussions with [Leo] Szilard, Jerome Wiesner, and [Igor] Usachev, who was the Soviet expert in Geneva at the time," Raskin stubbornly believed an international agreement on a test-ban treaty was possible, and he had gone to Geneva to push things along. Writing to the president in late April, Bundy told him, "That young menace, Marcus Raskin, has returned from Geneva," where he had "been a good staff officer in spite of—and perhaps partly because of—his insistent efforts to find ways of making progress in this most unpromising field."[39]

Raskin and Stone both independently noticed the delegation of "50 American women on a Quixotic mission, somehow to reach the hearts and minds of the diplomats here for the great Powers," as Stone put it. The women, who had flown to Geneva without a single appointment, brought with them a petition bearing 50,000 signatures demanding an immediate test ban and urging that the conference remain in session until real progress on disarmament had been made. After staging an illegal procession to the Palais des Nations, the group, whose ranks included Coretta Scott King and Anne Eaton, wife of the Cleveland industrialist and Pugwash benefactor Cyrus Eaton, was received in turn by the U.S. and Soviet negotiators, both of whom promptly came in for a scolding: "You are constantly concerned with national security, national sovereignty, national prestige. All these outmoded ideas must be abandoned," Dagmar Wilson, the delegation's leader, told the diplomats. "We are not interested in techniques of inspection of nuclear tests and the arms race . . . In your hands lies the fate of the human race. We have one great concern—our children."[40]

The name of Wilson's organization was Women Strike for Peace, and though he never knew it, I. F. Stone was practically the group's godfather.

•

Dagmar Wilson was a member of the Washington, D.C., chapter of SANE. (The chair of the chapter was Gerhard Van Arkel, Izzy's Haddonfield classmate.) A successful illustrator of children's books including *While Susie Sleeps* and *Casey the Utterly Impossible Horse*, Wilson was also a subscriber to *I. F. Stone's Weekly*. Driving back from summer vacation with her husband and children, she heard a radio news report on the confrontation between the two nuclear powers over Berlin. When the family arrived home in Georgetown, she found the September 11–18, 1961, issue of the *Weekly* on top of the pile of mail. Above the masthead, and taking up half the front cover, was a dramatic appeal from Bertrand Russell:

> The populations of East and West, misled by stubborn governments in search of prestige and corrupt official experts bent on retaining their posts, tamely acquiesce in policies which are almost certain to end in nuclear war . . . Kennedy and Khrushchev, Adenauer and de Gaulle, Macmillan and Gaitskell, are pursuing a common aim, the ending of human life. You, your families, your friends and your countries are to be exterminated, by the common decision of a few brutal but powerful men. To please these men, all the private affections, all the public hopes, all that has been achieved in art and knowledge and thought and all that might be achieved hereafter is to be wiped out for ever.

Izzy and Esther had stayed with Russell and Edith Finch, Russell's American fourth wife, at their house in London on the way back from an earlier trip to Geneva. Three days after the Stones returned to Washington, the eighty-nine-year-old peer began a seven-day jail sentence for refusing to call off his campaign of nonviolent civil disobedience. For Wilson, American-born but British-educated, Russell's imprisonment was an outrage. When she asked SANE how it planned to respond, she learned that no protest was planned. Wilson was stunned. Three days later, she and four other women gathered in her living room. "Perhaps, we told ourselves that night . . . it was time for women to speak out."

Leafing through their address books, Christmas card lists, and contacts in PTAs, church and synagogue groups, women's clubs, and old-line peace organizations, the five women spread the word from coast to coast. "We strike against death, desolation, destruction and on behalf of life and liberty," said their call to action. "Husbands or babysitters take over the home front. Bosses or substitutes take over our jobs!" For a group of housewives to presume to speak on questions of nuclear strategy was unprecedented. Just as remarkable, however, was what the early communiqués of Women Strike for Peace didn't say. There were no leaders or officers, no organizational structure. And though the group announced plans to present petitions to both Jacqueline Kennedy and Nina Khrushchev, WSP was open to any woman who supported its aims. Only two years earlier, Norman Cousins had fired a New York SANE organizer who took the Fifth Amendment before the Senate Internal Security Committee; after bitter debate SANE's board issued guidelines barring current or former Communists from membership. A. J. Muste resigned in protest. Linus Pauling and Bertrand Russell withdrew their sponsorship. Wilson and her friends, along with most of the Washington chapter, regarded the purge as a capitulation to the cold war, and they were determined that WSP would be different. There would be no political litmus tests, no formal requirements for membership, indeed no membership lists at all. Every chapter would have autonomy.[41]

"As a husband," Stone commented in the *Weekly*, "we are alarmed at this move toward the unionization of women but we hasten to approve." On November 1, 1961, some 50,000 women walked out of their kitchens or off their jobs. In dozens of local actions across the country, women pushed baby carriages, carried placards, marched, and rallied. In Los Angeles, 4,000 women assembled on the steps of the State Building; in Washington, 700 women, several children, and one dog picketed the White House. In New York, twin marches targeted both the Soviet embassy and the Atomic Energy Commission. Ten weeks later, when 3,000 WSP women filled both sides of Pennsylvania Avenue in front of the White House, I. F. Stone was there, too, wishing "every reader could have seen the demonstration . . . The good humor, the brightly painted signs smeared by the rain, the multi-colored balloons they carried made a vivid and inspiring sight."

"I recognized why they were here," President Kennedy told a news conference Stone attended that afternoon. "There were a great number of them, it was in the rain. I understand what they were attempting to say, therefore, I consider their message was received."[42]

Meanwhile, other currents were stirring. Later that spring, roughly between the WSP and Tocsin demonstrations in Washington, a graduate student named Richard Flacks attended a speech at the University of Michigan Union in Ann Arbor. The ostensible topic was in loco parentis—the rules colleges and universities use to regulate student behavior. But the speaker, Tom Hayden, a twenty-two-year-old student journalist, soon revealed he had more pressing matters on his mind than paternalism. Hayden, like Flacks, was an ardent admirer of C. Wright Mills. Reporting for the *Michigan Daily* on the Student Nonviolent Coordinating Committee (Sandra Cason, Hayden's wife, was a SNCC activist) and its voter registration campaign in Fayette County, Tennessee, Hayden had felt both inspired and existentially challenged. SNCC's black activists literally risked their lives for their beliefs; few white students had shown similar moral courage. "There is no willingness to take risks, no setting of dangerous goals, no real conception of personal identity except one made in the image of others," said Hayden. Instead of accepting their lot as passive fodder for the status quo, Hayden urged his audience to take democracy, citizenship, their universities, and themselves seriously. "We must have a try at bringing society under human control."[43]

Flacks went home buzzing with excitement. As the son of blacklisted Communist schoolteachers, he had an instinctive diffidence toward political organizations. Flacks didn't want his own political baggage—which, after Khrushchev's revelations and the Soviet invasion of Hungary, he had in any case abandoned in disgust—to be either held against him or used to damage groups he did support. His wife, Mickey, another "red-diaper baby" who also had rejected communism but remained on the left, had just joined WSP. Flacks subscribed to *I. F. Stone's Weekly* and was an avid reader of *Studies on the Left*, the journal produced by the circle around the historian William Appleman Williams at the University of Wisconsin.[44] Another important source was the British *New Left Review*, one of whose founders, Ralph Miliband, a professor at the London School of Economics, was a close friend of C. Wright Mills. It was in the pages of *NLR* that Mills's "Letter to the New Left," with its suggestion that intellectuals and students might be "real live agents of historic change," first appeared. "We are beginning to move again," promised Mills, whose premature death within a few days of Hayden's speech seemed like a cruel blow.[45] For years Flacks had kept his head down. But when he learned that Hayden had been asked to draft a manifesto for a new group, Students for a Democratic Society (SDS), to be debated that June at a United Auto Workers camp at Port Huron, Michigan, he decided to go along.

"We are people of this generation, bred in at least modest comfort, housed now in universities, looking uncomfortably at the world we inherit." Hayden's ringing opening cadences to the Port Huron Statement quickly entered the national mythology. But other aspects of the SDS founding document, less remarked on, are no less worthy of attention. One is the section on "Communism and Foreign Policy." Hayden's original draft outraged Michael Harrington, an organizer for the League for Industrial Democracy, SDS's parent organization. A veteran of Dorothy Day's Catholic Worker movement and rising man in the Socialist Party, Harrington's *The Other America*, the book on poverty that would make him famous, had just been published. For Harrington, who had entered the Socialists via Shachtman's Independent Socialist League (and who had considerable influence over SDS's funding), anticommunism was an article of faith, and Hayden, his friend and drinking companion, was risking heresy. Ironically, it was Flacks, the former young Communist, who drafted the language designed to mollify Harrington: "As democrats we are in opposition to the communist system. The Soviet Union, as a system, rests on the total suppression of organized opposition as well as a vision of the future in the name of which much human life has been sacrificed." Yet because SDS, like WSP, refused to compromise its commitment to a nonsectarian politics, Harrington remained implacably hostile.[46]

Another surprising influence was *The Liberal Papers*, and not just for the claim made by Riesman and his coeditor, Michael Maccoby (who had been Bundy's assistant at Harvard), that "as higher education expands and as blue-collar work gives way to white-collar work, the often denigrated bourgeois idealist, the pilot-fish of the Marxist theory of revolution, becomes a member of a class quite as large in number as the factory workers."[47] To SDS, Raskin and Waskow's Liberal Project, though "neither disciplined nor very influential," represented a key test of New Frontier good faith. Yet even as the SDSers gathered, controversy over Raskin's involvement in *The Liberal Papers* forced him out of his job at the NSC and, by the end of the summer, out of the administration altogether. Tom Hayden thought this was a "shameful end" to what had been "a hopeful beginning." Port Huron's condescending skepticism about the Kennedy administration was complete; its "feeble but desirable efforts . . . to be more flexible are coming perhaps too late, and are of too little significance to really change the historical thrust of our policies."[48]

The students' assumption that the administration was unable to change course at home or abroad was shared by Stone—and sharpened by what he viewed as Kennedy's persistent cowardice on civil rights. "When is the president going to mention racism?" demanded the *Weekly* after a white mob attacked not only James Meredith but three federal marshals whom JFK sent to escort him into the University of Mississippi to register on September 30, 1962. Slating Kennedy's "stale cold war rhetoric," Izzy argued, "Devotion to freedom should begin at home. If we can't have it in Mississippi, we won't win it defending dictators in Vietnam."[49]

In the fall of 1962, a book was published that seemed to embody the fears of a generation brought up to duck and cover. *Fail-Safe* is a novel about how the United States and the Soviet Union accidentally start a "limited" nuclear war. Though neither Eugene Burdick nor his coauthor, Harvey Wheeler (editor of that 1953 pamphlet *Lattimore, the Scholar*), was a nuclear strategist, Professor Groteschele, their combined caricature of Herman Kahn and Henry Kissinger, was easily recognizable. The novel's depiction of the Strategic Air Command's fail-safe system, whose breakdown triggers a nuclear exchange, was plausible enough to prompt an official Pentagon statement that such an accident was "virtually impossible," published in the *New York Times*.[50] Unfortunately for the nation's nerves, the very next day, October 22, 1962, in a televised address from the White House, President Kennedy announced the presence of Soviet nuclear missiles on Cuba. Kennedy also informed the country that he had imposed a naval "quarantine" around the island until the Soviet Union agreed to remove the missiles.

The president's speech was on a Monday. Richard and Mickey Flacks and Tom and Casey Hayden were in Ann Arbor, where attempts to protest the blockade—an act of war—were met with jeers, eggs, and stones. Todd Gitlin was in the basement of Quincy House at Harvard, where Tocsin debated whether opposing Kennedy meant defending Cuba. By Saturday, with the whole world still on tenterhooks, all of them were at the First Congregational Church in Washington along with Marc Raskin, Richard Barnet, and most of the Washington chapter of Women Strike for Peace. They had gathered to protest the end of the world—and to listen to I. F. Stone. "Six thousand years of human history is about to come to an end," he told them. "Do not expect to be alive tomorrow." Mickey Flacks believed him. So did Tom Hayden. So did most of the people in the church.[51]

It was a long time before the full story emerged of Attorney General Robert Kennedy's secret negotiations with Soviet Ambassador Anatoly Dobrynin that Saturday, in which Kennedy promised to remove American missiles from Turkey if the Russians agreed the deal would remain secret. And it was not until 1989 that McGeorge Bundy learned that he and Secretary of Defense Robert McNamara, who assumed in October 1962 that the Russians had not yet shipped their warheads and pressed Kennedy to launch an air strike before the missile bases became operational, were mistaken: There were already 36 medium-range and 158 tactical nuclear warheads on Cuba.[52] Late in the night of October 27, when the Soviet ships turned around and it was announced that Khrushchev had agreed to withdraw the missiles in return for an American promise not to invade Cuba, Izzy went home never knowing how close his apocalyptic remarks had come to the truth.

•

The subpoenas arrived at the beginning of December, summoning Dagmar Wilson and thirteen women from New York to testify before the House Committee on Un-American Activities. Three of the recipients weren't even WSP activists, belonging instead to a New York peace group formed by those who had resigned from or been expelled by SANE. One was Elizabeth Moos, who had already been named as a card-carrying Communist at the trial of her former son-in-law, William Remington.[53] That had been a decade earlier, but a HUAC subpoena was still a serious matter. A RAND Corporation study published that same December warned that after the Cuban missile crisis the peace movement was a "growing cause," singling out WSP for particular concern. "There is nothing spontaneous about the way the pro-Reds have moved in on our mothers," charged the Hearst columnist Jack Lotto. Midge Decter, writing in *Harper's*, smeared the group as "anti-U.S." dupes or worse.

When the hearings on Communist Infiltration into the Peace Movement opened on December 11, 1962, it soon became apparent that HUAC's members were about to get a lot more than they had bargained for. Chairman Francis Walter received more than a hundred cables from WSP women around the country *volunteering* to testify before his committee. The cables were in response to a suggestion in *Memo*, the group's newsletter, that WSP "Turn the Tables!" on HUAC.[54] Barbara Bick, the editor of *Memo*, had been a friend of I. F. Stone since he'd gotten her thrown out of college fifteen years earlier.* "I think he and Esther felt a little guilty—without any reason. They were always warm and protective of me," Bick said.

Bick had worked for the *People's World*, the CP's West Coast paper, but she and her husband left the party before they came back east. "We never became anti-Communists. We just didn't want to be part of that anymore." Bick didn't receive a subpoena, but it wouldn't have mattered if she had. WSP would not "make the error of initiating its own purges." As long as they agreed to oppose Soviet as well as U.S. tests, all the women subpoenaed would be supported.

As Bick points out, Dagmar Wilson "was (1) never a Communist, (2) not Jewish, (3) lived in Georgetown, and (4) spoke with a British accent."[55] Perhaps for that reason, when the hearings opened in the caucus room of the Old House Office Building, the subcommittee chairman, Clyde Doyle, reminding his colleagues that all "initiated" Communists

---

*In 1947, Bick was a student at Antioch College on a co-op job at the Office of the Alien Property Custodian. Her boss discovered that the office was about to return seized I. G. Farben assets to the firm's German managers and leaked the story to Stone at *PM*, but when a family emergency kept her from the appointment, she asked Bick to deliver the relevant documents. After conferring with her parents, Bick agreed, and with the story on the front page she and her colleagues were soon questioned by the FBI. Convinced by her mother to deny everything, Bick "made it through the interrogation" and returned to Antioch where, summoned by the administration, she told the whole story—and was promptly suspended.

know "the 'fight for peace' means . . . to destroy capitalism and its major
bastion, the United States of America," called Blanche Posner instead. A
former teacher at DeWitt Clinton High School in the Bronx, Posner, who
managed WSP's New York office, had already been identified as a Communist by an informant. Yet when she rose to testify, the audience of
WSP women from around the country rose to stand with her. "I don't
know why, sir, I am here, but I do know why you are here," she told Doyle.
"You don't quite understand the nature of this movement. This movement
was inspired by mothers' love for their children . . . When they were putting their breakfast on the table, they saw not only the Wheaties and milk,
but they also saw Strontium 90 and Iodine 131 . . . They feared for the
life and health of their children.* That is the only motivation." Posner
took the Fifth Amendment forty-four times, yet she never relinquished
the high ground.[56]

The WSP hearing was "the biggest such affair I can recall since Mc-
Carthy," Izzy reported. "It was also the dirtiest." This time, though, the
mud didn't stick. "I saw a lot of the Women Strike for Peace delegation in
Geneva last spring, and came away with great respect for them . . . This
was no gathering of party line dupes, and a Congressional committee
could learn a lot by talking with them in a serious atmosphere." Instead,
the women had been baited by committee investigators, "most of them
from the screwball fringe or ex-hotel dicks." This time the joke was on
HUAC. Doyle admonished the audience not to stand when witnesses
were called; instead they applauded each witness. Toddlers crawled in
the aisles, babies demanded and were given bottles, and when Dagmar
Wilson, resplendent in a red wool suit, rose to testify, a young woman
with an infant on her hip walked over and presented her with a bou-
quet.[57] Two years earlier, in San Francisco, HUAC's decision to exclude
students had triggered a scuffle inside the hearings and a riot outside.
The WSP hearings were altogether more decorous—"Ladies' Day at the
Capitol," said the *Chicago Daily News*. In terms of HUAC's credibility,
though, the results were devastating. "Peace March Gals Make Red
Hunters Look Silly," said the headline over Russell Baker's sympathetic
report in the *New York Times*. Herblock's cartoon showed a clueless

---

*In 1981, Blanche Posner's son Richard was appointed to the federal bench by Ronald Reagan. At
the time of his mother's testimony, Richard Posner was a clerk for Justice William Brennan on the
Supreme Court.

committee member asking, "I came in late. Which was it that was Un-American—Women or Peace?" When HUAC decides "to smear a half million angry women, it's in deep trouble," thundered the *Detroit Free Press*. "We wish them nothing but the worst." For all their matronly demeanor, WSP, as Eric Bentley later pointed out, represented "a new generation come to life." The end of HUAC as a malign force in American politics, wrote Bentley, "began with Women Strike for Peace" and Dagmar Wilson, "a woman with nothing to hide. A woman who disdained to conceal her views."[58]

With Castro's missiles on their way back to Moscow and Soviet ships tamely allowing inspection on the high seas to verify the agreement, President Kennedy made a revelation of his own. "We will not, of course," he told a press conference, "abandon the political, economic, and other efforts . . . to halt subversion from Cuba."[59] A "military invasion" was out, but what did the president mean by "other efforts"? Clearly the United States hadn't finished with Cuba. Neither had I. F. Stone. Lugging a suitcase full of medical supplies and "three boxes of weight-reducing Metrecal wafer in my capacious brief-case, in the happy expectation that a visit to Cuba should be a chance to get a little fat off," Stone flew to Havana shortly after Christmas 1962. His sixth visit to the island—his third since Castro came to power—began badly. At Havana airport an immigration officer with "a lean and hungry look, like Cassius," took him to a police station for questioning.

"I was poorly guarded, and could have run away if I knew where I was. But this would have meant leaving my bags behind and risking a shot from the pistols of the guards. In any case, it was much too interesting an experience to run away from." Stone spent the night under arrest, browsing the jailhouse library where, alongside works by Lenin and Liu Shaoqi's *How to Be a Good Communist*, he found several volumes by Trotsky as well as Plato's *Republic* and of course *Don Quixote*. In the morning, Stone's mood darkened. Informing his captors that he was one of the few U.S. newsmen still friendly to the revolution, and that Che Guevara, Foreign Minister Raúl Roa, and President Osvaldo Dorticós all knew him personally, he was told his case now rested with the security police. "I suddenly remembered the fate of my good friend Mordecai Oren," an Israeli newsman seized in 1952 on a visit to Prague and framed for espionage in connection with the Slansky affair. Oren had spent four years in Czech prisons.

Released the next day after the intercession of a friendly guard, Stone made his way to Sloppy Joe's, where he celebrated his liberation with "a Daiquiri, which cost only 90 cents and was first rate. Despite Marxism-Leninism, Cuba's Daiquiris remain the world's best." Much else, however, had changed since his last visit: "Cuba . . . is today unmistakably a part of the Soviet world, and Havana is a Soviet capital." Yet underneath this gray façade Stone still saw considerable complexity and some cause for hope. "In press relations with Western correspondents, Cuba is almost Stalinist . . . Cuba, as seen from the West, has lost considerable intellectual freedom but Cuba, as seen from the Soviet East, now has more artistic and intellectual freedom than any other member of the bloc." Stone was unable to meet with Guevara. Nor, he cautioned his readers, had he sought out "enemies of the regime. I did not visit the prisons, or study the workings of the block system which is supposed to give the Castroites eyes and ears everywhere against the threat of sabotage and our CIA, but which must work some injustice, too. The Cuba I picture is a Cuba as it appears through friendly eyes. This, of course, is not the whole truth . . . But I believe it is dangerously misleading to make policy and form opinion, as we do back home . . . almost exclusively on the basis of hostile views."[60]

Though he remained sympathetic, writing that "the courage of the people" still reminded him of Israel, I. F. Stone never returned to Cuba. Instead, the January 21, 1963, issue contained an announcement: After "a birthday which put me well beyond the age of consent," the *Weekly* was going biweekly. It wasn't much of a rest. That April, Stone reported from the Dominican Republic. In a memorandum for the president opposing the planned invasion of the Bay of Pigs, Arthur Schlesinger Jr. had asked, "Could we not bring down Castro and Trujillo at the same time?" Though "plausible deniability" was maintained, Rafael Trujillo, the Dominican dictator, was assassinated in May 1961. However, the subsequent victory of Juan Bosch in U.S.-supervised elections put America's "principled concern for human freedom" to the test. "The Dominican Republic can be a showcase of democratic socialism," said the *Weekly*, hailing Bosch as "a peaceful challenge to Castroism."[61] Instead, after only a few months in office, Bosch was deposed by a military coup that was welcomed, if not actually initiated, by the CIA.

In June, the *Bi-Weekly* ballooned to eight pages to accommodate a lengthy exposé of Pentagon mendacity on the dangers of nuclear fallout and atmospheric testing. Yet for all Stone's diligence on this area, his pas-

sion was clearly reserved for that issue's cover story, about the murder of
Medgar Evers, the NAACP field secretary in Jackson, Mississippi. A few
days earlier, in a speech at the American University, John Kennedy urged
his countrymen to "reexamine our attitude toward the Soviet Union." In
seeking peace, said the president, he did not mean "a Pax Americana enforced on the world by American weapons of war." It was, wrote Izzy, the
speech "we've all been asking for." Kennedy's call on television for a federal civil rights act the following evening should have been equally welcome. Instead, the news of Evers's assassination "made the president's
appeal seem little and late."

> No white man, from the President down, can really understand
> the Negro's feelings. For this, one must know what it is to feel re-
> jected from birth, and to be made to wonder in the dark night of
> our hearts whether we may not indeed be a nigger. Humiliation is
> a word which figures honorably in Mr. Kennedy's strategy of peace,
> not to back an opponent into that dangerous corner where he must
> knuckle under or unleash mutual suicide. But few of us seem to
> understand that humiliation is what the Negro's struggle is all
> about. To be deprived of manhood, to be deprived of the right to
> hit back, to have no job and depend on your wife's support, to be
> beaten by the cops with impunity, to be drafted for some crazy
> white folks' crusade for freedom far away when there's a bigger and
> more genuine one to be fought at home: how can a white man
> really know what it means to be inside a black skin in America?
>
> It would be refreshing, if for once, somebody made a speech on
> civil rights and skipped all that stuff about the Declaration of In-
> dependence and the Constitution, or admitted frankly that from
> the beginning they were as plainly marked "for whites only" as any
> Mississippi drinking fountain . . . In this perspective the shot that
> killed Medgar Evers, a hero slain seeking to liberate his people,
> was not simply the act of barbarity which the White House termed
> it. It was part of the system the South has used for a century to
> keep the Negro in his place.[62]

The president, Stone wrote two weeks later, "proposes to get the civil rights
battle 'out of the streets and into the courts' . . . With all due respect to the
President, the Negro can only win his struggle if he keeps it in the streets."

When the *Bi-Weekly* returned after a month's vacation, it was to a changed world. The United States and the Soviet Union announced agreement on a treaty barring nuclear tests in the atmosphere, beneath the oceans, and in space. Only underground testing would be allowed. Stone was exultant: "The President, the Secretary of State and the Secretary of Defense have been eloquently speaking the language one heard earlier only from fringe groups like SANE . . . Peace has broken out, and hope leaps up again."[63] The day after that issue went to press, August 28, 1963, Izzy stood in the early morning at Union Station watching the "thousands pouring in from New York and Pittsburgh and Chicago" for the great civil rights March on Washington. Suddenly he felt "no longer alone in this hothouse capital, but as if out in the country people did care."

The organizers were an uneasy coalition of old-line civil-rights groups and the radicals in SNCC and CORE (the Congress of Racial Equality). But the mood of the crowd was one of jubilation. Even Stone, who found Martin Luther King Jr.'s celebrated speech "a little too saccharine for my taste," was stirred by the sight he'd so often longed for: black America rising to its feet. "For me the heroes of the March—or heroines—were the gnarled old colored ladies on tired feet and comfortably broken shoes, the kind who walked into history in Montgomery." He was also gratified "to see amid the Marchers so many old-time radicals, the unquenchables of so many vanished movements, many of them long ago forced out of jobs and pulpits, now joyously turning up again, with the feeling that they were at last part of a mass upsurge, no longer lonely relics." And though he lamented the pressure that the Kennedy administration and the march organizers put on John Lewis, the young SNCC representative, to "tone down his speech," he found little to disagree with in Lewis's censored but widely circulated text, which also dismissed Kennedy's bill as "too little, too late." Until the very last minute the Kennedys tried to get the whole march called off.* "Mr. Kennedy," Lewis wanted to say, "is trying to take

---

*The president told the march leaders, "We want success in Congress, not just a big show at the Capitol." It was also during this period that both Kennedys put pressure on Martin Luther King Jr. to drop two key aides, Jack O'Dell and Stanley Levison, because of their alleged Communist ties. King, who was being vilified himself as a Communist on billboards throughout the South showing a photograph of him taken at the Highlander Folk School, resisted for months but in the end discharged O'Dell from the SCLC payroll. Levison, a radical lawyer who had grown wealthy through real-estate investments, temporarily distanced himself from King.

the revolution out of the street and put it in the courts." Lewis was able to urge the crowd of 250,000 to "get in and stay in the streets," until "the revolution of 1776 is complete." But the question that he and I. F. Stone saw as central was cut: "I want to know, which side is the Federal Government on?"[64]

That question was one of many left unanswered on November 22, 1963.

•

"Funerals are always occasions for pious lying," Stone wrote. "To watch the President at a press conference or a private press briefing was to be delighted by his wit, his intelligence, his capacity and his youth. These made the terrible flash from Dallas incredible and painful. But perhaps the truth is that in some ways John Fitzgerald Kennedy died just in time."

Describing an administration blocked by Southern intransigence at home and a cold war congress abroad, Stone felt "that in the tangled dramaturgy of events, this sudden assassination was for the author the only satisfactory way out." With an astringency that must have seemed shocking at the time, he reminded his readers that murder had become a routine tool of U.S. policy.

"How many Americans," he wrote, "have not assumed—with approval—that the CIA was probably trying to find a way to assassinate Castro? . . . How many applauded when Lumumba was killed in the Congo?" South Vietnam's Diem had been murdered less than three weeks earlier in a coup given the green light by U.S. officials.

> How many of us—on the Left now—did not welcome the assassination of Diem and his brother Nhu in South Vietnam? We all reach for the dagger, or the gun, in our thinking when it suits our political view to do so. We all believe the end justifies the means. We all favor murder, when it reaches our own hated opponents. In this sense we share the guilt with Oswald and Ruby and the rightist crackpots. Where the right to kill is so universally accepted, we should not be surprised if our young President was slain. It is not just the ease in obtaining guns, it is the ease in obtaining excuses, that fosters assassination.
>
> We all had a finger on that trigger.[65]

Though Lee Harvey Oswald's links with the Fair Play for Cuba Committee put an end to the group's fading efficacy, Stone was simply grateful that "the press . . . handled the fact that Oswald seems to have been some kind of a leftist with great restraint." Lyndon Johnson's appointment of Chief Justice Earl Warren to chair a commission on the assassination was a "wise move," Stone declared. As for the new president himself, Stone, who had known the Texan for decades, described him as "far below" his predecessor "in sophistication, breadth and taste." Johnson's "vanity, his thin skin and his vindictiveness make even the mildest criticism, or approach to objectivity, dangerous." Yet for all that, and despite the certainty that "Johnson like Truman will bring a lot of unseemly cronies to town," Stone refused to despair: "There may be surprises in Johnson, and we wish the new President luck."[66]

That Stone could be so hopeful in the midst of national mourning had less to do with any occupant of the Oval Office than with what he heard, and saw, at a conference at Howard University on the weekend after Kennedy's murder. "There is nothing wrong with our younger generation when it can produce a movement like SNCC," he reported. "I had the privilege over the past few years of getting to know a few of them. They are an impressive lot. Purity is the only word for their intrinsic quality— the absence of self-seeking or vanity. They are the stuff of saints. They are determined to change our country, and for them the most fundamental change of all is to win by non-violent means, to answer hate with love. They stand in a line that runs from Gandhi to Tolstoy to Thoreau to St. Francis to Jesus. I regard them with reverence."[67]

Stone genuinely liked young people and gladly accepted invitations to speak to college and even high school groups.[68] Young journalists found an especially warm welcome. Fred Graham came to Washington in 1963 as counsel to one of Estes Kefauver's subcommittees, having worked his way through Vanderbilt Law School on the *Nashville Tennessean*, where he had roomed with another young reporter, David Halberstam. Both of them had read the *Weekly* in Nashville, and in Washington they were eager to meet the editor despite his radical reputation. "In the culture I was raised in, people were being accused of communism all the time," said Graham.[69] They could see that Izzy, never a very patient man, had a diminishing tolerance for political cant. He publicly withdrew from moderating a panel on Student Travel to Cuba after hearing students on the panel, members of the Maoist splinter group Progressive Labor, express views that struck him as "a mixture of naiveté, Negro nationalists' distortions . . . and out of this world leftism." Reports of his condemnation in the *New York Times* and *Washington Post* quoted his refusal "to be identified with what I regard as hysterical exaggerations hurtful to an honorable settlement between the United States and Castro's Cuba."[70]

Nor would he, like some of his old comrades, chase a spurious relevance on the coattails of young activists. Just a few days after the SNCC conference, the Emergency Civil Liberties Committee gave its Tom Paine Award, which had gone to Bertrand Russell the previous year and to Izzy three years earlier, to a twenty-two-year-old folksinger. Bob Dylan wrote "Oxford Town" in response to James Meredith's ordeal; in July, he had joined Pete Seeger and Theodore Bikel at a SNCC voter registration drive in Greenwood, Mississippi, performing "Only a Pawn in Their Game," his dirge for Medgar Evers, for the first time (he sang it again at the March on Washington). Anointed as spokesman for a generation by the *National Guardian*, Dylan had been introduced to Clark Foreman by the singer Joan Baez, who was a close friend of Foreman's son Geno.[71] Yet as he gazed out at the ECLC audience of aging leftists, the young protest singer told them, "I only wish that all you people who are sitting out here today or tonight weren't here."

Feeling exploited, patronized, and apparently fortified by several drinks on the way to the banquet, Dylan continued, "I got to admit that the man who shot President Kennedy, Lee Oswald, I don't know exactly where—what he thought he was doing, but I got to admit honestly that I too—I saw some of myself in him." This elicited loud boos from the audience. Though Dylan accepted the award "in behalf of James Forman and the Student Nonviolent Coordinating Committee," his speech so outraged the ECLC audience that Clark Foreman later complained that it had cost the group $6,000 in donations. In a rambling reply, Dylan offered to repay any money lost by his remarks—"I accepted that award for all others like me who want t' see for themselves [but] I do not apologize for any statement."[72]

John Lewis, too, was in no mood to apologize, and he closed the SNCC conference with the speech he had been prevented from giving at the Lincoln Memorial: "We will march through the South, through the heart of Dixie, the way Sherman did . . . We shall fragment the South into a thousand pieces and put them back together in the image of democracy." After a weekend with Lewis, Robert Moses,* and other SNCC activists, Stone had little doubt these "sophisticated intellectuals" would prevail. "Cattle prods will not help," he told his readers, "any more than it once helped to feed them to the lions. The South has a right to be terrified."[73]

I. F. Stone's engagement with what came to be called the New Left was in many ways unique. For the ECLC and other survivors of McCarthyism, the young activists represented not only new blood but a possible ticket back to the mainstream. Nor was such wishful projection limited to the anti-anti-Communist left. A few weeks before the SNCC conference, Tom Hayden, Todd Gitlin, and some other SDS members were summoned for inspection by Irving Howe, editor of *Dissent*. At the Upper East Side town house of Joseph Buttinger, one of the magazine's patrons, two generations faced each other, in Howe's recollection, "fumbling to reach across the spaces of time." To Gitlin and his friends, though, it felt like bullying—particularly when the talk turned to Cuba. Yet even more than Hayden's "feckless" refusal to condemn Castro and Howe's "rigid anticommunism," the two generations were divided by history itself. Howe and his comrades seemed reconciled to their own marginality—to being, in a word, *dissenters*. Gitlin and Hayden were activists; their loyalty was to their peers in SNCC and—or so it seemed at the time—in Cuba, who were actually making history. It could be said that their sense of themselves as historical subjects was too precious, too thrilling, to exchange for Irving Howe's blessing. That Stone never subjected his young admirers to such a catechism—and indeed would have failed Howe's test himself—was doubtless a point in his favor.[74]

By the fall of 1963, the *Weekly* had more than 20,000 subscribers, and Stone himself had a new book out—*The Haunted Fifties*—issued by the impeccably mainstream Random House. Izzy's editor there, Larry Bensky, was a twenty-three-year-old Yale graduate from Brooklyn, the son of Jewish immigrants. Even as a student at Stuyvesant High School in New York, Bensky had been aware of the *Weekly*. "A lot of people I knew read it. So when I got promoted from proofreader to assistant editor, Izzy was one of the first writers I proposed." Bennett Cerf, the head of Random House (literally a household name thanks to his role on the popular television quiz show

*Not to be confused with the New York city planner, Robert Parris Moses was SNCC field secretary and director of its Mississippi Project to register black voters.

What's My Line?), was not immediately enthusiastic. "Cerf said to me, 'This guy is a Commie.' I said I didn't think he was. Then Cerf asked, 'Do you think a collection of his columns would sell?' I said I thought it might."[75]

Bensky went down to Washington. "We had lunch in the Monocle restaurant. Izzy turned to me and said, 'I don't know anybody in this town.'" Part of what made Stone so attractive to young activists of the New Left was precisely his status as an outsider. With Howe or Michael Harrington—as with their shared éminence grise, Max Shachtman—there was always a sense of other agendas, tactical calculations imposing a limit on what could be said, how much of the truth could be acknowledged, in order to hold on to the labor movement, white liberals, the Democratic Party. In his preface to *The Haunted Fifties*, James Newman* praised his friend's "passion for confrontation," his impulse, in the face of cruelty or injustice, to respond with "fundamental defiance." With Stone there was never any question which side he was on.

When John Perdew, a SNCC fieldworker in Georgia, faced a death sentence charged with insurrection, riot, and assault, Stone gave him two pages of the *Weekly* to explain the difficulties of organizing the poor.[76] Many of the very qualities that led Roy Wilkins and the NAACP to dismiss SNCC as a bunch of young hotheads and that exasperated Harrington, Howe, and the rest of the anti-Communist left about SDS attracted Stone's interest and encouragement. What looked to them like an irresponsible eagerness for direct action or a reckless lack of ideological rigor seemed to him just plain Popular Front common sense. Stone genuinely admired SNCC, and not just for its young activists' courage. "Bob Moses," he told his readers, "is a sober seer, and does not fool himself." Still, he said, "There will be a murder this summer in Mississippi."[†77]

Given the choice between the enthusiastic Stone and the scolding "futilitarians of the left," it is hardly surprising that the *Weekly*'s[‡] influ-

---

*Newman died before the Freedom of Information Act became law and may never have known that in October 1953, at the height of the "haunted fifties," the FBI followed Izzy to a lunch date with Newman, who was described in the surveillance report as "ring leader" of a "group with pro-Soviet leanings" among government employees responsible for the development of atomic energy.

†There were several. Only a week after Stone wrote those words, three SNCC activists—James Chaney, Andrew Goodman, and Michael Schwerner—were arrested in Mississippi and then turned over to the Ku Klux Klan. Their bodies were found on August 4, but it wasn't until June 21, 2005, exactly forty-one years after the three disappeared, that anyone was convicted of their murders.

‡Stone returned to weekly publication in January 1964.

ence on campus continued to grow. Yet there was another factor of perhaps even greater importance. Stone may have been, in the words of one young admirer, "a radical with an old-fashioned faith." But unlike so many of the young generation's tormentors, "his beliefs are so authentically American that they do not bear facile comparison to the radical creeds of Europe." Saluting *The Haunted Fifties* for its "lucid and crisp" style, this same reviewer, a Harvard social studies lecturer named Martin Peretz, insisted that Stone "has not permitted his pages to serve as an intellectual pastorate for oppression."[78]

Two events in August 1964 pushed liberals and radicals apart. In Atlantic City, the Mississippi Freedom Democratic Party presented its credentials to the Democratic convention. With 80,000 members and 17,000 completed voter registration forms (of which only 1,600 made it onto the voter rolls), the MFDP bid for recognition was the culmination of a strategy based on a radical wager by SNCC—that by pushing voter registration instead of civil disobedience, it could maneuver the federal government into enforcing the law. "The fact is," the *Weekly* had reported in June, "that the same Lyndon Johnson who made his debut in the Senate 15 years ago as an opponent of Federal civil rights legislation of any kind, even against lynching, has made his debut as President by successfully putting through Congress the most sweeping civil rights bill in a hundred years."[79] Mississippi's official delegation of die-hard segregationists had sworn undying hostility to the new Civil Rights Act; most were expected to support Barry Goldwater in November. Offered a choice between Governor Paul Johnson, who liked to say that NAACP stood for "Niggers, Alligators, Apes, Coons, and Possums," and MFDP vice chair Fannie Lou Hamer, a sharecropper's wife who'd been jailed and beaten for trying to register voters in Senator Eastland's hometown, there was every chance the convention would have voted to seat Hamer who, like all the MFDP delegation, had pledged allegiance to the Democratic Party and its platform.

But Lyndon Johnson, the master of procedure, made sure the convention never got to choose. As Hamer began describing her beatings on national television, Johnson called a press conference to preempt the networks. When Joseph Rauh, the MFDP lawyer, asked the credentials committee, "Are you going to throw out of here the people who want to work for Lyndon Johnson, who are willing to be beaten and shot and thrown in jail to work for Lyndon Johnson?" Johnson got Walter Reuther to threaten to fire Rauh, who when he wasn't volunteering for the MFDP was the UAW's general counsel. Finally Johnson offered to seat two of the MFDP delegates as "guests"; the votes would remain with the white Mississippians. Roy Wilkins urged Hamer to "pack up and go home," and Martin Luther King Jr. leaned on Bob Moses. But SNCC rejected all this as "tokenism." Hubert Humphrey said if they kept fighting he would lose the vice presidency. And then Walter Mondale, attorney general of Minnesota and chair of the credentials subcommittee, pushed through Johnson's plan. For SNCC and its supporters, Atlantic City taught a bitter lesson: Never turn your back on a liberal in a tight corner.[80]

I. F. Stone, typically, was more cheerful. His sympathies were with "the brave handful from Mississippi," but a victory in a floor fight that let delegates "express their moral revulsion against the murderous folkways of the deep South," however emotionally satisfying, "would also have torn the party apart." That mattered, Stone argued, because under Lyndon Johnson "our country is doing more about racism than any other country in the world . . . In this respect Johnson is not just a superb political tactician but serving the highest national and human purposes." Far from crying betrayal, he enthusiastically endorsed Johnson and Humphrey, "the chief architect of the nuclear test ban treaty," whose very nomination was an earnest of peace, from Cuba to Vietnam.[81]

Stone seems to have made his own kind of radical wager: "The White House is LBJ's last chapter, and he wants desperately to make it a great one . . . De Gaulle's genius at flim-flam enabled him to free Algeria against the wishes of those who brought him to power. Johnson's may reconcile the South to equality for the Negro."[82] And so, despite the defeat in Atlantic City, Stone still believed in Johnson's Grand Design.

Yet even before the convention came to order, Lyndon Johnson had already set in motion the forces that would turn his last chapter from triumph to tragedy. On August 6, the United States launched a reprisal raid against North Vietnam following reports of an attack on two American destroyers in the Gulf of Tonkin. In response to testimony from Defense Secretary McNamara claiming "unequivocal proof" of "unprovoked attacks" on the USS *Maddox* and the USS *Turner Joy*, Congress passed a resolution allowing the president "to take all necessary steps, including the use of armed force" in Southeast Asia. The vote in the House was unanimous. In the Senate, only Ernest Gruening of Alaska and Wayne Morse of Oregon opposed the president.

The press was at least as credulous. Wayne Morse is a "chronic dissenter," scoffed Richard Rovere in the *New Yorker*.[83] "Even those men here who had opposed Mr. Johnson in the past," gushed James Reston, "were saying now they had a Commander in Chief who was better under pressure than they had ever seen him."[84] With one exception.

The attack on the *Maddox* took place on August 2, apparently in response to raids by South Vietnamese commandos (trained and armed by the CIA) on a pair of North Vietnamese islands. The *Weekly* that went to press on August 4 put together fragmentary press reports of the raids to accuse the White House of "carrying on war behind our backs." As for the attacks that supposedly took place on August 4 itself, "one bullet embedded in one destroyer hull is the only proof we have been able to muster that the . . . attacks even took place." The absence of debris, the large scale of the U.S. response—sixty-four bombing sorties targeting an oil depot, a coal mine, and a significant portion of the North Vietnamese navy—taken together with the haste to retaliate and the history of U.S. covert operations in the area led Stone to conclusions very different from the picture of outraged innocence McNamara and Johnson presented to Congress. "Everything is discussed," said Stone, "except the possibility that the attack might have been provoked."[85]

Special Issue on The Indochinese War

The International Law We Violated in Our Reprisal Raids on North Vietnam

I. F. Stone's Weekly

VOL. XII, NO. 28   AUGUST 24, 1964 WASHINGTON, D. C.   15 CENTS

What Few Know About the Tonkin Bay Incidents

The American government and the American press have kept the full truth about the Tonkin Bay incidents from the American public. Let us begin with the retaliatory bombing raids on North Vietnam. When I went to New York to cover the UN Security Council debate on the affair, UN correspondents at lunch recalled cynically that four months earlier Adlai Stevenson told the Security Council the U.S. had "repeatedly expressed" its emphatic disapproval "of retaliatory raids, wherever they occur and by whomever they are committed." But none mentioned this in their dispatches.

When Britain Staged Reprisals

On that occasion, last April, the complaint was brought by Yemen against Britain. The British, in retaliation for attacks from Yemen into the British protectorate of Aden, decided to strike at the "privileged sanctuary" from which the raids were coming. The debate then might have been a preview of the Vietnamese affair. The British argued that their reprisal raid was justified because the Fort they attacked at Harib was "a centre for subversive and aggressive activities across the border." The Yemeni Republicans in turn accused the British of supporting raids into Yemen by the Yemeni Royalists. "Obviously," Stevenson said, "it is most difficult to determine precisely what has been happening on the remote frontiers of Southern Arabia." But he thought all UN members could "join in expressing our disapproval of the use of force by either side as a means of solving disputes, a principle that is enshrined in the Charter," especially when such "attacks across borders" could "quickly escalate into full-scale wars." The outcome was a resolution condemning "reprisals as incompatible with the purposes and principles of the United Nations." That resolution and Stevenson's words are as applicable to Southeast Asia as to Southern Arabia. Though the Czech delegate cited them in his speech to the Council on August 7 about the Vietnamese affair, no word of this appeared in the papers next day.

In the August 7 debate, only Nationalist China and Britain supported the U.S. reprisal raids. The French privately recalled the international uproar over the raid they had made under similar circumstances in February, 1958, into the "privileged sanctuary" afforded the Algerian rebels by Tunisia. They struck at the Sakiet-Sidi-Youssef camp just across the border. Senators Kennedy, Humphrey, Morse and Knowland denounced the raid and Eisenhower warned the French the U.S. would not be able to defend their action in the Security Council.

Reprisals in peacetime were supposed to have been outlawed by the League of Nations Covenant, the Kellogg Pact and the United Nations Charter. All of them pledged peace-

Whose Freedom? What Freedom?

"He (Stevenson) ventured to repeat that the peoples of Laos, Vietnam and Cambodia wished to be left alone. To whom was he addressing himself? Would he not do better in telling this to his Government, to the Pentagon, to the CIA? He alleged that the U.S. is in Southeast Asia for the purpose of helping friends to preserve their opportunity to be free. What kind of friends are these? Yesterday it was the Ngo family, with their torture chambers; then it was a military junta; and now it is Khanh who, in order to save himself from impending fall, has just now proclaimed martial law and suppressed the last vestiges of freedom in the remnant of the territory he holds with U.S. support, and is trying to create new provocation of war and following the example set by the aggression on the coast of the Democratic Republic of Vietnam, by unleashing aggressive actions against his neighbors. Tomorrow it may be perhaps another puppet, equally as corrupt or possibly even more so, and perhaps more brutal."

—*Czech delegate to the Security Council Aug. 7.*

ful settlement of disputes. Between nations, as between men, reprisals are lynch law. Some White House ghost writer deserves a literary booby prize for the mindless jingle he turned out to defend ours in Vietnam. "The world remembers, the world must never forget," were the words he supplied for Johnson's speech at Syracuse, "that aggression unchallenged is aggression unleashed." This gem of prose is a pretty babble. What the world (and particularly the White House) needs to remember is that aggression is unleashed and escalated when one party to a dispute decides for itself who is guilty and how he is to be punished. This is what is happening in Cyprus, where we have been begging Greeks and Turks to desist from the murderous escalation of reprisal and counter-reprisal. Johnson practices in Southeast Asia what he deplores in the Mediterranean.

More Reprisal Raids Coming?

Public awareness of this is essential because the tide is running strongly toward more reprisal raids in the Far East. The first was the raid by U.S. Navy planes in June on Pathet Lao headquarters in Laos in retaliation for shooting down two reconnaissance planes. We would not hesitate to shoot down reconnaissance planes over our own territory; such overflights are a clear violation of international law. But the U.S., now seems to operate on the principle that invasion of other people's skies is our right, and efforts to interfere with it (at least by weaker powers) punishable by reprisal. This is pure "might is right" doctrine.

The very day we took the Vietnamese affair to the Security

Ten

AN AMERICAN TRAGEDY

———•◆•———

They come in as newspaper men, trained to get the news and eager to get
it; they end as tin-horn statesmen, full of dark secrets and unable to write
the truth if they tried.   —H. L. Mencken, "Journalism in America"

The "war behind our backs" had been going on a long time. As early as
1942, the OSS, anticipating a protracted war with Japan, had established
relations with a group of Vietnamese partisans fighting against the Japanese occupation of Indochina. But it was not until the summer of 1945
that Archimedes Patti, the OSS major in charge of the operation, met the
guerrilla leader known to his men simply as "the general," a wizened man
in his fifties with a wispy beard whose baggy trousers were held up by a
length of string. In perfect English—learned when he had worked as a
pastry chef in London and Boston—the general introduced himself by his
latest nom de guerre: Ho Chi Minh.

As an exile in Paris during the 1920s, Ho Chi Minh had been a founding member of the French Communist Party, but to Patti and other American officials who met him during this period Ho seemed "first and
foremost a Vietnamese nationalist." The Viet Minh, which he had formed
in 1940, operated as a broad nationalist coalition. And with the United
States committed, under the 1941 Atlantic Charter, to "see sovereign
rights and self-government restored to those who have been forcibly deprived of them," Ho had every reason to expect American support.[1]

Indeed, on September 2, 1945, when Ho proclaimed the independent

Democratic Republic of Vietnam following the defeat of Japan, he asked Patti's assistance in drafting the document that, translated into English, began, "All men are created equal. They are endowed by their Creator with certain inalienable rights, among these are Life, Liberty, and the pursuit of Happiness." But as the Japanese occupiers left Vietnam, the French were determined to return. Under the formula agreed to by the Allies at the Potsdam Conference in July 1945, Vietnam was to be divided at the 16th parallel; the Kuomintang army would occupy the northern half of the country, while British troops would take the south. The British soon announced their intention to withdraw in favor of the French, who promised Ho and the Viet Minh independence within the French Union—and offered him help in getting the Chinese out of Hanoi.[2]

But the instability of the Fourth Republic and the rise of independence movements in Morocco and Algeria made withdrawal from Vietnam a political football in France. Maurice Thorez, the Communist Party leader, a vice premier in France's post-war government, declared he "did not intend to liquidate the French position in Indochina"—a stance reiterated by subsequent Socialist, Christian Democrat, and Gaullist ministers. Meanwhile, Ho wrote at least eight letters to President Truman and the State Department requesting American assistance in freeing his country from France's colonial empire; no one ever replied.[3] French participation in NATO was apparently more important than Vietnamese independence. Despite his evident willingness, Ho would not become an Asian Tito.*

Instead, both the Soviet Union and China granted Ho's government official recognition in 1950, shortly after the beginning of the Korean War. The Communist victory in China in 1949, and the ensuing purge of Asian experts from the State Department, left Truman and his successors determined not to "lose" Vietnam to communism, and the United States soon moved to prop up Bao Dai, the Vietnamese emperor who had been the figurehead for Japan's occupation government before performing a similar function for the French in the south. In June 1950, Dean Rusk, then deputy under secretary of state, told the Senate Foreign Relations Committee: "Because Ho Chi Minh is tied in with the Politburo, our pol-

*In early 1950, Ho requested—and received—recognition of his government by Tito's Yugoslavia.

icy is to support Bao Dai and the French in Indochina until we have time to establish a going concern."[4]

By May 1954, when French forces surrendered at Dien Bien Phu, the United States was bankrolling the French war effort in Indochina to the tune of $1.33 billion. Even as a four-power conference of France, Britain, the USSR, and China to discuss the future of Indochina began in Geneva on May 8, the CIA sent a psychological warfare team under Colonel Edward Lansdale, an American officer "advising" the new government of South Vietnam, to Hanoi, where it sabotaged the engines of the municipal bus company, spread rumors of an impending Chinese occupation, and hired astrologers to issue dire predictions for Ho Chi Minh and his colleagues and to detect favorable omens for Bao Dai and his prime minister, Ngo Dinh Diem.[5] Less whimsically, as I. F. Stone reported at the time, "American policy is designed to create a government strong enough to block the holding of the elections promised in the Geneva agreement." These nationwide elections, intended to unify the country, were set to be held in mid-1956.[6]

Though Vice President Nixon failed to persuade President Eisenhower to send troops, the military aid that formerly had gone to the French was now channeled directly to President Diem, who with Lansdale's advice and U.S. backing had deposed Bao Dai in the fall of 1955. By 1956, Diem's government was receiving more U.S. aid per capita than any other except those of South Korea and Laos. The American presence in South Vietnam grew from 350 advisers in the early 1950s to 948 at the beginning of the Kennedy administration. In October 1961 Kennedy sent General Maxwell Taylor, whom he had made his military aide only months before, to Saigon; Stone described the Taylor mission as "an assorted bag of men looking for trouble," noting that the general's companions included Lansdale, the columnist Joseph Alsop, and W. W. Rostow, "an amateur enthusiast of anti-guerrilla tactics."[7] A year later, with the "flood relief task force" recommended by Taylor growing from 5,000 men to more than 11,000, the *Weekly* reported "danger signals on Southeast Asia." Stone noted that U.S. Army helicopter pilots were being authorized, for the first time, to attack Viet Cong guerrillas—clandestine fighters of the National Liberation Front, linked to North Vietnam—rather than merely to return their fire.[8]

It almost seemed as if the United States became entangled in Vietnam in a fit of inadvertence. Early in the Kennedy administration, the journalist Stanley Karnow stopped by the Justice Department to see the attorney general. Karnow, who had lived in Paris through the French defeat and had been reporting from Southeast Asia since 1959, suggested that Vietnam could be a dangerous place for Americans. "Vietnam," Robert Kennedy replied dismissively, "Vietnam . . . We've got thirty Vietnams a day here."[9] Yet for anyone who bothered to pay attention, the snares were evident from the beginning. In early 1962, Bernard Fall visited Hanoi, where he obtained a rare interview with North Vietnam's prime minister, Pham Van Dong. Though U.S. aid to the South Vietnamese government was ratcheting sharply upward, far from being concerned by this largesse toward his adversary, Pham was amused. "Poor Diem," he told Fall. The more he relies on American support, the more unpopular he becomes—needing even more American support. Sounds like a vicious circle, said Fall. "Not a vicious circle," Pham replied, "a downward spiral."[10]

In 1963, Izzy weighed in on the side of Bertrand Russell, whose accusation that the United States was using "chemical warfare" in Vietnam was dismissed as "arrant nonsense" by the *New York Times*. The *Weekly* quoted a report by Dick Dudman for the *St. Louis Post-Dispatch*: "A troubling question is whether the use of poisonous sprays is a valid technique of warfare."[11] In September, as Maxwell Taylor went off to Vietnam on yet another fact-finding mission, this time with Robert McNamara in tow, Izzy remarked, "To the future historian, these missions will appear not as efforts to find the facts but to evade them. One fact is that a clique of rich Catholic mandarins* can't go on ruling a Buddhist country. Another fact is that you can't go on pouring napalm on villages and poisons on crops, uprooting people and putting them in prison-like compounds, and expect to be liked."[12]

When Lyndon Johnson assumed the presidency, 16,732 Americans were in South Vietnam, most of them engineers, technicians, or advisers.

---

*Diem and many of his political associates came from aristocratic families that had been Roman Catholic for centuries. But that Catholics comprised only a small minority—about 10 percent—of the South Vietnamese population was apparently news to Robert McNamara, who told a congressional committee in 1963 that there were three times as many Catholics as Buddhists there. "This was a real scoop," reported the *Weekly*, "comparable to the discovery that Ireland is populated largely by Protestants."

Roughly a hundred Americans had died there, and a National Security Action Memorandum prepared for the new president predicted that the aim of assisting "the people and government . . . to win their contest against the externally directed and supported Communist conspiracy" would be achieved by the end of 1965, with 1,000 troops already due for withdrawal at the end of 1963. Though the document remained secret, official optimism did not. Diem, who had seemed in danger of losing his grip on his reason as well as his country, had been assassinated in November. And with the troublesome mandarin out of the way, the war could at last be won, which makes I. F. Stone's verdict on the new administration's Vietnam policy all the more striking: "The war in Vietnam," he wrote in December 1963, "is being lost."[13]

What could Stone see that others could not? The year he'd spent living in Jouy-en-Josas, and his continued attention to the French press and to writers like Jules Roy, Philippe de Villiers, and Jean Lacouture, gave him a deeper awareness of the background to the conflict than most Americans. But unlike his friends Bernard Fall and Dick Dudman—or younger acquaintances like Neil Sheehan and David Halberstam—Izzy had never been to Vietnam. (Even Sheehan, a UPI correspondent later hired by the *New York Times* whose reporting was often cited by Stone, argued well into 1966 that the United States had no choice "but continue to prosecute the war" lest we "undermine our entire position in Southeast Asia."[14]) When he wanted to know more about Vietnamese society he asked Bernard Fall, or read Robert Guillain, *Le Monde*'s Asia specialist.

What Izzy knew was Washington. He knew how an administration could set limits not only on what was discussed but even on what counted as evidence. He knew the way domestic politics shaped and skewed debates on foreign policy, and he knew that the very subjects Truman and McCarthy made taboo—the relationship between nationalism and socialism, the legacy of colonialism and America's assumption of an imperial role in the world—were those most germane to understanding why we were in Vietnam. He also knew how to read a budget—the one place Johnson's war had to come out from the shadows. And though it had made him a pariah, *The Hidden History of the Korean War* had also given him an unmatched instinct for Pentagon prevarication.

Most of all, he wanted to know. In January 1964, Marine Corps Major General Victor Krulak had proposed a covert program of "destructive undertakings" designed to "result in substantial destruction, economic loss and harassment" against "targets identified with North Vietnam's economic and industrial well-being." Approved by President Johnson and supervised by Robert McNamara, this top secret program, known as 34-A, was a direct violation of the Geneva agreements that the United States, though not a signatory, had promised to support, which had explicitly outlawed the use of force. Operation 34-A included U-2 spy flights, sabotage and psychological warfare teams dropped into North Vietnam, and the bombardment of the North Vietnamese coast by PT boats, actions that increased in both magnitude and frequency throughout 1964. At the same time, CIA pilots flew bombing raids against North Vietnamese bases in Laos, while U.S. destroyers began patrolling the Gulf of Tonkin, collecting electronic intelligence on North Vietnamese radar and other coastal defenses.[15] Both McNamara and McGeorge Bundy realized immediately that whatever happened in the gulf that August was a response to the 34-A operations—that the North Vietnamese attacks had, indeed, been provoked. Not until the publication of the Pentagon Papers in 1971 would the *Weekly*'s coverage of Tonkin be completely vindicated. And it was only in 1995 that McNamara, after a meeting with the Vietnamese general Vo Nguyen Giap in Hanoi, finally conceded that the second "attack" on August 4, 1964—the "aggression unleashed" that Lyndon Johnson used to get his blank check from a pliant Congress—never happened. But as Kai Bird, biographer of the two Bundy brothers, observed, "the information Bundy and others were withholding from the American public was an open secret to anyone who wanted to know."[16] I. F. Stone wanted to know.

So did Paul Booth, director of the SDS Peace Research and Education Project. One of the youngest participants at Port Huron, Booth had spent the summer of 1963 working with Arthur Waskow at the Peace Research Institute, a project set up by James J. Wadsworth, a liberal Republican who had been Eisenhower's ambassador to the UN. By the time of the Gulf of Tonkin incident, Booth told the historian James Miller, SDS "had developed close ties with Izzy Stone. We depended on him to interpret all the events of the world for us. The moment his *Weekly* arrived, we devoured it."[17] Booth and Todd Gitlin decided to invite Stone to speak at the upcoming SDS National Council meeting in New York in December.[18]

But SDS was not the only game on campus. In October 1964, Jack Weinberg, a Mississippi Freedom Summer veteran whose disgust with the betrayal at Atlantic City led him to coin the phrase "Don't trust any-body over thirty," set up a table to recruit CORE volunteers on Sproul Plaza at the University of California at Berkeley, defying a ban on politi-cal activity on campus. Weinberg was arrested, hundreds of students sur-rounded the police car, and the Free Speech Movement was born. As the confrontation between students and university continued, another Free-dom Summer veteran, Mario Savio, told members of a sit-in that Decem-ber, "There's a time when the operation of the machine becomes so odious, makes you so sick at heart that you can't take part! . . . And you've got to put your bodies upon the gears and upon the wheels, upon the levers, upon all the apparatus—and you've got to make it stop!"

When I. F. Stone spoke to the leaders of SDS a few weeks later, his os-tensible topic was America and the Third World. Mainly, though, Izzy talked about Vietnam, offering a brief résumé of American involvement— "a history of lost opportunities"—and arguing that it was time for the United States to withdraw. In the past he had chided the peace move-ment for its lack of interest "in the one area where warfare is going on." Now he threw his considerable influence behind a proposal to hold an antiwar protest march on Washington the following spring.[19]

That the United States was at a crossroads in Vietnam became abun-dantly clear on the morning of February 7, 1965, when a company of Viet Cong troops launched a mortar attack against an air base at Pleiku, in the central highlands of South Vietnam. The attack itself was no different from dozens of similar actions, but this time the targets were Americans, as were the casualties: 8 dead, 126 wounded, and 10 planes destroyed. "Our Joint Chiefs . . . and the South Vietnamese military have agitated for months to widen the war," Izzy reported, and now they had their chance. Fourteen hours after Pleiku, U.S. jets were dropping bombs on North Vietnam.[20] The theory was that by applying pressure on the North, the war in the South could be, in Stone's phrase, "turned off like a faucet." This assumption that the Viet Cong, or National Liberation Front, was merely a tool of the North Vietnamese government nested in-side a further assumption that Hanoi's actions were dictated by Mao's China.

On February 27, the State Department issued a white paper on Viet-nam, a sixty-four-page justification for widening the war. Written by William Bundy, Mac Bundy's older brother, a veteran of the OSS and CIA

Debunking The State Dept.'s Slanted Version of The Vietnamese War, Pps. 1-4

If We're Not Careful, One of These Days We're Liable to Hit A Guerrilla

"The employment of jet aircraft has been a subject of controversy at the Pentagon. . . . It has been argued that fighting guerrillas with jet bombers in jungle areas will inevitably prove unproductive since in most instances the guerrilla forces can disappear easily."
—*New York Times Feb. 25 on the decision to use jets.*

"One risk in using supersonic bombers against ground targets is that inevitably some bombs will fall on innocent civilians, probably in more instances than when slower air-

craft are used."
—*Wall Street Journal same day.*

"B-57 air strikes against the Viet Cong have been halted in a Mekong delta area after the American bombers accidentally killed 4 South Vietnamese troops and wounded 13. . . . There were no reports of damage to the Viet Cong. . . . The B-57s and Vietnamese Air Force Skyraiders had been pounding the area for five days."
—*AP from Saigon in* Washington Evening Star *March 1.*

I. F. Stone's Weekly

VOL. XIII, NO. 9 MARCH 8, 1965   101   WASHINGTON, D. C.   15 CENTS

A Reply to the White Paper

That North Vietnam supports the guerrillas in South Vietnam is no more a secret than that the United States supports the South Vietnamese government against them. The striking thing about the State Department's new White Paper is how little support it can prove. "Incontrovertible evidence of Hanoi's elaborate program to supply its forces in the South with weapons, ammunition and other supplies," the White Paper says, "has accumulated over the years." A detailed presentation of this evidence is in Appendix D; unfortunately few will see the appendices since even the *New York Times* did not reprint them, though these are more revealing than the report. Appendix D provides a list of weapons, ammunition and other supplies of Chinese Communist, Soviet, Czech and North Vietnamese manufacture, with the dates and place of capture from the Viet Cong guerrillas, over the 18-month period from June, 1962, to January 29 last year when it was presented to the International Control Commission. The Commission was set up by the Geneva agreement of 1954. This list provides a good point at which to begin an analysis of the White Paper.

The Pentagon's Figures

To put the figures in perspective, we called the Pentagon press office and obtained some figures the White Paper does not supply—the number of weapons captured from the guerrillas and the number lost to them in recent years:

	Captured From Guerrillas	Lost to Them
1962	4,800	5,200
1963	5,400	8,500
1964	4,900	13,700
3-Year Total	15,100	27,400

In three years, the guerrillas captured from our side 12,300 more weapons than they lost to us.

What interests us at the moment is not this favorable balance but the number of guerrilla weapons our side captured during the past three years. The grand total was 15,100. If Hanoi has indeed engaged in an "elaborate program" to supply the Viet Cong, one would expect a substantial number of enemy-produced weapons to turn up. Here is the sum total of enemy-produced weapons and supplies in that 18-month

---

Little Support For Wider War

The polls show little support for a wider war but scant attention is being paid to this. Congressional debate continues to distort the latest Harris poll on the Vietnamese war (Washington Post, Feb. 22). The only figure being quoted is the 83% approval for the Pleiku retaliatory raids. A table showing decreasing support for a wider war is ignored. Those polled were asked to choose between three policies. One was to carry the war into North Vietnam at the risk of bringing China in. This got 20% last November, 17% in January and 12% in February. A second choice was to negotiate and get out. This got 20% in November, 23% in January and 35% in February. A third course, to hold the line in South Vietnam against a Communist takeover, had 40% in November and January, 46% in February. Similar results turned up in the last Gallup poll (New York Herald-Tribune, March 1) where 67% answered "yes" when asked whether they approved of "action taken by the U.S. in Vietnam in the last few days." When those who voted "yes" were asked whether they favored continuance even at the risk of nuclear war, only 31% said they did.

---

tally to the Control Commission—

- 72 rifles (46 Soviet, 26 Czech)
- 64 submachine guns (40 Czech, 24 French but "modified" in North Vietnam)
- 15 carbines (Soviet)
- 8 machine guns (6 Chinese, 2 North Vietnamese)
- 5 pistols (4 Soviet, 1 Czech)
- 4 mortars (Chinese)
- 3 recoilless 75.mm rifles (Chinese)
- 3 recoilless 57.mm guns (Chinese)
- 2 bazookas (1 Chinese, 1 Czech)
- 2 rocket launchers (Chinese)
- 1 grenade launcher (Czech)

179 total

This is not a very impressive total. According to the Pentagon figures, we captured on the average 7500 weapons each 18-months in the past three years. If only 179 Communist-made weapons turned up in 18 months, that is less than 2½% of the total. Judging by these White Paper figures,

(Continued on Page Two)

who as assistant secretary of state for the Far East was one of the war's principal architects, the white paper had two problems. The first was that Bundy himself didn't really believe the war was winnable. In a confidential memo to his brother, McNamara, Secretary of State Dean Rusk, and Under Secretary of State George Ball (another opponent of escalation) the previous October, he'd summarized the difficulties: "A bad colonial heritage of long standing, totally inadequate preparation for self-government by the colonial power, a colonialist war fought in half-baked fashion and lost, a nationalist movement taken over by Communism ruling in the other half of an ethnically and historically united country, the Communist side inheriting much the better military force and far more than its share of the talent." Just over four months elapsed between Bundy's superiors telling him his brief for withdrawal "won't wash" and the release of the white paper.[21]

"Unfortunately for the administration's case," writes Kai Bird, "Bill's effort attracted the attention of I. F. Stone." Dated March 8, 1965, two days after the first U.S. ground troops landed in Vietnam, "A Reply to the White Paper" was probably the single most important issue of the *Weekly* ever published. The white paper, Izzy wrote, "pictures the war as an attack from the North." That "North Vietnam supports the guerrillas in South Vietnam is no more a secret than that the United States supports the South Vietnamese government," Stone declared. Using statistics supplied by the Pentagon press office, Stone underlined what the white paper failed to mention: "The rebellion in the South may owe some men and materiel to the North but is largely dependent on popular indigenous support for its manpower, as it is on captured U.S. weapons for its supply." Seizing upon the figures in the white paper's Appendix D ("A good way to read a government document," he told Andrew Patner, "is backward"), Izzy showed that in the eighteen months between June 1962 and January 1964, out of approximately 7,500 weapons captured from the Viet Cong, only 179 were of either Chinese or Eastern Bloc manufacture. The embarrassing fact, which Bundy had hidden but could not deny, was that 95 percent of Viet Cong arms came from South Vietnam.[22]

Stone's report did more than "make a mockery of the State Department." In demolishing the white paper, he gave the antiwar movement something it desperately needed—credibility. No sooner had SDS invited "all students who agree with us that the war in Vietnam injures both

Vietnamese and Americans, and should be stopped" to come to Washington on April 17 than a coalition of older peace activists released a letter calling for "an independent peace movement, not committed to any form of totalitarianism nor drawing inspiration . . . from the foreign policy of any government." The signers, who must have believed that SDS was overly sympathetic to North Vietnam, included H. Stuart Hughes, A. J. Muste, Bayard Rustin, and Norman Thomas. Senator Ernest Gruening, who with I. F. Stone had agreed to address the SDS rally, was pressured to withdraw. And on the morning of the march, the *New York Post* editorialized against "attempts to turn the event into a pro-Communist production."

Gitlin and Booth hoped for "two or three thousand students." At 12:30, when the folksinger Phil Ochs sang "Love Me, I'm a Liberal," the tensions of the day threatened to burst into the open. The crowd was estimated at 15,000 to 25,000 people. "I've seen snot-nosed Marxist-Leninists come and go," said Izzy, telling them that he was a liberal and so was Senator Gruening. Content to leave radical rhetoric to the younger generation, Stone noted benignly that the revolutionaries of 1776 had been labeled dupes of a foreign power (France) in their day, too. The men now in charge of U.S. policy were "decent human beings" caught up in "monstrous institutions," he said, urging his young audience to set aside "hatred and self-righteousness. We have to get out of this reign of hatred." Finding himself cast as the voice of moderation was something new for I. F. Stone; so was speaking before such an enormous audience. A movement was again finding its feet—and its voices.

•

A month before the SDS protest, SNCC's chairman, John Lewis, was brutally beaten in Selma, Alabama, where Martin Luther King Jr. had been leading a massive voter registration drive for several months. State troopers had used tear gas, truncheons, and bullwhips to stop the Selma-to-Montgomery Walk for Freedom. A few days later, James Reeb, a white Unitarian minister from Boston, was clubbed to death in Selma. Lyndon Johnson thereupon summoned a nighttime session of Congress to introduce his Voting Rights Act. I. F. Stone was in the press gallery. Moved by Johnson's extraordinary address to Congress, in which he acknowledged that "the real hero of this struggle is the American Negro," Stone confessed that "even for the skeptical and the wary, it was a speech that made one want to stand in the darkness outside the White House and cheer the President when he drove back."[23] Never again would he feel so tender toward Lyndon Johnson, or be so willing to be distracted from a war he believed was destroying not just Vietnam but the United States as well.

During this domestic turmoil, the Vietnam War was always on the horizon, although, as David Halberstam wrote, "The forces of peace in 1965 were thin and scattered."[24] Halberstam's own dispatches from Vietnam in the early 1960s had so annoyed President Kennedy he'd tried to get the *Times* to transfer the reporter. Yet in 1965, Halberstam himself still viewed Vietnam as "a legitimate part" of America's "global commitment," arguing, "We cannot abandon our efforts to help these people no matter how ungrateful they may seem." Reviewing Halberstam's *The Making of a Quagmire* in April 1965, Izzy noted that both Halberstam and Malcolm Browne, an AP correspondent whose reporting he also admired, "were critics not of the war itself but only of the ineffective way it was conducted." Neither man favored withdrawal or the kind of "neutral" (i.e., nonaligned) government the United States tolerated in Laos and Cambodia. "Their books," said Stone, "disclose little contact with the Vietnamese."[25] Despite the presence of nearly a hundred thousand U.S. troops and the imminent arrival of a hundred thousand more, Vietnam remained for most Americans a faraway country of which they knew little.

The one place where opposition to the war, though still not a majority view, was vocal, visible, and spreading was the academy. In the spring of 1965, campus antiwar activists unveiled a new tactic in what Stone termed "the most important battle in South Vietnam . . . the fight to let the American people know what was going on": the teach-in.[26] The first teach-in was organized by faculty at the University of Michigan and held on the same March weekend as the third, triumphal Selma-to-Montgomery march. Arthur Waskow, one of the speakers, recalls looking out at 3:00 a.m. over "a sea of students" prepared to stay up all night to learn about Vietnam. When McGeorge Bundy accepted an invitation to a teach-in scheduled for May 15 in Washington, the idea gained national attention, prompting Lyndon Johnson to send Bundy on a last-minute trip to the Dominican Republic to keep him from appearing. Izzy, who served as a "resource person" for the Washington teach-in, called it "an inspiring occasion." Some of the proceedings were televised, including a speech by

Isaac Deutscher, who "spoke a language Washington has not heard in public since the cold war and the witch hunt began two decades ago."[27] A week later, Izzy joined Deutscher on the platform at Berkeley, where 30,000 people also heard from Norman Mailer, Robert Moses, Mario Savio, Benjamin Spock, Norman Thomas, and others during a marathon thirty-five-hour teach-in.

"I'm proud to be in Berkeley," Izzy told the crowd, "where for the first time in years students cared enough about free speech to fight for it." Summarizing the history of Vietnam as "a history of broken promises," he urged his audience "to call for an end to the fighting. We ought to call for an American withdrawal and free elections under international auspices." This was still very much a radical position; nor would most Americans have agreed with Izzy's claim that "the fight for peace abroad is a fight for freedom at home." But the crowd loved it, bringing him back for a second speech and sending him away to a standing ovation both times.[28] Stone enjoyed the adulation. Just as satisfying, though, was being on a platform with Thomas, the "invincible old lion," as he wrote afterward in an adoring note to his old mentor.[29]

"The intellectuals," reported the *Weekly*, "are beginning to do their duty." In Boston that summer, 2,000 people filled the Sanders Theatre to hear Izzy at a teach-in sponsored by the Harvard-Radcliffe chapter of SDS and chaired by Martin Peretz. "When the teach-ins began," said Arthur Waskow, "hardly anyone in America knew anything at all about Vietnam . . . After two months of teach-ins, hundreds of thousands of students had a basic working knowledge from an independent non-governmental perspective."[30] Waskow himself was now based at the Institute for Policy Studies, a new counterinstitution set up by Marcus Raskin and Richard Barnet, a fellow refugee from the Kennedy administration. Along with the Center for the Study of Democratic Institutions, a California think tank started in 1959 by Robert M. Hutchins, former president of the University of Chicago, IPS became the nucleus of a counterestablishment of scholars and activists generating a stream of facts and analyses challenging the status quo. Unlike RAND and the Brookings Institution, which owed their allegiance to government or corporations, IPS "is an institute for the rest of us," said Izzy, who became one of the first IPS fellows.

Stone also was becoming a frequent contributor to the *New York Review of Books*, the counterestablishment's house journal. Founded during the 1963 New York City newspaper strike, the *Review* rapidly developed a reputation for high literary standards and intellectual seriousness. When the editor Robert Silvers asked Izzy to review campaign biographies of Barry Goldwater, Hubert Humphrey, and Lyndon Johnson, he was aware of the risks. Ever since his encounter with the *Weekly* on a Paris kiosk, Silvers had wanted to publish Stone. A few years earlier, at *Harper's*, he'd proposed asking Izzy to write on the civil rights movement, but the editor, John Fischer, had vetoed the idea "because he didn't think he was independent. Meaning that he had some leftish commitments. And I felt strongly that he had no such constricting commitments because I'd been reading [the *Weekly*]."

Stone wrote his first piece for the *Review* at the house on Fire Island; he and Silvers went over the galleys in the waiting room of the Babylon station of the Long Island Rail Road. "I think he was very pleased I was willing to come out," Silvers recalled. After the election books, Stone turned to Bernard Fall's *Street Without Joy*, a sober history of the "first" (i.e., French) Indochina war that had been published in 1961, and Arthur Dommen's *Conflict in Laos*, published in 1964, followed a few months later by the essay on Halberstam and Browne. A few days after Stone's first article about Vietnam appeared, Silvers received a phone call from the White House. The presidential aide Richard Goodwin was on the line. While acknowledging that Izzy was "a decent fellow," Goodwin suggested the *Review* consider assigning the next set of Vietnam books to "someone like Joe Alsop."[31] But by using I. F. Stone as its expert on Vietnam, the *New York Review* was declaring its opposition to the war. At the *New Republic*, Gilbert Harrison sent a similar signal to his readers in the spring of 1965, inviting Izzy back onto the magazine's pages for the first time since the 1940s to explain why stepping up the bombing and sending combat troops to Vietnam will only "drag us further into the Asian morass."[32]

Was Izzy becoming respectable again, or were Americans becoming more radical? When Lyndon Johnson sent the Marines to the Dominican Republic in April to prevent Juan Bosch, that country's first democratically elected president, from returning to power after having been removed in a military coup, Izzy was not alone in his scathing assessment of the action: "We have again been made to appear in Latin American eyes not as a paper tiger but as an elephantine power with more muscle than brain." The *New York Herald Tribune* was equally dismissive, calling the deployment of 30,000 troops "ludicrous." "The U.S. press," reported Izzy with delight, "never showed itself more independent than in its coverage of the Dominican affair." The *New York Times* reporter Tad Szulc, who had broken the story, "deserves a Pulitzer Prize," wrote Izzy, and the *Times* editorial page "was magnificent."[33] Returning from a month's holiday in Europe to visit Italy, Switzerland, France, and Britain, Izzy found himself marching at the head of the Fifth Avenue Peace Parade in New York. (Such prominence came at a price. When "a small organized gang of louts" attacked the marchers, "I myself . . . got hit with an egg, fortunately fresh," he reported.) According to the *Guardian*, "clashes in political perspective and traditional liberal exclusion of the left were cast aside for the day," which may partially account for Izzy's sunny disposition.[34]

Another factor was the return of his hearing. In the autumn of 1964, Dr. Samuel Rosen, whose discovery of the "mobilization of stapes" procedure had revolutionized the treatment of hearing loss, operated on Stone's right ear. Even with just one good ear, "I go to the movies and don't have to use my Sonotone," the delighted patient reported.[35] A second operation the following year meant that now, after three decades of near deafness, Stone could hear again. It may have been this euphoria that prompted him to take "A Fresh Look at Lyndon Johnson" in September 1965. Acknowledging the president's "extraordinary accomplishments in the field of social legislation," Izzy admitted that "were it not for Vietnam and the Dominican Republic, Johnson would be the hero today of the left-of-center. Not since FDR has so much reform legislation been won from Congress." Responding to rumors that Johnson only intended to bomb his way to the negotiating table, Stone said that if "he now succeeds in negotiating peace in Vietnam," denunciations of the president by "angry peaceniks like this writer will turn out to be history's No. 1 case of mistaken identity. We hope it does."[36]

Instead, Johnson escalated, approving General William C. Westmoreland's shift to a "search-and-destroy" strategy in which progress would now be measured in enemy "body counts." Johnson also moved to increase troop numbers from 175,000 in June 1965 to 275,000 in July and 443,000 in December. The U.S. Air Force was now flying 1,500 sorties *a week* over North Vietnam.[37] Stone's burst of generosity prompted a telegram inviting him to a reception at the White House for a Presidential Conference on International Cooperation, but by then Izzy's mood had shifted. Attending a session devoted to the problems of homeless children in Vietnam, he remarked that if the panel "had only had a U.S. Air Force consultant he might have explained how easily, by a step-up in B-52 raids, we could reduce the number of both orphanages and orphans."[38]

Satire, however savage, was no match for reality. In March 1964, the first photograph ever printed in the *Weekly* showed what Johnson's air war was doing to Vietnamese children. Though the Associated Press refused to sell the picture to Stone—the *Weekly* ran a pirated copy—he kept the original wire service caption: "INNOCENT VICTIM—A Vietnamese child, body completely covered with burns from a napalm bomb, is held by father." The *Weekly*'s second photo, which appeared in March 1965, almost exactly one year later, showed a peasant woman, her child in her arms, pleading with a South Vietnamese soldier who was setting fire to her village. That November, the *Weekly* carried a report by the French journalist Jean Lartéguy about a Catholic priest whose church was destroyed by American bombers. "I have seen my faithful burned up in napalm. I have seen the bodies of women and children blown to bits. I have seen all my villages razed. By God, it's not possible."[39]

On November 2, 1965, Norman Morrison, a thirty-one-year-old Quaker and father of three children, cut out Lartéguy's article from the *Weekly* and put it in an envelope with a letter to his wife, saying he "must act for the children in the priest's village." Taking their infant daughter with him, Morrison made his way to the Pentagon, where, after setting his little girl down a safe distance away, and in sight of Robert McNamara's office windows, he doused himself with kerosene in the manner of Buddhist priests protesting in Vietnam and set himself alight.

Escalation in Vietnam made the *Weekly* indispensable; circulation rose from just over 20,000 in 1964 to 31,000 two years later. But the war—and the responsibility Stone felt in covering it—began to crowd out other issues. Just as the Free Speech Movement was beginning in Berkeley, a young Labor Department attorney approached Izzy with a damning dossier on the American auto industry. Preoccupied with Vietnam, Stone turned down the eager subscriber and would-be author, Ralph Nader. "I said, if all we had to worry about were inferior cars . . . it would be a very happy universe."[40]

Just keeping up with the war was more than Stone could manage on his own. For some time he'd employed young assistants to help get out the *Weekly*. Initially he asked David Riesman if he "could perhaps find a recent Harvard College graduate to serve as his assistant." Riesman sent him "several bright graduates—honors graduates, at that—who admired him greatly, but he found them all wanting." The problem, apparently, was their ignorance of history, classics, foreign languages, and bibliography.[41] Nor was Izzy a particularly understanding boss. The *Washington Times* columnist Suzanne Fields got her job at the *Weekly* through Marcus Raskin. "He never quite told you what he wanted. You were expected to read his mind." Married and with a husband in the service, Fields phoned one morning and said, "Izzy, my car is dead." He told her not to bother coming in again.[42] Neil Kotler, who succeeded Fields in early 1964, had a happier experience, but he still recalled a man whose existence was "run by those deadlines."[43]

"He was the toughest boss I ever had," said Phil Stanford, a newspaper columnist in Portland. "Izzy did give me a raise when our first child was born," says Stanford, but when he refused to make hotel reservations for his boss—"I thought it was beneath me"—Stone fired him. "He wasn't in the business of making my life happy," said Peter Osnos, who was so exhausted by his ten months at the *Weekly*—at $100 a week—he consulted a therapist. (Perhaps in recognition of his faults, Izzy persuaded his own niece Kathy Boudin to abandon her plan to drop out of Bryn Mawr and work for the *Weekly*.) Osnos, who later became a foreign correspondent and then a publisher, described Stone as "one of the most difficult people that walks the face of the earth" yet eventually became immensely fond of Izzy and Esther. "It was really the beginning of a friendship as well as the beginning of a career."[44]

Osnos was unusual among Izzy's assistants in actually writing for the *Weekly*, first under his initials and then with a full byline. More important, his competence allowed Stone to spend several weeks in the spring of 1966 reporting from Vietnam. "Those who have gone to Vietnam," Izzy told the Berkeley teach-in, "are not necessarily the best advisers," yet he still felt compelled to go and see the war for himself. When he returned, pressure to deliver the big story gave him writer's block for the first time in his life. "The first draft of the piece was really very weak," recalled Osnos. "All about girls in floating silk. [Esther and I] were kind of wringing our hands. What do we tell Izzy? But he knew it was no good. And he had a terrible time. He was blocked . . . And then he woke up in the middle of the night, jumped out of bed, raced into his study, and wrote the whole thing."[45]

"What I remember most of Saigon," Stone wrote, "is the heat, the squalor and the despair." Gone were the girls in their summer dresses (though he noted "how demurely seductive the Vietnamese woman's costume can be"). Instead, he offered a vivid chronicle of disintegration: "The guerrillas have cut the railroads and made the roads impassible everywhere—except for those who pay their fee and are granted passage. For Americans it is safe to travel only in the skies." And he evoked, unforgettably, the tone of empire, American-style:

> To watch the young Ivy Leaguers arriving briskly at the Embassy of a morning is to feel oneself on the eve of the Harvard-Yale game. The team spirit is bursting out all over; it demands optimism; patriotism is equated with euphoria . . . Under the supposed benevolence of our policy one soon detects a deep animosity to the Vietnamese and a vast arrogance. We assume the right to remold them, whether they choose to be remolded or not.
>
> It is significant that those like Gen. Lansdale and Colonel John Paul Vann who would approach the Vietnamese as people soon find themselves sidetracked, suspect and frustrated. The machine instinctively reacts against the human, and what we are running, or what is running us, is a bureaucratic war machine."[46]

The following issue was devoted to "What Vietnamese Say Privately in Saigon." Though most of Stone's informants insisted on anonymity, he reported a lengthy conversation with the Buddhist monk Thich Nhat Hanh,* who opposed the Communists but was "terrified by the U.S." Even more striking was Stone's interview with Dr. Phan Quang Dan, "one of the heroes of the democratic resistance . . . [but] also an advocate of continuing the war to victory, and of sharply restricting democratic rights in the process." Unlike so many "engaged" journalists, Stone insisted on hearing and taking seriously the arguments of those who disagreed with him.[47]

---

*Thich Nhat Hanh came to the United States later in 1966. It was during this trip that he met with Martin Luther King Jr., whom he had written to, and urged him to oppose the Vietnam War publicly, which King began doing with a speech at New York City's Riverside Church in April 1967.

A third week saw Stone again shunning embassy briefings for conversations with as many different shades of Vietnamese political opinion as possible. "The Vietnamese are neither defeated nor submissive," he reported. "They are as stubborn and fanatically determined as the Irish or the Jews. They'll fight us and themselves to exhaustion." Among "the U.S. leadership on the spot—military and civilian," Stone found "a sober realization that no quick solutions are in sight and that a long, long war lies ahead." Returning home, Izzy stopped in Phnom Penh, a "Paradiso" after the "Inferno" of Saigon. Savoring "the blessings of [Cambodia's] neutralist policy," Izzy was thoroughly charmed by Prince Sihanouk, "a Louis XIV, a Tito and a Harry Truman rolled into one. No one has been more skillful at getting aid from all sides. At home, 'Monseigneur' had managed to reconcile monarchy with a democratic facade, Five Year Plans, and enough 'socialism' to make Cambodia seem fraternal if confusing in Moscow and Peking. In his spare time he writes first-rate editorials for his French language press and composes popular songs. There's been nothing quite like him in all the annals of statecraft. He's genuinely popular." And the clincher was that "his country, unlike Laos and South Vietnam, is troubled by no Communist guerrillas."* Another two years passed before the Communist Party of Kampuchea, or Khmer Rouge, launched an insurgency revealing the limitations of Sihanouk's "wily" policy of "taking them [Cambodian Communists] into camp."[48]

Back in Washington, Izzy joined the congressmen Don Edwards and John Conyers and Reverend Channing Phillips (a politically prominent African-American pastor in Washington) in sponsoring a garden party benefiting the Mississippi Freedom Democratic Party. It was another garden party later that summer, however, that underlined the changes set in motion by the war. At a dinner at Bernard and Dorothy Fall's house, Izzy found himself chatting with Walter Lippmann, a writer whose Olympian perspective couldn't have been farther from his own. Indeed, ever since Lippmann lent his name to the whitewash of George Polk's murder, Izzy regularly damned him as a "stuffed shirt," the most severe denunciation in the Stone lexicon. Yet on the morning after their meeting at the Falls',

---

*Tom Hayden, in Cambodia the following autumn, also saw the country as "a pastoral island in the middle of all this," a view, he told James Miller, that retrospectively "haunts me. Because I assume that all of the people I met are skulls in a museum somewhere."

an engraved card arrived inviting Izzy and Esther to Lippmann's annual mint-julep lawn party, a fixture of the capital's social calendar. Guests who expected the usual assembly of cabinet members, columnists, and Supreme Court justices were greeted instead by the sight of their host, Walter Lippmann, the American establishment made flesh, in rapt conversation with that journalistic pariah I. F. Stone.[49]

•

To the Englishman Anthony Howard, in October 1966 a newly arrived Washington correspondent for the *Times* of London, Stone was one of the few reporters in the capital not seduced by or reduced to punditry. As a result, Howard wrote in the *New York Times Magazine*, the *Weekly* "is required reading in every embassy, not to mention the State Department itself."[50] After a decade of invisibility, Izzy relished his rising profile. So when Oleg Kalugin, press secretary of the Soviet embassy, invited him to lunch, Izzy made sure they went to Harvey's, J. Edgar Hoover's favorite restaurant (and, in the 1950s, the setting for the director's regular trysts with Joe McCarthy), "to tweak Hoover's nose."[51]

Though Hoover got the message—a report of the lunch was on his desk shortly afterward—Kalugin proved less receptive. The invitation had come in response to an article in the *Weekly* about Yuli Daniel and Andrei Sinyavsky, two Russian writers recently convicted and imprisoned for "anti-Soviet" activity. Hailing the writers' young Russian supporters as "the natural counterpart of our own New Left, rebels like ours against moral indifference," Izzy presumably hoped that Kalugin, whose true identity as a KGB agent was widely suspected among the press corps, might have some influence with Moscow. If so, the Russian was unwilling to use it; after their lunch Stone published an "Open Letter" to Ambassador Anatoly Dobrynin announcing he would boycott "all functions at the Soviet Embassy until these writers are free."[52]

Stone was less sympathetic to the plight of his former copyboy Ralph Ginzburg. Charged with violating federal obscenity statutes as editor of *Eros* magazine (which he advertised in mailings from Blue Ball and Intercourse, Pennsylvania, as well as Middlesex, New Jersey), Ginzburg assumed that his old boss, the noted champion of free speech, would rush to his defense, particularly since Izzy's sister, Judy Stone, worked on *Fact* magazine, another Ginzburg publication. Yet when the Supreme Court upheld Ginzburg's conviction, Stone was offended not by the five-year prison sentence but by "the posturing of Ralph Ginzburg . . . This effort to cloak himself in the mantle of Thomas Jefferson, and at the same time grab onto the coat-tails of the peace movement, was characteristic of a young man who seems straight out of *What Makes Sammy Run?*" To Izzy, squandering the moral capital of the First Amendment was "worse than pornography."[53] Izzy "was a bit of a prude," recalled Peter Osnos, who like Ginzburg credited Esther Stone with softening her husband's wrath. Though still convinced that "liberals who . . . make a fast and dirty buck" from pornography "betray the cause of freedom," as he wrote a few weeks later, he "did not believe one should send a man to jail because he disagrees."[54]

What really annoyed Izzy was not sex—this was, after all, a man who'd spent many happy hours watching burlesque—but Ginzburg's resolutely frivolous attitude. It was the moral courage of SNCC, the earnest idealism of SDS that drew Stone's support. Even Malcolm X, whose incendiary black nationalism had long rendered the Muslim minister anathema to most white liberals, engaged Izzy's sympathy by his evident seriousness of purpose. The author of *Underground to Palestine* had already seen one downtrodden people lift themselves up in response to a nationalist message. As a Jewish atheist, he understood "the tendency to dismiss Elijah Muhammad's weird doctrine. But it is not really any more absurd than the Virgin Birth or the Sacrifice of Isaac."[55]

When in May 1966 Stokely Carmichael, a younger man who was known to be sympathetic to the ideas of Malcolm X, succeeded John Lewis as chairman of SNCC, Izzy advised "white sympathizers [to] keep several things in mind. One is that in any movement the leverage exerted by the moderates depends on the existence of an extremist fringe. The second is that a certain amount of black nationalism is inevitable among Negroes; they cannot reach equality without the restoration of pride in themselves as Negroes. The third is that this cannot be achieved unless they learn to fight for themselves, not just as wards of white men."[56]

"It is not Stokely Carmichael, it is Mayor Daley and President Johnson who by their actions indoctrinate the Negro in violence," Stone wrote after riots had broken out in Cleveland, New York, Detroit, Watts, and Chicago during the long hot summer of 1966. "There is a hopeful side to the riots," he thought. "They indicate that the poor are no longer poor in spirit." Yet it is hard to miss the ambivalence in his remark that "the cry of 'black power' is less a program than an incantation to deal with the crippling effects of white supremacy . . . It is not practical politics; it is psychological therapy." Stone acidly dismissed Carmichael's call for "the coming together of black people" to pick their own representatives and at the same time to reject "most of the black politicians we see around the country today" as "typical New Left *narodnik* mysticism, albeit in Negro form." After all, he wanted to know, "who picked Adam Clayton Powell, Harlem's absentee landlord?"[57] (Adam Clayton Powell Jr. had represented Harlem in the House of Representatives since 1944 but in recent years had spent most of his time outside the district.)

However much he understood its origins, the turn toward black power was bound to make Stone uncomfortable. It was America's good fortune, he wrote, that "the Negro still wants in . . . But the time is short before hate shuts the doors." With the possible exception of Julius Hobson, a Tuskegee-educated pilot who spearheaded a campaign for equal educational opportunity in the D.C. schools, Izzy had no black friends. Yet his appraisals of black leaders new and old betrayed none of the pulled punches of a guilty liberal. W.E.B. Du Bois "was one of the great Negroes of our time," Izzy wrote after the NAACP founder's death. But his education in Germany had given him a "Prussian" temperament: "authoritarian and Stalinist by instinct long before he joined the Communist Party, [he] was prepared to accept and rationalize all the repressions and horrors committed by Stalin in the name of socialism." Though he believed the effort made in Congress in 1967 to deprive Powell of his seat* "had racist overtones," Izzy described the country's most outspoken black congressman as "the Nkrumah of Harlem, a brilliant man whose career was ruined by the temptations of power."[58] Which makes the eloquence and emotional power behind Stone's tribute to Malcolm X, assassinated in February 1965, all the more striking.

"Savagely uncompromising," the Black Muslim leader "drove home the real truth about the Negro's position in America. It may not be pleasant, but it must be faced . . . No man has better expressed his people's

---

*The resolution to bar Powell from Congress was introduced by Gerald R. Ford, Republican of Michigan.

trapped anguish," Stone wrote. Perhaps it was because, unlike the young advocates of black power, Malcolm X seemed to be moving away from racism toward the vision of brotherhood he brought back from his pilgrimage to Mecca. Or perhaps Stone recognized something of his own struggles "in the agony of this brilliant Negro's self-creation." His account of Malcolm X first tasting freedom in a prison library, "finding substantiation for the Black Muslim creed in *Paradise Lost* and in Herodotus," and his description of the convicted burglar's "passionate curiosity and voracious reading," suggest an unlikely yet unmistakable identification with the martyred leader.[59]

Izzy's relations with white student radicals, however, were beginning to fray. As the teach-ins spread across the country, he warned in June 1965 that "the peace movement may be divided into three groups," and activists might "find it useful first to determine to which of these three groups they belong. One wants to persuade, and to win public support for an end to the war"; a second was "not so much concerned with persuading as with *testifying* . . . These people want to demonstrate their moral disapproval of the war." And finally there were those who wanted "to express their solidarity with the Viet Cong . . . These may be termed the revolutionary forces." But, Stone went on, only the first group could "change public opinion for the better." Self-styled revolutionaries "can fulfill little more than the role of *agents provocateurs*, giving the government an excuse for repression." Besides, in a country as prosperous as the United States and with such a conservative labor movement, "they couldn't marshal enough men for a *putsch*; they'd be lucky to seize one post office!"[60]

Those students who scorned "middle-class liberals" and wanted a working-class third party might, Stone suggested, "reflect on the fact that in the North as well as in the South the bitterest resistance to the Negro's struggle comes from the white working class." In greater demand than ever as a campus speaker, Stone saw more and more students "who would like to opt out—just where they do not know, but *out* . . . Much of the New Left politics is an attempt in disillusion to secede from the American political system."[61]

At the Spring Mobilization against the war in April 1967, Stone found the New Left even more in need of a strong dose of Popular Front common sense: The movement "has to make up its mind. Does it want to per-

suade as large a section of the American people as possible, or to antagonize them? . . . Those who want to use the peace movement to preach
hate, race war and revolution ought to get out of the peace movement and
back to their own little war movements."[62] Yet he, too, felt a terrible frustration. By the fall of 1966, Arthur Schlesinger Jr. and Richard Goodwin
both publicly opposed "further escalation"; but neither was ready to advocate withdrawal from Vietnam. Privately even Robert McNamara admitted there was "no evidence" that increasing U.S. troop numbers would
change the course of the war, and "the Rolling Thunder program of bombing the North," he told Johnson, had not cracked Hanoi's morale. Yet
Westmoreland asked for another 200,000 men; in the meantime, Johnson's "spring air offensive" included bombing Haiphong and Hanoi.[63]
When Michael Padnos, an ADA lobbyist who occasionally wrote for the
Weekly, expressed surprise at the president's persistence, Izzy replied,
"You have to remember that ever since the time of Thucydides, the popular party has always been the war party."[64]

Stone could see only two possible routes out of Vietnam. One was
Robert Kennedy, who for all his infuriating caution—and his McCarthyite
baggage—seemed to be genuinely considering opposing the president on
the war. In February 1966, when Kennedy first proposed that the United
States accept a coalition government in South Vietnam that would include the Viet Cong, the *Weekly* printed the full text of his speech. But
when Kennedy followed this "political event of the first magnitude," as
Izzy called it, by voting in the Senate against a resolution to rescind the
Tonkin Gulf authorizations, Stone denounced him as "neither hawk nor
dove but chicken."

He was still more scathing in October, calling Kennedy "a trimmer"
who "put career ahead of duty." He didn't doubt Kennedy's sincerity, he
said, merely his courage. By the end of the year, however, he had tossed
aside even this politesse: "When I was a boy a certain kind of girl was
known as a certain kind of tease. She promised a lot but she never delivered. Robert Kennedy seems to be that kind of politician. He's always
flirting with the liberals but manages to avoid coming to the point . . . He
has 'reservations' about the bombing of the North . . . Kennedy seems to
feel that a 'reservation'—like an advance phone call to a busy night
club—will save him a seat with the anti-war forces." The death of
Bernard Fall in February 1967—he stepped on a land mine while accom-

panying a marine patrol in Saigon—made Stone even less tolerant of Kennedy's equivocation. "When Robert Kennedy is ready to risk his political future as others in Southeast Asia are risking their lives," he wrote in the issue of the *Weekly* that carried Fall's death notice, "he will deserve the leadership he so desperately wants.[65]

The other way out was military defeat. For I. F. Stone, as for most Americans, losing in Vietnam was inconceivable. Describing the war as unwinnable didn't mean he expected Johnson to accept defeat. Indeed, in the early years of the war, Stone worried more that the United States might succumb to the temptation of quick victory through nuclear weapons. Yet as it became increasingly clear that Johnson, for all his bellicosity, was not deranged enough to risk a nuclear confrontation with Moscow— or Peking, which had conducted its first nuclear test in October 1964— and that the president was nonetheless willing to destroy all of Vietnam on both sides of the 17th parallel, Stone's views began to change. "Johnson has ruined morally all who deal with him at home and he will ruin morally all who deal with him abroad," he wrote in October 1966. "If our military machine crushes the Vietnamese rebellion, it will mete out similar punishment wherever subject peoples seek their freedom from corrupt oligarchies linked with American interests. Vietnam is intended to be a lesson to . . . the disaffected everywhere; a training ground for the Legions of the Pax Americana. If our military win in Vietnam there will be no holding them elsewhere or at home."[66]

By the winter of 1967, the writer who'd warned the New Left against becoming cheerleaders for the Viet Cong found himself forced to choose. A Viet Cong victory would be, he thought, a rebuke to

everything America stands for . . . And not just America, but everything the modern world admires. And not just the capitalist world, but all that Lenin and his comrades aspired to ever since the days when *Fordismus* was the magic word of Bolshevism, its gleaming goal, a future of mass production . . . It is the Machine, it is the prestige of the machine, that is at stake in Vietnam. It is Boeing and General Electric and Goodyear and General Dynamics. It is the electronic rangefinder and the amphibious truck and the night-piercing radar. It is the defoliant, and the herbicide, and the deodorant, and the depilatory. It is the products and the brand names we have been conditioned since childhood to revere . . . This is the faith those uncouth guerrillas in Vietnam have placed in jeopardy.

It is worth noticing that Stone rationalized his acceptance of America's likely defeat by the Viet Cong not as a socialist but as a humanist: "Down there in the jungles, unregenerate, ingenious, tricky, as tiny as a louse or a termite, and as hard to get at, emerged a strange creature whose potency we had almost forgotten—Man. To sit down now and deal with him is to admit that the Machine lost to Man, that our beautifully computerized war, with the most complicated devices for killing ever assembled and the most overwhelming firepower ever mustered, had failed."[67]

A Viet Cong victory still seemed far from inevitable. "A nation of 30,000,000," he wrote, "cannot defeat a nation of 200,000,000 if the bigger nation cares enough to pay the price of victory and has the patience to pursue it."[68] But he had come to see it as desirable. The coup that installed a military junta in Greece in April 1967, just weeks before a center-left coalition, led by former prime minister George Papandreou, was expected to win a general election, offered a vivid reminder of where the Pax Americana could lead. "Greece was our first Vietnam," said Stone. "Now 20 years and $2 billion later the facade of success has crumbled."[69] It was time for Americans to wean themselves from the delusions of empire.

•

Defeat would be hard to accept. But victory had its own perils—as could be seen in Israel, where the Jewish state's repeated triumph over its Arab neighbors was encouraging a miniature version of imperial hubris. At the beginning of June 1967, however, the *Weekly* quoted from a statement by Jean-Paul Sartre and fifty other French intellectuals denouncing Egypt's recent closure of the Straits of Tiran to Israeli ships, affirming that "the security and sovereignty of Israel . . . are the bases of peace" and rejecting as "incomprehensible the identification of Israel with an imperialist and aggressive camp."[70]

The Egyptian blockade was, Israel had warned, a casus belli, and despite intense and numerous diplomatic efforts to head off a war, Israel struck on June 5. Six days later, as Jews around the world celebrated what

Stone called "Israel's swift and brilliant military victory," he warned that it only made

> reconciliation with the Arabs more urgent. [Israel's] future and
> world peace call for a general and final settlement now of the Pales-
> tine problem. The cornerstone of that settlement must be to find
> new homes for the Arab refugees, some within Israel, some outside
> it, all with compensation for their lost lands and properties . . . The
> challenge to Israel is to conquer something more bleak and forbid-
> ding than even the Negev or Sinai, and that is the hearts of its Arab
> neighbors. This would be greater and more permanent than any
> military victory. Abba Eban exultantly called the sweep of Israel's
> armies "the finest day in Israel's modern history." The finest day will
> be the day it achieves reconciliation with the Arabs.[71]

Equally prophetic, and equally destined to be disregarded in the after-glow of conquest, was his suggestion that Israel "make a virtue of necessity by offering to set up an Arab state in these areas, linked in a confederation with Israel and perhaps also with Transjordan. Why not do it with grace and magnanimity instead of grudgingly and in this context provide repara-tion and settlement?" More than two decades would pass before the Israeli Labor Party, whose dominance in 1967 seemed as impregnable as the state's new borders, recognized the force of Stone's comment that "in a sense the Arab refugees have been carrying on a sit-down strike for 19 years on Israel's borders. Now the sit-down strikers are inside."[72]

He made a similar argument in *Ramparts*, a Catholic monthly turned New Left glossy magazine that employed his sister, Judy, as a staff writer and whose New York office was run by his brother Marc. "By defeating Nasser, Israel did Lyndon Johnson an enormous favor, but it is a mistake to assume he will reciprocate." The United States would always be torn "between oil interests in the Arab states and the Jewish vote at home," he wrote, urging Israel to seek reconciliation with the Palestinians instead of becoming an American client. "Now is the time to right that wrong, to show magnanimity in victory."[73]

Stone's most considered response to the Six-Day War came in the *New York Review of Books* later that summer, in a review of *Le conflit israélo-arabe*, a special issue of Sartre's journal, *Les Temps Modernes*, the

first confrontation in print of Arab and Israeli intellectuals. Alas, he reported ruefully, it turned out "to be 991 pages not so much of dialogue as
of dual monologue." The issue's editor, Claude Lanzmann,* explained
that the Arab contributors, most of whom wrote after consultation with
their governments, defended a common position, while the Israelis, "as is
normal in a Western-style democracy," spoke for themselves or for various
political parties. There was also, Stone pointed out, the unavoidable
"asymmetry of the victorious and the defeated. The victor is ready to talk
if the latter will acquiesce in defeat. The defeated, naturally, is less inclined to this kind of objectivity."

Stone himself made no pretense to objectivity. Instead, he proposed
that his people, the Jews, undertake a "reexamination of Zionist ideology"
lest they succumb to the "moral imbecility [that] marks all ethnocentric
movements. The Others are always either less than human, and thus
their interests may be ignored, or more than human, and therefore so
dangerous that it is right to destroy them. The latter is the underlying
pan-Arab attitude toward the Jews; the former is Zionism's basic attitude
toward the Arabs." He harked back to the Hebrew philosopher Achad
Ha'am, Martin Buber, and other Zionist pioneers "who tried to preach
Ichud, 'unity,' with the Arabs," but he had little expectation, after nine visits to the Holy Land since 1945, that his advice would be heeded, "especially since the U.S. press is so overwhelmingly pro-Zionist.

"For me," he concluded, "the Arab-Jewish struggle is a tragedy. The
essence of tragedy is a struggle of right against right . . . When evil men
do evil, their deeds belong to the realm of pathology. But when good men
do evil, we confront the essence of human tragedy. In a tragic struggle,
the victors become the guilty and must make amends to the defeated."
The tragic consequences of Israel's road not taken—its insistence in re-
taining the West Bank and Gaza, making "facts on the ground" rather
than amends to the Palestinians—were eventually to be acknowledged
even by Ariel Sharon, who in 1967 was the victorious tank commander of
the Sinai campaign. But at the time, Stone's views were heretical. "If God
as some now say is dead," he quipped, "He no doubt died of trying to find
an equitable solution to the Arab-Jewish problem."[74]

---

*In 1985, Lanzmann directed the nine-and-a-half-hour documentary film *Shoah*, an oral history of
the Holocaust.

"There's nothing I like better than a good brawl," Izzy once told Norman Thomas, admitting that he deliberately tried to "annoy" his readers from time to time. "Otherwise you have escaped the larger prison only to land in theirs." His break with Bertrand Russell, a man he admired as much as anyone living, after the philosopher made what Izzy thought was a "hysterical and defamatory" attack on the Warren Commission in September 1964, was perhaps the most celebrated instance of Stone's refusal to genuflect. Stone's view that "the Warren Commission has done a first rate job" and that "the case against Lee Harvey Oswald as the lone killer" was "conclusive" cost him subscribers. He had already dismissed two early conspiracy-mongering works on the Kennedy assassination ("You couldn't convict a chicken thief on the flimsy slap-together of surmise, half-fact and whole untruth in either book"), and some held (and still hold) this against him. "There are a lot of people among our own Left-wingers," he wrote Thomas, "who are full of hate . . . You're a hero when you defend them but when you try to be humanly objective about 'the others' they're furious—even when theoretically they believe in co-existence." But nothing in his career made Stone so many new enemies—or cost him so many old friends—as his criticism of Israel.[75]

Michael Blankfort submitted a lengthy objection to Izzy's position that the *New York Review* declined to publish, running instead a ferocious denunciation by the literary critic and biblical scholar Robert Alter and the political scientist Amos Perlmutter, and a more temperate but long and tendentious letter from James Michener.[76] By custom Stone would have had the last word, but an editors' note said he "has recently been ill, and is therefore unable to reply." On August 7, he had been admitted to a hospital in New York for surgery on a detached retina. Two days later, still in the hospital, he had a heart attack. ("Zero Mostel came to see him in the hospital after the heart attack, but we had to keep him away," Christopher Stone recalled. "The laughter might have killed him.") Under doctors' orders, he suspended publication of the *Weekly* for three months. The day after his attack he wired a reply to Blankfort, who had sent him a copy of his letter: LAY ON MACDUFF.[77]

That Izzy's blistering pace should have taken a toll on his health wasn't a surprise. His schedule of reporting, writing, editing, and speaking wore out his young assistants, only one of whom lasted more than a year. He tried farming out sections of the *Weekly* to other writers—Robert

Sherrill, for one, who was introduced to Izzy by George Rucker, a researcher who kept tabs on the far right. Fired from a reporting job in Washington for the *St. Petersburg Times*, Sherrill went to work for the *Weekly*. "I desperately needed money. I think I had $500 in the bank," Sherrill recalled. Izzy published two articles by Sherrill in the *Weekly*, one on how Southern congressmen hobbled the food stamp program and one on the Senate's reluctance in 1967 to censure Thomas Dodd of Connecticut, paying him $100 for each.[78] Stone also plugged Sherrill's "newly published acid and ribald portrait of Lyndon Johnson, *The Accidental President*." But exhaustion had not made Izzy more tolerant, and when Sherrill turned in an article suggesting "the possibility that LBJ was bonkers, Izzy said, 'Well, we're all a little mad,' and instead of just cutting that bit out, he rejected the whole piece. We were living from day to day, and I'd worked on this piece all week . . . He paid me nothing. I couldn't afford to work for him after that."[79]

Andrew Kopkind, who also wrote for the *Weekly* during 1967, fared a little better. A graduate of Cornell and the London School of Economics, Kopkind had spent three years in California as a correspondent for *Time*. A job at the *New Republic* brought him to Washington, where he wrote some of the first mainstream coverage of SNCC's campaign in Alabama. "After that I was talking to Arthur Waskow," said Kopkind, "and I said, 'Is anyone doing this kind of thing up North?' and he said, 'Funny you should ask. There's this group called Students for a Democratic Society.' Waskow said, 'You should go to Cleveland and talk to my friends.' So off I went. This was the spring of 1965, and I became really emotionally involved with this whole experience."[80]

"To be white and a radical in America this summer," Kopkind wrote in September 1967, "is to see horror and feel impotence. It is to watch the war grow and know no way to stop it, to understand the black rebellion and find no way to join it, to realize that the politics of a generation has failed and that the institutions of reform are bankrupt, and yet to have neither ideology, programs, nor the power to construct them."[81] Kopkind's angle of vision was very different from Stone's. A few years older than his sources and readers in SDS and SNCC, he was a participant as well as an observer, and his cool reportorial detachment, as well as his LSE-honed analyses of forces and institutions, was offset by an existential excitement and a willingness to go out on a New Left limb farther than any other journalist. Yet his sense of where things were heading was similar to Izzy's. Cold war liberalism had been discredited, in part by recent revelations of its collaboration with the CIA. (Kopkind's first piece for the *Weekly*, in May 1967, was a profile of Thomas Braden, the agency's culture warrior in the early 1950s, whose international operations division subsidized *Encounter* and the National Student Association and bankrolled goons to break Communist-led dock strikes in Italy and France, and who in 1966 ran as a liberal Democrat for lieutenant governor of California.[82]) Mostly, though, by Vietnam. It was Murray Kempton, not Andrew Kopkind, who called that war "the logical consequence of anti-Communist liberalism."[83]

Izzy was still convalescing when the National Conference for New Politics met in Chicago over the Labor Day weekend. The brainchild of Arthur Waskow, the conference was intended as a combination pep rally and party convention, "to give new politics a higher order of visibility, and perhaps even do something about Lyndon Johnson" (the phrase is from Kopkind's report on the proceedings in the *New York Review of Books*). Disorganized and at times fatally divisive, the conference revealed a paradoxical truth about the state of the American opposition. The hostility between Jews and blacks over a motion critical of Israel was to poison the left for months and years to come.* "This should be a summer of despair," Kopkind wrote, adding, "It is doubtful that the radicals could affect the balance of power in national politics even if they tried."

And yet the energy of the movement "has not only been conserved but generated," as Kopkind put it.[84] Coffee houses where soldiers were advised on how to get to Canada sprang up; housewives rang doorbells canvassing opposition to the war; Benjamin Spock joined Marcus Raskin in urging young men to refuse the draft; the streets of Newark and Detroit saw a new kind of militant, "half guerrilla, half ward heeler"; the *New York Review of Books* ran Tom Hayden's diagram of a Molotov cocktail on the cover. "We have arrived," announced Kopkind in the same issue, "at an infrequent fulcrum of history."[85]

I. F. Stone was not so sure. When the *Weekly* finally reappeared in November, Izzy devoted most of the issue to a long and, at first glance, bizarre reconsideration of the Russian Revolution. Describing the Soviet Union as

---

*Martin Peretz gave a furious exit speech that was later published as "The American Left and Israel" in the November 1967 issue of *Commentary*.

"a dictatorship in which neither worker nor peasant dare speak freely," he sought to explain how Russian communism became "a gigantic caricature of what socialism was meant to be." The problem facing Lenin and his successors had been "how to get more out of the peasant. The right opposition, led by Bukharin, suggested the carrot. He was impressed by American agriculture. He wanted to stimulate greater farm production by offering the peasant more consumer goods and expanding industry on the basis of a prosperous agriculture. The left opposition led by the Trotskyists suggested the stick. Stalin adopted the program of the left."[86]

Yet "The Mujik as the Negro of the Russian Revolution" reveals more than a preference for Bukharin over Trotsky. With Detroit in flames during the terrible riots that broke out there in late July, Stone, too, saw "the tanks of colonial war appear in *our* streets and the helicopters in *our* skies" and wondered if "the bill for racial humiliation has come due. In the ghettoes and the *barrios* the striking change is that where the people once feared the cops, the cops now fear the people."[87] Inside this history lesson was a warning: "Lenin and Trotsky, before they took power, sometimes spoke in terms very similar to that 'participatory democracy' which our own New Left cherishes." And a reminder: "Freedom," he wrote, quoting Rosa Luxemburg's criticism of the Bolsheviks, "is always and exclusively freedom for the one who thinks differently."[88] If the hinge of history really was open, Stone wanted his readers to make sure that this time it didn't swing shut on a prison cell.

Perhaps his brush with mortality encouraged him to take a longer view. While he was still in the hospital, Izzy received more than a thousand cards and letters; the well-wishers ranged from old friends like Norman Thomas and Owen Lattimore to old foes like Joseph Starobin and James Wechsler.[89] Illness hadn't made him soft. The second issue of the *Weekly* after his convalescence was an unsparing exposure of State Department evasions on negotiations. "All we ask of the Viet Cong," he wrote, "is their surrender." But his illness—or the changes in American society that had detonated all through that summer—did seem to have made him venerable.

Like its immediate predecessors *The Truman Era* and *The Haunted Fifties*, Stone's seventh book, which appeared in November 1967, was a collection of previously published articles, mostly from the *Weekly* plus a handful from the *New York Review of Books*. While the two earlier books had been studiously ignored by the mainstream press, *In a Time of Torment* drew admiring notices. Ronald Steel in the *Washington Post* celebrated Izzy's "eternal hostility to bunk." The *Times Literary Supplement* hailed "an American Diogenes." And in the *New York Review of Books*, the historian Henry Steele Commager saluted "a modern Tom Paine, celebrating Common Sense and the Rights of Man, hammering away at tyranny, injustice, exploitation, deception, and chicanery with an eloquence that appeals even to the sophisticated who are most suspicious of eloquence." And on Thanksgiving morning, eighteen years almost to the day since his last appearance on national television, a jovial I. F. Stone bantered with Hugh Downs, host of NBC's *Today* show. His rehabilitation was nearly complete.[90]

•

The war was everywhere. And though opposition to it had now spread well beyond college campuses to city streets, suburban living rooms, even corporate boardrooms, President Johnson shut out his critics. In October, 30,000 people surrounded the Pentagon; hundreds were arrested,* several were beaten. At midnight, after the clouds of tear gas had been dispersed by the wind, the remaining protesters sang "Silent Night." Business Executives Move for Vietnam Peace released a statement in January 1968 calling for a halt to the bombing of North Vietnam that was endorsed by the former commandant of the Marine Corps, four other retired generals, and a rear admiral. The battle for public opinion was being won, and still the war went on.

"Now is the time to resist." Written by Marcus Raskin and Arthur Waskow, "A Call to Resist Illegitimate Authority" spurred thousands of young men to tear up their draft cards. The document also marked a turn in the antiwar movement's tactics from protest to resistance. "Resistance, properly conducted," argued Noam Chomsky in the *New York Review of Books*, "can serve to increase the domestic cost of American aggression."[91]

---

*Including Dagmar Wilson of Women Strike for Peace; David Dellinger; and Noam Chomsky, whose article "The Responsibility of Intellectuals" had recently appeared in the *New York Review of Books*. Norman Mailer, whose participation in the march is the subject of his comic masterpiece *The Armies of the Night*, was not arrested.

As Chomsky acknowledged, resistance could also backfire, alienating the portion of the population that opposed the war on "pragmatic" rather than principled grounds, and it was precisely this danger that preoccupied I. F. Stone. "It should never be forgotten," he wrote in January 1968, "that the ultimate appeal is to public opinion . . . It is essential that we keep cool. The peace movement must not become a vicarious war movement."[92] Yet the sense of mounting frustration drove many to desperation. Even as the *Weekly* went to press, the federal government moved to put Raskin, Spock, the Yale chaplain William Sloane Coffin, and two others on trial for conspiring to "aid, abet and counsel" violations of the Selective Service Act.

The entry of the Minnesota senator Eugene McCarthy into the presidential campaign as an antiwar candidate on November 30 changed nothing. "We have to support McCarthy," Izzy advised his readers. "A poor showing in the primaries for McCarthy will be a poor showing for peace. But he's also got to support us. And himself." That was the rub. As Kopkind wrote a few weeks later, "McCarthy is a sympathetic, intelligent man. If politics were nothing more than a show of sensibility, McCarthy would be counted a success . . . But of the uses of power he knows little, and cares less." Izzy agreed: "McCarthy gives one the uneasy feeling that he doesn't give a damn."[93]

"The enemy has been defeated in battle after battle," President Johnson boasted in his State of the Union address on January 17. Yet only two weeks later, in the early hours of the Vietnamese lunar New Year, Tet, the North Vietnamese army and Viet Cong troops launched a coordinated offensive against cities and towns across South Vietnam, including all thirty-six provincial capitals. In Saigon, the U.S. embassy was the scene of a six-hour firefight that took the lives of seven Americans and nineteen Viet Cong and made headlines around the world. "What the hell is going on!" Walter Cronkite, anchor of the *CBS Evening News*, was heard to shout in the studio as the first reports came in. "I thought we were winning this war!"

In conventional military terms—and General William Westmoreland, head of the Military Assistance Command Vietnam, was an extremely conventional strategist—Tet ended in a victory for the United States. Within ten days, Westmoreland claimed 37,000 enemy dead. But Vietnam, as Stone had been saying for years, was not a conventional war. After three years of bombing North Vietnam and three years of "interdiction" on the so-called Ho Chi Minh Trail that carried supplies through Laos to the South, the enemy had massed 80,000 troops for this offensive; most were Viet Cong, but 5,000 uniformed North Vietnamese army troops seized the old imperial capital of Hué; in Lang Vei, the NVA used tanks for the first time in the war to overrun a U.S. Special Forces base.[94] "It is no longer necessary to argue the mendacity of our leaders and the incompetence of our military," said the *Weekly*. "Mr. Johnson has assured us that the successful surprise attack on 100 South Vietnamese cities and towns was really a Viet Cong defeat; if they suffer a few more such defeats, we'll be lucky to settle for a coalition government in Hawaii."[95]

Most observers outside the Pentagon regarded the Tet offensive in the same way. *Time* described the attack as "a *tour de force*: the spectacle of an enemy force dispersed and unseen, everywhere hunted unremittingly, suddenly materializing to strike simultaneously in a hundred places throughout the country."[96] Cronkite, who'd seen some of the fighting at firsthand, now sounded like Stone: "To say that we are closer to victory today is to believe, in the face of the evidence, the optimists who have been wrong in the past." Instead, the most trusted man in America, as he was called, told viewers on February 27, "We are mired in a stalemate." Negotiation, he added in a rare personal note, is "the only rational way out."

For Stone, the scale of the Tet assault was not the only revelation. The U.S. response to it illustrated "what the Pax Americana really means for the people we claim to be protecting." The village of Bentre "was shelled 'regardless of civilian casualties . . . to rout the Vietcong.' A U.S. Major explained, 'It became necessary to destroy the town to save it.' This will go down in the history books as typical of our whole Vietnamese campaign."[97]

Westmoreland asked President Johnson for another 206,000 troops. For a moment Izzy, too, wondered if the president's heedless pursuit of a lost cause might spark an outright revolt among those expected to die because America had nothing to negotiate. "We could be in the first stage of what Mao has envisaged—a world-wide colonial uprising against American power, accompanied by a complementary and similar rising of blacks in the racial colonies that our ghettoes have become . . . So long as the war goes on it must deepen racial bitterness at home and abroad."[98] Apocalypse was in the air. It was Richard Nixon, after all, who had observed—

to the National Association of Manufacturers!—that "even as American troops attempt to pacify hamlets in Vietnam, special Army teams are now touring scores of our cities, making contingency plans for their pacification next summer."[99] On March 10, the *New York Times* published a leaked report on Westmoreland's troop request. Two days later, in the New Hampshire primary, McCarthy stunned President Johnson by winning 40 percent of the vote and a majority of delegates. By the end of the week, Robert Kennedy entered the race.

"The Vietcong made politics possible again," wrote Andrew Kopkind. "McCarthy made it thinkable; Kennedy made it seem workable." In other words, the political system "will have been seen to work. It has produced alternatives, which is its function," releasing "a surge of energy in the society which is essential if anything good is to happen."[100]

Stone wrote:

> I share the bitterness of many young people toward Bobby Kennedy for hastily plunging in to steal the limelight and the prize from McCarthy as soon as it looked promising. But this bitterness should not lead one to lose sight of the political realities. Bobby may be arrogant and power-hungry; he may be surrounded by the same group of opportunist-intellectuals who surrounded his brother when he got us into the Vietnamese mess; but he alone has the money, the fame, the organization, and the drive for taking the nomination away from Johnson and giving us some hope of negotiating peace.[101]

Like Izzy, Kopkind remained deeply suspicious of Kennedy. Yet to his friends in SDS beginning to flirt with revolution and to those who shared his and Stone's dislike of Kennedy's opportunism, Kopkind offered some blunt advice: "For anyone looking for a political way out of the Vietnamese disaster, it is impossible to reject the Bobby phenomenon, even if it is equally impossible to enjoy it. Kennedy is real. The radical protests, the Senate doves and even the McCarthy campaign are not."[102] On March 22, President Johnson promoted Westmoreland out of Vietnam—an implicit rejection of further escalation. On March 31, he announced, "I shall not seek, and I will not accept, the nomination of my party." The United States and North Vietnam agreed to begin negotiations. The war would finally come to an end. The revolution, it seemed, had been postponed.

To celebrate his recovery, and his sixtieth birthday, in January 1968 Izzy invited 1,500 well-wishers (at $1 a head) to Town Hall in New York City. Conor Cruise O'Brien, the Irish journalist and politician, was master of ceremonies; Murray Kempton, Leo Huberman, Robert Silvers, the *Village Voice* columnist Nat Hentoff, and the *Ramparts* editor Sol Stern also spoke. E. Y. "Yip" Harburg, lyricist for "April in Paris," "It's Only a Paper Moon," and 600 other songs, offered a musical tribute to his friend that was sung to the tune of "The Battle Hymn of the Republic":

> *HUAC rails at him and cites him*
> *Alsop hates him and indicts him*
> *Reston reads him and rewrites him*
> *And the Stone goes rolling on.*

Many of those present recalled how they had felt the previous August, when the obituary desk of the *New York Times* had telephoned them to gather anecdotes about Izzy, whose departure had been deemed imminent. "In the past I've demonstrated how to run a newspaper on your own," quipped the guest of honor. "Tonight I've shown how to run your own funeral service."[103] Stone also had an announcement: He was cutting back again to biweekly publication, this time for good. Earlier in the year, he'd offered to take on Kopkind as coeditor and designated successor, but his young colleague preferred to remain freelance. "At that point our politics were pretty compatible," Kopkind remembered, "but Izzy understandably wanted it to remain *I. F. Stone's Weekly*, and I wanted to do my own thing."[104]

The problem was that while Izzy was slowing down, events were speeding up. He welcomed Alexander Dubček's efforts to decentralize the economy and liberate the press in Czechoslovakia—the so-called Prague Spring: "For the first time public opinion in a Communist State has been strong enough to oust the leadership." The Czech revolt "must set off seismic tremors in every other Communist capital." Yet this "is not a revolt against socialism—no demand is heard to restore capitalism; it is a revolt for that right to speak which is the first essential of any good society. It is the triumph of Jefferson over Lenin."[105] But events at home quickly turned celebration to ashes.

"Saigon Afire Now—Will It Be Washington in April?" he'd wondered after the Tet battles. The euphoria on hearing of Johnson's withdrawal lasted less than a week before Martin Luther King Jr. was assassinated. This time, Izzy feared, "The Fire Has Only Just Begun." In the face of another "of those massive outpourings of hypocrisy characteristic of the human race," Stone wanted his readers to know that "the President and the Washington establishment had been working desperately up until the very moment of Dr. King's killing to keep him and his Poor People's March out of the capital . . . The masses they sang were not so much of requiem as of thanksgiving, that the nation's No. 1 Agitator had been laid to rest at last."[106] Stone did not view the riots after King's murder as an urban revolt. Liquor stores were a frequent target, so he suggested that this "might sourly be termed the debut of Marxism-Liquorism in revolutionary annals." What he heard amid the flames and broken glass was "the agony of a lost race speaking. If we cannot respond with swift compassion, this is the beginning of our decline and fall."[107]

Compassion was in short supply. In Chicago, Mayor Richard Daley ordered his police to "shoot to kill" looters. In Oakland, the nineteen-year-old Black Panther Bobby Hutton was shot twelve times as he walked out of a hideaway with his hands in the air. Army machine guns protected the steps of the Capitol; the Cherry Blossom Festival was canceled. And though Johnson had said on March 31 that all bombing of North Vietnam above the 20th Parallel would come to an end, raids over the rest of the country actually increased. Meanwhile, Johnson allowed the South Vietnamese government to obstruct negotiations. "The old fox hasn't given up power," warned Stone. "He has regained it." Instead of ending the war, he was merely handing some of it over to the South Vietnamese—though "there wouldn't be a half million U.S. troops in South Vietnam if the Saigon ruling clique over the past decade hadn't demonstrated its utter political and military incapacity."[108]

In New York, students opposed to Columbia University's sponsorship of war-related research at the Institute for Defense Analyses started a sit-in that became an occupation of college buildings. After several days of increasingly tense standoffs, the Columbia administration called in the police on April 30, and they indiscriminately beat students, faculty members, and bystanders—the first time force had been used against white college students on such a scale.[109] That same week, Vice President Hu-

bert Humphrey entered the race for the presidency, proclaiming "the politics of joy."

If Columbia students were playing at revolution, the *Weekly* reported
that their French counterparts, whose revolt began in May, posed a more
serious threat. Students who led protests and demonstrations against the
government and the universities were joined by striking workers; in Paris,
more than a million people were involved in ever more vehement action.
"The events we have just witnessed," Georges Pompidou told the National Assembly, "are not just a flash fire. Our civilization is being questioned, not the government, not the institutions, not even France, but the
materialistic and soulless modern society."[110] Andrew Kopkind, on his
way to Hanoi with the writer Susan Sontag, stopped off in Paris and heard
a striker wearing "a buttoned-down shirt and Levis" proclaim, "The unique
and essential enemy is America." Yet as Kopkind recognized, "American
radicals are Americans," children of a country, in I. F. Stone's words,
whose "working class is willing to give up its chains but not its washing
machines."[111]

While it lasted, Robert Kennedy's campaign seemed to offer, if not a
resolution of such contradictions, a way around them. Besides the appeal
of a Kennedy restoration and the power of his father's money (the *Weekly*
described the rivalry with McCarthy as a "race between college idealists
and the Kennedy credit cards"), the Kennedy campaign attracted support
from those long marginalized by electoral politics: blacks, Mexican Americans, poor whites. It didn't last long. Given the level of violence in America, Robert Kennedy's murder on June 5, just a day after his victory in the
California primary, might have been a death foretold. "We live in a huge
human abattoir," Izzy wrote, "but our nostrils are so conditioned to the
stink we no longer notice it." Something more than an illusion died that
night in Los Angeles. Reporting on Kennedy's funeral at St. Patrick's
Cathedral in New York, Stone "could not help but notice the symbolism
in the appearance" of four Green Berets from the John F. Kennedy Special Warfare Center in the vigil. Unremarked by Izzy, Tom Hayden was
also there, with a Cuban fatigue cap in his lap, weeping. In Hayden's
thoughts one refrain kept repeating: "On to Chicago" and the Democratic
convention.[112]

The Republican convention in Miami was like a cartoon short before
the feature. Its story line, wrote Izzy, "was clearly a victory for the working

class. A poor boy grew up to defeat a Rockefeller for the Republican nomination." The nomination of Richard Nixon and Spiro Agnew "was a humbling affair altogether for Us Ethnics. It was hard to listen to Senator Barry Goldwater and realize that a man could be half Jewish and yet sometimes appear to be twice as dense as the normal Gentile . . . If the race that produced Isaiah is down to Goldwater and the race that produced Pericles is down to Agnew, the time has come to give the country back to the WASPs."[113]

The passion unfolding on the streets of Prague, however, soon cut short his laughter. "The Czechs stood alone in 1938 against German imperialism. Today they stand alone against Russian imperialism." As Soviet tanks smashed what Dubček had called "socialism with a human face," Izzy told Kalugin, the Soviet press attaché in Washington, that he never wanted to see him again. "The consequences [of the invasion] will be felt for a long time," he wrote; Communism would never shed its capital letter. "The hopes of democracy under communism have been destroyed; the youth of the bloc will now begin to turn more openly against Communism as inevitably linked with the one-party state."[114]

And just as the protesting Czechs were forced to accept the presence of Warsaw Pact troops in their country, and just as their leaders were arrested, came the Democratic Party convention in Chicago. In the weeks after Kennedy's assassination, Izzy urged support for the sole remaining antiwar candidate: "Only McCarthy offers a way to escape, a way to make democratic processes meaningful again, a way to preserve peace at home by moving swiftly toward it in Vietnam."[115] But Americans weren't listening. Neither was McCarthy, who'd already met with Humphrey and offered to drop out in exchange for the vice president's making a statement against the war. Though Humphrey refused, McCarthy's presence in the race remained purely symbolic, unlike the 12,000-strong Chicago police force, 6,000 army troops, and 5,000 members of the Illinois National Guard who confronted less than half that many demonstrators over the barbed wire surrounding the International Amphitheatre. During the ensuing "police riot," which is how the National Commission on the Causes and Prevention of Violence later described it, the demonstrators chanted, "The whole world is watching." But they didn't have a chance.

"Daley's big and beefy police seemed to crack the skulls of the TV and press reporters with a special gusto," Stone reported. Lest his own account appear too partial, Izzy quoted from Hearst's *Chicago American*, whose reporter saw police beat a handicapped man:

> Clergymen, medics and this cripple were the special pigeons last night. At State and Adams a nightstick cracked open the head of a clergyman who didn't move fast enough . . . It sickens me to write this because I am on the police's side, and I went out at 1 o'clock yesterday to write exactly what I saw and I was sure it would bring credit to the police . . . This is the way it is done in Prague. This is what happens to candidates who finish second in Vietnam. This is not the beginning of the police state, it IS the police state.[116]

Stained seemingly beyond redemption by the violence in Chicago, electoral politics had failed. "When a country is denied a choice on the most burning issue of the time, the war in Vietnam, then the two-party system has become a one-party rubber stamp . . . The Pentagon won the election even before the votes are cast," Stone wrote. For exposing this charade, he added, "The country owes a debt of gratitude to the tatter-demalion army of yippies, hippies and peaceniks—and to their leaders David Dellinger, Tom Hayden and Jerry Rubin—who frightened the Establishment into such elaborate security precautions in Chicago. They made opposition to the war visible."

On the eve of the convention, Stone had been willing to defend Humphrey even at the cost of offending Robert Sherrill."* Afterward, when the nominee "stepped out as Daley's apologist," Stone decided that "Humphrey is no lesser evil than Nixon. A vote for Humphrey is a vote for Johnson's war and Daley's police state tactics. I confess I do not know what to do politically." McCarthy's supporters wanted to take over the Democratic Party; Marcus Raskin thought only a new party could bring change; the New Left, chanting "the streets belong to the people," called for insurrection. "If law and order really break down," Stone worried, "it is we of the Left, the anti-war forces and the intellectuals who will be the first to suffer." The politics of joy had given way to the politics of despair.[117]

"Hubert is as tricky as Dicky," Stone warned.[118] As for Edmund

---

*Coauthor of *The Drugstore Liberal*, an unsympathetic biography of the candidate.

Muskie, the Democrats' vice presidential nominee was "a safe and bridle-broken liberal. Johnson put a saddle on him long ago."[119]

Still, Stone was cheered in early October by the "living theatre" of the federal trial of the Catonsville Nine, Catholic antiwar activists who in May had broken into a Maryland draft board with homemade napalm and burned papers and records. One of them, Father Daniel Berrigan, explained when they were convicted of destroying government property that they were "guilty of burning paper instead of children."

On Election Day, Izzy had lunch with Julius Hobson, former head of the Washington, D.C., chapter of CORE. Hobson, who was equally depressed by the ballot, had a suggestion. "They decided they were going to vote for each other," remembered Andrew Moursund, Stone's assistant at the time.[120]

●

It was Moursund, knowing his boss's disenchantment with national politics, who precipitated Izzy's involvement in one of the thorniest local disputes of the time. "We were talking about the teachers' strike in New York"—a bitter struggle between the mostly black parents of pupils in the public schools of Ocean Hill and Brownsville, Brooklyn, and the largely Jewish membership of the United Federation of Teachers over community control of the schools. "He was pretty pro-UFT [United Federation of Teachers], but I said why don't you go up and listen before you make up your mind." The result was a special issue of the *Weekly* that called on all of Stone's experience as a foreign correspondent—and challenged some of his own prejudices. The community forces were backed by his old nemesis McGeorge Bundy, who after leaving Washington had become head of the Ford Foundation, which was supporting an experimental school district in Ocean Hill that gave control to local families and local educators. When these black district leaders charged some teachers with racism and had them transferred, the UFT protested that the move was anti-Semitic and went out on strike. For Izzy, both Popular Front common sense—"we don't cross picket lines"—and *landsmanschaft* inclined him to side with the union. "I asked [one] Brooklyn schoolteacher just what was the issue in the strike," he reported. Her reply? "Anti-Semitism." For Norman Podhoretz and a generation of New York Jewish intellectuals, Ocean Hill–Brownsville was the first turn on the road to neoconservatism. Not I. F. Stone. After interviewing parents, teachers,* students, and administrators, he decided that the union's rallying cry, with its demand for "due process," was "a monumental bit of hypocrisy." Parental anger was justified; the union *had* colluded with the city's Board of Education to "sabotage" desegregation. Pointing out that three-quarters of the nonstriking teachers were white—and that half of these were Jewish—he concluded, "If this great city is to be saved from race war, more Jewish intellectuals are going to have to speak up in ways that their own people will resent, just as white southerners resented those who spoke up for the Negro. The Teachers Union is exaggerating, amplifying and circulating any bit of anti-Semitic drivel it can pick up from any far-out black extremist, however unrepresentative, and using this to drive the Jewish community of New York into a panic."[121]

Returning to Washington in the new year, Stone was just as hard on another kind of special pleading. "I can still remember my own desperate feelings in Paris, on my way to Palestine on the eve of the 1948 war, when the airlines stopped flying into Lydda," he wrote. On December 29, Israel retaliated against a new Arab guerrilla tactic of airplane hijacking by bombing Beirut airport, and while both the hijackings and the reprisal seemed deplorable to Stone, what really bothered him was the reluctance of Israel and American Jewry

> to look some unpleasant truths squarely in the face . . . One is to recognize that the Arab guerrillas are doing to us what our terrorists and saboteurs of the Irgun, Stern and Haganah did to the British. Another is to be willing to admit that their motives are as honorable as were ours. As a Jew, even as I felt revulsion against the terrorists, I felt it justified by the homelessness of the surviving Jews from the Nazi camps, and the bitter scenes when refugee ships sank, or sank themselves, when refused admission to Palestine. The best of Arab

---

*Stone described a classroom where "Leslie Campbell in an African gown over his normal clothes teaches Afro-American studies" amid posters "showing 'Our Homeland' and 'Our Proud and Glorious Past.' They reminded me of Zionist posters in many Jewish Sabbath schools . . . Campbell after class was friendly and open." Shortly after Stone's visit, Campbell, in a discussion on radio station WBAI about the hatreds stirred up by the strike, read a poem by one of his students that included the lines, "Hey, Jew boy, with that yarmulke on your head / You pale-faced Jew boy, I wish you were dead." Though he'd indicated that the poem did not reflect his own views, the incident continued to haunt Campbell, who later changed his name to Jitu Weusi, for decades afterward.

youth feels the same way; they cannot forget the atrocities committed by us against villages like Deir Yassin, nor the uprooting of the Palestinian Arabs from their ancient homeland.[122]

Not even the advent of Richard Nixon's presidency dimmed the pleasure Stone took from his own return to work and health. "I'm having a wonderful time," he wrote the Durrs in Alabama, "and as long as I can go on with my pea shooter I'm happy." Indeed, the new administration was proving to be a target-rich environment: The *New York Review of Books* began a lengthy series by Izzy on Nixon and defense spending even before the president was sworn in. Izzy's association with Silvers, he told his friends, "has given me a wider audience and recognition. It's the best review in the English language and I'm the only Washington reporter who has been able to meet his standards," he boasted.[123] The *New York Times* ratified his newfound prominence with an admiring, if mildly patronizing profile, placing him in the "the honorable tradition of the uncommon scold."[124]

Yet he felt increasingly out of joint with the times. "If the CIA had set out to produce a savage burlesque of the peace movement, it could not have done better than the counter-inaugural staged by the National Mobilization Committee," he complained in January. Speakers from the "Women's Liberation Army" had sounded "as if they had been invented by Art Buchwald with an assist from Aristophanes."[125] The Summer of Love was long gone; this was the era of Abbie Hoffman and *Revolution for the Hell of It*, of People's Park and People's War, Black Panthers, the clenched fist, and the radical politics of Weatherman. Mark Rudd, who led the Columbia SDS chapter that became the nucleus of Weatherman, argues that those young people who turned to armed revolution did so not out of frustration—the antiwar movement was huge and growing; SDS itself claimed 100,000 members in 1968—but out of "wild optimism over the possibilities." Yet Rudd also looks back at a generation crazed by grief: "And the natural response to grief is rage and violence. Bring the war home!"[126]

Bliss was it in that dawn to be alive, But to be young was very heaven! I. F. Stone was thirty years over thirty. His friend Andrew Kopkind, at thirty-three still close enough to the zeitgeist to smell and taste it, started his own mimeograph version of the *Weekly* for the newly militant New Left. He called it *Mayday*. But Izzy himself was an inspirational figure and an avuncular presence at Liberation News Service, which aimed at being the AP of the movement. Stone's own children were themselves all over thirty: his daughter, Celia Gilbert, had become a poet; Chris, his youngest, was a law professor; Jeremy, who had long ago abandoned the Hudson Institute, was now a disarmament expert of sufficient renown—and skepticism about the Pentagon's new antiballistic missile system—to be cited as an authority in the *Weekly*.[127] The "generation gap" was more apparent in Izzy's relationship with his niece. As a girl, Kathy Boudin had idolized her uncle. "One year when I was very young I wanted to give him a present. So I cut out the little photographs of Izzy that appeared above his column in *Compass* until I had enough to cover the back of a legal pad, and then I gave that to him." Kathy had also once proposed dropping out of Bryn Mawr to do a "great books" reading program supervised by her uncle. But by the time she ran into Izzy in Chicago, shortly before she was arrested at the Democratic convention, Kathy had already graduated from Bryn Mawr, and was spending more time with her friends in SDS. When she and Izzy did meet, "it was clear there was a generational divide," she said. Her own father threw himself into defending Dr. Benjamin Spock and other antidraft defendants, but to Kathy anyone who relied on "legal rights" was guilty of ignoring "entirely the fundamental reality of a class society."[128]

Still, when Izzy, writing "In Defense of the Campus Rebels" in May 1969, protested that his "credentials as an expert are slim," he was being disingenuous. He knew very well what motivated young radicals: "Our own country is becoming a Vietnam." He might not approve of their tactics. "I do not like to hear opponents shouted down, much less beaten up. I do not like to hear any one group or class, including policemen, called pigs. I do not think four letter words are arguments." He did not agree with their analysis. Above all, he distrusted their wild optimism. "Lifelong dissent has more than acclimated me cheerfully to defeat. It has made me suspicious of victory. I feel uneasy at the very idea of a Movement. I see every insight degenerating into a dogma, and fresh thoughts freezing into lifeless party lines. Those who set out nobly to be their brother's keeper sometimes end up by becoming his jailer. Every emancipation has in it the seeds of a new slavery, and every truth easily becomes a lie." But he would not disown them. "I feel about the rebels as Erasmus did about Luther . . . While Erasmus could not join Luther, he dared not oppose him, lest haply, as he confessed, 'he might be fighting against the spirit of God.' I feel that the New Left and the black revolutionists, like Luther, are doing God's work, too, in refusing any longer to submit to evil, and challenging society to reform or crush them."[129]

After fifteen years of rowing his solitary craft against the current of history, Stone now found himself and his *Weekly* swept along into the mainstream. An August appearance on the *Dick Cavett Show*, ABC's countercultural challenger to the *Tonight Show*, brought him 4,500 new subscribers.[130] Sales of his books took off. "I used to take forty or fifty of those every goddamn day to the Post Office," said Moursund, who estimated Stone was easily clearing $100,000 a year. (His own weekly wage remained a less than princely $125.) The *Weekly* had long been a financial success. In the late 1950s, when Christopher Stone gave his father the forms to apply for a scholarship to Harvard, Izzy had shouted, "I have money! We don't need charity!" Until now, though, independence had been his only extravagance. Never an expert driver, Izzy traded in his battered 1963 Plymouth Valiant for a new 1969 Mustang. Also in 1969, he and Esther moved to a much larger house, a comfortable two-story colonial at 4429 29th Street, NW, that sat on a half-acre lot off a cul-de-sac nestled amid the trees of Soapstone Valley Park. It had space for a proper office for the *Weekly* and a separate study for Izzy. There was even a room on the ground floor where he could store multiple copies of his own books and have shelves enough for most of his library. The walls showed framed subscription checks from Einstein and Russell, which were soon joined by a host of honorary degrees.[131]

"Are We in the Middle of a Revolution?" wondered the *New York Times Magazine*. For answers, the paper turned to Andrew Kopkind, who on balance thought not. "The art of holding on to power is the American system's special grace," Kopkind wrote; his newsletter, in recognition of lengthening odds, had just changed its name to *Hard Times*.[132] The *Weekly*, too, reflected a grimmer view. "We believe there was a conspiracy to kill Dr. King," wrote Izzy, staunch defender of the Warren Report, after James Earl Ray pleaded guilty and the FBI insisted he had acted alone. J. Edgar Hoover, "who hated and once insulted King, should be challenged." The antiwar movement, too, needed to raise the stakes. "It is not enough to just get out of Vietnam. It is imperialism and militarism which must be recognized as our enemies." Imperialism, Izzy acknowledged, "is an impolitic word. It is only other countries which are imperialist. One's own is always engaged in some noble crusade . . . That is why we have to talk of militarism and imperialism and not just of Vietnam."[133]

The culture itself seemed to be coming apart at the seams. In July, a man walked on the moon. In August, while Izzy held forth on Cavett, Kopkind swam nude at Woodstock—"a model of how good we will all feel after the revolution."[134]

Only there wasn't going to be a revolution. Kopkind knew it, which didn't keep him from getting busted in Chicago during the Days of Rage, a confrontation staged by Weatherman to protest the trial of eight radicals charged with conspiracy and incitement to riot at the Democratic convention the year before.* There might not even be an end to the war. "The best argument for marching on Washington again—and again—is that nothing really is going on here," Izzy wrote at the beginning of November. "Unless the peace movement keeps the heat on, the Vietnamese war will drag on endlessly."[135] Yet the peace movement itself was now split. Veterans of the McCarthy campaign, the *Weekly* reported, "with 17 telephones and 11 outside lines, . . . plotted a campus Moratorium against the war" (it was held on October 15). One flight up in the same building on Vermont Avenue, "the more politically unkempt but equally vigorous New Mobilization Committee to End the War in Vietnam" called for a "March Against Death" on November 15.

Izzy watched the feuding with anguish. "*We support the Moratorium, and we support the Mobilization,*" he wrote, putting the message in italic type for emphasis. "*One is moderate, the other radical. Both are needed.*"[136] He dutifully attended both. "To march with the thousands in the candle-light procession that night," wrote the old Popular Fronter after the October 15 moratorium, "was a religious experience." Izzy was equally delighted by the mobilization, which, "despite the incendiary forecasts . . . proved as pacific as the Moratorium. The March of Death [*sic*] was a masterpiece of dramaturgy. Thanks to an army of marshals, and logistic preparations few armies could match, Saturday's parade went off without incident, the greatest outpouring of its kind in U.S. history."[137] Between 500,000 and 750,000 protesters came to Washington. Richard Nixon, the White House announced, spent the afternoon watching the Redskins game on television.

Buffeted by anger and fear, Stone held fast to the view that the movement's task was education, not provocation: "The country has grown sick

---

*The Chicago Eight defendants were: Rennie Davis, David Dellinger, John Froines, Tom Hayden, Abbie Hoffman, Jerry Rubin, Bobby Seale, and Lee Weiner. After Seale, a cofounder of the Black Panthers, was ordered bound and gagged by Judge Julius Hoffman, his case was severed from the other defendants and the trial became known as the Chicago Seven.

of violence, and of Vietnam as a form of violence." He was appalled when David Hilliard, the Black Panther chief of staff, threatened "to kill" President Nixon. "Such rhetoric is suicidal for a minority. It has no place in the peace movement. It invites the repression of which it complains."[138] Was anyone listening?

At the end of January 1970, Nixon made it clear that the "Vietnamization" of combat in Indochina did not mean peace—or even withdrawal. The Paris newspaper *Le Figaro* quoted Ambassador Ellsworth Bunker saying the only thing that would change was "the color of the corpses." In February, a coroner's jury in Chicago ruled that the police who had murdered the Black Panther Fred Hampton in his bed had acted reasonably. Later that month, Julius Hoffman, the judge in the Chicago conspiracy trial, imposed a four-year sentence for contempt of court on the defense lawyer William Kunstler (the charges were later reversed). In March, Ralph Featherstone, a SNCC activist who had waited in vain for Schwerner, Chaney, and Goodman to turn up in Neshoba, Mississippi, that day in the summer of 1964, was himself blown up by a car bomb in Bel Air, Maryland.

Though Featherstone's death made the front page of the *New York Times*, it barely dented the national consciousness, which was still reeling from a blast in New York City a few days earlier. Initially believed to be the result of a gas leak, the explosion in Greenwich Village was loud enough to have been heard ten blocks away at the Boudin's town house on St. Luke's Place.* As it happened, Jean Boudin was out that morning, shopping for underwear for her daughter. She ran into Ted Gold, a friend of Kathy's, a veteran of the Columbia strike and a leader of Weatherman. If their brief chat had lasted longer, Gold might be alive today. Instead, he went to 18 West 11th Street, where one of his comrades, assembling a bomb in the basement, crossed a wire just as Gold came in on the parlor floor. Jean first heard, then felt, an enormous explosion. If she had lingered a few more moments on Fifth Avenue, she might have recognized one of the two young women who emerged from the burning rubble, naked and bleeding, as her own daughter.[139]

It took the police nearly a week to name Kathy Boudin as the "unidentified young woman" seen fleeing the explosion. Ten days passed before the body of a third victim, Diana Oughton, was found in the wreckage.

---

*The exterior of the Boudins' house is known to millions of Americans as the home of Dr. Cliff Huxtable, Bill Cosby's television alterego.

But Jean knew of her daughter's narrow escape almost immediately. Shortly after the blast, Kathy and Cathlyn Wilkerson, whose father owned the house on 11th Street, had rung the Boudins' doorbell. Leonard was in Harrisburg, meeting with his clients Daniel and Philip Berrigan and the rest of the Catonsville Nine. Jean's brother-in-law Izzy was in Washington, having lunch with Leslie Gelb, a fellow at the Brookings Institution and former head of policy planning at the Pentagon, where he'd helped to assemble a top secret history of relations between the United States and Vietnam.* In the dining room at St. Luke's Place, Kathy told Jean she'd left her house keys somewhere in the burning building. For the Boudin family and the Stones, who were extremely fond of their niece, the war had come home with a vengeance.

•

It would be an overstatement to say that the town house explosion was the end of *I. F. Stone's Weekly*. The publication kept going for another eighteen months, and Izzy himself never stopped writing. But something had broken—for him and for a lot of others. He wrote in the *Weekly*:

> The Weatherman kids can be seen in various ways, and it is necessary to see them in as many as possible. The Weatherman faction of SDS, whence several different "direct action" splinter groups seem to derive, can be looked at like a distraught child. They can be viewed as spoiled brats, in a tantrum with a world which will not change overnight to suit them. But they are also the most sensitive of a generation which feels in its bones what we older people only grasp as an unreal abstraction, that the world is headed for nuclear annihilation and something must be done to stop it. The Weatherman manifesto from which they take their name is from one point of view a mishmash of ill-digested pseudo-Marxist rubbish, [which] spurns every normal base of revolutionary support and ends up squarely in the clouds . . . It sounded like the Children's Crusade come back to life, a St. Vitus dance of hysterical politics.

---

*Gelb's project, *United States–Vietnam Relations, 1945–1967: A Study Prepared by the Department of Defense*, was leaked by one of its contributors, Daniel Ellsberg, to the *New York Times* in 1971, when it became known as the Pentagon Papers.

Yet he also insisted, "Some of our young revolutionaries are chillingly sober and disconcertingly sensible. Their criticism of conventional dissenters like myself and our futility, as the war goes on, is hard to rebut." Their contempt for "'bourgeois pigs,' i.e. people exactly like their fathers and mothers," suggested to Stone that "the ultimate menace they fear is their own secret selves in their own parents. This is what they are acting out on the stage of national politics. But these psychological aspects are only a part of the whole complex picture. These wild and wonderful—yes, wonderful!—kids also serve quite rational political ends."[140] His niece's name never appeared in the *Weekly*.

Stone remained committed to the view he had held since the 1930s, that without pressure from less "responsible" quarters, liberals would never get a hearing. But evidence of the establishment's willingness to listen even to liberals was very thin on the ground. In her column in the *Catholic Worker*, Dorothy Day cited Izzy's remarks on the bombing with approval. "We cannot judge the young," wrote Day. "But we are challenged to answer."[141] Students still flocked to Izzy. A speech at Temple University in April had to be moved to a larger auditorium to handle the crowd. At Penn, the Philomathean Society (which had blackballed him in 1927) sponsored his appearance on campus. Seniors at Amherst voted him their commencement speaker, an invitation that prompted David Eisenhower, the president's son-in-law and a member of the class of 1970, to announce that he would skip his own graduation.

On April 30, President Nixon gave the country a lesson in geography and in his own version of political psychology. In order to safeguard "the lives of Americans remaining in Vietnam after our next withdrawal," he was ordering an "incursion," which was *not* an invasion, he claimed, of Cambodia, "a small country of seven million people," which he pointed out on a large map for the television audience. Draft-eligible students took any widening of the war personally, and campuses across the country erupted in protest. At Kent State University on May 4, Ohio National Guardsmen shot thirteen people, killing four unarmed students; ten days later, police shot and killed two students during protests at Jackson State College in Mississippi. Stone urged the students not to retreat. "The race is on between protest and disaster," he wrote. "The only hope is that the students can create such a Plague for Peace, swarming like locusts into the halls of Congress, that they stop all other business and make an end to the war the No. 1 concern it ought to be. Washington must no longer be the privileged sanctuary of the warmakers."[142]

Izzy wasn't the only one whose rhetoric was overheating. At a $500-a-plate Republican fund-raising dinner in Houston a few weeks after the murders at Kent State, Vice President Agnew denounced student protesters, who he claimed were led astray by "an effete core of impudent snobs who characterize themselves as intellectuals." Singled out for special mention were *Life*, the *New York Times*, the *Washington Post*, the *New Republic*, the *Arkansas Gazette*—and *I. F. Stone's Weekly*, "another strident voice of illiberalism."

At Amherst, where the sixty-two-year-old college dropout was made an honorary Doctor of Humane Letters, Stone told the students not to "do what we claim Spiro Agnew is doing and polarize the country." The United States was, he said, still "a free country." As if to illustrate his thesis, in July the *Wall Street Journal* printed on the front page an admiring profile by A. Kent MacDougall of "I. F. Stone, tireless pamphleteer and senior leftist." *Who's Who in America*, which had dropped Izzy during the McCarthy era, had recently reinstated him, the *Journal* reported, while "a Canadian filmmaker is producing a documentary on him." Success and respectability wouldn't spoil I. F. Stone, promised the *Journal*; "the maverick muckraker continues to rake muck."[143]

MacDougall's valedictory tone proved more accurate than his predictions. In October, Stone flew to Ohio, telling a rally in memory of the slain Kent State students that the twenty-five protesters arrested there on riot charges were "the heroes of tomorrow." Indeed, his trip to Kent inspired one final feat of muckraking: two special issues of the *Weekly* and an article in the *New York Review of Books* on "How Murder Went Unpunished." Izzy's prose was a blistering indictment of official indifference and as pungent as ever. He quoted a KSU faculty member describing his students as "the insurance salesmen of tomorrow," adding, "This is a campus where you meet activists who never heard of *The Nation* or read *The New Republic* and students who think themselves avant garde because they read *Time* and *Newsweek*." The President's Commission on Campus Unrest, Stone wrote, had "honestly and thoroughly shown that the killings were unjustified and unnecessary. The established order mustered its best and they fulfilled their moral and political obligation. *And yet there is not the slightest chance that anything will be done about it.*"[144]

The emphasis was his. "As a young newspaperman during the world depression I never felt the despair I am beginning to feel now about the future of our country," he wrote after a bombing in August of the Army Mathematics building at the University of Wisconsin in Madison killed a young man. The Penn undergraduate so inflamed by the murder of Sacco and Vanzetti had become a radical celebrity: On the *Dick Cavett Show*, Izzy held up a leaked FBI report showing that the Ohio National Guard had lied to the grand jury investigating the killings at Kent State. Yet even the personal vindication he felt after the publication of the Pentagon Papers in June 1971 was small consolation for his growing conviction that as a result of official mendacity on a monumental scale, the United States was now reaping the whirlwind.

"It begins to look as if it may be easy to break down the fabric of American society," he wrote. "To rebuild it will be very hard. Anarchy and barbarity, race war and gang rule, not utopia, lie at the end of the road on which our instant revolutionaries would put us." He was profoundly out of sympathy with the campus bombers—"There is no moral arithmetic to cancel out the crime of murder"—but also desperately uncomfortable preaching "to youth the sanctity of human life . . . How often have we heard it said here in Washington, in cold-blooded defense of bombing North Vietnam, that 'hurting them' would force them to make peace? Now our country is hurting."[145]

Stone, too, was hurting. He was losing his faith, as he never had in the 1930s, in the country's ability to redeem its promise. He struggled against succumbing to hysteria. When the Berrigans' attorney, William Kunstler, invoked the Reichstag fire in their defense in January 1971, Izzy reminded him, "Nixon is not Hitler; the Republicans are not Nazis; the Capitol has not been set afire." Likewise, though the activist and philosopher Angela Davis, on trial for murder following her abortive attempt to help free imprisoned Black Panthers, impressed Stone as "a brilliant young woman driven to revolutionary views and associations by the suffering of her people," he also insisted that "the seizure and killing of a Judge—and the supply of arms with which to do it—are not acts for which any society, regardless of *isms*, hands out medals."[146] But a sense of proportion was a poor substitute for hope.

His own reputation was at an all-time high. In February 1971, his final collection of essays, *Polemics and Prophecies*, was published to unanimously admiring notices. *Time* ran a two-column photo of "the old New Lefty" at work in his pajamas. The lead review in the *New York Times Book Review* called Izzy "a living lesson in the potential of the journalist as outsider." Written by Elizabeth Drew, Washington editor of the *Atlantic Monthly*, the article was essentially a two-page valentine (the issue was dated February 14) to "one of the finest fog-cutters in Washington."[147] The following month he received the prestigious George Polk Award—his first recognition from mainstream journalism since *Underground to Palestine* won a Newspaper Guild Front Page Award in 1947. (Among the other Polk honorees were Walter Cronkite, who collected an award on behalf of the *CBS Evening News*, and Charles Peters, a former Peace Corps official, for his new magazine the *Washington Monthly*.)

"I'm happy to receive my first establishment award," said Izzy, typically using his acceptance speech to object to an earlier speaker's "antiseptic reference" to Polk, "who seems to be forgotten at these affairs. I knew George very well, met him in Cairo on a number of trips after the war. He was a wonderful young man. And he was the first journalistic victim of the Cold War." The whole exchange was captured on film by Gerald Bruck Jr., the young Canadian filmmaker who helped assemble *Polemics and Prophecies* and whose documentary about the *Weekly* was rapidly turning into a eulogy.

Because by the time Bruck's film *I. F. Stone's Weekly* made its triumphant debut, the eponymous newsletter was no more. "I'd like to stick to sixty-five," Stone told an interviewer. "In December 1972 [the *Weekly*] will be twenty years old and I'll be sixty-five."[148] He didn't make it. Returning home from a cruise with Esther aboard the *Raffaello* in the summer of 1971, he'd been reading the book of Isaiah, his favorite prophet. "Zion shall be redeemed by judgment." For his beloved Israel, such redemption seemed farther off than ever: "While the Palestinian Arabs are beginning in their homelessness to talk like Jews in a new Diaspora, the Israeli leadership is beginning to sound more and more like unfeeling *goyim*. This reversal of roles is the cruelest prank God ever played on His Chosen People." The show trial in Cuba of the poet Heberto Padilla for "subversive writing" demonstrated how Castro's "vanity and megalomania have become enemies of a besieged revolution." Meanwhile, Stone's own country was beginning to inspire something close to disgust. The American dream, he wrote, "is becoming a nightmare of rotting cities, growing race revolt and a decline of the once almighty dollar as we continue to squander on our overgrown military establishment abroad the billions we need for re-construction at home."[149]

"My father capitalized anger," said Christopher Stone. "He drew it down. It was an animating resource." Izzy's pleasure in graduating from "a pariah to a character," as he told *Time*, did nothing to diminish his capacity for indignation. In April, the audience of the *Today* show witnessed a shouting match between Izzy and James Michener after the novelist tried to defend what Izzy thought was a whitewash of the murders at Kent State in *Reader's Digest*. Yet Stone's call for a senator, any senator, to block Nixon's nomination of Michener and the *Digest* editor Hobart Lewis to the board of the United States Information Agency went unheeded. He collected another honorary doctorate from Brown and a lifetime achievement award from the Columbia School of Journalism (Walter Lippmann had been the previous year's winner). But he had no answer to a twenty-seven-year-old navy veteran* who asked the Senate Foreign Relations Committee: "How do you ask a man to be the last man to die in Vietnam? How do you ask a man to be the last man to die for a mistake?"[150]

With peace "still a long, long march away," I. F. Stone decided he'd had enough. Feeling less like the young Wordsworth and more like a Herzen who'd seen the revolution curdle into Thermidor, he set about looking for a successor. Andrew Kopkind physically ejected Jerry Bruck from a Chinese restaurant after the filmmaker tried to capture his and Izzy's negotiations. "Andy thought it would mean more names [for *Hard Times*] and more money," recalled Robert Silvers, "and Izzy thought it would mean *I. F. Stone's Weekly* would go on but someone else would do all the worrying. In the end it didn't happen." Shortly after the town house explosion, Kopkind left his suits, ties, and Brooks Brothers shirts in a cardboard box on a D.C. street corner, got on his Honda 450, and joined a commune in Vermont.[151]

A "terrible illness" in October 1971 put Stone out of action for a month and convinced him to stop looking for an heir. Charles Peters thought he had a deal with Izzy—not to take over the *Weekly* but to buy his subscription list for the *Washington Monthly*. Instead, it was the *New York Review of Books* that acquired the *Weekly*'s 68,700 subscribers. The publisher, A. Whitney Ellsworth, negotiated the $58,392 purchase of all

*His name was John Kerry. "His testimony," Stone reported, "was the most moving and eloquent we have heard in 30 years as a Washington correspondent. He spoke with a firmness, a tact and a grace that made the Senators seem elderly fumblers."

the outstanding assets and liabilities of I. F. Stone's Weekly, Inc., and though Ellsworth later grumbled that "there were only about 38,000 valid subscribers" (the rest were expired subscriptions that Esther and Izzy kept on the list in hopes they'd eventually renew), Silvers was more than satisfied. The *Review*'s newest contributing editor was soon at work on a mammoth report on Soviet psychiatry.[152]

On December 6, Izzy sent a letter to subscribers announcing that the next issue of the *Weekly* would be his last. Thanking readers for their support and "affection," he explained that with his sixty-fourth birthday coming up, "the compulsion to cover the universe in four pages has become too heavy a burden." Though in recent issues he had depicted the United States as on "the fastest track to a repressive era," the "Notes on Closing, But Not in Farewell" in the December *Weekly* cast only an oblique glance at current events. A handful of boxes reprised warnings against Truman's cold war diplomacy, Izzy's farewell to Albert Einstein, his recent defense of campus rebels, and "My Article on the Six-Day War Which Has Been So Unfairly Distorted." For the most part, though, the temptation to re-fight old battles was resisted. Instead, Izzy offered an "autobiographical fragment," but that, too, was more an account of the *Weekly* than of its editor: "I wanted the paper to have readability, humor and grace. I dreamed of taking the flotsam of the week's news and making it sing. I had a vision of a paper which would be urbane, erudite and witty." The only truly personal notes were at the end: "I think every man is his own Pygmalion, and spends his life fashioning himself. And in fashioning himself, for good or ill, he fashions the human race." And on the front page, above the masthead, ran a dedication "in gratitude to my wife, Esther. Her collaboration, her unfailing understanding, and her sheer genius as a wife and mother, have made the years together joyous and fruitful." Ever the romantic, he repeated the tag from Tibullus he had used thirty-four years earlier in dedicating his first book to Esther: *Tu mihi curarum requies, tu nocte vel atra lumen, et in solis tu mihi turba locis* (You are the solace of my cares, light in the blackest night, and company in lonely places).

After nineteen years and more than 3.5 million words, the longest essay in single-handed journalism in American history was over. I. F. Stone's pilgrimage from outcast to institution was complete. The *New York Times*, reporting on the *Weekly*'s closing, described Izzy as "a prosperous free-enterpriser, 'a solid bourgeois' as he put it."[153] And though his farewell was in Latin, the remainder of his life would be lived, at least in part, in Greek.

Eleven

HELLENISTIC PERIOD

———◆◆◆———

This is really a fragment of what was meant to be a larger, a much larger
work.   —I. F. Stone, *The Trial of Socrates*

I. F. Stone's retreat into the cloistered precincts of classical scholarship
was as unorthodox as anything he'd ever done. For one thing, it began at
the Cannes Film Festival.

The year of Izzy and Esther's attendance, 1974, saw a particularly rich
group of films at Cannes. The Grand Prix was awarded to *The Conversa-
tion*, Francis Ford Coppola's prophetic evocation of the surveillance state;
Pasolini's *A Thousand and One Nights* won the Special Jury Prize. Jack
Nicholson stopped by to pick up his best actor award for *The Last Detail*,
though he had to compete for press attention with Linda Lovelace, star of
Deep Throat, whose presence at the festival offered an unlikely foil for
Susan Sontag, in Cannes to promote *Promised Lands*, her film about the
Arab-Israeli conflict. Robert Altman's *Thieves Like Us* was entered in the
competition, as were films by Luis Buñuel, Alain Resnais, and an obscure
young director named Steven Spielberg, just making the transition from
television to film with *Sugarland Express*. Prince Rainier of Monaco and
Princess Grace threw a big party for Elizabeth Taylor; Tony Curtis and
Jack Valenti posed for photographers. Federico Fellini's *Amarcord* was
shown outside the competition.

Yet *"la grande vedette du festival,"* according to the Paris daily *L'Aurore*,
was a sixty-seven-year-old American retiree. Or, as translated by Vincent

Canby, the *New York Times*'s film critic, "the great star of the 1974 festival is I. F. Stone."[1] Everywhere he and Esther went, from the shops along the rue d'Antibes to the lobby of the Carlton Hotel, they were the center of attention. Strolling down the Croisette, Izzy ran into Peter Davis, whose documentary about America's involvement in Vietnam, *Hearts and Minds*, premiered at Cannes that year. Both men felt a little incongruous amid the festival glamour, but Stone confided he was also really enjoying "being a Kosher ham."[2]

Though *I. F. Stone's Weekly* was also screened outside the festival competition, the Cannes audience's response to its eponymous hero turned the film into a worldwide phenomenon, with triumphant runs from Berlin to Tokyo. Ruled ineligible for an Oscar nomination because Bruck's shoestring budget covered only 16-mm prints* (instead of the more expensive 35-mm format then required under academy rules), the film's American debut the previous fall had already given Stone an extra round of public adulation. An "inspiration," said the *New York Post*; "funny, affectionate, absolutely riveting," agreed the *Washington Post*; "a lively, witty entertainment" was the verdict of the *Los Angeles Times* critic Charles Champlin. But such effusion paled beside Canby in the *Times*, who called *I. F. Stone's Weekly* "a thorough delight [that] left me feeling the way other people said they felt after seeing *The Sound of Music*. That is, quite high."[3]

The film opens with a military band playing "Hail to the Chief" as Izzy begins to speak over the music: "Now in the job of covering a capital, there's really certain basic assumptions you have to operate on. The first is that every government is run by liars, and nothing they say should be believed." Bruck shows Stone talking to students, putting the last issue of the *Weekly* to bed, and bidding a tearful good-bye to his printers.

The twenty-six-year-old director, a former history major and reporter for the *Yale Daily News*, never completed another film. But in editing his dozens of hours of interviews and archive material down to just sixty-two minutes, Bruck managed to capture many of his subject's essential qualities. A news clip showing a credulous Walter Cronkite describing Nguyen Cao Ky in July 1965 as "a hero to the Vietnamese people" who "doesn't

---

I. F. Stone's Weekly, surely a suitable candidate for release on DVD, is still available only on 16-mm film, though there are rumored to be a few pirate VHS copies in existence.

even go out to lunch but, like an American businessman, eats off the corner of his desk" is intercut with a quotation from a *Weekly* issue of the
time in which "the playboy Air Force general" says he has "only one" hero:
Adolf Hitler. We then see Cronkite putting on a flak jacket and riding
along on a bombing run, followed by Izzy telling a student audience,
"Isn't it wonderful that human beings can resist all that murderous tech-
nology of ours"; the sequence ends, mischievously, with both men collecting their Polk Awards. Stone's praise for CBS's coverage of the war clearly
makes the anchorman uncomfortable—an elegant reminder of Izzy's talent for disturbing the peace even at his most innocuous.

There is nothing innocuous about the next sequence, though. After
sitting through a tirade at the awards banquet by the president of the Associated Press about how "the journalist's task is to be clear, cool, and objective," Izzy turns his own acceptance speech into a memorial for the
murdered George Polk, "one of those few American journalists who was
not afraid to see beyond the murk of the cold war," and an indictment of
"the Pax Americana" and "our imperialist oppression."

Yet even as the film celebrates Stone's courage and perspicacity, it also
turns him into a myth: the maverick who wouldn't quit. The narrator, Tom
Wicker, has evident respect and affection for Stone. What's missing is a
sense of Stone's own political history, and how his brand of independent
radicalism was shaped by larger movements. This is not entirely Bruck's
fault. In one sequence we see Al Bernstein, described simply as a subscriber to the *Weekly* and a former union official but who seems to have
been included as a link to his son, Carl, whose articles in the *Washington
Post* were shortly to lead to Nixon's resignation. A montage of Watergate
stories introduces Carl telling the camera, "Anybody who goes into what's
known as 'investigative reporting'—you can't help being influenced by
Izzy." That Al Bernstein and his wife had been members of the Communist Party, part of a generation of radicals for whom *I. F. Stone's Weekly*
was both talisman and bush telegraph, is left unsaid—and perhaps in
1973 was still unsayable.

By suggesting that it was Stone's "opposition to the loyalty purges of
the fifties" that "made him untouchable in Washington" rather than his
own long involvement in radical causes, the film sanitizes him. And
though audiences in the 1970s might have known the *Weekly* or remembered Izzy's early, outspoken opposition to the Vietnam War, later viewers

are unlikely to see past the journalistic icon, endorsed by Wicker of the *Times* and Bernstein of the *Post* whose comments, like those of Peter Osnos (also then a reporter at the *Washington Post*), depict Stone as a curmudgeonly character for whom politics was secondary to the thrill of the chase. In other words as merely an exemplary journalist.

Another factor that contributed to the domestication of I. F. Stone was his work for the *New York Review of Books*. By 1972, when Izzy appeared in its pages nineteen times, the *Review* had long since attained not merely intellectual respectability but intellectual preeminence, and Stone himself was an agent of that transformation. The unabashed Henry Wallace supporter who had once dared to suggest that General MacArthur deliberately prolonged the Korean War in hopes of involving China, and who had been the lone American newsman to realize that the Gulf of Tonkin attacks had been provoked, now turned his muckrake on Brezhnev's Soviet Union. Izzy was not alone in endorsing the dissident Russian historians Roy and Zhores Medvedev, whose critical books on Stalin and Stalinism began to appear in English in the early 1970s, but his endorsement helped to create a climate in which the left could no longer evade either the enormity of Stalin's crimes or the persistent brutality of his successors.

Stone's reports in 1972 on the perversion of psychiatry to suppress dissent in the Soviet Union gave the nascent movement for international human rights crucial credibility, providing an instant rebuttal to anyone tempted to dismiss such reports as cold war propaganda. He approached the subject with customary thoroughness, and the articles he wrote were a coup for both Robert Silvers and the magazine,[4] as were Izzy's subsequent analyses of the scandal about ITT, the giant holding company, Nixon's constitutional crimes, and the politics behind Kissinger's diplomacy. John Leonard, then editor of the *Times Book Review*, waspishly observed that now he had to read the competition, adding that "any magazine that gives a home to I. F. Stone is eminently worth publishing."[5] Izzy's new choice of targets also made him palatable to some of his oldest adversaries. Arthur Schlesinger Jr. thought his fellow *Review* contributor's pieces on the Pentagon budget in 1972 were "brilliant." Schlesinger's wife was also a fan of the *Weekly*. "But what really brought us together," said Schlesinger, "was the change in his own view" regarding the Soviet Union.[6]

Another figure in the *Review*'s orbit who warmed to Stone was the British philosopher Isaiah Berlin. At their first meeting, in the British embassy in Washington during World War II, Berlin was warned, "This man is a Communist." Though drawn to Stone personally—"He looked a very nice cozy little Jew"—Berlin (himself Jewish) had been "rather shocked by his leftism." After the war, "people like Joe Alsop were very against him, thought he was a traitor." A rabid cold warrior, Alsop was a close friend of Berlin's, and his prejudices were enough to encourage the philosopher to keep his distance.* Still, Berlin read the *Weekly* from time to time; even in the 1940s as a British government official, he'd been impressed by Stone's reporting from Palestine. And of course Stone's vindication on Vietnam made him respectable, as did endorsements from Silvers and Richard Wollheim, a British philosopher active in anti–Vietnam War circles in London who used to arrange meetings between Izzy and senior figures in the Labour Party to stiffen Prime Minister Harold Wilson's resistance to President Johnson's repeated requests for British troops.[7] Izzy and Esther stayed with Berlin and his wife at Headington House, their elegant Queen Anne home just outside Oxford. "Once over lunch we were talking about the Holocaust and Izzy mentioned the way some of the children, before they were put on the trains, were given potatoes—*kartoffeln*, he said—to put in their pockets. He just burst into tears," recalled Berlin.[8]

Stone treasured his friendship with Berlin. "He had the Jewish reverence for learning," said the philosopher, "and the joy of the self-educated man." To be treated as an intellectual equal by such a famous scholar was as much a delight for Stone as the invitation, which came during his 1974 visit to Oxford, to address the fellows of St. Antony's College. "The liveliest, the most relevant, original and unaffected American intellect since H. L. Mencken," raved the *Guardian*, whose reporter also noted Izzy's newfound relish for the groves of academe. "One feels that he came to Oxford," the paper observed, "for the acceptance, the camaraderie, the after-dinner conversation of Learned Men of Distinction."[9] Yet in the winter of 1975, Stone's relationship with Berlin suffered a breach that was to take a long time to heal. The argument was not over the many areas where the two men had long records of disagreement, but on a topic that was a mutual passion: the survival of the Jewish people.

---

*During the war, Berlin had briefly shared a house in Washington with E. F. Prichard, among others. If, as I suggested earlier, Prichard was indeed the *Nation*'s mysterious Mr. "XXX," Berlin and Stone had another friend in common. Unfortunately, Isaiah Berlin died before I could ask him about the Prichard connection.

•

Isaiah Berlin and I. F. Stone both rejoiced in Israel's victory in the 1973 Yom Kippur War, just as both men had been glad to see Israel win its previous wars. But for Stone, Israel's military victory over Egypt and Syria, in 1973 as in 1967, however necessary, still left unanswered the crucial question of Israel's relations with the Palestinians. And in the crisis that followed the Organization of Arab Petroleum Exporting Countries' decision to stop shipments of oil during the fighting, and concurrent moves by the Organization of Petroleum Exporting Countries to push up the price of oil over the long term, Izzy saw new and potentially terrifying consequences for both Israel and the United States.

The Arab willingness to use oil as a political weapon outraged many Americans.* And though even Secretary of State Henry Kissinger ruled out the use of military force "in the case of a dispute over price," he made an explicit exception "where there's some actual strangulation of the industrialized world." In the wake of this public pronouncement, *Commentary* published an article in early 1975 advocating the military seizure of Persian Gulf oil fields in order to break the OAPEC cartel and lower the price of fuel in the West. In its sober embrace of America's imperial prerogatives, in its advocacy of military means for political ends, and above all in its sponsors' identification of American and Israeli national interests, Robert Tucker's "Oil: The Issue of American Intervention" was a pioneering work of neoconservative foreign policy.[10] It was also, thought Izzy, a pernicious fantasy.

His reply, "War for Oil?" in the *New York Review* pointed out that Kissinger's statement "was not a ringing call for war. Nor was it especially new." In any case, "The idea that you can slice away a coastal strip of a country's territory, containing most of its wealth, and just sit there, happily enjoying the fruits of occupation and shipping out the oil spurting from its wells, belongs in an anthology of military-political delusions." Isaiah Berlin agreed. Nor did he take issue with Stone's contention that "this is exactly the kind of rescue operation of which some Israeli hardliners may have been dreaming."

What bothered Berlin was Stone's observation that "one of the worst

---

*During the Arab embargo, the retail price of gasoline in the United States, which had been roughly 39¢ a gallon in May 1973, rose to 55¢ a gallon in June 1974.

aspects of this inflammatory proposal is the place where it appeared. *Commentary* is published by the American Jewish Committee. Nothing could be more dangerous for American unity, for the future of the American Jewish community, and for Israel itself than to have it look as if Jewish influence were trying to get the US into war with the Arabs, and to take their richest resource from them."[11] "I, too wish that *Commentary* had not accepted the article," Berlin wrote in a letter he drafted to Stone as soon as he finished reading. "But when you say . . . that such attitudes are likely to incite anti-semitism, in short that it is not for Jews to advocate or even to publish such policies—I disagree; I simply cannot believe that you mean it." Berlin compared Stone's argument with "that which was used by [Charles] Lindbergh . . . when he warned the Jews against inciting America into war." "You would not, I feel sure," he added pointedly, "use this argument in warning Jews . . . against being socialists or communists because this would identify Jews with subversion and compromise the entire community?"*

Perhaps sensing the wounding nature of his response, Berlin sent his comments not directly to Izzy, but to their mutual friend Silvers, whose eight-page reply to Berlin's four-page draft is a masterpiece of editorial tact from its opening sentences: "Of course you should send that letter to Izzy. He will find it troubling, as I did, and struggle with the questions that you raise, as I have, and that is what we should do."†[12]

Berlin did send his complaint to Izzy, and though he avowed that he

---

*This same argument was used by Walter Goodman, author of *The Committee*, a blame-the-victims account of the Hollywood blacklist, in the March 1975 article "Jews, Israel, and I. F. Stone" for the *New Leader*. Declaring that "America's Jews have lately been put on notice that they had better watch what they say about events in the Middle East," Goodman asked readers to "set aside the question of whether I. F. Stone's sympathies for the State of Israel are equal to those he held for Henry Wallace." His conclusion: "The precincts where anti-Semitism has probably grown as a result of the Arab-Israeli troubles are on the Left, among the admirers of I. F. Stone."

†It is eerie to read Berlin arguing that "the mood of the [Israeli] majority is very, very unlike that of the minority of hawks into whose hands the PLO are playing; they are ready for large concessions to live in peace with the Arabs." And it is equally haunting to read Silvers, in 1975, taking comfort from the fact that Ariel Sharon "is not the government, nor the voice of the Israelis." One passage in particular is likely to resonate with many contemporary readers. To the charge that Stone is advocating Jewish self-censorship, Silvers replies, "Suppose I envisage opprobrium attaching to Jews or even suffering by them, at the hands of politicians or populists etc., as they are held responsible for encouraging and launching into public discussion strategies that might end up, to imagine a lurid example, with boys from Iowa and Harlem futilely dying in Kuwait." Should one then keep silent? he asks.

would "continue reading you, whatever you may say, because I feel deep personal affection and great respect," his letter, with its reference to "the same consideration that caused fears in the breasts of many highly-placed American Jews in 1939–40 about protesting too vehemently against Hitler, for fear of being thought warmongers," couldn't but sting.[13] It took Stone nearly a month to reply, and while he, too, tried to be conciliatory, his reference to Berlin's "service in the British Embassy" having "touched old wounds of controversy" gave new grounds for offense. Berlin, who had been terribly torn during the 1940s by the conflict between loyalty to his adopted (and beloved) Britain and the Zionist cause he supported, now accused Stone of seeking to "make me smart," prompting a further, still more placatory, response from Izzy. But Stone's assurance that "the reference was not intended to be wounding but understanding" was only partly successful. As he acknowledged during their first exchange, their disagreements on Israel ran on "a well-worn track of debate." And though both men saw the *Commentary* campaign as dangerously wrongheaded, for Stone there was a larger issue involved—one that would continue to divide Berlin, faithful familiar to the great and good, from his friend. "It is time," Izzy insisted, "we American Jews balked [at] the tail-wag-the-dog tactics of drift and hard-line Israeli politics."[14]

Given the assiduous efforts he made to mediate between two favorite writers, it is perhaps surprising that Robert Silvers himself was the object of Izzy's next public quarrel. The article that touched it off was Allen Weinstein's April 1976 dismissal of Alger Hiss's latest defender. The one-time organ of radical chic was abandoning its war paint and marching boots for the sober, if still chic, tones of academic bohemia. Andrew Kopkind's May 1975 gloss on the impending bicentennial celebrations was the last appearance for the *Review*'s most radical contributor. Even Noam Chomsky, whose essay "The Responsibility of Intellectuals" was as influential as anything published during the *New York Review*'s first decade (and whose criticisms of Israeli policy Berlin had denounced in his letter to Stone as "a depressing form of self-induced vanity and blindness"), now seemed confined to the correspondence pages.

Izzy bore no particular brief for Hiss. "I talked to Alger when he came out of jail," he told Andrew Patner, "and I really admired him for his composure." But he told the same interviewer that Whittaker Chambers's *Witness* "had a lot of verisimilitude in his picture of life inside the party," while

Hiss's version, *In the Court of Public Opinion*, "was not much of a book." And he'd been reluctant to defend Hiss in either his newspaper columns or the *Weekly*. The issue now was fairness. In 1976, Stone told Patner, "a *Herald Tribune* man [John Chabot Smith] had just published his own book on the Hiss case and before that book had a chance to be evaluated, even read, it was really destroyed by the Weinstein *review*![15] I thought that was unfair. He [Weinstein] had his book coming out and he was given a chance to destroy the other book [Smith's]." Stone asked Silvers to take his name off the masthead. "I didn't want to be a dummy director."[16]

Years later, an unapologetic Silvers explained that it was precisely Weinstein's own researches on Hiss that made him uniquely qualified to review Smith's *Alger Hiss: The True Story*. In any case, he said, Izzy never stopped writing for the *Review*.[17] The very next month saw a major essay on Senator Frank Church's committee report on abuses by the Central Intelligence Agency, and in the following year the *Review* published Izzy's "Confessions of a Jewish Dissident," the preface to a reissue of *Underground to Palestine* and the occasion for still further abuse from those who objected to his plea for justice for the Palestinians. The *New Republic*, which under its new owner, Martin Peretz, had become aggressively, even obsessively pro-Israel, derided Stone's "PLO apologetics" while the journal *Midstream* condemned him as a "Universalist" and "the comrade of those who call openly for the massacre of all Jews in Israel."[18]

Though such attacks pained him to the end of his life, they were far from the whole story. The younger generation continued happily to embrace Izzy, who had become a grandfather figure to a whole new generation of crusading journalists. *[MORE]* magazine, the *Editor & Publisher* of the underground press, feted him at the very first A. J. Liebling Counter-Convention. Before a crowd of 3,000 people, including Jack Anderson, Murray Kempton, Dan Rather, and Studs Terkel, Izzy accepted his Liebling Award with the defiant proclamation that "to be a pariah is to be left alone to see things your own way, as truthfully as you can."[19]

He could perhaps be forgiven for stretching a point. Even synagogues were asking him to speak again—though they were sometimes shocked by his outspokenness. At Temple Sinai in Washington, a questioner reminded him that the Jews remained "a moral light in this world" even after obeying the biblical injunction to destroy Canaan. "I really ought to make my answer in German," Izzy replied.[20] At Rodeph Shalom in downtown Philadelphia, he repeatedly compared Palestinian refugees with the Jewish Diaspora. "How can you want something for yourself that you won't extend to someone else?" he asked, and when the audience audibly rejected his claim that Palestinians had been "driven to terror," he insisted, "We are not fighting Adolf Hitler. We are a kindred people fighting over the same land."[21]

The surest sign that, at least as far as official Washington was concerned, I. F. Stone had completed his predicted transit from pariah to colorful character to national institution was the coverage of his and Esther's fiftieth wedding anniversary. On July 9, 1979, the front page of the *Washington Post* Style section featured a six-column spread on the festivities, topped by a photo of the happy couple flanked by their wedding pictures. Myra MacPherson's affectionate portrait cited fans from Marilyn Monroe to Albert Einstein. While Esther Stone's total devotion to her husband's career might have caused a few feminist eyebrows to rise, the *Post* awarded Izzy the mainstream media's supreme benediction: "Stone managed to enrage both the right and the left through the years." His 1956 critique of the Soviet Union was duly cited, along with Vice President Agnew's denunciation of him, contributing to the overall impression of a successful "mom-and-pop operation" with "pop" not only safe but celebrated—"to the point of becoming immortalized as New Yorker cartoons."

Izzy was quoted insisting, "I've had enough journalism to last me." The Stones filled their days, the *Post* reported, with reading, long walks, and disco dancing, "although Esther Stone will volunteer that 'sex is madly important in a good marriage.'" The key to enjoying retirement, said Izzy, was to "have something new, such as my Greek studies." Bemused by Stone's passion for "ancient, musty tomes in Greek," MacPherson assured readers that "he is also writing a book on freedom of thought." The "puckish little man with thick glasses" still had one last surprise left in him.[22]

•

In 1971, a few months before the end of the *Weekly*, the *Washington Post Book World* interviewed Stone on his life as a reader. The list of books and writers cited is lengthy and, for a newspaperman, extraordinarily catholic, with warm evocations of Izzy's personal canon: Kropotkin, Whitman, Keats, Shelley, Bertrand Russell, Spinoza, and George Santayana. Recently, he said, he'd been reading Gide (in French), *Death in Venice* ("in German, a rather baroque and difficult German"), and the book of Isaiah (in Hebrew and English). "The Bible is one thing I would read if I had time. Another ambition is to read Proust all the way through in French. And I'd like to read all the Prophets. And I'd like to read a beautiful edition I bought of Maimonides' *Guide for the Perplexed*, but I haven't had the chance." The only mentions of the language that would actually consume his final years came in a lament that "I'll probably never be able to read Aeschylus and Sophocles in the original," and a reference to his beloved Gibbon, who "had the dirty parts in Latin and the real dirty parts in Greek."[23]

It is tempting to treat I. F. Stone's Greek studies as simply a final bravura piece of reporting. Stone, interviewing himself for the *New York Times Magazine*, admitted, "I am drawn by the hope of one last scoop." Yet his knowing reference to Sigmund Freud in that same interview—"we overlook what we do not wish to see"—and the passion he brought to his labors suggest that something more was going on beyond a simple desire to break "the Socrates story."[24] The invocation of the Viennese father of psychoanalysis is a reminder of what Stone's journalistic admirers all too often overlook: his sense of himself as an intellectual, a man who, though self-educated, is not only conversant with contemporary debates in philosophy, history, literature, and psychology but fully capable of participating in the controversy. Freud, too, was a Jewish writer and sometime pariah who used his own classical learning both to gain entry into the realm of secular scholarship and as a means to exert his own authority, through the power of his arguments, over his critics.[25]

Stone described his immersion in the Greek world as something of a happy accident, a delightful detour from his intended aim of writing a history of freedom of thought. "I began . . . by spending a year studying the two English revolutions in the seventeenth century, which played so large a part in the development of the American constitutional system." From John Milton's *Areopagitica* and the Putney debates of the English Civil War, it was "a natural regression" to the Reformation, then the Middle Ages, "and finally I landed back in the Athens of the fifth and fourth centuries B.C."[26]

Once in Athens, Izzy immediately noticed that his sources—the standard works of classical Greek thought—were seldom in agreement. Just like the cub reporter who turned up at halftime and had to have the game explained to him, he found himself on the sidelines of a ferocious contest, only this time the players lived 2,500 years before he arrived, and the referees' explanations were not only contradictory but incomprehensible without an understanding of the rules—which in this case meant the rhetoric, grammar, and language of ancient Greece. "I decided in retirement to learn enough Greek to be able to grapple with conceptual terms for myself. I started on my own with a bilingual edition of the Gospel of St. John, then went to the first book of the *Iliad*."[27] Even without invoking Freud it seems obvious that Stone was on a quest, though whether heroic or quixotic would remain to be seen. That more than mere scholarly diligence was involved is clear from his language: "Like so many before me, I fell in love with the ancient Greeks."[28]

It was a love that had deep roots. Stone had completed only a single semester of Greek at college (for which he received a mark of P for Pass), unlike Latin, which he'd studied through four years of high school and two years at Penn. But in the spring of 1927, shortly before he dropped out, he bought a copy of the Earl of Cromer's *Paraphrases and Translations from the Greek*, which remained in his library all his life. It was also in some way an illicit passion. For the newly emancipated Jews of the Austro-Hungarian empire, the safely defunct deities of the classical world may have offered "religiously neutral ground for constructing a secular liberal culture."[29] But for *Ostjuden* from the shtetl like the Feinsteins, to be a "Hellenist" was akin to apostasy.* Indeed, the opposition between "Hellenism and Hebraism" was a well-established convention.

Stone was not the first Jewish renegade to make his stand in ancient Athens. Moses Finley, an American who was professor of ancient history at Cambridge, had lost his job at Rutgers University in 1953 for pleading the Fifth Amendment before the Senate Internal Security Subcommittee. Stone's copy of Finley's *The Ancient Economy* was heavily underlined and annotated.[30] Izzy also sought out Pierre Vidal-Naquet, the French Jewish classicist whose parents had been murdered at Auschwitz and

*Hence *Midstream*'s denunciation of Stone as a "Universalist"—the secular equivalent of "Hellenist" and precursor to the "self-hating Jew" wheeled out by modern-day enforcers of Jewish conformity.

who himself had been one of the most outspoken critics of France's use of torture during the war in Algeria.

Were Stone's Athenian excavations partially intended as a riposte to his own people? With Nixon and Agnew finally in disgrace by 1974, the journalistic establishment's embrace of the man whom it had once ostracized was complete; even the National Press Club eventually welcomed him back to the fold. He still had enemies on the right, but his most fervent critics were now Jews who found his advocacy of Palestinian rights heretical.

Are we—and was he—overlooking what we do not wish to see by failing to consider the connection between history's most famous suicide and the man whose mother also swallowed poison?

Or was his assault on Plato and Socrates a way for this self-described "Red Jew son-of-a-bitch" to thumb his nose at a world that had excluded him since his childhood on the wrong side of the tracks in Haddonfield? Though deficient in credentials, he was blessed with an ample supply of chutzpah, and he plunged into ancient controversies where classicists feared to tread.

The result, *The Trial of Socrates*, was a cross between a detective story and a courtroom thriller. Our intrepid narrator, I. F. Stone, finds his researches on the history of free thought derailed by a paradox: Why should Athens, "a city famous for free speech," have executed Socrates, "a philosopher guilty of no other crime than exercising it"?[31] Even if his fellow citizens didn't like Socrates or his ideas, "he had been teaching there all his life, unmolested. Why did they wait until he was 70, and had only a few years to live, before executing him?"[32]

And so Stone begins to dig. The eyewitnesses are all dead, the paper trail stretches back to 399 B.C., and there is a suggestion that not all the documents are genuine (i.e., Plato's *Seventh Letter*, "which may or may not be authentic").[33] Undaunted, Stone strolls over to the local library— at American University, where he is made a visiting scholar with a desk and borrowing rights—and to Washington's Center for Hellenic Studies, whose director, Bernard Knox, a British veteran of the International Brigade, he impresses with his knowledge of Plato. "I had him to lunch with the fellows of the institute, many of whom were Platonists," said Knox, "and he absolutely bowled them over. He knew all the textual references. Especially the Germans."[34]

Relying principally on the accounts by Plato and Xenophon and the comedies of Aristophanes, with a scattering of references in Aristotle, Stone takes his readers back to an Athens riven by conflict and beset by enemies both within and without the city gates. His Socrates is a brilliant writer, inspiring teacher, and master propagandist whose deep hostility to Athenian democracy, taken up by his student disciples Alcibiades and Critias, leads to a succession of bloody dictatorships that render the city defenseless before its Spartan enemies. This legacy—and the fact that Socrates remained in the city throughout the oligarchic rule of the infamous Tyranny of the Thirty*—led, according to Stone, a newly restored democracy to try its most famous critic as an enemy of the people. In Stone's account, it is Socrates himself who manipulates the jury into sentencing him to death. Offered the chance to escape into exile, as dramatized in Plato's *Crito*, Socrates refuses. "Socrates needed the hemlock, as Jesus needed the Crucifixion, to fulfill a mission. The mission left a stain forever on democracy."[35]

How original was Stone's case for the prosecution? "I think he put his finger on a real problem, which had been understated," said Knox. "The Athenians had a real case [against Socrates]. Not for death, of course. I don't think they ever meant to put him to death." In interviews and articles Izzy always pointed out his debt to "my hero," the nineteenth-century British scholar George Grote, "the first to write Greek history from a prodemocratic point of view."[36] And he had other predecessors. Richard Crossman, the British politician and journalist whom he had known in the 1950s, had described Plato's philosophy as "totalitarian," "the most savage and profound attack upon liberal ideas which history can show," in his 1937 study *Plato Today*. Crossman's remark was quoted by Karl Popper in his magisterial *The Open Society and Its Enemies*, a work that, though never cited by Stone, foreshadowed many of his conclusions.[37]

So did *The Ancient City*, by the nineteenth-century French historian Fustel de Coulanges. Though Stone relied heavily on Fustel's depiction of unceasing class struggle in the ancient world (Stone's copy of the book contains more than a hundred underlined or annotated passages), neither Fustel nor his book is mentioned in *The Trial of Socrates*.[38]

---

*In 404 B.C., the victorious Spartan general Lysander dissolved the popular assembly of Athens and replaced it with an oligarchy of thirty men. In the revolt that followed, 1,500 people were executed and 5,000 were forced to flee the city or were exiled. The next year, the Spartan king Pausanias restored democracy.

Certainly Stone would have recognized the force of Popper's observation that "the enemies of freedom have always charged its defenders with subversion."[39] And just as Popper, an Austrian refugee writing in the shadow of World War II, used the ancient world to explore his own ideas about fascism, communism, and democracy, so Izzy's interest in the subject seems as much allegorical as historical. With his references to an "un-Athenian Activities Investigating Committee" and his remark that Plato's celebration of Sparta's totalitarian society "provides Leninist dictatorships with a precedent they cannot find in Marx or Engels," Stone, too, had one eye fixed firmly on the not-so-distant past.[40]

For all their similarities, *The Trial of Socrates* is far from an imitation of Popper. Indeed, Stone entirely rejects one of Popper's crucial premises, the view that every antidemocratic sentiment voiced by Socrates is actually attributable not to him but to his chronicler and biographer, Plato. Popper's radical solution to what is known as "the Socratic problem" allows him to portray Socrates as not only "a martyr to free speech," a phrase that also occurs in Stone, but also "a man who would criticize any form of government for its shortcomings . . . As it happened, he spent his life largely under a democratic form of government, and as a good democrat he found it his duty to expose the incompetence and windbaggery of some of the democratic leaders of his time."[41] In other words, Popper's Socrates bears a striking resemblance to I. F. Stone.

Yet in the end both depictions are perhaps less interesting for what they tell us about Socrates than about their authors. To Popper, what is important is "the contrast between two worlds—the world of a modest, rational individualist and that of a totalitarian demi-god."[42] Stone, with both Soviet communism and the American Red Scare in mind, has a more exigent view of the obligation to dissent. Thus he explicitly rejects the theory advanced by Popper that there is anything heroic in the less-than-passive resistance offered by Socrates to the Thirty Tyrants. Ordered to help arrest Leon of Salamis, an innocent "resident alien," Socrates simply goes home. What Popper describes as "courageous" Stone sees as "merely avoiding personal complicity."[43]

Stone's distaste for Socrates is hardly disguised: The Athenian's attacks on the Sophists Stone calls merely "class prejudice" against their clients, the rising merchants and middle classes that wanted to learn rhetoric in order to challenge the old aristocracy (Socrates' friends and patrons). Socrates is arraigned for hypocrisy (describing himself as a poor man when, thanks to his inherited wealth, he never had to earn a living) and even for male chauvinism: "Socrates' cold and unfeeling attitude toward his devoted wife, Xanthippe . . . has too long been passed over in silence by reverent scholars."[44]

But the ultimate grounds of difference are philosophical and political. For the ancient Athenians, "participation in 'politics'—managing the city—was a right, a duty, and an education. But all the Socratics, from Antisthenes to Plato, preached withdrawal from it." Stone saw this withdrawal from politics, in his own time as in ancient Athens, as inimical to the survival of democracy. "The negative dialectic of Socrates—if the city had taken it seriously—would have made equity and democracy impossible. His identification of virtue with an unattainable knowledge stripped common men of hope and denied their capacity to govern themselves."[45] Allegory, political archaeology, historical muckraking, and personal mythology—*The Trial of Socrates* is all these things. But above all it is a plea for engagement.

•

His timing was all wrong.

Eager to get his "scoop" into print as soon as possible, he wrote "I. F. Stone Breaks the Socrates Story" for the *New York Times Magazine* in April 1979. Apart from its undoubted effectiveness in scaring any would-be competitors off the Socrates beat, Izzy's preliminary report had a more tangible consequence: He acquired an agent. Andrew Wylie was a thirty-one-year-old graduate-school dropout who had recently begun renting desk space in the office of a New York literary agency. He had no actual clients yet but plenty of nerve. "Izzy was one of the first calls I made. I'd been a subscriber to the *Weekly.* I saw his article on Socrates—I'd studied Greek at Harvard. So I phoned and said I was going to be in Washington tomorrow and could we meet."

Stone was reluctant. But Wylie, a former student of Albert Lord, whose book *The Singer of Tales* argued for the oral roots of Homeric epic, starting singing the *Iliad* into the telephone and Stone's resistance dissolved. "We went to a cafeteria near Izzy's house," and Wylie explained his theory of literary economics. "The most important thing, I assured him, is to get paid. If you get $100,000, the publisher will print a lot of copies and will make sure the bookstores put your book in the front of the stores." By the end of lunch, Wylie had his first client. "I think Izzy let me be his agent in order to get me to leave town."[46]

For the past decade, Stone's books had been published by Random House, and as it happened his old assistant, Peter Osnos, had recently become an editor there. "I thought I'd found the right person," said Wylie. "But when I went to see Osnos, he said, 'Look, this is the Reagan era. No one is going to buy a book about Socrates by I. F. Stone.' In the end, Random House gave up the rights to all of Izzy's books."

It took some time, but eventually Wylie got Stone his money— $105,000 for the Socrates book and the rights to his backlist from the Boston publishers Little, Brown. "The problem was Izzy didn't want to let go of the book," Wylie recalled. "I think he thought the moment he hands in the manuscript he's going to die."

Ronald Reagan was still president in January 1988 when *The Trial of Socrates* went on sale. With Esther's encouragement, Wylie had finally coaxed his reluctant client. "I told him: 'Why don't you allow yourself the pleasure of having the book appear?'"

At first the pleasure was mixed. Reviews of *The Trial of Socrates* were considerably less ecstatic than for *Polemics and Prophecies* or *In a Time of Torment*. Though Christopher Lehmann-Haupt, the daily *New York Times* critic, found the book "impressive . . . Mr. Stone's scholarship is alive and engaging," the paper's Sunday reviewer, Julia Annas, a classicist, was distinctly underwhelmed. As was the classicist Allan Bloom, who invoked Mel Brooks's 2000 Year Old Man and compared Stone to "a beady-eyed, mean spirited prosecutor" in the course of dismissing "this often tiresome book" in the *Washington Post*. Sidney Hook in the *Wall Street Journal* called Stone a "cultural Philistine."[47]

Hook was an old antagonist, a defender of exactly the kind of witch hunt—when the hunted were American Communists—that gave Stone's narrative half its allegorical bite. (But he was hardly the only reviewer not to realize that it was precisely because Socrates'—or Plato's—ideas really might have threatened Athenian democracy that Stone found his case so interesting.) As for Bloom, the disciple of the conservative classicist Leo Strauss had a host of possible reasons for closing his mind to Stone's arguments. As pessimistic as his mentor about the very possibility of enlightened democratic deliberation—the basis of Stone's Jeffersonian credo—Bloom was also a translator of Plato's *Republic*. And in arguing against Bloom's claim that the totalitarian prescriptions of the *Republic* are not meant to be taken seriously, Stone had misspelled his adversary's first name as "Alan." But not all of the book's critics could be so easily impeached.

The *Philadelphia Inquirer* reviewer, Carlin Romano, mounted a merciless attack on Stone's scholarship that was all the more deadly for its apparent lack of motive. "*The Trial of Socrates* is a hatchet-job," he complained, concluding "Stone owes Socrates an apology." The classicist Gregory Vlastos introduced his own reservations by avowing that "for I. F. Stone, I have long had respect verging on reverence . . . For many of us, *I. F. Stone's Weekly* was a beacon in a darkened landscape." But this did not prevent Vlastos from debunking Stone's claim to have "scooped" historians, or from labeling much of his argument "inadvertently misleading."[48]

On the whole, the scholarly reviewers were mostly hostile—but with significant exceptions. The poet-translator (and Oxford classicist) Peter Levi rejected Stone's claim to have uncovered "the real Socrates," but he was otherwise warmly approving: "Whatever he says is truer than its opposite, and the picture of Athens that he paints seems to me substantially true and worth having." And in the pages of the *New York Review*, the philosopher Miles Burnyeat, though regretfully reporting that "Stone has little patience with philosophy," found much to admire in this "lively, provocative and sometimes exasperating book." The Scottish journalist Neal Ascherson, picking up on the parallels between the Athenian gadfly and his American antagonist, was one of the few critics to realize that despite the ferocity of his assault on Socrates as a foe of democracy, Stone believed such "negative critics" should be protected by any free society worthy of the name. (Ascherson himself was unconvinced, warning that there are some gadflies "whose sting paralyses the muscle of liberty. Socrates was one of those.")[49]

Such scholastic disputation was entertaining, but as a spur to public interest attacks were apparently as effective as applause. On April 10, 1988, *The Trial of Socrates* entered the *New York Times*'s nonfiction bestseller list at tenth place, just below Richard Ellmann's biography of Oscar Wilde and two slots above *The Closing of the American Mind* by Allan Bloom. A month later, it had lost ground to Michael Jackson's *Moonwalk* and Stephen Hawking's *A Brief History of Time* but was still hanging on. Without a blacklist to hold him back, Stone no longer needed the critics' approval. In all, *The Trial of Socrates* spent nine weeks on the best-seller list. A Book-of-the-Month-Club edition sold more than 25,000 copies; total sales approached 100,000. "We had no idea the goddamned thing would sell like that," said Roger Donald, Stone's editor at Little, Brown.[50]

Neither did Izzy. For the first few years of his Greek studies, Izzy had tried to supplement his earnings from the *New York Review* by syndicating his own material. Though he complained to his friend Morton Mintz that he found it "easier to get his stuff into the old Hearst paper in San Francisco, the *Examiner*, than into *The Washington Post*," the problem had long since ceased to be acceptability.[51] The *New York Times* happily printed an essay describing the rise of Solidarity in Poland as "the birth pangs of a revolution not so unlike our own 1776" and commending the writings of Rosa Luxemburg to "our Polish brothers."[52] It was just that syndication took too much of his time.

Then, on a visit to New York shortly after he had finished *The Trial of Socrates*, Izzy and Esther attended a dinner party for George Seldes. Also present was Victor Navasky, who had taken over as editor of the *Nation* from Izzy's friend Carey McWilliams. Walking the Stones back to their customary room at the Tudor Hotel, Navasky listened eagerly as the journalist, whose last contribution to the *Nation*, "New Facts on Korea," had appeared in December 1951, now proposed a return to his old stand. Navasky, an admirer of Stone's since *PM* days, who still cherished the memory of a chance meeting over the card catalog at the Library of Congress before the launch of the *Weekly*, was thrilled. Though Izzy's penchant for pushing a deadline—a process that could also see his 150-word paragraph balloon into a full-fledged cover story in the course of a week—exasperated the magazine's hard-pressed young staffers, Navasky promised them that someday they would be grateful for the association. The legendarily tight-fisted Navasky didn't even balk when, having persuaded Izzy to give the keynote speech at a conference for investigative journalists in Amsterdam that May, he and the magazine ended up paying for Izzy and Esther, who preferred to travel by sea, to make their way to Amsterdam via Southampton and London on the *Queen Elizabeth II*.[53]

"Izzy and Esther liked to travel by ocean liner because they loved to dance," his London agent, Felicity Bryan, recalled. "They would arrive in

London giddy after four nights on the dance floor." Bryan, who first met the Stones in Washington in the late 1960s, said that shortly after she moved back to Britain she and Izzy met for lunch at the Ritz. At the time, he was just beginning his Athenian investigations. "I think I'm on to something," he told her. "Let's just say I fancy myself the Woodward and Bernstein of Periclean Greece." At the end of the meal, Stone paid the check and turned to Bryan with tears in his eyes. "Oh Felicity, this has been such a lovely meal. When the revolution comes we'll eat here every day!"[54]

•

He never did get to see the revolution. Or Czechoslovakia's Velvet Revolution, either, an equally unimaginable event—though perhaps not to the man who'd written "what happened in Budapest will one day happen in Moscow."

His eightieth birthday in 1987 was marked by a quiet family celebration at Jean and Leonard Boudin's house—and another round of adulatory profiles. Andrew Patner, a twenty-eight-year-old Chicago journalist, wrote *I. F. Stone: A Portrait*, whose transcribed conversations allowed his subject to reflect on topics ranging from Socrates and Plato to Yiddish, the Rosenbergs, and his apprenticeship with J. David Stern. Even *Rolling Stone* joined the celebration, with a staff writer, William Greider, introducing the magazine's young readers to "the most radical, independent and effective investigative reporter in Washington."[55]

Being anointed a cult figure in his ninth decade after so many years of ostracism and isolation was an irony Stone did his best to enjoy. He'd been faithfully recording his blood pressure since the late 1960s. Now taking nitroglycerin pills for his heart and slowed down by a detached retina in one eye and cataracts in the other, he still managed a five-mile walk most days—though increasingly dependent on a cane to maintain his balance. Forced to relinquish his driver's license, he was delighted to let young admirers like Eric Alterman, who had interviewed Izzy for a college paper and become a close friend, ferry him and Esther to the movies. At the Herbst Theatre in San Francisco, built on the site where, forty-two years earlier, he'd reported on the signing of the United Nations covenant, a capacity crowd interrupted his remarks on peace in the Middle East to sing "Happy Birthday." Gesturing toward the huge cake wheeled out on stage, he wondered, "What the hell does eighty years mean in the life of the human race?" Then, brightening, he reminded them that Michelangelo, who also lived into his eighties, had remarked near the end of his life, "What a shame. I was just beginning to learn the alphabet of my art." Back home in Washington, he and Esther went for a walk together every evening, the two of them holding hands.[56]

There were frustrations, not all of them due to physical infirmity. Ever since Israel's invasion of Lebanon in 1982, he'd been active in trying to arrange behind-the-scenes meetings between Israelis and Palestinians, and between liberal Arabs and Jews. He'd also been part of an attempt, with Noam Chomsky, the philosopher Sidney Morgenbesser, and the Palestinian writer and activist Edward Said,* to hammer out a joint position on how to move toward a just peace in the Middle East. Despite their mutual respect, the four men were unable to find sufficient common ground.[57] And after several months relishing his renewed connection to the *Nation*, he phoned Navasky to say he had to stop. Journalism was too tempting, and he had his own work to do.

Having disposed of the Greeks, he now turned his attention to the Hebrews. Though still a "devout Jewish atheist," his interest in spiritual matters had been growing for some time. He'd even sent the *New York Review* a poem about *Star Wars* chasing God from the heavens (Silvers returned it with a polite note).

Thanks to the 24-point Chicago font on the screen of his Apple Macintosh computer, **which looks like this**, and to Esther, who lovingly pasted blown-up letters on the keys, he could still just about manage to type. But reading was a more complex operation, requiring him to bring the page up to a circular lens in the middle of one side of his glasses. So he commissioned a neighbor, a man not much younger than himself, to track down and photocopy material on the history of the idea of original sin.[58]

His aim was "a series of biographical essays on the seminal figures involved in the freedom of thought."[59] Beginning, it seemed, with Isaiah, his favorite of the Hebrew prophets. A cataract operation early in 1989 re-

---

*Said told me that Stone had known his parents. On a train from New York to Washington, Izzy noticed an older couple in the seat behind him. Hearing them converse in a foreign tongue, he leaned over and asked if they were French. On being told that they were speaking Arabic, he delightedly asked where they were from. His pleasure increased when Said's father said he was from Jerusalem and had owned the stationer's shop that had been a regular stop on Izzy's visits to Palestine.

stored the sight in one eye, and his library at home was well stocked with Bibles in English, Hebrew, Greek, and Aramaic, including the one he'd been given at his bar mitzvah.

The direction of his thought can be seen from material he left in his study. One note card contained a quotation from Karl Marx's doctoral dissertation calling the titan Prometheus "the most eminent saint and martyr in the philosophical calendar." On another Izzy had copied a speech from Aeschylus's *Prometheus Bound*, also cited by Marx: "Be sure of this, I would not change my state of evil fortune for your servitude. Better to be the servant of this rock than to be faithful boy to Father Zeus." Nearby, a small blue spiral notebook bearing the handwritten title "Searchers After God" begins:

> Man's effort to create God is an effort to create order, to make a little clearance in the chaos of the universe, to humanize whatever force may drive its incessant turbulence, to lend this the features of man's compassion and sense of justice, to fashion an idol less indifferent than the awful reality which he feels around him. Religion is in this perspective the highest form of art. Man creates God in his own image, and in perfecting the image perfects himself. The search for God is man's effort to transcend himself, to make an angel of the beast.

But he'd scarcely begun work when he was back in the hospital. And this time the problem wasn't just his heart. After months of stomach cramps, Izzy was finally prevailed upon to see a doctor.

On May 21, 1989, a day after the Chinese government, responding to student protesters at Tiananmen Square, declared martial law in Beijing, I. F. Stone was admitted to the Brigham and Women's Hospital in Boston. Exploratory surgery revealed that he was suffering from colon cancer. The initial prognosis was good, but a few days later his heart began to falter and he moved into intensive care. Coming out of cardiac surgery surrounded by his children and grandchildren, he demanded, "What's going on in China?" Curious to the last, I. F. Stone died on June 18, 1989.

Twelve

LAST WRITES

———◦•◦———

I don't want to be buried in this goddamned town.
—I. F. Stone on Washington, D.C.

On the day before he died, I. F. Stone called his daughter, Celia Gilbert, into his hospital room. He had instructions for her, as his oldest child, on a matter he considered of great importance: the disposition of his books. His library, especially his collection of Greek and Latin texts, was to be sent to his favorite bookstore, William Allen, a dark, dusty warren of a shop in center city Philadelphia, so that they might continue to be of use. His other worldly goods went to Esther under the terms of a will he'd had drawn up twenty years before. (In the spring of 1968, a few months after his first heart attack, he went to New York to see Jeremiah Gutman, a *Weekly* subscriber and civil rights lawyer. "I think he picked me for the sake of privacy," said Gutman.) Though he left a considerable estate, the struggle over I. F. Stone's posterity would not be about property.[1]

It was Lenin who observed that however much great revolutionaries may be persecuted and slandered during their lifetimes, once safely in the grave "attempts are made to turn them into harmless icons." I. F. Stone was only a radical newspaperman, but his mummification into respectability had been under way for some time. All four major television networks made Stone's death an item on the evening news broadcast; his death was front-page news in the *New York Times* (which called him an "iconoclast of journalism"), the *Washington Post* ("a dogged investigator and a concise and clever writer"), the *Philadelphia Inquirer* ("Like Sunday doubleheaders and the five-cent cigar, I. F. Stone was an American institution"), the *Los Angeles Times* ("the conscience of investigative journalism"), and dozens of smaller newspapers. The day after Stone died, Peter Jennings, anchor-man of ABC's *World News Tonight*, the top-rated news program in the country, ended his broadcast with a tribute to the man he called "a jour-nalist's journalist." Quoting from Izzy's credo in *Who's Who*—"To write the truth, to defend the weak against the strong, to fight for justice . . ."—Jennings told his audience, "For many people, it's a rich experience to read or reread Stone's views on America's place in the world."

In the days to come, the *Times*, whose obituary had, in typical *Times* fashion, balanced "admirers" (who hailed his "wit and lucidity") with "crit-ics" (of Stone's "wrongheadedness"), also published an editorial celebrat-ing "a great dissident," a warm remembrance of his old boss by Peter Osnos and tributes from the columnists Tom Wicker and Anthony Lewis. The *Washington Post* ran cartoons by Jules Feiffer and Pat Oliphant and an "appreciation" by one of its writers (and future Clinton aide), Sidney Blumenthal. *Le Monde*, *Libération*, the *Guardian*, the *Independent*, the *Times,* and the *Daily Telegraph* all weighed in on the passing of the man the impeccably conservative *Telegraph* called, in a remarkably generous and lengthy obituary, "the most notable radical publicist of his time." The *Nation* put its longtime correspondent's death on the cover, the *Progres-sive* ran a fond farewell by Erwin Knoll, its editor and a friend of Izzy since the 1960s, and the *New Yorker* offered readers an affectionate sketch by Adam Gopnik of the aged muckraker probing the mysteries of men's fashion.

A few dissonant notes were sounded. The *New Republic* saluted Stone's courage but patronizingly described him as "the establishment's favorite oppositionist," with "a rather uncomplicated attitude toward America . . . There was hardly a problem in the world for which the United States gov-ernment was not to blame." Even the *National Review* marked Stone's passing with an editorial, though there was nothing ambivalent about the conservative weekly's dismissal of a "lockstep leftist" who "predictably . . . embraced the Palestinian cause." But the chorus canonizing I. F. Stone as the patron saint of journalism, an eccentric character with Coke-bottle glasses and a slightly louche political past, was mostly harmonious. Of his many admirers, only John R. MacArthur, writing in the socialist weekly *In These Times*, hinted at the reasons for Stone's long isolation or the threat he posed to mainstream journalism when he was still alive and report-ing news that his newfound acolytes wouldn't even recognize as news. As usual, his enemies served him better than his friends, with Mona Charen, a right-wing syndicated columnist, rushing to attack "Stone's stubborn fantasies about the 'progressive' forces in the world." Though mistaken in almost every particular, Charen's rant at least reminded her readers that I. F. Stone had been a feared opponent.[2]

As befitted a man who, though a fixture of the capital, was never truly at home there, I. F. Stone had two memorials. In Washington, the two hundred celebrants at the Friends' Meeting House heard eulogies from Peter Osnos, Robert Kaiser of the *Washington Post*, Marcus Raskin, Richard Dudman, and Felicity Bryan, Izzy's British literary agent and a former Washington correspondent for the *Financial Times*. Bryan also read a message from Isaiah Berlin—the two men had long since reconciled—that said, "He was not invariably right, but his motives were always pure. As Bishop Wilberforce [the nineteenth-century Anglican bishop of Oxford] said about himself, he was always in hot water and his hands were always clean." Celia Gilbert told the gathering that her father's hospital bedside reading was an anthology of Greek verse, with his final bookmark at the Stoic poet Cleanthes' hymn to Zeus: "Master of the bright thunderbolt, save men from painful ignorance." Esther wept quietly throughout the proceedings.

The New York City memorial was bigger. A crowd of nearly 600 people jammed into the Ethical Culture Society on a sweltering July afternoon. And here the audience, which included Stone's son-in-law, Walter Gilbert, who had been awarded the Nobel Prize in Chemistry in 1981, his fellow laureate James Watson, and a gallery of Pulitzer Prize–winning journalists, was at least as distinguished as the speakers. "Izzy would have preferred that we all be just a little bit uncomfortable," said Peter Osnos, apologizing for the lack of air-conditioning. But apart from Christopher Stone's admission that his father could be "a rather difficult man"—a hint, perhaps, of the toll on family life taken by Izzy's dedication to his work—the event was, like the Washington memorial (also organized by Osnos), a celebration not only of Stone's life and achievements but of the extent to which, in his final years, he'd become a kind of mascot for his profession. Robert Silvers recalled his days as a young serviceman in Paris stopped in his tracks by the phrase "The American Negro needs a Gandhi to lead him, and we need the American Negro to lead us" in *I. F. Stone's Weekly*. Leonard Boudin paid a warm tribute to his brother-in-law, "the

only genius I knew of with a functioning sense of humor." And he recalled
Izzy's description of Franklin D. Roosevelt as "a master of the art of
changing the subject." But when it came to the many lonely campaigns
the two had waged on behalf of radicals and their rights, he, too, changed
the subject. Judith Miller* of the *New York Times* described Izzy's passionate commitment—to ballroom dancing!

Victor Navasky told a funny story about Izzy's business acumen. Celia
Gilbert recalled her father's love of poetry—and his admonition that
"typos are worse than fascism!" Even Murray Kempton, who over the
preceding four decades had gone from Izzy's red-baiting competitor to
comrade in arms in any number of lost causes, obscured their mutual history under a blanket of benign rhetoric. In his introduction to *In a Time
of Torment*, Kempton had written that "Stone's is the tone of the man who
sets his face against king and court; it strikes us as special because we are
not used to hearing the voice of the opposition."[3] But in an assemblage
packed with court reporters, Kempton confined himself to the observation that "our children's children will refer to Izzy Stone as we do to
Mencken and Macaulay," a prediction that managed both to flatter and to
skewer his audience at the same time.

•

It was left to his opponents to rescue I. F. Stone from the condescension
of posterity. Fortunately, they did not disappoint. The first attack came
from the fringes: In the summer of 1992, fewer than three years after his

---

*Initially drawn to I. F. Stone by her interest in the Middle East, Miller seems to have missed her
mentor's warning that reporters who start by attending off-the-record briefings and go on to socialize
with their sources end up "in the God-damnedest mess of crap." An eager collaborator with the Pentagon, Miller wrote exclusive stories for the *Times* on Saddam Hussein's supposed weapons of mass
destruction that were used by Donald Rumsfeld and White House officials to justify the invasion of
Iraq in March 2003. Miller was also the chief American booster of Ahmed Chalabi, the exiled leader
of the Iraqi National Congress who promised that American troops would be welcomed with sweets
and flowers by the Iraqi people. In the summer of 2005, Miller served eighty-five days in jail for refusing to cooperate with federal prosecutors. Though she sought to portray herself as a martyr to the
First Amendment, the confidential source whose identity Miller withheld was no lowly whistleblower
but I. Lewis Libby, Vice President Dick Cheney's chief of staff, who'd disclosed to her the identity of
Valerie Plame, a covert operative in the CIA; he had done this in order to discredit the agent's husband, Ambassador Joseph Wilson, after Wilson had publicly criticized the Bush administration for
"twisting" the evidence to justify the Iraq war.

death, the conservative weekly *Human Events* charged that I. F. Stone had been "a paid KGB agent." The article was based partly on a British newspaper report, in March 1992, of a speech in Exeter by Oleg Kalugin, by then a retired general of the KGB, during which he recounted the story of an unnamed "agent—a well-known American journalist" who had been so incensed by "the invasion of Czechoslovakia . . . he said he would never again take any money from us."

Herbert Romerstein, who wrote this article, was not a figure to inspire confidence. A Communist at seventeen and a professional informer since the age of nineteen, when his testimony naming two of his former teachers at Samuel Tilden High School in Brooklyn led to a career as an expert witness on Communist summer camps, in the 1950s Romerstein also worked as a researcher for *Counterattack*, the blacklisters' handbook. At first the only outlet to take his charges seriously was Accuracy in Media, a pressure group devoted to exposing the supposed leftist slant of the mainstream American media. AIM broadened the smear to include five more Washington journalists who, some anonymous KGB source claimed, had been Soviet "agents of influence."* And then AIM's reliable echo chamber of right-wing pundits went to work.

The shift from "agent" to "agent of influence" was just slippery enough to evade a libel suit. But dead men can't sue for libel, and for a few weeks it was open season on I. F. Stone. One factor in keeping the controversy alive was Kalugin, who'd been feverishly trying to peddle his memoirs after his American publisher canceled his contract. Why a man who spread disinformation for a living should be treated as an unimpeachable source is a question best left to Kalugin's collaborators, the more so since his track record included the claim—during his first effort to find an American publisher—that the Soviets had held on to American POWs in Vietnam for years beyond the end of the war.[4]

In the fall of 1992, after he'd found a new publisher, Kalugin decided to clean up the mess he'd created, telling Andrew Brown, who had written the original account of Kalugin's speech for the *Independent,* that while he had indeed been referring to I. F. Stone, any suggestion that

---

*The five were the columnists Joseph Kraft and Jack Anderson, the *Washington Post* reporters Murray Marder and Chalmers Roberts, and Walter Lippmann, who AIM claimed the KGB referred to as "our man in Washington."

Stone had ever been a Soviet intelligence operative was "just a malicious misinterpretation."[5] Kalugin now said that he had met with Stone as he had met with many American journalists* in the course of his official job as press attaché at the Soviet embassy. Sometimes he paid, sometimes they picked up the check. But after the invasion of Czechoslovakia, he told Brown, Stone was so angry he wouldn't even let him pay for lunch. "Never did I mention Stone as a man who was paid as a Soviet agent," Kalugin explained. "He refused to be paid for the lunch. That's all."[6]

Kalugin told a similar story to Martin Garbus, an American constitutional lawyer who met him at the Journalists' Club in Moscow in September 1992. Garbus asked Kalugin whether, so far as he was in a position to know, Stone had ever been paid by the KGB or any other branch of the Russian government. Kalugin replied that that he "was never involved with [Stone] as an agent" nor did he know of any evidence that Stone had "ever received any money from the KGB or the Russian government."[7] And though Kalugin's denials may have been no more credible than his purported allegations, his contention that in describing Stone as an "agent" he'd simply meant someone who was willing to meet with him from time to time—a source or a contact, not an intelligence asset—received support from an unexpected quarter. In late September, William Safire, language maven at the *New York Times* and a former speechwriter for President Nixon, asked an anonymous CIA officer about the difference between an "agent" (i.e., a spy) and an "agent of influence." "That's a Russian term," Safire's CIA contact explained. "When a KGB man found a source, even one that took no money and would have been furious to be considered helpful to a foreign power, he would claim to have developed an agent of influence. It made the KGB man look good in his reports, as if he had half-recruited a well-placed American."[8]

The question of Kalugin's credibility was perhaps most pointedly posed by Mikhail Kazachkov, who spent fifteen years as a prisoner in the Soviet gulag before becoming president of the Freedom Channel, a not-for-profit Russian television company. "These guys, even when they tell

---

*Both Nicholas Daniloff, the former *U.S. News & World Report* writer arrested by the Soviets in 1986, and Stephen Rosenfeld, an editor at the *Washington Post*, told me they'd had many contacts with Kalugin during the 1960s. "In those years it would have been perfectly normal and ordinary for a correspondent to have lunch with Kalugin," said Daniloff.

the truth they only do it for their own interest . . . He is trying to retain visibility. From time to time he pushes out some information—whether it is disinformation or [genuine] information is irrelevant. The whole game is about control. And control is achieved through the dissemination of plausible information."[9]

Unfortunately, very few of Stone's American accusers or defenders understood Kazachkov's warning. Thus Myra MacPherson, seeking further clarification from Kalugin in 2003 for a biography of Stone, elicited only the same equivocal demurrals, plus the seemingly careless aside that Stone had been "willing to perform tasks" for the Soviets! Kalugin was of course well aware of the way the KGB used "tasks" as a term of art in a whole array of unsavory contexts. His stock had been in decline, so his interview with MacPherson offered a brief chance to make headlines once again, especially when reviewers noticed his little slip.[10] It seems not to have occurred to Kalugin's publicists to ask whether a lifetime of service in the organization that slandered Andrei Sakharov and Josef Brodsky should commend a man as a character witness in the case of I. F. Stone (who as it happened was an eloquent defender of both those Russians).[11]

To any regular reader of *I. F. Stone's Weekly*, the charges were preposterous. Long before his famous 1956 denunciation of Khrushchev's Russia—"This is not a good society and it is not led by honest men"— Stone reported the repression, stultification, anti-Semitism, and worship of power that turned the Soviet Union into a vast prison. Even earlier, from his defense of American Trotskyists in 1940 to his war-mongering editorials for *PM* and the *Nation* during the Hitler-Stalin pact to his enthusiastic support for the Marshall Plan, he'd shown a consistent contempt for the dictates of the Communist Party line. "The loss of liberty began with Lenin, as Rosa Luxemburg, Martov, Kautsky and Emma Goldman saw quite early. Leninist democracy is a Trotzkyist myth," he wrote in 1964, a time when some of his latter-day inquisitors were still in thrall to that myth. In 1966, just as his second jaunt on the Kremlin gravy train was meant to be gathering steam, he complained, "American anti-Communism has become such a dirty tool that it is hard to draw the attention of our best youth to the real injustices of the Soviet system." This was said in protest at the arrest of Andrei Sinyavsky and the silencing of Yuli Daniel (for whose persecution it was Oleg Kalugin's job to furnish glib rationalizations). "If peace can be preserved," Izzy wrote in November 1961, "a new generation in Russia will get rid not just of Stalin's mummy but of his system." Abelard Stone may have longed for a Soviet America, but for I. F. Stone Russian communism was always "a gigantic caricature of what socialism was meant to be."[12]

When in 1996 the National Security Agency declassified the Venona transcripts of intercepted KGB cable traffic, Stone's enemies tried to resurrect the controversy, but with little success. Between the Venona decrypts and Stone's FBI file—released in response to requests by this writer and others under the Freedom of Information Act—all of the government's cards were now on the table. It remains theoretically possible that Izzy was BLIN, the evasive journalist with three children who, when approached by the KGB in 1944, did not go running to the FBI. But it is most unlikely, given that by 1944 Stone was already a public antagonist of J. Edgar Hoover who, far from avoiding attracting the FBI's notice, repeatedly challenged both the bureau and its untouchable director. Certainly it is difficult to conceive of any circumstance in which Stone would have looked on Hoover as a potential rescuer. And after reading his mail, tapping his phone, rifling through his garbage, and following him around for months, making him the target of a full-blown espionage investigation over a period of years when his supposed fealty to Moscow hadn't yet been disturbed by events in Budapest, the FBI didn't find a single piece of evidence to suggest that I. F. Stone was anything other than he seemed—an unrepentant radical who concentrated his fire on his own government's failings. As much as it may annoy his critics, when Stone told Andrew Patner that he was never hauled up before HUAC or the McCarthy committee because "like Gypsy Rose Lee, I was taking it off every week. There was nothing left to expose," he appears to have been telling the truth.[13]

•

But what if he hadn't been? In his book *Writing Lives*, Leon Edel, Izzy's former colleague on *PM*, recounts a tale whose allegorical thrust any biographer will recognize. Edel's great subject was Henry James, whose ghost story "A Romance of Certain Old Clothes" revolves, in part, around a key kept in a secret desk drawer. And of course Douglas, the narrator of "The Turn of the Screw," sets up his strange yarn with a disclosure: "The story's written. It's in a locked drawer—it has not been out for years." So it is not difficult to imagine Edel's excitement when he learned that

Henry James himself had equipped his own desk with a secret drawer. Or to sympathize with Edel's disappointment when that drawer, opened after the writer's death, was found to contain only a prescription for spectacles and some gout medicine![14]

To a biographer, the image of the secret drawer is both a temptation and a warning. Anyone who attempts the weird transubstantiation of lived experience into words on the page knows the terror of the overlooked detail, the neglected source, the archive that, if only one had bothered to look, contained a treasure trove of revelatory detail. Nor is it ever possible to escape the knowledge that no matter how assiduous the search, there will always remain a region of unmappable mystery. The temptation is to insist that the most profound truths are invariably hidden from sight, whether deliberately encoded or merely concealed by the profusion of accessible—and therefore less valuable—information. When the subject is I. F. Stone, a man who (like all good investigative reporters) seldom troubled to ask whether he was entitled to the information he sought, who consorted with sources (not all of them model citizens), and whose relationship with the secret world of American communism was never one of simple enmity, the temptation of the secret drawer is all the more powerful. Indeed, the compulsion to explain what we cannot know can lure us far beyond the reach of mere empirical fact. That the drawer turned out to be empty, or its contents innocuous—perhaps some pills or a pair of glasses—is by no means sufficient reason to abandon the quest.

I. F. Stone's desk did not have a secret drawer. I mean his actual desk, which I inspected in his study after his death. Nor does the available evidence—which at this point is probably substantial enough to be conclusive—suggest the existence of a secret life of any kind. Unlike Walter Lippmann, whose Olympian detachment masked the feelings that made him capable of running off with his best friend's wife, I. F. Stone seems to have kept his marriage vows. And from the moment he made a name for himself, Stone's political commitments, however unorthodox, were entirely in line with his professed opinions. That some people—not all of them political opponents—remain unconvinced would not surprise him. "There are some charges," he wrote in 1954, "which must be laughed off or brushed off. They cannot be disproved. If a man charges that he saw Eisenhower riding a broomstick over the White House, he will never be convinced to the contrary by sworn evidence that the President was in bed reading a Western at the time."

Yet because, despite the facts, the evidence, and the consistent clarity of Stone's own writings throughout the fifty years following his denunciation of the Nazi-Soviet pact, the question is likely to persist, it may be worth considering how much it would matter if it were true. Some of those who profess to admire Stone or claim to have been fond of him suggest that if some future unsealing of former Soviet archives should reveal I. F. Stone to have been party to a regular, covert, financial relationship with Soviet intelligence, we should be neither surprised nor dismayed. After all, goes this argument, Stone had no access to secrets. He was in no position to betray his country. And his public pronouncements against the cold war and American imperial arrogance, in favor of a modus vivendi with the Soviet Union, remained persistently radical. If Moscow was willing to overlook Izzy's regular animadversions on the brutal stupidity of Soviet communism in order to subsidize the *Weekly*, why shouldn't he have taken the money? Other left-wing publications supposedly accepted a secret subvention. The CIA's funding of a number of journals—*Encounter*, *Tempo Presente*, *Der Monat*—which gave the agency a kind of shop window in the cultural cold war, has long been known.

My own view is that it would matter very much indeed. I. F. Stone was no plaster saint. He'd earned his hireling's wages on the *Post*, helped Tommy Corcoran pull wires for the White House, and used his column at *PM* to hammer the CIO's enemies and help his friends in the Haganah. His stance was engagement, not detachment. But his causes were always his own, freely chosen, freely espoused. By November 1952, Stone's Washington contacts were all but useless, his career as a big-city newspaper columnist at an end. Yet with his access cut off, Stone gained his independence. Freed at last from publishers, patrons, party loyalties, or party lines, Stone promised his readers "uninhibited commentary and let-the-chips-fall-where-they-may reporting." It was that independence, and the intelligence with which he used it, that kept *I. F. Stone's Weekly*, however well written, from being just another piece of junk mail. A journalist who accepts a hidden subsidy from a foreign power betrays not his country but his readers (as does a reporter who accepts a secret subsidy from his own government). He also betrays himself.

This is not about objectivity. Stone did not believe in objective journalism. "What they call 'objectivity' usually is seeing things the way everybody else sees them," he once told interviewers.[15] This is about honesty. And credibility. The attacks on Stone help to remind us not just of what he was, but of what he represented—an independent radical who kept hold of his ideals, and kept faith with his comrades, without renouncing his freedom to speak his mind. Destroy that credibility and you have destroyed more than a man, more than a reputation. But grant his credibility—grant him the compatibility of his beloved Jefferson and his equally beloved Marx— and I. F. Stone remains, even in death, a dangerous man.

•

I. F. Stone is not buried in Washington. Several months after his death, his ashes were interred at Mount Auburn Cemetery in Cambridge, Massachusetts, the picturesque final resting place of McGeorge Bundy, Oliver Wendell Holmes Sr., and the senators Henry Cabot Lodge *grand-père et petit-fils*. Besides its Brahmin population, Mount Auburn holds the remains of Felix Frankfurter, Arthur Schlesinger Jr., the novelist Bernard Malamud, and poets from Henry Wadsworth Longfellow and Amy Lowell to Robert Creeley. Whatever your vision of the hereafter, Mount Auburn probably qualifies as a good address.

As a figure in the culture, Stone's place seems secure. This is the fourth book devoted to his life, and his work appears in numerous collections (though, scandalously, only once in the Library of America anthologies of American journalism, for his June 1944 plea to admit Jewish refugees; his reporting on and from the Vietnam War, which did as much to galvanize opposition to that war as any work of journalism, is missing from the *Reporting Vietnam* collection). A panel of thirty-six journalists and historians (whose political biases ranged from Todd Gitlin on the left to George Will on the right) asked by New York University in 1999 to list the 100 greatest feats of journalism in the twentieth century put *I. F. Stone's Weekly* at number 16 on the list—below John Hersey's reports from Hiroshima (number 1), Bernstein and Woodward's Watergate investigation (3), and the *New York Times*'s publication of the Pentagon Papers (13), but above Norman Mailer's *Armies of the Night* (19), Hannah Arendt's coverage of the Eichmann trial (20), Truman Capote's *In Cold Blood* (22), and anything by A. J. Liebling, Murray Kempton, Damon Runyon, or Walter Cronkite.[16] The Kronos Quartet, a San Francisco–based string ensemble, commissioned a "Cold War Suite" from the composer Scott Johnson in which each piece uses Stone's recorded voice! His putative claim to the title "first blogger" has become a cyberspace cliché.

His legacy as a writer, though, is more difficult to trace. Murray Kempton said that our children's children would "refer to I. F. Stone as they do to Mencken or Macaulay."* But will they read him? "I had a vision of a paper that would be urbane, erudite, and witty; with substance, but as light as a soufflé," he wrote in the last issue of the *Weekly*. Yet he could wound with either hand, as in his devastating verdict on the presidential campaign chronicler Theodore H. White: "A writer who can be so universally admiring need never lunch alone." Or his remark that the *Washington Post* was such an exciting newspaper because "you never knew on what page you would find a page one story." He could make you cry, too. "It's not so much the killings as the lack of contrition," he wrote in 1964, after a bomber murdered four little girls in a Birmingham, Alabama, church. Even so, sentence by sentence, his claim on posterity is not as a stylist.

He was a very great investigative reporter, probably the greatest solo practitioner ever. But there are limits to what one man can do, even a man as gifted and tenacious as I. F. Stone, especially when he can't or won't cultivate the insider sources who are ultimately essential for the most spectacular Washington scoops. Stone had no false modesty: "Establishment reporters undoubtedly know a lot of things I don't," he often said. "But a lot of what they know isn't true." Still, the reporter's craft is an ephemeral one, with today's front page lining somebody's hamster cage the day after tomorrow.

Yet even Stone's most hastily written pieces hold up remarkably well. His *Nation* account of how Washington reacted to D-day, which stops to note "the darkened Navy Department, the lonely sentries before the White House, the couples making love across the way in Lafayette Park," belongs in any anthology of his best work. So, too, does his front-page *PM* report of Franklin Roosevelt's death, with its admission that "not a few of us cried yesterday when the first flash came over the wire." Sadly, neither of the published collections of Stone's journalism includes any of his work for *PM*, yet it was on those tabloid-size pages, even more than in the *Nation*, that he first exhibited the streetwise, lapel-grabbing voice that

---

*Measured quantitatively, Kempton was absolutely right. If you put "I. F. Stone" into the Google search engine, which counts how often a term is referred to on the World Wide Web (and is the reference of first resort for my children's generation), you get (as of December 2008) approximately 237,000 "hits"—fewer than H. L. Mencken (860,000) but considerably more than Thomas Babington Macaulay (117,000).

was to resonate so powerfully in *I. F. Stone's Weekly*. It was also the *PM* audience, with all its prejudices and preoccupations, that formed the core of Stone's readership. They may have been insufficiently numerous to finance a daily newspaper, but their willingness to pay for what I. F. Stone had to say, week after week, enabled him to survive and even prosper as the Truman era gave way to the haunted fifties. (Stone's ability to muster a paying audience amid such adverse conditions also makes his frequent invocation by today's bloggers misleading self-flattery.)

The great fear that swept the country in the 1950s probably did save Stone from punditry; he was forced instead into a kind of internal exile whose enforced silences allowed him to hone his craft—and his cunning. Cut off from daily journalism, let alone television or radio, he fell back on readers who, like him, represented (depending on how you look at it) either the surviving remnant of the New Deal faith or the hard core of Popular Front delusion. Cast out from the corridors of power he had strode so confidently under Franklin Roosevelt, he became, in Victor Navasky's phrase, an "investigative reader," prospecting through the public record for the nuggets of awkward fact that all governments hide, not locked away in secret archives but in plain sight.

"The key to good reporting," he often said, is the ability to notice "what Galsworthy called the significant trifle." He was a superb reporter, and, rare in the newsrooms of Stone's day and practically unheard of in ours, a superb historian—literate, curious, conscientious. His consciousness of history, and the sense of himself and his subjects as participants in a complex and long-unfolding drama, give his best work a pace and solidity that will outlast any headline.

Though currently out of print, *Underground to Palestine*—his best book, partly because it is his most personal—will remain relevant as long as Israel contends with its neighbors. Unique among the early chronicles of the Jewish state, written like an adventure story but with the force of prophecy, *Underground to Palestine* shows both Israel's desperation and her fateful inability to acknowledge the terrible consequences of that desperation for the Palestinian Arabs. Stone was famously once asked how he could maintain such admiration for the slave owner Thomas Jefferson. "Because history is a tragedy, not a melodrama," he replied. In *Underground to Palestine*, Stone's powers of observation and sympathy are at their highest pitch; so, too, is his sense of tragedy.

Until the United States abandons its dreams of empire, *The Hidden History of the Korean War* will always find and reward readers. Stone's anatomy of American military power in thrall to domestic politics remains so much better than anything else written at the time that it would be worth reading purely as a work of history, even if the Vietnam War hadn't transformed his portrait of a weak president led into the quagmire by a dissembling, disastrously self-deceiving war machine into yet another prophecy. If what's past is indeed prologue, then *The Hidden History of the Korean War* remains an indispensable introduction to all our subsequent follies, its astringent skepticism setting a standard that our embedded media seldom even aspire to reach.

Then there is *I. F. Stone's Weekly*. Read today, the boxes whose contents Stone and his assistants worked so hard to find often fall flat, their intended ironies rendered either heavy-handed or indecipherable by the passage of time. Here, too, Stone has been ill served by his anthologists. A handful of pieces, particularly his firsthand reportage on the struggle for civil rights both in the South and in the Congress (long a Southern plantation) will always repay rereading, likewise his deadly dissections of Kennedy and Johnson's liberal interventionism (still the model for American adventures abroad). His exposé of Pentagon fabrications in the Gulf of Tonkin and his demolition of the State Department's white paper on Vietnam will be studied as long as governments lie. Yet to judge the *Weekly* by its highlights is to miss the essence of Stone's achievement, which was cumulative.

The best way really to grasp what Stone was up to in the *Weekly* is to open the bound volumes and read through them. This is not a recommendation made lightly, but the issues of the *Weekly* read in proper sequence acquire a narrative momentum and scope rivaling the works of Francis Parkman, epic chronicler of the Oregon Trail and the Anglo-French struggle for North America (who also is buried in Mount Auburn). As an activist, Stone remains a prisoner of his times—and of his causes, many of which have come to seem even more radical now than in his day. (Who of us, at the dawn of the twenty-first century, actually expects the United States or Russia or China to renounce nuclear weapons? Which of us would dare suggest that the CIA, despite a half century of bloody incompetence stretching from the Bay of Pigs to the World Trade Center, be put out to pasture?) But as an account of two of the darkest and at the same time most ecstatically hopeful decades in American history, *I. F. Stone's Weekly* has no peer.

To read through even a single year of the *Weekly* is to understand why, despite his scores of imitators and self-appointed disciples, I. F. Stone was unique. In a career that began in the era of *The Front Page*, when reporting was a trade and reporters semiskilled workers on a par with bartenders and policemen, and ended in the age of the celebrity journalist, his longevity itself was a kind of curiosity. Yet the *Weekly* is no mere artifact. Instead, it maps a branch of the American river, a short stretch of the tributary that begins in Boston under British rule and flows through revolt and resistance from Tom Paine and Daniel Shays to the abolitionists, the Populists, Progressives, and subversives right through the twentieth century, bending, like the arc of the universe, toward justice. At times reduced to a trickle or even driven underground, in Stone's lifetime it burst forth as a mighty stream not once but twice, in the 1930s and the 1960s. Each time the floods rose, I. F. Stone was there amid the waters, in right up to his neck. Most of today's journalists are far too sophisticated to risk such embarrassment.

Fortunately, there are still activists who write, and even some writers who would act, often with all of Stone's dedication, if with only some of his talent. What they chiefly lack, though, is Stone's public, the movement to which he gave a voice and which gave him direction. We can perhaps aspire to Stone's courage, but in all honesty we can only envy his confidence—at least for now, though any reader of *I. F. Stone's Weekly* knows not to expect the end of history. The stenographers of power will always find work. As will the trumpeters of fame. I. F. Stone wrote not to create a sensation, or to promote himself (or his "brand"), but to change the world. We read and work—and wait.

A NOTE ON SOURCES

I. F. Stone left little of what biographers and historians think of as "papers." He did, of course, publish several million words in newspapers, magazines, and books. He also left behind what might best be described as "personal effects." During my research, Stone's older son, Jeremy Stone, granted me generous access to his late father's study, where I consulted various materials, including a black ring binder with notes for *The Hidden History of the Korean War*, Stone's address books, and his appointment diaries for the last thirty years of his life.

Unsigned *Nation* articles and editorials attributed to Stone have been verified by checking the annotated set of the *Nation* deposited in the New York Public Library or the set contained in the *Nation* Collection at Harvard. Identifying Stone's unsigned newspaper editorials is more difficult, but in the case of the *New York Post* I have relied principally on the memory of Samuel Grafton, who ran the paper's editorial page with Stone from 1934 to 1938.

With the exception of a very few notes from Albert Einstein and Bertrand Russell, Stone saved none of his own correspondence. I was therefore obliged to trawl for his letters in the papers of his friends and associates, and was immeasurably cheered to find a sizable cache of Stone material in the Michael Blankfort Papers at Boston University. Blankfort was a prodigious correspondent and a lifelong friend of Stone, and his papers include a wealth of material on their whole circle at the University of Pennsylvania.

The following additional manuscript collections were consulted for this book:

American Federation of Musicians, Local 802 Collection, Wagner Labor Archives, New York University
American Newspaper Guild, New York Guild Archives, New York
Newton Arvin Collection, Smith College Library, Northampton, MA
Isaiah Berlin Archive, Wolfson College, Oxford, England
Earl Browder Collection, Smith College Library, Northampton, MA
Irving Caesar Collection, Wisconsin Historical Society, Madison, WI

V. F. Calverton Collection, Rare Books and Manuscripts Division, New York Public
    Library, Astor, Lenox and Tilden Foundations
Columbia University Oral History Project, Columbia University; interviews with:
    Paul Appleby
    Robert Bendiner
    Heather Booth
    Leonard Boudin
    Kenneth Crawford
    Thomas Emerson
    Gardner Jackson
    Corliss Lamont
    Kenneth McCormick
    Richard Rovere
    William Sennett
    J. David Stern
    Norman Thomas
    Henry Wallace
    Colston Warne
Edward U. Condon Collection, American Philosophical Society, Philadelphia, PA
Thomas Corcoran Collection, Manuscript Division, Library of Congress
Malcom Cowley Collection, Newberry Library, Chicago, IL
Virginia Durr Collection, Schlesinger Library, Radcliffe College, Cambridge, MA
James T. Farrell Collection, Van Pelt Library, University of Pennsylvania, Philadelphia, PA
Louis Fischer Collection, Princeton University Library, Princeton, NJ
Jerome Frank Collection, Sterling Library, Yale University
Felix Frankfurter Papers, Mugar Memorial Library, Boston University
Haganah Archives, Tel Aviv, Israel
E. Y. Harburg Collection, Mugar Memorial Library, Boston University
Harold L. Ickes Diaries and Harold L. Ickes Collection, Manuscript Division, Library of
    Congress
Ralph Ingersoll Collection, Mugar Memorial Library, Boston University
V. J. Jerome Papers, Sterling Library, Yale University
Matthew Josephson Collection, Beinecke Library, Yale University
Freda Kirchwey Collection, Schlesinger Library, Radcliffe College, Cambridge, MA
James Kutcher Civil Rights Committee Collection, Wisconsin Historical Society,
    Madison, WI
Owen Lattimore Collection, Manuscript Division, Library of Congress
Max Lerner Collection, Sterling Library, Yale University
Dwight Macdonald Collection, Manuscript Division, Library of Congress
Margaret Marshall Collection, Beinecke Library, Yale University
J. B. Matthews Papers, Special Collections, Duke University, Durham, NC
Meet the Press Collection, Motion Picture, Broadcasting and Sound Division, Library of
    Congress
Alexander Meiklejohn Collection, Wisconsin Historical Society, Madison, WI
Nation Collection, Houghton Library, Harvard University
Newspaper Guild of Philadelphia Collection, Temple University Library, Philadelphia, PA
Harvey O'Connor Collection, Walter Reuther Library, Wayne State University, Detroit, MI

Palestine Statehood Group Collection, Manuscript Division, Library of Congress
Drew Pearson Collection, Lyndon Baines Johnson Library, Austin, TX
Richard Rovere Papers, Wisconsin Historical Society, Madison, WI
Bertrand Russell Archives, McMaster University, Hamilton, Ontario, Canada
Dorothy Schiff Collection, New York Public Library
George Seldes Collection, Van Pelt–Dietrich Library, University of Pennsylvania,
       Philadelphia, PA
Socialist Party Collection, Tamiment Institute Library, New York University
Lawrence Spivak Collection, Manuscript Division, Library of Congress
Joseph R. Starobin Collection, Wisconsin Historical Society, Madison, WI
Kenneth Stewart Collection, American Heritage Center, University of Wyoming, Lara-
       mie, WY
I. F. Stone File, Central Intelligence Agency, Langley, VA
I. F. Stone File, Temple University Library, Philadelphia, PA
Norman Thomas Papers, Rare Books and Manuscripts Division, New York Public Library,
       Astor, Lenox and Tilden Foundations
Shepard Traube Collection, Mugar Memorial Library, Boston University
Harry S. Truman Presidential Personal File and Post-Presidential General File, Harry S.
       Truman Library, Independence, MO
U.S. Department of State, Washington, D.C., Office of Passport Services and Central
       Foreign Policy Records
U.S. Military Intelligence Reports: Surveillance of Radicals, 1917–41, Tamiment Insti-
       tute Library, New York University
James Wechsler Papers, Wisconsin Historical Society, Madison, WI
White House Central Name File, Lyndon Baines Johnson Library, Austin, TX

WORKS BY I. F. STONE

BOOKS

The Court Disposes. New York: Covici, Friede, 1937 (as Isidor Feinstein)
Business as Usual: The First Year of Defense. New York: Modern Age, 1941
Underground to Palestine. New York: Boni and Gaer, 1946. Reprint, Pantheon Books, 1978
This Is Israel. New York: Boni & Gaer, 1948
The Truman Era. New York: Monthly Review Press, 1952. Reprint, Little, Brown, 1988
The Hidden History of the Korean War. New York: Monthly Review Press, 1953. Reprint,
       Little, Brown, 1988
The Haunted Fifties. New York: Random House, 1963. Reprint, Little, Brown, 1989
In a Time of Torment. New York: Random House, 1967. Reprint, Little, Brown, 1989
Polemics and Prophecies. New York: Random House, 1970. Reprint, Little, Brown, 1989
The Killings at Kent State: How Murder Went Unpunished. New York: New York Review, 1971.
The Trial of Socrates. Boston: Little, Brown, 1988.

OTHER WRITINGS

"Haddonfield: A Sketch of Its Early History," in Borough Directory of Haddonfield, N.J.
       (1931)

*Propaganda Analysis: A Bulletin to Help the Intelligent Citizen Detect and Analyze Propa-
ganda.* New York: Institute for Propaganda Analysis, 1939 (pamphlet)
Your Investments. I:vi–viii (July–September 1940). New York: American Investors Union
(written and edited by Stone)
The CIO and National Defense. New York, 1941 (pamphlet)
 I. F. Stone's newspaper and magazine articles and the secondary sources consulted in
writing this book are cited in the notes.

INTERVIEWS

Shana Alexander, Sara Alpern, Eric Alterman, Richard Barnet, Harriet Baskin, Samuel H.
Beer, Arnold Beichman, Sally Belfrage, Robert Bendiner, Larry Bensky, Elmer Berger,
Chip Berlet, Isaiah Berlin, Carl Bernstein, Barbara Bick, Kai Bird, Dorothy Blankfort,
Laurie Blankfort, Jean Boudin, Kathy Boudin, Michael Boudin, Jerry Bruck Jr., Felicity
Bryan, Michael Buckley, SJ, Marvin Caplan, Terence Carroll, Alexander Cockburn,
Roberta Garfield Cohn, Sidney Cohn, Joe Conason, Tom Cornell, I. Edward Cutler,
Nicholas Daniloff, Sigmund Diamond, Elizabeth Dixon, Art D'Lugoff, Roger Donald,
Maurice Donohue, Jim Doyle, Richard Dudman, Virginia Durr, Leon Edel, A. Whitney
Ellsworth, Amos Elon, Margaret Farrington, Creekmore Fath, Suzanne Fields, Franklin
Folsom, Mairi Foreman, Graydon Forrer, Simon Gerson, Celia Gilbert, Ralph Ginzburg,
Arthur Goldschmidt, Reba Goodman, Adam Gopnick, Nathalie Bodanskaya Gorman,
Sanford Gottlieb, Edith Grafton, Samuel Grafton, Fred Graham, John Greenya, Jeremiah
Gutman, Simon Head, Nat Hentoff, Christopher Hitchens, Palmer Holloway, Anthony
Howard, Doug Ireland, Michael Janeway, Marvin Kalb, Oleg Kalugin, Jamie Kalvan,
Stanley Karnow, Shirley Kasdon, Mikhail Kazachkov, Murray Kempton, Penn Kimball,
Bernard Knox, Andrew Kopkind, Neil Kotler, David Kraslow, Amos Landman, David Lat-
timore, Paul Lehmann, Max Lerner, Robert Levin, Nelson Lichtenstein, Stuart Loory,
Jesse Zel Lurie, Christopher Lydon, Paul Lyons, Norman MacKenzie, A. B. Magil, Jere
Mangione, Stephen J. Marmon, Ruth Matthews, Neville Maxwell, Ben Menin, Helen
Goldberg Menin, Karl Meyer, Neil Middleton, Morton Mintz, Jonathan Mirsky, Sidney
Morgenbesser, Andrew Moursund, Victor Navasky, Janet Neschis, Jack O'Dell, Peter Os-
nos, Mark Pavlick, J. R. Pole, Marcus Raskin, Doug Rauschenberger, Sidney Roger, Sum-
ner Rosen, Stephen Rosenfeld, Isador Rosenthal, Steve Rosner, Andrew Roth, Martha
Rountree, Mark Rudd, Edward Said, Arthur Schlesinger Jr., Eleanor Milgrim Schneider,
Zita Schwarcz, Cynthia Scollon, Jack Seigle, George Seldes, Robert Sherrill, Susan
Shicone, Clancy Sigal, Albert Silverman, Robert Silvers, Joshua Sommer, Joseph Spear,
Phil Stanford, Jill Stern, Tommy Stern, Christopher Stone, Esther Stone, Jeremy Stone,
Louis Stone, Peter Stone, Paul Sweezy, Edith Tiger, Sigmund Timberg, Mildred Traube,
Dan Wakefield, Arthur Waskow, Gertrude Weber, Rae Weimer, Nathaniel Weyl, Frank
Wilkinson, Richard Wollheim, Andrew Wylie

NOTES

ABBREVIATIONS

IFS I. F. Stone
IFSBW *I. F. Stone's Bi-Weekly*
IFSW *I. F. Stone's Weekly*

PREFACE

1. "What's Nixon Up To?" *IFSBW*, September 6, 1971.
2. Jerry Buckley, "I. F. Stone: Journalist and Prophet" (B.A. honors thesis, Fordham University, 1977).
3. IFS, interviewed by Graydon Forrer and Elise Glickman, 1979.
4. "The Price at Home of the Destruction We Wreak Abroad," *IFSW*, December 13, 1965; "Slow-Fuse Sarajevo," *IFSW*, February 7, 1966.
5. Murray Kempton, Introduction to I. F. Stone, *In a Time of Torment* (New York: Random House, 1967), p. ix.
6. I. F. Stone et al., "For Solidarity," *New York Review of Books,* April 16, 1981; see also *IFSW,* July 9, 1956, and January 28, 1957.

1: FEINSTEIN'S PROGRESS

1. Louis Stone and Marcus Stone, "The Family (Where and When It Began)" (manuscript); "I. F. Stone," Federal Bureau of Investigation, Headquarters File 100-37078, Document 60, p. 2; interview with Louis Stone, March 13, 1991.
2. Interview with Louis Stone.
3. Ibid. Judah Feinstein's wife was Rachel Tonkonogy, whose first cousin Abraham Tonkonogy was the grandfather of the publisher George Delacorte, who was born George Tonkonogy and took his wife's name.

4. Henry James, "Philadelphia," in *The American Scene* (1907; Bloomington: Indiana University Press, 1968), p. 286.
5. John Lukacs, *Philadelphia: Patricians & Philistines* 1900–1950 (New York: Farrar, Straus, 1981), pp. x–1.
6. Caroline Golab, "The Immigrant and the City: Poles, Italians, and Jews in Philadelphia, 1870–1920," in Allen F. Davis and Mark H. Haller, eds., *The Peoples of Philadelphia: A History of Ethnic Groups and Lower-Class Life, 1790–1940* (Philadelphia: Temple University Press, 1973), pp. 204–205.
7. Edward P. Johanningsmeier, *Forging American Communism: The Life of William Z. Foster* (Princeton: Princeton University Press, 1994), p. 40.
8. Maxwell Whiteman, "Philadelphia's Jewish Neighborhoods," in Davis and Haller, *Peoples of Philadelphia.*
9. Andrew Patner, *I. F. Stone: A Portrait* (New York: Anchor Books, 1990), p. 117.
10. Interview with Jeremy Stone, November 20, 1991.
11. Henry Clay Fox, ed., *Memoirs of Wayne County and the City of Richmond, Indiana* (Madison: Western Historical Association, 1912), pp. 519–26; *Richmond Directory* (Indianapolis: R. L. Polk, 1912), p. 143.
12. Lance Jonathan Sussman, *The Emergence of a Jewish Community in Richmond, Indiana* (Fort Wayne: Indiana Jewish Historical Society, 1981), p. 52.
13. Douglas B. Rauschenberger and Katherine Mansfield Tassini, *Lost Haddonfield* (Haddonfield: Historical Society of Haddonfield, 1989).
14. Marcus Stone, "Max" (manuscript).
15. Louis Stone and Marcus Stone, "The Family."
16. Marcus Stone, "Max."
17. Ibid.; interview with Isador Rosenthal, March 3, 1994; Douglas Rauschenberger, letter to the author, December 7, 1994.
18. Interview with Margaret Farrington, November 25, 1991; interview with I. Edward Cutler, March 3, 1994; *Public Press*, Haddonfield, July 26, 1923.
19. Interview with Louis Stone; Jeffrey M. Dorwart and Philip English Mackey, *Camden County, New Jersey, 1616–1976: A Narrative History* (Camden: Camden County Cultural and Heritage Commission, 1976); Louis Stone and Marcus Stone, "The Family"; interview with I. Edward Cutler.
20. Dick Polman, "Outcasts and Icons," *Philadelphia Inquirer*, January 28, 1968, p. C1; IFS, *The Truman Era* (Boston: Little, Brown, 1952), pp. 100–101; interview with Margaret Farrington.
21. Interview with Margaret Farrington; interview with Palmer Holloway, November 23, 1992.
22. John Greenya, "Portrait of a Man Reading," *Washington Post Book World*, February 14, 1971, p. 2.
23. IFS to a Mr. Erickson, May 3, 1968; ibid.
24. Greenya, "Portrait of a Man Reading"; Malcolm Cowley, "Books That Changed Our Minds," *New Republic* 95 (December 21, 1938): 205–206; Jack London, *Martin Eden* (New York: Library of America, 1982), p. 849.
25. London, *Martin Eden*, pp. 849, 650.
26. Peter Kropotkin, *The Conquest of Bread and Other Writings* (1906; New York: Cambridge University Press, 1995), p. 34.
27. Buckley, "I. F. Stone."
28. Kropotkin, *Conquest of Bread*, pp. 35–36.

29. See any of Stone's articles (writing as Abelard Stone) in *Modern Monthly*, particularly "Roosevelt Moves Toward Fascism," vol. 7, no. 5 (June 1933): 261–74.

30. Greenya, "Portrait of a Man Reading"; *The Shield*, Haddonfield High School, 1924.

31. IFS, "I. F. Stone on Bertrand Russell on Bertrand Russell," *Ramparts*, April 1970, 64–73.

32. Louis Stone and Marcus Stone, "The Family"; Marcus Stone, "Max"; interview with Isador Rosenthal.

33. Louis Stone and Marcus Stone, "The Family"; Marcus Stone, "Max"; IFS eulogy for Ithamar Feinstein, 1934, reproduced in *Your Family Flyer*, a Feinstein family newsletter, vol. 1, no. 2, October 25, 1989.

34. *Your Family Flyer* 4, no. 3; Patner, *I. F. Stone*, p. 118.

35. Patner, *I. F. Stone*, p. 118; Marcus Stone, "Max"; Louis Stone and Marcus Stone, "The Family."

36. Interview with Louis Stone; Malcolm Cowley, "Books That Changed Our Minds"; Ronald Steel, *Walter Lippmann and the American Century* (Boston: Little, Brown, 1980), p. 75.

37. Robert Cottrell, *Izzy: A Biography of I. F. Stone* (New Brunswick, NJ: Rutgers University Press, 1992), p. 24; interview with Louis Stone; IFS, "Notes on Closing, But Not in Farewell," *IFSW* 19, no. 21–22 (December 14, 1971): 1.

38. *Progress* 1, no. 1 (February 1922); interview with Margaret Farrington.

39. *Progress* 1, no. 2 (March 1922); interview with Palmer Holloway.

40. IFS, interviewed by Forrer and Glickman; *IFSW* 3, no. 36 (October 3, 1955): 2; *Progress* 1, no. 3 (April 1922).

41. *Progress* 1, no. 3 (April 1922); Marcus Stone, "Max."

42. Isadore Feinstein transcript, Haddonfield High School; Greenya, "Portrait of a Man Reading"; interview with Karl Meyer, December 12, 1991; interview with Margaret Farrington.

43. Louis Stone and Marcus Stone, "The Family"; interview with Louis Stone; interview with Jill Stern, December 9, 1992.

44. J. David Stern, *Memoirs of a Maverick Publisher* (New York: Simon & Schuster, 1962), pp. 113, 127.

45. Bernard Feinstein deeds on file in Camden County, NJ, Courthouse.

46. Stern, *Memoirs*, p. 9; Patner, *I. F. Stone*, pp. 32–34. The byline Isadore Feinstein does not appear in the *Camden Courier* during 1923.

47. Interview with Jill Stern.

48. E. Digby Baltzell, Allen Glicksman, and Jacqueline Litt, "The Jewish Communities of Philadelphia and Boston," in Murray Friedman, ed., *Jewish Life in Philadelphia: 1830–1940* (Philadelphia: Ishi Publications, 1983), p. 310; Michael Blankfort, draft autobiography, Michael Blankfort Papers, Box 59, folder 4.

49. Blankfort, autobiography; Isadore Feinstein transcript, University of Pennsylvania.

50. Blankfort, autobiography.

51. Ibid.

52. Ibid.; interview with Mildred Traube, August 27, 1991; interview with Nathalie Bodanskaya Gorman, November 5, 1991.

53. IFS to Michael Blankfort, July 21, 1926, Blankfort Papers, Box 83, folder 3. Interview with Janet Neschis, March 21, 1995; "Pirandello a Disappointment," *Camden Courier,* July 2, 1926; *Camden Morning Post*, July 2, 1926, p. 1.

54. IFS to Michael Blankfort, July 21, 1926.

55. Edward Abrahams, *The Lyrical Left* (Charlottesville: University Press of Virginia, 1986), pp. 166–67.

56. Interview with Louis Stone; Malcolm Cowley, *Exile's Return* (1934; New York: Penguin, 1994), p. 9; Isadore Feinstein, *Junto*, May 1928, pp. 24–28.

57. Interview with Helen Goldberg Menin, June 1992.

58. Interview with Jean Boudin, March 27, 1991; interview with Eleanor Milgram Schneider, June 4, 1992.

59. IFS to Esther Roisman, May 17, 1927.

60. IFS to Michael Blankfort, July 21, 1926.

61. IFS to Esther Roisman, May 17, 1927; interview with Sidney Cohn, July 1991; interview with Janet Neschis.

62. Robert Gershon, interview with IFS, December 29, 1982.

63. IFS, "Notes on Closing."

64. Gardner Jackson, Oral History, Columbia University Oral History Project, p. 115; David Felix, *Protest: Sacco-Vanzetti and the Intellectuals* (Bloomington: Indiana University Press, 1965), pp. 212–13.

65. Robert Strauss Feuerlicht, *Justice Crucified: The Story of Sacco and Vanzetti* (New York: McGraw-Hill, 1977), pp. vii–ix; Louis Joughin and Edmund Morgan, *The Legacy of Sacco and Vanzetti* (Princeton: Princeton University Press, 1948), pp. 238, 274; Felix, *Protest*.

66. Cottrell, *Izzy*, pp. 30–31. Louis Stone told Cottrell that Izzy never made it out of Camden. Bernard, he said, headed his son off at the ferry landing. Izzy told the same interviewer that he did leave town, but when he stopped to visit a relative in New York he learned of the reprieve and decided to continue north to stay with a friend, Vernon Rich, an actor from Camden who was spending the summer in Bellows Falls, Vermont. Neither of these accounts is wholly satisfactory. For one thing, the first strong indication that there might be a reprieve came less than two hours before midnight on the tenth—the time originally scheduled for the executions (Felix, *Protest*, p. 213). Anyone hoping to reach Boston in time would have already left New York. Louis Stone told me about his brother's sojourn in Vermont but couldn't recall his route. Given the importance Stone obviously attached to the incident, and the fact that a half century later he still remembered the name of his Vermont friend—who was indeed a native of Bellows Falls—I'm inclined to believe he made it to New England.

67. Jackson, Oral History, p. 242; IFS to Esther Roisman, May 17, 1927.

68. Seymour Michael Blankfort, "A Final Appeal," in Lucia Trent, ed., *America Arraigned!* (New York: Dean, 1928), p. 48.

69. Malcolm Cowley, "Echoes of a Crime," *New Republic* 134, no. 79 (August 28, 1935).

70. The expression is from IFS, "In Defense of the Campus Rebels," *IFSW* 17, no. 10 (May 19, 1969): 1.

71. John Dos Passos, *U.S.A.: The Big Money* (New York: Harcourt, 1961), pp. 521–22.

2: PUBLISHER'S APPRENTICE

1. William G. Shepherd, "The Price of Liquor," *Collier's*, December 1, 1928, pp. 8–41.

2. Thomas H. Coode and John F. Bauman, *People, Poverty and Politics: Pennsylvanians During the Great Depression* (Lewisburg: Bucknell University Press, 1981), p. 176; Bonnie Fox Schwartz, "Unemployment Relief in Philadelphia, 1930–1932: A Study of the Depression's Impact on Voluntarism," in Bernard Sternsher, ed., *Hitting*

Home: The Great Depression in Town and Country (Chicago: Ivan R. Dee, 1989), p. 65.

3. Schwartz, "Unemployment Relief," p. 64; Philip Scranton, *Figured Tapestry: Production, Markets, and Power in Philadelphia Textiles, 1885–1941* (New York: Cambridge University Press, 1989), p. 11.

4. Coode and Bauman, *People, Poverty*, pp. 52–53.

5. Henry Tetlow, "Philadelphia Acquires a Good Newspaper," *American Mercury* 28 (February 1933): 185–87.

6. Russell Davenport, *Fortune* 13, no. 6 (June 1936): 186.

7. Schwartz, "Unemployment Relief."

8. IFS to Esther Roisman, May 17, 1927; Isadore Feinstein transcript.

9. Robert Cottrell, interview with IFS, October 16, 1981, transcript made available by Robert Cottrell.

10. Ibid.

11. Ibid.

12. IFS, "Notes on Closing."

13. Daniel Leab, *A Union of Individuals: The Formation of the American Newspaper Guild, 1933–1936* (New York: Columbia University Press, 1970), pp. 120–25.

14. Buckley, "I. F. Stone," p. 14.

15. *Junto*, May 1928, pp. 2–4; Michael Blankfort to Mr. Lyle, September 9, 1972, Blankfort Papers. In the same letter, Blankfort says that "Auerbach disappeared into the radical movement . . . and I don't know what happened to him." According to Harvey Klehr in *The Heyday of American Communism* (New York: Basic Books, 1984), pp. 422–23, after leaving Penn, Auerbach adopted the party name of Jim Allen, later becoming editor of the *Southern Worker*.

16. IFS to Esther Roisman, May 17, 1927.

17. "Pepito the Clown Stars on Fox Bill," *Camden Evening Courier*, July 17, 1928.

18. Ibid.

19. "Civic Theatre Opens in Play by Tchekoff," *Evening Courier*, April 8, 1930.

20. "Movie Dramatizes Undersea Disaster," *Evening Courier*, November 6, 1928.

21. "Max, Have Moissi!" *Evening Courier*, December 11, 1928.

22. "Word or Flesh," *Evening Courier*, December 4, 1928.

23. "Better Than Ben Jonson," *Evening Courier*, December 18, 1928.

24. "To Be Witty or to Be Pure," *Evening Courier*, November 20, 1928.

25. "Another Gangster Finds Salvation," *Evening Courier*, October 16, 1928.

26. "Who Might Doris Vinton Be?" *Evening Courier*, December 18, 1928; Walter Hart to Michael Blankfort, n.d., Blankfort Papers.

27. "Editorial Note," *American Mercury* 29 (May 1933): xxiv.

28. David A. Shannon, *The Socialist Party of America: A History* (New York: Macmillan, 1955), p. 187; interview with Ben Menin, June 1992.

29. Irving Howe, *Socialism and America* (New York: Harcourt, 1985), pp. 3–4, 49–50.

30. Ibid.; IFS, "Notes on Closing." He was not, however, the youngest state official in the party. That distinction probably belonged to David George, an eighteen-year-old who served as secretary of the Virginia party in 1928 when no one else could be found to take the job (Shannon, *Socialist Party*, p. 200).

31. Roy Rosenzweig, "'Socialism in Our Time': The Socialist Party and the Unemployed, 1929–1936," *Labor History* 20 (1979): 488–89.

32. Cottrell, *Izzy.*

33. See Lawrence Goodwyn, *The Populist Moment: A Short History of the Agrarian Revolt in America* (New York: Oxford University Press, 1978), for an enlightening discussion of the relationship between politics and "movement culture."
34. Norman Thomas, "The Thirties in America as a Socialist Recalls Them," in Rita James Simon, ed., *The Thirties: Essays on Social and Political Movements of a Decade* (Urbana: University of Illinois Press, 1967), p. 115.
35. Cottrell, *Izzy.*
36. Gershon interview with IFS.
37. Floyd Dell, *Liberator* 3 (January 1920): 46.
38. Margaret Brenman-Gibson, *Clifford Odets: American Playwright* (New York: Atheneum, 1981), pp. 122–23; interview with Jean Boudin.
39. Eric A. Gordon, *Mark the Music: The Life and Work of Marc Blitzstein* (New York: St. Martin's Press, 1989), pp. 24, 33.
40. Friedman, *Jewish Life in Philadelphia*, pp. 21–22.
41. Interview with Samuel Grafton, April 25, 1991.
42. Interview with Jean Boudin.
43. John P. Diggins, *Mussolini and Fascism: The View from America* (Princeton: Princeton University Press, 1972), p. 141.
44. Patner, *I. F. Stone*, p. 37; Robert Jewett and John Shelton Lawrence, *The Myth of the American Superhero* (Grand Rapids: William B. Eerdmans, 2002), pp. 132–33; Diggins, *Mussolini*, p. 40. See also Benjamin L. Alpers, *Dictators, Democracy, & American Public Culture: Envisioning the Totalitarian Enemy, 1920s–1950s* (Chapel Hill: University of North Carolina Press, 2003).
45. *Philadelphia Jewish Exponent*, July 12, 1929, p. 12.
46. Interview with Jean Boudin.
47. Bernard Feinstein deeds.
48. Dorwart and Mackey, *Camden County*, pp. 217–20.
49. John F. Bauman and Thomas H. Coode, *In the Eye of the Great Depression: New Deal Reporters and the Agony of the American People* (DeKalb: Northern Illinois University Press, 1988), p. 42.
50. Cottrell, *Izzy.*
51. Walter Hart to Michael Blankfort, April 1929, Blankfort Papers.
52. George Seldes, *The Years of the Locust: America 1929–1932* (1933; New York: Da Capo Press, 1973), p. 42.
53. "Ethel Barrymore, a Cleo Conquered in 'Love Duel,'" *Evening Courier*, March 18, 1930.
54. "Hop This Finale," *Evening Courier*, July 27, 1930; "Colored Swindler Turns Messiah in 'Sweet Chariot,'" ibid., October 7, 1930.
55. *Evening Courier*, June 17, September 9, and December 30, 1930.
56. Seldes, *Years of the Locust*, p. 25; "'The Apple Cart' Opens at Garrick," *Evening Courier*, December 9, 1930.
57. "'Once in a Lifetime' Thumps the Talkies," *Evening Courier*, September 2, 1930.
58. Schlesinger and Warshow quoted in Robert S. McElvaine, *The Great Depression: America 1929–1941* (New York: Times Books, 1984), pp. 208–209.
59. Seldes, *Years of the Locust*, p. 57.
60. Interview with Louis Stone.
61. Interview with Kathy Boudin, September 2007.
62. Ben Hecht, *A Child of the Century* (New York: Signet Books, 1955), pp. 117–18,

136. Though the job title has fallen out of use, city editors still send reporters out with the admonition not to return without a photo of the newsworthy deceased.

63. "De Rohan Is Sentenced," *New York Times*, January 29, 1926, p. 5.

64. Stephen M. O'Keefe, "Stone 'Unturned' in 50 Years," *Courier-Post*, December 10, 1971, p. 1.

65. Gershon interview with IFS. The epigraph to this chapter is from the same source.

66. Henry Demarest Lloyd quoted in Harvey Swados, *Years of Conscience: The Muckrakers* (Cleveland: Meridian Books, 1962), pp. 13–14.

67. Quoted ibid., pp. 12–13.

68. Ray Stannard Baker, *American Magazine* 72 (1911): 61, quoted in David Mark Chalmers, *The Social and Political Ideas of the Muckrakers* (Salem, NH: Ayer Company, 1964), p. 74.

69. Justin Kaplan, *Lincoln Steffens* (New York: Simon & Schuster, 1974).

70. Goodywn, *Populist Moment*, pp. xiv–xvii.

71. Russell F. Weigley, ed., *Philadelphia: A 300-Year History* (New York: Norton, 1982), p. 584.

72. Sam Bass Warner Jr., *The Private City: Philadelphia in Three Periods of Its Growth* (Philadelphia: University of Pennsylvania Press, 1968), pp. 217–18. While not denying Vare's kleptocratic tendencies, Warner argues that Vare was "instrumental in guiding the final bills through the Pennsylvania legislature for workman's compensation, child labor, hours of labor for women, Mother's Assistance welfare payments, and the constitutional amendment giving women the vote," and that Vare also unsuccessfully sponsored an old-age pension bill.

73. Davenport, *Fortune,* June 1936: 194; E. Digby Baltzell, *Philadelphia Gentlemen: The Making of a National Upper Class* (Glencoe, IL: Free Press, 1958), pp. 379–80.

74. Coode and Bauman, *People, Poverty*, pp. 224–25; Sandra Featherman, "Jewish Politics in Philadelphia, 1920–1940," in Friedman, *Jewish Life in Philadelphia*, p. 278.

75. Weigley, *Philadelphia*, pp. 620–21.

76. The *Philadelphia Record* reporters' assignment books are at the Historical Society of Pennsylvania. Isidor Feinstein first appears in the entry for September 23, 1931.

77. Schwartz, "Unemployment Relief," p. 65; Coode and Bauman, *People, Poverty*, p. 178; *Philadelphia Record*, October 4, 1931, p. 1.

78. See William L. Phillips and Bernard Sternsher, "Victims of the Great Depression: The Question of Blame and First-Person History," in Sternsher, *Hitting Home*, pp. 267–85.

79. Klehr, *Heyday*, p. 41.

80. Coode and Bauman, *People, Poverty*, pp. 55, 57, 62–63.

81. Ibid., p. 180.

82. Mauritz A. Hallgren, "Mass Misery in Philadelphia," *Nation* 134 (March 9, 1932), 275–77.

83. Cottrell, *Izzy*.

84. Coode and Bauman, *People, Poverty*, p. 63.

85. *Philadelphia Record*, February 13, 1931, p. 8.

86. Schwartz, "Unemployment Relief," pp. 60–61, 78.

87. Seldes, *Years of the Locust*, pp. 188–91.

88. *Philadelphia Record*, August 5, 1932, p. 8.

89. Weigley, *Philadelphia*, p. 612.

90. *Philadelphia Record*, October 23, 1932, p. 1.
91. *Philadelphia Record*, August 8, 1932.
92. Klehr, *Heyday*, p. 91.
93. A. B. Magil, "Toward Social Fascism—The 'Rejuvenation of the Socialist Party,'" *Communist* 2 (April 1930): 309–20.
94. Blankfort, autobiography.
95. Leonard Wilcox, *V. F. Calverton: Radical in the American Grain* (Philadelphia: Temple University Press, 1992), pp. 31, 49, 99, 147.
96. Blankfort, autobiography.
97. Alfred Kazin, *Starting Out in the Thirties* (Boston: Little, Brown, 1965), pp. 61–65.
98. V. F. Calverton to Isidor Feinstein, January 6, 1933, Rare Book and Manuscripts Division, New York Public Library.
99. Henry Tetlow, "Philadelphia Acquires a Good Newspaper," *American Mercury* 28 (February 1933): 185–87.
100. IFS, interviewed by Forrer and Glickman; Isidor Feinstein, "A Gentleman in Politics," *American Mercury* 29 (May 1933): 82–85.
101. IFS to Michael Blankfort, July 21, 1926, Blankfort Papers; Feinstein, "A Gentleman in Politics," p. 83.
102. Feinstein, "A Gentleman in Politics," p. 85.
103. Abelard Stone, "Roosevelt Moves Toward Fascism," *Modern Monthly* 7, no. 5 (June 1933): 261–74.
104. League of Professional Groups for Foster and Ford, *Culture and the Crisis: An Open Letter to the Writers, Artists, Teachers, Physicians, Engineers, Scientists and Other Professional Workers of America* (New York: Workers Library Publishers, 1932), pp. 17, 23.
105. Wilcox, *V. F. Calverton*, pp. 14–50.
106. Abelard Stone, "Morgan & Co.: A House of Ill Fame," *Modern Monthly* 7, no. 6 (July 1933): 344.
107. Blankfort, autobiography.
108. Isidor Feinstein, "Back to Autocracy," *Philadelphia Record*, January 22, 1933, p. 9; Abelard Stone, "Who Pays for Inflation?" *Modern Monthly* 7, no. 3 (April 1933): 135–37.
109. "The Twilight of Capitalism and Democracy in Germany," *Philadelphia Record*, January 31, 1933, p. 8.
110. Abelard Stone, "The Literary Caravan," *Modern Monthly* 7, no. 3 (April 1933): 189.
111. Isidor Feinstein, "Social Democracy Surrenders," *Philadelphia Record*, April 4, 1933, p. 8.
112. Abelard Stone, "Literary Caravan"; Klehr, *Heyday*, p. 102; Abelard Stone, "Morgan & Co.," p. 345.
113. Frank A. Warren III, *Liberals and Communism: The "Red Decade" Revisited* (Bloomington: Indiana University Press, 1966), p. 44.

3: MANHATTAN TRANSFER

1. J. David Stern, Oral History, Columbia University Oral History Collection, p. 80.
2. Interview with Samuel Grafton.
3. "New York Loyal to Its Own," *New York Evening Post*, December 11, 1933, p. 1.
4. Ibid.

5. Cottrell, interview with IFS.

6. Rauschenberger and Tassini, *Lost Haddonfield*, p. 62.

7. Interview with Louis Stone.

8. Earl Bond, *Dr. Kirkbride and His Mental Hospital* (Philadelphia: Lippincott, 1947), p. 152.

9. Federal Writers' Project, *New York Panorama* (1983; New York: Pantheon, 1984), p. 3.

10. Robert A. M. Stern, Gregory Gilmartin, and Thomas Mellins, *New York 1930: Architecture and Urbanism Between the Two World Wars* (New York: Rizzoli, 1987).

11. Dos Passos, *U.S.A.: The Big Money*, p. 65.

12. Ann Douglas, *Terrible Honesty: Mongrel Manhattan in the 1920s* (New York: Farrar, Straus and Giroux, 1995), p. 15.

13. Federal Writers' Project, *New York Panorama*, p. 76.

14. Robert Caro, *The Power Broker: Robert Moses and the Fall of New York* (New York: Vintage Books, 1975), p. 354.

15. Cottrell, *Izzy*; Isidor Feinstein, "Warning," *New York Evening Post*, December 28, 1933, p. 1.

16. Norman Thomas and Paul Blanshard, *What's the Matter with New York: A National Problem* (New York: Macmillan, 1932), p. 3.

17. Ibid., pp. 177–78.

18. Moshe R. Gottlieb, *American Anti-Nazi Resistance, 1933–1941: An Historical Analysis* (New York: KTAV, 1982), pp. 57, 131, 222.

19. "A Good Beginning," *New York Evening Post*, December 14, 1933, p. 10.

20. Isidor Feinstein, "Pension Graft," ibid.

21. "O'Brien Is on Warpath; Reads Editorial in Post and Goes for Our Scalp," *New York Evening Post*, December 16, 1933, p. 1.

22. Michael Blankfort to Karen Malpede, n.d., Blankfort Papers.

23. Charles Shipman, *It Had to Be Revolution: Memoirs of an American Radical* (Ithaca, NY: Cornell University Press, 1993), pp. 189–92.

24. Federal Writers' Project, *New York Panorama*, p. 275.

25. Shipman, *It Had to Be Revolution*.

26. Ibid.

27. Cottrell, *Izzy*.

28. Buckley, "I. F. Stone," p. 34.

29. Cottrell, *Izzy*.

30. "Barricades Against Brown Shirt Barbarism," *New York Evening Post*, February 13, 1934, p. 8.

31. "Reds Mass at Pier to Boo Austrians Arriving Tonight," *New York Evening Post*, February 17, 1934, p. 2; Howe, *Socialism and America*, p. 60.

32. "Disgraceful," *New York Evening Post*, February 19, 1934, p. 6.

33. Buckley, "I. F. Stone," p. 36.

34. "Thunder on the Left," *New York Evening Post*, November 30, 1934, p. 8.

35. Cottrell, *Izzy*.

36. Kazin, *Starting Out in the Thirties*, p. 15.

37. Bernard Karsh and Phillips L. Garman, "The Impact of the Political Left," in Milton Derber and Edwin Young, eds., *Labor and the New Deal* (Madison: University of Wisconsin Press, 1957), p. 86.

38. Ibid., p. 98.

39. McElvaine, *Great Depression*, pp. 225–26.
40. Mark Naison, "Remaking America: Communists and Liberals in the Popular Front," in Michael E. Brown, Randy Martin, Frank Rosengarten, and George Snedeker, eds., *New Studies in the Politics and Culture of U.S. Communism* (New York: Monthly Review Press, 1993), p. 51.
41. Anthony J. Badger, *The New Deal: The Depression Years, 1933–1940* (New York: Hill and Wang, 1989), p. 130.
42. Meridel Le Sueur, "I Was Marching," in *Ripening: Collected Work 1927–1980* (Old Westbury, NY: Feminist Press, 1982), pp. 158, 162.
43. Michael Denning, *The Cultural Front: The Laboring of American Culture in the Twentieth Century* (New York: Verso, 1998), p. 68.
44. Hal Draper, "The Student Movements of the Thirties: A Political History," in Simon, *The Thirties*, p. 170; see also Robert Cohen, *When the Old Left Was Young: Student Radicals and America's First Mass Student Movement, 1929–1941* (New York: Oxford University Press, 1993).
45. Klehr, *Heyday*, p. 350.
46. "The Showdown," *New York Evening Post*, July 17, 1934, p. 6; "Sinclair in California," *New York Evening Post*, August 30, 1934, p. 6.
47. Isidor Feinstein, "How to Make a Riot," *New Republic*, June 27, 1934, pp. 178–80.
48. Ibid.
49. Interview with Simon Gerson, October 3, 1991. Gerson was the *Daily Worker*'s City Hall bureau chief in the 1930s; the relief worker was his wife, Sophie.
50. Isidor Feinstein, "O'Ryan Must Go," *New York Post*, August 12, 1934, p. 6.
51. Cottrell, *Izzy*; Elizabeth Dilling, *The Red Network: A "Who's Who" and Handbook of Radicalism for Patriots* (Kenilworth, IL: Elizabeth Dilling, 1934), pp. 297–98.
52. Simon Gerson, *Pete: The Story of Peter V. Cacchione, New York's First Communist Councilman* (New York: International Publishers, 1976), p. 54.
53. Cottrell, *Izzy*, p. 56.
54. Interviews with Arnold Beichman, April 1994 and October 1996.
55. Interview with Samuel Grafton.
56. Quoted in Stefan Kanfer, *A Journal of the Plague Years* (New York: Atheneum, 1973), p. 34.
57. Michael Blankfort, *A Time to Live* (New York: Harcourt, 1943), p. 162.
58. "Justice at Scottsboro," *Philadelphia Record*, November 9, 1932, p. 8.
59. "Too Dumb to Be Dangerous," *New York Post*, August 12, 1935, p. 8.
60. "The Case Against Dictatorship," *New York Post*, June 24, 1935, p. 10.
61. Ibid.; "About the Red Bogey," *New York Post*, August 6, 1934, p. 6.
62. "The Wild and Visionary Theorist," *New York Post*, August 14, 1934, p. 8.
63. "Fight the Un-American with American Methods," *New York Post*, February 6, 1935, p. 6; Isidor Feinstein, "About That Red Scare on Relief," *New York Post*, October 17, 1935, p. 14.
64. Warren, *Liberals and Communism*, pp. 45–48.
65. Interview with Nathaniel Weyl, November 19, 1996; see also Earl Latham, *The Communist Controversy in Washington: From the New Deal to McCarthy* (Cambridge, MA: Harvard University Press, 1966), pp. 102–23.
66. Klehr, *Heyday*, p. 74.
67. Naison, "Remaking America," pp. 55, 59.
68. Howe, *Socialism and America*, pp. 60–61.

69. B. J. Field, "The Viewpoint of the Left (Trotsky) Opposition," *Modern Monthly* 7, no. 5 (June 1933): 280.

70. Klehr, *Heyday*, pp. 167–68.

71. Morgan Himelstein, *Drama Was a Weapon: The Left-Wing Theatre in New York, 1929–1941* (New Brunswick, NJ: Rutgers University Press, 1963), p. 41; Isidor Feinstein, "They Played It Safe," *New York Post*, May 8, 1935, p. 12.

72. Denning, *Cultural Front*, pp. 442–43.

73. "A Victory for World Opinion," *New York Evening Post*, December 26, 1933, p. 6.

74. Isidor Feinstein, "The People's Front in France," *New York Post*, April 28, 1935, p. 12; "Poor Little Ethiopia," *New York Post*, August 16, 1935, p. 10.

75. Isidor Feinstein, "Jitters in the Kremlin," *New York Post*, August 18, 1936, p. 8; "Borsch," *New York Post*, December 1, 1936, p. 8.

76. Latham, *Communist Controversy*, pp. 46–48.

77. Howe, *Socialism and America*, pp. 88–89. As usual, Howe's densely contentious prose contains several strands of argument, many of them debatable. Talk of motives is fair enough, but noble motives should not be equated with admirable policies, nor should one assume that out of base motivations higher goals cannot be attained—indeed, the liberal apologia for capitalism is founded on the converse assumption. While the Popular Front may well have been "conceived in bad faith," Howe's rhetoric about its execution is contradicted by his own assertion that "much of the credit for the success of the Popular Front must go to [CP leader] Earl Browder," who did not merely accept "the Popular Front line; he warmed to it, he enjoyed it, and he came, with evident sincerity, to believe in it" (p. 96).

78. Maurice Isserman, *Which Side Were You On? The American Communist Party During the Second World War* (Middletown, CT: Wesleyan University Press, 1982).

79. Ibid., p. 22.

80. Klehr, *Heyday*, pp. 91, 413.

81. "The Totalitarian God," *New York Post*, December 31, 1935, p. 6.

82. Feinstein, "About That Red Scare on Relief."

83. Isidor Feinstein, "Racketeering in the A. F. of L.: I. The Poultry Racket," *Nation* 141, no. 3662 (September 11, 1935): 288–91.

84. Isidor Feinstein, "Racketeering in the A. F. of L.: II. Skulduggery in New York," *Nation* 141, no. 3663 (September 18, 1935): 316–18.

85. Harvey Klehr, John Earl Haynes, and Fridrikh Igorevich Firsov, *The Secret World of American Communism* (New Haven, CT: Yale University Press, 1995), p. 9. The authors promised that in a subsequent volume they will "reproduce documents definitely establishing Bridges's membership in the CPUSA" (p. 104).

86. Louis Adamic, *My America* (New York: Harper, 1938), pp. 316–23. Adamic, a fervent anti-Stalinist who was nonetheless a key Popular Front figure, provides shrewd yet sympathetic contemporary portraits of both Lewis and Harry Bridges.

87. Ibid., p. 394; interview with Jill Stern.

88. Leo Huberman, *We, the People* (New York: Harper, 1947), p. 317; Adamic, *My America*, pp. 386, 394.

89. Badger, *New Deal*, pp. 132–33.

90. Klehr, Haynes, and Firsov suggest that Lewis personally negotiated an agreement with the CPUSA leadership to allow party members to work for the CIO—an arrangement that, given Lewis's well-known preference for going to the top, seems plausible (*Secret World*, p. 106).

91. Feinstein, "Skulduggery in New York."
92. Isidor Feinstein, "Spying on the Jobless: Tsarist Methods in New York," *New Republic*, October 30, 1935, pp. 328–31.
93. Katie Louchheim, *The Making of the New Deal: The Insiders Speak* (Cambridge, MA: Harvard University Press, 1983), pp. 67–70.
94. Joseph P. Lash, *Dealers and Dreamers: A New Look at the New Deal* (New York: Doubleday, 1988), p. 60.
95. Jordan A. Schwarz, *The New Dealers: Power Politics in the Age of Roosevelt* (New York: Knopf, 1993), pp. 126–27; Louchheim, *Making of the New Deal*, p. 25.
96. Arthur M. Schlesinger Jr., *The Politics of Upheaval: 1935–1936*, Vol. III, *The Age of Roosevelt* (Boston: Houghton Mifflin, 2003), p. 227.
97. Page Smith, *Redeeming the Time: A People's History of the 1920s and the New Deal* (New York: McGraw-Hill, 1987), p. 424.
98. Schwarz, *New Dealers*, p. 139.
99. William E. Leuchtenberg, *Franklin D. Roosevelt and the New Deal: 1932–1940* (New York: Harper, 1963), p. 149.
100. Isidor Feinstein to Thomas Corcoran, May 28, 1936, Thomas Corcoran Papers, Box 198.
101. Interview with Christopher Stone, June 25, 1998.
102. Lash, *Dealers and Dreamers*, pp. 9–10.
103. Abelard Stone, "Roosevelt Moves Toward Fascism"; Isidor Feinstein, "A Bad Boy Grows Older," in *Press Time: A Book of Post Classics* (New York: Books, Inc., 1936), pp. 300–301.
104. Thomas Corcoran to Isidor Feinstein, September 8, 1936, Corcoran Papers; interview with Samuel Beer, March 1994.
105. Interview with Samuel Beer, March 1994.
106. Samuel Beer, "Memoirs of a Political Junkie," *Harvard Magazine*, September/October 1984, pp. 65–70. Beer says the phrase "economic royalists" was not his.
107. Isidor Feinstein, "Bedtime Story for Radicals," *New York Post*, February 5, 1936, p. 10.
108. IFS to Michael Blankfort, September 11, 1938, Blankfort Papers.
109. Interview with Jean Boudin, June 28, 1991.
110. Isidor Feinstein to Thomas Corcoran, December 19, 1936, Corcoran Papers; "Gashouse Trio," *Time*, September 19, 1938.
111. "Mr. Roosevelt's Blank Check," *New Republic*, November 11, 1936, p. 31; Latham, *Communist Controversy*, pp. 51–52, 77; Gerson, *Pete*, p. 58; "Democracy Triumphs," *New York Post*, November 4, 1936, p. 18; Heywood Broun, "The President Needs a Gadfly," *Nation*, November 14, 1936, p. 577.
112. Alan Brinkley, *The End of Reform: New Deal Liberalism in Recession and War* (New York: Knopf, 1995), p. 18.
113. Lash, *Dealers and Dreamers*, pp. 218, 291–95.
114. Cottrell, *Izzy*, p. 59; the outline is in the Corcoran Papers.
115. Thomas Corcoran to Lincoln Filene, December 17, 1936, Corcoran Papers.
116. Isidor Feinstein, "A Lucky Toss of the Judicial Dice," *New York Post*, November 24, 1936, p. 10. A split decision sustains the lower court ruling, which in this case upheld the law.
117. Isidor Feinstein, "'Unpacking' the Supreme Court," *New York Post*, February 8, 1937, p. 6.

118. Isidor Feinstein, "The Worst That Can Happen Is—Democracy," *New York Post*, February 9, 1937, p. 6.
119. Isidor Feinstein, *The Court Disposes* (New York: Covici, Friede, 1937), pp. 87, 99.
120. Ibid., p. 20.
121. Isidor Feinstein, "Human Rights vs. Property Rights," *Philadelphia Record*, May 3, 1932.
122. Feinstein, *The Court Disposes*, pp. 114, 127.
123. Theodore Draper, *The Roots of American Communism* (Chicago: Ivan R. Dee, 1989), p. 57. In 1905, Boudin had been thrown out of the founding convention of the Industrial Workers of the World (IWW) on the grounds that "no attorney of law could be anything but a parasite." Victor Rabinowitz, "The Radical Tradition in the Law," in David Kairys, ed., *The Politics of Law: A Progressive Critique* (New York: Pantheon Books, 1982), p. 310.
124. Feinstein, *The Court Disposes*, pp. 42, 78–79.
125. Matthew Josephson, "Review and Comment," *New Masses* 23 (June 8, 1937): 22.
126. Thomas Reed Powell, "The Court, the Constitution, and the Country," *Saturday Review of Literature* 16, no. 6 (June 5, 1937): 3–5.
127. Isidor Feinstein, "The Supreme Court and Civil Liberties," *Nation*, February 6, 1937, pp. 151–53.
128. Arthur D. Pierce, "Clears the Air," *Philadelphia Record*, June 26, 1937.
129. Brinkley, *End of Reform*, pp. 19–20.
130. Ibid.; Isidor Feinstein, "A Defeat More Glorious Than Victory," *New York Post*, August 26, 1937, p. 6.
131. Thomas Corcoran to Isidor Feinstein, May 5 and May 14, 1937, Corcoran Papers.
132. Interview with Celia Gilbert, September 30, 1991; Isidor Feinstein to Mr. and Mrs. Matthew Josephson, June 1, 1937, Matthew Josephson Collection.

4: POPULAR FRONT

1. J. David Stern, Oral History, Columbia University Oral History Project, pp. 88–89.
2. Malcolm Cowley to Isidor Feinstein, n.d., Malcolm Cowley Collection; Louis Stone and Marcus Stone, "The Family"; Isidor Feinstein to Thomas Corcoran, August 20, 1937, Corcoran Papers; IFS to Jerome Frank, June 22 and July 22, 1938, Jerome Frank Collection.
3. "Browder Tells of Bribe Offer in '36 Election," *New York Post*, September 6, 1939, p. 1. Browder went to Heywood Broun first, then, when Broun took no action, sought out Izzy, who introduced Browder to a colleague on the news desk. Unable to substantiate the story, the *Post* never published it, and nothing further was heard of the incident until Browder testified before the Dies Committee (HUAC) in 1939. Ironically, it was during this appearance that Browder was asked if he'd ever traveled under a false passport. His admission that he had was later to land him in federal prison.
4. Denning, *Cultural Front*, p. 13; interview with Celia Gilbert, September 31, 1991.
5. Franklin Folsom, *Days of Anger, Days of Hope: A Memoir of the League of American Writers, 1937–1942* (Boulder: University Press of Colorado, 1994), pp. 266–333.
6. Interview with Nathalie Bodanskaya Gorman.
7. Isidor Feinstein to James Henle, January 8, 1937, and Isidor Feinstein to James T. Farrell, January 15, 1937, James T. Farrell Collection.
8. See William Barrett, *The Truants: Adventures Among the Intellectuals* (New York:

Anchor Press, 1982), pp. 75–78, for a mendacious and self-serving recitation of the myth.

9. Isidor Feinstein, "The Two-Edged Sword of Terror," *New York Post*, December 7, 1934, p. 10.

10. "Hobgoblins in Moscow," *New York Post*, January 10, 1935, p. 8.

11. Such "realism" about Stalin was common on the American left. As Frank Warren points out, liberals like the *Nation* editor Freda Kirchwey "based their sympathy for Russia on their belief in Russian economic democracy and in her consistent striving for peace in opposition to Fascism. Political and civil liberty did not play an important part. This is precisely why the trials were not a shattering blow . . . They only demonstrated Russia's lack of something these liberals did not look for in Russia." (*Liberals and Communism*, p. 190.)

12. Cottrell, interview with IFS.

13. "Jitters in the Kremlin," *New York Post*, August 18, 1936, p. 8.

14. Klehr, Haynes, and Firsov, *Secret World*, p. 96.

15. Nathaniel Weyl to author, September 13, 1996; interview with Nathaniel Weyl.

16. Isidor Feinstein, "?????????" *New York Post*, January 26, 1937, p. 6.

17. Isidor Feinstein, "The Real Question Behind the Russian Trials," *New York Post*, June 14, 1937, p. 6.

18. See David Caute, *The Fellow-Travellers: A Postscript to the Enlightenment* (New York: Macmillan, 1973), p. 300, for an acute discussion of the ironies inherent in such postures.

19. Archibald MacLeish, "Spain and American Writers," in Henry Hart, ed., *The Writer in a Changing World* (New York: Equinox Cooperative Press, 1937), p. 57.

20. Isidor Feinstein, "The People's Front in Spain," *New York Post*, February 21, 1936.

21. "A Business Man on the Popular Front," *New York Post*, July 23, 1936, p. 6.

22. Isidor Feinstein, "Democracy Fights for Its Life in Spain," *New York Post*, August 1, 1936, p. 6.

23. "A Perversion of Neutrality," *New York Post*, August 6, 1936, p. 6.

24. "The Lesson of Spain," *New York Post*, September 10, 1936, p. 6; "Russia Refuses to Cooperate," *New York Post*, January 10, 1937, p. 6; "The Rape of Spain," *New York Post*, January 3, 1937, p. 6.

25. "The Fight For Peace," *New York Post*, February 8, 1937, p. 6.

26. "Rape of Spain."

27. Ronald Fraser, *Blood of Spain: An Oral History of the Spanish Civil War* (New York: Pantheon, 1979), p. 419.

28. Stern, *Memoirs*, pp. 175–76.

29. Thomas Corcoran to Felix Frankfurter, n.d., Felix Frankfurter Papers. Stern complained to Corcoran about the move.

30. Dan Rottenberg, "The Rise of Albert M. Greenfield," in Friedman, *Jewish Life in Philadelphia*, p. 232; Stern, *Memoirs*, pp. 244–45; J. David Stern, Oral History, pp. 79–80.

31. Patner, *I. F. Stone*, pp. 37–38.

32. "Salute to Heroes," *New York Post*, February 9, 1937, p. 6.

33. Nathalie Robins, *Alien Ink* (New York: William Morrow, 1992), p. 88; Julia Dietrich, *The Old Left in History and Literature* (New York: Twayne, 1996), p. 131.

34. "The Lines Shift in Spain," *New York Post*, May 21, 1937, p. 10.

35. Friedman, *Jewish Life in Philadelphia*, p. 20.

36. Interview with Samuel Beer.

37. Denning, *Cultural Front*, pp. 285–95.

38. Adamic, *My America*, p. 409. Adamic cites Italian factory workers and Yugoslavian and Polish coal miners as precedents.

39. Badger, *New Deal*, p. 131.

40. McElvaine, *Great Depression*, p. 294.

41. Edward Levinson, "Labor on the March," *Harper's Magazine* 174 (May 1937): 642–46.

42. Badger, *New Deal*, p. 130.

43. McElvaine, *Great Depression*, p. 294.

44. Levinson, "Labor on the March."

45. Marc Blitzstein, *The Cradle Will Rock*, quoted in Swados, *American Writer*, p. 407.

46. Badger, *New Deal*, pp. 132–33.

47. John J. Abt, *Advocate and Activist: Memoirs of an American Communist Lawyer* (Urbana: University of Illinois Press, 1993), p. 61.

48. Ibid., pp. 66–68; Badger, *New Deal*, p. 135.

49. Denning, *Cultural Front*, pp. 286–87.

50. "Presenting 'One-Sixth of the Earth,'" *Daily Worker*, November 12, 1937, p. 3.

51. Virgil Thomson, "In the Theatre," *Modern Music*, January–February 1938, pp. 112–14, quoted in Gordon, *Mark the Music*, p. 165.

52. See Klehr, *Heyday*, p. 414, for a typically strenuous depiction of the party's marginality. For an account of the Popular Front that goes beyond plausibility into paranoia but contains interesting tidbits of information, see Stephen Koch, *Double Lives: Spies and Writers in the Soviet Secret War of Ideas Against the West* (New York: Free Press, 1994).

53. Ellen Schrecker, "McCarthyism and the Decline of American Communism, 1945–1960," in Brown et al., *New Studies*, pp. 123–33.

54. Denning, *Cultural Front*, pp. 116–28, contains an acute, persuasive discussion of these issues.

55. Isserman, *Which Side Were You On?* pp. 19–23, offers both the grounds for this belief and a sense of the internal contradictions.

56. As a student in the last years of Trilling's tenure, I can still recall the Columbia English department's mandarin dismissal of any work of American literature beyond a tiny canon of some half dozen classics (Twain, Hawthorne, Melville, etc.). The personal motives for the rebirth of an American Jew as an English gentleman are not obscure, but the politics behind the *Partisan Review* critics' distaste for Popular Front culture is brilliantly elucidated by Denning, *Cultural Front*, pp. 116–28.

57. Isidor Feinstein, "Make It a Civil Rights Act," *New York Post*, January 25, 1938, p. 10.

58. Brinkley, *End of Reform*, pp. 28–29.

59. Nelson Lichtenstein, *Labor's War at Home: The CIO in World War II* (New York: Cambridge University Press, 1982), pp. 18–19; Isidor Feinstein, "Shuffle the Cards," *Nation*, September 24, 1938, p. 286.

60. Brinkley, *End of Reform*, p. 86.

61. Hart, *Writer in a Changing World,* p. 239. Of course, the Trotskyists, who opposed the Popular Front, fastidiously condemned any accommodation with capitalism.

62. Isserman, *Which Side Were You On?*, p. 25.

63. Morris Schonbach, *Native American Fascism During the 1930s and 1940s* (New York: Garland Publishing, 1985), p. 297; Dale Kramer, "The American Fascists," *Harper's Magazine* 181 (September 1940): 380–93.

64. Schonbach, *Native American Fascism*, pp. 183, 317.

65. Ibid., p. 245.

66. Kramer, "American Fascists."

67. Brinkley, *End of Reform,* p. 55; Schonbach, *Native American Fascism*, pp. 160, 232.

68. Schonbach, *Native American Fascism*, p. 193n; Isidore Feinstein to Thomas Corcoran, February 5, 1938, Corcoran Papers.

69. League of American Writers, *Writers Take Sides: Letters About the War in Spain from 418 American Authors* (New York: League of American Writers, 1938), p. 58.

70. Isidor Feinstein, "Fascism in America," *New York Post*, November 21, 1934, p. 8.

71. Schwarz, *The New Dealers*, pp. 144.

72. Dick Polman, "Outcasts and Icons," *Philadelphia Inquirer*, January 28, 1968, p. C1; Patner, *I. F. Stone*, p. 13. Most of Stone's profilers were too polite to raise the question, but those who did seldom failed to elicit the note of regret.

73. Geoffrey Stone, "Neutrality—a Dangerous Myth," *Nation,* September 18, 1937, pp. 283–85.

74. Interview with Murray Kempton, December 15, 1991.

75. Denning, *Cultural Front*, p. 153.

76. IFS, "The Romans Would Understand," *Nation*, October 2, 1937, pp. 345–46.

77. Interview with Nathaniel Weyl.

78. Isadore Feinstein et al., Supreme Court, New York County, M309-38, January 6, 1938. Leonard Boudin was lawyer for the petitioner.

79. Interview with Louis Stone.

80. Interview with Jeremy Stone; Blankfort, autobiography; interview with George Seldes, May 24, 1991; interview with Jill Stern.

81. Interview with Nathaniel Weyl.

82. Felix Frankfurter to IFS, January 24, 1938, Frankfurter Papers.

83. IFS, "1937 Is Not 1914," *Nation*, November 6, 1937, pp. 495–97.

84. Ibid.

85. Kazin, *Starting Out in the Thirties*, p. 85.

86. Brinkley, *End of Reform*, p. 48.

87. Ibid., p. 294n3.

88. IFS, "Our Reigning Families," *New Republic*, December 29, 1937, p. 233.

89. Brinkley, *End of Reform*, pp. 56–57.

90. IFS, "Hyde Park, Tennessee Style," *New Republic*, October 20, 1937, pp. 317–18.

91. Brinkley, *End of Reform*, p. 48.

92. Ibid., pp. 57–58; Lash, *Dealers and Dreamers*, pp. 352–53; IFS to Thomas Corcoran, "Monday nite" [January 1938], Corcoran Papers.

93. Lash, *Dealers and Dreamers*, pp. 291–95; Brinkley, *End of Reform*, p. 55.

94. Latham, *Communist Controversy*, p. 52.

95. Ellen Schrecker, *Many Are the Crimes: McCarthyism in America* (Boston: Little, Brown, 1998), p. 14. As Schrecker points out elsewhere, party members "did not advertise their affiliation at the time; even today many of them remain reluctant to reveal that part of their lives . . . Ironically, contemporary historians need the same kinds of confessions the congressional investigators of the 1950s did." *No Ivory Tower: McCarthyism and the Universities* (New York: Oxford University Press,

1986), p. 25. Anyone who thinks, as I once did, that the end of the cold war might make such inquiries less contentious hasn't had much experience interviewing former Communists.

96.	Schrecker, *Many Are the Crimes*, pp. 41, 110–11.

97.	IFS, "Company in the Doghouse," *New Republic*, January 5, 1938, p. 251.

98.	Cottrell, interview with IFS.

99.	IFS, "Russia's Editors Follow Her Generals," *New York Post*, July 28, 1937, p. 8.

100.	"Stalin Takes Off His Mask," *New York Post,* February 15, 1938, p. 1; "Thunder from the Left," *New York Post*, February 18, 1938, p. 18.

101.	Stern, *Memoirs*, pp. 245–47.

102.	Cottrell, interview with IFS.

103.	Heywood Broun, "The New York Post Handicap," *New Republic*, March 9, 1938, p. 127.

104.	John Gunther, *Inside U.S.A.* (New York: Harper, 1947), p. 592.

105.	Dayton McKean, *The Boss: The Hague Machine in Action* (Boston: Houghton Mifflin, 1940).

106.	IFS, "Judicial Brief," *New Republic*, August 31, 1938.

107.	Stephen Becker, *Marshall Field III* (New York: Simon & Schuster, 1964), p. 194.

108.	IFS to Freda Kirchwey, "Tuesday" [1938]; Freda Kirchwey to IFS, April 8, 1938, *Nation* Collection.

109.	IFS to Suzy Blankfort, September 11, 1938, Blankfort Papers.

110.	Ibid.; IFS to Matthew Josephson, September 24, 1938, Josephson Collection; Cottrell, interview with IFS.

111.	IFS, "Jerome Frank's Dilemma," *Southern Review* 4, no. 2 (Autumn 1938).

112.	IFS to Jerome Frank, June 23 and 25, 1938, Frank Collection.

113.	Harry T. Saylor to Newspaper Guild of New York, March 28, 1939, Newspaper Guild Archives.

114.	John W. Hevener, *Which Side Are You On? The Harlan County Coal Miners, 1931–39* (Urbana: University of Illinois Press, 1978), p. 147.

115.	IFS, "It Happened in Harlan," *Current History*, September 1938, pp. 29–31.

116.	Ibid.

117.	[IFS], "Bloody Harlan Reforms," *Nation*, August 6, 1938, p. 121; Hevener, *Which Side Are You On?* p. 151. The New York Public Library's collection of bound volumes of the *Nation* contain handwritten annotations giving authorship of unsigned editorials.

118.	IFS to Suzy Blankfort, September 11, 1938.

119.	IFS, "Max Lerner's Capitalist Collectivism," *Southern Review* 4, no. 4 (Spring 1939): 649–64.

120.	Ibid.

121.	IFS to Matthew Josephson, November 1, 1938, Josephson Collection.

122.	Patner, *I. F. Stone*, pp. 30–32.

123.	Interview with Samuel Grafton. Grafton mistakenly places the incident in June 1939, six months after Stone left the editorial desk. Recounting the same story to Robert Sherrill, Grafton said that Stone "tried to solicit support from the other writers, but apparently he'd laid into them so often they were happy to be rid of him" (Interview with Robert Sherrill, July 29, 1998). Newspaper Guild records show that Grafton was the only other editorial writer on the *Post* at the time.

124.	J. David Stern, Oral History, pp. 89–90.

125. IFS, "When Wall Street Goes Socialist: The End of New York's Five-Cent Fare," *New Republic*, August 10, 1938, pp. 10–12.

126. "Keep Politicians—Any Kind—from Running the Unions," *New York Post*, January 21, 1939, p. 6.

127. Patner, *I. F. Stone*, p. 35.

128. IFS to Joint Newspaper Guild–New York Post Grievance Committee, March 22, 1939, Newspaper Guild Archives.

129. IFS to Matthew Josephson, November, 1938; IFS to Suzy Blankfort, September 11, 1938.

130. Louis Boudin to Abraham Isserman, April 1, 1939; Francis Biddle, *In re Newspaper Guild of New York and New York Post, Inc.*, Case of I. F. Stone, July 7, 1939, both in Newspaper Guild Archives.

131. IFS, "The New York 'Post' Changes Hands," *Nation*, July 1, 1939.

132. Memorandum to the Secretary[, March 15, 1939, Harold] L. Ickes Collection.

133. Patner, *I. F. Stone*, p. 36; Cottrell, *Izzy*, p. 72.

134. IFS to Michael Blankfort, October 15, 1939, Blankfort Papers.

135. James Wechsler, "Stalin and Union Square," *Nation*, September 30, 1939, pp. 342–45.

136. Denning, *Cultural Front*, pp. 299–309.

137. Ibid., pp. 325–27.

138. Ibid., pp. 335–36.

139. Dizzy Gillespie, *To Be or Not to Bop* (New York: Da Capo Press, 1979), p. 377.

140. "Monsieur Minsky's Deshabilleuses Tentatrices," in *Press Time*, pp. 308–10; *Nation*, May 6, 1939, p. 541.

141. IFS, "Class Conflict, Sunkist Style," *Nation*, August 5, 1939, pp. 150–51.

142. IFS, "The Associated Farmers," *Propaganda Analysis* 2, no. 12 (August 1, 1939): 1–12.

143. Whittaker Chambers, *Witness* (New York: Random House, 1952), p. 472.

144. IFS, "Remedies for Monopoly," *Nation*, April 15, 1939, pp. 420–21; Feinstein, "Shuffle the Cards."

145. IFS, "Liberals Never Learn," *Nation*, March 18, 1939, p. 308; IFS, "The Greatest Strike-Breaker of All," *Nation*, March 25, 1939; Freda Kirchwey to IFS, n.d., *Nation* Collection.

146. IFS, "America and the Next War: II," *New Republic*, June 21, 1939, pp. 175–77.

147. "Manifesto," and Freda Kirchwey, "Red Totalitarianism," *Nation*, May 27, 1939, pp. 626, 605–606.

148. Kirchwey, "Red Totalitarianism."

149. Sidney Hook, "Red Totalitarianism Reply—," and Freda Kirchwey, "And Rebuttal," *Nation*, June 17, 1939, pp. 710–11.

150. Kirchwey, "Red Totalitarianism."

151. Letter to the editor, *Nation*, August 24, 1939, p. 228.

152. "The Moscow Trials: A Statement by American Progressives," *New Masses* 27 (May 3, 1938): 19.

153. IFS to Freda Kirchwey, n.d. [October 1939], Freda Kirchwey Collection.

5 : WAR YEARS

1. IFS to Michael Blankfort, October 15, 1939, Blankfort Papers.

2. Cottrell, *Izzy*, p. 85; telephone interview with Louis Stone, May 1999.

3. Junius Scales, for example, joined the Communist Party in March 1939. The party always had a high turnover, and like many new recruits, Scales was on the verge of dropping out after a few months when his experiences organizing cotton-mill workers in Greensboro convinced him to stay. Compared to "my first picket line" with its "vision of the revolution to come," the pact barely registered. Junius Scales, *Cause at Heart: A Former Communist Remembers* (Athens: University of Georgia Press, 1987).

4. Paul Lyons, *Philadelphia Communists, 1936–1956* (Philadelphia: Temple University Press, 1982); Isserman, *Which Side Were You On?*, pp. 38–54.

5. Denning, *Cultural Front*, p. 343; Isserman, *Which Side Were You On?* p. 55; Alan Wald, *The Responsibility of Intellectuals: Selected Essays on Marxist Traditions in Cultural Commitment* (Atlantic Highlands, NJ: Humanities Press, 1992), p. 88.

6. Richard Rovere, *New Masses* (September 5, 1939): 5–6.

7. IFS, "Chamberlain's Russo-German Pact," *Nation*, September 23, 1939, pp. 313–16; [IFS], "Hitler Will Be Addressing," *Nation*, September 23, 1939, p. 305; [IFS], "With Organized Minorities Deluging," *Nation*, September 30, 1939, p. 335.

8. IFS to Freda Kirchwey, n.d. [October 1939], Kirchwey Collection. *Soviet Russia Today* ran an identical text—but without Stone's name.

9. [IFS], "Dictators at Work," *Nation*, September 30, 1939, pp. 337–38.

10. Granville Hicks, "New Directions on the Left," *New Republic*, June 17, 1940, pp. 815–18. Whether Hicks was right about Stone's willingness to join the CP will never be known, but the "G-string" was a staple of Stone's rhetoric, as was the twice-sold gold brick. Given that Hicks was writing about a tiny group of left intellectuals that included both Stone and himself, there is little doubt about his correspondent's identity.

11. [IFS], "Blackmailer's Peace," *Nation*, October 14, 1939, p. 401.

12. IFS to Michael Blankfort, October 21, 1939, Blankfort Papers.

13. Stephen J. Whitfield, *A Critical American: The Politics of Dwight Macdonald* (Hamden, CT: Archon Books, 1984); *Labor Action*, May 27, 1940, p. 1, and July 22, 1940, p. 1. Howe, who at least had the excuse of extreme youth (he was nineteen), soon was drafted into the army, where he revised his views. But Macdonald never renounced his "plague on both your houses" approach to the Nazis and the British. Both men went on to greater achievements, and their early lapses of judgment, of whatever magnitude, would not be worth mentioning were it not for the legions of mythologizers who persist in depicting the Trotskyists of the 1930s and 1940s as clear-sighted anti-Stalinists instead of sectarians who, though right about Stalin (frequently for the wrong reasons), were hardly models of political prescience. Anyone doubting the adage that there is no mythologizer like a self-mythologizer need only turn to *The Truants*, William Barrett's memoir of *Partisan Review*, where (on p. 76) he describes the period following the pact as the magazine's "most shining hour—certainly its period of greatest courage." This of a time when *PR*'s July 1941 "10 Propositions on the War," by Macdonald and Clement Greenberg, closed with the bland assertion that "all support of whatever kind must be withheld from Churchill and Roosevelt."

14. IFS, "Chamberlain's Russo-German Pact"; IFS, "The Chicken or the Egg?" *Nation*, November 4, 1939, pp. 500–501; James T. Farrell to Freda Kirchwey, October 30, 1939, Kirchwey Collection.

15. Granville Hicks, "The Fighting Decade," *Saturday Review of Literature* 12 (July 6, 1940): 3–17.

16. Sanford Lakoff, *Max Lerner: Pilgrim in the Promised Land* (Chicago: University of Chicago Press, 1998), p. 108.

17. Michael Harank to author, November 14, 1992. When Dorothy Day, editor of the *Catholic Worker*, died in November 1980, Stone traveled to New York from Washington for her funeral. After the wake he approached the *Catholic Worker* associate editor, Michael Harank, to whom he acknowledged that during the Spanish Civil War he had received reports that Republican forces had committed atrocities on the civilian population outside Barcelona. "It was the only time in my life as a journalist that I did not print the truth about what was happening in Spain," Stone said.

18. Richard Rovere, *Final Reports: Personal Reflections on Politics and History in Our Time* (New York: Doubleday, 1984), p. 67.

19. Granville Hicks to Richard Rovere, November 8, 1939, Richard Rovere Papers.

20. Ibid.

21. IFS, "Justice Frankfurter," *Nation*, October 14, 1939, pp. 443–44.

22. Daniel Aaron, *Writers on the Left: Episodes in American Literary Communism* (New York: Harcourt, 1961), p. 376.

23. IFS to Michael Blankfort, October 15, 1939, Blankfort Papers.

24. "Shaw Says We Bear Guilt in New War," *New York Times*, December 2, 1939, p. 1.

25. Carl Rollyson, *Lillian Hellman: Her Legend and Her Legacy* (New York: St. Martin's Press, 1988), p. 148.

26. Isserman, *Which Side Were You On?* pp. 53–54; [IFS], "The Finns at Geneva," *Nation*, December 16, 1939, pp. 667–68.

27. IFS, "They Cry War," *Nation*, November 4, 1939, p. 483.

28. IFS, "Nineteenth-Century Bogeywoman," *Nation*, October 14, 1939, p. 418.

29. IFS, "Portrait of a Dollar-a-Year Man," *Nation*, September 30, 1939, pp. 345–47.

30. IFS, "Mercy and Statesmanship," *Nation*, November 25, 1939, p. 568.

31. Deborah E. Lipstadt, *Beyond Belief: The American Press and the Coming of the Holocaust 1933–1945* (New York: Free Press, 1986), cites the *Nation* and *PM* as among a handful of publications that attempted to warn America of the magnitude of the Holocaust.

32. Isidor Feinstein, "For an Investors' Union," *Nation*, May 22, 1937, pp. 597–98.

33. Interview with Shirley Kasdon, January 29, 1993.

34. Ibid.

35. IFS, "Defense Hysteria and the Investor," *Your Investments* 1, no. 6 (July 1940): pp. 4–5.

36. Feinstein, "For an Investors' Union."

37. Gordon, *Mark the Music*, p. 136.

38. Robert D. Leiter, *The Musicians and Petrillo* (New York: Octagon Books, 1974), pp. 149–64.

39. [IFS], "The Worst Enemies of Labor," *Nation*, September 7, 1940, p. 182.

40. Leiter, *Musicians and Petrillo*.

41. Freda Kirchwey to IFS, September 18, 1940, *Nation* Collection.

42. Federal Writers' Project, *The WPA Guide to Washington D.C.* (1942; New York: Pantheon, 1983), p. 6.

43. Interview with Creekmore Fath, August 14, 1998.

44. Interview with Mairi Foreman, December 5, 1991; interview with Virginia Durr, September 12, 1991.

45. Brinkley, *End of Reform*, p. 145.

46. Interview with Virginia Durr.

47. Ibid. Ironically, it was Michael Straus who had talked Ickes out of hiring Izzy when he first left the *Post*.

48. "Memorandum for Mr. [Clyde] Tolson," January 12, 1941, Federal Bureau of Investigation, New York Field Office File 100-NY-90640 (I. F. Stone).

49. Interview with Steve Rosner, January 27, 1994.

50. C. A. MacDonald, *The United States, Britain, and Appeasement, 1936–1939* (New York: St. Martin's Press, 1981), pp. 120–21.

51. Douglass Aircraft, for example, which sold $18 million worth of planes in the first quarter of 1941, had a backlog of $332 million, while Boeing, which had net sales of $9 million in the first quarter, had a backlog of $207 million according to I. F. Stone, *Business as Usual: The First Year of Defense* (New York: Modern Age, 1941), p. 37.

52. Eliot Janeway, *The Struggle for Survival: A Chronicle of Economic Mobilization in World War II* (New Haven, CT: Yale University Press, 1951), p. 221.

53. Ibid.

54. Philip Murray, "For Full Production," in Philip Murray, John Brophy, James Carey, and I. F. Stone, *The CIO and National Defense* (Washington, D.C.: American Council on Public Affairs, 1941), p. 7.

55. Lichtenstein, *Labor's War*, pp. 84–85.

56. IFS, "The Long View of Air Defense," *New York Post*, December 29, 1938, p. 10.

57. Lichtenstein, *Labor's War*.

58. IFS, "Labor's Plan: 500 Planes a Day," *Nation*, December 21, 1940, pp. 624–25; Louis Stark, "500 Planes a Day by Auto Plant Use Proposed by C.I.O.," *New York Times*, December 23, 1940, p. 1.

59. Lichtenstein, *Labor's War*, p. 269n9; also my telephone interview with Nelson Lichtenstein.

60. Brinkley, *End of Reform*, p. 208; Lichtenstein, *Labor's War*, pp. 41, 85–87.

61. The *New York Times*, for example, editorialized, "The main issue is purely a technical one . . . Airplane engines and other essential parts must be made by machine tools which are highly specialized" (January 31, 1941, p. 18).

62. Lichtenstein, *Labor's War*, p. 88; Brinkley, *End of Reform*.

63. Bruce Catton, *The Warlords of Washington* (New York: Harcourt, 1948), pp. 91–93.

64. Lichtenstein, *Labor's War*.

65. Brinkley, *End of Reform*, p. 212.

66. John Kenneth Galbraith, *A Life in Our Times: Memoirs* (Boston: Houghton Mifflin, 1981), pp. 157–58.

67. David Brinkley, *Washington Goes to War* (New York: Knopf, 1988), pp. 172–73.

68. Ralph Ingersoll, "A Proposition to Create a New Newspaper," in Roy Hoopes, *Ralph Ingersoll* (New York: Atheneum, 1985), Appendix 1, p. 399.

69. Hoopes, *Ralph Ingersoll*; David Margolick, "*PM*'s Impossible Dream," *Vanity Fair*, January 1999, pp. 118–32.

70. The photographer Morris Engel, quoted in Margolick, *"PM's* Impossible Dream,"
    p. 122.

71. Penn Kimball, *The File* (New York: Harcourt, 1983), p. 80.

72. Ingersoll, "Proposition," p. 401.

73. Paul Milkman, *PM: A New Deal in Journalism* (New Brunswick, NJ: Rutgers University Press, 1997), p. 66.

74. IFS, "Labor Formulates Plane Speed-Up Plan to Help President End Defense Log
    Jam," *PM*, December 22, 1940, pp. 1, 9. See also IFS, "Labor Seeks President's Answer Today on Plan," *PM*, December 23, 1940, and issues for December 24–30.

75. IFS, "His Majesty—Martin Dies," *PM*, February 24, 1941, p. 8.

76. Ingersoll, "Proposition."

77. J. Anthony Lukas, "Where Are You Now, PM Spinney?" *New Republic*, September 9, 1972, pp. 26–30.

78. Benjamin Stolberg, "Muddled Millions," *Saturday Evening Post*, February 15, 1941,
    pp. 9–10, 88–93.

79. Marshall Field quoted in Lukas, "Where Are You Now?"

80. *PM*, April 26, 1942, p. 19. See also Philip Nel, "'Said a Bird in the Midst of a
    Blitz . . .': How World War II Created Dr. Seuss," *Mosaic: A Journal for the Interdisciplinary Study of Literature* 34, no. 2 (June 2001): 65–85, and Richard H. Minear,
    Dr. Seuss Goes to War: The World War II Editorial Cartoons of Theodor Seuss Geisel
    (New York: New Press, 1999).

81. Ralph Ingersoll to the staff of *PM*, June 18, 1940, reproduced in Federal Bureau of
    Investigation, Headquarters File on *PM*, 100–36, pp. 37–38.

82. Ralph Ingersoll, "Volunteer Gestapo," *PM*, July 12, 1940, p. 8.

83. IFS, "Murphy Puts Shoe on Wrong Foot," *PM*, February 21, 1941, p. 8; IFS, "Making Defense Safe for Alcoa," *Nation*, September 27, 1941, pp. 271–73; October 4,
    1941, pp. 299–301; and October 18, 1941, pp. 363–64.

84. Interview with Penn Kimball, December 13, 1991. In his memoir *The Age of Suspicion* (New York: Random House, 1953), Wechsler wrote that he "felt personally
    sorry for Huberman and uncertain about the propriety of replacing him" (p. 167),
    but Wechsler's protégé, Arnold Beichman, in an interview with the author, described Huberman's dismissal, with evident satisfaction, as "a purge."

85. Kenneth Stewart, "The People Who Made PM and the Star" (manuscript), Kenneth
    Stewart Collection.

86. Milkman, *PM*, p. 111.

87. IFS, "Louis D. Brandeis, the Attorney for the People, Is Dead," *PM*, October 6,
    1941, p. 9.

88. Leon Edel to author, March 28, 1992.

89. IFS to Michael Blankfort, January 15, 1941, Blankfort Papers.

90. Lichtenstein, *Labor's War*, pp. 61–62. Lichtenstein writes that there were 4,288
    strikes involving 2.4 million workers in 1941, more than any year since 1919 (p. 46).

91. Wechsler, *Age of Suspicion*, p. 172.

92. According to Milkman, *PM*, p. 67, Stone believed it was the sinking of the *Reuben
    James* that really forced America into the war; IFS to Michael Blankfort, January 15,
    1941, Blankfort Papers.

93. Clement Greenberg and Dwight Macdonald, "10 Propositions on the War," *Partisan
    Review*, July–August 1941, p. 275.

94. IFS, "F.D.R.'s First Task," *Nation*, August 23, 1941, pp. 155–56.

95. Turner Catledge, *New York Times*, June 24, 1941, cited in IFS, *Truman Era*, pp. 14–15.
96. George Orwell, "Letter from London," *Partisan Review* 8, no. 6 (November–December 1941): 498.
97. IFS, "The G-String Conspiracy," *Nation*, July 26, 1941, pp. 66–67.
98. IFS, "War Comes to Washington," *Nation*, December 13, 1941.
99. Schwarz, *New Dealers*, p. 152.
100. IFS, "In the First Line of Defense," in *The CIO and National Defense*, p. 1.
101. IFS, *Business as Usual*, pp. 258, 265.
102. Janeway, *Struggle for Survival*, p. 170.
103. Brinkley, *End of Reform*, pp. 240–41.
104. Michael Straight, "The First Year and the Next," *New Republic*, September 1, 1941, p. 284; Lewis Corey, "Monopoly and Defense," *Nation*, September 6, 1941, p. 204; Dwight Macdonald, "Democracy and the War Effort," *Partisan Review* (September–October 1941): 438–39.
105. IFS to Freda Kirchwey, "Weds. nite" [December 1940]; Freda Kirchwey to IFS, February 27, 1941; Stephen Early to Freda Kirchwey, March 1, 1941; IFS to Freda Kirchwey, "Wednesday morning" [September 1941]; Freda Kirchwey IFS, September 25, 1941, *Nation* Collection.
106. Schwarz, *New Dealers*, p. 303; Harold Ickes to IFS, September 27, 1941, and Ickes, *Secret Diary*, p. 6187 (January 4, 1942), Harold L. Ickes Collection; Freda Kirchwey to IFS, May 23, 1941, *Nation* Collection.
107. Ickes, *Secret Diary*, p. 6187.
108. Joseph Borkin, *The Crime and Punishment of I. G. Farben* (New York: Free Press, 1978), pp. 77–82.
109. Freda Kirchwey to IFS, March 31, 1942, *Nation* Collection.
110. IFS, "An Open Letter to John D. Rockefeller, Jr.," *PM*, April 5–12, 1942.
111. Borkin, *Crime and Punishment*, pp. 91–94; interview with Creekmore Fath.
112. Schwarz, *New Dealers*; Ickes, *Secret Diary*, pp. 6702–704 (June 14, 1942); IFS, "The Baruch Report," *Nation*, September 19, 1942, pp. 227–28; IFS, "*PM* Expose Breaks Russian Aid Blockade," *PM*, September 29, 1942, p. 11; Harold Ickes to IFS, September 28, 1942; Harold Ickes to IFS, September 30, 1942, Ickes Collection.
113. Ickes, Secret Diary, pp. 7037–39 (October 4, 1942) and pp. 7070–71 (October 10, 1942).
114. IFS, "F.D.R. and the May Bill," *Nation*, July 19, 1941, pp. 46–47; IFS, "Ask U.S. Probe of Eugene Cox," *PM*, March 29, 1942, p. 12; see also *PM*, May 14, 1943, p. 3, and IFS, "Mr. Biddle Is Afraid," *Nation*, May 22, 1943, pp. 735–36.
115. Or so it seemed. The FCC's champion in Congress was Clifford Durr's close friend Lyndon Johnson, who according to Robert Caro used his influence with Sam Rayburn to counter Cox. During the FCC fight, Johnson kept his distance from Durr, but (again according to Caro) conferred constantly with Durr's chief assistant, Red James. Caro argues persuasively that Johnson acted neither out of friendship nor political principle but rather to further Lady Bird's application to purchase KTBC, the Texas radio station that was the foundation of the Johnsons' personal fortune. Robert Caro, *The Years of Lyndon Johnson*, Vol. 2, *Means of Ascent* (New York: Knopf, 2002), pp. 89–93.
116. Freda Kirchwey to IFS, September 9, 1941, *Nation* Collection; IFS, "Next Step on Bridges," *Nation*, October 11, 1941, pp. 329–30.

117. Freda Kirchwey to IFS, July 15, 1941, and December 20, 1943, *Nation* Collection.
118. Interview with Robert Bendiner, 1994.
119. IFS to Max Lerner, March 27, 1943, Max Lerner Collection.
120. Celia Gilbert, "The Sacred Fire," in Sara Ruddick and Pamela Daniels, eds., *Working It Out* (New York: Pantheon, 1977), pp. 306–19.
121. Robert Bendiner to IFS, January 28, 1943, *Nation* Collection.
122. "I. F. Stone," Federal Bureau of Investigation, Headquarters File 100-90640. The program for the Artists' Front to Win the War benefit is in the files of J. B. Matthews, research director of the Dies Committee, J. B. Matthews Papers.
123. Interview with Albert Silverman, April 15, 1994.
124. IFS, "Washington Notes," *Nation*, May 23, 1942, p. 591.
125. Hugo Black, *Fred Korematsu v. United States*, 323 U.S. 214, 65 S. Ct. 193, 89 L. Ed. 194; [IFS], "The Supreme Court and Racialism," *Nation*, December 30, 1944, pp. 788–89.
126. IFS, "Biddle and the Facts," *Nation*, June 13, 1942, pp. 674–77.
127. IFS to Freda Kirchwey, "Wednesday morning" [September 1941], Kirchwey Collection.
128. IFS, "The Case of the Trotskyites," *PM*, December 31, 1943, p. 2.
129. "American Monopolies and the War," *Daily Worker*, April 24, 1942; IFS, "Our Slacker Patents," *Nation*, May 2, 1942, p. 506.
130. Paul Willen, "Who 'Collaborated' with Russia?" *Antioch Review*, Fall 1954: 259–83. Willen also cites James Reston, Wendell Willkie, and Walter Winchell.
131. Luncheon program and list of sponsors from Newspaper Guild Archives.
132. Brinkley, *Washington Goes to War*, pp. 246–47; H. G. Nichols, ed., *Washington Despatches, 1941–1945* (Chicago: University of Chicago Press, 1981), p. 146.
133. IFS, "Capital Notes," *Nation*, April 10, 1943, pp. 51–513. Stone's departure was noted by W.E.B. Du Bois in "A Chronicle of Race Relations," *Phylon* 4, no. 3 (1943): 270–89. His resignation was also covered extensively in the black press, prompting the Capital Press Club, an association of black journalists, to offer Izzy a membership, which he accepted.
134. IFS, "Aid and Comfort to the Enemy," *Nation*, January 3, 1942, pp. 6–7.
135. IFS, "Fighting the Fighting French," *Nation*, November 28, 1942, pp. 565–66.
136. IFS, "Who OK'd Franco Deal?" *PM*, February 18, 1942, p. 12; blind memo, April 30, 1942, re: Joseph L. Rauh Jr., Federal Bureau of Investigation, Headquarters File 100-90640 (I. F. Stone), Section 2, p. 49.
137. IFS, "Did Hull and Welles Tell the Truth?" *Nation*, January 9, 1943, pp. 42–44; memo from W. D. Puleston, January 14, 1943, Federal Bureau of Investigation, Headquarters File 100-90640 (I. F. Stone). Puleston, a security officer for the BEW, wrote, "It is believed that a crime as provided in the Espionage Act has been committed." But Under Secretary of State Sumner Welles informed J. Edgar Hoover that the cable, though in the secret "brown" code, was not itself classified Secret or Confidential.
138. IFS, "Peyrouton, Vichy Anti-Semite, Was Named Governor of Algeria with Approval of U.S. Minister," *PM*, January 22, 1942, p. 3.
139. "Hull Lets African Tick Get Under His Skin," *PM*, January 29, 1943.
140. *Congressional Record*, 89th Cong., 478 (February 1, 1943), and 89th Cong., 511 (February 2, 1943), remarks of Rep. John Rankin. Cited in Cottrell, *Izzy*, p. 332n14.

141. Michael Straus, "Memorandum for the Secretary," October 31, 1942; Harold Ickes to Freda Kirchwey, November 2, 1942; Michael Straus to Harold Ickes, January 29, 1943; Harold Ickes to IFS, January 30, 1943; IFS to Harold Ickes, February 4, 1943, all in Ickes Collection. A copy of the official State Department transcript of the press conference is also in the Ickes Collection.

142. "I. F. Stone," Federal Bureau of Investigation, Headquarters File 100-90640, Documents 1 and 2 (July 1941).

143. XXX, "Washington Gestapo," Nation, July 17, 1943, pp. 64–66, and July 24, 1943, pp. 92–95.

144. "I. F. Stone," Federal Bureau of Investigation, Headquarters File 100-90640, Hoover to Tolson and Nichols, November 18, 1943; Morris Ernst, "Another Witness," Nation, September 25, 1943, p. 362.

145. IFS, "XXX and the F.B.I.," Nation, September 25, 1943, p. 342.

146. Harold Ickes, Secret Diary, p. 7534 (March 14, 1943) and p. 7267 (April 10, 1943); IFS, "Shipsaw: Jesse Jones Finances Public Power Plant for Aluminum, Ltd., but Public Projects in U.S.A. Are Stalled," PM, March 22, 1943, p. 3; IFS, "The Shipsaw Scandal," Nation, April 3, 1943, pp. 475–77.

147. IFS interviewed by Forrer and Glickman.

148. Harold Ickes, Secret Diary, p. 7704 (May 9, 1943), pp. 7779–80 (May 23, 1943), pp. 8244–45 (October 10, 1943); Harold Ickes to IFS, "PERSONAL," May 21, 1943; IFS to Harold Ickes, May 22, 1943, Ickes Collection.

149. IFS, "Wallace Betrayed," Nation, July 24, 1943, pp. 89–90. Freda Kirchwey was particularly distressed by "the violence of your [IFS's] language." In a letter dated July 29, 1943, she said "you sounded as if you let your anger override every other consideration."

150. IFS, "What F.D.R. Forgot," Nation, January 8, 1944, pp. 34–35; IFS, "Some Facts of Life," PM, April 14, 1944, p. 2.

151. IFS, "One Year After Pearl Harbor," Nation, December 12, 1942, pp. 639–40.

152. R. Harris Smith, OSS: The Secret History of America's First Central Intelligence Agency (Berkeley: University of California Press, 1972), pp. 12, 70.

153. IFS, "Cordell Hull and the Peace," PM, November 27, 1944, p. 2.

154. Lipstadt, Beyond Belief.

155. "Jews Reveal Story of Slaughter by Nazis . . . FDR Is Shocked by Verified Records," PM, December 9, 1942, pp. 12, 18–20.

156. Philip S. Bernstein, "The Jews of Europe: The Remnants of a People," Nation, January 2, 1943.

157. [IFS], "Hitler's Subtlest Poison," Nation, February 27, 1943, p. 293.

158. Freda Kirchwey, "While the Jews Die," Nation, March 13, 1943, pp. 366–67.

159. IFS, "The Indian Skeleton at Atlantic City," Nation, December 11, 1943, pp. 686–87.

160. PM, February 15, 1943, p. 14; August 27, 1943, pp. 12–13; December 10, 1944, p. 2.

161. IFS, "For the Jews—Life or Death?" Nation, June 10, 1944, pp. 670–71.

162. IFS, "How Washington Took the News," Nation, June 17, 1944, pp. 700–701.

163. IFS, "Rescuers or Accomplices," PM, August 2, 1944, p. 2.

164. IFS, "Washington Underground," PM, April 5, 1945, p. 2.

165. IFS for the Editors of PM, "Franklin Delano Roosevelt," April 13, 1945, p. 1; IFS, "Farewell to F.D.R.," Nation, April 21, 1945, pp. 436–37.

6: UNDERGROUND TO PALESTINE

1. IFS, "The New President Speaks," *PM*, April 17, 1945, p. 2; IFS, "Farewell to F.D.R."
2. IFS, "Saluting the Red Army," *PM*, February 1, 1945, p. 2.
3. R. Alton Lee, *Truman and Taft-Hartley* (Lexington: University of Kentucky Press, 1966), p. 18.
4. *PM* staff chart, Ralph Ingersoll Collection.
5. Stewart, "The People Who Made *PM*," p. 92; R.I. [Ralph Ingersoll] to J.P.L [John Lewis] and M.L. [Max Lerner], March 31, 1946, Ingersoll Collection.
6. IFS, "The Dies Challenge to Free Speech," *PM*, March 22, 1944, p. 2; Ralph Ingersoll, "Complete Index of PM Accomplishments," p. 20, Ingersoll Collection.
7. IFS, "The Same Old Codgers," *Nation*, May 5, 1945, pp. 506–507.
8. Michael Blankfort to IFS, May 14, 1945, Blankfort Papers.
9. IFS, "Same Old Codgers."
10. IFS, "Pie in the 'Frisco Sky," *Nation*, May 19, 1945, pp. 561–63; IFS, "Trieste and San Francisco," *Nation*, May 26, 1945, pp. 589–90.
11. Interview with Sidney Roger, January 31, 1994.
12. Harvey Klehr and Ronald Radosh, *The Amerasia Spy Case: Prelude to McCarthyism* (Chapel Hill: University of North Carolina Press, 1996), p. 53; Robert P. Newman, *Owen Lattimore and the "Loss" of China* (Berkeley: University of California Press, 1992).
13. Pacificus, "Dangerous Experts," *Nation*, February 3, 1945, pp. 128–29.
14. IFS, *Underground to Palestine* (New York: Pantheon, 1978), p. 7.
15. Philip Rosen, Robert Tabak, and David Gross, "Philadelphia Jewry and the Holocaust," in Friedman, *Philadelphia Jewish Life*, pp. 42–47.
16. Interview with Jesse Zel Lurie, May 25, 1993.
17. Eliahu Elath, *Zionism at the UN: A Diary of the First Days* (Philadelphia: Jewish Publication Society, 1976), pp. 242, 246.
18. IFS, "Back in Washington," *PM*, May 29, 1945, p. 2.
19. Ronald Steel, *Walter Lippmann and the American Century* (Boston: Little, Brown, 1980), pp. 420–22.
20. IFS, "Back in Washington."
21. Though far from an objective account, Klehr and Radosh's *Amerasia Spy Case* is an invaluable reference to which I am indebted here and in the following paragraphs relating to the case.
22. "I. F. Stone," Federal Bureau of Investigation, Headquarters File 100-37078, Section 1, Document 30 A, p. 113; see also Klehr and Radosh, *Amerasia Spy Case*, p. 77.
23. Interview with Andrew Roth, November 18, 2004.
24. IFS, "What's Behind the Arrest of the Six?" *PM*, June 8, 1945, p. 2.
25. IFS, "Arrest of 'the Six,'" *Nation*, June 16, 1945, pp. 666–67.
26. *New York Times*, June 8, 1945, p. 1, cited in Klehr and Radosh, *Amerasia Spy Case*, p. 98.
27. Klehr and Radoch, *Amerasia Spy Case*, p. 99.
28. IFS, "The Red Issue and the Six," *PM*, June 11, 1945, p. 2.
29. Klehr and Radosh, *Amerasia Spy Case*, p. 131.
30. Ibid., p. 135; David McCullough, *Truman* (New York: Simon & Schuster, 1992), p. 475; "Out Swinging," *Time*, December 10, 1945.

31. IFS, "The Red Issue and the Six."
32. Interview with Christopher Stone, May 8, 1994; IFS, "What About the Emperor?" *PM*, August 13, 1945, p. 2.
33. Gar Alperovitz, *The Decision to Use the Atomic Bomb, and the Architecture of an American Myth* (New York: Knopf, 1995), p. 428; IFS, "What Russia's Participation Means," *PM*, August 9, 1945, p. 2.
34. IFS, "Inside Palestine, How the Jews and Arabs Get Along," *PM*, November 8, 1945, p. 2.
35. IFS, "The Harrison Report: A Revelation and a Challenge," *PM*, October 1, 1945, p. 2.
36. IFS, "Anti-British Campaign Won't Help Palestine," *PM*, December 7, 1945, p. 8.
37. IFS, "Palestine Pilgrimage," *Nation*, December 8, 1945, pp. 615–17.
38. IFS, "Palestine—Town and Country—Is at Peace," *PM*, November 9, 1945, p. 3.
39. IFS, "Why Palestine Is 'Home' to Jews," *PM*, December 4, 1945, p. 4; also "Palestine Pilgrimage."
40. IFS, "Bi-Nationalism as Solution for Palestine," *PM*, December 24, 1945, p. 6.
41. IFS, "Russia—and the British Policy in Palestine," *PM*, December 11, 1945, p. 7.
42. IFS, "Palestine Pilgrimage"; see also IFS, "Egypt's Misery a Contrast to Rebirth in Palestine," *PM*, December 23, 1945, p. 6.
43. IFS, "Jewry in a Blind Alley," *Nation*, November 24, 1945, p. 543.
44. IFS, "Bi-Nationalism as Solution for Palestine."
45. Ibid.
46. R.I. to J.P.L. and M.L., March 31, 1946.
47. Stewart, "The People Who Made *PM*," pp. 114–18; interview with Arnold Beichman.
48. "The Press," *Time*, February 25, 1946; IFS, "Salute to Harold Ickes," *PM*, February 14, 1946, p. 2.
49. IFS, "Where There Is No Vision," *Nation*, February 2, 1946.
50. IFS, *Underground to Palestine*, p. 3.
51. Akiva Skidell, "'Illegal Immigration': Laying the Groundwork," in Jonathan Jeremy Goldberg and Elliot King, eds., *Builders and Dreamers: Habonim Labor Zionist Youth in North America* (New York: Herzl Press, 1993), pp. 103–108.
52. IFS, *Underground to Palestine*, p. 8.
53. Victor Bernstein, "*Underground to Palestine* Now a Book," *PM*, November 21, 1946, p. 11.
54. IFS, *Underground to Palestine*, pp. xi, 19.
55. Ibid., p. 53.
56. Enzo Sereni, "Towards a New Orientation of Zionist Policy," in Enzo Sereni and R. E. Ashbery, eds., *Jews and Arabs in Palestine: Studies in a National and Colonial Problem* (New York: HeChalutz Press, 1936), p. 63.
57. IFS, *Underground to Palestine*, pp. 112–16.
58. Skidell, "Illegal Immigration," p. 109.
59. Yehuda Arazi interview, October 12, 1949, Haganah Archives, Document 6.10. Translated from the Hebrew by Daphna Baram.
60. IFS, *Underground to Palestine*, pp. 118–19.
61. Ada Sereni interview, n.d., Haganah Archives, Document 19.40. Translated from the Hebrew by Daphna Baram. The American naval historian Paul Silverstone's

website www.paulsilverstone.com/immigration/primary/index.html is a useful resource for information about the Aliyah Bet.

62. Yehuda Arazi interview, December 5, 1955, Haganah Archives, Document 6.18.
Translated from the Hebrew by Daphna Baram.

63. Ibid.

64. Ada Sereni interview.

65. IFS, *Underground to Palestine*, pp. 173–74.

66. Ibid., p. 182.

67. Bezalel Drori interview, n.d., Haganah Archives, Document 16.36. Translated from
the Hebrew by Daphna Baram.

68. IFS, *Underground to Palestine*, pp. 206–208.

69. Lewis Gannett, "Books and Things," *New York Herald Tribune*, November 26, 1946;
Meyer Berger, "Living Nightmares," *New York Times Book Review*, January 19, 1947,
p. 20; "Elsa Maxwell's Party Line," *New York Post*, January 3, 1947, p. 12.

70. Bartley Crum, "Escape from Europe," *Nation*, January 25, 1947, pp. 104–105; *New
York Post*, November 20, 1946, p. 5.

71. Lord Inverchapel No. 4597 to F.O., July 17, 1946, FO files, Public Record Office,
Kew, UK.

72. IFS, "Confessions of a Jewish Dissident," *New York Review of Books*, March 9,
1979. The essay is appended to the 1978 reprint of *Underground to Palestine* on
pp. 229–40.

73. Judah Magnes to IFS, February 14, 1947, in Arthur A. Goren, ed., *Dissenter in Zion:
From the Writings of Judah L. Magnes* (Cambridge, MA: Harvard University Press,
1982), pp. 445–47.

74. Rose Conway to IFS, January 8, 1947, Harry S. Truman Presidential Papers, President's Personal File 9 "S," January–April 1947.

75. D. D. Guttenplan, "The Death of a Reporter," *Media Studies Journal* 10, no. 4 (Win-
ter 1996): 173–83. See also Edmund Keeley, *The Salonika Bay Murder* (Princeton,
NJ: Princeton University Press, 1989); Kati Marton, *The Polk Conspiracy* (New
York: Farrar, Straus and Giroux, 1990); and Elias Vlanton, *Who Killed George Polk?*
(Philadelphia: Temple University Press, 1996).

76. Marton, *Polk Conspiracy*, p. 23.

77. IFS, "Wallace Won't Quit—Unless Asked To," *PM*, September 16, 1946, p. 3; "Wal-
lace's Appeal to Truman—For Peace," *PM*, September 18, 1946, p. 3; "The Story of
Truman versus Wallace," *PM*, September 22, 1946, p. 2. See also Richard J. Walton,
Henry Wallace, Harry Truman, and the Cold War (New York: The Viking Press, 1976).

78. George F. Kennan, "The Long Telegram," February 22, 1946. Published in *Foreign
Relations of the United States*, 1946, Vol. VI; full text at www2.gwu.edu/~nsarchiv/
coldwar/documents/episode-1/kennan.htm.

79. X [George F. Kennan], "The Sources of Soviet Conduct," *Foreign Affairs* 26, no. 2
(July 1947): 566–82.

80. Interview with Martha Rountree, May 26, 1994.

81. IFS, "Some Questions for J. Edgar Hoover," *PM*, October 6, 1946, p. 2.

82. "I. F. Stone," Federal Bureau of Investigation, Headquarters File 100-37078, Section
1, Document 30 A, p. 150. According to the file entry, the CIO attorney Lee Pressman
and his wife were also invited but were unable to attend. However, David Karr, one
of Drew Pearson's legmen, and his wife, Madeline, who wrote for the *Nation*, were
present.

83. The best account of Whittaker Chambers is Sam Tanenhaus, *Whittaker Chambers: A Biography* (New York: Random House, 1997), which I found largely persuasive, including on the contentious question of Alger Hiss. Of the dissenters, the most credible are Kai Bird and Svetlana Chervonnaya, "The Mystery of Ales," *American Scholar*, Summer 2007, and John Lowenthal, "Venona and Alger Hiss," *Intelligence and National Security* 15, no. 3 (Autumn 2000): 98–130.

84. John Earl Haynes and Harvey Klehr, *Venona: Decoding Soviet Espionage in America* (New Haven, CT: Yale University Press, 1999), pp. 93–115, 129–52. For background on Bentley, see Kathryn S. Olmsted, *Red Spy Queen: A Biography of Elizabeth Bentley* (Chapel Hill: University of North Carolina Press, 2002).

85. "I. F. Stone," Federal Bureau of Investigation, Headquarters File 100-37078, Section 1, Document 34, pp. 66–67. The document, a summary of Remington's testimony before a federal loyalty board, goes on to say that Bentley handed him articles from *PM* written by Stone and Crawford, with the implication that she had been assisting both writers—a scenario that, given Crawford's vigorous anticommunism, seems unlikely.

86. Haynes and Klehr, *Venona*, pp. 218–21. The authors note that "several dozen International Brigades veterans served in the OSS units that worked with resistance forces in enemy-occupied areas," though given what happened to Marzani, who ended up serving a thirty-two-month prison sentence for perjury, it was perhaps inevitable that very few of them felt inclined to come forward after the war. Klehr and Haynes also note (p. 219) that the CPUSA general secretary, Eugene Dennis, himself negotiated with Donovan the details of the party's collaboration with the OSS.

87. IFS, "Indicted Ex–U.S. Aide Wrote 'Radical' Film," *PM*, January 19, 1947, p. 6.

88. IFS, "Portrait of a Witch Hunt," *PM*, January 27, 1947, p. 3; IFS, "Labor Dept., Unlike War Dept., Grants Hearing to 4 Accused," *PM*, January 29, 1947, p. 3.

89. IFS, "Patterson Replies: 'We're Still at War,'" *PM*, February 2, 1947, p. 4.

90. Schrecker, *Many Are the Crimes*, pp. 122–29.

91. IFS, "The Eisler Affair as Spectacle and Warning," *PM*, February 9, 1947, p. 5.

92. *Daily Worker*, February 20, 1947, pp. 5, 8; "I. F. Stone," Federal Bureau of Investigation, Headquarters File 100-37078, Section 1, clipping of I. F. Stone, "Is the District of Columbia Becoming Police State?" *PM*, June 15, 1947, p. 8.

93. Arnold Offner, *Another Such Victory: President Truman and the Cold War, 1945–1953* (Stanford: Stanford University Press, 2002), pp. 197–99. For a more sympathetic view, see Walter Isaacson and Evan Thomas, *The Wise Men: Six Friends and the World They Made* (New York: Simon & Schuster, 1986).

94. Carl Bernstein, *Loyalties: A Son's Memoir* (New York: Simon & Schuster, 1989), pp. 190–98.

95. IFS, "It's Not the Heat, It's the Hysteria," *PM*, July 2, 1947, p. 2.

96. IFS, "Palestine Quiet, but British Are Afraid," *PM*, February 25, 1947, p. 6.

97. *PM*, February 23, 1947, p. 7, and February 26, 1947, p. 6; *Daily Compass*, August 29, 1949.

98. IFS, "Round Trip to Cyprus on Deportation Ship," *PM*, March 17, 1947, p. 7.

99. Rick Hellman, *Kansas City Jewish Chronicle*, November 29, 2001.

100. IFS, *PM*, May 16, 1948, p. 4; May 17, 1948, p. 3; May 24, 1948, p. 2.

101. IFS, *PM*, May 24–31, 1948.

102. IFS, "Refugees Just off Ship Swell Israeli Army," *PM*, May 21, 1948, p. 2. For figures on the order of battle, see Benny Morris, *The Birth of the Palestinian Refugee Problem*

Revisited (New York: Cambridge University Press, 2004), pp. 216–18, and Ahron Bregman, *Israel's Wars: A History Since 1947* (New York: Routledge, 2002), p. 24.

103. Stone did, however, go into considerable detail on Israel's war production capacity in *This Is Israel* (New York: Boni and Gaer, 1948), the coffee-table book he wrote with photographs by Robert Capa, Jerry Cooke, and Tim Gidal. See especially p. 68.
104. Ibid., p. 89.
105. IFS, "Trip to Jerusalem on Israel's 'Burma Road,'" *PM*, June 14, 1948, p. 2; Alex Kershaw, *Blood and Champagne: The Life and Times of Robert Capa* (New York: St. Martin's Press, 2003), pp. 205–206. For a fuller account of Marcus's life and death, see Ted Berkman, *Cast a Giant Shadow* (New York: Doubleday), 1962.
106. IFS, "I. F. Stone Reports from Israel," *Daily Compass*, August 29, 1949.
107. IFS, *This Is Israel*, pp. 26, 91.
108. Ibid., pp. 57–58.
109. Ibid., p. 68.
110. Patner, *I. F. Stone*, p. 67; see also Patricia Bosworth's memoir of her parents, *Every Little Thing Your Heart Desires: An American Family Story* (New York: Touchstone Books, 1998).
111. IFS, "Confessions of a Dupe," *New York Star*, August 25, 1948.
112. Ibid., p. 13.
113. IFS, *Truman Era*, p. 161.
114. IFS, "Washington Perspective," *New York Star*, June 30, 1948, p. 19.
115. IFS, "Confessions of a Dupe."
116. IFS, "The Last Chance," *PM*, December 21, 1947, p. 16, and "The Wallace Plan and the Communists," *PM*, January 2, 1948, p. 10.
117. IFS, "Mr. Truman's Police State," *Nation*, October 25, 1947, pp. 436–37.
118. IFS, "Count Me In, Too," *PM*, March 15, 1948, p. 8.
119. "Gerhard P. Van Arkel, 77, Former NLRB Counsel," *Washington Post*, October 19, 1984, p. D6.
120. Lee, *Truman and Taft-Hartley*, p. 50.
121. IFS, "The Case of the Legless Veteran," in *Truman Era*, pp. 86–88.
122. Murray Polner, review of James Kutcher, *The Case of the Legless Veteran*, posted on HNN, January 9, 2005: http:hnn.us/roundup/comments/9491.html.
123. IFS, "The Shadow Cast at Foley Square," in *Truman Era*, pp. 93–96.
124. Arthur Schlesinger Jr., "History of the *Week*," *New York Post*, July 7 and September 2, 1951, cited in Victor S. Navasky, *Naming Names* (New York: The Viking Press, 1980), pp. 53–54.
125. Was White a spy? For the most persuasive version of the affirmative case, see John Earl Haynes and Harvey Klehr, *In Denial: Historians, Communism and Espionage* (San Francisco: Encounter Books, 2003), pp. 182–92. For the most convincing rebuttal, see James M. Boughton and Roger Sandilands, "Politics and the Attack on FDR's Economists," *Intelligence and National Security*, Spring 2002. For a nuanced, credible account somewhere between the two, see R. Bruce Craig, *Treasonable Doubt: The Harry Dexter White Spy Case* (Lawrence: University of Kansas Press, 2004).
126. Interview with Simon Gerson; see also Gerson, *Pete*, p. 203.
127. Selma R. Williams, *Red Listed: Haunted by the Washington Witch Hunt* (Reading, MA: Addison-Wesley, 1993), pp. 218–20; "I. F. Stone," Federal Bureau of Investigation, Headquarters File 100-37078, Section 1.

7: THE GREAT FREEZE

1. Patricia Sullivan, *Days of Hope: Race and Democracy in the New Deal Era* (Chapel Hill: University of North Carolina Press, 1996).
2. Interview with Mairi Foreman.
3. *Meet the Press*, May 6, 1949, *Meet the Press* Collection.
4. *Meet the Press*, November 26, 1949, ibid.
5. IFS, "Palestine Run-Around," *Nation*, March 18, 1944, pp. 326–28. For a more sympathetic portrayal of Hurley as an "anti-imperial imperialist," see Christopher Hitchens, *Blood, Class and Nostalgia: Anglo-American Ironies* (New York: Farrar, Straus and Giroux, 1990), pp. 227–28.
6. *Meet the Press*, August 15, 1949, Lawrence Spivak Collection.
7. "Below-Belt Video," August 17, 1949, Spivak Collection.
8. John Crosby, "Temper, Temper, on the Air," *New York Herald Tribune*, August 20, 1949, Spivak Collection.
9. Cottrell, *Izzy*, pp. 157–58; *Meet the Press* audience information from an April 1994 interview with Susan Shicone of A. C. Nielsen.
10. IFS to Kenneth Stewart, January 26, 1950, Kenneth Stewart Collection.
11. A. J. Liebling, "Toward a One-Paper Town," in *The Press* (New York: Pantheon, 1975), pp. 45–55.
12. Patner, *I. F. Stone*, pp. 76–78; Cottrell, *Izzy*, p. 148.
13. Cottrell, *Izzy*; IFS, "Can America Plan Without Planning?" *New Republic*, January 24, 1949, pp. 11–12; Harold Field to IFS, January 17, 1949, *Nation* Collection.
14. "I. F. Stone," Federal Bureau of Investigation, Headquarters File 100-37078, Correlation Summary, p. 345.
15. IFS, "Agit-Prop Defense," *New York Post*, March 14, 1949, p. 37; "Decorum and Frame-Ups," *Daily Worker*, n.d.
16. IFS, "Lenin and Locke," *New York Post*, February 28, 1949, p. 48.
17. "I. F. Stone," Federal Bureau of Investigation, Headquarters File 100-37078, Section 3. For evidence that Smedley spied for the Soviets, see Ruth Price, *The Lives of Agnes Smedley* (New York: Oxford University Press, 2005).
18. "Red Visitors Cause Rumpus," *Life* 26, no. 14 (April 4, 1949): 40–43.
19. Dwight Macdonald, "The Waldorf Conference," *Politics* 6 (Winter 1949): 32A–D. Though Macdonald predictably found himself beset by villains on all sides, the lone hero of his account, excepting himself, was a fledgling novelist named Norman Mailer. Mailer's determination to plow his own furrow was signaled by his presence, months before the Waldorf affair, on the letterhead of the Kutcher Civil Rights committee, along with I. F. Stone.
20. IFS, "Has the ADA Stopped Being a Truman Front?" *Daily Compass*, April 6, 1950, p. 5; "I. F. Stone," Federal Bureau of Investigation, New York Field Office File 100-NY-90640, Document 10.
21. Finding Aid, Dorothy Schiff Collection, www.nypl.org/research/chss/spe/rbk/faids/schiff.html.
22. T. O. Thackrey, "The Compass Story—Some Lessons Learned in Failure," *Editor and Publisher*, December 26, 1953, pp. 9, 50–51.
23. Ibid.
24. Interview with Christopher Stone, May 8, 1994.
25. Michael J. Ybarra, *Washington Gone Crazy: Senator Pat McCarran and the Great American Communist Hunt* (Hanover, NH: Steerforth Press, 2004), pp. 433–58.

26. Williams, *Red Listed*, p. 218.

27. "I. F. Stone," Federal Bureau of Investigation, Headquarters File 100-37078.

28. IFS, *Truman Era*, p. xxi.

29. J. Edgar Hoover to George E. Allen, May 29, 1946, file "FBI-Atomic Bomb," in subject file "President's Secretary's File," Truman Papers, cited in Daniel Patrick Moynihan, *Secrecy: The American Experience* (New Haven, CT: Yale University Press, 1998), pp. 63–68.

30. Moynihan, *Secrecy*, p. 68.

31. Jessica Wang, "Edward Condon and the Cold War Politics of Loyalty," *Physics Today* 54, no. 12 (December 2001): 35–41.

32. Galbraith, *A Life in Our Times*, p. 23. Silvermaster's Berkeley PhD thesis was titled "Lenin's Economic Thought Before the October Revolution."

33. Haynes and Klehr, *Venona*, pp. 158–60; Schrecker, *Many Are the Crimes*, pp. 175–76; Susan Braudy, *Family Circle: The Boudins and the Aristocracy of the Left* (New York: Knopf, 2003), pp. 58–66. In differing degrees all these sources are problematic. Though Klehr and Haynes offer a detailed account of the evidence against Coplon, they skate over FBI misconduct with cryptic references to "the complex standards of U.S. criminal justice" and "legal technicality." There is nothing either technical or complex about the law guaranteeing the confidentiality of attorney-client communications. Schrecker is frank about Coplon's espionage but doesn't go into detail about her legal strategy. Braudy is so often unreliable on other matters that I have used her only as a last resort, and because the detailed account she gives of Leonard Boudin's approach is backed up by contemporary reports.

34. *United States v. Coplon*, 185 F.2d 629 (2d Cir. 1950); IFS, "Vice Squad Methods in the Coplon Case," *Daily Compass*, June 23, 1949, p. 5; IFS, "The Coplon Verdict," *Daily Compass*, July 3, 1949, p. 5.

35. IFS, "Whittaker Chambers: Martyrdom Lavishly Buttered," *Daily Compass*, February 12, 1952, p. 5.

36. Interview with Nathaniel Weyl; also Nathaniel Weyl, "I Was in a Communist Unit with Hiss," *U.S. News & World Report* 34 (January 9, 1953): 22–40.

37. Patner, *I. F. Stone*, p. 85.

38. IFS, "The Curtain Rises on the UN at San Francisco," *PM*, April 26, 1945.

39. "I. F. Stone," Electronic Surveillance (ELSUR) summaries (November 1949), Federal Bureau of Investigation, Headquarters File 100-37078.

40. *Meet the Press*, November 11, 1949, Spivak Collection.

41. IFS, "Me and Marxism: Invitation to a Dog-Fight," *Daily Compass*, November 14, 1949.

42. Ibid.

43. IFS, "The CIO Purges Labor's Own Liberties," *Daily Compass*, December 22, 1949. The American Jewish Congress launched a similar purge, which was striking, given that up until 1948 the AJC was the most left-wing of the mainstream Jewish organizations, with councils in Detroit, Los Angeles, and several boroughs of New York City controlled by Communists or radicals. Though the immediate effect was hard to discern, the silencing of radical voices within the politically active American Jewish community was of almost as much long-term significance as organized labor's self-mutilation. See Schrecker, *Many Are the Crimes*, pp. 39–40, and Paul Lyons, "Philadelphia Jews and Radicalism," in Friedman, *Philadelphia Jewish Life*, pp. 114–20.

44. IFS, "Has the ADA Stopped Being a Truman Front?"

45. Albert Fried, *McCarthyism: The Great American Red Scare—A Documentary History* (New York: Oxford University Press, 1997), pp. 78–80; Schrecker, *Many Are the Crimes*, pp. 240–45, 248.

46. Newman, *Owen Lattimore and the "Loss" of China*.

47. Owen Lattimore, "New Road in Asia," *National Geographic* 86 (December 1944): 641–76, cited in Elinor Lipper, *Eleven Years in Soviet Prison Camps* (Chicago: Regnery, 1951), pp. 114–16. In Patner, *I. F. Stone*, Izzy describes Lipper's exposé as "a terrific book" (p. 49).

48. IFS, "Budenz: Portrait of a Christian Hero," *Daily Compass*, April 23, 1950; also IFS, *Truman Era*, pp. 190–93.

49. [IFS], "There is no divinity . . . ," *Nation*, March 30, 1940, p. 405.

50. Herbert L. Packer, *Ex-Communist Witnesses: Four Studies in Fact Finding* (Stanford, CA: Stanford University Press, 1962), p. 129.

51. Kenneth McCormick, Oral History, Columbia University Oral History Collection, pp. 61–63.

52. Haywood Patterson and Earl Conrad, *Scottsboro Boy* (Garden City, NY: Doubleday, 1950). According to the cultural historian Alan Wald, Earl Conrad (whose real name was Earl Cohen), though celebrated by American Communists for his part in *Scottsboro Boy*, was later driven from party circles for allegedly portraying blacks as degraded in his antiracist novel *Rock Bottom*. See Alan Wald, "The Urban Landscape of Marxist Noir," www.crimetime.co.uk/features/marxistnoir.php.

53. IFS, "Fugitive's Book Tells of Nazi-Like Horror Camps in Southland, U.S.A.," *Daily Compass*, June 2, 1950.

54. IFS, "A Look at the South," *Daily Compass*, June 7, 1950.

55. IFS, "Tribute to Joe Brodsky," letter to *Daily Worker*, August 2, 1947, p. 7. Brodsky was the party lawyer who headed the ILD at the time of the Scottsboro campaign. Izzy wrote that he had "served justice and the working class faithfully according to his lights."

56. IFS, "Gov. Folsom Last Hope to Wipe Slate Clean of Scottsboro Case," *Daily Compass*, June 5, 1950.

57. U.S. Congress. Senate. 81st Cong., 2nd Sess., *Congressional Record*, pp. 10708–12.

58. "I. F. Stone," Federal Bureau of Investigation, Headquarters File, Section 2, Part 2, p. 397; also New York Field Office File NY 100-90640-14A.

59. Interview with Celia Gilbert, September 31, 1991.

60. Interview with Christopher Stone, May 8, 1994; interview with Jeremy Stone.

61. IFS, "Nehru's Job Harder Than Gandhi Faced," *Daily Compass*, September 12, 1950, p. 5.

62. IFS, "Marshall Tito Grants Interview," *Daily Compass*, October 19, 1950, p. 5; "Freedom of Speech Found in Yugoslavia," *Daily Compass*, October 24, 1950, p. 5; "Tito's Dilemma: The Bureaucracy," *Daily Compass*, October 31, 1950, p. 4; "Labor Has Real Say in Big Yugoslav Plant," *Daily Compass*, November 8, 1950, p. 4.

63. IFS, "Looking at America from 3,000 Miles," *Daily Compass*, October 1, 1950, p. 5.

64. Interview with Celia Gilbert; Cottrell, interview with IFS.

65. Interviews with Celia Gilbert, Christopher Stone, and Jeremy Stone.

66. Interview with Stanley Karnow, July 12, 2005.

67. Patner, *I. F. Stone*, p. 64.

68. Ibid., p. 62.

69. Interview with Ralph Ginzburg, spring 1992. Ginzburg later gained infamy, and a footnote in Supreme Court history, when he served a prison sentence for obscenity as the publisher of *Eros*, "America's first major magazine of mass circulation that took a psychologically mature view of sex."

70. IFS, "On July 4, 1951," *Daily Compass*, July 4, 1951, p. 4.

71. Interview with Paul Sweezy, April 10, 1992. See also Leo Huberman and Paul Sweezy, "Publisher's Foreword," in IFS, *The Hidden History of the Korean War* (New York: Monthly Review Press, 1952), p. xiii. Brought into being to publish *The Hidden History*, Monthly Review Press went on to publish works by Régis Debray, Eduardo Galeano, and Ernest Mandel, as well as Sweezy and Paul Baran's classic study, *Monopoly Capital*.

72. IFS, "Les Origines de la Guerre de Corée," *L'Observateur*, March 8, 1951, pp. 12–14. See also Huberman and Sweezy, "Publisher's Foreword," p. ix.

73. Cottrell, *Izzy*, p. 166.

74. W. Macmahon Ball, "Some Questions on Korea," *Nation*, July 5, 1952, pp. 14–15; John Pittman, "I. F. Stone's 'Hidden History' Debunks Korean War Myths," *Daily Worker*, June 29, 1952, p. 9; Art Preis, "A Trotskyist Defends New I. F. Stone Book," *Daily Compass*, May 26, 1952, p. 12.

75. Interview with Murray Kempton. Kempton's hunch—really more of a certainty—is borne out by James Wechsler to Richard Rovere, April 29, 1952, Rovere Papers, in which Wechsler responds to Rovere's first draft, suggesting a few changes and apparently correcting Rovere's implication (no copy of the first draft survives) that Izzy had also once been a party member. Wechsler also credits Stone with "a sense of humor and a kind of ebullience not characteristic of the fellow traveller," an emendation ignored by Rovere, perhaps because, according to Kempton, "Dick really hated Izzy."

76. Norman Kaner, "I. F. Stone and the Korean War," in Thomas G. Paterson, ed., *Cold War Critics: Alternatives to American Foreign Policy in the Truman Years* (Chicago: Quadrangle Books, 1971), pp. 240–65.

77. For the full text of NSC-68, see www.fas.org/irp/offdocs/nsc-hst/nsc-68.htm. Drafted, largely by Paul Nitze, in April 1950, the document remained on Truman's desk, unsigned, for more than six months, until events in Korea rendered Nitze's proactive approach irresistible.

78. IFS, *Hidden History*, p. 44.

79. Kathryn Weathersby, "To Attack, or Not to Attack: Stalin, Kim Il Sung, and the Prelude to War," *Cold War International History Project Bulletin* 5 (Spring 1995): 1–9. Weathersby argues that the war was indeed Stalin's blunder, though Bruce Cumings's robust response (*CWIHP Bulletin* 6–7 [Winter 1995/1996], pp. 120–21) makes it clear that even this question is not settled. My own view is that comparing Stalin's role in the Korean War to the starter of a race, as Adam Ulam does in his December 10, 1993, letter to the CWIHP, and as Weathersby appears to accept in her response (*CWIHP Bulletin* 4), is misleading. In Vietnam, for example, the ARVN staged numerous raids and the United States shelled repeatedly offshore; any of these could have been seen as starters' guns, though as it turned out in Tonkin Gulf the runners were off the mark with only a fictive firing of the gun. War is not a race; in order for a war to start, both sides need to believe that they are indeed at war. It

may have been the difficulty of applying such analogies to the situation in Korea that led Cumings, in his response to Weathersby, to describe the controversy over who started the Korean War as "the question we ought to all try to forget."

80. John Lewis Gaddis, *We Now Know: Rethinking Cold War History* (New York: Oxford University Press, 1997), p. 70. See also Sergei Goncharov, John W. Lewis, and Xue Litai, *Uncertain Partners: Stalin, Mao and the Korean War* (Stanford, CA: Stanford University Press, 1993), pp. 130–68.

81. Stephen E. Ambrose, "Preface to the Second Paperback Edition," in IFS, *The Hidden History of the Korean War* (New York: Monthly Review Press, 1971), p. xii.

82. Bruce Cumings, "Preface," IFS, *The Hidden History of the Korean War* (Boston: Little, Brown, 1988), pp. ix–xx.

83. IFS, *Hidden History*, pp. 193, 196.

84. Ibid., p. 75.

85. I. F. Stone, Department of State File, Document PO 56.

86. Interview with Stanley Karnow; Klehr and Radosh, *Amerasia Spy Case*, p. 30; Ybarra, *Washington Gone Crazy*, pp. 633–35.

87. IFS to Willis Young, November 2, 1951, in I. F Stone, Department of State File, Document PO 16.

88. "Acheson to AmConsul, Jerusalem," in I. F. Stone, Department of State File, Document PO 51.

89. IFS, *Hidden History*, pp. 23–27. Bruce Cumings observed that "Dulles's own memoranda now show that Stone was exactly on the money in saying that after Dulles joined the Truman administration in April 1950, he 'discreetly but unmistakably joined forces with MacArthur on Formosa policy'" (Cumings, *CWIHP Bulletin*).

90. IFS, *Hidden History*, pp. 203–206.

91. Haynes and Klehr, *Venona*, pp. 25–26; see also the interview with Meredith Gardner on the PBS documentary *Secrets, Lies, and Atomic Spies*, transcript at www.pbs.org/wgbh/nova/transcripts/2904_venona.html.

92. Haynes and Klehr, *Venona*; Moynihan, *Secrecy*, pp. 60–62. The message decoded in December 1946 is reproduced by Moynihan as Figure 6 on p. 151.

93. Haynes and Klehr, *Venona*, pp. 304–11.

94. Venona 1433, 1435 KGB New York to Moscow, October 10, 1944. All the Venona decrypts that have been released to date by the National Security Agency are available at www.nsa.gov/venona/venon00017.cfm.

95. Venona 1313 KGB New York to Moscow, September 13, 1944.

96. Venona 1506 KGB New York to Moscow, October 23, 1944.

97. "Isidor Feinstein Stone," blind memorandum dated February 1, 1951, Document Number 51-010, released to the author by the FBI in response to a Freedom of Information request to the National Security Agency.

98. Venona 1506; "I. F. Stone," Federal Bureau of Investigation, Headquarters File 65-6065, Section 1, Document 1, which includes a copy of Washington Field Office File 65-5685, SAC Washington to Director, March 30, 1951. In 1944, Izzy's combined salary from the *Nation* and *PM* was $975 a month.

99. "I. F. Stone," Federal Bureau of Investigation, Headquarters File 65-6065, Section 1, Document 1; see also New York Field Office File NY 100-90640, Document 33, SAC New York to Director, April 9, 1951, and Document 34, SAC New York to Director, April 20, 1951.

100. "I. F. Stone," Federal Bureau of Investigation, Washington Field Office File 100-22286-22.

101. "I. F. Stone," Federal Bureau of Investigation, Headquarters File 65-6065, Section 1, Document 1, Director to SAC New York, August 1, 1951.

102. "I. F. Stone," Federal Bureau of Investigation, Headquarters File 65-6065, Section 1, Document 1, SA Scheidt to Director, August 22, 1951.

103. "I. F. Stone," Federal Bureau of Investigation, Headquarters File 65-6065, Section 1, Document 1, SAC New York to Director, September 18, 1951.

104. Ibid.

105. "BLIN=I. F. Stone," in "Top Secret Umbra," untitled ms., pp. 422–24, released by the National Security Agency in response to my Freedom of Information request. This appears to be an excerpt from Robert Louis Benson and Michael Warner, eds., *Venona: Soviet Espionage and the American Response 1939–1957* (Washington, D.C.: National Security Agency/Central Intelligence Agency, 1996; Laguna Hills, CA: Aegean Park Press, 1996).

106. Even J. Edgar Hoover had his doubts. In a May 1952 memo he cautioned, "Stone has only been tentatively identified as Soviet agent 'Blin' and . . . investigation conducted to date has developed no indication that Stone may currently be engaged in espionage activity." See "I. F. Stone," Federal Bureau of Investigation, New York Field Office File NY 100-90640, Document 81, Director to SAC New York, May 15, 1952. The extensive Venona Project material released by the National Security Agency since 1995 adds nothing to Lamphere's four-pronged argument (which initially failed to convince even his own colleagues). And though it may have escaped notice, BLIN also appears in Allen Weinstein and Alexander Vassiliev's 1999 *The Haunted Wood* (p. 31), where he is described as "a *New York Post* reporter" who "volunteered information" about William Randolph Hearst. Though *The Haunted Wood* didn't mention Stone, in 2009 Vassiliev and two new coauthors claimed not only that BLIN was Stone but that during the mid-1930s he served as an "agent" and "talent spotter" for the KGB. Leaving aside the fact that Stone was never a *Post* reporter, there are ample grounds for skepticism—not least because the only source for the charge is Vassiliev's purported notes on what he claims to have read in KGB files now closed to researchers. (In 2003 a British jury ruled against Vassiliev in a libel action based on his handling of evidence regarding Alger Hiss.) See John Earl Hayes, Harvey Klehr, and Alexander Vassiliev, *Spies: The Rise and Fall of the KGB in America* (New Haven: Yale University Press, 2009), pp. 146–52.

107. Venona 1805 KGB New York to Moscow, December 23, 1944.

108. Ronald Radosh, e-mail to author, September 24, 1996.

109. "I. F. Stone," Federal Bureau of Investigation, New York Field Office File NY 100-90640, Sub A. Ironically, the "Surveillance Log" for March 26, 1952, shows Izzy, Esther, and Celia going to the movies but fails to note that the film was made by Buñuel, a Communist.

110. "I. F. Stone," Federal Bureau of Investigation, Headquarters File 100-37078, Section 3, Document 33.

111. Having his phone calls bugged was not a new experience for Izzy. His file in the FBI's Washington Field Office, WMFO 100-22286, Section 10, contains 295 pages of transcribed wiretaps of calls either made by I. F. Stone or where he is mentioned. The targets include Harry Bridges, the United Federal Workers Union in Washing-

ton, a lawyer's office (probably Leonard Boudin, judging from the tone of his conversations with Izzy), the Washington Cooperative Bookshop, and several figures in the *Amerasia* case. All of the hundreds of calls in this file date from before 1951; that is, before Stone himself became a target of federal investigators.

112. Interview with Jeremy Stone; "I. F. Stone," Federal Bureau of Investigation, Washington Field Office File WMFO 100-22286, Section Sub B, Volume IC, Serial B-48.

113. "I. F. Stone," Federal Bureau of Investigation, Headquarters File Document 177; also Department of Justice File, "Raymond Farrell to J. Edgar Hoover," December 17, 1953.

114. M. Wesley Swearingen, interviewed for CNN series *The Cold War*, transcript available at www.gwu.edu/~nsarchiv/coldwar/interviews/episode-6/swearingen1.html.

115. Ybarra, *Washington Gone Crazy*, pp. 518–23.

116. Christopher Phelps, "Introduction: A Socialist Magazine in the American Century," *Monthly Review* 51, no. 1 (May 1999), or www.monthlyreview.org/599phelp.htm.

117. Michael Blankfort to George Sokolsky, Blankfort Papers.

118. House Committee on Un-American Activities, *Communist Infiltration of Hollywood Motion Picture Industry: Hearings*, 82nd Cong., January 24, 1952, Part 7, cited in Navasky, *Naming Names*, pp. 101–102, 377, 445. According to Victor Navasky, Blankfort's remark naming his ex-wife and cousin, though expunged from the record at the request of Blankfort's attorney, Marvin Gang, was widely reported at the time. In 1950, Blankfort and Maltz had been close enough for Blankfort to serve as the "front" for his blacklisted friend's screenplay for *Broken Arrow*, which was nominated for an Academy Award. But after Blankfort appeared before HUAC as a "cooperative witness," Maltz never forgave him.

119. "I. F. Stone Speaks," *New York Herald Tribune*, November 4, 1951, p. 11; IFS, "Me and the Red Underground," *Daily Compass*, November 11, 1951, p. 5.

120. Ogden R. Reid, *New York Herald Tribune*, March 23, 1952, p. 9; IFS, *Daily Compass*, March 25, 1952, p. 5.

121. IFS, "The Right to Travel and the ACLU's Split Personality," *Daily Compass*, February 22, 1952, and "What Are the Links Between the ACLU and the FBI?" *Daily Compass*, September 2, 1952, p. 5: "Many of us have wondered whether the dual role of Morris L. Ernst had led to undercover relations between the FBI and the ACLU." Stone was right to wonder. In the 1950s, Ernst went from advising Hoover to informing for him. See Anthony Marro, "F.B.I. Files Disclose '50s Tie to A.C.L.U.; F.B.I's Files Disclose A.C.L.U. Gave Data on Activities and Members to Bureau in 1950's," *New York Times*, August 4, 1977, p. 1.

122. Max Gordon and Howard Rodman, "National Emergency Civil Liberties Committee: The First Quarter Century," *Bill of Rights Journal* 9 (December 1976): 4–30.

123. Interview with Edith Tiger, September 20, 1991.

124. Sidney Hook to Richard Rovere, April 2, 1952, and Sidney Hook to Arthur Schlesinger Jr., April 16, 1952, both in Rovere Papers.

125. Interviews with Paul Lehmann, October 18 and 24, 1991.

126. IFS, "The Man Who Protects Budenz," *Daily Compass*, October 13, 1951, p. 5, and "The Ethics of the Knife in the Back," *Daily Compass*, October 14, 1951, p. 5.

127. IFS, "The Rosenberg Case," *Daily Compass*, October 15, 1952, p. 5.

128. IFS, "What's the Government Afraid Of?" *Daily Compass*, July 14, 1951, p. 5.

129. Dashiell Hammett to IFS, March 18, 1952, V. J. Jerome Papers. Stone's refusal is handwritten on the bottom of the letter—his habitual method of replying to correspondents.
130. IFS, *New York Star*, October 20, 1948, cited in Vlanton, *Who Killed George Polk?* p. 89.
131. Vlanton, *Who Killed George Polk?* pp. 91–92.
132. Ibid., pp. 16–17; Keeley, *Salonika Bay Murder*, pp. 102–104.
133. IFS, "I. F. Stone Exposes Polk Murder Case Whitewash," *Daily Compass*, August 6–10, 1952; see also Guttenplan, "Death of a Reporter."
134. Vlanton, *Who Killed George Polk?* pp. 147–48, 267n73.
135. IFS, "Devoted Teacher's Reward," *Daily Compass*, October 3, 1952, p. 5. Mildred Flacks was also the mother of the SDS activist and historian Richard Flacks, co-drafter of the Port Huron Statement and author of *Making History*. In the 1970s, the New York City Board of Education, in settlement of a suit brought by Mildred Flacks, her husband, and a number of other blacklisted teachers, agreed to pay a substantial sum to each teacher as well as issue a public apology for the dismissals.
136. IFS, "What Are YOU Going to Do About School Witch Hunt?" *Daily Compass*, October 8, 1952, p. 5.
137. IFS, "Yale May Be Weak on God, But It Still Believes in Man," *Daily Compass*, February 19, 1952, p. 5.
138. IFS, "Eisenhower, Korea, and World Peace," *Daily Compass*, June 3, 1952, p. 5.
139. IFS, "Adlai's Stand Offers Chance for Peace," *Daily Compass*, October 1, 1952, p. 5.
140. IFS, "Progressives Kick Off Campaign," *Daily Compass*, July 7, 1952, p. 1.
141. C. B. Baldwin to Editor, *Daily Compass*, July 20, 1950.
142. IFS, "Memo on How to Function as a Peace Party," *Daily Compass*, August 3, 1952, p. 5.
143. IFS, "Democrats Little Man's Party," *Daily Compass*, July 23, 1952, p. 5, and "Dead Past Still Rules Dems," *Daily Compass*, July 24, 1952, p. 5.
144. IFS, "Why I'm for Adlai Stevenson," *Daily Compass*, September 21, 1952, p. 5.
145. IFS, "Why You Should Vote for Corliss Lamont," *Daily Compass*, October 26, 1952, p. 5.
146. Corliss Lamont to Virginia Durr, December 5, 1952, Virginia Durr Collection.
147. Thackrey, "Compass Story."
148. Freda Kirchwey to IFS, April 16, 1952; IFS to Freda Kirchwey, November 19, 1952, Kirchwey Collection. See also Cottrell, *Izzy*, p. 171.
149. Interview with Jeremy Stone.
150. Stone, *Truman Era*, p. xvii.

8: COMING UP FOR AIR

1. George Seldes, *Tell the Truth and Run* (New York: Greenberg, 1953), pp. 262–63. Also interview with George Seldes. Seldes may never have known that when J. Edgar Hoover first put Seldes in the FBI's crosshairs, he was acting at the behest of Seldes's idol, Franklin Roosevelt. See Steve Early to the President, February 18, 1941, Official File 4185, Franklin D. Roosevelt Library, Hyde Park, NY, cited in Kenneth O'Reilly, *Hoover and the UnAmericans: The FBI, HUAC, and the Red Menace* (Philadelphia: Temple University Press, 1983), p. 303n32.

2. George Seldes, interviewed by Robert Gershon, 1982.

3. George Seldes, "Draft Farewell," Seldes Collection. See also letter from Claud Cockburn (n.d., 1945 or 1946) asking for advice on mailing lists and offering Seldes stock in the *Week*.

4. Interview with Jeremy Stone; "A Personal Letter from I. F. Stone," copy in J. B. Matthews Papers; interview with Christopher Stone.

5. Interview with Carey McWilliams, in Buckley, "I. F. Stone," pp. 21–22.

6. James Boylan, *Columbia Journalism Review*, September/October 1998, p. 67, reviewing Matthew Passmore and Chip Robertson, eds., *Forgive Us Our Press Passes: Selected Works by Daniel Schorr* (Berkeley: University of California Press, 1998).

7. The FBI, which had Stone under nearly continuous surveillance, promptly opened a file on Weiner. "I. F. Stone," Federal Bureau of Investigation, Headquarters File 100-37038, Section 8, Document 212, May 24, 1954. See also Cottrell, *Izzy*, pp. 175–76; Patner, *I. F. Stone*, p. 78; "*Weekly* ledgers," accounts for November 17, 1952–December 31, 1952.

8. Interview with Sidney Roger. Also see Sidney Roger, Oral History, Bancroft Library, University of California, Berkeley, 1998, p. 429.

9. IFS to Harvey O'Connor, December 20, 1952, Harvey O'Connor Collection; Cottrell, interview with IFS.

10. Anti–Smith Act Rally, Polk Hall, San Francisco, August 1951, tape furnished by Sidney Roger.

11. Jeremy Stone to Michael Blankfort, February 8, 1953, Blankfort Papers; "Hats Off," *IFSW*, February 14, 1953.

12. "Those Diabolic Doctors," *IFSW*, February 7, 1953; "Anti-Zionism or Anti-Semitism," *IFSW*, February 21, 1953.

13. "Making America a Police State," *IFSW*, May 2, 1953; "The Jenner Report and Those Panicky Liberals," *IFSW*, September 12, 1953.

14. "A New and Safe Form of Popular Front," *IFSW*, February 21, 1953.

15. Christopher Stone to Robert Newman, May 24, 1992.

16. Braudy, *Family Circle*, pp. 86–87 (see my earlier caveat about this source, but Leonard's infidelities were widely discussed).

17. Navasky, *Naming Names*, p. 79.

18. Ibid., pp. 268–70, 340–41.

19. Bernard Weinraub, "Recalling John Garfield, Rugged Star KO'd by Fate," *New York Times*, January 29, 2003; interview with Roberta Garfield Cohn, July 1991.

20. "The Case of the Cooperative Teacher," *IFSW*, March 21, 1953.

21. U.S. Senate, Subcommittee to Investigate the Administration of the Internal Security Act, Testimony of Frederick Palmer Weber, New York, NY, April 21, 1953, 83rd Cong., p. 194; interview with Gertrude Weber, March 2006.

22. Max Gordon and Howard Rodman, "National Emergency Civil Liberties Committee: The First Quarter Century," *Bill of Rights Journal* 9 (December 1976): 10; Joseph R. McCarthy, Address to the Sons of the American Revolution, May 15, 1950, *Congressional Record*, 81st Cong., 2nd sess., A3787.

23. Executive Sessions of the Senate Permanent Subcommittee on Investigations of the Committee on Government Operations, 83rd Cong., 1953, made public January 2003, available at www.gpo.gov/congress/senate/mccarthy/83870.html.

24. Ibid.

25. Interview with Celia Gilbert, September 30, 1991.
26. Federal Bureau of Investigation, Washington Field Office File 100-22286, Subsection B, Volume 1C, Serials B1–B48 (I. F. Stone Surveillance Logs), and Serial 152. The Washington Field Office's code name for Stone was GREELEY.
27. Ibid.
28. "I. F. Stone," Federal Bureau of Investigation, Washington Field Office File 100-37078 (I. F. Stone), Section 4, Serial 155, p. 14; Newman, *Owen Lattimore*, p. 312; interview with Andrew Roth.
29. "Morale Builder," *IFSW*, May 30, 1953.
30. *IFSW* corporate records, minutes of March 6, 1953.
31. Interviews with Jeremy Stone and Christopher Stone.
32. Interview with Richard Dudman, March 15, 1991.
33. U.S. Senate, Subcommittee to Investigate the Administration of the Internal Security Act, Testimony of Victor Perlo, Flushing, NY, May 12, 1953, 83rd Cong., pp. 418–20. Perlo's anxiety about self-incrimination was well founded. According to the *Venona* decrypts, Perlo, code-named "Raider," was an energetic, productive source for Soviet intelligence. Yet Perlo, who repeatedly denied having engaged in espionage, was never prosecuted. When he died in December 1999, his *New York Times* obituary, though noting his service from the 1960s onward as chief economist of the CPUSA, referred only to "accusations."
34. *IFSW*, February 28, 1953.
35. Schrecker, *No Ivory Tower*, pp. 8–9.
36. *IFSW*, March 22, 1954.
37. *IFSW*, September 5, 1953.
38. Richard Rovere, *Senator Joe McCarthy* (New York: Harper, 1973), p. 262.
39. *IFSW*, May 2 and May 16, 1953.
40. *IFSW*, May 2, 1953.
41. *IFSW*, May 9 and May 30, 1953.
42. *IFSW*, May 16 and July 4, 1953.
43. Harvey Wheeler, "Recollections of a Meeting with I. F. Stone in 1953," communication with the author, July 27, 1992.
44. Executive Sessions of the Senate Permanent Subcommittee on Investigations of the Committee on Government Operations, 83rd Cong., 1953, www.gpo.gov/congress/senate/mccarthy/83870.html.
45. " 'Refuse to Testify,' Einstein Advises Intellectuals Called in by Congress," *New York Times*, June 12, 1953, p. 1.
46. John J. Simon, "Albert Einstein, Radical: A Political Profile," *Monthly Review* 57, no. 1 (May 2005). See also Fred Jerome, *The Einstein File: J. Edgar Hoover's Secret War Against the World's Most Famous Scientist* (New York: St. Martin's Press, 2002).
47. "Professor Einstein's Theory," *New York Times*, June 13, 1953, p. 14.
48. "Who Will Take the 'Einstein Pledge'?" *IFSW*, June 20, 1953.
49. Mary Sperling McAuliffe, *Crisis on the Left: Cold War Politics and American Liberals, 1947–1954* (Amherst: University of Massachusetts Press, 1978), pp. 116–20. See also Kai Bird and Martin J. Sherwin, *American Prometheus: The Triumph and Tragedy of Robert J. Oppenheimer* (New York: Knopf, 2005), pp. 372, 379–82, 487–90.
50. Albert Einstein to IFS, March 21, 1954.
51. Murray Kempton, "A Prevalence of Witches," *New York Post*, March 16, 1954.

52. *IFSW*, March 15, 1954; the fraught atmosphere behind Murrow's documentary was itself the subject of the Academy Award–winning film *Good Night, and Good Luck*.

53. *IFSW*, March 8, 1954.

54. Haynes Johnson, *The Age of Anxiety: McCarthyism to Terrorism* (Orlando: Harcourt, 2005), pp. 351, 358–60, 389.

55. *IFSW*, March 15, 1954.

56. *IFSW*, September 6, 1954. The complete text of the bill is printed in *IFSW*, September 13.

57. *IFSW*, October 25, 1954.

58. IFS, "Mr. O and Mr. X," *PM*, March 30, 1948, p. 3; *IFSW*, May 9 and June 15, 1953.

59. Hal Draper, "The Strange Case of I. F. Stone," *Labor Action*, November 8, 1954, p. 6. By far the best brief résumé of the extremely strange case of Max Shachtman is Maurice Isserman, *If I Had a Hammer: The Death of the Old Left and the Birth of the New Left* (Urbana: University of Illinois Press, 1993), pp. 37–75.

60. Hal Draper, "The Imperialist Apologetics of Max Lerner," *Labor Action*, July 5, 1954; *IFSW*, June 21 and December 6, 1954. Nor was Izzy impressed by the removal of Mohammed Mossadegh, the left-leaning Iranian prime minister who had nationalized the country's oil resources. "The net effect . . . ," he wrote, "seems to be Americanization of Iranian oil" (*IFSW*, December 14, 1953).

61. Robert Scheer, *How the United States Got Involved in Vietnam* (Santa Barbara, CA: Center for the Study of Democratic Institutions, 1965), cited in James Aronson, *The Press and the Cold War* (New York: Monthly Review Press, 1970), pp. 183–85. Buttinger was also a minor angel for *Dissent*. For a sense of his effect on the magazine and on Irving Howe's responses to Vietnam, see Isserman, *If I Had a Hammer*, p. 107. See also Phillipe de Pirey, "The Indo-Chinese War—As Seen in a French Soldier's Diary," *IFSW*, March 1, 1954.

62. *IFSW*, March 15, 1954.

63. *IFSW*, March 29, 1954.

64. Bird and Sherwin, *American Prometheus*. Much was made of the fact that Oppenheimer had given conflicting accounts of an approach by his Berkeley friend Haakon Chevalier soliciting information to be passed to the Soviets. But Oppenheimer did report the approach to General Groves in 1943, and Groves, an arch-conservative, kept Oppenheimer at Los Alamos.

65. *IFSW*, April 19 and April 5, 1954.

66. *IFSW*, July 18 and December 5, 1955; Susan E. Tifft and Alex S. Jones, *The Trust: The Private and Powerful Family Behind the* New York Times (Boston: Little, Brown, 1999), pp. 267–70.

67. "The Moral Collapse of the *New York Times* and the *Washington Post*," *IFSW*, July 25, 1955. See also Michael Cross-Barnet, "The New York Times Shafted My Father," *Los Angeles Times*, June 26, 2005.

68. "Witness Ejected at Hearing; Ex-Red's Story Starts Fight," *New York Times*, March 21, 1954, p. 1; Jennings Perry, "The Congressional Inquisition Moves South," *IFSW*, March 29, 1954, pp. 2–3; interview with Virginia Durr. See also Taylor Branch, *Parting the Waters: America in the King Years, 1954–63* (New York: Simon and Schuster, 1988), pp. 121–22, for the impact of the Eastland hearings on the Durrs' finances.

69. *IFSW*, May 24, 1954.

70. Anita Krajnc and Michael Greenspoon, "Singing Together for Social Change: Interview with Pete Seeger," *Peace Magazine*, July–August, 1996, p. 6.

71. Catherine Fosl, *Subversive Southerner: Anne Braden and the Struggle for Racial Justice in the Cold War South* (New York: Palgrave Macmillan, 2002), pp. 183–90. Walter Millis, author of both *Nation* pieces, was a former editorial writer for the *New York Herald Tribune* and a staff member of the Fund for the Republic.

72. *IFSW*, October 5, 1955.

73. Interview with Christopher Stone, May 8, 1994.

74. Interview with Robert Silvers, February 11, 1992.

75. Dorothy M. Zellner, "They Stood Up: Rosa Parks and Virginia Durr, Heroines of the Civil Rights Movement," *Jewish Currents*, May 2006, pp. 14–18. For more on Rosa Parks at Highlander, including photos, see www.highlandercenter.org.

76. *IFSW*, February 20, 1956; Jennings Perry, "A First Hand Report from Montgomery, Once the Capital of the Confederacy . . . Now the 'Capital' of the Southern Negro's New Gandhi-Style Revolt," *IFSW*, March 5, 1956, pp. 2–3.

77. John Salmond, *A Southern Rebel: The Life and Times of Aubrey Willis Williams, 1890–1965* (Chapel Hill: University of North Carolina Press, 1983), pp. 240–55. In his memoir *A Life in Our Times*, John Kenneth Galbraith writes that Johnson later told him that "one of his proudest Senate accomplishments was telling Joe McCarthy and another witch-hunter, William E. Jenner of Indiana, to lay off the Durrs or suffer the full if unspecified consequences of the Johnson wrath. McCarthy, he told me, 'frightened good.'" (p. 447).

78. *IFSW*, December 5, 1955.

79. IFS to James Wechsler, December 8, 1955; James Wechsler to IFS, December 12, 1955, Wechsler Papers.

80. *IFSW*, December 19, 1955.

81. *IFSW*, January 9, 1956; "Eastland v. the *Times*," *Time*, January 15, 1956; Tifft and Jones, *The Trust*, pp. 268–70.

82. Schrecker, *Many Are the Crimes*, pp. 312–13; see also Robert M. Lichtman and Ronald D. Cohen, *Deadly Farce: Harvey Matusow and the Informer System in the McCarthy Era* (Urbana: University of Illinois Press, 2004).

83. Lichtman and Cohen, *Deadly Farce*, p. 22; Albert Kahn, *The Matusow Affair: Memoir of a National Scandal* (Mt. Kisco, NY: Moyer, Bell, 1987), pp. 121–22, 295n21; Murray Kempton, *America Comes of Middle Age* (Boston: Little, Brown, 1963), pp. 3, 324; *IFSW*, February 7 and 28, 1955.

84. *IFSW*, February 28, 1955.

85. House Committee on Un-American Activities, *Hearings*, 84th Cong., 1st Sess., October 14, 1955; Mostel FBI file, http://foia.fbi.gov/foiaindex/mostel_zero.htm; Schrecker, *No Ivory Tower*, p. 130.

86. "I. F. Stone," Federal Bureau of Investigation, Washington Field Office File WFO 100-22286, Section 12, Serial 337, p. 6.

87. "I. F. Stone," Federal Bureau of Investigation, Washington Field Office File WFO 100-22286, Section 10A, Serial 267A, p. 49.

88. Edward U. Condon to IFS, October 27, 1955, Edward U. Condon Collection; *IFSW*, November 7, 1955.

89. *IFSW*, January 23, 1956.

90. I. F. Stone, Department of State File, Passport Division, Documents PO 13 and PO 14.

91. "I. F. Stone," Federal Bureau of Investigation, Washington Field Office File WFO 100-37078-224, J. Edgar Hoover to Special Agent in Charge, August 30, 1954: "The bureau feels that consideration should be given to the closing of this case [Espionage-R investigation]." In January 1956, an informant phoned the FBI and said that Stone had asked his assistance in finding a secretary. See Washington Field Office File WFO 100-37078, Section 13, Serial 382.
92. Interview with A. B. Magil, spring 1992.
93. Isaac Deutscher, "Communism Now," *Partisan Review* 23 (Fall 1956): 513.
94. Yossi Melman, "Trade Secrets," *Ha'aretz*, March 10, 2006 (English-language edition).
95. *IFSW*, March 26, 1956.
96. *IFSW*, April 30, 1956; http://news.bbc.co.uk/2/hi/middle_east/4855056.stm.
97. Interview with Dan Wakefield, 1994.
98. *IFSW*, May 15, 1956.
99. *IFSW*, May 28, 1956.
100. Anna Louise Strong, "Critique of the Stalin Era," *Monthly Review*, July–August, 1956, cited in Patner, *I. F. Stone*, p. 39.
101. "I. F. Stone," Federal Bureau of Investigation, Headquarters File 100-37078, Documents 239, 250; Joseph Clark, "I. F. Stone's Appraisal of Lenin," *Daily Worker*, June 17, 1956, p. 5.
102. IFS to Norman Thomas, June 8 and November 27, 1956; Norman Thomas to IFS, November 26, 1956, Norman Thomas Papers.
103. *IFSW*, May 21, 1956, and March 14, 1953.
104. *IFSW*, June 4, 1956.
105. *IFSW*, July 23, 1956.
106. Sidney Hook, "Socialism and Liberation," *Partisan Review* 24 (Fall 1957): 501; *IFSW*, March 25, 1957.
107. *IFSW*, March 7, 1953; *IFSW*, October 18, 1954; IFS to Earl Browder, October 29, 1954, November 14, 1954, December 20, 1954, and June 2, 1957, Earl Browder Collection.
108. *IFSW*, July 9, 1956, and January 28, 1957.
109. *IFSW*, October 29, 1956.
110. *IFSW*, April 30, August 6, August 13, and August 20, 1956.
111. *IFSW*, November 5, 1956.
112. *IFSW*, November 12, 1956.
113. *IFSW*, November 19, 1956.
114. Interview with David Kraslow, January 27, 1994.
115. Buckley, "I. F. Stone," pp. 132–33.
116. *IFSW*, October 15 and November 5, 1956.
117. Clancy Sigal, *The Secret Defector* (New York: Harper, 1992), p. 9; e-mails from Clancy Sigal, 2006.
118. Isserman, *Which Side Were You On?* p. 173, describes the meeting between Thomas and Browder.
119. *IFSW*, June 25 and July 2, 1956.
120. *IFSW*, January 28 and February 25, 1957.
121. Interview with Cynthia Scollon, 1994.
122. Irving Caesar to IFS, February 20, 1958, Irving Caesar Papers.
123. Braudy, *Family Circle*, pp. 99–100; *IFSW*, April 21, 1958.

124. The whole of *IFSW*, July 22, 1957, is devoted to the Pugwash statement, which according to Stone "not a single newspaper in the United States" would publish.

125. *IFSW*, December 9, 1957.

126. *IFSW*, February 24, 1958.

127. Gladwin Hill, "First Atomic Blast Set Off in Tunnel," *New York Times*, September 20, 1957, p. 1. Patner, *I. F. Stone*, pp. 55–58, includes Stone's definition of a shirt-tail: "little paragraphs following the paper's own story. They hang down at the end like a shirt-tail."

128. *I. F. Stone's Weekly* (1973), a film by Jerry Bruck Jr., transcript, pp. 2–3.

129. *IFSW*, March 24, March 31, and May 12, 1958.

130. IFS, "Hill-billies from Morningside Heights," *Nation*, March 16, 1940, p. 350; Russell-Stone correspondence, Bertrand Russell Archives.

131. "How Sane the SANE?" *Time*, April 21, 1958, pp. 13–14, cited in Isserman, *If I Had a Hammer*, pp. 149, 180–81.

132. Isserman, *If I Had a Hammer*, pp. 127–69, is a characteristically lucid account of the pacifist and antinuclear movements.

133. *IFSW*, January 20, 1958.

134. *IFSW*, February 11 and July 15, 1957.

135. *IFSW*, August 12, 1957.

136. *IFSW*, October 7, 1957.

137. *IFSW*, May 26 and August 11, 1958.

138. *IFSW*, September 22, 1958.

139. Interview with Frank Wilkinson, May 1, 1992.

140. "First Amendment," *New York Times*, October 5, 1960, p. 40; "Coming to Life," *Washington Post*, May 17, 1960.

141. *IFSW*, September 1, 1958.

142. *IFSW*, June 23, 1958.

143. *IFSW*, February 29 and April 11, 1960.

144. "Mighty Steve Young," *Time*, December 21, 1962.

145. *IFSW*, July 21, 1958, and July 18, 1960.

146. I. F. Stone, Department of State File, Documents PO 8 and PO 12.

147. *IFSW*, April 6, 1959.

148. *IFSW*, April 20, 1959.

149. *IFSW*, April 27, 1959.

150. "Humanist Abroad," *Time*, May 4, 1959; "Castro and Communism," *New Leader*, July 4–11, 1960.

151. *IFSW*, July 18, 1960.

152. *IFSW*, August 1, 1960.

153. *IFSW*, August 8, 1960; IFS, "The Legacy of Che Guevara," *Ramparts*, December 1967, pp. 20–21. It is probably worth noting that a year earlier the *New York Times* described the Cuban leadership as "out of another century—the century of Sam Adams and Patrick Henry and Tom Paine and Thomas Jefferson" (April 17–20, 1959), cited in Van Gosse, *Where the Boys Are: Cuba, Cold War America and the Making of a New Left* (New York: Verso, 1993), p. 114.

154. *IFSW*, March 25 and April 1, 1957; January 25, 1960.

155. *IFSW*, August 25, 1958; August 10, 1959; May 23, July 18, and October 3, 1960.

156. *IFSW*, October 10 and November 7, 1960.

157. *IFSW*, November 28, 1960, and January 30, 1961.
158. *IFSW*, February 6, 1961.

9: THE IMPERIAL THEME

1. John F. Kennedy, *The Strategy of Peace* (New York: Harper, 1960), pp. 167–68.
2. "Castro Visit Triumphant," *Harvard Law Record*, April 30, 1959, pp. 3–4.
3. Gosse, *Where the Boys Are*, pp. 144–51.
4. Ibid., p. 61.
5. Ibid., pp. 147–48. Louis, under pressure from the IRS, publicly renounced his support for Cuba, and Langston Hughes decided to boycott the reception at the Theresa. See Richard E. Welch Jr., *Response to Revolution: The United States and the Cuban Revolutions, 1959–1961* (Chapel Hill: University of North Carolina Press, 1985), p. 128.
6. "Castro's Going to College," *New York Journal-American*, December 24, 1960; Gosse, *Where the Boys Are*, pp. 161–62, 211.
7. *IFSW*, October 31, 1960.
8. *IFSW*, January 16 and February 6, 1961.
9. Interview with David Kraslow; Peter Wyden, *Bay of Pigs: The Untold Story* (New York: Simon & Schuster, 1980), pp. 45–46; interview with Karl Meyer, December 12, 1991; Harrison E. Salisbury, *Without Fear or Favor: The New York Times and Its Times* (New York: Times Books, 1980), pp. 150–51; "Are We Training Cuban Guerrillas?" *Nation*, November 19, 1960, pp. 378–79; *New York Times*, January 10, 1961, p. 1.
10. *IFSW*, February 27, 1961.
11. *IFSW*, March 13 and 27, 1961.
12. Foreign Relations of the United States, 1961–1963, Vol. XI, Cuba, Document 79. Schlesinger's February 11 memorandum is Vol. X, Document 31M, in the same series.
13. *IFSW*, April 17, 1961.
14. Gosse, *Where the Boys Are*, p. 215.
15. *IFSW*, April 24, 1961.
16. Gosse, *Where the Boys Are*, p. 194.
17. Ibid., pp. 215–21.
18. Ronald Steel, *Walter Lippmann and the American Century* (Boston: Little, Brown, 1980), p. 530; Gosse, *Where the Boys Are*, pp. 223–24.
19. Gosse, *Where the Boys Are*, pp. 225, 231. See also Schrecker, *No Ivory Tower*, and Sigmund Diamond, *Compromised Campus: The Collaboration of Universities with the Intelligence Community, 1945–1955* (New York: Oxford University Press, 2001). The latter contains a devastating account of Diamond's own encounter with McGeorge Bundy at Harvard.
20. Interview with Frank Wilkinson.
21. IFS to Michael Blankfort, July 3, 1961, Blankfort Papers; *IFSW*, March 6, May 1, and June 12, 1961.
22. *IFSW*, May 1 and 8, 1961. The Kennedy speech is at www.jfklibrary.org/Historical+Resources/Archives/Reference+Desk/Speeches/JFK/003POF03NewspaperPublishers04271961.htm.

23. *IFSW*, May 15, May 22, and October 23, 1961. See also Slavko N. Bjelajac, "Unconventional Warfare: American and Soviet Approaches," *Annals of the American Academy of Political and Social Science* 341 (May 1962): 74–81.

24. Bernard Fall, "Solution in Indochina: Cease-fire, Negotiate," *Nation*, March 6, 1954, p. 193; Dorothy Fall, *Bernard Fall: Memories of a Soldier-Scholar* (Washington, D.C.: Potomac Books, 2006), pp. 154–55.

25. *IFSW*, May 22, 1961.

26. Interview with Karl Meyer; interview with Neville Maxwell, January 9, 1992; interview with Sanford Gottlieb, January 17, 2007.

27. Interview with Sanford Gottlieb.

28. Arthur Waskow, "The Theory and Practice of Deterrence," in James Roosevelt, ed., *The Liberal Papers* (New York: Quadrangle Books, 1962), pp. 121–55.

29. Interview with Arthur Waskow, January 22, 2007; Jeremy J. Stone, *Every Man Should Try: Adventures of a Public Interest Activist* (New York: PublicAffairs, 1999), pp. 4–7.

30. Interview with Jeremy Stone.

31. *IFSW*, June 25, 1962.

32. "The Need to Speak Out," *Time*, February 23, 1962; *Life*, September 15, 1961.

33. Kai Bird, *The Color of Truth: McGeorge Bundy and William Bundy: Brothers in Arms* (New York: Simon & Schuster, 1998), pp. 145, 187–88.

34. Interview with Marcus Raskin, November 20, 1991; e-mail from Marcus Raskin, December 1, 2006.

35. Bird, *Color of Truth*, p. 200.

36. *IFSW*, February 26, 1962; *Time*, February 23, 1962.

37. Interview with Arthur Waskow; Todd Gitlin, *The Sixties: Years of Hope, Days of Rage* (New York: Bantam, 1987), pp. 91–94.

38. *IFSW*, September 11–18, 1961; April 9 and 16, 1962.

39. Marcus Raskin, e-mail to author; Bird, *Color of Truth*, p. 219.

40. Amy Swerdlow, *Women Strike for Peace: Traditional Motherhood and Radical Politics in the 1960s* (Chicago: University of Chicago Press, 1993), pp. 203–208; *IFSW*, April 16, 1962.

41. Swerdlow, *Women Strike for Peace*, pp. 18, 44–48.

42. Ibid., p. 15; *IFSW*, October 30, 1961, and January 22, 1962.

43. James Miller, *"Democracy Is in the Streets": From Port Huron to the Siege of Chicago* (New York: Simon & Schuster, 1987), pp. 100–102; Tom Hayden, *Student Social Action* (Chicago: Students for a Democratic Society, 1966).

44. Miller, *"Democracy Is in the Streets,"* p. 117; e-mail from Richard Flacks, June 12, 2005.

45. C. Wright Mills, "Letter to the New Left," *New Left Review* 5 (September–October 1960). Mills died on March 20, 1962, at the age of forty-five.

46. Miller, *"Democracy Is in the Streets,"* pp. 112–17; Kirkpatrick Sale, *SDS* (New York: Random House, 1973), pp. 58–61.

47. David Riesman and Michael Maccoby, "The American Crisis," in Roosevelt, *Liberal Papers*, pp. 13–48.

48. "The Port Huron Statement," appendix to Miller, *"Democracy Is in the Streets,"* pp. 329–74. For Raskin's departure, see Bird, *Color of Truth*, p. 219.

49. *IFSW*, October 8, 1962.

50. Jack Raymond, "Pentagon Backs 'Fail-Safe' Setup," *New York Times*, October 21, 1962, p. 69.

51. Miller, "*Democracy Is in the Streets*," p. 164; Gitlin, *Sixties*, pp. 98–101; interview with Marcus Raskin; interview with Richard Barnet, November 20, 1991; interview with Barbara Bick, November 18, 1991.

52. Bird, *Color of Truth*, p. 245.

53. Named by Elizabeth Bentley and convicted of perjury after two trials in which his ex-wife had been forced to testify for the prosecution, Remington was murdered in prison in 1954. For a judicious account of Remington's guilt and innocence, see Gary May, *Un-American Activities: The Trials of William Remington* (New York: Oxford University Press, 1994).

54. Amy Swerdlow, "Ladies' Day at the Capitol: Women Strike for Peace Versus HUAC," *Feminist Studies* 8, no. 3 (Autumn 1982): 493–520.

55. Barbara Bick, "How I Lost College but Found Knowledge," undated manuscript in author's possession; interview with Barbara Bick.

56. Swerdlow, "Ladies' Day."

57. *IFSW*, December 16, 1962; Swerdlow, "Ladies' Day."

58. Eric Bentley, ed., *Thirty Years of Treason* (1971; New York: Nation Books, 2002), pp. 950–51.

59. John F. Kennedy, press conference, November 20, 1962. By the end of 1962, the budget for Operation Mongoose, the CIA program to overthrow or assassinate Fidel Castro, was in excess of $50 million a year. Bird, *Color of Truth*, pp. 242–43.

60. *IFSW*, January 7, 14, and 21, 1963. Even such restrained sympathy was too much for Antonio de la Carrera of the Junta Revolucionario Cubana, who in the February 6, 1963, issue of the Socialist Party magazine *New America* denounced Stone for "Castro traveling." Betty Elkins, the SP's national administrative secretary, wrote to Izzy apologizing for Carrera's "intemperate language and not really giving your side of the controversy" with the hope that he would "not be too angry." Betty Elkins to IFS, April 10, 1963, Socialist Party Archives.

61. *IFSBW*, April 1, 1963. The phrase "principled concern for human freedom" comes from Schlesinger's memo to the president, February 11, 1961.

62. *IFSBW*, June 24, 1963.

63. *IFSBW*, September 2, 1963.

64. *IFSBW*, September 16, 1963. Interview with Jack O'Dell, August 2004. See also Branch, *Parting the Waters*, pp. 208–12, 850–51. For Lewis's proposed text, see www.hartford-hwp.com/archives/45a/641.html, and for what he actually said, see www.npr.org/news/specials/march40th/part1.html.

65. *IFSBW*, December 9, 1963.

66. Ibid.

67. Ibid.

68. George G. Weickhardt to author, January 21, 1993, was just one of several letters I received describing Stone's interest in and kindness to high school students.

69. Interview with Fred Graham, 1994.

70. *Washington Post*, September 14, 1963, p. A4.

71. David Hajdu, *Positively 4th Street: The Lives and Times of Joan Baez, Bob Dylan, Mimi Baez Fariña and Richard Fariña* (New York: North Point Press, 2001), pp. 76, 168. Oddly, though Dylan's alienation from politics is one of Hajdu's principal themes, his book makes no mention of the ECLC dinner.

72. For the text of Dylan's speech and his letter, see www.corliss-lamont.org/dylan.htm or Robert Shelton, *No Direction Home: The Life and Music of Bob Dylan* (New

York: William Morrow, 1989), pp. 200–205. According to Shelton, Foreman made several attempts to take up Dylan's offer, but the money was never paid.

73. *IFSBW*, December 9, 1963.

74. Irving Howe, *A Margin of Hope* (New York: Harcourt Brace, 1983), pp. 291–93, cited by Gitlin, *Op. cit.*, pp. 170–75, which gives ample space to both contemporary and retrospective accounts from all sides—the very opposite of special pleading.

75. *IFSW*, October 14, 1963, gives paid circulation as 20,242. Interview with Larry Bensky, November 27, 2006.

76. *IFSW*, December 9, 1963.

77. *IFSW*, June 15, 1964.

78. Martin Peretz, "As He Saw It," *Dissent*, Summer 1964: 368–69.

79. *IFSW*, June 22, 1964.

80. The saga of the MFDP deserves a book of its own. I've drawn on accounts in Clayborne Carson, *In Struggle: SNCC and the Black Awakening of the 1960s* (Cambridge, MA: Harvard University Press, 1981), pp. 106–16; David Garrow, *Bearing the Cross* (New York: Vintage, 1988), pp. 345–51; Harvard Sitkoff, *The Struggle for Black Equality, 1954–1980* (New York: Hill and Wang, 1981), pp. 175–85. I also found a session with Robert Moses at the Socialist Scholars' Conference in the late 1980s useful. But the account that best captures the emotional meaning as well as the backroom maneuvering, and on which I relied most heavily, is Gitlin, *The Sixties*, pp. 151–62.

81. *IFSW*, September 7, 1964.

82. IFS, "Biography as Facial Surgery," *New York Review of Books*, July 30, 1964.

83. Richard Rovere, "Letter from Washington," *New Yorker* 40 (August 22, 1964): 102.

84. James Reston, "Washington: The Illuminating Flash in Southeast Asia," *New York Times*, August 9, 1964, p. E8.

85. *IFSW*, August 10 and 24, 1964.

10: AN AMERICAN TRAGEDY

1. Stanley Karnow, *Vietnam: A History* (New York: The Viking Press, 1983), pp. 147–49. The description of Ho Chi Minh as a Vietnamese nationalist is from Abbot Low Moffat, a State Department official who met Ho shortly after Patti, and is in Michael Maclear, *The Ten Thousand Day War: Vietnam: 1945–1975* (New York: St. Martin's Press, 1981), pp. 1–17.

2. Karnow, *Vietnam*, pp. 162–75.

3. Neil Sheehan et al., *The Pentagon Papers: As Published by the* New York Times (New York: Bantam Books, 1971), pp. 4, 8, 26–27.

4. Karnow, *Vietnam*, pp. 184, 194.

5. Ibid., pp. 16–17; Frances FitzGerald, *Fire in the Lake: The Vietnamese and the Americans in Vietnam* (New York: Vintage, 1972), p. 597n42.

6. *IFSW*, May 9, 1955.

7. FitzGerald, *Fire in the Lake*, p. 113; *IFSW*, October 23, 1961.

8. Larry Berman, *Planning a Tragedy: The Americanization of the War in Vietnam* (New York: Norton, 1982), p. 29; *IFSW*, October 22, 1962.

9. David Halberstam, *The Best and the Brightest* (New York: Random House, 1972), p. 77, cited in Karrow, *Vietnam*, p. 265.

10. Halberstam, p. 183.

11. *IFSW*, May 3, 1963.

12. *IFSW*, September 30, 1963.

13. Sheehan, *Pentagon Papers*, pp. 81, 232–33; *IFSW*, December 23, 1963. The phrase itself was the lede of a September roundup on the war by Charles Mohr, *Time*'s chief correspondent in Southeast Asia. Killed by *Time*'s editors, Mohr's piece was never published, but David Halberstam told the story in an article in the January 1964 issue of *Commentary* on the stands when Izzy wrote.

14. Bird, *Color of Truth*, p. 359.

15. Sheehan, *Pentagon Papers*, pp. 238–42.

16. Bird, *Color of Truth*, pp. 286–88, 447n53.

17. Miller, "*Democracy Is in the Streets*," pp. 218–21.

18. Ibid., p. 222; Gitlin, *Sixties*, pp. 179.

19. Miller, "*Democracy Is in the Streets*," pp. 223–28; Gitlin, *Sixties*, pp. 164, 179–80; *IFSW*, July 23, 1962. No transcript exists of Stone's talk to SDS, but the October 23, 1963, issue of the *Weekly*, an eight-page special on Vietnam, contains a summary of U.S. involvement. For the full text of Savio's speech, see www.american rhetoric.com/speeches/mariosaviosproulhallsitin.htm.

20. *IFSW*, February 15, 1965; Halberstam, *Best and the Brightest*, pp. 591–93.

21. Bird, *Color of Truth*, pp. 290–96, 312.

22. Ibid., p. 313; Patner, *I. F. Stone*, p. 101.

23. *IFSW*, March 22, 1965.

24. Halberstam, *Best and the Brightest*, p. 593.

25. IFS, "Vietnam: An Exercise in Self-Delusion" (review of *The Making of a Quagmire* by David Halberstam and *The New Face of War* by Malcolm W. Browne), in *Time of Torment*, pp. 307–16.

26. *IFSW*, May 24, 1965.

27. Arthur Waskow, "40 Years Ago, the First Teach-In," www.shalomctr.org/node/1027; Bird, *Color of Truth*, pp. 318–19; *IFSW*, May 24, 1965.

28. *National Guardian*, May 29, 1965, pp. 1, 8. *New York Times*, May 23, 1965, p. 26, gives a crowd estimate of 10,000. A recording of I. F. Stone's principal remarks, which were later broadcast over station KPFA, is available in the Pacifica Archive, www.pacificaradioarchives.org, and at http://sunsite.berkeley.edu/videodir/pacificaviet/ifstone.ram.

29. IFS to Norman Thomas, May 22, 1965, Thomas Papers.

30. Waskow, "40 Years Ago, the First Teach-in."

31. Interview with Robert Silvers, February 11, 1992.

32. IFS, "An Official Turns State's Evidence," *New Republic*, May 29, 1965, reprinted in IFS, *Time of Torment*, pp. 316–20.

33. *IFSW*, May 24 and 31, 1965.

34. *IFSW*, November 8, 1965; *National Guardian*, October 23, 1965, p. 6.

35. IFS to Norman Thomas, February 18, 1965, Thomas Papers.

36. *IFSW*, September 6, 1965.

37. Sheehan, *Pentagon Papers*, pp. 459–61.

38. *IFSW*, December 6, 1965.

39. *IFSW*, March 30, 1964; March 8 and November 1, 1965. Stone noted that the *New York Times*, which also ran the first photo, "left out the reference to napalm."

40. IFS, interviewed by Forrer and Glickman. Nader's information about the auto industry was the basis for his 1965 best-seller *Unsafe at Any Speed*.

41. David Riesman, "Society's Demands for Competence," in Gerald Grant, ed., *On Competence: A Critical Analysis of Competence-Based Reforms in Higher Education* (San Francisco: Jossey-Bass, 1979), p. 45.
42. Interview with Suzanne Fields, December 2006.
43. Interview with Neil Kotler, December 2006.
44. Interview with Phil Stanford, December 2006; *I. F. Stone's Weekly* film transcript, p. 14; interview with Peter Osnos, June 1991.
45. Interview with Peter Osnos.
46. *IFSW*, May 9, 1966.
47. *IFSW*, May 16, 1966.
48. *IFSW*, May 23 and 30, 1966.
49. Interview with Celia Gilbert, September 1991; Steel, *Walter Lippmann*, p. 576. Stone saved the invitation, which I found in his study.
50. Anthony Howard, "Behind the Bureaucratic Curtain," *New York Times Magazine*, October 23, 1966, pp. 34–36; interview with Anthony Howard, November 1994.
51. Curt Gentry, *J. Edgar Hoover: The Man and the Secrets* (New York: Norton, 1991), p. 719. For Hoover's meetings with McCarthy, see Johnson, *Age of Anxiety*, p. 163.
52. "I. F. Stone," Federal Bureau of Investigation, Washington Field Office File 100-22286, SA Joseph Keller to Director, March 16, 1966; *IFSW*, January 24 and February 21, 1966.
53. *IFSW*, March 28, 1966; interview with Ralph Ginzburg, spring 1992.
54. *IFSW*, June 6, 1966; interview with Peter Osnos.
55. IFS, "The Pilgrimage of Malcolm X," *New York Review of Books*, November 11, 1965.
56. *IFSW*, June 6, 1966.
57. *IFSW*, July 25 and September 19, 1966. The latter article, titled "Why They Cry Black Power," was a response to Carmichael's essay "What We Want" in the September 22, 1966, issue of the *New York Review of Books*.
58. *IFSW*, March 14, April 11, and October 3, 1966; January 17, 1967.
59. IFS, "Pilgrimage of Malcolm X."
60. *IFSW*, June 28, 1965.
61. *IFSW*, October 10, 1966.
62. *IFSW*, May 29, 1967.
63. *IFSW*, September 26, 1966; Sheehan, *Pentagon Papers*, pp. 512–17.
64. Michael Padnos, e-mail to author, June 14, 2006.
65. *IFSW*, February 18, March 7, and October 24, 1966; February 20 and March 13, 1967.
66. *IFSW*, October 17, 1966.
67. *IFSW*, February 13, 1967.
68. *IFSW*, May 1, 1967.
69. *IFSW*, May 8, 1967.
70. *IFSW*, June 5, 1967.
71. *IFSW*, June 12, 1967.
72. *IFSW*, June 19 and July 3, 1967.
73. IFS, "The Future of Israel," *Ramparts* 6, no. 1 (July 1967): 41–44.
74. IFS, "Holy War," *New York Review of Books*, August 3, 1967.
75. IFS to Norman Thomas, October 9, 1964, Thomas Papers; "The Left and the Warren Commission," *IFSW*, October 5, 1964.

76. "Letter: Israel and the Arabs," *New York Review of Books*, September 28, 1967.
77. IFS to Michael Blankfort, August 10, 1967, Blankfort Papers.
78. Robert Sherrill, *IFSW*, May 1, 1967, p. 3, and May 8, 1967, p. 3.
79. Interview with Robert Sherrill.
80. Interview with Andrew Kopkind, 1994.
81. Andrew Kopkind, "They'd Rather Be Left," *New York Review of Books*, September 28, 1967.
82. Andrew Kopkind, "He Claims to Have Fought with Ideas but He Bought Them for Cash," *IFSW*, May 15, 1967, p. 3.
83. Murray Kempton, *New York Post*, April 4, 1967, reprinted in *IFSW*, April 10, 1967.
84. Kopkind, "They'd Rather Be Left."
85. Andrew Kopkind, "Soul Power," *New York Review of Books*, August 24, 1967, reprinted in Kopkind, *The Thirty Years' Wars* (New York: Verso, 1995), pp. 87–94.
86. *IFSW*, November 13, 1967.
87. *IFSW*, July 31, 1967.
88. *IFSW*, November 13, 1967.
89. Owen Lattimore Collection; Joseph R. Starobin Collection; Norman Thomas Papers; James Wechsler Papers.
90. Ronald Steel, "Eternal Hostility to Bunk," *Washington Post Book World*, March 17, 1968, pp. 6–7; "A Prophet, Not a Gadfly," *Times Literary Supplement*, October 3, 1968, p. 1099; Henry Steele Commager, "Common Sense," *New York Review of Books*, December 5, 1968, pp. 3–4.
91. Noam Chomsky, "On Resistance," *New York Review of Books*, December 7, 1967, and "An Exchange on Resistance," *New York Review of Books*, February 1, 1968.
92. *IFSW*, January 22, 1968.
93. *IFSW*, December 11, 1967; Andrew Kopkind, "The McCarthy Campaign," *Ramparts*, March 1968.
94. Maclear, *Ten Thousand Day War*, pp. 189–205.
95. *IFSW*, February 19, 1968.
96. *Time*, February 9, 1968, p. 22.
97. *IFSW*, February 19, 1968.
98. Ibid.
99. *IFSW*, December 18, 1967.
100. Andrew Kopkind, "A Cord Snaps," *New York Review of Books*, April 25, 1968.
101. *IFSW*, April 1, 1968.
102. Andrew Kopkind, "The Importance of Kennedy," *New Statesman*, March 29, 1968, reprinted in Kopkind, *America: The Mixed Curse* (London: Penguin, 1969), pp. 160–64.
103. Interview with Robert Silvers; E. Y. Harburg to IFS, January 19, 1968, E. Y. Harburg Collection, Boston University Library; Michael D. C. Macdonald, "Izzy at 60," *Village Voice*, January 25, 1968, p. 9.
104. Interview with Andrew Kopkind.
105. *IFSW*, April 1, 1968.
106. *IFSW*, April 15, 1968.
107. Ibid.
108. *IFSW*, April 29, 1968.
109. Kopkind, "The American Nightmare," in *America*, pp. 50–54; Jerry L. Avorn et al., *Up Against the Ivy Wall* (New York: Atheneum, 1968).

110. *IFSW*, May 27, 1968.

111. Ibid.; Andrew Kopkind, "Are We in the Middle of a Revolution?" in *Thirty Years' Wars*, pp. 148–54.

112. *IFSW*, April 1, June 10, and June 24, 1968; Miller, *"Democracy Is in the Streets,"* pp. 293–94.

113. *IFSW*, August 19, 1968.

114. *IFSW*, August 5 and September 9, 1968. Interview with Oleg Kalugin, August 19, 1992; Andrew Brown, "The Attack on I. F. Stone," *New York Review of Books*, October 8, 1992, p. 21.

115. *IFSW*, June 24, 1968.

116. *IFSW*, September 9, 1968.

117. Ibid.; IFS, "Who Are the Democrats?" *New York Review of Books*, August 22, 1968. The version reprinted in IFS, *Polemics and Prophecies, 1967–1970* (New York: Random House, 1970), pp. 3–21, includes an angry letter from Sherrill accusing Stone of trying "to inflate his reputation as an unsnobbish democrat at my expense" and Stone's apology.

118. *IFSW*, October 7, 1968.

119. *IFSW*, September 9, 1968.

120. Interview with Andrew Moursund, April 7, 1992.

121. *IFSW*, November 4, 1968. See also Jerald E. Podair, *The Strike That Changed New York: Blacks, Whites, and the Ocean Hill–Brownsville Crisis* (New Haven, CT: Yale University Press, 2004).

122. *IFSW*, January 13, 1969.

123. IFS to Virginia and Clifford Durr, December 20, 1968, Durr Collection.

124. Israel Shenker, "I. F. Stone: Gadfly Likes People and Sometimes Angers Readers," *New York Times*, November 19, 1968, p. 33.

125. *IFSW*, January 27, 1969.

126. Mark Rudd, e-mail to author, August 2004.

127. *IFSW*, November 14, 1966, and July 14, 1969.

128. Interview with Kathy Boudin, August 31, 2007; *The Bust Book: What to Do Till the Lawyer Comes* (New York: New York Regional SDS, 1969).

129. *IFSW*, May 19, 1969.

130. *IFSW*, October 6, 1969.

131. Interview with Andrew Moursund; interview with Christopher Stone. According to public records, the Stones sold the Nebraska Avenue house for $31,000, and paid $80,000 for the house on 29th Street.

132. Andrew Kopkind, "Are We in the Middle of a Revolution?" *New York Times Magazine*, November 10, 1968.

133. *IFSW*, March 24 and November 3, 1969.

134. Andrew Kopkind, "Coming of Age in Aquarius," *Hard Times*, reprinted in *Thirty Years' Wars*, pp. 171–75.

135. *IFSW*, November 3, 1969.

136. Ibid.

137. *IFSW*, December 1, 1969.

138. *IFSW*, November 3, 1969, and January 26, 1970.

139. Interview with Jean Boudin; Braudy, *Family Circle*, pp. 200–210.

140. *IFSBW*, March 23, 1970.

141. Dorothy Day, *Selected Writings*, ed. Robert Ellsberg (Maryknoll, NY: Orbis Books, 1992), pp. 342–44.
142. *IFSBW*, May 18, 1970.
143. A. Kent MacDougall, "Gadfly on the Left: I. F. Stone Achieves Success, Respectability but Keeps Raking Muck," *Wall Street Journal*, July 14, 1970, p. 1.
144. IFS, *The Killings at Kent State: How Murder Went Unpunished* (New York: New York Review, 1971), p. 15.
145. *IFSBW*, September 21, 1970.
146. *IFSBW*, January 25, 1971.
147. "The Press," *Time*, February 8, 1971, p. 47; Elizabeth Drew, *New York Times Book Review*, February 14, 1971, p. 3.
148. "The Press," *Time*, February 8, 1971, p. 47.
149. *IFSBW*, September 7, 1970; May 17 and 31, 1971.
150. Interview with Christopher Stone; *IFSBW*, May 3 and 17, 1971.
151. Interview with Robert Silvers; interview with Andrew Kopkind.
152. A. Whitney Ellsworth to author, January 31, 1993.
153. Christopher Lydon, "I. F. Stone to Suspend 19-Year-Old Leftist Biweekly," *New York Times*, December 7, 1971, p. 43.

11: HELLENISTIC PERIOD

1. Vincent Canby, "New Cannes Festival Star: I. F. Stone," *New York Times*, May 23, 1974, p. 50.
2. Peter Davis to author, July 27, 1992.
3. Charles Champlin, "Portrait of a Muckraker," *Los Angeles Times*, January 25, 1974, p. IV:1; Vincent Canby, "*I. F. Stone's Weekly* Is a Film Delight," *New York Times*, October 19, 1973, p. 52.
4. IFS, "I. F. Stone Reports: Betrayal by Psychiatry," *New York Review of Books*, February 10, 1972; and "I. F. Stone Reports: Can Russia Change?" *New York Review of Books*, February 24, 1972.
5. John Leonard quoted in Cottrell, *Izzy*, p. 295.
6. Interview with Arthur Schlesinger Jr., December 1995.
7. Interview with Richard Wollheim, 1993.
8. Interview with Isaiah Berlin, 1992.
9. T. D. Allman, "A Giant in the Academic Pond," *Guardian*, June 15, 1974.
10. Robert C. Tucker, "Oil: The Issue of American Intervention," *Commentary* 59 (January 1975): 21–31. See also Stanley Hoffmann, "The Response to Tucker," in *Commentary* 59 (1975): 4–5, for a more restrained critique.
11. IFS, "War for Oil?" *New York Review of Books*, February 6, 1975: 10.
12. Robert Silvers to Isaiah Berlin, February 5, 1975, Oxford, Bodleian Library, MS. Berlin 279, folio 243.
13. Isaiah Berlin to IFS, February 13, 1975, ibid., MS. Berlin 209, folios 262–63.
14. IFS to Isaiah Berlin, March 9 and 20, 1975, ibid.
15. Allen Weinstein, "Was Alger Hiss Framed?" *New York Review of Books*, April 1, 1976.
16. Patner, *I. F. Stone*, pp. 84–86.
17. Interview with Robert Silvers.

18. Marie Syrkin, "Underground to Palestine and Reflections Thirty Years Later," *New Republic* 180 (January 27, 1979): 28–30; Marvin Maurer, "I. F. Stone—Universalist," *Midstream* 25 (February 1979): 2–12.

19. Cottrell, *Izzy*, pp. 290–91.

20. Ibid., p. 298.

21. John J. Farmer, "Izzy Stone Sparks Jewish Ire . . . Again," *Philadelphia Bulletin*, November 20 1978; Rick Nichols, "Izzy Stone Thrives on Controversy," *Philadelphia Inquirer*, November 22, 1978.

22. Myra MacPherson, "Gathering No Moss: The I. F. Stones: Marking 50, Still Going Like Sixty," *Washington Post*, July 9, 1979, p. B1.

23. Greenya, "Portrait of a Man Reading," p. 2.

24. IFS, "Izzy on Izzy," *New York Times Magazine*, January 22, 1978.

25. For a brilliant and endlessly provocative examination of Freud's relationship with antiquity, see Carl E. Schorske, "Freud's Egyptian Dig," *New York Review of Books*, May 27, 1993.

26. IFS, *The Trial of Socrates* (Boston: Little, Brown, 1988), pp. x–xi; "Izzy on Izzy."

27. IFS, *Trial of Socrates*, p. xi.

28. Ibid.

29. Schorske, "Freud's Egyptian Dig."

30. M. I. Finley, *The Ancient Economy* (Berkeley: University of California Press, 1973). Stone's copy is in the author's possession.

31. IFS, *Trial of Socrates*, p. 197.

32. IFS, "Izzy on Izzy."

33. IFS, *Trial of Socrates*, p. 64.

34. Interview with Bernard Knox, November 15, 1991.

35. IFS, *Trial of Socrates*, p. 230.

36. IFS, "Izzy on Izzy."

37. Karl Popper, *The Open Society and Its Enemies* (London: Routledge, 2002), p. 111. This is the one-volume edition of a work first published in 1945.

38. Fustel de Coulanges, *The Ancient City* (New York: Doubleday, 1956). Stone's copy is in the author's possession.

39. Popper, *Open Society*, p. 97.

40. IFS, *Trial of Socrates*, pp. 129, 197.

41. Ibid., p. 197; Popper, *Open Society*, p. 140.

42. Popper, *Open Society*, p. 144.

43. Ibid., p. 140; IFS, *Trial of Socrates*, pp. 112–14.

44. IFS, *Trial of Socrates*, pp. 41, 118.

45. Ibid., pp. 60, 97–99.

46. Interview with Andrew Wylie, 1996; also see Andrew Wylie, "An International Agent Argues for a Global Approach to Selling Serious Literature," *Washington Post*, May 9, 2004, p. BW 13.

47. Christopher Lehmann-Haupt, "Books of the Times," *New York Times*, January 18, 1988, p. C20; Julia Annas, "Down with Democracy!" *New York Times Book Review*, February 7, 1988, p. 7; Allan Bloom, "Dateline Athens: I. F. Stone Reopens the Socrates Case," *Washington Post Book World*, February 14, 1988, p. 1; Sidney Hook, "Making the Case Against Socrates," *Wall Street Journal*, January 20, 1988.

48. Carlin Romano, "Thoughts About the Crimes of Socrates," *Philadelphia Inquirer*,

January 28, 1088, p. I-1; Gregory Vlastos, "On the Socrates Story," *Political Theory* 7, no. 4 (November 1979): 533–36.

49. Peter Levi, "Athens on Trial," *Independent* (London), September 21, 1988; M. F. Burnyeat, "Cracking the Socrates Case," *New York Review of Books*, March 31, 1988, pp. 12–16; Neal Ascherson, "Sting Like a Gadfly," *Observer*, September 25, 1988.

50. Interview with Roger Donald, 1994. Sales figures courtesy of the Wylie Agency.

51. Interview with Morton Mintz, 1991.

52. IFS, "On Rosa Luxemburg," *New York Times*, April 5, 1981.

53. Interview with Victor Navasky, 1990; see also Victor S. Navasky, *A Matter of Opinion* (New York: Farrar, Straus and Giroux, 2005), pp. 194–97, 289–91.

54. Interview with Felicity Bryan, 1994.

55. Larry Bensky, "No Stone Unturned," *Sun* (Berkeley), June 30, 1988; William Greider, "National Affairs," *Rolling Stone*, April 21, 1988, p. 38.

56. Kate Regan, "Izzy at 80: Wisdom Through the Ages," *San Francisco Chronicle*, February 6, 1988, p. C3.

57. J. R. Pole to author, October 11, 1991; interview with Sidney Morgenbesser, 1994; interview with Edward Said, 1994.

58. Albert Friedman to author, January 8, 1992.

59. David E. Rosenbaum, "Gentle Gadfly's Classic Scoop," *Chicago Tribune*, January 26, 1989, p. 3.

12: LAST WRITES

1. Last Will and Testament of Isidor F. Stone; interview with Jeremiah Gutman, 1993.

2. John R. MacArthur, "Life in the U.S.," *In These Times*, August 2–29, 1989, p. 24; Mona Charen, "Two Obits Reveal Press' Leftist Slant," *NY Newsday*, July 19, 1989, p. 56.

3. Murray Kempton, Introduction to IFS, *In a Time of Torment*, p. x.

4. Elaine Sciolino, "K.G.B. Telltale Is Tattling, But Is He Telling U.S. All?" *New York Times*, January 20, 1992, p. 1.

5. A record of my own dealings with Kalugin can be found in D. D. Guttenplan, "Izzy an Agent?" *Nation*, August 3–10, 1992, pp. 124–25, and "Stone Unturned," *Nation*, September 28, 1992, pp. 312–13.

6. Andrew Brown, "The Attack on I. F. Stone," *New York Review of Books*, October 8, 1992, p. 21.

7. Martin Garbus to *New York Observer*, October 8, 1992, made available to the author by Martin Garbus.

8. William Safire, "On Language," *New York Times Magazine*, September 27, 1992, p. 20. Safire's column merely "attributed" these remarks to his source, who was "on background" and hence not quotable.

9. Interview with Mikhail Kazachkov, January 26, 1994. See also Kazachkov, letter to the editor, *New York Times*, August 31, 1992.

10. Paul Berman, "The Watchdog," *New York Times Book Review*, October 1, 2006.

11. For Stone on Sakharov, see IFS, "The Sakharov Campaign," *New York Review of Books*, October 18, 1973; for Brodsky, see *IFSW*, July 6, 1964. For my own perspective on Kalugin's latest, see D. D. Guttenplan, letter to the editor, *New York Times Book Review*, October 22, 2006.

12. *IFSW*, November 6, 1961; September 11, 1964; January 24, 1966; and November 13, 1967.
13. Patner, *I. F. Stone*, p. 121.
14. Elinor Langer, "The Secret Drawer," *Nation*, May 30, 1994, pp. 752–60.
15. IFS, interviewed by Forrer and Glickman.
16. Felicity Barringer, "Journalism's Greatest Hits," *New York Times*, March 1, 1999, p. 1.

ACKNOWLEDGMENTS

It wasn't supposed to take this long.

When I started this book in 1990, I was a thirty-three-year-old newspaperman, newly married with a baby on the way. A biography seemed like a good antidote for the reporter's *déformation professionelle*—the glib certainty that comes from constantly having to write without having time to learn about anything in depth. I was too young to have known *I. F. Stone's Weekly*, but I'd been an avid reader of Stone's essays in the *New York Review of Books* and later in the *Nation*. After he died in 1989, I volunteered to cover his memorial service for my paper, the late, lamented *New York Newsday*. So when my friend Deborah Karl, then a literary agent at the Wylie Agency, telephoned and said her colleagues had seen my article and wondered if I'd be interested in becoming Stone's biographer, I was intrigued—especially since my union had recently lost its fight for paid paternity leave. I figured I'd spend a couple of years reading through Stone's personal papers and published work, interview his family, friends, and enemies, and write up the result while the baby gurgled happily on a sheepskin at my feet. I figured three years, maybe four years max. I had no idea.

So began my real education—and, in a way, my adult life. I was a graduate of two venerable universities and had thoroughly enjoyed my adventures in the reporter's trade: I'd exposed a few bad guys, written a weekly column, worked the police beat, fought City Hall, even shared a Detroit steam bath with George H. W. Bush (where I learned that Bob Dylan was right: the president of the United States sometimes must have to stand naked). Nothing I had done prepared me for the labor-intensity of fatherhood. Or for the sheer complexity of the biographical task I'd taken on.

Letters and diaries normally form the skeleton of a biography, but I. F. Stone never kept a diary, and from the mid-1940s on, when he held down two full-time jobs at *PM* and the *Nation*, he had little time for personal correspondence, which in any case he didn't save. Typically he'd reply to a letter by scribbling a brief response on the bottom and returning it to his correspondent. After 1953, when he had to produce all the copy for *I. F.*

Stone's Weekly, he seldom had the time even to do that, which made writing the first half of his life akin to assembling a mosaic out of thousands of tiny fragments scattered around the world. And in those pre-Internet days, countless telephone calls, letters, and hours of peering at card indexes might be required before I could even be sure a given fragment existed. Stone's life after 1953 posed a difficult problem: How to extract a narrative from the literally millions of words he published?

Four years went by before I wrote so much as a sentence. My interest in Stone, as both a man and a historical figure, only increased with the passage of time. Indeed, after eighteen years in his company I still return to his writings with immense pleasure and often with surprise at the depth of his perspicacity and the vigor of his prose. There were interludes: I took two years off to write another book; I also produced a couple of documentaries and did a fair amount of radio work. Even when Stone's biography was my day job, I never stopped writing journalism. Yet my acknowledgments ought to begin with my good fortune in happening on a subject so rich and rewarding as to make such a sustained effort seem less like folly and more like fascination.

So I remain grateful to Deborah Karl for making that telephone call and for encouraging me. Andrew Wylie has stuck by me all these years; as I. F. Stone's agent, he took a personal interest in this book from the first and never wavered as the usual vicissitudes of publishing were compounded by what must have seemed my glacial pace. He and his associates Jin Auh and Tracy Bohan, and former associate Zoë Pagnamenta, were always superbly effective as well as patient, for which they have my thanks.

When I contacted I. F. Stone's family, they were perhaps properly wary. But eventually all three of his children made themselves available for my questions, as did his widow, Esther, before her death in November 2000. Over the years, Celia Gilbert, Jeremy Stone, and Christopher Stone have all been generous with their time, recollections, and family photographs; Jeremy's wife, B.J., kindly copied the remembrances of Izzy sent to the family after his death; Jeremy and Esther allowed me to work in Stone's study. Louis Stone, Izzy's youngest brother—my first real advocate within the family and a lovely man whom I feel very lucky to have known—gave me a copy of the unpublished family history he'd written with his brother Marc. However, no member of the Stone family saw a single page of this book before it was published.

Jean Boudin, Esther Stone's younger sister, was more than just a source. Sharp, self-deprecating, pixieish, and remarkably attractive (she was not quite eighty years old when I first met her), she was wonderfully indiscreet; by the time of her death in 1994 we had become friends. I was very happy, too, that I was able to interview both her son, Michael Boudin, and her daughter, Kathy Boudin, some years later.

My dear friends and teachers Andrew Kopkind, Sidney Morgenbesser, and Edward Said died before this book was finished. They all had known Stone: Sidney and Edward through their involvement in the cause of peace and justice in the Middle East; Andy as a close journalistic colleague. Each of them put aside their abundant reserves of skepticism to offer warm encouragement for this project; their advice and approval were a source of sustenance over the long haul. I also want to acknowledge my late father-in-law, Pandias Margaronis, whose generosity meant that we could keep a roof over our heads despite the increasingly dismal economics of writing biography. My own father, Mitchell Guttenplan, remembered reading Stone's column in *PM*. He died before this book was finished, but not before I could thank him for his love and support.

Fortunately, the majority of my debts are to the living. Victor Navasky was the first person I interviewed, and he was indispensable, opening the Nation's files and offering sage advice on navigating the snares and pitfalls of the American left. It was also Victor who, as editor of the Nation, commissioned my reporting on Stone, Oleg Kalugin, and the KGB.

This book would have been impossible without Scott Sherman, who applied to be my research assistant before I had any thought of hiring such a person or any money to pay his salary. Now a distinguished journalist himself, in those days Scott was the perfect researcher, tracking down Stone's contributions to long-defunct journals and doggedly writing to every name in Stone's address book. Scott's grasp of the historical context made it a pleasure to discuss matters great and small, and his organizational skills enabled me to complete the archival stage of my research before I moved to London in 1994.

The Freedom Forum Media Studies Center at Columbia University awarded me a research fellowship (and research assistant stipend) for the 1993–94 academic year. I am delighted finally to thank Everette Dennis for supporting my candidacy, and to thank him, Duncan MacDonald, John Pavlik, Shirley Gaszi, and the rest of the center's staff for making my year there so pleasant. That it was also productive is in large part due to the influence of such stimulating colleagues as Alan Brinkley, Jim Clad, Donna Demac, Oscar Gandy Jr., Bob Jeffrey, Sig Gissler, Johanna Neumann, John Tierney, and Dai Qing. I am grateful to Alan Brinkley in particular, both for his own clear-sighted work on the New Deal and for smoothing the path for me in London by introducing me to his friend Anthony Badger.

Within journalism, investigative reporters form a kind of priesthood: ascetic, obsessive, suspicious characters who feel with some justification that they are Jefferson's true heirs. All the investigative reporters I've ever met regarded Izzy as one of them. I thank Lewis Lapham for long ago bidding me to follow the money, and the web of political favors, behind New York's Times Square redevelopment, an inquiry that also served as my introduction to the Village Voice, which in the mid-1980s was indeed a very heaven, giving its writers a real, measurable, and almost instant impact on the city's cultural and political life. David Schneiderman, who hired me there to carry on investigating Times Square and then kept me on to edit news and politics, and his successors, Robert Friedman (who lured me to Newsday) and Martin Gottlieb, shielded us from interference by the paper's owners, tolerating and even encouraging a level of creative insubordination that would have driven lesser men mad. Richard Goldstein, Thulani Davis, and Ellen Willis turned editorial meetings into seminars on the personal and the political. Geoffrey Stokes taught me how to read the daily papers, a discipline he'd learned in part by reading Stone. Pete Hamill showed me the difference between telling the story and writing the story; he also taught me to take our shared craft seriously. And if I. F. Stone's analysis of the defense budget was our model, Jack Newfield and Paul Du Brul's book Abuse of Power: The Permanent Government and the Fall of New York (1977) was our textbook. Both veteran Village Voice writers, Jack and Paul welcomed me to the fold, as did Joe Conason, Bill Bastone, Maria Laurino, Tom Robbins, and Murray Waas, all of whom taught me a great deal. So did Wayne Barrett, with whom I had weekly shouting matches but who is still, for my money, the best documents man in the business.

New York Newsday, where I worked after the Voice, was a great metropolitan newspaper whose crusading spirit and refusal to condescend to its readers made it easier for me to understand the appeal of that other late, great tabloid, PM. The many arguments I had with Anthony Marro, who edited its parent paper on Long Island and supervised my coverage of the media, helped me understand Stone's often strained yet affectionate relations with his bosses. Both Tony and Don Forst, editor of the New York City edition, were patient with my youthful excesses and taught me much about the strengths and limits of mainstream journalism. To share a newsroom with Sidney Schanberg, whose reports of the Cambodian killing fields had made history and who sustained an adamant skepticism toward the claims of power, and with Jimmy Breslin, whose newspaper work combined a novelist's sense of the epic with a bookie's feel for track record and particular conditions, was a privilege. As for Murray Kempton, he could (and would) tell you why today's mafiosi represented such a lamentable falling off in character from their godfathers, how H. L. Mencken liked to vent his spleen, and which judges owed their careers to Roy Cohn. Murray was a higher education in journalism all by himself. In the long interview he gave me about Stone, he offered as hardheaded an assessment as he would have about any politician; that it was largely positive was a tribute to the genuine admiration he felt for a former competitor. More than anyone else, Murray helped me see what a sense of history could give a reporter. Kevin Flynn, my former reporting partner, taught me how little the experts know; he also made even the tedium of a Bronx stakeout a pleasant experience.

All biographers are indebted to their predecessors, but my gratitude to Robert Cottrell, who wrote the first full-length Stone biography, goes beyond the norm. Cottrell opened his files to me, sent me not just the notes of his own interviews with Stone but the actual tapes, and in every way was a model of scholarly generosity. Andrew Patner, whose *I. F. Stone: A Portrait* is an affectionate, indispensable record of Izzy's abiding preoccupations and conversational rhythms, subjected me to rigorous vetting before taking me under his wing. Then we became friends. I'm also grateful to Myra MacPherson—and not just for taking nearly as long to write her biography of Stone as I have taken with mine. I didn't read her book until I'd finished this one, but I know her efforts brought new readers to Stone's writings and generated new interest in his life and times.

My friend Eric Alterman has always been helpful and supportive, trusting me with his own I. F. Stone file despite what happened when he lent me his material on Lee Atwater. Max Holland shared his research on Stone and the *Nation*'s CIA files, and Brian Hill sent me his copy of Stone's State Department file, which differed in slight but interesting ways from the material released to me. I apologize to John Greenya for borrowing his Stone file for fifteen years, and thank Joseph Spear for letting me see the raw material he had from Stone's FBI file.

Raymond Schroth, SJ, a descendant of the family that once owned the *Brooklyn Eagle*, got his former student Jerry Buckley to send me a copy of his Fordham undergraduate thesis on I. F. Stone, which included an extremely useful interview. Graydon Forrer sent me cassette tapes of the unpublished interview he and Elise Glickman recorded with Stone in 1979. The broadcaster Sidney Roger, a great source and a delightful conversationalist, sent me audiotapes of Stone speaking against the Smith Act in 1952 and against the Vietnam War in Berkeley in 1965. Robert Gershon made me a copy of his videotaped 1982 interview with Stone as well as his own film profile of George Seldes. Jerry Bruck arranged a special showing of his wonderful film *I. F. Stone's Weekly* for me and gave me a transcript of it. Franklin Folsom mailed me early proofs of his memoir, *Days of Anger, Days of Hope*, and was a patient instructor on the intricate politics of the League of American Writers. Paul Milkman was kind enough to hand-deliver a manuscript copy of his brilliant *PM: A New Deal in Journalism*. Anya Schiffrin lent me her copy of *PM*'s FBI file and gave me a copy of her senior thesis on *PM*. I am deeply grateful to all of them.

This book couldn't have been written without the Freedom of Information Act. On the other hand, it might have been written a lot faster if that law were properly enforced. I made my first FOI request to the FBI, with Les Payne at *Newsday* sponsoring it, in July 1990; I received my last release in 2005. David Garrow, biographer of Martin Luther King Jr., advised me on what to expect and when to expect it. Scott Armstrong and Lynda Davis at the National Security Archive told me I needed to make a separate request to each agency and helped frame the inevitable appeals, many of which were successful. Emil Moschella, chief of the Freedom of Information section at the Justice Department, and his successors J. Kevin O'Brien and Richard L. Huff, eventually released some 6,000 pages of material. At first much of it was heavily redacted, but my appeals coincided with the Clinton presidency, which had a policy presumption in favor of disclosure, and the material released in those years was mostly legible. As a result, it became possible to see the full florid lunacy of J. Edgar Hoover's obsession with Stone, one of the few journalists who dared to criticize the FBI director by name. Hoover's agents illegally tapped Stone's telephone and opened his mail, rummaged through his garbage, interviewed his employers, and for some years put him under daily personal surveillance. The result of all this wasted manpower is a treasure trove of material, and though Hoover should never be forgiven, I am grateful to the FBI for holding on to it and to Alice Grasewicz and her fellow analysts for eventually releasing so much of it.

Most of my other FOI requests finally bore fruit, and I thank Kathleen Siljegovic, chief of the FOIA Section at the State Department; James B. Sealock, chief of the Freedom of Information Office at the Department of the Army; Cecil Fry, director of records management at the Department of the Air Force; Ave Sloane, chief of the FOIA/PA Unit at the Immigration and Naturalization Service; Milton O. Gustafson, chief of the Civil Reference Branch at the National Archives; William H. Davis at the Center for Legislative Archives; John H. Wright, information and privacy coordinator at the Central Intelligence Agency; and C. R. Clauson, chief postal inspector, for the material they released. Retrospective gratitude is surely due to Abe Goff, solicitor of the Post Office, who in February 1954 resisted an attempt to deny *I. F. Stone's Weekly* second-class mail privileges.

The National Security Agency was another story. My correspondence with the NSA, which began in May 1993, produced nothing but pro forma denials until 1995, when at the behest of Senator Daniel Patrick Moynihan the NSA went public with the existence of the Venona project, its effort to decode hundreds of intercepted cables sent by Soviet intelligence agents in the 1940s. I am grateful to the historian Ronald Radosh, who alerted me to the presence of material potentially relevant to I. F. Stone among the Venona decrypts, and to Joanne H. Grube, deputy director of policy at the NSA, who released the material to me in 1998.

While I'm on the subject of Venona and historians with whom I don't always agree, I thank John Earl Haynes, twentieth-century political historian at the Library of Congress (one of Izzy's favorite haunts), for his many kindnesses. Thanks to John and his colleagues James Hutson, chief of the Manuscript Division, and Jeff Flannery, also of the Manuscript Division, and Janet McKee of the Motion Picture, Sound and Broadcasting Division, I came away with what I needed.

Peter Filardo at the Tamiment Library at New York University has been helpful in countless ways over the years, as has Ruth Dar, formerly curator of the United States collection at University College London library. Douglas Rauschenberger, director of the Haddonfield Public Library, helped me get my bearings in Stone's hometown. At the Pennsylvania Historical Society, Lee Arnold and Janice Dockery allowed me to examine not just Stone's contributions to the *Philadelphia Record* but that paper's reporters' assignment books as well. Margaret Jerrido at Temple University Library was my guide to the archives of the Philadelphia Newspaper Guild. Phil Joyce, editorial page editor of the *Philadelphia Inquirer*, arranged access to that paper's excellent library. Gail Pietrzyk, public services archivist at the University of Pennsylvania, provided Stone's college transcript and financial records. Tom Pernacchio of the Newspaper Guild of New York allowed me to rummage through the guild's basement until I found the original transcript of Stone's guild grievance when he was fired from the *Post*. The late Jerry Nachman, editor of the *Post*, forgave me for the occasional rough treatment I'd given him in my column and let me, in the early 1990s, have the run of that paper's morgue, then still kept on paper in a forest of metal file cabinets. The late Eric Breindel, the *Post*'s editorial page editor, graciously printed my side of the controversy over Stone and the KGB. My thanks also to the *New York Times Book Review*, the *New York Review of Books*, and the *Nation* for printing my author's query, and to all of those who wrote in response.

Charles Greifenstein of the American Philosophical Society copied Izzy's correspondence with Edward Condon for me; Henry Hardy was helpful in obtaining access to Stone's correspondence with Isaiah Berlin; the Bertrand Russell Archive at McMaster University sent me Stone's correspondence with Lord Russell. Dr. Howard Gotlieb at the Mugar Memorial Library of Boston University arranged access to both the Ralph Ingersoll and Michael Blankfort archives; Amy Sliwinski, archivist at the Wisconsin Historical Society, was similarly accommodating. At the Morrisson-Reeves Library in Richmond, Indiana, Doris Ashbrook kindly searched through deeds and county court records to flesh out the Feinstein family's Hoosier period. I am also grateful to the staff at the Brooks Memorial Library in Brattleboro, Vermont, who requested interlibrary loans, arranged Internet access, and, even more important, provided a quiet, air-conditioned place to work over several steamy summers.

Fred Karl and Ken Silverman welcomed me to the Biography Seminar at New York University (or, as we used to call it, Biographers Anonymous). These two eminently sane men made the vertiginous emotional life of solitary toil seem bearable, even admirable. I'm grateful to Elizabeth Harlan for the comment by George Sand that I quote in Chapter 3. Early on I was the beneficiary of some useful how-to advice from Michael Shnayerson and Jean Strouse. Michael Massing tried to warn me.

In London, I was fortunate to be sent (by Tony Badger) to Rick Halpern, then at University College London, who not only became my academic mentor but also hired me to teach a survey course in American history, thus forcing me to learn it myself. Rick was happily complicit in my scheme to reverse the customary order of events and turn a book—or half a book—into a doctorate; Andrew Hemingway allowed me to do so with a minimum of academic hoop jumping and a maximum of genuine intellectual stimulation. I am grateful to Marybeth Hamilton for inviting me to teach at Birkbeck College and to my students there and at UCL for their curiosity and intelligence. Rick, Andrew, Tony, Marybeth, and Scott Sherman all read portions of this book, which has been improved by their suggestions.

Maurice Isserman and Alan Wald encouraged me to take an expansive view of I. F. Stone's life and times. I remain indebted to them for welcoming my interest and for their own pioneering work. Two other scholars whom I don't know personally, but whose influence merits acknowledgment, are Michael Denning and Ellen Schrecker.

The names of the 130-plus people interviewed for this book are listed elsewhere. I am obliged to all of them, particularly to the tiny handful of Communists or former Communists who spoke to me candidly and on the record. I. F. Stone was never a member of the Communist Party. But in the 1930s and 1940s, he was often close to the party and to party members, and it seemed important to understand the nuances of that complex, shifting relationship. Ellen Schrecker has pointed out that "ironically, contemporary historians need the same kinds of confessions the congressional investigators of the 1950s did, including, if at all possible, the naming of names." Any assumptions I might have had about how readily, after the end of the cold war, such answers might be obtained were shattered by the sociologist Sigmund Diamond, who threw me out of his apartment for asking the question. (He later relented, allowing me access to the material he'd collected on McCarthyism and the press.) So it was with a mixture of relief, gratitude, and astonishment that I listened to Amos Landman calmly and credibly recount his experiences as a Communist newspaperman on the *Daily Mirror* and *PM*. He and Albert Silverman, a veteran Philadelphia Communist, and A. B. Magil, a former editor of *New Masses*, were a joy to interview. I am also grateful to Nathaniel Weyl and Arnold Beichman, committed anti-Communists, for their careful, patient testimony.

The Israeli journalist and historian Tom Segev, one of my intellectual heroes, steered me to the Haganah Archives, who located interviews with several of the organizers of Stone's underground odyssey to Palestine. My chaver Jonathan Freedland put me in touch with the intrepid Jonathan Cummings, who tracked down further material in Israel. Daphna Baram ably translated the Haganah interviews.

Rob Snyder asked me to write about I. F. Stone and George Polk for *Media Studies Journal*; I'm grateful to him, and to Elsa Dixler and Sam Tanenhaus at the *New York Times Book Review*, for publishing my letter about Stone and the KGB.

This book has had more editors than I can count, but only two of them matter. The late Aaron Asher commissioned it for a new imprint he was starting. Learned, witty, and thoughtful, Aaron paid enough to allow me to quit my job, but was himself a casualty of corporate restructuring before I had anything to show him. Elisabeth Sifton had been the most interesting person I met when discussing the book with potential publishers; that she remained just as interested twelve years later was an enormous stroke of luck. I still remembered her comments on the social world of the New Dealers from our first meeting, and it has been a huge comfort (if also a sometimes daunting stimulus) to know that I can always expect a frank and well-informed response to anything I send her. Her patience, tact, and personal warmth have made the writing a pleasure; I am delighted and honored to be in her company of authors. Charles Battle, Elisabeth's assistant at FSG, guided me through the editorial process with élan, and Gena Hamshaw, who took over from Charles, kept me, and the book, on schedule. Cynthia Merman tried valiantly to rescue me from solecism.

I was fortunate, several years after leaving daily journalism, to find myself back at the *Nation*, where I'd begun as an intern and whose longtime books editor, Betsy Pochoda, had been my first patron. Thanks to the *Nation*'s editor in chief, Katrina vanden Heuvel, my friend before she became my boss, I've never felt that being 3,000 miles away from the office meant that my relationship with the magazine was detached. She and my editors Karen Rothmyer and Roane Carey have been available, enthusiastic, and incredibly indulgent about the constraints imposed on my time by this book.

I have also been indulged and sustained by my friends. Steve Ackerman, Peter Cariani and Becky Heaton, Patti Cohen, Larry Friedman, Sid Holt, Jeff Klein, Nanci Levine, Christian McEwen, Rosemary Moore and Josh Shneider, Marie Nahikian, Patti Nolan and David Rabkin, Verandah Porche, Joel Sanders, John Scagliotti and Dave Hall, Don Share, and Carl Strehlke have allowed me to pretend that the Atlantic Ocean really is just a pond. Gene Seymour, culture maven extraordinaire, put me on to the connection between Dizzy Gillespie and Charles Roisman. Rick MacArthur is perhaps the only one of my old friends who would read this book solely out of interest in the subject; he's also one of the few journalists to understand Stone's radicalism.

Life in London has been made not only bearable but rich and strange thanks to Sarah Dunant, Edward Fox, Jonny Freedland, Ben Freedman, Caroline Johns, Jonny Levy, Mando Meleagrou, Andy Metcalf, Susie Orbach, Daniel and Isobel Pick, Joe Schwartz, and Gillian Slovo. My cousins Jennifer and Sam Guttenplan always make London feel less foreign. Now that I'm done I hope you can all come out to play!

That I have a home to come home to is largely due to my wife, Maria Margaronis, who also proved my toughest editor. By inclination more Rosalind Russell (or Katharine Hepburn) than Esther Stone, the other half of the Nation's London bureau has kept every word of the vows she made nearly twenty years ago, on a spring day in Prospect Park, when she promised to be "truthful, generous, and kind," to be with me "and to keep the faith." In turn I promised "to go on adventures" with her and to love her fiercely, which I do. Our big adventure turned out to be family life, for which the credit must go to our children, Alexander, Zoe, and Theo. I hope that if any of them read these words, and go on to read this book, they will not begrudge their father the years he spent cooped up in his study. Also that they will come to see the wisdom, in Stone's life and someday in their own, of Dante's advice: Segui il tuo corso, e lascia dir la gente: Follow your path, and let people talk.

I began this book in part as a way to rationalize spending more time at home with Alexander, who as a very small boy once asked me, "Is I. F. Stone's son called Izzy Pebble?" Now I find that I'm finishing as he's about to leave home for university—not just a man but a real mensch of whom I'm tremendously proud. He and his sister and brother give me great hope for the future, and it is to them, as well as to the memory of my friend and rabbi Andy Kopkind, that this book is dedicated.

Park Slope, Brooklyn, 1991–94
Islington, London, 1994–96
Guilford, Vermont, 1995–2008
Hampstead, London, 1997–2008

INDEX